Teaching Mathematics in Secondary and Middle School
An Interactive Approach

SECOND EDITION

Teaching Mathematics in Secondary and Middle School

An Interactive Approach

James S. Cangelosi

Utah State University

MERRILL, An imprint of Prentice Hall

Englewood Cliffs, New Jersey   Columbus, Ohio

Library of Congress Cataloging-in-Publication Data

Cangelosi, James S.
    Teaching mathematics in secondary and middle school : an
interactive approach / James S. Cangelosi. — 2nd ed.
      p. cm.
    Includes bibliographical references and index.
    ISBN 0-13-439233-7
    1. Mathematics—Study and teaching (Secondary) I. Title.
QA11.C23 1996   95-30511
510'.71'2—dc20
                                       CIP

Editor: Bradley J. Potthoff
Editorial/production supervision: WordCrafters Editorial Services, Inc.
Design coordinator: Julia Z. Van Hook
Cover design: Proof Positive/Farrowlyne Associates, Inc.
Cover photo: Jeffrey Muir Hamilton/Liaison International
Production manager: Laura Messerly
Text photos: Ted Hansen

This book was set in Century Schoolbook by Carlisle Communications, Ltd.,
and was printed and bound by Quebecor/Semline. The cover
was printed by Phoenix Color Corp.

 © 1996 by Prentice Hall, Inc.
A Simon & Schuster Company
Englewood Cliffs, NJ 07632

Earlier edition © 1992 by Macmillan Publishing Company.

Printed in the United States of America

10 9 8 7 6 5 4 3

ISBN 0-13-439233-7

Prentice-Hall International (UK) Limited, *London*
Prentice-Hall of Australia Pty, Limited, *Sydney*
Prentice-Hall Canada Inc., *Toronto*
Prentice-Hall Hispanoamericana, S.A., *Mexico*
Prentice-Hall of India Private Limited, *New Delhi*
Prentice-Hall of Japan, Inc., *Tokyo*
Simon & Schuster Asia Pte. Ltd., *Singapore*
Editora Prentice-Hall do Brasil, Ltda., *Rio de Janeiro*

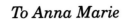

To Anna Marie

Preface

Contrary to popular belief, mathematics is a human endeavor in which otherwise ordinary people of all ages construct concepts, discover relationships, invent methods, execute algorithms, communicate, and solve problems posed by their own real worlds. New mathematics are discovered and invented every day as illustrated by the students in Ms. Lowe's class as they work with "Nortons" (see page 18). In Case 3.1, which begins on page 49, 15-year-old Brenda demonstrates that creative applications of mathematics are not limited to the efforts of professional mathematicians working on extraordinary problems. Brenda and Ms. Lowe's students find mathematics exciting and relevant to their personal interests as they confidently use it to address problems. How do these students acquire these attitudes about and abilities with mathematics? According to consistent findings of numerous research studies (see e.g., Davis, Maher, & Noddings, 1990; Grouws, 1992; Steffe & Kieren, 1994; Suydam & Brosnan, 1994), students acquire these attitudes and abilities by experiencing (a) inquiry lessons that lead them to reason inductively to construct concepts as well as discover relationships, (b) direct-instructional lessons that lead them to gain knowledge of conventions and facts as well as to develop and polish algorithmic skills, (c) comprehension lessons for learning how to communicate with and about mathematics, and (d) inquiry lessons that lead them to reason deductively to devise solutions to real-life problems.

However, most students acquire a considerably different view of mathematics, perceiving it as a boring string of terms, symbols, facts, and algorithms, truly understood only by rare geniuses. In stark contrast to Brenda and Ms. Lowe's students, it is typical for students only to memorize mathematical content—never to discover, invent, or creatively apply it (Dossey, Mullis, Lindquist, & Chambers, 1988; McLeod, 1994; Romberg, 1992; Schoenfeld, 1992). The unhealthy attitudes and the inability to extend mathematics beyond what is memorized are perpetuated by the most dominant method of teaching mathematics in our schools from kindergarten through college. Typically, mathematics lessons begin with the teacher telling the students a fact or giving them the steps in an algorithm. The teacher then works a textbook example and assigns students to work exercises from the textbook to help them remember the fact or process. The lessons are void of experiences whereby students discover, invent, or apply mathematics to problems they find meaningful (Fuson, 1992; Jesunathadas, 1990; Rowley, 1995).

For at least the past century, mathematics education specialists have encouraged teachers to practice the research-based approaches rather than the more commonly practiced approaches. The recent widespread dissemination and support for the National Council of Teachers of Mathematics (NCTM) plan for school mathematics curriculum reform as articulated in *Curriculum and Evaluation Standards for School Mathematics* (NCTM, 1989a) provides promise for bringing typically practiced mathematics teaching in line with the research-based approaches. *Professional Standards for Teaching Mathematics* (NCTM, 1991) represents a unified effort of exemplary mathematics teachers, mathematicians, and educators to spell out what mathematics teachers must be able to do to take advantage of the research-based approaches and teach in harmony with NCTM's *Curriculum and Evaluation Standards*.

Teaching Mathematics in Secondary and Middle School: An Interactive Approach is designed to lead you to develop the competencies set forth in NCTM's *Professional Standards for Teaching Mathematics* so that you, as a teacher, successfully lead your students to eagerly construct concepts for themselves, discover relationships, acquire and retain knowledge of conventions and facts, develop and maintain algorithmic skills, communicate with and about mathematics, and devise solutions to real-life problems. Introducing topics in a spiral fashion, this book actively involves you in learning activities throughout 12 chapters:

Chapter 1, "$T_i(S) = L$: A Set of Messy Functions," points out the complexities of teaching, examines variabilities among students, and demonstrates that whether students find mathematics mystifying or understandable depends largely on the approaches employed by their teachers.

Chapter 2, "Developing Mathematics Curricula," distinguishes between typical and research-based curricula, describes the NCTM *Standards,* and explains how you as a mathematics teacher can develop curricula you consider appropriate for your secondary or middle school students.

Chapter 3, "Designing Mathematics Courses and Teaching Units," serves as an advanced organizer for Chapters 4–6, which deal with specifics of lesson design; it also leads you to extend your understanding of real-world problem solving and teacher planning.

Chapter 4, "Leading Students to Construct Concepts and Discover Relationships," explains and illustrates how to design lessons that lead students to construct concepts, as well as lessons that lead students to discover mathematical relationships. Strategies for developing performance assessment items for obtaining formative feedback relative to how well students achieve construct-a-concept and discover-a-relationship objectives are emphasized. Throughout the chapter there are integrated activities that will engage you in formulating objectives, designing lessons, and devising assessments for conceptual and discovery learning.

Chapter 5, "Leading Students to Develop Knowledge, Comprehension, and Algorithmic Skills," explains and illustrates how to design lessons that lead students to acquire and remember mathematical information, comprehend mathematical expressions, and develop algorithmic skills. Strategies for developing performance assessment items for obtaining formative feedback relative to how well students achieve simple-knowledge, comprehension, and algorithmic-skill objectives are emphasized. Activities are integrated throughout the chapter that will engage you in formulating objectives, designing lessons, and devising assessments for skill-level and comprehension-level learning.

Chapter 6, "Leading Students to Solve Problems, Be Creative with Mathematics, and Willingly Do Mathematics," explains and illustrates how to design lessons that lead students to apply mathematics to real-life situations, foster their creativity with mathematics, and develop an appreciation for and willingness to do mathematics. Strategies for developing per-

formance assessment items for obtaining formative feedback relative to how well students achieve application, creativity, and affective objectives are emphasized. Activities are integrated throughout the chapter that will engage you in formulating objectives, designing lessons, and devising assessments for two cognitive (application and creativity) and two affective (appreciation and willingness to try) learning levels.

Chapter 7, "Resources and Technology for Teaching Mathematics," provides an overview of resources and technologies (textbooks, inservices opportunities, trade books, professional associations, journals, calculators, computers, video and audio equipment, multimedia networks, measuring instruments, and classroom arrangements) to help you lead students to do meaningful mathematics.

Chapter 8, "Gaining Students' Cooperation in an Environment Conducive to Doing Mathematics," suggests and illustrates methods for establishing a classroom climate that is conducive to learning mathematics, gaining and maintaining students' cooperation, and efficiently dealing with student off-task behaviors.

Chapter 9, "Engaging Students in Learning Activities," demonstrates how to design, organize, and conduct different types of learning activities (large-group presentations, cooperative-learning sessions, question/discussion sessions, and independent-work sessions). Further, suggestions for responding to students' questions and assigning homework are explained and illustrated.

Chapter 10, "Monitoring Student Progress and Evaluating Achievement," examines fundamental principles and strategies for assessing and reporting student progress in a manner consistent with NCTM's *Assessment Standards for School Mathematics* (NCTM, 1993).

Chapter 11, "Theory into Practice: Casey Rudd, First-Year Mathematics Teacher," affords you the opportunity to experience vicariously the thoughts, plans, classroom activities, decisions, professional associations, disappointments, and successes of a high school mathematics teacher as he attempts to implement the suggestions from Chapters 1 through 10 of this text.

Chapter 12, "A Profession in Transition," is intended to stimulate your thinking about the current movement to reform the way mathematics is typically taught in schools and to reflect on your professional role in that movement.

Teaching Mathematics in Secondary and Middle School: An Interactive Approach is an unusual book in that it not only presents research-based principles for teaching mathematics, but also demonstrates each via realistic classroom-based examples and also contrasts them with examples that violate the principle. Furthermore, throughout the text it integrates topics like defining learning goals, designing lessons, motivating students' cooperation, and evaluating achievement by using over 150 cases that follow teachers' thoughts, actions, and reactions as they design, organize, conduct, evaluate, and redesign lessons. The book is structured to use the same type of research-based teaching strategies it suggests you use with your students. In other words, (a) the book uses inductive structures with carefully orchestrated examples to lead you to construct key concepts and discover principles, (b) it incorporates direct instructional strategies in the presentations to expose you to information and techniques, and (c) it uses deductive structures to lead you to apply principles and techniques. Throughout, the text uses comprehension strategies to introduce technical terms and advanced organizers.

One consequence of such an approach is that topics treated separately from one another in other mathematics teaching methods texts are integrated throughout this text. For example, there is no separate chapter or section on "motivating students' interest in mathematics" nor on "gender issues in mathematics." However, those two topics are inextricably meshed throughout all 12 chapters, as are topics such as accommodating multiple achievement levels within one classroom, teaching mathematics to middle school students, teaching algebra, teaching geometry, teaching discrete mathematics, teaching consumer mathematics, teaching calculus, teaching trigonometry, and other topics enumerated in the index and the table of contents. Even topics that have complete chapters devoted to them (e.g., classroom management and assessment) are integrated throughout the book. The art of teaching is far too complex to treat its aspects independently of one another, as is commonly done in other teaching methods books which are organized linearly.

Since the first edition of this text was published in 1992, an abundance of print, electronic, and audiovisual instructional and resource materials have become available for teachers to use in their efforts to implement the NCTM *Standards* (e.g., NCTM's *Addenda Series* and The Learning Team's CD-ROM *MathFinder*). Furthermore, a new generation of powerful calculators and computer software for doing mathematics has been developed. This second edition suggests and illustrates strategies for taking advantage of these advances as you develop mathematics curricula and teach your students. The second edition is an update of the first edition, and recent contributions to the research literature, with particular emphasis on the constructivist perspective, are incorporated throughout this volume. For example, the taxonomy of cognitive and affective learning levels described in Chapters 3 and 4 of the first edition has been reworked and explained in Chapters 3, 4, 5, and 6 in this edition.

The second edition is designed to be more user friendly than the first, and it should be easier for you to locate cross-referenced material—a complication necessitated by the spiral organization of the book. The longer vignettes in the first edition have been subdivided into several cases in the second. Furthermore, the book has been rewritten so that it is truly interactive. For example, rather than having only Self-Assessment Exercises at the end of each chapter, you will engage throughout the chapters in activities that are integrated with the narratives, cases, and exhibits. At the end of each chapter you will engage in Transitional Activities that are designed to set the stage for and prepare you for the subsequent chapter.

Also new to the second edition is an *Instructor's Manual,* available from Merrill/Prentice Hall. The manual provides suggestions for designing mathematical teaching methods courses that utilize *Teaching Mathematics in Secondary and Middle School: An Interactive Approach* (Second Edition). Also included is a course syllabus and a sample sequence of 108 course activities, including in-class sessions, cooperative-learning activities, out-of-class assignments, formative feedback experiments, field-based activities, and microteaching sessions. A midterm exam and final exam, accompanied by detailed criterion-based scoring keys, provide examples of applications of alternative assessment strategies for a mathematics teaching methods course.

I am particularly grateful to the numerous but proportionally rare mathematics teachers who have demonstrated that research-based teaching strategies are practical in realistic classroom situations. They are the people who provided me with the bases for the examples and cases, without which I could not have written a book that uses inductive and deductive teaching strategies. Outcomes from three research and development studies had a major influence on this work, the first sponsored by the National Science Foundation, the second and third by the U.S. Office of Education: *Mathematics Teacher Inservice Project, Underprepared Mathematics Teacher Assessment Project,* and the *Mathematics Teacher Network.* I am indebted to those two funding agencies as well as to the numerous researchers cited throughout the book.

Expert reviews of the manuscript were provided by Joel Bass of Sam Houston State University, Linda Cronin Jones of the University of Florida, William Croadale of the University of Rhode Island, Ed Dickey of the University of South Carolina, Thomas Gibney of the University of Toledo, Jay Graening of the University of Arkansas, Boyd Holton of West Virginia University, Virginia Horak of the University of Arizona, Mark Klespis of St. Xavier (Chicago), Mary M. Lindquist of Columbus College, William L. Merrill of Central Michigan University, Nancy Minix of Western Kentucky University, E. Alexander Norman of the University of North Carolina-Charlotte, Sandra J. Olson of Winona State University, Katherine Pederson of Southern Illinois University, Ken Stillwell of Northeast Missouri State University, William K. Tomhave of Concordia College, Stephen F. West of State University of New York at Geneseo, and Earl J. Zwick of Indiana State University.

Credit for this work is shared with the many professionals of Merrill/Prentice-Hall Publishing and WordCrafters Editorial Services, including Linda Zuk, Cynthia Hausdorff, Brad Potthoff, Linda Montgomery, Mary Irvin, and Linda James Scharp.

To my best friend Barb Rice, I extend my sincerest appreciation for her expert copyreading, support, and counsel.

Contents

CHAPTER 3
Designing Mathematics Courses and Teaching Units   49

CHAPTER 4
Leading Students to Construct Concepts and Discover Relationships   79

CHAPTER 5
Leading Students to Develop Knowledge, Comprehension, and Algorithmic Skills   117

CHAPTER 6
Leading Students to Solve Problems, Be Creative with Mathematics, and Willingly Do Mathematics,   157

CHAPTER 9
Engaging Students in Learning
Activities   271

CHAPTER 10
Monitoring Student Progress and Evaluating Achievement   307

CHAPTER 11
Theory into Practice: Casey Rudd, First-Year Mathematics Teacher,   339

1

$T_i(S) = L$: A Set of Messy Functions

Teaching is a set of functions you design and control. Whether your students find mathematics mystifying or understandable, boring or exciting, useless or useful, depends largely on how you teach them. Chapter 1 is designed to help you:

1. Explain how students' perceptions of mathematics and abilities with mathematics are dependent on (a) the learning experiences provided by their teachers, and (b) the individual characteristics the students bring to those experiences.

2. List student variables (for example, aptitudes for abstract reasoning, prior experiences, and personal biases) that you will need to take into consideration whenever you design and execute teaching functions.

3. Explain why the most commonly practiced method of teaching mathematics leads students to perceive mathematics as a mysterious sequence of symbol and word meanings, facts, and algorithms to be memorized.

4. Explain the general differences between (a) the most commonly practiced method of teaching mathematics, and (b) methods that lead students to perceive mathematics as a human pursuit they can creatively apply to solve problems from their own real world.

5. Describe the differences between those aspects of mathematics that are discoveries and those that are inventions.

A SET OF TIDY FUNCTIONS (f_i)

Let x be a variable such that $x \in \{-3, -.5, 0, 0.01, \sqrt{3}, 2\}$. Consider four functions of x, f_1, f_2, f_3, and f_4, defined as follows:

$$f_1(x) = 3x^2 - 8$$

$$f_2(x) = -10x^2 + 1$$

$$f_3(x) = x$$

$$f_4(x) = 3x$$

f_1, f_2, f_3, and f_4 are all well defined; the result of substituting each value of x in each function is completely predictable. Thus, you can make the following statements with certainty:

$f_1(-3) = 19$	$f_2(0) = 1$	$f_3(\sqrt{3}) = \sqrt{3}$
$f_1(-.5) = -7.25$	$f_2(.01) = .999$	$f_3(2) = 2$
$f_1(0) = -8$	$f_2(\sqrt{3}) = -29$	$f_4(-3) = 9$
$f_1(.01) = -7.9997$	$f_2(2) = -39$	$f_4(-.5) = -1.5$
$f_1(\sqrt{3}) = 1$	$f_3(-3) = 3$	$f_4(0) = 0$
$f_1(2) = 4$	$f_3(-.5) = -.5$	$f_4(.01) = .03$
$f_2(-3) = -89$	$f_3(0) = 0$	$f_4(\sqrt{3}) = 3\sqrt{3}$
$f_2(-.5) = -1.5$	$f_3(.01) = .01$	$f_4(2) = 6$

Furthermore, the following conclusions are indisputable:

- $f_i(-.5) < 0$ for $i = 1, 2, 3, 4$.
- Substituting x in f_3 does not yield values different from x.
- $f_2(-.5) = f_4(-.5)$.
- $f_1(2) > f_2(2)$.

- The arithmetic mean of $f_3(x)$ is greater than the arithmetic mean of $f_2(x)$.
- The standard deviation of $f_2(x)$ is greater than the standard deviation of $f_3(x)$.
- The values of $f_i(-3)$ vary according to the value of i to a greater degree than do either $f_i(-.5)$, $f_i(0)$, $f_i(.01)$, $f_i(\sqrt{3})$, or $f_i(2)$.
- $f_i(\sqrt{3})$ is rational for $i = 1, 2$.
- $0 < f_i(.01) < 1$ for $i = 2, 3, 4$.
- f_i for $i = 1, 2, 3, 4$ is a set of *tidy* functions because:

1. The characteristics of the domain $\{-3, -.5, 0, .01, \sqrt{3}, 2\}$ are well understood. For example:
   (a) Each element is a real number.
   (b) $-3 < -.5 < 0 < .01 < \sqrt{3} < 2$.
   (c) Each element except for $\sqrt{3}$ can be expressed as the ratio of two integers.
   (d) The square of each number, except for 0 and .01, is greater than the number.
2. The result of substituting each of value of x in any one of these functions is completely predictable; the outcome is certain.
3. The resulting range of each of these functions consists of real numbers and the range is as well understood as the domain. You understand why each result occurs (for example, why substituting -3 for x in $f_1(x) = 3x^2 - 8$ yields 19).
4. Each of these functions can be consistently executed. For example, tripling the square of -3 and then subtracting 8 from that result always yields 19. Any other result can be traced back to a failure to follow the rules of f_1, not to some inherent changes in either x or $f_1(x)$.
5. The characteristics of the domain of these functions remain constant over time. You can be assured, for example, that since -3 is less than $-.5$ today, -3 will be less than $-.5$ tomorrow.

MESSY FUNCTIONS

All functions are not as tidy as f_1, f_2, f_3, and f_4. Some are rather *messy* because:

1. The characteristics of the domain are too complicated to be completely understood.
2. The result of submitting each value from the domain to such functions cannot be confidently predicted.
3. The resulting range of such functions cannot always be readily identified, nor can the impact of the function always be explained.
4. The execution of such functions cannot necessarily be repeated at will.
5. The domain of such functions may vary with time.

Why would anyone choose to work with messy functions instead of tidy functions? You are in a po-

sition to answer that question because when you decided to be a teacher, you chose to join a profession of people who devote their time to designing and executing extremely messy functions.

TEACHING AS A SET OF FUNCTIONS (T_i)

Teaching is a set of functions $T_1, T_2, T_3, \ldots, T_i$, with a domain consisting of students, S, and a range, L, comprising different types and levels of student learning. In other words, $T_i(S) = L$.

Just as the value of f_i depends on which function is used (whether $i = 1, 2, 3,$ or 4) and which element of the domain is used (whether $x = -3, -.5, 0, .01, \sqrt{3}$, or 2), so do learning outcomes (L) depend on (a) how teaching is designed and executed, and (b) the students. Consider Case 1.1.

CASE 1.1 _____

Ms. O'Farrell uses *direct* instructional methods (Darling-Hammond & Snyder, 1992, pp. 65–66; Joyce, Weil, & Showers, 1992, pp. 308–323; Secada, 1992, pp. 649–650; Woolfolk, 1993, pp. 481–484) almost exclusively to teach her students mathematics. To conduct these lessons, she follows a typical direct instructional pattern:

1. First, she names the skill students are to acquire ("Today, we are going to learn how to graph linear functions using slopes and *y*-intercepts.").
2. Then she explains the skill and, with the aid of an overhead projector, lists each step in the process the students are to follow.
3. She uses at least two examples to demonstrate the skill.
4. She addresses students' questions.
5. She assigns exercises from the textbook for the students to begin in class and complete for homework.
6. She circulates among the students as they work on the exercises, responding to individual questions.
7. The next day, homework is checked and she uses the overhead projector to explain homework exercises with which students said they experienced difficulties.
8. She tests students on the skill.
9. She decides either to reteach or to move to the next lesson.

Maxine and Ron are both 15-year-old students in one of Ms. O'Farrell's geometry classes. Maxine is motivated by a desire to maintain a high grade-point average, which she believes will help her obtain a college scholarship. Ron realizes that with his current grade-point average he has virtually no chance of receiving a scholastic scholarship and, besides, "life after high school" seems like a lifetime from now. Although Ron would like to improve his grades, he's not motivated to work hard on lessons *solely* for grades. He's willing to work only on lessons that appear to be relevant to the life he's living at the moment.

Following her direct instruction formula, Ms. O'Farrell opens a lesson by announcing to the class, "Today, we're going to learn how to compute the lateral surface area of a right cylinder." On an overhead transparency she displays Exhibit 1.1.

She explains, "As you can see by the formula, to find the lateral surface area of a right cylinder you multiply 2π times the radius of the base times the height. Here, let me work an example for you. Suppose the cylinder's height is 20 centimeters and. . . ."

Maxine assiduously follows the step-by-step explanation without bothering to think about why the area can be found by completing the prescribed multiplication or why anyone would ever want to compute the lateral surface area of a right cylinder. After completing the exercises Ms. O'Farrell assigned near the end of the lesson, Maxine has mastered the algorithm for computing lateral surface areas of right cylinders.

Ron, on the other hand, fails to follow Ms. O'Farrell's explanation from the moment she writes out the formula. As she is working through the first example, he is busy thinking to himself, "Just what I wanted to know, lateral surface areas of right cylinders! I don't even know what a wrong cylinder is! Two-pi-*r*-*h*! Who thinks up this stuff? I'd better get this anyway; she's going to quiz us tomorrow." But Ron's heart isn't in the lesson, and by the time he gets his mind-wandering under control and tries to follow the explanation, Ms. O'Farrell is midway through the presentation. He fails to complete the exercises accurately and doesn't acquire the skill as Ms. O'Farrell intended.

Ms. O'Farrell designed and executed a teaching function (T_1) with her students (S) that resulted in certain learning outcomes (L) by planning and conducting the lesson on lateral surface areas of right cylinders. The lesson's effects on Maxine were different from its effects on Ron. Because T_1 is a messy function, its effects are not completely predictable. On another day (one on which Maxine is distracted by an argument she had with a friend or on which,

by chance, Ron realizes that the drums he loves to play are cylindrical), the responses of the two students to the lesson may be at odds with what occurred in Case 1.1.

Although teaching functions is messy, research studies in the areas of mathematics education and cognitive science do provide us with a basis for predicting the learning outcomes of certain types of lessons. The type of instructional strategies Ms. O'Farrell employed tend to:

- Effectively lead self-motivated students (for example, Maxine) to acquire memory-level skills in executing algorithms (Beyer, 1987, pp. 99–105; Good & McCaslin, 1992; Phye, 1986).
- Neglect both comceptual-level understanding of relationships (e.g., why $A = 2\pi rh$) and the ability to apply mathematics to real world situations (Ferinni-Mundy & Graham, 1991; Linn, 1986; von Glasersfeld, 1990).
- Leave the impression that mathematics is a magical "bag of tricks" that students memorize in school (Ball, 1988a; Cangelosi, 1989a).
- Be time-efficient in that explanations and discussions are relatively brief, but time-inefficient in that students are apt to forget the algorithm shortly after the test (Schoenfeld, 1985, pp. 358–360; Yassin, 1992).

The teacher's instructional strategies in Case 1.2 deviate from Ms. O'Farrell's in Case 1.1; consequently, the learning outcomes differ dramatically.

CASE 1.2

Ms. Lowe uses *inquiry* instructional methods (Cangelosi, 1992, pp. 69–115; Joyce, Weil, & Showers, 1992, pp. 107–257; Woolfolk, 1993, pp. 455–456) almost exclusively to teach mathematics to her students. To conduct these lessons, she often follows a relatively complex pattern:

1. She initially confronts students with a perplexing problem, for example, a lesson to lead students to discover how to graph linear functions using slopes and y-intercepts. Ms. Lowe says, "Suppose you just took a job. You want to project how much you will have earned at any point in time after taking the job. How might you picture your predicted earnings from the job?"
2. She raises open-ended questions that lead students to address the problem.
3. The first two phases of the lesson are repeated with two or three more problems exemplifying the usefulness of the mathematical content of Ms. Lowe's lesson.
4. She engages the students in a question-and-discussion session designed to lead students to make mathematical generalizations from their experiences in problem solving.

Exhibit 1.1
Ms. O'Farrell's overhead transparency display

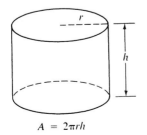

$$A = 2\pi rh$$

5. The students engage in writing and discussion activities designed to stimulate them to formulate a general method for solving any problems of this type in the future.
6. The students summarize their conclusions and articulate their hypotheses.
7. Ms. Lowe assigns exercises and engages students in activities that lead them to test and refine their hypotheses.
8. After assessing how well students can explain and apply their discovery, Ms. Lowe determines whether to reteach or to move to the next lesson.

In one of her geometry classes, Ms. Lowe begins a lesson on the lateral surface areas of right cylinders by telling students, "With the permission of Mr. Duke (the head custodian for the school), I've asked Izar and Elaine to bring in one of the trash barrels that are placed about the school grounds." The two students, Izar and Elaine, stand the barrel up in front of the classroom. Ms. Lowe continues, "Mr. Duke told me he plans to repaint all these barrels. He thought instead of using this drab gray again, he'd try to make them a bit more decorative this time. Yes, Parisa, you have the floor."

Parisa: What has this got to do with us?
Ms. Lowe: Mr. Duke thought you might have some ideas on what colors he should use. Yes, Izar?
Izar: Could we have pictures and stuff drawn on them?
Ms. Lowe: Mr. Duke said each of the three sections of the barrels could be different colors, but nothing fancier than that. He also said he'd let us choose the colors in exchange for providing him with an estimate of the amount of paint he has to buy. If he's going to use colors other than the gray he has now, it's going to be expensive and he doesn't want to buy more than he needs.

Further discussions lead the students to recognize the need to find the lateral surface area of the barrels. No one has a formula for computing it, but Ms. Lowe continues, "We may not know how to figure the area of this barrel, but there are some shapes with areas we can compute. Everyone, please write down the names of three shapes for which you have area formulas." Observing that everyone has written something, she continues, "In the order I call your names, read your lists: Elaine, Mark, Eli, and Norton."

Elaine: Square, rectangle, triangle.
Mark: Rectangle, triangle, and other polygon.
Eli: Same as theirs.
Ms. Lowe: Read them.
Eli: Rectangle, square, triangle.
Norton: Rectangle is the only one I put.
Mark: But a square is a rectangle, so you didn't also need to list a square.
Ms. Lowe: Isn't that also true for this barrel?
Michelle: No, a barrel isn't a type of rectangle.
Ms. Lowe: Hmmm, maybe that's so. I was just thinking about the part of this barrel that needs to be painted.
Izar: Well we said only the outside needs to be painted.

Ms. Lowe: What if we just covered the outside of the barrel with colorful contact paper?
Michelle: That would never hold up.
Ms. Lowe: Yeah, too bad! It's just that seeing our butcher paper over here in the corner gave me that idea. It seemed so simple just to wrap paper around the barrel. Too bad it wouldn't hold up!
Ebony: Ms. Lowe, may I try something with our butcher paper?

Ebony wraps a section of the paper around the barrel, cuts it, unwraps it, and then displays the rectangular shape to the rest of the class. Eyes light up around the room as students begin to understand what Ebony demonstrated: the lateral surface area of the barrel is equivalent to the area of a rectangle whose dimensions can be obtained from the barrel.

The lesson continues with Ms. Lowe playing upon Ebony's discovery to lead students to associate the circumference of the base of a right cylinder with a rectangle's width and the height of the cylinder with the rectangle's length. By the end of the class period, most students understand why the lateral surface area of a barrel is $2\pi rh$.

Over the next two days, Ms. Lowe conducts learning activities that help students apply the formula they discovered to various real-life problems. Almost all of the students gain an understanding of why the formula works and how to decide when to use it to solve real-life problems. Some students, however, do not respond well to the frustration of being confronted with a perplexing problem before being provided with the tools for solving it. Consequently, their attention during the first part of the lesson wavers, and they never feel confident that they ever had the "right" formula. Also, Ms. Lowe never provides enough practice exercises for all students to master the skill of computing with the algorithm.

The teaching function (T_2) that Ms. Lowe designed and executed had different effects on different students. T_2, like Ms. O'Farrell's T_1, is a messy function. But research findings do suggest that the type of instructional strategies Ms. Lowe employed in Case 1.2 tends to:

- Intrinsically motivate students to engage in mathematical learning activities (Ames & Ames, 1984; Brophy, 1986; Cangelosi, 1990a, pp. 21–27; 1993, pp. 141–149).
- Effectively lead students to construct concepts for themselves, discover relationships, and apply mathematics to solve meaningful problems (Cobb, 1988; Goldin, 1990; Schoenfeld, 1992).
- Neglect mastery of algorithmic skills (Beyer, 1987, pp. 124–137; Cooney, Davis, & Henderson, 1983, pp. 174–201; Good, Grouws, & Ebmeier, 1983).

- Leave students with the impression that mathematics is a doable endeavor, discovered and invented by ordinary humans for human purposes (Ball, 1988a; Cangelosi, 1989b; Milosheff, 1992; National Council of Teachers of Mathematics, 1991, pp. 104–109).
- Be time-efficient in that explanations and discussions are relatively time consuming, but time-efficient in that students are apt to retain what they learn over an extended period of time (Joyce, Weil, & Showers, 1992, pp. 141–179; Post & Cramer, 1989; Wittrock, 1992).
- Depend on the teacher's creative use of examples, understanding of the students as individuals, and classroom management strategies (Brown, Cooney, & Jones, 1990; Cangelosi, 1993, pp. 297–303; National Council of Teachers of Mathematics, 1991, pp. 25–44, 144–167).

Of course, as a teacher you will need to design and execute your own teaching functions (T_3, T_4, T_5, . . . , T_k) that (a) combine the more effective features of both Ms. O'Farrell's and Ms. Lowe's approaches, (b) are appropriate for your unique set of students, and (c) match your unique personality and capabilities. Designing and executing successful teaching functions requires you to utilize your expert understanding of your students, pedagogical principles, and mathematics as you carry out the following instructional responsibilities:

- Organize for teaching
- Develop curricula
- Determine learning goals
- Design lessons
- Manage student behavior and the learning environment
- Conduct lessons and engage students in learning activities
- Monitor student progress and assess their achievements

STUDENTS AS AN INDEPENDENT VARIABLE (DOMAIN OF T_i)
Variations Among Students

This book is intended to help you effectively integrate and perform the complex operations inherent in teaching functions. The book began, however, by introducing you to the algebraic functions, f_i for $i =$ 1, 2, 3, 4, that combine some straightforward operations (e.g., squaring x, multiplying by 3, and subtracting 8) on a familiar domain, $\{-3, -.5, 0, .01, \sqrt{3}, 2\}$. Why begin with f_i when the focus is to be T_i?

One thing certain about you is that you've chosen to make teaching mathematics your profession, so it may be assumed that you are attracted to the field of mathematics. Thus, the book opened with a treatise on some familiar algebraic functions in an attempt to use your interest in mathematics to seduce you into thinking about how different instructional approaches influence students in various ways. You, too, need to play on the interests of your students to entice them into doing mathematics. But to accomplish this, you need to learn from them what they consider important.

Students are the independent variable in your teaching functions; you have little, if any, influence over who your students are. Of course, you exert some control when you decide where you will teach (whether you join the faculty of an urban junior high, a suburban middle school, or a rural high school) and you may even express a choice in the courses to which you are assigned (prealgebra, consumer mathematics, or advanced-placement calculus). Historically, however, beginning teachers' options are limited. Typically, first-year teachers plan on teaching only college-preparatory courses, but in most cases they are assigned at least some sections involving what many—but not all—teachers consider the more mundane aspects of mathematics curricula.

The first thing to remember about your students is that each is a unique individual, unlike any other. They range in age from 11 (younger middle school students) to 20 (older high school students). Thus, most are adolescents. However, there is extreme variation among adolescents regarding factors that have an impact on how you should design and execute your teaching functions.

Interest in Mathematics

Adolescents' interest in mathematics ranges from obsessive avoidance to obsessive pursuit. Your students will come to you with a wide variety of interests within those two extremes. Most (i.e., over half) people's interest in mathematics deteriorates between the ages of 8 and 15 (Anderman & Maehr, 1994; Cangelosi, 1984b; Dossey, Mullis, Lindquist, & Chambers, 1988). Consequently, you can expect that most of your students will initially arrive in your classroom with a distaste for the subject. This creates some tension between your interests and theirs. After all, you chose to pursue a career working with mathematics. Most students are not so inclined—at least not until they've benefited from your tutelage. One mathematics teacher's comment reflects the attitude held by some: "Mathematics is beautiful; everyone should enjoy it. I expect my students to like it." You may also think mathematics is beautiful, but you must understand that beauty is in the eye of the beholder. If you expect your students to be interested in mathematics simply because you think they should, you will be disillusioned and will probably fail to provide them with the type of experiences that can eventually build their interest.

Perception of Mathematics

One of the reasons most students' interest in mathematics seems to wane between the ages of 8 and 15 is that their view of mathematics narrows; they no longer see it as a wide range of activities (quantifying, grouping, and ordering) that are an integral part of everyday life but instead view it as an exacting, school-based skill involving manipulating symbols (numerals and geometric representations) (Schoenfeld, 1988). Unfortunately, most mathematics teachers tend to view mathematics as a narrow school-bound sequence of vocabulary and symbol meanings, rules, algorithms, and theorems that are not applicable to the outside interests of adolescents (Brown, Cooney, & Jones, 1990, pp. 648–649; Jesunathadas, 1990).

Aptitude for Reasoning with Abstractions

Consider the exchange between the teacher and the algebra student in Case 1.3.

CASE 1.3 _____

Ms. Cook: Is point three-three-three and so on [.3333 . . .] rational or irrational?

Martin: Irrational.

Ms. Cook: Why?

Martin: Because the 3s go on forever; it's a nonterminating decimal.

Ms Cook: Is 1/3 rational or irrational?

Martin: Rational.

Ms. Cook: Why?

Martin: Because it's the ratio of two integers.

Ms. Cook: What is the decimal equivalent of 1/3?

Martin: .3333 . . . .

Ms. Cook: So is 1/3 equal to .333. . . ?

Martin: Yes.

Ms. Cook: Well, since 1/3 equals .333 . . . and 1/3 is rational, can't we conclude that .333 . . . is rational?

Martin: No, because it doesn't terminate.

Ms. Cook [to herself]: Aggaahh!!!!

_____

Before Ms. Cook's frustration got the best of her, she attempted to lead Martin to recognize the contradiction in his statements. But her strategy depended on Martin being able to reason with abstractions. An abstraction is an intangible such as a number, set, or function that exists in the form of an idea (a concept or generalization), rather than a specific that can be empirically detected—smelled, seen, felt, tasted, or heard. Reasoning about intangibles is an arduous task for some adolescents, but it is readily accomplished by others. Because the study of relations among abstractions is paramount in mathematics, you will have to continually contend with this student variable.

The formal operational stage of Jean Piaget's stages of cognitive development (Pintrich, 1990, pp. 830–831; Stewart & Hafner, 1994, pp. 284–286) is associated with students' abilities to reason with abstractions. Sometimes people try to convert a complex theory into a few simple rules for teaching practice. Piaget's theory for stages of cognitive development has suffered much abuse via the oversimplification that students cannot reason with abstractions until they have matured from Piaget's concrete operational stage into the formal operational stage between the ages of 11 and 15. Consequently, some argue that students are incapable of learning so-called abstract subjects such as algebra prior to age 11, but are perfectly capable of doing so after 15. In truth, many children under the age of 11 successfully reason with abstractions (Baroody, 1989; Battista, 1994; Kouba, 1989), whereas some over 15 struggle tremendously (Shoenfeld, 1985, pp. 11–45).

An oversimplified version of another theory, left and right hemispheric learning (Orlich, Harder, Callahan, Kauchak, & Gibson, 1994, pp. 44–45) suggests that students are either left-brain learners or right-brain learners. Supposedly, left-brain learners have an easier time with mathematics because they are better able to cope with the "cold" logic of abstract reasoning, whereas right-brain learners are more inclined to "warmer" aesthetic pursuits. In truth, mathematics is not the cold and exacting technical endeavor that some purport it to be. Mathematics includes both left-brain functions (logical thinking and calculations) and right-brain functions (sensory patterns and creativity). Thus, the teaching of mathematics needs to provide experiences that appeal to both sides of the brain for all students.

In Case 1.2, Ms. Lowe began the lesson with a concrete operational reasoning task that appealed to students' aesthetic and sensory inclinations by having the students empirically examine the barrel. In a subsequent stage of the lesson, students were challenged with an abstract reasoning task when they attempted to formulate a general rule for finding lateral surface areas of right cylinders.

Perception of What Is Important

Your students are more likely to work eagerly on mathematical tasks that relate to what they consider important than on tasks they perceive as irrelevant to their immediate interests (Brophy, 1986). Thus, you need to capitalize on students' existing values to design lessons that focus on problems that they consider important. But since what is important to one student is not necessarily important to another, how can such lessons be designed for any one group of students? This question is addressed in subsequent chapters.

Experiences upon Which You Can Build

Different students bring different backgrounds to your classroom. Participating in sports, caring for younger children, repairing motors, raising gardens, doing carpentry work, working in stores, traveling, moving from residence to residence, purchasing a motorcycle, planning parties, engaging in debates, conducting science experiments, taking surveys, operating cash registers, applying for jobs, serving in school clubs, dieting, doing charity work, caring for ill family members, cooking, programming computers, playing music, watching television, surfing, driving an automobile, and raising animals are a small sampling of the types of student experiences to which you can relate mathematics. Mr. Pepper considers his students' interests in Case 1.4.

CASE 1.4 ─────────────

Mr. Pepper thinks to himself as he plans on solving first-degree open sentences: "Before demonstrating methods for solving these algebraic sentences, I should first have them analyze some application-level problems. Let's see, what kind of word problems does the textbook offer? Looks as if they involve the mathematics I want to teach, but they're not very motivating for my ninth graders. I'll rewrite them so the mathematics stays the same but the situations are more in line with their interests. Okay, the first one reads:

> An exotic tribe has a rule that the number of guards protecting the tribe must be at least one-tenth the number in the tribe less 50. According to this rule, how many tribespeople can be protected by 40 guards?

"Great! An exotic tribe—just what my students can identify with! To what should I make this relate? Something where one number depends on another. Phil has experience racing dirt bikes. Maybe I could do something with the relation between tire size and power instead of guards and tribespeople. Oh, I've got it! Most of these kids love to go to music concerts—rap, rock, whatever they like. I'll change the guards in the word problem to security people for a concert and the tribespeople to concert goers. I've got to work this out. Okay, here's the problem:

> The number of security guards working at a rock concert depends on the number of people expected to attend. One rule of thumb stipulates that the number of security guards must be at least one-tenth the number of concertgoers less 50. According to the rule, how many people can attend a concert with 40 security guards?

"But I don't know if that rule of thumb is all that realistic. It doesn't make any more sense to me than the one for the exotic tribe. Oh, another brilliant idea! Naomi loves to read those rock magazines. I'll bet she could be our resource person for coming up with the rule. There's bound to be something about that in her magazines. This is perfect! Naomi isn't real fond of mathematics, but this time she can

be the one to provide the formula we use in the word problem. Okay, I'll make this next one relate to something different. Let's see. . ."

─────────────

Prior Mathematical Learning

Look at the first chapters of middle, junior high, and high school mathematics textbooks. Note how each book begins with remedial material that overlaps the content for three or four prior grades. Simple whole-number computational tasks ($138 + 48 = ?$) greet prealgebra students as they open their textbooks. Algebra textbooks begin with scores of exercises such as "Find the value of $(12 - 8) + 3$" or "Show that each number is rational by naming it as the quotient of two integers: $-13, 9.3, 0.06$."

Apparently the authors of these textbooks recognize that having been exposed to mathematical topics in prior courses does not guarantee that those topics were learned by all students. Most of your students will lack some mathematical skill that is prerequisite to what you plan to teach them, but the gaps will vary from student to student. Furthermore, many students, although lacking some skills, may have already acquired an understanding of some advanced topics that you are expecting to introduce.

Communication Skills

Mathematics lessons typically require students to receive messages by listening to the teacher and to one another, and by reading explanations, examples, and directions appearing in textbooks, on visual classroom displays, worksheets, computer screens, and tests, and send messages by speaking, writing, drawing, and entering information in computers or graphing calculators. Schools typically provide students with extensive exposure to lessons targeting general communications skills (reading, writing, and speaking) in language arts courses (English, spelling, and reading). However, communications skills in the language of mathematics are too often blatantly neglected, and many of your students will need you to provide remedial work in many areas, such as:

1. The technical vocabulary of mathematics.
2. How mathematical language differs from conventional languages with respect to precision and structure.
3. Comprehending mathematical text content.
4. Reading shorthand symbols, numerals, and formulas (for example, English narratives normally appear in rectangular arrays to be read row by row from left to right, but as illustrated in Exhibit 1.2, mathematical communications are often meant to be read from the bottom up, right to left, and diagonally.

5. Structuring and linking precise, rigorous mathematical statements.
6. Expressing mathematical arguments.
7. Illustrating mathematical relationships (Cobb, 1988; National Council of Teachers of Mathematics, 1991, pp. 45–54; Nunes, 1992).

Coursework in Other Academic Areas

Real-life problem-solving applications of mathematics are most efficiently taught via mathematics lessons that are integrated with lessons from other disciplines (e.g., social studies, language arts, physical education, and physics) (Romberg & Carpenter, 1986). Integrated curriculum efforts, in which teachers from various disciplines coordinate their lessons so that students apply what they are learning in one class to a problem presented in another, have proven successful [e.g., *Connected Mathematics Project*, *Six Through Eight Mathematics*, and *Interactive Mathematics Project*] (National Science Foundation, 1993, pp. 14–15, 28). Although not all of your mathematics students will necessarily be taking the same courses, some integration is possible whenever you can find a willing collaborator among your colleagues from other disciplines. When you read Chapter 11, you'll note how mathematics teacher Casey Rudd manages to integrate his mathematics curricula with those of other content areas.

Self-Confidence

The effort students are willing to invest in a mathematical task depends not only on the value they recognize in the task, but also on their perception of the likelihood that they will successfully complete the task (Ames & Ames, 1985: National Council of Teachers of Mathematics, 1991, pp. 57–61). Solving problems, discovering relationships, proving theorems, analyzing situations, and interpreting mathematical communications are all cognitive tasks that require students to work through perplexing moments. Those who are not confident in their own mathematical abilities tend to stop working on such tasks as soon as they become perplexed; more confident students tolerate perplexity longer and are more likely to continue with the tasks.

Attitude Toward Learning

Some students view learning tasks as opportunities to acquire new skills and abilities. Others feel that learning tasks present competitive situations in which their existing abilities and skills are challenged. Unlike the latter group, the former are not burdened by the fear that their mistakes will be ridiculed, so they are willing to pursue even perplexing tasks and to learn from their mistakes.

Study Skills

Consider Case 1.5.

CASE 1.5

"Would you show us how to do number 7 from the homework assignment? I couldn't do it," Linda asks Mr. Childress, who responds, "Please write it on the board and we'll think it through together." Linda writes the following:

> When the angle of elevation of the sun is 27°, the shadow of a tree is 75 feet long. What is the height of the tree?

Mr. Childress: Think aloud for us as you begin
Linda: I did it wrong; my answer didn't check with the back of the book.
Mr. Childress: That's okay; just show us what you did. Linda writes:

$$\sin 27° = h/75$$
$$0.45399 = h/75$$
$$h = (75)(0.45399)$$
$$h \approx 34.05 \text{ ft}$$

Exhibit 1.2
Reading mathematical expressions does not proceed in the usual left-to-right, top-to-bottom order.

The expression $\frac{7}{x} - (5 - 3x)^2$ is read in this order:

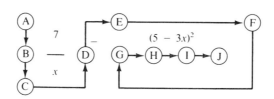

Begin at (A), reading "7," go down to (B) to read "divide by"; then continue down to (C) to read "x" and up to (D) for "subtract." Go over to (E) for "quantity of," up and over to (F) for "square the quantity," down to (G) for "5," right to (H) to "subtract," right to (I) to "three times," and right to (J) for "x."

Linda: I used my calculator so I don't know why it doesn't come out to be 38 feet like the back of the book.

Mr. Childress: Why did you use sine?

Linda: Because that's what you did when you worked one yesterday. I copied it down.

Mr. Childress moves to his computer display station and calls up a picture of a tree he's stored in a graphic file.

Mr. Childress: This is our tree. It casts a shadow how long?

Linda: 75 feet.

Mr. Childress depicts the 75-foot segment on the screen as shown in Exhibit 1.4 and asks, "And what's the angle of elevation of the sun?" Linda says, "27 degrees."

With the computer, Mr. Childress finishes the sketch so it looks like Exhibit 1.3 and asks, "What's the sine of the angle of elevation?"

Linda: Like I wrote, 0.45399.

Mr. Childress: Yes, but I didn't ask my question right. What's our definition of sine?

Linda: Oh, opposite over hypotenuse.

Mr. Childress: Look at the picture on the screen. Is h over 75 opposite over hypotenuse?

Linda: No, in your picture it's opposite over adjacent.

Mr. Childress: And what trigonometric function is opposite over adjacent?

Linda: That's tangent. Oh, so we were supposed to use tangent!

Mr. Childress: Try it.

Linda: But there wasn't any picture to go by so I just did what you did yesterday.

Mr. Childress: Next time, draw a picture.

Linda: I didn't know we were supposed to draw one—not without a computer like you've got.

Linda attempted the homework exercises Mr. Childress assigned, but she seemed to lack some study skills that might have helped her gain more from the experience. She may not know how to study efficiently. Research studies suggest that knowledge of how to study is a skill that varies widely among students and needs to be systematically taught (Weinstein, Goetz, & Alexander, 1988).

Use of Drugs

Inadequate study skills, boredom, lack of confidence, fatigue, hyperactivity, and nonacademic interests are just some of the many factors hindering students' willingness to engage in mathematical learning activities. Being either high or depressed on drugs at school or when trying to study is just one more factor that hinders students' academic work (Cangelosi, 1990a, pp. 64–66). Because it has become so pervasive in so many of today's schools, drug abuse is likely to influence some of your students' engagement in lessons. Information on and suggestions for dealing with drug abuse in schools are now widely available (Cangelosi, 1993, pp. 256–263; Rogers & McMillin, 1989; Towers, 1987).

Home and Social Life

Adolescents are under continual domestic and social pressures. The parenting your students receive ranges from supportive to neglectful, healthy to abusive, and constant to absent. For most students, peer acceptance is of paramount concern (Santrock, 1984, pp. 277–321). Some have friends who encourage their pursuit of mathematics and cooperation with your efforts. Others may perceive that they risk acceptance of those whose friendships they value most by being studious and cooperative with you.

Although it is important that you understand the pressures and influences with which adolescents live, you should keep two things in mind:

- Each student is a unique individual. Do not apply the aggregate results from demographic studies to judge individuals. For example, as a group, Japanese children tend to value academic activities more than western children (Allen, 1988), but that doesn't mean that any particular student from a Japanese family will be more motivated toward mathematics than a student of, say, Native American heritage. Nor will any one student living in an inner-city housing project be any more inclined to abuse drugs than a student from a suburb.
- Unfortunately some students live with disadvantages such as abusive parents or the influence of gangs. However, that does not mean that they cannot control their own behaviors, nor does it imply that you should expect less of them than of students living in an enriched, supportive environment (Cangelosi, 1993, pp. 28–36).

Exhibit 1.3
Mr. Childress' display on the classroom screen

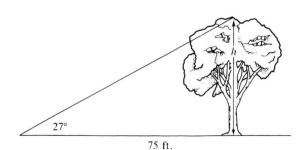

27°

75 ft.

Time and Place Available for Studying Mathematics

Due to differences in home and social life, some students have more time and a better environment for studying mathematics than others. Many students' out-of-class time is dominated by jobs or nonacademic school-sponsored activities such as athletics or service organizations. Understanding restrictions on the time students have for doing mathematics helps you diagnose difficulties and plan assignments. Many students need to be taught how to set priorities, schedule their time, and faithfully complete assignments.

Access to Calculators, Computers, and Other Needed Tools

Technologic tools like computers and graphing calculators are as necessary for mathematical work today as are paper and pencil. Although the *Curriculum and Evaluation Standards for School Mathematics* (National Council of Teachers of Mathematics, 1989a, p. 8), a document explained in Chapter 2, emphasizes the necessity for all students to have access to computers and calculators, the availability of such tools varies considerably from home to home as well as from school to school (Struyk, Cangelosi, & Ehlert, 1993).

Attitude Toward School

Some of your students greet you as their friend, expecting to benefit from the experiences you provide. Others arrive with little regard for how you might help them and view you as an authority figure who interferes with activities they would prefer to be doing. As explained in Chapters 8 and 11, the beginning of a school term is an opportune time to reinforce desirable attitudes and lead students to modify negative attitudes.

Classroom Citizenship

Dealing with uncooperative, disruptive, and off-task student behaviors generally presents teachers, especially beginning teachers, with their most difficult challenges (Doyle, 1986; Steere, 1988, pp. 5–9; Tobin, Tippins, & Gallard, 1994; Weber, 1994). Classroom management strategies that work well with one student don't necessarily work well with others. Some students cooperate with one teacher but present discipline problems for others. How to elicit students' cooperation and keep them on-task and engaged in learning activities is the focus of Chapter 8 and is also dealt with throughout the text.

Special Needs and Students in the Mainstream

Although you may not be a special education teacher, you can expect to have a few students mainstreamed into your mathematics classes whose special needs have been formally identified. Included among the labels are *learning disabled, hearing impaired, hard of hearing, blind, visually handicapped, orthopedically impaired, behaviorally disordered, emotionally handicapped, gifted,* and *multihandicapped* (Lewis & Doorlag, 1991, pp. 49–69). The number of such exceptional students mainstreamed into regular classrooms has increased dramatically since Congress passed the Education for All Handicapped Children Act of 1975 (P.L. 94–142). P.L. 94–142 mandates that free, appropriate public education be available to all handicapped students between the ages of 3 and 18, that they be educated to the maximum extent possible, and that their education take place in the "least restrictive" learning environment. For each handicapped student, an Individualized Education Program (IEP) is to be designed collaboratively by the special education and regular classroom teachers, parents, and the student himself or herself. The IEP is a description of the student's individualized curriculum, including statements of learning goals, prescriptions for educational services related to those goals, timelines for delivery of those services, and delineation of the assessment procedures to be used for placement decisions and evaluations of the program's success. Coolican (1988, p. 216) states:

> It is important to realize that handicapped children are often socially ignored or even ridiculed by their nonhandicapped peers (Sabornie, 1985). Teachers of mainstreamed students should therefore attempt to establish positive attitudes toward the handicapped and to encourage appropriate interactions between their disabled and nondisabled students. For example, students in a class that includes a hearing-impaired child could be taught the manual alphabet (for "finger spelling") and rudimentary sign language. To further reduce social isolation of mainstreamed students, teachers might develop a social skills training program or, if necessary, a self-care program. Such a program could be developed with the assistance of the handicapped student's special education teacher.

Many of the educational needs of handicapped students are similar to the needs of other students in your classroom. As a result of improved identification and placement procedures, emphasis is being directed toward each child's educational characteristics. This could eventually prove to be a useful way of assessing all learners. In addition, the classroom teacher is in a key position to recognize those students who have special needs. A comprehensive diagnosis, however, is not the classroom teacher's responsibility, but that of specialized personnel in the school system. You should be prepared to communicate learners' problems and work cooperatively with the professionals assigned to diagnose disabilities and prescribe treatments.

Besides addressing these students' special needs, you can be assured that your so-called normal students also vary considerably in their abilities to hear, see, perform mental tasks, control their emotions, concentrate, and perform physical tasks. For example, it is estimated that at any one point in time, 25 percent of students with "normal" hearing are suffering a temporary hearing loss (perhaps because of an infection) serious enough to interfere with their ability to follow an oral presentation (Berg, 1987, pp. 22–38).

Cultural Background and Ethnicity

Schools in the United States serve a pluralistic society bestowed with multiethnic, multicultural communities. Your understanding of cultural diversity will serve you well as you develop strategies for motivating students to be on-task and engaged in learning activities. Furthermore, you are hardly in a position to elicit students' cooperation unless you are aware of differences that cause an action or communication to be perceived as a compliment by one subculture and as an insult by another (Boutte & McCormick, 1992; Drake, 1993; Woolfolk, 1993, pp. 154–193).

Personal Values

People who misunderstand the nature of mathematics often think of it as a cold, impersonal subject void of human values. To the contrary, the history of mathematics is filled with interplays among religion, philosophy, politics, psychology, science, and mathematics. See, for example, Barrow's (1992, pp. 178–226) account of the brutal arguments between nineteenth and twentieth century mathematicians Georg Cantor and Leopold Kronecker to make infinities and transfinite arithmetic a legitimate part of mathematics. Furthermore, using mathematics to solve real-life problems raises emotional issues involving politics, human rights, ethics, environmental matters, civic responsibilities, family, and so on. Your students' personal values and beliefs vary tremendously. You may value the pursuit of accurate information (a primary purpose for doing mathematics), whereas some of your students may appreciate fantasy and the defense of existing beliefs more than truth. This is a reality with which you must contend as you design your teaching functions.

STUDENT LEARNING AS A DEPENDENT VARIABLE (RANGE OF T_i)

Teaching functions result in two types of student learning: (a) achievement of stated curriculum objectives, and (b) side effects or extraneous outcomes.

Achievement of Stated Objectives

Case 1.1 alludes to a lesson Ms. O'Farrell conducts to teach her students to compute lateral surface areas of right cylinders. Helping students acquire that skill was the objective of the lesson. Case 1.2 relates a lesson in which Ms. Lowe attempts to help her students achieve two objectives: (1) explain why the lateral surface area of a right cylinder equals $2\pi rh$, and (2) given a real-life problem, determine whether or not computing the lateral surface area of a right cylinder is applicable to solving that problem.

Lessons are designed for the purpose of helping students achieve learning objectives. Each learning objective specifies both a *mathematical content* and an *achievement level*. The mathematical content is the topic about which the student is to learn (for example, definition of rational number, division of two rational numbers expressed in decimal form, graphs of quadratic relations, volume of spheres, proof by mathematical induction, conditional probabilities, convergent sequences, and derivatives of exponential functions). The achievement level is the cognitive or affective behavior students are to display with the content by achieving the objective. For example:

- The content of Ms. O'Farrell's objective in Case 1.1 is *lateral surface areas of right cylinders*. The achievement level is *remembering the steps in an algorithm,* which you'll refer to as "knowledge of process" after studying Chapter 5.
- The content of Ms. Lowe's first objective in Case 1.2 is *lateral surface areas of right cylinders*. The achievement level is *discovering a relationship,* which you'll refer to as "discover a relationship" after studying Chapter 4.
- The content of Ms. Lowe's second objective in Case 1.2 is *lateral surface areas of right cylinders*. The achievement level is *discriminating between problems to which the content applies and those to which it does not* (which you'll refer to as "application" after studying Chapter 6).

How you design a lesson depends on the type of learning objective you intend your students to accomplish. The success of the lesson depends on how well students achieve that objective.

Side Effects or Incidental Outcomes

Besides achieving learning objectives, students are influenced in other, often unanticipated, ways by the experiences orchestrated by mathematics teachers. Some of these side effects or incidental outcomes are desirable; others are undesirable.

Desirable Effects. Consistently engaging in appropriately designed, research-based lessons leads students to the following desirable outcomes:

1. Enjoyment of mathematics.
2. Perception of mathematics as a useful tool that they can creatively apply to enhance their own lives.
3. Development of confidence in their own abilities to work through perplexing problems.
4. Use of systematic thought processes for decision making.
5. Pursuit of careers in mathematics related fields.
6. Increase opportunities for success both within and outside of school.

Undesirable Effects. Unfortunately, the type of teaching that dominates mathematics classrooms in today's schools (Jesunathadas, 1990) tends to produce undesirable side effects, including leaving students with the following impressions:

1. Mathematics is a boring sequence of technical vocabulary, rules, and algorithms to be memorized for the purpose of passing tests in school.
2. It is more important for males to succeed in mathematics that females.

3. Only people with an exceptional aptitude for mathematics can creatively do mathematics.
4. Mathematics is a complex, mystifying subject that was handed down to us by some ancient mystics (from Greek mythology). (See Exhibit 1.4.)

THE MYSTIFICATION OF MATHEMATICS

Did you ever attend a social gathering where it became known that you plan to be a mathematics teacher? If so, you probably heard comments such as, "Math?!! So you're some kind of genius! I was never any good at math!" "Gosh, I avoid every math course possible!" "Math! How can you learn all that stuff? It's impossible for me!" "I can't imagine teaching math! How can you possibly learn to work all those problems? I can't even balance my checkbook!" "Really, mathematics? My roommate is smart too. He does math all the time; I think he's studying to be an accountant."

Exhibit 1.4
Many people confuse the origins of mathematics with ancient Greek mythology.

Why is mathematics commonly thought of as a mystifying subject that is virtually impossible for most people to learn? There are at least four contributing factors: (1) a failure to link mathematics to its historical origins; (2) a failure to comprehend the language of mathematics with its shorthand symbols; (3) the fragmentation of mathematical topics into seemingly disconnected subtopics; and (4) the failure to construct mathematical concepts and discover mathematical relationships for oneself.

Misunderstanding the Historical Foundations of Mathematics

Mathematical vocabulary, symbols, concepts, relations, and algorithms are typically presented in school without reference to their origins. Without an understanding of who, why, when, and where a relationship (for example, the area of circular region = πr^2) was discovered or a convention [for example, $P!$ is a shorthand notation for $P(P-1)(P-2)(P-3)\ldots(1)$] was invented, mathematics is perceived as some sort of magic. Most students' exposure to the origins of mathematics is limited to either a passing mention of ancient Greeks (usually Euclid or Pythagoras) in a geometry course, captioned pictures inserted in textbooks, or a wall poster of a few of the "great *men* of mathematics" (like Carl Friedrich Gauss) who lived many years ago. Some students confuse the ancient Greek mathematicians with the Greek gods they read about in language arts courses. The fact that today mathematics is a living dynamic area for discoveries and inventions by modern and otherwise ordinary people (not only men and not only geniuses) is lost.

Miscomprehension of the Language of Mathematics

A glance through virtually any mathematics textbook reveals shorthand notations and symbols that appear strange to the uninitiated. Exhibit 1.5 contains a relatively minute number of examples. However the meanings of the vocabulary, expressions, or symbols are a mystery to anyone who has not learned the rules for translating them. The following shorthand expression is incomprehensible to those who are unaware of the rules for simplifying (or translating) it:

$$\int_1^2 (2x^3 - 3/x^2)dx$$

But, as you learned from your study of calculus and as illustrated in Exhibit 1.6, the expression simply denotes the whole number 6. Note that the algorithm for simplifying this expression can be boiled down to nothing more than permutations of the four fundamental operations of addition, subtraction, multiplication, and division with whole numbers. Most people do not think of adding, subtracting, multiplying, and dividing whole numbers as difficult, but integrating a function is mystifying to them.

Fragmentation of Mathematical Topics

The number of topics listed in the table of contents of most mathematics textbooks appears overwhelming. Examine the list from a prealgebra textbook (see, e.g., Lowry, OcKega, & Rucker, 1992) that appears in Exhibit 1.7. At first glance there appears to be a plethora of concepts to be learned. But a more careful examination reveals that only a few concepts are introduced and that much of the content involves different ways of expressing and relating those concepts. For example, Chapters 1 and 2 focus on decimals, Chapters 6 and 7 on fractions, and Chapter 9 on ratio, proportion, and percent. Typically, students perceive these three topics as if each is a concept unrelated to the other two (Cangelosi, 1989b). However, in reality, decimals, fractions, and percents are simply three different ways of expressing *one* concept, namely, rational numbers.

Exhibit 1.5
A sample of conventional mathematical shorthand notations.

$\sqrt{a}$, or $a^{1/2}$ means "The nonnegative number whose square is a."

$A \cap B = \varnothing$ means "Sets A and B have no elements in common."

$\sum_{i=3}^{6} (i^2 - 4)$ means "$(3^2 - 4) + (4^2 - 4) + (5^2 - 4) + (6^2 - 4)$."

$\prod_{i=3}^{6} (6 + i)$ means "$(6 + 1)(6 + 2)(6 + 3)(6 + 4)(6 + 5)(6 + 6)$."

$\forall$ means "for each," or "for every."

$\exists$ means "there exist."

Exhibit 1.6
An algorithm for integrating a function reduces to four fundamental operations with whole numbers.

$$\int_1^2 \left(2x^3 - \frac{3}{x^2}\right)dx$$

$$=\int_1^2 \left(2x^3 - 3x^{-2}\right)dx$$

$$= 2\int_1^2 x^3\,dx - 3\int_1^2 x^{-2}\,dx$$

$$= 2\left(\frac{x^4}{4}\right)\Big|_1^2 - 3\left(\frac{x^{-1}}{-1}\right)\Big|_1^2$$

$$= 2\left(\frac{16}{4} - \frac{1}{4}\right) - 3\left(\frac{2^{-1}}{-1} - \frac{1}{-1}\right)$$

$$= 2\left(4 - \frac{1}{4}\right) - 3\left(-\frac{1}{2} + 1\right)$$

$$= 6$$

Redundancy of expressions and multiple methods of reaching the same results are ubiquitous in mathematics. Virtually everything in the field of calculus revolves around only one concept: limits. Yet a typical sequence of college calculus courses requires students to read between 750 and 1200 textbook pages. Fortunately, things are changing as the calculus-reform movement toward a "leaner and livelier" calculus flies in the face of that tradition (Cole, 1993; Culotta, 1993; Rowley, 1995).

Failure to Construct Concepts and Discover Relationships for Oneself

Concepts such as rational numbers and relationships such as the product of two negative integers is positive, are presented in the most commonly conducted type of mathematics lesson (for example, Ms. O'Farrell's in Case 1.1) as ideas and facts without providing students with the experiences that lead them to construct concepts or understand why the relationships exists (Post & Cramer, 1989). Mathematics will not be meaningful to students unless they develop certain key concepts in their own minds and discover key relationships for themselves (Cooper, 1993; Koehler & Grouws, 1992).

DEMYSTIFYING MATHEMATICS
Human Discoveries and Human Inventions

From Where Does Mathematics Come? Mathematics seems far less mystifying once one understands that it originates with mortal, mistake-prone human beings attempting to solve their problems and explain the world in which they live. For example:

- The Greek mathematician Archimedes (287 B.C.–212 B.C.) invented methods of experimenting with physical models for the purpose of discovering relationships. For example, to find the area or volume of a figure, he would cut up a model of the figure into a great number of thin, parallel, planar strips and hang the pieces at one end of a large lever in such a way as to be in equilibrium with a figure whose content and centroid are known. This method of equilibrium discovered relationships that lead to some of today's familiar formulas (such as that for surface area and volume of a sphere). To demonstrate the validity of formulas he discovered through equilibrium and other experimental methods, Archimedes invented the cumbersome, indirect method of exhaustion based upon ideas that centuries later became fundamental to the development of integral calculus. Much of Archimedes' work was motivated by the need to solve real-world problems of his times (for example, the development of weaponry during the siege of his home state of Syracuse by Roman armies) (Aaboe, 1964, pp. 73–99; Eves, 1983b, pp. 83–95).

- Amundson (1989) provides the following account of the origins of expressing ratios as percents:

  Percent has been used since the end of the fifteenth century in business problems such as computing interest, profit, and taxes. However, the idea had its origin much earlier. When the Roman emperor Augustus levied a tax on all goods sold at auction, *centesima rerum venalium,* the rate was 1/100. Other Roman taxes were 1/20 on every freed slave and 1/25 on every slave sold. Without recognizing percentages as such, they used fractions easily reduced to hundredths.

  In the Middle Ages, as larger denominations of money came to be used, 100 became a common base for computation. Italian manuscripts of the fifteenth century contained such expressions as "20 p 100," "x p cento," and "vi p c°" to indicate 20 percent, 10 percent, and 6 percent. When commercial arithmetic appeared near the end of the century, use of percent was well established. For example, Giorgio Chiarino (1481) used "xx.per .c." for 20 percent and "viii in x perceto" for 8 to 10 percent. During the sixteenth and seventeenth centuries, percent was used freely for computing profit, loss, and interest.

Exhibit 1.7.
Table of contents of *Heath Pre-Algebra*
Source: *Health Pre-Algebra* by D.W. Lowry, E.C. OcKenga, and W.E. Rucker, 1992. Copyright 1992 by D.C. Health. Copied with permission.

Exhibit 1.7
Continued

Exhibit 1.7
Continued

The percent sign, %, probably evolved from a symbol introduced in an anonymous Italian manuscript of 1425. Instead of "per 100," "P 100," or "P cento," which were common at the time, this author used "P ℅." By about 1650, the ℅ had become ÷ , so "per ÷ " was often used. Finally, the "per" was dropped, leaving ÷ or %.

- In 1984, Narendra Karmarker formulated a new algorithm for linear programming that has the potential of obtaining the most efficient solutions for optimizing systems of thousands of equations in thousands of unknowns (Peterson, 1988, pp. 11–112).

- How to evaluate the validity and estimate the error of achievement and aptitude tests used in schools is a problem that has been pursued since 1845, when Horace Mann attempted to defend written examinations for groups of students (Strom, 1969, pp. 270–345). Developments in statistical and numerical analytical models for the purpose of assessing the validities and reliabilities of mental measurements have advanced from E. L. Thorndike's (1904) initial work and continue feverishly today [see, for example, Keeves (1988) or any recent issue of *Journal of Educational Measurement*].

- In 1985, while exploring figures with the aid of a computer, Rob Stringer, a tenth grader, discovered a new theorem in Euclidean geometry for partitioning the interior of a triangle into five regions of equal area (Kidder, 1985).

- Several days after Ms. Lowe conducted the lesson on lateral surface area of a right cylinder alluded to in Case 1.2, her students figured out how to compute the surface area of a fish bowl that one student, Norton, had brought to class. The shape is depicted in Exhibit 1.8. Over the course of the following week, they discovered relationships that they used to invent the following formula for estimating the surface area of any size figure with the shape of that fish bowl; they named the figure a "Norton":

Area of a Norton = $2\pi(2s^2 + 2sw - t^2)$ where

s = the radius of one of the circled side panels

w = the width of one of the curved sides

t = the radius of the opening at the top

- About 1637, the French jurist and mathematician Pierre de Fermat wrote in the margin of a copy of Diophantus' *Arithmetic* that he had a "truly marvelous" proof that the equation $x^n + y^n = z^n$ has no solution in positive integers for any integer $n > 2$. Unfortunately, the margin was too narrow to contain the proof. Since then, professional number theorists and amateurs alike have struggled unsuccessfully to prove what is now known as "Fermat's last theorem." Calling Fermat's proposition a theorem was misleading because, although the proposition appears to be true, today's number theorists and historians of mathematics generally doubt that Fermat ever formulated a valid proof. In 1993, Andrew Wiles, a British mathematician on the Princeton University faculty, announced that he had developed a possible proof of the intriguing proposition. Wiles and other mathematicians continue to diagnose and repair holes in the logic of the "proof." While only professional mathematicians are aware of the vast majority of mathematical discoveries and inventions, the debate over Fermat's last theorem is routinely reported in publications for general consumption (Devlin, 1994).

- Allison is working hard to earn and save enough money to buy a car in two years when she turns 18. To help her determine the best buy for her needs, budget, and desires, she designs a mathematical function for assessing the value of cars available. Her function accepts a number of variables (size, gas mileage, age, appearance, extra features, horsepower, and guarantee) weighted according to importance to her and yields a value-to-cost ratio. She writes a computer program to execute the function.

New mathematical discoveries and inventions are being made today at a rate far exceeding any time in the past. Vos Savant (1993, pp. 32–33) estimated that in recent years nearly 200,000 formal theorems per year are published in mathematics research journals.

Mathematical Discoveries.   Concepts—areas of figures, whole numbers, ratios, angles, finite sets, circles, and irrational numbers—and relationships—the ratio of the circumference of any circle to its diameter is a little greater than 3; ($x \in$ {reals} $\ni 0 < x < 1$) $\Rightarrow (x^2 < x)$; $17 \div 4 = 4.25$; $\lim_{x \to 3}(x^2 - 9)/(x - 3) =$

Exhibit 1.8
A Norton.

6—exist in our world. One goal of doing mathematics is to discover such concepts and relationships so that we can better control our existence. Archimedes' discovery of a relationship between the radius of a sphere and its volume provided him with insights he used in the design of weapons. Ms. Lowe's students discovered that they needed to make only three measurements to calculate the area of a Norton. Mathematical discoveries can be explained via logic and reasoning. From your study of Chapters 3 through 5, you will understand how a mathematical discovery should be taught differently from a mathematical invention.

Mathematical Inventions. Methods (step-by-step algorithmic procedures), conventions (criteria for a valid proof), and mathematical language are inventions. Archimedes invented his method of equilibrium for discovering relationships about areas and volumes. Ms. Lowe's students discovered the relationship area of a Norton $= 2\pi(2s^2 + 2sw - t^2)$ after inventing the name for any figure shaped like Norton's fish bowl. Generally speaking, invented methods and conventions, unlike discoveries, need to be remembered. Understanding why a method (for example, an algorithm for using the quadratic formula to solve quadratic equations) works, requires discovery and reasoning, but knowing how to execute it taxes primarily the memory.

Teaching Comprehension of Mathematical Language

Communications within any specialty field (chemistry, carpentry, aeronautics, or mathematics) depend on three types of vocabulary:

1. *General-usage* terms are words and symbols with conventional meanings listed in standard dictionaries and understood by people both within and outside the specialty. With regard to mathematics, "friend," "red," and "horse" are examples.
2. *Special-usage* terms consist of words and symbols from the general vocabulary whose meaning changes when used in the context of the discipline or specialty. With respect to mathematics, "field," "union," "derivative," "imaginary" and "power" are examples.
3. *Technical-usage* terms consist of words and symbols that have meaning only within the context of the discipline or specialty. With respect to mathematics, "cosine," "polyhedron," and "vector space" are examples.

Both special- and technical-usage terms hinder communications within any field—welding, electronics, football, or mathematics—until the contextual meaning of those terms is understood. Imagine how mystifying football would seem to anyone who had never been taught that a *clip* is neither something done with scissors nor a device that holds objects in place.

Besides its special and technical vocabulary, the nuances of reading mathematics require special attention if students are to derive meaning from their textbooks. Much of the mystery associated with mathematics evaporates when research-based methods for teaching comprehension of its language are incorporated in mathematical lessons (Guzzetti, Snyder, Glass, & Gamas, 1993; Santa & Alvermann, 1991). Strategies for teaching students to comprehend mathematical language are explained in Chapter 5.

Connecting and Integrating Mathematical Topics

The popularity of precision teaching, direct instruction, and mastery learning (Bowden, 1993; Hunter, 1982; Joyce, Weil, & Showers, 1992, pp. 299–323) have encouraged teachers and curriculum designers to present topics in small, fragmented segments with easier skills preceding those more difficult to learn. Some textbooks, for example, explain multiplication of fractions before addition of fractions. Presumably, multiplication is treated first because the algorithm is simpler than that for addition, in which one must bother with finding common denominators. When the two are presented as unrelated algorithms, remembering one tends to interfere with—rather than enhance—the learning of the other (Chance, 1988, pp. 205–238). Consequently, the following error pattern is likely to emerge in representative samples of students' work (Ashlock, 1990):

Seventh grader:

$$\frac{17}{10} + \frac{4}{7} = \frac{21}{17}$$

Ninth grader:

$$\frac{x+1}{x-1} + \frac{3}{x+7} = \frac{x+4}{2x+6}$$

If addition of fractions is treated first and multiplication is then presented simply as a special case of addition, students are more likely to relate the two so that the learning of one enhances the learning of the other. Methods for connecting and integrating topics so that students have fewer concepts and relationships with which to contend are explained and illustrated throughout this book. But to give you some semblance of the idea, consider Case 1.6.

CASE 1.6

Mr. Sanchez has just used direct instructional methods to develop his algebra students' skills in adding two polynomial fractions by the method used in the following example:

$$\frac{x-9}{4} + \frac{2x+3}{x-5}$$

$$= \frac{(x-9)(x-5)}{(4)(x-5)} + \frac{(2x+3)(4)}{(4)(x-5)}$$

$$= \frac{(x-9)(x-5) + (2x+3)(4)}{(4)(x-5)}$$

$$= \frac{(x^2 - 14x + 45) + (8x + 12)}{4x - 20}$$

$$= \frac{x^2 - 6x + 57}{4x - 20}$$

Now, to introduce multiplication of polynomial fractions, he tells his class, "Consider *multiplying* these two numbers." He writes on the board;

$$\frac{2x-1}{4} \cdot \frac{4}{x-2}$$

He continues, "Since we already know how to add polynomial fractions, let's turn this into an addition problem. Multiplication is repeated addition, so we can write the following:"

$$\frac{2x-1}{x+3} \cdot \frac{4}{x-2} =$$

$$\underbrace{\frac{2x-1}{x+3} + \frac{2x-1}{x+3} + \frac{2x-1}{x+3} + \cdots + \frac{2x-1}{x+3}}_{\frac{4}{x-2}\ \text{times}}$$

Mr. Sanchez: But $4/(x-2)$ times doesn't make a lot of sense to everyone. So, let's rework what we've done to this point with a constant in place of x. Pick an odd whole number for us, Gretchen.

Gretchen: 7.

Mr. Sanchez adds to the illustration on the board:

$$\underbrace{\frac{2(7)-1}{7+3} + \frac{2(7)-1}{7+3} + \frac{2(7)-1}{7+3} + \cdots + \frac{2(7)-1}{7+3}}_{\frac{4}{7-2}\ \text{times}}$$

$$\underbrace{\frac{13}{10} + \frac{13}{10} + \frac{13}{10} + \cdots + \frac{13}{10}}_{\frac{4}{5}\ \text{times}}$$

Mr. Sanchez: I know what adding 13/10 to itself 4 times means, but what in the world does adding 13/10 to itself 4/5 times mean? Cam-Loi.

Cam-Loi: You add 1/5 of 13/10 four times itself.

Mr. Sanchez: Oh! So you mean . . .

He writes,

$$\left[\frac{13}{10} \div 5\right] + \left[\frac{13}{10} \div 5\right] + \left[\frac{13}{10} \div 5\right] + \left[\frac{13}{10} \div 5\right]$$

$$= \frac{13}{50} + \frac{13}{50} + \frac{13}{50} + \frac{13}{50}$$

$$= \frac{(13 + 13 + 13 + 13)}{50} = \frac{(13)(4)}{50} = \frac{52}{50}$$

Mr. Sanchez: Now, let's use the same process to work out an answer in variable form.

Together, they complete the following:

$$\frac{2x-1}{x+3} \cdot \frac{4}{x-2} =$$

$$\underbrace{\frac{2x-1}{x+3} + \frac{2x-1}{x+3} + \frac{2x-1}{x+3} + \cdots + \frac{2x-1}{x+3}}_{\frac{4}{x-2}\ \text{times}}$$

Which is,

$$\left[\frac{2x-1}{x+3} \div (x-2)\right](4)$$

Or simply,

$$= \frac{(2x-1)(4)}{(x+3)(x-2)} = \frac{8x-4}{x^2+x-6}$$

Mr. Sanchez: By the way, what is $(8x-4)/(x^2+x-6)$ if x is 7?

The lesson continues with the rule being specifically stated and practice exercises assigned.

Leading Students to Discover and Invent Mathematics

Mr. Sanchez in Case 1.6, like Ms. Lowe in Case 1.2, did not simply tell students a rule (for multiplying polynomial fractions or for computing lateral surface areas of right cylinders). Students need to engage in Archimedean-type reasoning if concepts, relationships, rules, and algorithms are to appear intelligible rather than as some sort of "other world" magic (Schoenfeld, 1985, 1989). Most people who remember the following rules after being told them in school have no idea as to why they work:

- $\frac{a}{b} \times \frac{c}{d} = \frac{ac}{bd}$ $\forall\, a, b, c, d \in$ {reals} such that $b \neq 0$ and $d \neq 0$.
- The product of two negative integers is positive.
- If a function f is integrable on the interval $[a, b]$ and is such that $D_xF(x) = f(x)$ for each $x \in (a, b)$, then

$$\int_a^b f(x)dx = F(b) - F(a)$$

Being required to memorize and then use rules that work for reasons that are not understood adds to the mystery of mathematics. When you read Chapter 2, you'll become acquainted with Case 2.4, in which Mr. Cocora's lesson leads his students to discover for themselves why the product of two negative integers is positive. Such lessons tend to demystify mathematics.

MONITORING YOUR OWN ATTITUDES

As long as school mathematics is divorced from the present, real worlds of students, remains couched in a language that is not specifically taught, and students do not discover and invent mathematics for themselves, mathematics will continue to be perceived as a boring, mystifying subject to be understood only by extraordinary people. As long as that perception is widespread, you and I can continue to enjoy reputations as "extraordinary" people who know something most people don't. If the teaching functions you design and conduct for students are intended to perpetuate that myth, you will spend more time defending your mathematical expertise than enjoying your students' development into creative users of mathematics. To avoid that trap born of the insecurities we all suffer, routinely check your motives for teaching the way you do.

TRANSITIONAL ACTIVITIES FROM CHAPTER 1 TO CHAPTER 2 _____

The transitional activities from one chapter to the next are intended to (a) help you evaluate your achievement of the chapter's objectives so that you can identify your areas of proficiency and the topics you need to review, (b) reinforce and extend what you've learned from the chapter, and (c) set the stage for your work in the next chapter. Another purpose is to encourage you to articulate your thoughts about teaching mathematics in both written and oral discourse. Understanding is enhanced through such activities (Connolly & Vilardi, 1989; Santa & Havens, 1991).

Following are the transitional activities from Chapter 1 to Chapter 2.

1. Observe a mathematics class with a colleague who is either a preservice or inservice mathematics teacher. Independent of one another, you and your partner are to (a) select two students on whom you will focus your attention, (b) describe the activities within the classroom and the students' apparent involvement in those activities, and (c) assess for each of the two students how you think the activities affected her or his abilities with and attitudes about mathematics. Distinguish activities that were the result of the teacher using direct instructional strategies from those that resulted from the teacher using inquiry instructional strategies. Also distinguish each student's achievement of objectives targeted by the teacher from side effects. Report your findings in writing and exchange your report with that of your partner. Compare the two reports and discuss observed differences in the two students that might have influenced them to respond differently to the learning activities.

2. Look over a mathematics textbook currently being used in a middle, junior high, or high school. Select any two topics and examine how the book presents each. Label aspects of each topic as to whether they originated as a discovery or invention. For example, here's how I labeled some aspects of two topics from the text whose table of contents appears in Exhibit 1.9:

Topic: Formula for perimeter

- The concept *perimeter* exists in nature and was discovered by people. The name for that concept, "perimeter," is an invented convention.
- The following method of depicting the dimensions of a rectangle is an invention:

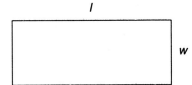

- The concepts rectangle, length, and width are discoveries. Their names, "rectangle," "length," and "width," are inventions.
- The relationship $P = 2l + 2w$ is a discovery, but the expression of that relationship is an invention.

Topic: Graphing equations

- The *Cartesian plane* is an invention for illustrating relations that are discovered.
- The *procedure for graphing a linear equation* is an invention.

- The fact that the graph of any linear equation expressed as $ax + by = c$, where a, b, and c are real constants and x and y are real variables, in a line is a discovery.

Now write a brief paragraph describing one way the two topics are related. For example, here's what I wrote for the two topics I chose:

> The perimeter of a rectangle is dependent on two variables: length and width. One type of problem that the formula can be used to solve involves determining the possible dimensions of a rectangle with a given perimeter (for example, in the case of a fixed amount of fencing available for a garden). For such situations the perimeter formula is of the form $ax + by = c$, where c is the given perimeter and $a = b = 2$. Thus, the possibilities for the length and width can be illustrated via the graph of a linear equation.

3. Interview an adolescent student and ask the following questions:
   a. If it were not a required subject, would you choose to study mathematics?
   b. Is mathematics more or less interesting than other school subjects you take? Why?
   c. Is mathematics more or less difficult to learn than other school subjects? Why?
   d. From where do you think the mathematics we study in school comes? Explain why you believe what you just told me.
   e. What is the most interesting thing about learning mathematics?
   f. What is the most boring thing about learning mathematics?
   g. What is the easiest thing about learning mathematics?
   h. What is the hardest thing about learning mathematics?
   i. How often and for what reasons do you use mathematics outside of school?
   j. Do you read your mathematics textbook any differently than you read any of your other textbooks? Explain.
   k. Do you have a routine for doing homework? Describe when, where, and how you completed your last mathematics homework assignment.
   l. How many of your friends really like to do mathematics? How many of your friends really hate doing mathematics?

Record the responses from the interview, and if you obtain the student's permission to share the answers, compare the responses you got to those of a colleague who completes the experiment with another student.

4. Following are two passages, one by Stewart (1992b, pp. 9–10), the other by Fowler (1994, p. 12). Read one of the passages yourself and have a colleague read the other. When you have finished, summarize what you read for your colleague and have your colleague summarize the other selection for you. Discuss strategies for narrowing the gap between "schoolmath" and "real mathematics."

Stewart's passage:

One of the biggest problems of mathematics is to explain to everyone else what it is all about. The technical trappings of the subject, its symbolism and formality, its baffling terminology, its apparent delight in lengthy calculations: these tend to obscure its real nature. A musician would be horrified if his art were to be summed up as "a lot of tadpoles drawn on a row of lines"; but that's all that the untrained eye can see in a page of sheet music. The grandeur, the agony, the flights of lyricism and discords of despair: to discern them among the tadpoles is no mean task. They are present, but only in coded form. In the same way, the symbolism of mathematics is merely its coded form, not its substance. It too has its grandeur, agony, and flights of lyricism. However, there is a difference. Even a casual listener can enjoy a piece of music. It is only the performers who are required to understand the antics of the tadpoles. Music has an immediate appeal to almost everybody. But the nearest thing I can think of to a mathematical performance is the Renaissance tournament, where leading mathematicians did public battle on each other's problems. The idea might profitably be revived, but its appeal is more that of wrestling than of music.

Music can be appreciated from several points of view: the listener, the performer, and the composer. In mathematics there is nothing analogous to the listener; and even if there were, it would be the composer, rather than the performer, that would interest him. It is the creation of new mathematics, rather its mundane practice, that is interesting. Mathematics is not about symbols and calculations. These are just tools of the trade—quavers and crotches and five-finger exercises. Mathematics is about *ideas*. In particular, it is about the way that different ideas relate to each other. If certain information is known, what else must necessarily follow? The aim of mathematics is to understand such questions by stripping away the inessentials and penetrating to the core of the problem. It is about understanding why an answer is possible at all, and why it takes the form that it does. Good mathematics has an air of economy and an element of surprise. But, above all, it has *significance*.

Fowlers' passage:

What is mathematics? The answer you will get to this question depends on whom you ask. What most people in the United States have experienced is not mathematics—it is not even an elementary or student version of mathematics. It is an entirely different subject—one that could be called "schoolmath." Schoolmath has its own terminology. The rational numbers between 0 and 1 are called The Fractions. The multiplicative inverses of these numbers are called The Improper Fractions. Students are taught that the Improper Fractions exist in a sort of unstable equilibrium and should always be reduced to Mixed Numbers. [An article by Hassler Whitney (1987) got me thinking of this.]

Schoolmath has its own protocol ranging from the Story Problem to the Two-Column Proof, the latter taught in a course called Geometry. And schoolmath has its own set of beliefs about the working world—for example, beliefs about how people in all professions use schoolmath to solve problems. A typical belief is that carpenters spend a great deal of time sawing long boards into many short boards, and must therefore be skilled at dividing one mixed number by another. The truth about carpenters is that their work requires highly developed spatial visualization skills—skills they don't get from schoolmath at any grade level, and certainly not Geometry. The cognitive psychologist Robert Schank (1987) compiled a collection of similar beliefs in an article titled "Let's Eliminate Math from Schools."

Although many people survive schoolmath and may even become mathematicians, most people end up—as Keith Devlin (1993) has pointed out in an article in the *Notices of AMS*—thinking of what they studied as "mathematics."

Is schoolmath a necessary step to learning mathematics? No. In fact, schoolmath prevents most people from doing mathematics in any real way, just as contrived "schoolmusic" pieces discourage most people from being musicians. During the period 1962–72 in the U.S.A., mathematicians and some mathematics educators attempted to replace schoolmath with a version of mathematics that was generally called "new math." This did not work for several reasons; in fact, it inspired a "back-to-basics" movement that returned to schoolmath with a vengeance.

In 1972, Seymour Papert introduced Logo, and argued in a paper called "Teaching Children To Be Mathematicians Versus Teaching About Mathematics" that children could be mathematicians in an authentic sense, just as children could be artists or musicians. Papert was not talking about prodigies. His attempt was not to produce little Bourbakists, as many of the new math people had seemed inclined to do, nor was it to set up phony "discovery" situations where children

somehow always came to the conclusion the teacher had previously prepared. Papert used the example of a child trying to construct a Logo procedure for some form that the child wanted the turtle to draw, such as a "squiral," and argued that children engaged in such activities were doing mathematics. In some cases, Logo is now taught as Papert intended. In other cases, teachers are suggesting that Logo be replaced by a "better drawing program," which suggests that the original purposes for Logo were not universally understood.

The mathematics reform movement, whose constitutional document is the NCTM *Curriculum and Evaluation Standards* (NCTM, 1989a), offers a rational plan for evolving from schoolmath, first to better schoolmath, and eventually to a version of real mathematics. This plan is, in fact, the official agenda for mathematics education.

5. In preparation for your work with Chapter 2, discuss the following questions with two or more of your colleagues:

   a. Who controls the design of mathematics curricula?

   b. In what ways should the lessons you, as a mathematics teacher, design and conduct differ from the lessons you experienced as a student? In what ways should they be the same?

   c. What is the NCTM *Curriculum and Evaluation Standards* alluded to in Stewart's passage? How would a mathematics curriculum designed in harmony with these standards differ from a traditional mathematics curriculum? How would it be the same?

   d. How have advances in instructional technology (including graphing calculators and computer-enhanced instruction) influenced mathematics curricula? How should it influence mathematics curricula? How will it?

   e. What do you need to do to prepare yourself to design and activate teaching functions that demystify mathematics for students? (By this we mean to teach in a way that leads students to (a) link mathematics to its historical origins, (b) comprehend the language of mathematics, (c) connect and integrate mathematical topics, and (d) construct mathematical concepts and discover mathematical relationships for themselves.)

2

Developing Mathematics Curricula

This chapter focuses attention on your impact on curricula, the discrepancy between traditional and research-based curricula, and ideas of how you might go about developing curricula, specifically, chapter 2 is designed to help you:

1. Define *"curriculum"* and *"curriculum guidelines"* and explain the relationship among school, course, mathematics, school-district, and state-level curricula.
2. Describe how teachers develop and control curricula as they design and conduct lessons.
3. Explain the differences between (a) a curriculum based on the view that students should learn mathematics for the purpose of learning more mathematics, and (b) a curriculum based on the view that students should learn mathematics for the purpose of solving real-life problems.
4. Describe a mathematics curriculum that is based on the NCTM *Standards* and contrast it to a more traditionally based mathematics curriculum.
5. Define *"teaching unit,"* explain the interrelationships among the components of a teaching unit, and describe how a course is composed of a sequence of teaching units.

A CURRICULUM

Many teachers, instructional supervisors, and school administrators perceive a curriculum as "the textbook series adopted, mandated state or local curriculum guides, and/or content and skills appearing on mandated tests" (Zumwalt, 1989, p. 174). Definitions range from that very narrow view to the broad, all-encompassing view forwarded by Brubaker (1982, p. 2) that the "curriculum is defined as what persons experience in a setting. This includes all the interactions among persons as well as the interactions between persons and their physical environment."

Herein, the meaning of "curriculum" falls between those two extremes (Cangelosi, 1991, pp. 135–136):

- A *school curriculum* is a system of the planned experiences—coursework, school-sponsored social functions, and contacts with school-supported services designed to educate students.
- A *course curriculum* is a sequence of teaching units designed to provide students with experi-

ences that help them achieve specified learning goals. A *teaching unit* consists of (a) a learning goal defined by a set of specific objectives, (b) a planned sequence of lessons, each consisting of learning activities designed to lead students to achieve specific objectives, (c) mechanisms for monitoring student progress and utilizing feedback to guide lessons, and (d) summative evaluation of student achievement of the learning goal.

- A *mathematics curriculum* is a sequence of mathematics courses, plus any other school-sponsored functions for the purpose of furthering students' achievement with and attitudes about mathematics. This definition is consistent with the one from the NCTM's *Curriculum and Evaluation Standards for School Mathematics:* "A curriculum is an operational plan for instruction that details what mathematics students need to know, how students are to achieve the identified curricular goals, what teachers are to do to help students develop their mathematical knowledge, and the context in which learning and teaching occur" (NCTM, 1989a, p. 1).

- A *school district curriculum* is the set of all school curricula within that school district.
- A *state-level curriculum* is the set of all school district curricula within a state.

State-level, district-level, school-level, and mathematics curricula guidelines are articulated in documents housed in the files of virtually every school. The consistency between official curricula guidelines and actual school curricula varies considerably (Goodlad & Su, 1992). Obviously, a school's curriculum can be no more in line with official guidelines than the composite of the course curricula developed by its teachers.

Because mathematics is widely misunderstood to be a linear sequence of skills to be mastered one at a time in a fixed order, some people think teaching mathematics is a matter of following a prescribed curriculum guide or mathematics textbook. In reality, there are three reasons you must creatively develop curricula to succeed as a mathematics teacher. First of all, state-level and district-level guidelines typically list objectives for mathematics courses (see Appendix A for an excerpt from the Utah curriculum guidelines relative to elementary algebra), but leave the responsibility of designing lessons for achieving those objectives up to individual teachers. Textbooks present information and exercises on mathematical topics. However, each teacher needs to select, supplement, complement, and organize text content so that the objectives listed in curriculum guidelines are addressed. Furthermore, the teacher should tailor lessons to the unique characteristics of her or his students.

Second, although understanding of one mathematical topic (for example, solving first-degree equations) is requisite to the understanding of another (solving quadratic equations), there is no fixed linear sequence that is optimal for all groups of students. Effective teaching requires teachers to arrange topics in response to feedback on their students' progress, diagnoses of the students' needs, and the students' interests (National Council of Teachers of Mathematics, 1991, pp. 110–119; Romberg, 1992).

Third, the design and how you conduct lessons usually influences what your students learn about mathematics more than which mathematical topics are addressed in the lessons. Compare Cases 2.1, 2.2, 2.3, and 2.4 with each other.

CASE 2.1

Mr. Jackson's algebra students have learned to solve quadratic equations by factoring, providing the left side of the equation in standard form can be factored easily (e.g., $x^2 - 6x - 16 = 0$). To teach them how to solve any quadratic equation (for example, $3x^2 + 5x + 1 = 0$), he introduces the quadratic formula by displaying it on an overhead transparency and saying, "Here is a formula for finding the solution of any quadratic equation. For example, suppose we want to solve for $3x^2 + 2 = 7$. Watch how much easier it is to use the formula than to try to factor the polynomial. First, we rewrite the equation in standard form, and then. . . ."

Mr. Jackson continues, working through several examples, and then assigning some exercises in which the students practice using the formula.

CASE 2.2

Ms. Youklic's algebra students have learned to solve quadratic equations by factoring, providing the left side of the equation in standard form can be factored easily (e.g., $x^2 - 12x + 32 = 0$). She wants to teach them to solve any quadratic equation (e.g., $x^2 + 6x + 4 = 0$) using the quadratic formula. But instead of simply stating the quadratic formula, she introduces a real-world problem whose solution requires finding roots to quadratic equations. Because of some students' interest in baseball, she takes an idea from the *Mathematics Teacher* article (Eisner, 1986) that appears in Appendix B and uses baseball-related situations to establish a need for solving quadratic equations. Most of the equations are not easily factored, so she leads them through the process by which they solve them by completing the square.

Using inductive questioning strategies (explained and illustrated in Chapters 4 and 9, see Cases 4.7–4.10), she leads them to generalize from their experiences in completing the square to discovering the quadratic formula. After agreeing to and articulating the formula, Ms. Youklic uses direct teaching strategies to improve their algorithmic skills with the quadratic formula.

CASE 2.3

Ms. Estrada tells her students, as she lists the rules for multiplying signed numbers on the chalkboard, "A positive times a positive is positive. A positive times a negative is negative. A negative times a positive is negative. A negative times a negative is positive. Zero times any number is zero; any number times zero is zero. Do you understand?"

She directs the students to complete a worksheet at their places as she circulates among them looking at their work, correcting errors, and individually responding to questions. She notices that Bonita's paper includes the following:

$17 \times 10 = 170$	$.3347 \times 0 = 0$
$-4.1 \times 3 = -12.3$	$(1/4)(-2/3) = -2/12$
$-20 \times 9 = -180$	$(-5)(-10) = -50$
$(0)(-19) = 0$	$(-11)(-1/17) = -11/17$
$4\pi(8) = 32\pi$	

They engage in the following conversation:

Ms. Estrada: Bonita, what is -5 times -10?
Bonita: Minus 50, it's right here.

Ms. Estrada: But a negative times a negative is a positive.
Bonita: Why?
Ms. Estrada: Because that's the rule. See, I have it listed on the board and it's right here on page 23 of the text.

CASE 2.4

With an overhead projector, Mr. Cocora displays Exhibit 2.1 to his class and says, "A friend of mine works for the city's Traffic Control Department. She asked if I could help her solve a problem. I said I could with the class' help. Here's the situation. The department wants to estimate when and where city traffic is likely to be congested. They're collecting data at the observation point marked here on the screen. The post is located at Highway 30, right at the west edge of the city. My friend tells me most of the traffic entering from west of the city passes this observation point.

"Here's the deal. Using a radar gun, the observer measures the direction and rate in miles per hour of a vehicle traveling on Highway 30. They want some rules for using this one observation to estimate where the vehicle will be or was at any point in time. Do you think we can help?"

A discussion ensues in which the problem is clarified and Mr. Cocora explains that at traffic control (a) travel into the city is coded as a positive (+) number of miles per hour, (b) travel out of the city is coded as a negative (−) number of miles per hour, (c) locations on the city side of the observation point (that is, to the east) are coded as positive (+) miles, (d) locations to the west, outside of the city are coded as negative (−) miles, (e) time in the future is coded as positive (+) hours, and (f) time in the past is coded as negative (−) hours.

Moving a toy car over the highway on the transparency, Mr. Cocora confronts the students with each of the following questions:

1. Where will a red Chevrolet that is headed into the city at 60 miles per hour be located 6 minutes from now?

Exhibit 2.1
Mr. Cocora's overhead transparency for his conceptual-level lesson on rules for multiplying signed numbers.

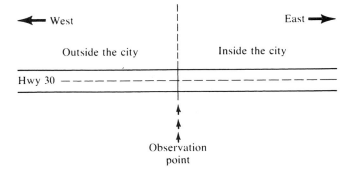

2. Where will a dump truck that is headed out of the city at 60 miles per hour be located 6 minutes from now?
3. Where was the red Chevrolet 6 minutes ago?
4. Where was the dump truck 6 minutes ago?
5. Where is a green Toyota that is passing the observation point right now?
6. Where will a yellow van that is broken down and not moving in front of the observation point be in 5 minutes?

Mr. Cocora directs his class into collaborative task groups that are to answer the six questions and then generalize rules for the Traffic Department to use. All the groups answer the question by applying the relationship *rate × time = distance* as follows:

1. $(+60)(+0.1) = +6$ (6 miles east of the observation point)
2. $(-60)(+0.1) = -6$ (6 miles west of the observation point)
3. $(+60)(-0.1) = -6$ (6 miles west of the observation point)
4. $(-60)(-0.1) = +6$ (6 miles east of the observation point)
5. $(?)(0) = 0$ (in front of the observation point)
6. $(0)(+5) = 0$ (in front of the observation point)

After further discussion led by Mr. Cocora, the students settle on rules for the Traffic Department that are tantamount to the usual rules for multiplying signed numbers.

The next day Mr. Cocora restates the rules devised in the exercise into more conventional textbook form. He then uses direct instructional techniques to help them remember the rules.

Both Mr. Jackson and Ms. Youklic taught lessons on the quadratic formula, so their students learned about a different mathematics topic than Ms. Estrada's and Mr. Cocora's students. However, Mr. Jackson's and Ms. Estrada's lessons were similar in that both their classes learned to think of mathematics as a set of rules to be remembered and used but not necessarily understood. Ms. Youklic's and Mr. Cocora's students experienced discovering and inventing mathematics. Thus, although according to a curriculum guideline or textbook section, Mr. Jackson and Ms. Youklic were "covering" the same topic, student outcomes were vastly different.

TWO VIEWS

Learn Mathematics to Learn More Mathematics

Over the past 20 years, I have asked hundreds of mathematics teachers and others who have been instrumental in the development of mathematics curricula why students should learn mathematics. Virtually all the answers were given without hesitation and could hardly be contested. For example:

- "Mathematical literacy is a necessity in today's world. It's needed for everything from budgeting, to being a wise consumer, to holding down many jobs. The mathematically able have more options available to them. If we didn't teach mathematics, we would deny opportunities to individuals and fail to produce the brainpower society needs for scientific, sociological, and technological advancement."

- "Obviously, fundamental mathematical skills are needed as basic survival tools for life. Furthermore, the world is changing so rapidly that we don't know what kinds of problems today's children will be facing tomorrow. So above all, they need to be able to be systematic, logical problem solvers. Appropriate experiences with mathematics enhance that ability."

However, most of those I queried were much slower to respond to questions about why selected topics are included in mathematics curricula. For example:

- "Why do you spend so much time on factoring polynomials in algebra?"
  "Well, the book really emphasizes it. And then, the students need it when they get into solving second-degree and higher equations and inequalities."
- "Why are compound interest formulas included in your consumer mathematics course?"
  "Almost everyone needs to understand banking and financing to survive today. Some of my students are in the process of buying a car. It's useful to them right now!"
- "What's the point of having students prove so many theorems in your geometry course?"
  "I've wondered about that myself. There's some logic to be learned, but, more importantly, I guess they need to see how a mathematical system evolves."
- "Why do you include this "application" section from the trigonometry book? Do your students really need to be able to find the angle of the shadow cast by flagpoles?"
  "Very funny! There are two very good reasons. One, these kind of problems are on the standardized tests that they need to pass. Second, they'll need this stuff when they get into calculus."

After listening to hundreds of such comments, it became obvious that many teachers and other curriculum developers recognize intrinsic value in mathematics; thus, mathematics courses, except for consumer, business, and general mathematics courses, are viewed as preparation for subsequent courses. To many, a primary goal of precollege school mathematics is preparing students to pass calculus.

Mathematics curricula based on the goal of preparing students to learn more mathematics are justifiable in light of the following:

- Generally speaking, the further individuals advance in school mathematics, the greater the variety of occupational opportunities available to them (Steen, 1987, 1988).
- Society needs a mathematically literate citizenry, as well as mathematicians, scientists, engineers, and other mathematically expert professionals (National Council of Teachers of Mathematics, 1989a, pp. 3–5).

Learn Mathematics to Solve Real-Life Problems

Although the inclusion of mathematics in school curricula can be justified solely on the intrinsic value of doing mathematics, a curriculum based only on such a rationale is likely to fail for three reasons:

1. Most students do not make the connection between mathematics learned in school and the application of that mathematics outside of school unless they learned the mathematics in a real-world problem-solving context (that is, they don't make the transfer from strategies for solving textbook word problems to strategies for solving problems they confront in their outside-of-mathematics-class real world) (Hiebert & Carpenter, 1992).
2. Students are likely to retain algorithmic skills and knowledge of rules only as long as they continue to use them. Unless they've learned to apply them to solve problems from their own real worlds, they're hardly motivated to continue to use them once the skill has been tested and they have moved on to other lessons (Schoenfeld, 1989). Hence, it is typical for a mathematics topic to be repeatedly cycled through curricula, being taught initially and reviewed each time it is a prerequisite to another topic.
3. Most adolescents are simply not highly motivated to work toward goals whose benefits appear only to be long-range (Santrock, 1984, pp. 553–563; Woolfolk, 1993, pp. 366–397). "Learn this now so you'll be able to pass calculus next year," seems reasonable to most 16-year-olds, but pales as a motivator in comparison to immediate concerns.

As new topics are introduced, students need to be provided with experiences that lead them to (a) connect each new topic to previously learned topics, and (b) apply their understanding of the topic to solve problems they consider real-life. Adherence to this curriculum design principle does not preclude teaching mathematics for the purpose of learning more mathematics, but it does rule out isolating topics from one another and from students' real worlds.

REAL-LIFE PROBLEMS

According to Merriam-Webster (1986, p. 1807), a *problem* is "an unsettled matter demanding solutions or decision and requiring usually considerable thought or skill for its proper solution or decision: an issue marked by usually considerable difficulty, uncertainty, or doubt with regard to its proper settlement: a perplexing or puzzling question . . . a source usually of considerable difficulty, perplexity, or worry."

Because problems are associated with difficulty and perplexity, some people consider them distasteful. However, the existence of problems serves as a strong motivator for human endeavor. A perfectly satisfied person, one who feels no need to solve a problem, lacks the motivation to change, and thus to learn (Cangelosi, 1993, pp. 141–149; Gagne, Yekovich, & Yekovich, 1993, pp. 425–448).

Do not confuse *mathematical problems* with *mathematical textbook exercises*. Schoenfeld (1989, pp. 87–88) states:

> For any student, a mathematical *problem* is a task (a) in which the student is interested and engaged and for which he wishes to obtain a resolution, and (b) for which the student does not have a readily accessible mathematical means by which to achieve resolution.
>
> As simple as this definition may seem, it has some significant consequences. First, it presumes that engagement is important in problem solving; a task isn't a problem for you until you've made it *your* problem. Second, it implies that tasks are not "problems" in and of themselves; whether or not a task is a problem for you depends on what you know. Third, most of the textbook and homework "problems" assigned to students are not problems according to this definition, but exercises. In most textbooks, the majority of practice tasks can be solved by direct application of procedures illustrated in the chapter—e.g., solving quadratic equations after you have been taught the quadratic formula, or a "moving trains" problem when the text has illustrated the specific procedures for solving "distance-rate-time" problems. In contrast, real problem solving confronts individuals with a difficulty. They know where they are, and where they want to get—but they have no ready means of getting there. Fourth, the majority of what has been called "problem solving" in the past decade—introducing "word problems" into the curriculum—is only a small part of problem solving.

Who outside of school is ever moved to engage in mathematics unless they have a problem to solve? People have to solve problems when they have questions they want answered. Before you are in a position to design mathematics lessons around problems which are of interest to students, you need to identify the problems they perceive in their real worlds. Strategies for identifying such problems are illustrated in Chapter 6 (Mr. Polonia's approach in Case 6.10). Exhibit 2.2 is a list of problems adolescent students identified as important to them. These problems were successfully incorporated into lessons relevant to mathematical topics included in middle, junior high, and high school curricula.

THE NATIONAL COUNCIL OF TEACHERS OF MATHEMATICS (NCTM) *STANDARDS*
The Gap Between Research-Based Curricula and Typical Practice

In the early 1900s, experimental studies of teaching and learning (James, 1890; Thorndike & Woodworth, 1901) undermined the faculty psychology and formal discipline principles upon which the prevailing mathematics curricula of the day were based (Strom, 1969, pp. 147–208). Unfortunately, a gap still exists between how mathematics is typically taught and how research-based principles indicate it should be taught (Brophy, 1986; Romberg, 1992). Even in today's secondary schools, the most commonly practiced method of teaching mathematics follows a tiresome pattern (Jesunathadas, 1990):

> The teacher introduces a topic by stating a rule or definition and then demonstrating it with textbook examples on the chalkboard or on overhead transparencies. Students work on exercises at their seats, with the teacher providing individual help to those experiencing difficulties. Similar exercises are completed for homework and checked as "right" or "wrong" at the beginning of the next class period. Homework exercises that were particularly troublesome are worked out for the class, either by the teacher or student volunteers.
>
> Emphasis is almost entirely on algorithmic skills. Neither understanding of why rules and algorithms work nor applications to real-life problems are stressed. The teacher's expectations for all but a few students are very low. The pace of lessons is slow, with plodding, repetitive exercises.

Research-based principles do not suggest that these expository, drill, and review lessons should be eliminated, but rather that they should not continue to be the dominant form of instruction. Acquiring algorithmic skills should not be the primary goal of school mathematics curricula.

Numerous curriculum-reform efforts have attempted to bring the teaching of mathematics more in line with research-based principles indicating that students need experience in discovering and inventing

Exhibit 2.2
Problems identified as important by adolescents that have been incorporated into mathematics lessons (Cangelosi, 1989a, 1990c).

Art and Aesthetics

- While thinking about how to sketch a picture: At what angles should I make these lines intersect to give the illusion I'm trying to create?
- In deciding how to decorate a room: What color combinations do people tend to associate with being happy?

Cooking

- While planning a meal: How should I expand this recipe so all my guests get enough to eat, but I don't have a lot of food left over?
- What, if any, functions can I formulate (and then write a computer program for) for relating recipe ingredients to output variables such as calories, fat content, nutrients, sweetness, and sourness?

Earning Money

- In considering a fund-raising class project: Would we net more money with a car wash, a bake sale, a "run for donations," used-book sale, or "rent-a-teenager" offer?
- Is this offer to sell greeting cards I just received in the mail a good deal for me?

Electronics

- How can I efficiently link this cable television, videotape recorder, and computer?
- What, if any, functions can I formulate for maximizing amplification of this sound system while minimizing reverberations?

Employment

- Considering time on the job, travel, expenses, opportunity for advancement, security, and benefit from experiences, which of these three jobs should I take?
- Is my paycheck accurate, considering my hours and overtime?

Environmental Concerns

- What's the most efficient way for us to get our message across to the most-influential people?
- In preparing for a field trip: How can we minimize our impact on the flora and fauna of the forest?

Family

- In response to the claim that too much time is spent listening to music and watching television and not enough time working on school work and doing chores: How much time do I usually spend a day on each of those four things?
- How can I help my brother manage his time better?

Friends

- Do people really care how their friends dress?
- What factors create friendships?

Gardening and Growing Plants

- What, if any, rules can I formulate (and then write a computer program for) to maximize the growth of beans as a function of soil composition, space, exposure to sun, moisture, etc.?
- What effect does varying the amount and frequency of watering have on plant's health?

Health

- What's the best exercise program for me?
- How should I change my diet?

Managing Money

- How should I go about saving money to buy a car when I'm 16?
- How should I budget my money?

Music

- Who is the hottest music group right now?
- Since I eventually want to work in a rock group, would I be better starting off learning to play the piano, guitar, or drums?

Parties

- How many people should we invite?
- What kind of food should we serve?

Personal Appearance

- What's the best way to treat pimples?
- How do different people respond to "muscular" women?

Exhibit 2.2
Continued

Personal Planning

- How should I budget my time?
- Would I be better off taking more college prep or business courses in high school?

Pets and Raising Animals

- What kinds and numbers of fish can this aquarium support?
- Is the behavior modification I've started with my cat working?

Politics

- What strategies should we employ to get Allison elected to the student council?
- What can we do to sway people's thinking on this gun-control issue?

School Grades

- What's the relation between the amount of time I study and the grades I get?
- Is it best to "cram" the night before a test or spread test preparation out over a longer period of time?

School Subjects Other than Mathematics

- In response to a problem assigned in science class: How much does it cost to leave a light bulb burning?
- In response to a health and physical education assignment: How many push-ups would I need to do to burn up 100 calories?

Social Issues

- Considering the composition of our student body with respect to ethnicity and gender, did ethnic or sex bias influence the outcome of the last school election?
- What can we do to discourage drug abuse in our school?

Sports and Games

- What kind of tennis racquet should I buy?
- What strategy (e.g., regarding lap times) should I use to minimize my time in the 1500-meter run?

Television, Movies, and Videos

- How does gun use in movies compare to gun use in real life?
- In what ways are people influenced by television commercials?

Travel

- What is the most efficient way for me to get from here to Tucson?
- In planning a class trip: Where should we plan to stop along the way?

Vehicles

- Which of these two skateboards is better for speed, control, and durability?
- Regarding a remote-control model car: How are speed, acceleration, maneuverability, and response time affected by battery power and distance between controller and car?

---

mathematics and utilizing mathematics to solve real-life problems [The 1908 Committee of Fifteen on the Geometry Syllabus (Kinney & Purdy, 1952, pp. 22–23); The Joint Commission to Study the Place of Mathematics in Secondary Education (NCTM, 1940); The School Mathematics Study Group (Begle, 1958); *An Agenda for Action: Recommendations for School Mathematics of the 1980s* (NCTM, 1980); *Educating Americans for the 21st Century* (National Science Board Commission on Precollege Education in Mathematics, Science, and Technology, 1983); *The Mathematical Science Curriculum K-12: What Is Fundamental and What Is Not* (Conference Board of the Mathematical Sciences, 1983a); *New Goals for Mathematical Sciences Education* (Conference Board of the Mathematical Sciences, 1983b)].

The impact of these curriculum-reform projects on actual mathematics curricula has been disappointing. However, the NCTM-sponsored project that produced the *Curriculum and Evaluation Standards for School Mathematics* (NCTM, 1989a) has and is continuing to make a profound impact on what actually goes on in classrooms. The document was developed with broad input from mathematics teachers, mathematics education specialists, mathematicians, cognitive scientists, and instructional supervisors and has been endorsed by scores of relevant professional associations (Mathematical Association of America, American Mathematical Society, School Science and Mathematics Association, and Association for Women in Mathematics). Clearly, it now serves as a national mathematics curriculum guideline. It states (NCTM, 1989a, v, 1):

The *Standards* is a document designed to establish a broad framework to guide reform in school mathematics in the next decade. In it a vision is given of what the mathematics curriculum should include in terms of content priority and emphasis. The challenge we issue to all interested in the quality of school mathematics is to work collaboratively to use these curriculum and evaluation standards as the basis for change so that the teaching and learning of mathematics in our schools is improved. . . .

These standards are one facet of the mathematics education community's response to the call for reform in the teaching and learning of mathematics. They reflect and are an extension of the community's responses to those demands for change. Inherent in this document is a consensus that all students need to learn more, and often different, mathematics, and that instruction in mathematics must be significantly revised.

As a function of NCTM's leadership in current efforts to reform school mathematics, the Commission on Standards in School Mathematics was established by the Board of Directors and charged with two tasks:

1. Create a coherent vision of what it means to be mathematically literate, both in a world that relies on calculators and computers to carry out mathematical procedures and in a world where mathematics is rapidly growing and is extensively being applied to diverse fields.
2. Create a set of standards to guide the revision of the school mathematics curriculum and its associated evaluation toward this vision.

Curriculum and Evaluation Standards for School Mathematics

The 265-page document lists, explains, and illustrates (a) 13 curriculum standards for grades K–4, (b) 13 curriculum standards for grades 5–8, (c) 14 standards for grades 9–12, and (d) 14 evaluation standards.

The two types of standards are described as follows:

Curriculum Standards. When a set of curricular standards is specified for school mathematics, it should be understood that the standards are value judgments based on a broad, coherent vision of schooling derived from several factors: societal goals, research on teaching and learning, and professional experience. Each standard starts with a statement of what mathematics the curriculum should include. This is followed by a description of the student activities associated with that mathematics and a discussion that includes instructional examples. (NCTM, 1989a, p. 7)

The Evaluation Standards. The evaluation standards are presented separately, not because evaluation should be separated from the curriculum but because planning for the gathering of evidence about student and programs outcomes is different. The difference is most clearly illustrated in comparing curriculum standards titled Connections and the evaluation standards titled Mathematical Power. Both deal with connections among concepts, procedures, and intellectual methods, but the curriculum standards are related to the instructional plan, whereas the evaluation standards address the ways in which students integrate connections intellectually so that they develop mathematical power. (NCTM, 1989a, p. 11)

Both the curriculum and evaluation standards are listed in Appendix C. However, without the explanations of student activities and the examples, the ideas behind each standard are lost. Thus, you should obtain your own personal copy of *Curriculum and Evaluation Standards for School Mathematics* from NCTM as a guide for developing curricula.

A curriculum developed with the *Standards* as a guide emphasizes the following far more than traditional mathematics curricula:

- Real-life problem solving
- Conceptualization of why rules and algorithms work
- Experiences with mathematical discovery and invention
- Integration across mathematical topics
- Use of calculators and computers
- Comprehension of the language of mathematics
- Writing and speaking about mathematics
- Testing for guiding instruction
- Testing for comprehensive, conceptual, and application levels of learning

Furthermore, compared to traditional curricula, a *Standards*-based curriculum places somewhat less emphasis on the following:

- Word problems that do not reflect real-world situations
- Paper-and-pencil calculations
- Segregation of topics and subdisciplines of mathematics
- Memorization of formulas
- Verification by appeal to authority
- Mindless exercises
- Problems with one exact solution
- Testing at the cognitive knowledge level, that is, for memory
- Testing solely for grades

Since publishing the *Standards* in 1989, the NCTM has produced a number of other documents and instructional materials (for example, videotape programs) to support teachers, teacher educators, and curriculum designers' attempts to implement the *Standards*. The following are included among these documents:

- The *Professional Standards for Teaching Mathematics* (NCTM, 1991) describes the competencies and practices of teachers who design and implement curricula based on the *Curriculum and Evaluation Standards for School Mathematics*. Furthermore, standards for evaluating the teaching of mathematics, for the professional development of mathematics teachers, and for support of mathematics teaching are spelled out. The goals and objectives listed near the beginning of the chapters of the textbook you are now reading are consistent with NCTM's *Professional Standards for Teaching Mathematics*.

- *Assessment Standards for School Mathematics: Working Draft* (NCTM, 1993, p. 5) "succinctly summarizes the assessment vision of the National Council of Teachers of Mathematics in its efforts to guide reform in the teaching and learning of mathematics. NCTM has produced this document on assessment for two reasons: the first is to present teachers of mathematics with a vision of assessment that is consistent with the earlier *Standards* documents produced by NCTM—*Curriculum and Evaluation Standards for School Mathematics* (1989a) and *Professional Standards for Teaching Mathematics* (1991). The second reason is to align this vision of assessment with different educational purposes."

- *Curriculum and Evaluation Standards for School Mathematics Addenda Series* include a number of resource books filled with sample learning activities that exemplify ideas advocated in the *Standards*. Among the titles from the addenda series for grades 5–8 are *Dealing with Data and Chance* (Zawajewski, 1991); *Developing Number Sense in the Middle Grades* (Reys, 1991); *Geometry in the Middle Grades* (Geddes, 1992); *Measurement in the Middle Grades* (Geddes, 1994); *Patterns and Functions* (Phillips, 1991); and *Understanding Rational Numbers and Proportions* (Curcio & Bezuk, in press). The addenda series for grades 9–12 include titles such as *Connecting Mathematics* (Froelich, 1991); *A Core Curriculum: Making Mathematics Count for Everyone* (NCTM, 1992a); *Data Analysis and Statistics Across the Curriculum* (NCTM, 1992b); and *Geometry from Multiple Perspectives* (Coxford, 1991). Exhibit 2.3 provides an example from *A Core Curriculum: Making Mathematics Count for Everyone*.

These and other resources to help you teach in harmony with the *Standards* (for example, the professional journals *Mathematics Teacher* and *Mathematics Teaching in the Middle School*) are referred to throughout the remainder of this text.

MATHEMATICS CURRICULA OUTCOMES
Elementary School-Level Outcomes

Traditional Curriculum. As a middle or secondary school mathematics teacher, you need to understand what your students experienced and achieved while in elementary school. After all, you are responsible for building on those experiences and advancing those achievements. Of course, there are considerable differences among students on these two variables. Beside the differences among students in how they respond to similar experiences, the differences among teachers are also great. Some students will have enjoyed the benefits of effective teachers who provided them with enriching experiences discovering and inventing mathematics. But most may not be so fortunate.

Typically, students engage in activities with hands-on manipulatives for counting, sorting, measuring, and naming objects in kindergarten and the beginning of first grade. By second grade such concrete activities are often replaced by skill-level drills for memorizing addition and subtraction facts and algorithms. Some conceptual work in identifying geometric figures and fractions is included, but fluency with fractions and algorithms involving the four fundamental operations is paramount through the fifth grade.

On the average, but with wide variation about this average, the impact of traditional elementary school mathematics curricula on students is as follows:

- Most students exit fifth grade with an arsenal of memorized algorithms for adding, subtracting, multiplying, and dividing whole numbers and rational numbers expressed in decimal form. Their facility for manipulating numbers expressed as fractions is typically limited to one- and two-digit numerators and denominators whose prime factors are obvious to them. Computational skills with numbers expressed as percentages are emphasized by some teachers and ignored by many others. However, having topics accurately presented in textbooks and by teachers does not imply that most students learn them accurately. What is "covered" is not necessarily what is learned. Many students' arsenal of algorithms include memorized error patterns (Ashlock, 1990; Hiebert & Carpenter, 1992, pp. 88–89) that produce incorrect computational results. Analyze, for example, the sample of Phil's work on a "review exercise" administered by his teacher on the first day of sixth grade; it appears in Exhibit 2.4.

Phil faithfully follows the algorithm he remembers, not even bothered by the fact that the product

Exhibit 2.3
Pages 95–97 from *Core Curriculum* (NCTM, 1992). (Reproduced by Permission.)

♦   ♦   ♦   ♦   ♦   ♦   ♦   ♦

REASONING IN INTUITIVE CALCULUS

Location in sample syllabus: Year 3, Unit 7

Major standard addressed: Underpinnings of calculus

Objectives: ♦ To write a function to describe cost on the basis of given information

♦ To find the minimum of a function graphically

♦ To interpret a discontinuity of a function

♦ To realize the pitfalls of uncritical reliance on technology

Prerequisites: ♦ Using the Pythagorean theorem

♦ Understanding the minimum or maximum value of a function over an interval

♦ Using a graphing utility to graph functions and to zoom in to find an extremum of the function

♦ Understanding continuity of a function

Materials: Graphing calculators, spreadsheets (optional), programmable calculators (optional), computer with BASIC (or other) programming capability (optional)

Motivating question: A pipeline is to be built from a point R to a point S as shown on the map. Points R and S are connected by roads as shown.

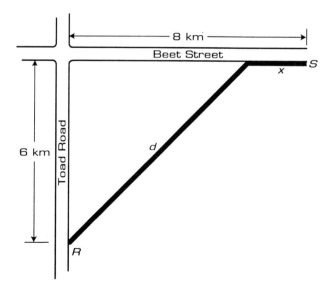

The pipeline will be built either across the land to a point x kilometers from S and then along Beet Street to S, as shown in the sketch, or entirely along Toad Road and Beet Street. If the cost is $12 000 a kilometer along the road or street and $37 000 a kilometer across the land, find x so that the cost will be minimal.

Exhibit 2.3
Continued

Directions for the initial activity:

Level 1

1. How much will it cost to build—
   a. 10 km of pipeline along the road?   [$120 000]
   b. 10 km of pipeline across the land?   [$370 000]
   c. 3.5 km of pipeline along the road and 7.5 km of pipeline across the land?   [$319 500]

2. How much will it cost to build the pipeline when *x* is—
   a. 0 km?   [$370 000]   d. 6 km?   [$306 009]
   b. 2 km?   [$337 955]   e. 7.9 km?   [$316 831]
   c. 4 km?   [$314 811]   f. 8 km? (Hint: be careful!)   [$168 000]

3. Write a formula for the cost when the pipeline is built—
   a. entirely along Toad Road and Beet Street.   [*C* = $168 000]
   b. across the land to a point *x* kilometers from *S* and then along Beet Street to *S*.   [See class discussion.]

4. Use your graphing utility to plot the function you wrote for part 3b.
   a. What is the domain of this function? This is VERY important.
      [$0 \leq x < 8$]
   b. Zoom in to find the minimum cost for this function to the nearest dollar.   [$306 000]
   c. What is the minimum cost for the pipeline?   [$168 000]

5. Solve the problem as if Toad Road were not there, so that the pipeline *must* be built across land to a point *x* kilometers from point *S*.
   [$306 000]

Class discussion:

In exercises 1–4, what is the minimum value suggested by zooming in on the graphing utility? [$306 000] Is this the minimum cost? Explain. [No, the minimum cost of $168 000 occurs when the entire pipeline is built along the road. The graph drawn by the graphing utility, $C = 12x + 37\sqrt{36 + (8 - x)^2}$, where *C* is the cost in thousands of dollars, is valid only when $0 \leq x < 8$. When *x* = 8, the entire pipeline is along the road, so the cost is $168 000, less than the minimum value obtained by zooming in.]

Follow-up activities:

Level 2

Have students use a spreadsheet, a programmable calculator, or a computer program to find the cost when *x* = 1, 2, 3, 4, 5, 6, and 7. (Recall that the cost for *x* = 8 is $168 000.) They should interpret their results to find the value of *x*, to the nearest whole number, producing the least cost when the pipeline goes across the land and then along Beet Street. Next, direct them to use a refined search (for example, by tenths between *x* = 4 and *x* = 6) to find the value of *x* to the nearest tenth, which produces the least cost.

Answers:

x	1	2	3	
cost	$353 123	$337 955	$324 979	
x	4	5	6	7
cost	$314 811	$308 203	$306 009	$309 062

Teaching Matters: Bring out with students that if we rely on the graphing calculator without interpreting its information in terms of the real-world situation, we may forget that the cost function is discontinuous at x = 8. Consequently, we might miss the actual minimum— a mistake that in this problem would cost an extra $138 000! (In exercise 5, the graphing utility does give the answer directly.)

Assessment Matters: Today's sophisticated calculators raise many issues concerning paper-and-pencil testing. For an interesting discussion of these issues, see The Use of Calculators in the Standardized Testing of Mathematics *(1989), a book of readings edited by John Kenelly from the College Entrance Examination Board.*

Exhibit 2.3
Continued

◆   ◆   ◆   ◆   ◆   ◆   ◆   ◆

Ask students to solve the problem as if Toad Road were not there, so that the pipeline *must* be built across land to a point x kilometers from point S.

Level 3

Make up a similar problem by changing the values of the distance from R to Beet Street (now 6 kilometers) and the cost a kilometer along the roads (now $12 000 a kilometer) so that it *is* cheaper to build part of the pipeline across the land. Students can use a graphing utility, a spreadsheet, a programmable calculator, or a computer program to evaluate $C = Lx + 37\sqrt{A^2 + (8 - x)^2}$ for various values of L and A. For example, when A is 5 kilometers from Beet Street and the cost along the road is $30 000 a kilometer, then x = 1.1 (to the nearest tenth), giving a minimum cost of about $348 000, which is cheaper than going along the roads at a cost of $390 000.

Level 4

Have advanced students apply the derivative concept in calculus to solve the original problem. (This gives rise to a cubic equation $37x^3 - 888x^2 + 8436x - 29\,588 = 0$, which is still difficult to solve analytically.)

Teaching Matters: The levels in this lesson permit a teacher to choose which approach or combination of approaches best fits a particular group of students and the available classroom resources. Regardless of the technology chosen, all students should work through exercises 1 and 2 to get a "feel" for the problem and the real-world aspects that the mathematics will model. "Grubbing with data" will enhance their consideration of constraints imposed on the mathematical model by the actual situation. This lesson carries two messages: (1) it illustrates that although technology can be helpful in solving problems, we must rely on our own thinking to apply and interpret results correctly; and (2) it illustrates how a problem may be solved in many ways by using different applications of technology.

Exhibit 2.4
Phil's responses to a "review exercise" administered by his teacher on the first day of sixth grade.

he got for 197 and 18 is larger than the one he got for 230 and 23. He is likely to continue this error pattern until a teacher diagnoses that he is adding carried digits one step too soon. For instance, in the second exercise, he begins by thinking, "Eight times 7 is 56. Put down the 6 and carry 5. Five plus 9 is 14. Fourteen times 8 is . . . " Although most of Phil's products are not even approximately correct,

he correctly executes the vast majority of the steps in the algorithm; he simply executes one repeated step out of order. Typically, students' computational errors are not random.

- Students fail to detect their own error patterns because they have learned to execute algorithms faithfully with a myopic, step-by-step view, never conceptualizing the whole process or bothering to predict a reasonable outcome (Fuson, 1992, pp. 777–782; Schoenfeld, 1989). Case 2.5 illustrates the phenomenon.

CASE 2.5

For the purpose of stimulating discussion and getting some insights about his students as they begin sixth grade, Mr. Stokes displays the following on the overhead screen and directs the class, "Simplify this."

$$\frac{8.47 + 8.47 + 8.47 + 8.47}{4}$$

Without hesitation 23 of the 26 students begin the process of adding 8.47 to itself four times and dividing the sum by four. One asks, "May we use a calculator?" Another inquires about the number of decimal places Mr. Stokes wants in the answer.

Mr. Stokes asks, "Why did you go to all that trouble when you could see that adding the same number four times divided by four is the number?"

Brad: "That's not the way we learned do it."
Molina: "Yeah, the rule is to simplify the numerator first and then . . ."

- Students are generally proficient in completing one-step skill-level tasks (such as recalling facts, associating names with figures, and executing one step of an algorithm) alluded to in curriculum guidelines. However, there is a dramatic drop in proficiency for multistep tasks like working two-step word problems (Schoenfeld, 1992, "U.S. Teens Lag Behind in Math, Science," 1989).

- Most students have access to calculators at home but not in school. In general, students are able to use calculators for trivial tasks such as checking answers to computational exercises, but use them neither to save time spent in computing nor in ways that take advantage of special functions (e.g., Σ) or features such as memory storage. (Struyk, Cangelosi, & Elhert, 1993).

- Only a small proportion of students appears to possess the conceptual understanding necessary to explain (a) why the algorithms they know work (that is, why, when multiplying 84 by 3, one should first multiply 4 by 3 and then carry the 1 from the 12), or (b) why relationships they've memorized (for example, area of a rectangle = length × width) hold (Schoenfeld, 1992; "U.S. Students Again Rank Near Bottom in Math and Science," 1989).

- Only a small proportion of students appears to possess the application-level understanding necessary to distinguish among appropriate and inappropriate mathematical procedures when confronted with a problem-solving task (Carpenter, Lindquist, Brown, Kouba, Silver, & Swafford, 1986; Schoenfeld, 1992).

- By the time students enter sixth grade they tend to believe mathematics has little or nothing to do with real-life problem solving, mathematical tasks are completed either quickly or not at all, and only geniuses can be creative with mathematics (McLeod, 1992; Schoenfeld, 1985, p. 43).

- Although most students perceive mathematics to be composed mainly of rule memorization and do not expect to use mathematics outside the classroom, those with more favorable attitudes tend to be more skillful with mathematics and also learn mathematics at more sophisticated cognitive levels; they are able to discover and invent, not simply remember, mathematical content. (Dossey, Mullis, Lindquist, & Chambers, 1988; McLeod, 1992).

NCTM *Standards*-Based Curriculum. In response to the question, "What in the *Standards* is new compared with current practice?" NCTM's 1988–1990 president, Shirley Frye (1989a, p. 7; 1989b, p. 316) states:

These new major themes are woven throughout all levels: communications, reasoning, and connections. New topics include data analysis and discrete mathematics, and the usual content topics are either expanded or modified. The *Standards* makes specific recommendations about the increased and decreased emphasis that should be placed on certain topics, skills, and procedures at all levels.

The evaluation standards focus on assessment of students' performance and curricular programs, with an emphasis on the role of evaluative measures in gathering information on which teachers can base subsequent instruction. A key factor in the general assessment section is alignment, the agreement of the assessment with the curriculum.

For all students to be mathematically literate, the instructional strategies must include collaborative experiences, use of calculators and computers, exploration activities that enable students to hypothesize and test, applications of mathematics, and experience in problem posing and writing.

Finally, the challenges to teach mathematics as an integrated whole and to link mathematics to the physical world are the relatively new focal points of the standards.

Some teachers—but not most—have been adhering to the principles put forward by the *Standards* for years. The NCTM continues its efforts to influence elementary school mathematics curricula so that, consistent with the *Standards,* there will be an increased emphasis on the items listed in Exhibit 2.5, while those in Exhibit 2.6 will be deemphasized (NCTM, 1989a, pp. 20–21).

Middle School- and Junior High School-Level Outcomes

Traditional Curriculum. In most school systems, middle school encompasses grades 6, 7, and 8; junior high encompasses grades 7, 8, and 9. Traditional middle or junior high school mathematics curricula impact students in ways very similar to those listed for traditional elementary school curricula. There are, however, some differences:

- There is much more formal treatment of algebra (often labeled prealgebra) and geometry.
- More emphasis is placed on percents, ratios, proportions, and formulas (for rate of speed, interest, area, volume, perimeter, and averages).
- There is even more separation among topics and mathematical subdisciplines, for example, between algebra and geometry.

Exhibit 2.5
Points for increased emphasis in the elementary grades according to the *Standards*.

Emphasize

Conceptual understanding of numbers and relationships between numbers (e.g., between numbers expressed as fractions and numbers expressed as decimals)

Estimation of quantities

Work with approximate figures

Conceptual understanding of fundamental operations

Conceptual understanding of why algorithms work

Mental computations

Application-level understanding of how to select appropriate algorithms

Prediction of computational results

Arithmetic work with numbers resulting from empirical measurements (as opposed to textbook numerals)

Integration of geometry, arithmetic, probability, and data gathering (i.e., measurement)

Exploration of patterns

Use of variables to express relationships

Word problems with a variety of structures

Applications to real-life problems

Problem-solving strategies

Concrete activities with manipulatives

Cooperative work among students

High cognitive-level question/discussion sessions (i.e., thought provoking as opposed to recitation)

Writing, speaking, and reading about mathematics

Use of calculators and computers to reduce time spent in complex algorithms

Use of calculators and computers as learning tools

Exhibit 2.6
Points for decreased emphasis in the elementary grades according to the *Standards*.

Deemphasize

Early attention to reading, writing, and ordering numbers symbolically

Complex paper-and-pencil computations

Treatment of algorithms in isolation from their applications

Use of rounding or other memorized processes for estimating numbers

Addition and subtraction without renaming

Long division without remainders

Paper-and-pencil computations with fractions

Naming geometric figures

Memorization of equivalence between units of measurements

Use of clue words to determine which operations to use in solving word problems

Rote memorization

One-answer-only, one-method-only problems to solve

Teaching by telling

- There is even less emphasis on manipulatives and concrete experiences.
- Perceptions of students about mathematics deteriorates even further (Dossey, Mullis, Lindquist, & Chambers, 1988).

Students' myopic views and lack of inclination to make sense out of mathematical tasks are illustrated by the beginning ninth graders in Case 2.6.

CASE 2.6 _____

For the purpose of stimulating discussion and getting some insights about her students on the first day of Algebra I class, Ms. Koa asks one student, Barbara, to multiply 307 by 4/5 at the board. Exhibit 2.7 displays what Barbara wrote on the board.

After Ms. Koa says, "Thank you, Barbara," Barbara starts to erase her work. But Ms. Koa intervenes, "No, please leave it there and work one more next to it. This time find 80% of 307." Exhibit 2.8 shows Barbara's second computation.

Ms. Koa: So you fund 4/5 of 307 to be $245\frac{3}{5}$, but 80% of 307 is 24.56. Does that seem okay to you?

Barbara: I think I did it right. You want me to rework it?

Dudley: The second one's not right because you didn't put the decimal in the right place.

Barbara: But you're supposed to have as many decimal places in the answer as there are in the problem. See! Two here, so I put two here.

Dudley: But that's because you didn't bring the zero down.

Exhibit 2.7
Barbara's initial computation.

Exhibit 2.8
Barbara's second computation.

Barbara: I thought you were supposed to . . .

Ms. Koa: Wait a minute. Doesn't anyone care whether or not the answer makes sense? About what would 50% of 300 be?

Lucy: 150.

Ms. Koa: Then should 80% of 307 be more or less than 150?

The discussion continues, with most of the students focusing on steps in algorithms and Ms. Koa striving to get them to make sense out of the task.

_____

The failure of Ms. Koa's algebra students to recognize that 4/5 of 307 is the same as 80% of 307 is not surprising considering how traditional mathematics curricula isolate topics. Students tend to disassociate fractions from percents, arithmetic from algebra, geometry from numbers, and measurements from numerals that appear in textbooks.

NCTM *Standards*-Based Curriculum. In the middle and junior high school classroom where the principles of *Standards* are put into practice, the items in Exhibit 2.9 are emphasized, whereas those in Exhibit 2.10 are deemphasized (NCTM, 1989a, pp. 70–73).

High School-Level Outcomes

Traditional Curriculum. Traditional high school curricula impact students in ways similar to those enumerated for elementary, middle, and junior high grades. But the following also occur at the high school level:

- Differences among students' mathematical competence and attitudes are further exaggerated as students tend to be separated into (a) 3-, or 4-year course sequences for the "mathematically inclined" college-bound, (b) 1- or 2-year course sequence for the "less mathematically inclined" college-bound, (c) 1- or 2-year sequences of business and consumer mathematics courses, or (d) "remedial" mathematics courses.
- The separation among traditional mathematics subdisciplines (algebra, geometry, trigonometry, statistics, business mathematics, arithmetic, analytic geometry, and calculus) becomes even more distinct in the minds of students.
- The treatment of mathematics, except in the consumer and business mathematics courses, becomes even more formalized, abstract, and removed from real-life situations.

The tendency of students to adhere faithfully and mindlessly to the execution of algorithms continues in high school, even in courses that are considered advanced. Case 2.7 provides an illustration.

Exhibit 2.9
Points for increased emphasis in the middle and junior high grades according to the *Standards*.

Emphasize

Investigation of open-ended problems

Problem-solving projects that extend for weeks

Representations of a problem and possible solutions verbally, numerically, graphically, geometrically, and symbolically

Speaking, writing, listening, and reading about mathematical ideas

Higher-order cognitive processes (e.g., inductive, deductive, analytic, and divergent thinking)

Interrelating mathematics with other school subjects and to the real world outside of school

Interrelating topics within mathematic and across mathematical specialties

Real-life problem solving

Conceptual understanding of rational numbers and their relations among themselves and other variables

Inventing algorithms and procedures

Predicting problem solutions and results of algorithms

Discovering concepts and relationships

Distinguishing between *representations of numbers and concepts* and the *numbers and concepts themselves*

Identifying functional relationships and associating mathematical functions to real-world situations

Using a variety of methods to solve linear equations and inequalities

Informal investigation of nonlinear relationships

Exploration and application of experimental and theoretical probability models

Application of descriptive statistical methods to real-life decision making

Problem-solving applications of geometric relationships

Acquisition of numbers through measurement and measurement approximations

Using technology (e.g., computers, calculators, and video) for exploration

Using computers and calculators to reduce time spent executing algorithms

Cooperative and group learning activities

Using concrete models and manipulatives

Exhibit 2.10
Points for decreased emphasis in the middle and junior high grades according to the *Standards*.

Deemphasize

Practicing routine, one-step tasks

Practicing solving problems categorized by type (e.g., coin, age, and reversed-digit problems)

Recitations and worksheets requiring only rote, one-step memory

Relying on appeal to authority (e.g., the teacher or textbook answer key) for solutions

Learning about topics in isolation from other topics

Developing skills out of context

Memorizing rules, formulas (e.g., in statistics) and algorithms (e.g., cross-multiplication or for manipulating algebraic symbols) without understanding why or how they work

Tedious paper-and-pencil computations

CASE 2.7

Twelfth grader Rosario diligently follows his calculus teacher's explanation of how to use the derivative of a quadratic function to find maximum and minimum y values. For homework, Rosario works a number of strictly computational exercises and then gets to the "application" word problems assigned by the teacher. The first one reads:

> If a rock is tossed upward with an initial velocity of 112 decameters per second from an altitude of 700 decameters above the surface of Mars, its altitude above the surface s seconds later is given by $h = -5.6s^2 + 112s + 700$. What is the maximum altitude reached by the rock?

Automatically, Rosario writes "$h(s) = -5.6s^2 + 112s + 700$," but then he pauses and thinks to himself, "I wonder what I'm supposed to do with that first part about velocity of 112 decameters and altitude of 700 decameters. The teacher didn't show us what to do with that. Oh, well, all these are maximum and minimum problems, so I know I've got to take the derivative." He writes as he thinks, "The rule is to multiply the coefficient by the exponent and then reduce the exponent by one and just drop the constants." He writes:

$$h(s) = -5.6s^2 + 112s + 700$$

$$h'(s) = (2)(-5.6)s + 112$$

$$h'(s) = -11.2s + 112$$

He continues, "Now, I've got to equate this to zero and solve for s, and that should give me the answer." He writes:

$$0 - -11.2s + 112$$

$$11.2s = 112$$

$$s = \frac{112}{11.2}$$

Using his calculator, he divides 112 by 11.2 and writes:

$$s = 10$$

He thinks, "So my answer is 10; better check it in the back of the book. 1260 decameters! Aw, no, I'm not even close! What'd I do wrong? Oh! I wonder if I should have plugged my 10 in for s and solved the function from there. I'll try that. He writes:

$$h(s) = -5.6s^2 + 112s + 700$$

$$h(10) = -5.6(10^2) + 112(10) + 700$$

After using his calculator to simplify the right side, he writes 1260 and exclaims to himself, "Now it's right! So I should work the rest this way. I wonder why I didn't have to use all of the given! Whatever, this way'll work for all the rest. Okay, next . . . ."

_____

Exhibit 2.11
Points for increased emphasis in high school according to the *Standards*.

Emphasize

The use of real-world problems to motivate the exploration and application of traditional topics from algebra, geometry, trigonometry, and analysis, as well as topics recently introduced into the curriculum from probability, statistics, and discrete mathematics

The use of computers to facilitate conceptual understanding of relations (e.g., with computer-based methods of successive approximations and multidimensional geometric representations)

Integration of both geometry and discrete mathematics within other specialty areas and across grade levels

Integration of functions in all specialty areas

Use of calculators and computers to facilitate the execution of algorithms

Deductive arguments expressed in natural rather than artificially rigid forms of communications

Interrelations among topics and specialties

Construction of functions as models for real-world problems

Exhibit 2.12
Points for decreased emphasis in high school according to the *Standards*.

Deemphasize

Word problems by type, such as coin, digit, and work

The simplification of radical expressions

The use of factoring to solve equations and to simplify rational expressions

Logarithmic and trigonometric calculations using tables

Solving systems of equations using determinants

Conic sections

Euclidean geometry as a complete axiomatic system

Algorithmic-like approaches to providing theorems (e.g., with two-column format)

Distinctions between analytic and Euclidean geometries

Inscribed and circumscribed polygons

Paper-and-pencil calculations

Memorization and formulas and identities

Graphing of functions by hand, using table values

Unexplained formulas given as models of real-world problems (e.g., the one given to Rosario in Case 2.7)

NCTM *Standards*-Based Curriculum. As you and other teachers develop curriculum and teach in harmony with the *Standards,* high school mathematics courses will tend to emphasize the items in Exhibit 2.11 and deemphasize those in Exhibit 2.12 (NCTM, 1989a, pp. 126–127).

MATHEMATICS COURSES

The mathematics curriculum in most schools consists primarily of a sequence of courses. Ordinarily, a middle, junior high, or high school mathematics teacher is responsible for four or five class periods a day. In a small school, the five class periods may involve five different courses, (ranging from beginning algebra to geometry to intermediate algebra to general mathematics, and precalculus). In a larger school, the assignment is more likely to include multiple sections of the same course, for example, two sections of general mathematics and three sections of geometry. Course titles vary among school districts; the following list includes some of the more common titles:

- In *sixth-grade mathematics* arithmetic operations with nonnegative rational numbers are the primary concern. Geometric and measurement topics are also emphasized.

- In *seventh-grade mathematics* the emphasis on the arithmetic of rational numbers continues. Applications of arithmetic are extended into areas such as probability and statistics. Negative integers are introduced, as is a more formal treatment of Euclidean geometry. (Due to the influence of the NCTM *Standards,* the trend is for seventh-graders to take prealgebra rather than traditional seventh-grade mathematics.)

- In *eighth-grade general mathematics* the focus is still on the arithmetic of rational numbers. Some elements of number theory are introduced, as are linear algebraic equations and the Cartesian coordinate system. The study of geometry emphasizes constructions, areas, and volumes. (Eighth-grade general mathematics is more and more being supplanted by prealgebra or elementary algebra; it may be an extinct course in the near future.)

- *Prealgebra* is ordinarily intended to provide more advanced work for seventh and eighth graders or basic work for ninth and tenth graders. In any case, it is a preparation for elementary algebra, and its content overlaps that of general eighth-grade mathematics and the first half of elementary algebra.

- In *elementary algebra* or *Algebra I,* the real numbers system is developed. Variable expressions, linear equations, linear inequalities, and operations with polynomials (including those with exponents) are emphasized. Work with quadratic relationships may also be included, depending on the pace of the course.

- *Consumer mathematics* is designed to provide high school students with fundamental mathematical skills needed in everyday life. Such courses are not intended to be a preparation for more advanced work in mathematics. Topics include applications of arithmetic and algebra to problems in the areas of homemaking, budgeting, banking, marketing, traveling, financing, and purchasing.

- *Basic mathematics* is designed to provide high school students with a review of mathematical work ordinarily included in elementary and middle school courses.

- In *geometry,* Euclidean geometry is studied as a system. Logic, constructions, and proofs of theorems are emphasized, but in recent years informal and hands-on approaches have also been included. Non-Euclidean systems may be visited and applications of trigonometry and coordinate geometry are typically included.

- In *intermediate algebra* or *Algebra II* ideas studied in elementary algebra are extended. Systems of linear equations, quadratic equations, and higher-order relationships are emphasized. Work with statistics, permutations and combinations, probability, complex numbers, sequences and series, trigonometry, coordinate geometry, and vectors are included. Conceptual understanding of limits, without a formal ϵ-δ definition, is a goal.

- *Trigonometry* is usually a half-year course for students who have completed intermediate algebra. Content hardly varies among trigonometry courses. Trigonometric functions, trigonometric identities, inverses of trigonometric functions, circular functions, and polar coordinates are standard fare.

- *Advanced algebra, precalculus,* or *Algebra III* is usually a half-year course in which topics from intermediate algebra are reviewed, with applications extended. Topics such as binomial expansion, determinants, and theory of equations are usually added. Considered a preparation for calculus, analytic geometry is emphasized.

- *Calculus* is often designed to help students pass the Advanced Placement Examination for college credit (College Board Publication, 1990). Topics from algebra and analytic geometry are reviewed, followed by treatises on limits of sequences, limits of functions, derivatives and their applications, and integrals and their applications.

- In *probability and statistics* students with a background in algebra study probability models, and the application of both descriptive and differential statistical models for interpreting data. (A proliferation of courses in probability and statistics may be one way some school districts respond to the *Standards* emphasis on discrete mathematics. However, the authors of the *Standards* emphasize other aspects of discrete mathematics as well, and suggest that statistics and probability be integrated throughout mathematics curricula.)

- *Mathematical connections* is a relatively new course some schools offer as part of their efforts to adhere to the *Standards.* It is usually offered in lieu of prealgebra. The content is similar to a traditional prealgebra course, but there is more emphasis on interrelations among arithmetic, algebra, and geometry.

In response to both the *Standards* and the middle education movement, there is a trend toward middle schools integrating mathematics and science courses (Kellough, in press).

Mathematics teachers are sometimes asked to teach courses in computer science. However, such courses are more appropriately conducted by teachers with special preparation in computer science education.

TEACHING UNITS

Each course is organized into teaching units. Exhibit 2.13 lists titles for a sample sequence of teaching units that might comprise an Algebra II course.

Each teaching unit consists of (a) a learning goal, (b) a set of specific objectives that define the learning goal, (c) a planned sequence of lessons, each consisting of learning activities designed to help students achieve specific objectives, (d) mechanisms for monitoring student progress and utilizing feedback in the design of lessons, and (e) a summative evaluation of student achievement of the learning goal.

The Learning Goal

The learning goal is the overall purpose of the teaching unit. The learning goal indicates what students are expected to learn if the teaching unit is successful. In other words, the student-learning outcomes targeted by the unit's teaching functions—this is, the intended range of $T_i(s)$—are defined. For example, the learning goal of Unit 6 from Exhibit 2.14, entitled "Systems of Linear Equations and Inequalities," might be as follows:

> Students can formulate and efficiently use systems of linear equations to solve real-life problems and ex-

Exhibit 2.13
Sample sequence of teaching units for an Algebra II course.

1. Variables, constants, and relations
2. Binary operations with real numbers
3. Variable expressions
4. Open sentences with real-number variables
5. Linear functions
6. Systems of linear equations and inequalities
7. Further applications of linear equations and inequalities
8. Simple operations with polynomials
9. Intermediate operations with polynomials
10. Advanced operations with polynomials
11. Quadratic equations and inequalities
12. Quadratic functions
13. Further applications of quadratic equations and inequalities
14. Complex numbers
15. Exponential and logarithmic functions
16. Systems of higher-order relations
17. Sequences
18. Further applications of sequences
19. Probability functions
20. Further applications of probability functions
21. A look ahead

plain the interrelationships within those systems that facilitate problem solving.

The Set of Specific Objectives That Defines the Learning Goal

The learning goal provides direction for designing the teaching unit by identifying the overall student outcomes. However, teaching is a complicated art. Leading students from where they are to where they can "formulate and efficiently use systems . . . that facilitate problem solving" involves a complex set of different learning stages requiring varying teaching strategies. For students to achieve a learning goal such as the one for the unit on systems of linear equations and inequalities, they must acquire a number of specific skills, abilities, and attitudes. Thus, the learning goal is defined by a *set of specific objectives,* each indicating the particular skill, ability, or attitude that is a necessary but insufficient component of learning-goal achievement. The union of the objectives equals the learning goal. For example, the aforementioned learning goal might be defined by the objectives listed in Exhibit 2.14. Keep in mind that the terminology and mathematical notations used in the statement of the objectives are for the teachers' benefit and do not necessarily reflect the terminology or notations to which the students will be exposed.

The Planned Sequence of Lessons

The paramount components of teaching units are the *lessons* you design and conduct for the purpose of achieving stated objectives and, thus, the learning goal. Each lesson consists of *learning activities.* For the sample Algebra II unit on systems of linear equations and inequalities, a teacher might engage students in lessons for three weeks to help them achieve Objectives A through I listed in Exhibit 2.14. Exhibit 2.15 is an example.

Mechanisms for Monitoring Student Progress and Utilizing Feedback in the Design of Lessons

When you plan a teaching unit, you design its lessons. However, because teaching functions are messy, with a highly complex and unstable domain, you need to routinely monitor students' progress throughout the unit. The feedback from your assessments of their progress should determine the pace of lessons and influence the design of learning activities. Case 2.8 is an example.

Exhibit 2.14
Sample set of objectives defining the goal for Unit 6 from Exhibit 2.14

Goal: Students can formulate and efficiently use systems of linear equations to solve real-life problems and explain the interrelationships within those systems that facilitates problem solving.

A. Given a problem whose solution is facilitated by solving for an equation of the form $f_1(x) + f_2(x) + f_3(x) + \cdots + f_n(x) = 0$, the student explains why the solution is also facilitated by a system of equations of the following form:

$$a_{1,1}x_1 + a_{1,2}x + a_{1,3}x_3 + \cdots + a_{1,n}x_n = 0$$

$$a_{2,1}x_1 + a_{2,2}x + a_{2,3}x_3 + \cdots + a_{2,n}x_n = 0$$

$$a_{3,1}x_1 + a_{3,2}x_3 + a_{3,3}x_3 + \cdots + a_{3,n}x_n = 0$$

.

.

.

$$a_{n,1}x + a_{n,2}x_2 + a_{n,3}x_3 + \cdots + a_{n,n}x_n = 0$$

B. The student describes situations, both real-life and mathematical, that are reflected by each of the following types of pairs of linear equations: (1) simultaneous, (2) inconsistent, and (3) equivalent.

C. Given a system of n n-variable linear equations or inequalities, the student solves for the n variables via the substitution method.
D. Given a system of two two-variable linear equations or inequalities, the student solves for the two variables via the graphing method.
E. Given a system of n n-variable linear equations or inequalities, the student solves for the n variables via the addition method.
F. Given a system of n n-variable linear equations or inequalities, the student solves for the n variables by using matrices.
G. The student explains the difference between problems with solutions that are efficiently facilitated by linear programming and those that are not.
H. The student solves linear programming problems.
I. Given a problem, the student (a) determines whether or not the solution is facilitated by formulating and solving for a system of linear equations or inequalities, and, if so, (b) formulates the system.

CASE 2.8

On the second day of Mr. Boyer's unit on systems of linear equations and inequalities, Jessica says, "The new method is the same as the old; it's just working with many small parts rather than one big part." To try to assess whether other students have also made this connection, Mr. Boyer organizes the class into cooperative groups of three each. Within each group, one student is designated the "judge," a second the "single-variable strategist," and the third the "two-variable strategist." The single-variable strategist and the two-variable strategist then debate for the judge which is the more efficient way to solve the following word problem, by using a single, one-variable linear equation or a system of two, two-variable equations:

A chemist has one solution that is 24% acid and a second that is 50% acid. How many liters of each should be mixed together to get 10 liters of a solution that is 40% acid?

The judge listens to the arguments, decides the winner of the debate and reports the judgment to the rest of the class.

Based on listening in on the debates of the cooperative groups, and on the judges' reports, Mr. Boyer is pleasantly surprised to find that most students are able to relate what they're learning about systems of linear equations to their prior work with one-variable linear equations. Thus, he de-

cides to spend less time discussing the purpose of systems of linear equations than he originally planned. However, he noted a number of unanticipated error patterns in some of the students' computations during the cooperative group activity—errors that prevented some of the one-variable strategists from getting the same solution as the two-variable strategists. Consequently, he spends an extra day remediating selected computational skills.

The assessments of your students' progress that you make for the purpose of guiding the design and conduct of teaching units are referred to as *"formative evaluation."* Strategies for conducting useful formative evaluations are a primary focus of Chapter 10.

A Summative Evaluation of Student Achievement of the Learning Goal

As a teacher, you are expected to make periodic reports to communicate to students, their parents, and your supervisors how well your students are achieving learning goals. Consequently, most teaching units terminate with a test of students' achievement of the learning goal. Your judgments of students' successes are referred to as *"summative evaluations."*

Exhibit 2.15
Sample sequence of lessons targeting Exhibit 2.14's objectives

---

A. The lesson for Objective A includes the following learning activities:
  1. Students are confronted with three rather complicated problems and are directed to formulate a single equation for each to solve the problem. The students work at the task.
  2. The teacher conducts an inductive questioning/discussion class session during which students reflect upon their work on the three problems and determine that the work could be accomplished more efficiently by formulating a system of simpler equations rather than trying to maintain all the relations between variables in one equation of one unknown.
  3. As homework, students work with additional problems, attempting to formulate both a single one-variable equation and a system of equations for each problem.
  4. The results of the homework are discussed in class, with the students concluding that the single one-variable equation contains exactly the same information as the corresponding system of equations.

B. The lesson for Objective B includes the following learning activities:
  1. As planned by the teacher, one of the previously assigned homework problems had no solution and another had infinite solutions, so the aforementioned discussion and subsequent inductive questioning session leads students to categorize problems according to whether they lead to pairs of simultaneous, inconsistent, or equivalent equations.
  2. Using direct instruction, the teacher informs the students of the conventional names for the three categories they discovered (*simultaneous, inconsistent,* and *equivalent*) and provides practice using the names.

C. The lesson for Objective C includes the following learning activities:
  1. The teacher directs one of the students to solve one of the homework problems using the original, single, one-variable-equation method. As the students work through the solution, the teacher explains and lists each step of the process. A discussion then ensues, in which an analysis of those steps leads to the formulation of the substitution algorithm for solving systems of simultaneous equations.
  2. Using direct instructional strategies, the teacher explains each step in the substitution method.
  3. For homework . . .
     .
     .
     .

I. The lesson for Objective I includes the following learning activities:
  1. The teacher engages the students in a deductive questioning/discussion session in which three problems are . . .

DESIGNING, ORGANIZING, AND CONDUCTING COURSES AND TEACHING UNITS

Comprehending research-based principles (for example, those presented by the *Standards*) for designing mathematics curricula and organizing teaching units is necessary to being an effective mathematics teacher. However, it's not sufficient. You also need to develop and refine your strategies for:

1. Selecting content
2. Sequencing units
3. Writing goals and objectives
4. Designing, organizing, and sequencing lessons
5. Selecting and using textbooks and other instructional materials such as manipulatives and concrete mathematical models, reference sources, audiovisual equipment, technology such as graphing calculators and computer software, and facilities (for example, classroom arrangements)
6. Managing student behavior and keeping them engaged in your learning activities

7. Making formative and summative evaluations of student achievement.

In other words, you need to work on improving your ability to actually do these things, not simply understand that they need to be done. Chapters 3 to 6 are designed to help you develop your abilities with respect to the first four items in the above list. Chapter 7 focuses on item 5. Chapters 8 and 9 are concerned with item 6, while Chapter 10 focuses on item 7. Chapter 11 is intended to help you pull together all these complicated components of teaching

TRANSITIONAL ACTIVITIES FROM CHAPTER 2 TO CHAPTER 3 _____

1. If you can conveniently do so, examine either a state- or district-level curriculum guide. Select a list of topics that could conceivably be included in a teaching unit. Describe a unit encompassing those topics as if it were designed solely for the purpose of teaching students

mathematics to prepare them to learn more mathematics. Describe the unit again, but this time as if it were designed for the purpose of teaching students to apply mathematics to real-life situations. If you are unable to conveniently obtain a copy of such a guide, then complete this activity using the table of contents from a middle or secondary school mathematics textbook (or use the table of contents in Exhibit 1.7). Compare your two descriptions with those of a colleague and discuss similarities and differences between them.

2. Following is a list of suggestions for mathematics curricula. Which of these suggestions are consistent with the NCTM *Standards*? Which are not? Feel free to refer to Appendix C as you categorize each.

   a. The distinction between geometry and algebra should be maintained throughout coursework in mathematics.

   b. Calculators may be used as a tool for executing an algorithm but only after students have mastered the algorithm using paper and pencil.

   c. Discrete mathematical problems should be integrated throughout the study of mathematics in grades 6 through 12.

   d. Students' abilities to estimate computational results should be afforded at least as much attention as their abilities to find exact numerical answers.

   e. Students should appeal to authoritative sources (for example, people with more sophisticated understanding than themselves) to validate their own hypotheses.

   f. Graphing should be taught along with other forms of expressing relationships, such as algebraic sentences and tables, rather than as a distinct topic.

   g. Euclidean geometry should be taught as a complete rational system separate from applied mathematics, which tends to distort its purity.

   h. Students should read about, write about, and discuss mathematics as an integral part of everyday life.

   i. Students should learn to appreciate the unique genius of those who gave us the precise mathematical system we use today.

   j. Coordinate geometry should be included in the curriculum only after algebra and before calculus.

   k. Topics from probability and statistics should be emphasized in school mathematics more than they have been in the past.

   l. Conceptual-level learning objectives are appropriate for students only after they have reached Piaget's formal operation stage, somewhere between ages 11 and 15.

   m. The use of determinants to solve systems of equations should be emphasized less than it has been in traditional curricula.

   n. Dependence on scientific calculators is preferable to dependence on tables.

   o. Mathematical instruction should proceed in small linear increments to avoid student perplexity.

   p. Students' invalid hypotheses should be corrected immediately.

   q. Although it may complicate lessons, connections among mathematical topics should be a paramount concern of instruction.

   Compare your responses to these: Parts c, d, f, h, k, m, n, and q are consistent with the *Standards:* the others are not.

3. Familiarize yourself with the learning activities described in Exhibit 2.3. In collaboration with a colleague who is also familiar with these activities, develop and implement a plan for engaging two or three secondary school students in these activities. Afterwards, discuss with each other, as well as with other pairs of colleagues who completed this activity with other students, what the students with whom you worked learned. Also discuss what you and your colleagues as teachers learned from this experience.

4. Exhibits 11.9, 11.32, 11.33, and 11.34 in Chapter 11 provide examples of plans for teaching units produced by teacher Casey Rudd. With several colleagues, examine these four unit plans and address the following questions in a discussion:

   a. For each unit goal, do the objectives define the goal as you would expect? Did Casey Rudd include objectives that don't seem appropriate to you or leave out objectives you would include?

   b. What do you suppose is the purpose of the parenthetical labels ("construct a concept," "discover a relationship," "comprehension," "algorithmic skill," "application," and "creativity") Casey put on his objectives?

   c. What do you suppose is the purpose of Casey weighting each objective with a percentage?

   d. What kinds of information does Casey include in his unit plans?

   e. For some of the objectives, Casey plans to use direct instruction, for others the plan implies inquiry instructional strategies. How are the objectives targeted by direct instruction, B and C in Exhibit 11.32, similar to each other but dissimilar from objectives A and D in

Exhibit 11.32, which are targeted by inquiry instruction?

5. Discuss the following questions with two or more of your colleagues:

a. What's the difference between a student simply learning about mathematics and a student learning to *do* mathematics that is *meaningful* to her or him?

b. How should courses be designed and lessons sequenced so that students don't simply learn about mathematics but learn to do meaningful mathematics?

3

Designing Mathematics Courses and Teaching Units

This chapter serves as an advanced organizer for Chapters 4–6, which deal with the specifics of lesson design; it is also designed to extend your understanding of real-world problem solving and teacher planning. Chapter 3 will help you:

1. Explain the nine-stage process which people use to apply mathematics in solving real-life problems.
2. Explain the types of learning activities students need to experience so that they are able to apply mathematics efficiently and creatively to solve real-life problems.
3. Describe how mathematics courses differ according to

whether they are designed by teachers who use a (a) follow the textbook approach, (b) contrived problem-solving approach, (c) real-world problem-solving approach, or (d) a combination of the three approaches.

4. Describe four levels of teacher planning and the purpose of each: (a) course, (b) unit, (c) lesson, and (d) daily.
5. Explain why each learning objective should specify both a mathematical content and a cognitive or affective learning level.

REQUISITES FOR LEARNING TO APPLY MATHEMATICS TO REAL-LIFE PROBLEM SOLVING

Problem Solving in the Students' Real World

Before addressing questions on how to design mathematics courses and teaching units that can lead students to apply mathematics to real-life problems, examine the process by which the student in Case 3.1 develops a solution to a problem from her real world.

CASE 3.1

Fifteen-year-old Brenda and her two brothers have just been told by their dad that he's tired of them leaving lights on in the house while he has to pay "outrageous" electric bills. He will therefore charge them 25¢ each time he catches one of them leaving lights on unnecessarily. Brenda retires to her

room and thinks to herself: "Twenty-five cents just for leaving a light on isn't fair! It doesn't cost that much to burn a light bulb, or does it? I ought to be able to figure what it costs and show Dad that 25¢ just isn't fair. Let's see, for a problem in school, Mr. Martinez (her mathematics teacher) has us write down the question we want to answer. Okay, here it is: How much does it cost to leave on a light bulb? Then from that I should be able to identify the main variable to solve. The variable is the number of dollars the electric company charges us for burning one bulb.

"So how should I solve for that variable? I could do an experiment. On the first of next month, I'll put a brand new bulb in my lamp and keep it on for a whole month. The next month, I'll keep the lamp off. Then I can find the difference between the electric bill for the month with the lamp on and the one for when it was off. Oh! What size bulb should I use? That's a variable that'll influence the results. Let's see, it's got a 60-watt one now. I'll stick with that and do the experiment for 60-watt bulbs, so size of the bulb will be constant rather than another variable to deal with.

"Oh! Oh! This experiment will take more than two months and I'll have to convince Dad to not charge me for leaving the lamp on all month. He should agree since it's necessary for the experiment and he's charging us only for unnecessary lights. But two months is too long to make my point. There must be some way to shorten this."

"I've got it! I could use last month's bill for the 'off' month and then I'd only have to wait for the 'on' month. That'd get me the results in half the time! Naw, that's not going to work because I used the lamp for some of the time last month. This is going to have to take two months. . . . But even with the two months, there are still too many variables to worry about, like differences in how much we run the heat and electric fans and stuff. I've got to find a better way to do this. I don't know, but maybe if I looked at some old electric bills I might get some ideas."

Brenda collects some old electric bills like the one in Exhibit 3.1; she examines them at her desk and thinks: "This gives me an idea! Maybe I don't have to do an experiment after all. Last month, they charged us $53.51. And it says we used 733 kilowatt hours. From that I ought to be able to figure how much they charge us by the kilowatt-hour. Let's see, the rate must be less than 25¢. I'll divide 733 by 53.51. Here's my calculator; okay, 733 divided by 53.51 is . . . What? $13.70! That can't be! Electricity can't be that expensive. Oh, I know? I should've divided the dollar amount by the kilowatt-hours instead of into them. So, it's 53.51 divided by 733 equals 0.073. So the rate is 7.3¢." Brenda's computation of the electric rate is shown in Exhibit 3.2.

Brenda continues to think: "Maybe from this I can solve for my variable, the cost of burning one 60-watt bulb, without having to do an experiment. But what's a kilowatt-hour? It's in my science book, better look it up. . . . It's, uhh, 'power consumption of 1000 watts for 1 hour.' This bulb is 60 watts, so it burns . . . 60 divided by 1000 watts per hour. So, if the rate is 7.3¢ per kilowatt-hour, it costs 0.06 times 0.073 dollars to burn the bulb for an hour. That's about $0.0044 every hour."

Exhibit 3.1
Brenda's data source.

> **CITY OF LOGANA**
>
> Electric & Utilities Company
> Billing date: 12/27/96   Account no.: 32-260-01-2
>   description
>
> Electric Meter Billing
> Date: 12/20   Reading: 75698   Kilowatt-hours: 733
> Charge for electricity: $53.51
> Charge for sewer: $11.00
> Waste charge: $4.75
> Utility tax: $3.24
>
> TOTAL AMOUNT DUE: $72.52
> DATE DUE: 1/16/97

Exhibit 3.2
Brenda's computation of the electric rate.

$$\text{Kilowatt - hours} = 733$$
$$\text{Cost to customer} = \$53.51$$
$$\cancel{733} \div \cancel{53.51} = \cancel{13.70}$$
$$53.51 \div 733 = 0.073$$
$$\text{Rate} = \$0.073 \text{ per Kilowatt-hour}$$

"So to leave one light bulb on all day would be 24 times 0.0044 or 0.1056, which isn't much more than a tenth of a cent. Gosh! Is that all it cost? It doesn't seem right for Dad to charge us 25¢. Oh, no! I've been doing this in dollars, so that's 0.1056 of a dollar, not a cent. So, it's really about 10½¢. And that's for only one 60-watt bulb." Brenda's computation is shown in Exhibit 3.3. She continues, "Let's see, my overhead light has three 60-watt bulbs . . . leaving lights on can get pretty expensive. But 25¢ is still too high for him to charge us. I'll show him these figures and see if we can negotiate this down."

Brenda hurries out of her room but quickly returns to shut off the lights before speaking to her father.

Research studies suggest that most people do not confidently address problems, nor do they systematically formulate solutions as Brenda did in Case 3.1 (Cangelosi, 1990c; Schoenfeld, 1985). Brenda's confident, systematic pursuit of a solution grew out of her experiences with a mathematics teacher who consciously taught her a process that includes nine stages:

1. *The person is confronted with a puzzling question or questions about how to do something or explain a phenomenon that has to be answered. In Brenda's case, the overall question was: Is it fair*

Exhibit 3.3
Brenda's computation of the cost of burning one 60-watt bulb for a day.

$$A \text{ Kilowatt-hour} =$$
$$\text{the power consumption of 1000 watts for one hour.}$$
$$\text{The light bulb is 60 watts.}$$
$$60 \div 1000 = 0.06$$
$$\text{Rate} = \$0.073 \text{ per Kilowatt-hour.}$$
$$0.06 \times 0.073 = 0.0044.$$
$$\text{It cost } \$0.0044 \text{ each hour to burn a 60 watt light bulb.}$$
$$24 \times 0.0044 = 0.1056.$$
$$\text{It cost about 1.05 cents to burn a 60 watt bulb for a day.}$$
$$\text{It cost about 10.5 cents to burn a 60 watt bulb for a day.}$$

for her dad to charge her and her brothers 25¢ each time they leave a light bulb on unnecessarily?

2. *The person clarifies the question or questions posed by the problem, often in terms of more specific questions about quantities.* Brenda refined the overall question about the fairness of 25¢ per incident to the more mathematical question: How much does it cost to leave a light bulb on?

3. *The principal variable or variables to be solved are identified.* Brenda inferred the variable number of dollars the electric company charges us for burning one bulb from the question: How much does it cost to leave on a light bulb?

4. *The situation is visualized so that relevant relationships involving the principal variable or variables are identified and possible solution designs are considered.* Brenda thought about how a bulb's wattage rating affects the cost of burning the bulb and how burning a bulb impacts the total monthly electric bill. This led her to consider experimenting with one 60-watt bulb for two months. After judging her plan impractical, she identified a relationship involving the rate the company charges for electricity. From there, she decided she could determine the rate from a previous monthly bill and figure the cost of burning the 60-watt bulb.

5. *The solution plan is finalized, including (a) selection of measurements (that is, how data are to be collected), (b) identification of relationships to establish, and (c) selection of algorithms to execute.* For this stage, Brenda decided to use a previous bill as the data source for the dollars charged and the kilowatt-hours consumed. Those figures were used to calculate the rate and then the cost of burning the 60-watt bulb.

6. *Data are gathered or measurements taken.* Brenda read the relevant information from the bill.

7. *The processes, formulas, or algorithms are executed with the data.* Brenda completed the computations leading to the figures of $0.073 per kilowatt-hour and 10.56¢ per day for burning a 60-watt bulb.

8. *Results of the executions of processes, formulas, or algorithms are interpreted to shed light on the original question or questions.* Brenda compared the 10.5¢ per day figure to the 25¢ figure per incident her father was charging.

9. *The person makes a value judgment regarding the original question or questions.* Brenda decided she had a reasonable chance of using her findings to negotiate successfully with her father.

Requisite Attitudes, Skills, and Abilities

Students' successes in applying the nine-stage process to solving problems from their own real worlds depends on how well they have acquired the five attitudes, skills, or abilities listed below.

Confidence and Willingness to Pursue Solutions to Problems. The dogged pursuit of problem solutions requires (a) confidence in the potential for success, (b) freedom from fear of the consequences of failure, and (c) an appreciation for truth. "Appreciation for truth" may appear corny, but Brenda probably would not have systematically persisted in addressing the light-bulb problem had she been more interested in fooling her father into changing his mind than in presenting him with accurate information. Such persistence and appreciation are learned behaviors.

Conceptual-Level Understanding of the Mathematical Concepts, Relationships, and Processes from which Problem Solutions Are Drawn. Unless students understand how examples and nonexamples of concepts differ and why relationships and processes work, they won't recognize how to apply concepts, relationships, and processes in novel situations with real-world clutter, that is, when information irrelevant to the problem or its solution is present. Brenda, for example, had never before tried to solve for an electric rate, but because she had previously constructed the concept of *rate* in her mind and discovered why relationships such as *rate* × *time = distance* and *rate* × *principal = interest* work, she was able to associate that understanding with the question about leaving on lights. (Davis, Maher, & Noddings, 1990).

Comprehension of Necessary Language and Structural Conventions for Organizing, Retaining, and Relating Mathematics to Problem Solving. Language and process conventions provide a means for (a) organizing and storing concepts, relationships, and processes, and (b) communicating about them. Brenda, for example, retrieved mathematics she had conceptualized and stored under such labels as "rate" and "multiplication of rational numbers" for use in solving her problem. Her knowledge of conventions helped her organize what she understands, use tools such as a calculator, and report her findings to her father.

Skills in Recalling or Retrieving Formulas and Executing Algorithms and Other Processes. Accuracy of solutions depends not only on selecting appropriate mathematics but also on correctly executing processes by hand, calculator, or computer. Brenda didn't remember the meaning of kilowatt-hour, but she knew where to look it up. Also, she knew how to compute with her calculator and how to use estimation for monitoring answers.

Ability to Discriminate Between Appropriate and Inappropriate Mathematical Concepts, Relationships, and Processes According to Problem Situations. How to decide when to use the mathematics one understands is a learned ability (Gagne, Yekovich, & Yekovich, 1993, pp. 347–385). Brenda, for example, recognized certain features of her problem situation that led her to use one type of mathematics rather than another.

Requisite Learning Experiences

Relative to the mathematical content of any teaching unit, students acquire requisite attitudes, skills, and abilities for applying that content to real-world problem solving by engaging in learning activities that provide them with the following:

- Successful experiences working with the content on problems from their own real worlds.
- Inquiry instruction leading them to use inductive reasoning to construct concepts and discover relationships (for example, the learning activity on the surface area of right cylinders in which Ms. Lowe engaged her students in Case 1.2).
- Comprehension-level instruction leading them to use the conventions of the language of mathematics.
- Direct instruction leading them to develop and polish memory-level and algorithmic skills (for example, Ms. O'Farrell's lesson in Case 1.1).
- Inquiry instruction leading them to use deductive reasoning to assess what mathematics to apply to different problem-solving situations.

Students learn mathematics that is *meaningful* when they are led to apply mathematics to solve problems from their own real worlds. Thus, meaningful teaching of mathematics provides students with the aforementioned requisite learning experiences.

APPROACHES TO DESIGNING COURSES

Teachers use at least four approaches to designing courses. Not all of them provide students with requisite learning experiences for learning meaningful mathematics.

The Follow a Textbook Approach

Some teachers "design" courses by faithfully following prescribed textbooks page by page; teaching units are equated to textbook chapters. Case 3.2, for example, is a glimpse into Ms. McCuller's thoughts as she begins planning a two-semester elementary algebra course.

CASE 3.2

Ms. McCuller thinks to herself, "Let's see, where's the table of contents? . . . Okay, it looks like I've got 16 chapters to cover, from Chapter 1, 'The Language of Algebra' to Chapter 16, 'Trigonometry.' I don't remember anything about trigonometry in the district curriculum guide for elementary algebra. I wonder if it's okay to skip that. Probably so, since it's the last chapter so nothing else would be depending on it. . . . Oh well, I'll cover it only if we have time for it at the end of the year.

"Let's see just how many instructional weeks are available per semester. Where's the district calendar? . . . All right, we've got a total of 36 weeks. But there's one week each semester for finals, so that leaves only 34. And then there's standardized test week in the spring, so we've got 17 weeks for the first semester and 16 for the second to cover 16 chapters. So, we should average about two weeks per chapter.

"Chapter 1, 'The Language of Algebra' . . . it won't take us but a week to get through this. Same with Chapters 2 and 3; it's all review. So we'll get through the first three chapters in three weeks. Now, Chapter 4 on inequalities—this will take us longer. Let's see, pages 114 to 140. That's 26 pages, not too many for two weeks. Let's see how involved this gets. . . . This is mostly new content for these students. I thought with the NCTM *Standards,* we were supposed to start emphasizing applications! There's not much real-life application in here. How are we supposed to follow the *Standards* if the textbooks don't? Of course, by the time the textbooks catch up, they'll be telling us to do something else! Anyway, two weeks for Chapter 4. . . ."

When Ms. McCuller gets to Chapter 9, "Factoring and Rational Expressions," she exclaims to herself, "This is just the kind of stuff the *Standards* suggests we deemphasize and yet I've got to cover a whole chapter on it. It'll probably take us four weeks to get through all these algorithms!"

During the school year, Ms. McCuller manages to cover the book page by page, skipping only the brief "Extending Your Knowledge" and "Computer Excursion" inserts near the end of each chapter. Faithfully, she assigns the even-numbered exercises for every section covered. Student learning is limited mostly to memory-level skills with virtually no conceptual- or application-level achievement. However, most students take comfort in being able to appeal to a single source, the textbook, for all they need to know about mathematics.

Contrived Problem-Solving Approach

To provide students with heuristic experiences discovering and inventing mathematics, some teachers incorporate concrete mathematical models or problem-solving tasks into every teaching unit. The same topics as are listed in curriculum guides and the textbook table of contents may well be included, but each topic relating to a concept or relationship is introduced through problem-solving or model-analysis experience. Cases 3.3, 3.4, and 3.5 are examples.

CASE 3.3

Mr. Theron is just beginning a teaching unit intended to help his algebra students extend their abilities to (a) apply arithmetic and geometric sequence formulas they discovered in a previous unit, (b) discover new relationships among integers, and (c) invent new algorithms with integers. He introduces the unit by confronting the students with the following problem, which he first read in a book by Posamentier and Stepelman (1990, pp. 252–253):

> Form a 3 × 3 matrix with whole numbers 1, 2, . . . , 9, so that the sum of the elements in each row, column, and diagonal is the same.

He tells them that any $n \times n$ matrix of real numbers, in which the sum of the numbers in each row, column, and diagonal is the same, is called a "magic square" (Sobel & Maletsky, 1988, pp. 123–129). Exhibit 3.4 has two examples.

Working in small cooperative groups, the students' trial-and-error method succeeds in producing magic squares with the desired attributes. Mr. Theron then conducts a question and discussion session leading students to reason inductively to discover that they can utilize the formula for the sum of an arithmetic series $\left[\sum_{i=1}^{n} a_i = (n/2)(a_1 + a_n)\right]$ that they discovered in a previous unit to formulate magic squares.

CASE 3.4

To provide students with experiences in discovering relationships in addition to inventing algorithms, as well as achieving the goal of a unit on Platonic solids, Mr. Pitkin integrates activities described in Exhibit 3.5, an article by Hopley (1994) from *Mathematics Teacher*.

CASE 3.5

To provide his students with experiences discovering relationships, inventing algorithms, and applying technology, as

Exhibit 3.4
Two Examples of "magic squares."

2	7	6
9	5	1
4	3	8

7	2	16	9
12	13	3	6
1	8	10	15
14	11	5	4

well as to achieve the goal of a unit on power and exponential functions, Ms. Bohrer integrates activities described in Exhibit 3.6, an article from *Mathematics Teacher* by Rahn & Berndes (1994).

The Real-Life Problem Solving Approach

In Case 3.6, Ms. Asgil uses an approach similar to those in Cases 3.3, 3.4, and 3.5; however, she has her students analyze real-life situations instead of contrived problems.

CASE 3.6

Ms. Asgil thinks, as she begins designing an algebra course: "In order for these students to appreciate the utility of mathematics they have to discover its power to help them solve their own real-life problems. I ought to have a year-long project that they all work on and to which they'd apply the algebra as they learn it. I once heard about a whole high school curriculum that revolved around a year-long project to build and sell a house. That would be great! Virtually everything I teach them about algebra could be applied. There would be functions to formulate and equations to solve to assess costs, work time, construction questions, carpentry decisions, purchasing questions, and on and on. That's a way to really teach math at the application level! But I've got to be realistic. This school won't be ready for that for another 300 years. Then maybe I'll try it!

"Okay, so we can't build a house, but maybe we could try something a little more realistic—like running a school store. That would involve work time, wages, buying, interest, and so on. But, now that I think about it, students would only learn to apply the algebra to store-related problems. What they need is a variety of real-life situations for analysis. . . .

I've got it! I'll begin the year by conducting a survey to find out what interests them and come up with a list of problems from their real worlds to which we can apply algebra (see Exhibit 2.2, as well as the first-day questionnaires that Casey Rudd uses in Exhibits 11.5–11.8). Then I'll introduce each unit with three or four problems built from that list. I could, for example, have those interested in motor vehicles discover functional relations from working on things like effects of tire size on acceleration. Those concerned with body fitness could examine diet and exercise variables against body-fat and muscle-mass variables. They might work on those in separate groups and report to the large group; then we could abstract what's common to the solution of all problems. They'd be doing real mathematics that was motivated from their own concerns! . . . Oh, another brilliant idea! If I could get some of the other teachers in on this, we could coordinate some of the problems we're working on with what they're doing in social studies, science, physical education, and so on. Maybe I could. . . ."

Exhibit 3.5
An article by Hopley from *Mathematics Teacher* (1994).

Ronald B. Hopley

Nested Platonic Solids: A Class Project in Solid Geometry

Several years ago at a regional NCTM conference in Phoenix, the author was fascinated by a set of cardboard Platonic solids that were nested inside each other. The Platonic solids are polyhedra whose faces are congruent regular polygonal regions, such that the number of edges that meet at each vertex is the same for all vertices; only five are possible. Since the set is no longer commercially available, the author decided to make a nested set for classroom demonstrations and instructions for students to make their own.

Making the nested set is an activity that takes students through many levels of geometric experience. It is a hands-on activity with angle and linear measurement. Students use applications of algebraic equations to geometric relations that result in physical products and gain more experience working with three-dimensional geometry. When they are finished, students have a set of Platonic solids to keep. These solids have interested mathematicians for thousands of years.

Determining the relative sizes of the polyhedra is trivial if the only goal is to make the inner ones smaller than the outer ones. However, the relationships between pairs of these figures is quite inter-esting if the vertices of the inner figures intersect the outer figures in the right places, as revealed in Pugh's table of relationships (see **table 1**). From 120 possible permutations of the five Platonic

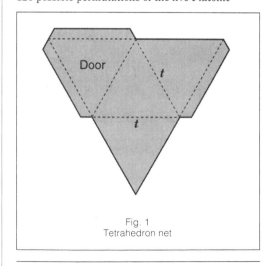

Fig. 1
Tetrahedron net

Ron Hopley teaches at Tucson High Magnet School, Tucson, AZ 85705. He is currently creating files of geometric solids for a three-dimensional computer-graphics program.

Exhibit 3.5
Continued

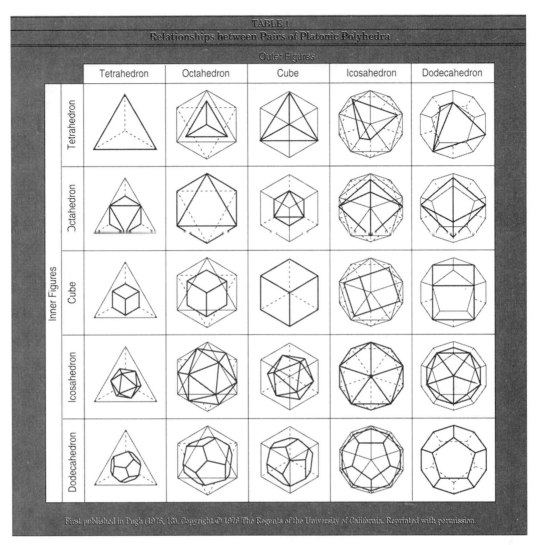

		Outer Figures				
		Tetrahedron	Octahedron	Cube	Icosahedron	Dodecahedron
Inner Figures	Tetrahedron					
	Octahedron					
	Cube					
	Icosahedron					
	Dodecahedron					

TABLE 1
Relationships between Pairs of Platonic Polyhedra

First published in Pugh (1976, 13). Copyright © 1976 The Regents of the University of California. Reprinted with permission.

solids, the set chosen, from innermost out, consists of octahedron, tetrahedron, cube, dodecahedron, and icosahedron. Another octahedron was added on the outside to show that the sequence of solids could continue. The calculations are at the level of high school geometry students. Building the tetrahedron is a good place for students to begin, since that solid has the fewest faces.

Each solid requires approximately one class period to build, except the icosahedron, which takes a little more time for a full discussion of the calculations. Students are supplied with lightweight poster board, scissors, rulers, and glue sticks. Students should have studied right triangles before making the cube and should have been introduced to trigonometry before making the dodecahedron and icosahedron. Thus they do not spend five consecutive class periods building the set. This past year the activity was broken up into two sessions, and next year four or five sessions will be tried.

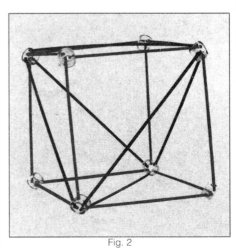

Fig. 2
Cube surrounding tetrahedron. Each edge of the tetrahedron is a diagonal of each face of the cube.

Exhibit 3.5
Continued

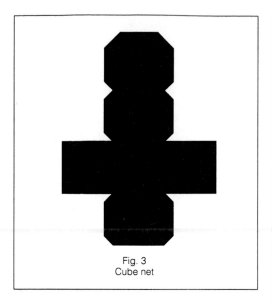

Fig. 3
Cube net

Several days a year we build the solids until we have five

For a follow-up assignment, students make an Archimedean solid on their own.

TETRAHEDRON

The teacher holds up a tetrahedron in front of the class and asks what it would look like if it were cut along the three edges from the "top" vertex to the base and folded open. If none of the responses would work, select one face of the tetrahedron and call it the base. Then point out that each lateral face is attached to the base, which results in the net in **figure 1.** Then draw the net on the chalkboard and discuss with the class the placement of the flaps and the length of the sides of the triangles. An edge length of 8 cm works well for the

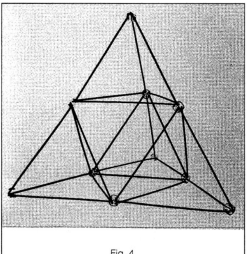

Fig. 4
Tetrahedron surrounding octahedron. Each vertex of the octahedron is the midpoint of each edge of the tetrahedron.

tetrahedron. Let t be the length of the side used in the calculations that follow.

As a class, calculate the dimensions of the smallest rectangle to contain the net without flaps, then add 3 to 5 centimeters for the flaps and minor errors. The calculation requires that the students know how to determine the altitude of an equilateral triangle. Have the students cut rectangles out of the poster board before drawing any of the nets. This step enables every student to get a quick start. With the net on the chalkboard as a guide, students use the rulers and either protractors or compasses to draw their own.

The face with two flaps attached is the door. It should be creased inward to help it stay closed. The single flap attached to the other face is the only flap that should be glued. For crisper edges, use a compass and ruler to score the net before folding.

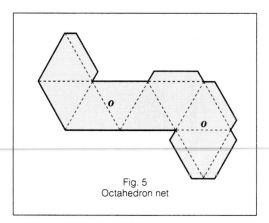

Fig. 5
Octahedron net

CUBE

The cube fits around the tetrahedron with each edge of the tetrahedron a diagonal of each square face of the cube (see **fig. 2**). Since the diagonal of a square is $\sqrt{2}$ times the length of its side, the length of the square's side, c, becomes $(t\sqrt{2})/2$. Thus the edge length of the cube is

$$c = \frac{t\sqrt{2}}{2} \approx 0.707t.$$

Have students add 2 millimeters to the edge length of the tetrahedron before calculating the cube's edge length. This addition takes care of minor errors and the thickness of the poster board.

To determine the net, hold up a cube and have students tell what the net should look like. Most of them are already familiar with it (see **fig. 3**). Leave one face unglued for the door. Make sure that this face has flaps on it to hold it closed.

INNER OCTAHEDRON

The octahedron fits inside the tetrahedron (see **fig. 4**). Its edge length, o, is half the edge length of the

Exhibit 3.5
Continued

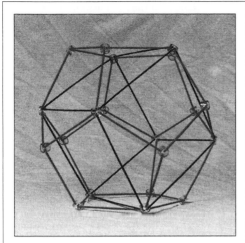

Fig. 6
Dodecahedron surrounding cube. Each edge of the cube is a diagonal of each face of the dodecahedron.

tetrahedron.

$$o = 0.5t$$

By this time, students have had experience visualizing the nets of two of the solids. They can be asked to draw the net of the octahedron as part of a homework assignment the night before they make it. As a start, have the class put four or five of their solutions on the chalkboard, making sure both correct and incorrect nets are selected. Many different correct versions are possible. The most common incorrect net has five triangles sharing a common vertex instead of four. One correct net is presented in **figure 5.**

Because this solid fits inside one that is already made, subtract 2 millimeters from the edge length of the tetrahedron before calculating the octahedron's edge length. It is the innermost figure, so no need arises for a door and thus all flaps can be glued.

DODECAHEDRON

The dodecahedron fits around the cube with each edge of the cube a diagonal of each pentagonal face of the dodecahedron (see **fig. 6**). The interior-angle measure of a pentagon is 108 degrees (see **fig. 7**). Since $\triangle ACB$ is isosceles, if a perpendicular is dropped from C to $\overline{AB}$, both $\overline{AB}$ and $\angle ACB$ are bisected.

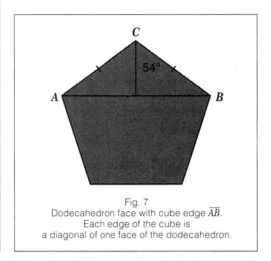

Fig. 7
Dodecahedron face with cube edge $\overline{AB}$.
Each edge of the cube is
a diagonal of one face of the dodecahedron.

Students gain experience in visualizing nets

Exhibit 3.5
Continued

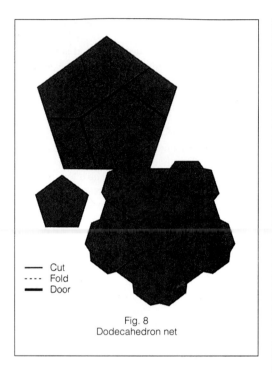

— Cut
- - - Fold
— Door

Fig. 8
Dodecahedron net

Elementary trigonometry gives the equation

$$\sin 54° = \frac{0.5c}{d},$$

where c is the length of an edge of the cube and d is the length of an edge of the dodecahedron. So

$$d = \frac{c}{2\sin 54°} \approx 0.618c.$$

The calculation of the edge length of the icosahedron is more involved than earlier calculations

Add 2 millimeters to the edge length of the cube before calculating the edge length of the dodecahedron.

Students are at first reluctant to offer suggestions on the net of a dodecahedron. When they focus on one face as a base surrounded by pentagons and the opposite face as another base also surrounded by pentagons, they quickly come up with the net in **figure 8.**

Students carefully draw one pentagon on scrap poster board to use as a template and then trace out the net. The pentagon template should be saved to glue on the door as a flap to help keep it closed. After cutting out the net, glue the five pentagons around each base first. Then cut the three diagonals for the door. Finally, glue the two halves of the dodecahedron together and add the spare pentagon to the door.

ICOSAHEDRON

The icosahedron fits around the dodecahedron (see **fig. 9**). These solids mirror each other. The dodecahedron's vertices are the centers of the faces of the icosahedron. In **figure 10a,** $\triangle WXY$ and $\triangle XYZ$ are

adjacent triangles of the icosahedron with A and B being the circumcenters of the triangles (and two adjacent vertices of the dodecahedron). Point C is the midpoint of $\overline{XY}$; $\overline{AB}$ is an edge of the dodecahedron. The calculation of the edge length of the icosahedron is more involved than the previous calculations. It is worthwhile to work through it with

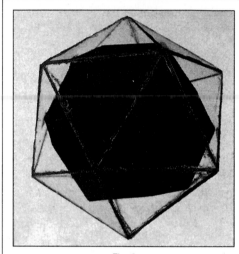

Fig. 9
Icosahedron surrounding dodecahedron.
Each vertex of the dodecahedron is
the circumcenter of each face of the icosahedron.

students because they are accustomed to short solutions to problems.

Calculate the length of $\overline{AC}$, an apothem of $\triangle WXY$. Then calculate the length of $\overline{XY}$, an edge of the icosahedron. AC is calculated by focusing on $\triangle ABC$. Besides being a part of the triangle, $\angle ACB$ is also a

Exhibit 3.5
Continued

dihedral angle of the icosahedron ($\angle A\text{-}CY\text{-}B$). Its measure is 138 degrees 11 minutes 22 seconds (Williams 1979, 67). As before, $\triangle ABC$ is isosceles, so trigonometry can again be used to determine the length of $\overline{AC}$:

$$AC \approx \frac{d}{2\sin 69°\,6'}$$

Now that AC is known, because $\triangle ACY$ is a 30-60-90 triangle, $CY = AC\sqrt{3}$ (**fig. 10b**). And since $XY = 2CY$, then $XY = (2\sqrt{3})AC$. By substituting into the foregoing equation and using i to represent the edge length of the icosahedron,

$$i = \frac{d\sqrt{3}}{\sin 69°\,6'} \approx 1.854\,d.$$

Add only 0.5 millimeters to the edge length of the dodecahedron before calculating the icosahedron.

To help students figure out the net of an icosahedron, point out five triangles meeting at a vertex "on top" of the solid and five meeting "on the bottom." The remaining ten triangles form a belt, alternating up and down, around the middle (see **fig. 11**).

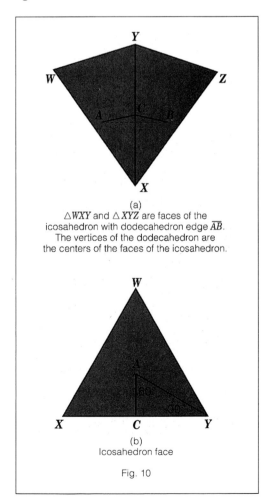

(a)
$\triangle WXY$ and $\triangle XYZ$ are faces of the icosahedron with dodecahedron edge $\overline{AB}$. The vertices of the dodecahedron are the centers of the faces of the icosahedron.

(b)
Icosahedron face

Fig. 10

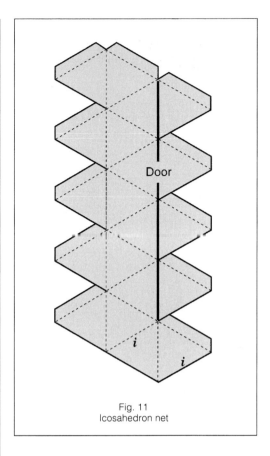

Fig. 11
Icosahedron net

A door for this solid can be cut from its edges. Choose any vertex. The five triangles that share the vertex form the door. Cut along four of the edges and fold along the fifth. Add extra flaps to hold it closed.

OUTER OCTAHEDRON

Students need not necessarily make this second octahedron, but it adds to the set. **Figure 12** shows how the icosahedron nests face to face inside the octahedron. The interesting aspect about this pair is that the vertices of the inner triangle cut the edges of the outer triangle in the golden ratio (Pugh 1976, 13). In the figure,

$$AD{:}DB = BE{:}EC = CF{:}AF = 1{:}\frac{1+\sqrt{5}}{2} \approx 1{:}1.618.$$

Let $AD = x$. Then

$$DB = \frac{1+\sqrt{5}}{2}\,x$$

and

$$AB = x + \frac{1+\sqrt{5}}{2}\,x = \frac{3+\sqrt{5}}{2}x.$$

Since $DB = AF$, then

$$AF = \frac{1+\sqrt{5}}{2}\,x.$$

Exhibit 3.5
Continued

			Outer Figures			
		Tetrahedron	Octahedron	Cube	Icosahedron	Dodecahedron
Inner Figures	Tetrahedron	$\dfrac{x\sqrt{3}}{\sin 35^\circ 16'}$	$\dfrac{x\sqrt{6}}{\sin 54^\circ 44'}$	$\dfrac{x\sqrt{2}}{2}$		
	Octahedron	$2x$		$x\sqrt{2}$		
	Cube	$\dfrac{x\sqrt{6}}{2\sin 35^\circ 16'}$	$\dfrac{x\sqrt{3}}{\sin 54^\circ 44'}$			$\dfrac{x}{2\sin 54^\circ}$
	Icosahedron		$\dfrac{x(3\sqrt{2}+\sqrt{10})}{4}$			$\dfrac{x}{(\sin 58^\circ 17')(\tan 54^\circ)}$
	Dodecahedron		$\dfrac{x\sqrt{3}(\sqrt{5}+1)}{2\sin 54^\circ 44'}$		$\dfrac{x\sqrt{3}}{\sin 69^\circ 6'}$	

TABLE 2
**Formulas to Calculate the Edge Length of the Outer Figure as a
Function of the Edge Length of the Inner Figure (x)**

Calculations are based on the relationships in **table 1.**

Let $i = FD$. From using the law of cosines,

$$i^2 = x^2 + \left(\frac{1+\sqrt{5}}{2}x\right)^2 - 2x\frac{1+\sqrt{5}}{2}x(0.5)$$

$$= x^2 + \frac{3+\sqrt{5}}{2}x^2 - \frac{1+\sqrt{5}}{2}x^2$$

$$= 2x^2.$$

So

$$x = \frac{i\sqrt{2}}{2}.$$

Then

$$AB = \frac{3+\sqrt{5}}{2}x$$

$$= \left(\frac{3+\sqrt{5}}{2}\right)\left(\frac{i\sqrt{2}}{2}\right)\sqrt{2}$$

$$= \frac{3\sqrt{2}+\sqrt{10}}{4}i$$

$$\approx 1.851i.$$

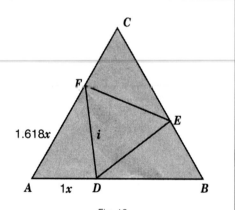

Fig. 12
Icosahedron face $\triangle DEF$ inside octahedron face
$\triangle ABC$. The vertices of the icosahedron cut
the edges of the octahedron in the golden ratio.

Thus the edge length of the outer octahedron is approximately 1.851 times the edge length of the icosahedron. Add 1 millimeter here before calculating. Instead of a door, locate four edges that form a square. Cut three of these and use the fourth as a hinge. The octahedron will open up into two square-based pyramids. Add flaps to keep it closed.

A summary of these and additional calculations is included in **table 2.** Nine cells are blank because the calculations haven't been determined yet. The author is interested in seeing these cells filled, with explanations from readers who would like to work on them.

REFERENCES

Pugh, Anthony. *Polyhedra: A Visual Approach.* Berkeley and Los Angeles: University of California Press, 1976.

Williams, Robert. *The Geometrical Foundation of Natural Structure.* New York: Dover Publications, 1979.

Exhibit 3.6
An article from *Mathematics Teacher* by Rahn & Berndes (1994).
Source: Copied with permission from J.R. Rahn and B. A. Berndes, "Using Logarithms to Explore Power and Exponential Functions,"
in *Mathematics Teacher,* 87: pp. 161–170. Copyright 1994 by National Council of Teachers of Mathematics.

Using Logarithms to Explore Power and Exponential Functions

Power functions and exponential functions often describe the relationship between variables in physical phenomena. Power functions are equations of the form $y = kx^n$ (see **fig. 1**), where k is a nonzero real number and n is a nonzero real number not equal to 1. Exponential functions are equations of the form $y = kb^x$ (see **fig. 2**), where k is a nonzero real number and b is a positive real number. Students should be able visually to recognize these functions so that they can easily identify their appearance when experimental data are graphed. When physical phenomena appear to describe exponential and power functions, logarithms can be used to locate approximate functions that represent the phenomena. This article will share—

1. some activities that have helped our students make visual generalizations about power functions and exponential functions,

2. some methods that have helped our students determine an approximate function represented by data,

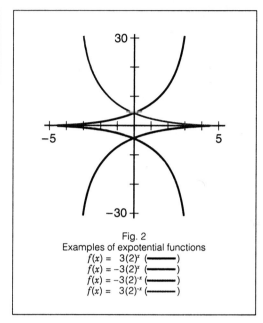

Fig. 2
Examples of expotential functions
$f(x) = 3(2)^x$ (——)
$f(x) = -3(2)^x$ (——)
$f(x) = -3(2)^{-x}$ (——)
$f(x) = 3(2)^{-x}$ (——)

3. several hands-on activities that our students have performed that apply the ideas and techniques described in items 1 and 2, and

4. **activity sheets** that students can complete.

As students apply these ideas, they develop their graphing sense, their understanding of logarithms, and their knowledge of two important functions that are used to represent many physical phenomena. Including this exploration in mathematics courses will help broaden the high school curriculum in the area of functions, graphing sense, and model-

Students make conjectures about the constants

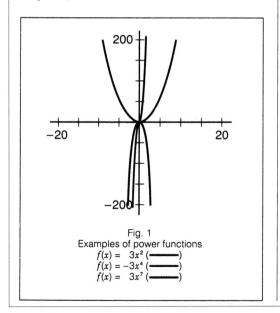

Fig. 1
Examples of power functions
$f(x) = 3x^2$ (——)
$f(x) = -3x^4$ (——)
$f(x) = 3x^7$ (——)

James Rahn teaches at Southern Regional High School, Manahawkin, NJ 08050. Barry Berndes is a mathematics and physics teacher at the Latymer School, Edmonton, London N9 9TN. He was a Fulbright Exchange Teacher to Southern Regional High School. Together they developed activities that helped their students understand key mathematical relationships.

Exhibit 3.6
Continued

What happens if you plot (x, log y)?

ing, as called for in the NCTM's *Curriculum and Evaluation Standards for School Mathematics* (1989, 154).

DEVELOPING A VISUAL COMPREHENSION OF POWER FUNCTIONS AND EXPONENTIAL FUNCTIONS

Through discovery and inductive reasoning, students can make conjectures about the relationships of the constants to the position of the curve on the coordinate axis. Such discoveries might be made when analyzing functions like $y = 2^x$, $y = e^{-x}$, $y = 4x^2$, and $y = 0.25x^{0.5}$. Today graphing calculators and computer graphing programs can be used to remove the tedious work of point-by-point graphing and make it easier to compare many different functions of the same form. Using these graphing tools, students can draw their own conclusions about the constants in $y = kx^n$ and $y = kb^x$ through the following exploration activities.

Activity 1

Have students use a graphing calculator or graphing program to graph the functions in the chart on

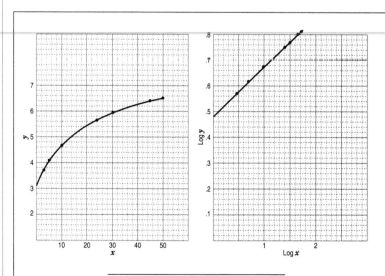

x	y	log x	log y
3	3.73	0.477	0.572
5	4.13	0.699	0.616
10	4.75	1.000	0.677
24	5.66	1.380	0.753
30	5.92	1.477	0.772
45	6.42	1.653	0.807
50	6.56	1.699	0.817

Fig. 3
The power function $y = 3x^{0.2}$ and the corresponding logarithmic graph

activity sheet 1, record a sketch of the graph, and conjecture about the effects on the graph of k and n in the function $y = kx^n$.

As the functions are graphed and compared with each other, students should conjecture about the effect of positive and negative k values, the effect of values of n where $0 < n < 1$, the effect of values of n where $n > 1$, and the effect of odd and even values on n. As our students have explored, they have asked, "What happens when $n = $ '1'?" When $n = 1$, a linear function, $y = kx$, is produced. Therefore, after students complete the investigations, I ask them to sketch

$$y = 2x^2,$$
$$y = -2x^3,$$
$$y = 2x^{1/2},$$
$$y = -2x^{1/3}$$
$$y = 2x^{-1/2},$$

and

$$y = -2x^{-1/2}$$

without the calculator or graphing program to be sure that they have made correct generalizations.

Activity 2

Have students use a graphing utility to graph the functions in the chart on **activity sheet 2,** record a sketch, and write conjectures about the effects on the graph of various values of k and b in the function $y = hb^x$.

As these graphs are compared and contrasted, students should describe the effects of a positive and negative k value, values of b between 0 and 1, and values of b greater than 1. Again, some students have wondered, "What happens when $b = $ '1'?" The result is a horizontal line of the form $y = k$. To confirm that the students understand the exponential functions, I have them make sketches of

$$y = 2^x,$$
$$y = (1/2)^x,$$
$$y = 5e^x,$$

and

$$y = -e^x$$

without a graphing utility.

EXPONENTIAL OR POWER FUNCTION?

Students begin to encounter graphs that appear to be power and exponential functions as they are given opportunities to collect data and graph the data. However, exactly which power or exponential function is being represented still remains a question.

Logarithms can be used to determine if a nonlinear equation is an exponential function ($y = kb^x$) or a power function ($y = ax^n$). They can also be used to determine the constants a, b, and k in these functions.

Exhibit 3.6
Continued

Power functions

Have students look at the power functions

(1) $\qquad y = ax^n$

in quadrant I. These quantities are equal, so their logarithms are equal.

$$\log y = \log ax^n$$
$$\log y = \log a + \log x^n$$
$$\log y = \log a + n \log x$$

Making substitutions of $Y = \log y$ and $X = \log x$ yields

(2) $\qquad \begin{aligned} Y &= \log a + nX, \\ Y &= nX + \log a. \end{aligned}$

This result is an equation of a straight line with a slope of n and a y-intercept of $\log a$. It also means that the *data fit a function of the form $y = ax^n$ if and only if the graph formed by plotting (log x, log y) produces a straight line.*

Students next consider a set of data and its corresponding graph (see **fig. 3**) to see how power functions can be analyzed.

The graph of these data seems to be a power function of the form $y = ax^n$ with n a nonzero real number not equal to 1. To test the conjecture, have students look at a new set of data, (log x, log y), and the corresponding logarithmic graph (see **fig. 3**).

By holding the logarithmic graph (**fig. 3**) horizontally at eye level, the new graph appears to be linear. After drawing a line that passes close to most data points, students should calculate the slope and y-intercept.

$$n = m\,\overline{_{AB}} = \frac{0.85 - 0.65}{1.8 - 0.9}$$
$$= \frac{0.2}{0.9}$$
$$\approx 0.222$$
$$y\text{-intercept} = \log a$$
$$= 0.48$$
$$a = 3.01$$

Using these constants in equation (1), students should predict the function represented in **figure 3.** (The actual function we used to generate the data was $y = 3x^{0.2}$.)

Exponential functions

A similar technique can be used with an exponential function; the investigation is restricted to quadrant-I values.

(3) $\qquad y = kb^x$

These quantities are equal, so their logarithms are also equal.

$$\log y = \log kb^x$$

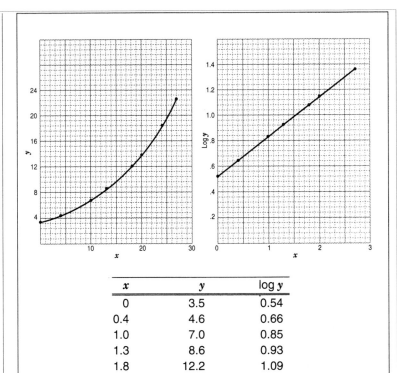

x	y	$\log y$
0	3.5	0.54
0.4	4.6	0.66
1.0	7.0	0.85
1.3	8.6	0.93
1.8	12.2	1.09
2.0	14.0	1.15
2.4	18.5	1.27
2.7	22.7	1.36

Fig. 4
The expotential function $y = 3.5(2)^x$ and the corresponding logarithmic graph

The logarithm of a product is the sum of the logarithms of the factors, therefore,

$$\log y = \log k + \log b^x.$$

Using the exponent rule for logarithms yields

$$\log y = \log k + x(\log b).$$

Making a substitution of $Y = \log y$ and reversing the factors in the last term yields

(4) $\qquad Y = \log k + (\log b)x.$

By observation, this equation is that of a straight line with a slope of $\log b$ and a y-intercept of $\log k$. Students should conclude that *the graph of the data is an exponential function of the form $y = kb^x$ if and only if the graph formed by plotting (x, log y) produces a straight line.*

Give students data and ask them to plot a graph (see **fig. 4**). The graph of the data appears to be an exponential function of the form $y = kb^x$. To test their conjecture have students look at a new set of data, $(x, \log y)$, and the corresponding graph (see **fig. 4**).

Exhibit 3.6
Continued

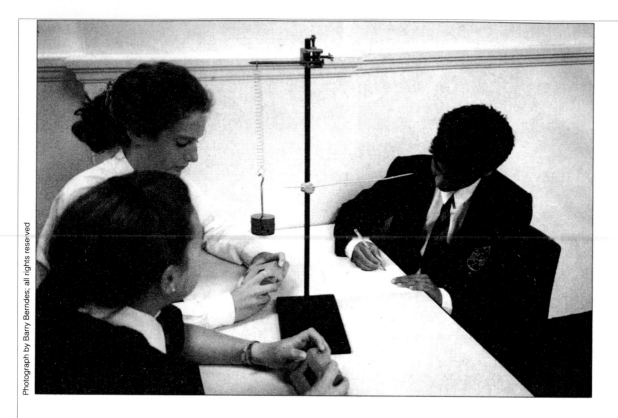

By observation, this new graph appears to be linear. Have students draw a line so that it passes close to most of the data points when measured in a vertical direction. Then ask them to calculate the slope and y-intercept for this line. Students can choose two lattice points, such as $P(0.55, 0.71)$ and $T(1.0, 0.84)$, on the line and calculate the slope.

$$m_{\overline{PT}} = \frac{0.84 - 0.71}{1.0 - 0.55}$$
$$\approx 0.289$$

From equation 4 students know that the slope of the straight line is $\log b$, so $\log b = 0.289$, or $b = 1.945$. The graph of the y-intercept is read to be 0.54, so by equation 4, $\log k = 0.54$, or $k = 3.5$.

Using these constants in equation 3, students should make a prediction for the function represented in **figure 4**. (The actual data in **figure 4** were generated using the function $y = 3.5(2)^x$.) Students note that the procedure arrives at an extremely close approximation of the actual function.

HANDS-ON ACTIVITY 1

"What is the relationship between the period of an oscillating spring and the mass suspended on the spring?" Students can investigate this question by collecting data, studying the graph, and using the techniques just described to analyze the graph.

Set up a spring, with a mass attached, as illustrated in **figure 5**. Then have students oscillate the

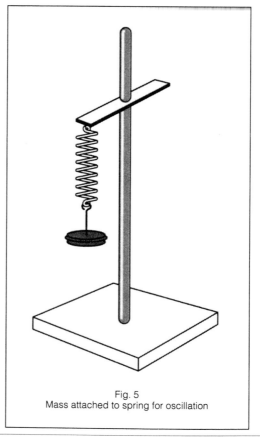

Fig. 5
Mass attached to spring for oscillation

Exhibit 3.6
Continued

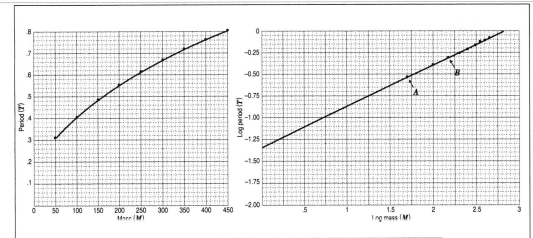

Time for 30 Oscil- lations	Mass **M** (Grams)	Log Mass (**M**)	Period **T** (Seconds)	Log Period **T**
9.3	50	1.70	0.310	−0.509
12.2	100	2.00	0.404	−0.394
14.5	150	2.17	0.483	−0.316
16.7	200	2.30	0.556	−0.255
18.4	250	2.40	0.613	−0.213
20.0	300	2.48	0.667	−0.175
21.7	350	2.54	0.723	−0.141
22.9	400	2.60	0.764	−0.117
24.2	450	2.65	0.807	−0.093

Fig. 6
The period, *T*, of a spring as a function of the mass, *M*, suspended on a spring and its corresponding logarithmic graph

Students collect and graph data

spring and keep a record of the time for thirty oscillations and the mass used. After completing this record for about ten different masses, students should calculate the time for one period by dividing by 30.

The data in **figure 6** represent those collected for one spring. Using the period (*T*) and the mass (*M*), students can complete a graph for the period as a function of mass (see **fig. 6**). Since this graph appears to be a power function, $T = aM^n$, a new set of data, (log x, log y), should be computed and graphed (**fig. 6**).

Students should notice that this new line closely approximates a straight line. The slope is determined using two points, *A* (1.75, −0.50) and *B* (2.25, −0.273).

$$n = m_{\overline{AB}} = \frac{-0.50 - (-0.273)}{1.75 - 2.25}$$
$$= \frac{-0.227}{-0.5}$$
$$= 0.454$$
$$\approx 0.5$$

The *y*-intercept from the graph is read to be −1.325, so log a = −1.325, or a = 0.0473 ≈ 0.05. The results yield an equation,

$$(5) \qquad T = 0.05M^{0.5}.$$

The class should note, from physics, that the period for a spring is described by the equation

$$(6) \qquad T = 2\pi\sqrt{\frac{M}{k}},$$

where *M* is the mass suspended by the spring and *k* is the force constant for the given spring. So by combining the information gathered from (5) and (6),

$$\frac{2\pi}{\sqrt{k}} = 0.05,$$

which yields a force constant, *k*, of 15 791 for the spring used.

HANDS-ON ACTIVITY 2
An activity that our students have used to model exponential decay is rolling dice and continually

Exhibit 3.6
Continued

PROGRAM 1

```
Program
RollTheDice(input,output);
        {by Mark Seibel}
Uses Crt, Printer;
Var numdice, randnum,
numsixs, counter, onetwo
hardcopy:Integer;
        enter:char;

Procedure GetInput(var onetwo:integer);  {input info}
Begin
    Writeln('Would you like <1>  Statistical numbers');
    Writeln('Or would you like <2> Randomly picked numbers?');
    Writelin('Statistical meaning one-sixth of number of dice entered
removed;);
    Writeln('Randomly meaning random computer generated numbers');
    Write( 'Enter choice <1 > or <2> -->);
    Readln(onetwo);
    Writeln:
    Write('Would you like a hard copy? Enter <1 > for NO; <2> for YES-->');
    Readln(hardcopy);
    Writeln;
    If hardcopy=2 then
        {printer message} begin
        Write('Prepare printer for a hardcopy.
Press <enter> when ready -->');
        readlin(enter end;
End;

Procedure RollDiceStat(var numdice, numsixs: integer);
{roll the dice w/stats} Var x:real;

Begin:
    x:=(1/6)*numdice;
    numsixs:=trunc(x);
End:

Procedure RollDice(var numdice, numsixs:integer);
{roll dice randomly) Var x:integer;

    Begin
        {begin random sequence}
        numsixs:=0;
        For x:=numdice downto 0
do
        begin
            randnum:=random(6)+1;
            If randnum=6 then
                numsixs:=numsixs+1
                end
        End:

Procedure ShowChart;
        {top of chart}
Begin
    Writelin ( '# of Rolls  # of dice rolled   # of 6"s that occurred
        # dice remaining');

Writeln('-------------------------------------------------------------------
------------------------------------------------------------------------');
```

```
End;

Procedure ShowResults(var numdice,numsixs,counter:integer);
Begin
                    {show results}

Writeln(counter:4,numdice:12,numsixs:21,numdice-numsixs:24);
End;

Procedure ShowChartHard;
                    {hard copy of top}
Begin
    Writeln(1 st,'# of Rolls # of dice rolled   # of 6"s that occurred   # dice
remaining');

Writeln(1st,'--------------------------------------------------------------------
--------------------------------------------------------------------------');
End;

Procedure
ShowResultsHard(var numdice,numsixs,counter:integer);
Begin
                    {hard copy of numbers}

Writeln(1st,counter:4,numdice: 1 2,numsixs:21 ,numdice-numsixs:24);
End.];

Procedure RemoveDice(var numdice, numsixs:integer);
{remove 6's}
Begin
    numdice:=numdice-numsixs;
End;

Begin
                    {begin main program}
    randnum:=0;
    counter:=1;

    ClrScr;
    Randomize
    GetInput(onetwo);
    Write('Enter how many dice you would like rolled-->');
Readln(numdice);
                    {num of dice to be rolled}
    ClrScr;
    If hardcopy=1 then
                    {screen output}
        Begin
            If onetwo=2 then
                    {begin random sequence}
        Begin

RollDice(numdice,numsixs);
                    ShowChart;

ShowResults(numdice,numsixs,counter);

RemoveDice(numdice,numsixs);
                    Repeat
counter:=counter+1;
```

Exhibit 3.6
Continued

PROGRAM 1—*(Continued)*	

RollDice(numdice,numsixs);
 	
ShowResults(numdice,numsixs,counter);
 	
RemoveDice(numdice,numsixs);
                 Until numdice<=3
        End
            {end random}
      Else
         Begin
           {begin stat roll}
 	
RollDiceStat(numdice,numsixs);
         ShowChart;
 	
ShowResults(numdice,numsixs,counter);
 	
RemoveDice(numdice,Numsixs);
         Repeat
 	
counter:=counter+1;
 	
RollDiceStat(numdice,numsixs);
 	
ShowResults(numdice,numsixs,counter);
 	
RemoveDice(numdice,numsixs);
        Until numdice=6;
     End
        {end stat}
   End
Else
     Begin
         {begin hard copy}
       If onetwo=2 then
        Begin
          {roll dice randomly}
 	
RollDice(numdice,numsixs);
       ShowChartHard;
	ShowResultsHard(numdice, numsixs, counter);
	
	RemoveDice(numdice,numsixs);
	        Repeat
	
	counter:=counter+1;
	
	RollDice(numdice,numsixs);
	
	ShowResultsHard(numdice,numsixs,counter);
	
	RemoveDice(numdice,numsixs0;
	         Until Numdice<=3
	      End
	         {end random}
	       Begin
	         {begin statroll}
	
	RollDiceStat(numdice,numsixs);
	        ShowChartHard;
	
	ShowResultsHard(numdice,numsixs,counter);
	
	RemoveDice(numdice,numsixs);
	        Repeat
	
	counter:=counter+1;
	
	RollDiceStat(numdice,numsixs);
	
	ShowResultsHard(numdice,numsixs,counter);
	
	RemoveDice(numdice,numdixs);
	
	        Until numdice=6
	      End
	        {end stat}
	    End
	End.
	        {end main program}

removing all "decayed" dice. Distribute 300 dice to the class (10 dice for each student in a class of 30). Preselect one number on the dice to represent decay. When this number appears on a rolled die, that die is removed from the sample. Students begin by rolling all 300 dice. After each roll students count and remove all "decayed" dice. They also record the number of remaining dice. The number of remaining dice indicates the portion of the sample that has not decayed. This procedure continues until only six or fewer dice remain. Students then create a graph of the number of dice remaining, D, as a function of the number of rolls, N.

One student, Mark Seibel, wrote a Pascal Turbo computer program (**program 1**) that generated these data using a random-number generator. The program continued until the number of dice remaining was six or fewer.

After observing the graph of D as a function of N (**fig. 7**), students should sense that it appears to represent an exponential function. A new set of data, $(N, \log D)$, should then be computed, graphed (**fig. 7**), and investigated.

Using two points, A (8, 1.85) and B (19, 1), on the straight line in **figure 7**, have students calculate the slope.

$$m_{\overline{AB}} = \frac{0.85}{-11}$$
$$\approx 0.077$$

The slope of line $AB = \log b$, from equation 4, so $\log b = -0.077$. Therefore $b = 0.837$, or 0.84 to two decimal places. From the graph the y-intercept is read to be 2.48, so

Exhibit 3.6
Continued

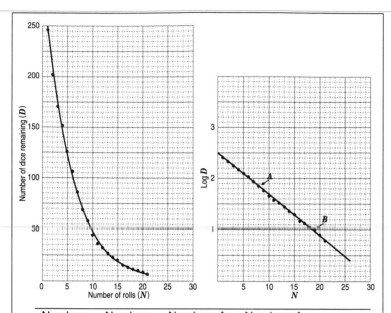

Fig. 7
The number of dice remaining, D, as a function of the number of rolls, N,
and its corresponding logarithmic graph

Number of Rolls (N)	Number of Dice Rolled	Number of Sixes That Occurred	Number of Dice Remaining (D)	Log D
1	300	54	246	2.39
2	246	44	202	2.31
3	202	32	170	2.23
4	170	18	152	2.18
5	152	26	126	2.10
6	126	20	106	2.03
7	106	20	86	1.93
8	86	18	68	1.83
9	68	10	58	1.76
10	58	14	44	1.64
11	44	8	36	1.56
12	36	4	32	1.51
13	32	5	27	1.43
14	27	4	23	1.36
15	23	3	20	1.30
16	20	5	15	1.18
17	15	2	13	1.11
18	13	2	11	1.04
19	11	1	10	1.00
20	10	2	8	0.90
21	8	2	6	0.78

$$\log k = 2.48,$$
$$k = 302.$$

By compiling the information from **figure 7**, students should conjecture the number of dice remaining, D, after n rolls. The actual function generated using probability was $D = 300\,(0.83)^n$.

As our students have applied these ideas, they have continued to develop their graphing sense, their understanding of logarithms, and their knowledge about two common functions that are used to represent many physical phenomena. At the same time the high school curriculum has been enriched and broadened, as recommended by the NCTM's *Curriculum and Evaluation Standards for School Mathematics* (1989) in the areas of functions, graphing sense, and modeling.

REFERENCE

National Council of Teachers of Mathematics. *Curriculum and Evaluation Standards for School Mathematics.* Reston, Va.: The Council, 1989.

Exhibit 3.6
Continued

ACTIVITY SHEET 1   Name _____

A Study of the Power Function $y = kx^n$

Using a graphing calculator or a graphing program, complete the following:

1. Study the effects of k and n in the Power Function $y = kx^n$.

2. Record a sketch for each category.

3. Make a conjecture about the effects of k and n in the Power Function $y = kx^n$.

	$k > 0$	$k < 0$
n even $n > 0$	$y = 3x^2$ $y = 3x^4$	$y = -3x^2$ $y = -3x^4$
n odd $n > 0$	$y = 3x^3$ $y = 3x^5$	$y = -3x^3$ $y = -3x^5$
nth root n even $n > 0$	$y = 3x^{1/2}$ $y = 3x^{1/4}$	$y = -3x^{1/2}$ $y = -3x^{1/4}$
nth root n odd $n > 0$	$y = 3x^{1/3}$ $y = 3x^{1/5}$	$y = -3x^{1/3}$ $y = -3x^{1/5}$
n even $n < 0$	$y = 3x^{-2}$ $y = 3x^{-4}$	$y = -3x^{-2}$ $y = -3x^{-4}$
n odd $n < 0$	$y = 3x^{-3}$ $y = 3x^{-5}$	$y = -3x^{-3}$ $y = -3x^{-5}$
nth root n even $n < 0$	$y = 3x^{-1/2}$ $y = 3x^{-1/4}$	$y = -3x^{-1/2}$ $y = -3x^{-1/4}$
nth root n odd $n < 0$	$y = 3x^{-1/3}$ $y = 3x^{-1/5}$	$y = -3x^{-1/3}$ $y = -3x^{-1/5}$

CONJECTURE: _____

_____

_____

_____

Exhibit 3.6
Continued

ACTIVITY SHEET 2   Name _____

A Study of the Exponential Function $y = kb^x$

Using a graphing calculator or a graphing program, complete the following:

1. Study the effects of k and b in the Exponential Function $y = kb^x$.

2. Record a sketch for each category.

3. Make a conjecture about the effects of k and b in the exponential function $y = kb^x$.

	$k > 0$	$k < 0$
$b > 1$	$y = 3(5)^x$	$y = -3(5)^x$
	$y = 3(6)^x$	$y = -3(6)^x$
	$y = 3(10)^x$	$y = -3(10)^x$
$0 < b < 1$	$y = 3(1/2)^x$	$y = -3(1/2)^x$
	$y = 3(1/5)^x$	$y = -3(1/5)^x$
	$y = 3(1/10)^x$	$y = -3(1/10)^x$

CONJECTURE: _____

_____

_____

_____

Combining Approaches

To learn to do meaningful mathematics, to apply mathematics to address real-life problems as Brenda did in Case 3.1, students need to engage in learning activities that provide the experiences listed in this section in this chapter entitled Requisite Learning Experiences. Each of the three approaches to course design provides some but not all of those experiences.

In addition to activities such as engaging in question sessions, students should work on four types of mathematical tasks:

- *Solving contrived problems.* Contrived problems, such as those the teachers incorporated in their lessons in Cases 3.3, 3.4, and 3.5, are a convenient complement to real-world problems and can stimulate students to reason inductively to discover and invent mathematics. As you will learn from your work in Chapter 4, contrived problems are particularly useful in leading students to construct mathematical concepts and discover mathematical relationships for themselves.
- *Executing skill-level exercises.* Mathematics textbooks are filled with this kind of exercises, which are necessary for polishing students' skills with algorithms. They provide practice in computation, in solving open sentences, translating expressions from one form to another (for example, from algebraic form to graphic form), re-forming expressions (factoring a polynomial), simplifying expressions, and using mathematical language.
- *Solving real-life problems.* Real-life problems are used to motivate students to work on the mathematical content of the unit and to help them bridge school mathematics with real-world mathematics. However, with 15 to 40 students per class, it is impractical to restrict problem-solving activities to real-life situations. Thus, real-world problems used in application-level lessons are complemented with textbook word problems.
- *Solving textbook problems.* Solving textbook word problems like the one in Case 1.4 involves students in some, but not all the aspects of real-life problem solving.

Compare the nine stages of real-world problem solving (as listed earlier in this chapter in the section titled, Problem Solving in the Students' Real World) to the task of solving textbook word problems:

1. With a real-life problem, students are confronted with puzzling questions they want to answer. Textbook word problems (for example, What is the height of a tree if it casts a 75-foot shadow when the angle of elevation of the sun is 27°?) present puzzling questions, but rarely are they questions students feel a need to answer.
2. To solve a real-life problem, students must clarify the questions posed by problems, often in terms of more specific questions about quantities. With textbook word problems, the specific questions involving quantities (What is the maximum possible area of the patio?) are typically articulated for students. Thus, instead of taxing students' abilities to formulate questions, what is tested is the students' reading comprehension skill.
3. With both real-world and textbook word problems, principal variables to be solved must be inferred from the questions about quantities.
4. To solve real-life problems, student must visualize situations so that relevant relationships involving the principal variables are identified and possible solution designs are considered. Typically, this step is unnecessary for solving textbook word problems because all relevant data are given and open sentences can be formulated by simply following the pattern established by the examples and other word problems in the text section where the problem appears.
5. The solution plan for real-life problems needs to be finalized, but this is unnecessary for textbook word problems, as alluded to in point 4.
6. Numbers used in real-life problem solving result from measurements. Numbers used in textbook word problems are usually given.
7. Both real-life and textbook word problems require students to execute processes, formulas, or algorithms.
8. Results of executions of processes, formulas, or algorithms are interpreted to shed light on the original questions posed by real-life problems. Simply obtaining the results, not interpreting them, is all that is typically required for textbook word problems (e.g., finding the height of the tree that casts the 75-foot shadow is sufficient; it is not necessary to decide if it is practical to move the tree).
9. Unlike real-life problems, solving textbook word problems does not require students to make value judgments.

Exhibit 3.7 summarizes some of the principal similarities and differences between solving real-life problems and textbook word problems. Techniques for modifying textbook word problems so they are more representative of real-world problems are explained and illustrated in Chapters 6 and 11.

Casey Rudd's Combined Approach to Designing Courses

Considering the trips you've made into Chapter 11 (for example, when you engaged in Transitional Activity 5 near the end of Chapter 2), you understand by now that Chapter 11 walks you through the professional life of Casey Rudd during his first year as a mathematics teacher. Mr. Rudd designs a course that depends on the textbook without following it page by page nor allowing it to dictate the course units (as did

Exhibit 3.7
Solving real-life problems compared to solving textbook word problems.

Characteristic	Real Problems	Textbook Word Problems
Problem is personalized with student having felt a need to solve it	Yes	No
Questions posed by the problem are clarified and articulated for the student	No	Yes
Reading comprehension skills are likely to be taxed	No	Yes
Principal variables must be inferred from questions posed by the problem	Yes	Yes
Type of problem is categorized for the student according to the type of mathematics needed	No	Yes
Student is likely to have to select the type of mathematics to be used	Yes	No
Measurement procedures must be selected and data collected	Yes	No
Irrelevant data and information (i.e., clutter) are present	Yes	No
Student needs to execute formulas, processes, or algorithms	Yes	Yes
Solutions have pat answers	No	Yes
Student must interpret results and make value judgments	Yes	No

Ms. McCuller in Case 3.2). The textbook is a significant influence on his choice of mathematical content and it is the primary source of skill level exercises, word problems, and a few contrived problems. But he also uses aspects of the contrived and real-life problem-solving approaches. Once again, jump ahead to Chapter 11 by quickly reading the section titled Planning and Organizing the Courses by Writing Syllabi. There is no need at this reading to attend to details to the degree you will when you actually study Chapter 11. Do, however, note what Mr. Rudd includes in the syllabus that is displayed in Exhibit 11.6.

PLANNING TEACHING UNITS

Chapter 2 outlined the components of a teaching unit: (a) a learning goal, (b) a set of specific objectives that define the learning goal, (c) a planned sequence of lessons, each consisting of learning activities designed to help students achieve specific objectives, (d) mechanisms for monitoring student progress and utilizing feedback in the design of lessons, and (e) a summative evaluation of student achievement.

When you engaged in Transitional Activity 5 near the end of Chapter 2, you examined a sample of four teaching unit plans Casey Rudd wrote (Exhibits 11.9, 11.32, 11.33, and 11.34). Note the parts of each written unit plan and the decisions Mr. Rudd makes in order to write a unit plan.

The Title and Goal

You determine the title and goal of each teaching unit when you plan the course during *long-range planning* prior to the opening of the school term or

year. Examples of titles of teaching units, along with their respective learning goals are shown in Exhibit 3.8.

Exhibit 3.8
Examples of unit titles and learning goals.

1. *Multiplying signed numbers* (seventh-grade mathematics). Understands why (a) $A \bullet B > 0$ if $A > 0$ and $B > 0$, (b) $A \bullet B > 0$ if $A < 0$ and $B < 0$, (c) $A \bullet B < 0$ if $A > 0$ and $B < 0$, (d) $A \bullet B < 0$ if $A < 0$ and $B > 0$, and (e) $A \bullet B = 0$ if $A = 0$ or $B = 0$, and applies these rules for multiplying signed numbers to solve real-life problems.
2. The number π (prealgebra). Understands that $\pi = C/d$ for any circle and utilizes that relationship in the solution for real-life problems.
3. *Interest on savings* (consumer mathematics). Understands both simple and compound interest formulas and applies them to solve real-life problems.
4. *Congruence of triangles* (geometry). Understands the rationale underlying certain triangle congruence postulates and theorems, utilizes them to develop and prove additional theorems, and applies triangle congruence relations to solve real-life problems.
5. *Probability of compound events* (intermediate algebra). Establishes appropriate sample spaces for compound events, understands fundamental probability formulas for compound events, and applies the formulas to solve real-life problems.
6. *Analyzing quadratic functions* (algebra II). Understands why the $f(x) = a(x - h)^2 + k$ form of a quadratic function facilitates graphing the function and applies that understanding to the solution of real-life problems.

The Objectives

The Need for Specificity. The learning goal indicates what you intend your students to gain from a teaching unit. Just how should the unit's lessons be designed so that students will achieve the goal? Before answering that question, the goal needs to be defined in greater detail, so that both its mathematical content and the learning levels that students must display to reach the goal are spelled out. You provide that detail by defining the goal with a set of specific objectives.

The teachers who formulated the six learning goals in Exhibit 3.8 detailed the mathematical content and indicated the specific skills, abilities, or attitudes their students are to display by listing objective A, B, C, ... for each goal as shown in Exhibit 3.9.

Mathematical Content. You write each objective to specify a mathematical content, so that you clearly know the mathematical topics students are to learn. Reread, for example, the sixth learning goal in Exhibit 3.9 (the one for the unit on analyzing quadratic functions). What "methods for facilitating graphing of quadratic functions" are to be included? Objectives A, C, and F specify three methods: (a) converting the function to the form $f(x) = a(x - h)^2 + k$ by completing the square and then identifying the graph's axis of symmetry and other features by inspecting a, h, and k, (b) inspecting x where $f(x) = 0$, and (c) inspecting $f(0)$.

Objectives need to be stated so that you know what types of numbers, operations, algorithms, terms, and the like are to be dealt with in the unit's lessons. How those lessons should be designed depends upon, among other things, the type of mathematical content specified in the objectives. As you shall see in Chapter 4, you design learning activities differently for teaching about one type of content (for example, a concept) from another type (e.g., an algorithm). Thus, before designing a lesson for leading students to achieve a particular objective, you need to consider whether the content is (a) a *concept* (for example, a rational number), (b) a *discoverable relationship* (for example, the Pythagorean theorem), (c) a *convention* (e.g., "$|x|$" is read as the "absolute value of x"), or (d) an *algorithm*.

Concepts and discoverable relationships are defined and elaborated upon in Chapter 4, conventions and algorithms in Chapter 5.

Learning Level. Compare the following five objectives for similarities and differences:

1. Willingly attempt to develop a general formula for making it easier (than either factoring or completing the square) to solve quadratic equations.

2. Explain why the quadratic formula yields the roots of any one-variable quadratic equation with real coefficients.
3. State the quadratic formula.
4. Given a one-variable quadratic equation with real coefficients, find the roots of the equation using the quadratic formula.
5. Given a real-life problem, determine how, if at all, a solution to that problem is facilitated by setting up and solving for a quadratic equation.

All five of these objectives specify the same mathematical content—namely the quadratic formula, which is a discoverable relationship that leads to an algorithm for solving quadratic equations. However, no two of the five objectives are the same. The objectives differ in the way the students are expected to think about and deal with the quadratic formula. Objective A is concerned with the students' willingness to develop the formula. Objective B's concern focuses on the students' understanding of why the formula works. Objective C strives to have the students remember the formula. Objective D targets the students' abilities to apply the formula to solve real-life problems. Each objective differs from the other four in the learning level it specifies. By definition:

> An objective's *learning level* is the manner in which students will interact with the objective's mathematical content once the objective is achieved.

Just as an objective's mathematical content influences how you go about teaching to that objective, that is, you teach about the quadratic formula differently than you teach about conditional probabilities, so should how you teach depend on the objective's learning level.

Familiarity with one of the published schemes for classifying objectives according to their targeted learning levels will help you clarify your own objectives. The scheme suggested to you in this text is especially adapted from a variety of sources (Bloom, 1984; Cangelosi, 1980, 1982, pp. 90–95, 1990b, pp. 7–19; Guliford, 1959; Krathwohl, Bloom, & Masia, 1964) for teaching mathematics in harmony with the *Standards* (NCTM, 1989). It takes into account the need for inquiry instruction from the constructivist perspective (Davis, Maher, & Noddings, 1990; Guzzetti, Snyder, Glass, & Gamas, 1993), as well as for direct instruction for skill building.

Two learning domains are included: *affective* and *cognitive*. If the intent of the objective is for students to develop a particular attitude or feeling (e.g., a desire to prove a theorem or willingness to work toward the solution of problems) the learning level of the objective falls within the *affective domain*.

Exhibit 3.9
Examples of sets of objectives teachers used to define the goals from Exhibit 3.8.

I. *Multiplying signed numbers* (seventh-grade mathematics): Understands why (a) $A \cdot B > 0$ if $A > 0$ and $B > 0$, (b) $A \cdot B > 0$ if $A < 0$ and $B < 0$, (c) $A \cdot B < 0$ if $A > 0$ and $B < 0$, (d) $A \cdot B < 0$ if $A < 0$ and $B > 0$, and (e) $A \cdot B = 0$ if $A = 0$ or $B = 0$, and applies these rules for multiplying signed numbers to solve real-life problems. The student's achievement of this goal depends on how he or she does the following:

A. When presented with two positive rational numbers, illustrates with a variety of paradigms why the product of those two numbers is positive.

B. When presented with two rational numbers, one positive and one negative, illustrates with a variety of paradigms why the product of those two numbers is negative.

C. When presented with two negative rational numbers, illustrates with a variety of paradigms why the product of those two numbers is positive.

D. When presented with two rational numbers, one of which is zero, illustrates with a variety of paradigms why the product of those two numbers is zero.

E. Given a rational constant A, explains why $A^2 > 0$ if $A \neq 0$ and $A^2 = 0$ if $A = 0$.

F. Recites the laws for multiplying signed numbers.

G. With the aid of a calculator, simplifies expressions involving nested operations (multiplication and addition) with rational constants, such as

$$12.3 + (30 - 33) \times (-101.1) \times (8.5 - 11.9)$$

H. Given a real-life problem, determines how, if at all, a solution to that problem is facilitated by multiplying signed numbers.

I. Describes novel paradigms illustrating the rules for multiplying signed numbers that he or she created.

II. *The number π* (prealgebra): Understands that $\pi = C/d$ for any circle and utilizes that relation in the solution of real-life problems. The student's achievement of this goal depends on how he or she does the following:

A. Provides an inductive argument for concluding that the ratio of the circumference of any circle to its diameter is π.

B. Displays a willingness to attempt to develop a method for obtaining a rational approximation of π.

C. Explains at least three methods for obtaining rational approximations of π: (a) a method for averaging measurements that the students themselves invent, (b) an ancient method (e.g., one listed by von Baravalle (1969), and (c) a computer-based method.

D. States the following: (a) π is the ratio of the circumference of any circle to its diameter, (b) π is an irrational number, (c) $\pi \approx 3.1415929$.

E. Explains why $C = \pi d = 2\pi r$ for a circle with circumference C, diameter d, and radius r.

F. Solves for the circumference of a circle given either its radius or diameter.

G. Solves for the diameter and radius of a circle given its circumference.

H. Given a real-life problem, determines how, if at all, a solution to that problem is facilitated by using the relation $\pi = C/d$.

III. *Interest on savings* (consumer mathematics): Understands both simple and compound interest formulas and applies them to solve real-life problems. The student's achievement of this goal depends on how he or she does the following:

A. Defines the following terms with respect to savings plans: interest, simple interest, and compound interest.

B. Explains the rationale underlying the formula for calculating simple interest, $I = Prt$.

C. For situations involving simple interest on savings, solves for the unknown variables when exactly three of the following four are given: I, P, r, and t.

D. Given a real-life problem, determines how, if at all, a solution to that problem is facilitated by using the relation $I = Prt$.

E. Explains the rationale underlying the following formula for calculating the accumulated amount, A, in a compound interest savings plan:

$$A = P\left(1 + \frac{r}{k}\right)^{kn}$$

where $P =$ the principal, $r =$ the annual rate, $k =$ the number of times per year the interest is compounded, and $n =$ the number of years.

F. For situations involving compound interest on savings, solves for the unknown variables when exactly four of the following five are given: A, P, r, k, and n.

G. Given a real-life problem, determines how, if at all, a solution to that problem is facilitated by using the relation

$$A = P\left(1 + \frac{r}{k}\right)^{kn}$$

IV. *Congruence of triangles* (geometry): Understands the rationale underlying certain triangle congruence postulates and theorems, utilizes them to develop and prove additional theorems, and applies triangle congruence relations to solve real-life problems. The student's achievement of this goal depends on how he or she does the following:

A. Explains the meaning of $\triangle ABC \cong \triangle DEF$, $\overrightarrow{AD}$ bisects $\angle BAC$, and median of a triangle.

B. Provides both an inductive and rational argument (but not necessarily a deductive proof) for why the following relations hold:

Exhibit 3.9
Continued

1. The theorem that congruence between triangles is an equivalence relation
2. The side-angle-side postulate
3. The theorem that if two sides of a triangle are congruent, then the angles opposite them are congruent
4. The theorem that if $\overline{AB}$ and $\overline{CD}$ bisect each other at F, then $AC = BD$
5. The angle-side-angle theorem
6. The side-side-side theorem
7. The theorem that if two angles of a triangle are congruent, the sides opposite these angles are congruent
8. The angle-bisector theorem
C. Explains deductive proofs for the seven theorems just listed.
D. Recognizes the value of a system of postulates and theorems as a means of verifying relations.
E. Prefers to verify a theorem for himself or herself rather than accepting it on faith in some authority.
F. Originates hypotheses based on the eight relations listed in B.
G. Develops deductive proofs of corollaries to the relations listed in B and to theorems based on student-generated hypotheses.
H. Finds lengths of line segments and measures of angles by executing algorithms based on postulates and theorems formulated in this unit.
I. Given a real-life problem, determines how, if at all, a solution to that problem is facilitated by using relations derived from triangle congruence postulates and theorems.

V. *Probability of compound events* (intermediate algebra): Establishes appropriate sample spaces for compound events, understands fundamental probability formulas for compound events, and applies the formulas to solve real-life problems. The student's achievement of this goal depends on how he or she does the following:
A. Distinguishes between examples and nonexamples of each of the following: sample space, compound event, independent events, dependent events, mutually exclusive events, empirical sample space, theoretical sample space, complement of an event, and conditional probability.
B. Defines the terms sample space, compound event, independent event, dependent events, mutually exclusive, empirical sample space, theoretical sample space, complement of an event, and conditional probability.
C. Translates the symbols $P(A)$, $P(A')$, A', $A \cap B$, $A \cup B$, and A/B.

D. Explains why the following relations hold:
1. The law of large numbers
2. $P(A') = 1 - P(A)$
3. The addition rule for mutually exclusive events
4. The addition rule for events that are not mutually exclusive
5. The multiplication rule for independent events
6. The multiplication rule for dependent events
E. Computes probabilities using algorithms based on relations 2, 3, 4, 5, and 6 of Objective D.
F. Given a real-life problem, determines how, if at all, a solution to that problem is facilitated by using probability principles and methods for compound events.

VI. *Analyzing quadratic functions* (algebra II): Understands why certain methods for facilitating the graphing of quadratic functions work and applies that understanding to the solution of real-life problems. The student's achievement of this goal depends on how he or she does the following:
A. Give $f(x) = a(x - h)^2 + k$, where x is a real value and a, h, and k are real constants, explains why the following is true regarding the parabolic graph of f:
1. The line of the axis of symmetry is given by $x = h$.
2. The vertex is (h, k).
3. If $a > 0$, then k is the minimum function value and the graph opens upward.
4. If $a < 0$, then k is the maximum function value and the graph opens downward.
B. Recites the four relations listed in A.
C. Given a quadratic function expressed in standard form, uses the algorithm for completing the square to express the function in the form $f(x) = a(x - h)^2 + k$.
D. Explains why the algorithm for completing the square works in changing the form of a quadratic function as indicated in C.
E. Explains why
1. Solving for $f(x) = 0$ yields the x-intercepts of f.
2. $f(0)$ provides the y-intercept.
3. The discriminant indicates the number of x-intercepts.
F. Defines maximum values of a function, minimum values of a function, x-intercept and y-intercept.
G. Given a quadratic function, describes its graph using the intercepts and the $f(x) = a(x - h)^2 + k$ form without actually plotting points.
H. Given a real-life problem, determines how, if at all, a solution to that problem is facilitated by analyzing a quadratic function.
I. Recognizes the advantages of being able to analyze a function without having to plot very many points of its graph.

If the intent of the objective is for students to be able to do something mentally (e.g., remember a formula or deduce a method for solving a problem) the learning level of the objective falls within the *cognitive domain.*

This scheme for classifying learning levels under the two domains is explained and its uses illustrated in Chapters 4, 5, and 6. However, to give you a preview of what you'll be working with, Exhibit 3.10 provides an outline of the scheme.

Revisit any one of Casey Rudd's unit plans from Exhibits 11.9, 11.32, 11.33, and 11.34. Note that Mr. Rudd specifies the learning level of each objective by labeling it according to Exhibit 3.10's scheme. Objectives listed in the remainder of this text are also labeled according to that scheme.

Sequencing the Objectives and the Overall Plan for Lessons

Each lesson is designed to lead students to achieve an objective. Casey Rudd's unit plan in Exhibit 11.10 lists objectives A through L in the approximate order in which he plans to conduct lessons for those objectives. I say "approximate," because the lesson for one objective often overlaps lessons for other objectives if two lessons share a common learning activity. Casey's Overall Plan for Lessons also indicates something about how objectives, and thus lessons, will be sequenced. Following are some general principles to keep in mind when you sequence objectives for a unit; how to apply these principles is explained and illustrated in Chapters 4, 5, 6, and 11:

- Ordinarily, conventional names for concepts or relationships should not be introduced before students have engaged in inquiry lessons leading them to construct the concepts or discover the relationships for themselves. Memorizing words such as "sample space" or "Pythagorean theorem" to attach to the concept sample space or the relationship Pythagorean theorem before the concept or relationship is conceptualized is meaningless for students.
- Comprehension objectives relative to certain messages (for example, the proof of the side-angle-side theorem as presented in a textbook) or to certain technical expressions like the use of the summation notation Σ, should be taught before conducting learning activities that depend on those messages or technical expressions. Students experience considerable difficulty engaging in lessons that include either messages they've yet to comprehend or technical expressions they've not learned to use.
- Ordinarily, the statement of a relationship, for example, that $a^2 + b^2 = c^2$, or that the product of two negative integers is positive, should not be com-

mitted to memory before students discover why that relationship exists.
- Students are ready to engage in inquiry lessons for an application-level objective only after they have conceptualized the content and relationships underlying the objective and acquired relevant comprehension and knowledge skills.
- If creativity or affective objectives are targeted by a unit, then lessons for them are ordinarily scattered throughout the unit and integrated with lessons for other objectives. Both creative and affective behaviors are usually acquired by experiences that extend over the entire course of a unit rather than tending to appear near the beginning (as with construct a concept or discover a relationship learning), the middle (as with comprehension, simple knowledge, and algorithmic skill learning), or the end (as with application learning).

A unit's overall plan for lessons provides only general ideas about how the lessons will be taught. You develop a detailed plan for a lesson a day or two before you actually plan to teach it.

Formative Feedback Plan and Summative Evaluations of Student Achievement

How to gather formative feedback on student progress throughout a unit, as well as how to assess students' achievement of a unit's goal, are addressed in Chapter 4, 5, 6, 10, and 11.

Equipment, References, Instructional Materials, and Technology

You need to anticipate what equipment, references, instructional materials, and technology you will need to conduct each lesson earlier enough to have them ready before the unit begins. Selection and application of resources such as, computer software or graphing calculators are the major focus of Chapter 7.

LESSON PLANNING AND DAILY PLANNING

Generally speaking, you should expect to plan courses, organizing each into units, just before the start of a school year or term. Planning for a specific unit needs to be done about a week or so before you anticipate beginning that unit. Skim the section Designing a Unit on Factoring Polynomials in Chapter 11.

You need to complete the detailed plan for a lesson a day or two before you plan to initiate the lesson. That phase of teaching is explained and illus-

Exhibit 3.10
Scheme for categorizing learning levels specified by objectives.

COGNITIVE DOMAIN

Construct a Concept

Students achieve an objective at the *construct-a-concept learning level* by using inductive reasoning to distinguish examples of a particular concept from nonexamples of that concept.

For example: Divide a set of relations into functions and nonfunctions and, for each of the given relations, explain why it was so classified (*construct a concept*)

Given a geometric figure (either concrete or abstract), discriminate between its surface area and other quantitative characteristics (e.g., height, volume, and angle size) (*construct a concept*)

Distinguish between examples and nonexamples of each of the following: sample space, compound event, independent events, dependent events, mutually exclusive events, empirical sample space, theoretical sample space, complement of an event, and conditional probability (*construct a concept*)

Discover a Relationship

Students achieve an objective at the *discover-a-relationship learning level* by using inductive reasoning to discover that a particular relationship exists or why the relationship exists.

For example: Explain why the area of a rectangle equals the product of its length and width (*discover a relationship*)

Explain why $x \in \mathbb{R}$ such that $0 < x < 1 \Rightarrow x^2 < x$ (*discover a relationship*)

Explain the rationale underlying the following formula for calculating the accumulated amount, *A,* in a compound interest savings plan:

$$A = \left(P + \frac{r}{k}\right)^{kn}$$

where P = the principal, r = the annual rate, k = the number of times per year the interest is compounded, and n = the number of years (*discover a relationship*)

Simple Knowledge

Students achieve an objective at the *simple-knowledge learning level* by remembering a specified response (but not multiple-step process) to a specified stimulus.

For example: State the definition of the six trigonometric functions (*simple knowledge*)

Associate the notation "$a|b$" where $a, b \in \{$integers$\}$, with the statement "a is a divisor of b" (*simple knowledge*)

State that the ratio of the circumference of any circle to its diameter is π (*simple knowledge*)

Comprehension

Students achieve an objective at the *comprehension learning level* by extracting and interpreting meaning from an expression.

For example: Explain in their own words the ϵ, δ definition of the limit of a sequence (*comprehension*)

Explain how to translate summation notation in the form

$$\sum_{i=a}^{n} f(i)$$

where a and n are integers such that $a \le n$ (*comprehension*)

Explain the rationale of the proof of the Pythagorean theorem as presented in the textbook (*comprehension*)

Algorithmic Skill

Students achieve an objective at the *algorithmic-skill learning level* by remembering and executing a sequence of steps in a procedure.

For example: Given the dimensions of a triangle, compute the area of its interior (*algorithmic skill*)

Use the chain rule to compute the derivative of $f(g(x))$, where f and g are algebraic functions such that g has a derivative at x and f has a derivative at $g(x)$ (*algorithmic skill*)

Bisect any given angle with a straightedge and compass (*algorithmic skill*)

Application

Students achieve an objective at the *application learning level* by using deductive reasoning to decide how to utilize, if at all, a particular mathematical content to solve problems.

For example: Given a real-life problem, determine how, if at all, a solution to that problem is facilitated by setting up a system of linear equations (*application*)

Given a real-life problem, decide if the solution requires computing the area of a polygonal region and, if so, determine how to find that area (*application*)

Given a real-life problem decide how, if at all, a solution to that problem is facilitated by using the relationship

$$A = \left(P + \frac{r}{k}\right)^{kn}$$

(*application*)

Creativity

Students achieve an objective at the *creativity learning level* by thinking divergently to originate concepts, conjectures, algorithms, or solution strategies.

For example: Describe novel paradigms they originate for illustrating the following relationship:

If $f(x) = ax^2 + bx + c$, where x is a real variable and $a,$ $b,$ and c are real constants, then $f'(x) = 2ax + b$

(*creativity*)

Generate novel conjectures about angle construction using a straightedge and compass, and either prove or disprove them (*creativity*)

Describe novel paradigms illustrating the rules for multiplying signed numbers that they originated (*creativity*)

Exhibit 3.10
Continued

AFFECTIVE DOMAIN

Appreciation

Students achieve an objective at the *creativity learning level* by believing that the mathematical content specified in the objective has value.

For example: Believe that an understanding of systems of linear equations can help solve problems they care about (*appreciation*)

Prefer to formulate algebraic open sentences when solving word problems rather than having the sentence set up by someone else (*appreciation*)

Recognize the advantages of being able to analyze a function without having to plot very many points on its graph (*appreciation*)

Willingness to Try

Students achieve an objective at the *willingness-to-try learning level* by choosing to attempt a mathematical task specified by the objective.

For example: Attempt to formulate algebraic open sentences to solve word problems before turning to someone else to set them up (*willingness to try*)

When executing a paper-and-pencil algorithm for using trigonometric relations to solve problems, list sequential results of the process neatly and in an orderly manner so that the work can readily be checked for errors (*willingness to try*)

Choose to use graphing calculators or computer software (e.g., *Derive or Mathematica*) to explore behavior of functions (*willingness to try*)

---

trated in Chapters 4, 5, 6, and 11. Then, of course, there is daily planning, during which you put the finishing touches on the details of what you and your students will do during a school day. Chapter 11 illustrates daily planning.

TRANSITIONAL ACTIVITIES FROM CHAPTER 3 TO CHAPTER 4

1. Recall a real-life problem you once solved. Analyze the process by which you solved it. Describe exactly what you did for each of the nine stages listed on pages 50–51. Exchange your description with that of a colleague and discuss the similarities and differences in the ways you, your colleague, and Brenda in Case 3.1 addressed the respective problems.

2. Solve one of the word problems in a mathematics textbook. Analyze the process by which you solved it. Now compare the process to the one you described for Activity 1. List the similarities and differences between the processes. Exchange your list with that of a colleague. Discuss them in light of Exhibit 3.7.

3. Familiarize yourself with the learning activities described in either Exhibit 3.5 or Exhibit 3.6. In collaboration with a colleague, develop and implement a plan for engaging two or three secondary students in these activities. Afterward, discuss with each other, as well as with other pairs of colleagues who completed this activity with other students, what the students with whom you worked learned. Also discuss what you

and your colleagues as teachers learned from this experience. Compare the experiences to those you acquired from completing Transitional Activities 3 and 4 in Chapter 2.

4. Examine a mathematics textbook for middle, junior, or high school students. If the book were to be the primary text for a course you were to teach, to what degree would you follow the sequence of content and presentations in the book? How, if at all, would you deviate from it as you planned your teaching units? Explain the rationale for your decision. Compare your response to those of colleagues.

5. Recall the work you did for the fifth transitional activity from Chapter 2 to Chapter 3. Discuss with those same colleagues how, if at all, you might respond to those questions differently now that you've studied Chapter 3.

6. Discuss the following questions with two or more of your colleagues:

   a. What strategies should teachers employ to lead their students to construct mathematical concepts for themselves? How should lessons be designed for construct-a-concept objectives?

   b. What strategies should teachers employ to lead their students to discover mathematical relationships for themselves? How should lessons be designed for discover a relationship objectives?

   c. How should teachers deal with students' misconceptions about mathematics?

Leading Students to Construct Concepts and Discover Relationships

This chapter explains how to design lessons that lead students to construct mathematical concepts and lessons that lead students to discover mathematical relationships. In particular, Chapter 4 is designed to help you:

1. Distinguish among examples of (a) concepts, (b) discoverable relationships, and (c) other types of mathematics content specified by learning objectives. (*construct-a-concept*)
2. Describe the inductive reasoning process by which students construct concepts for themselves. (*comprehension*)
3. Formulate construct-a-concept objectives that, for a given group of middle or secondary school students, are consistent with the NCTM *Standards.* (*application*)
4. Design lessons for construct-a-concept objectives. (*application*)

5. Design measurement items that are relevant to student achievement of construct-a-concept objectives. (*application*)
6. Describe the inductive reasoning by which students discover relationships for themselves. (*comprehension*)
7. Formulate discover-a-relationship objectives for a given group of middle or secondary school students that are consistent with the NCTM *Standards.* (*application*)
8. Design lessons for discover-a-relationship objectives. (*application*)
9. Design measurement items that are relevant to student achievement of discover-a-relationship objectives. (*application*)

CONCEPT

Conceptualizing

In addition to the transitional activities in each chapter, activities for you to engage in yourself are scattered throughout Chapters 4 to 10. Engage in Activity 4.1.

_____ ACTIVITY 4.1 _____

Purpose: To continue refining your notion of a concept.

You Need: A box, any 15 objects from your immediate environment that can all fit in the box, pen or pencil, and notebook paper.

Procedure: Place the 15 objects you've collected in the box. List each of the 15 objects separately on a sheet of paper. Name each entry so that it is unmistakably unique. For example, to list the book you are now reading, don't simply write "a book," because there are not only other book titles but also other copies of the title *Teaching Mathematics in Secondary and Middle School: An Interactive Approach.* Write, for example, "The copy of the book from which I read the directions for this activity."

Now, make a second list with exactly three entries; include each of the 15 objects named on the first list, but do not necessarily list them separately.

Although you may be confused by the directions for this assignment, make your two lists following your best guess as to what these directions are intended to mean.

Now, compare your lists to those of colleagues, and in light of those comparisons, help each other comprehend the directions and revise your lists so the intended directions have been followed.

In Case 4.1 a preservice mathematics teacher engages in Activity 4.1.

CASE 4.1 _____

After collecting 15 objects from her room, Tina Huerta thinks to herself: "Okay, first of all, there are these three pencils I dumped out of my pencil box. But I'm supposed to list each separately so that it is unmistakably unique. It sure would be easier to write, 'three pencils, but. . . .' "

Six minutes later, after realizing that describing unique entities is not as simple a task as she initially perceived, Tina completes the following list:

1. The yellow pencil I'm using to write this list that was in the cardboard box on my floor a minute ago.
2. The never-before sharpened pencil that was in my pencil box on my desk just before I dumped the pencils in the cardboard box that's on my floor right now.
3. The green pencil that was in my pencil box 10 minutes ago.
4. My copy of the book *Another Fine Math You've Got Me Into.*
5. The copy of the book *Pi in the Sky: Counting, Thinking, and Being* that I borrowed from Bill.
6. My copy of the *Random House College Dictionary.*
7. The paper clip in the cardboard box on my floor.
8. My pencil box that's now in the cardboard box on the floor of my room right now.
9. The rubber band that's farthest to the left side in the cardboard box on my floor.
10. The rubber band that's farthest to the right side in the cardboard box on my floor.

11. The rubber band that's second from the left in the cardboard box on my floor.
12. The rubber band that's second from the right in the cardboard box on the floor of my room.
13. The pair of scissors in the cardboard box on my floor.
14. The copy of the book *A Guided Tour of the T-85 Graphics Programmable Calculator with Emphasis on Calculus* that I checked out of the Math Department library.
15. The brown, shiny-looking, oddly-shaped, odorless thing that's about two centimeters long that I picked up off the floor of my room and put in the cardboard box on my floor.

She thinks, "Now my task is to collapse some of these specifics so I end up with a list of three categories. Let's see, I've got four pencils, and. . . ." Quickly, she collapses the list of 15 into the following:

1. Three pencils
2. A pencil box
3. Four books
4. Four rubber bands
5. A paper clip
6. A pair of scissors
7. The brown, shiny-looking, oddly-shaped, odorless thing that's about two centimeters long that I picked up off the floor of my room and put in the cardboard box on my floor.

"That brown, shiny thing must have broken off of something; I have no idea what it is or what to call it. I don't see a way to group it with any of the other stuff—*stuff!* That's a category that includes all of these things. But I'll follow the directions and get these down to exactly three," she thinks before finalizing the following lists:

1. Office supplies
2. Books
3. The brown, shiny-looking, oddly-shaped, odorless thing that's about two centimeters long that I picked up off the floor of my room and put in the cardboard box on my floor.

Our real world is composed of *specifics* we detect with our empirical senses. Specifics are far too numerous for us to deal with efficiently or think about each one as a unique entity. Thus, we categorize and subcategorize specifics according to certain commonalities or attributes. The categories provide a mental filing system for storing, retrieving, and thinking about information. The process by which a person groups specifics to construct a mental category is referred to as "*conceptualizing.*" The category itself is a *concept.* Here are two definitions to keep in mind:

- A *specific* is a unique entity, something that is not abstract.
- A *concept* is a category people mentally construct by creating a class of specifics possessing a common set of characteristics; in other words, a concept is an abstraction.

Of the three items in Tina's final list in Case 4.1, two refer to more than one specific thing. Thus, those two items, office supplies and books, are concepts. Exhibit 4.1 illustrates how concepts can relate to one another, with broader concepts including narrower subconcepts.

The task of listing 15 specific objects for Activity 4.1 was greatly facilitated by having conventional names associated with categories, concepts that you, Tina in Case 4.1, and I recognize (for example, pencil, book, box, or rubber band). You've never seen Tina's pencil box, but you have a reasonable vision of what it's like because you've see other pencil boxes. On the other hand, the fifteenth item on her initial list did not fit any concept for which I know a conventional name (other than "thing" and that's not very informative). Thus, Tina used more words to describe the fifteenth entry than for the ones that fit preconceived categories.

In the second phase of Activity 4.1 you clustered specific examples of a concept such as, office supply and reported them as a single category. That required a higher level of thought, but was not as tedious as listing each one specifically; it also provided an easier list to read. Of the three sets in Tina's final list, two contain more than one element. Thus, those two sets, the office supplies in the box and the books in the box, are *variables*. The set that contains only

Exhibit 4.1

A concept relates to its subconcepts as a set relates to its subsets. Examples of a concept relate to the concept as elements in a set.

A polygon is a concept; it is a set with more than one element.

polygon

Each of the following concepts is a subconcept of a polygon: triangle, quadrilateral, pentagon, hexagon, heptagon, etc.

triangle

Special types of triangles (e.g., isosceles), quadrilaterals (e.g., rectangles), pentagons (e.g., regular), are subconcepts of triangle, quadrilaterals, pentagons, respectively (i.e., subsets of subsets).

isosceles triangle

A specific example of a concept is not a concept but a constant; it is the specified elements of a set.

The unique isosceles triangle
determined by the following three points:

•

•   •

the brown, shiny-looking . . . thing is a one-element set and thus is not a variable but a *constant*.

The terms *"variable"* and *"concept"* mean the same thing—namely, a set with more than one element or value. The following terms or expressions all refer to a unique entity: *"constant," "specific example of a set," "element of a set,"* and *"value of a variable."*

Return your attention to Exhibit 3.9. Read Objective A of the fifth unit. The mathematical content specified by that objective are the concepts *sample space, compound event, empirical sample space* (a subconcept of sample space), *theoretical sample space* (also a subconcept of sample space), *complement of an event,* and *conditional probability.* Sample space is defined as the set of all possible outcomes of an experiment. Consider, for example, the following experiment:

> Joseph and Charog each shoot two foul shots on the basketball court. The number of successful shots for each is recorded.
>
> The following is a sample space for the experiment: {all possible ordered pairs (j, c), where j = the number of successful foul shots Joseph makes and c = the number of successful shots Charog makes}, that is {(0, 0), (1, 0), (2, 0), (0, 1), (1, 1), (2, 1), (0, 2), (1, 2), (2, 2)}.

Because experiments differ, sample spaces vary. Furthermore, more than one sample space can be set up for a single experiment. Thus, the idea of sample space is a concept. Similarly, the topics specified by Exhibit 3.9's Objective A of the fifth unit (compound event) all vary from situation to situation, thus each is a concept.

Engage in Activity 4.2.

——————————— **ACTIVITY 4.2** ———————————

Purpose: To continue refining your notion of a *concept*.

Procedure: Examine the following list and (a) determine which entries are concepts and which are constants, (b) for each constant identify those concepts on the list for which it is an example, and (c) identify pairs of concepts in which one is a subconcept of the other:

1. Number
2. Geographic feature
3. 9.013
4. Rational number
5. Irrational number
6. Mountain
7. Miles
8. Former baseball player
9. Mount Olympus
10. Line segment
11. The line segment determined by the following two points: (a) the most extreme top corner of the textbook page you are now reading, and (b) the most extreme point at the right top corner of the same textbook page
12. Limit of a function
13. Baseball Hall of Fame celebrity
14. $7(x + 4)/(3x)$, where $x \in$ {real numbers}
15. Degree
16. Standard unit of measure
17. Rectangle
18. Jackie Robinson
19. Real number
20. Square (geometric)
21. Derivation of a function
22. Polynomial
23. Meter

Compare how you grouped the 23 items to the following:

1. Number: a concept
2. Geographic feature: a concept
3. 9.013: a constant that is an example of the concepts listed as items 1, 4, and 19 (9.013 could also be considered an example of item 12, limit of a function, but such second-step examples are not included in this list)
4. Rational number: a concept that is a subconcept of items 1 and 19
5. Irrational number: a concept that is a subconcept of items 1 and 19
6. Mountain: a concept that is a subconcept of item 2
7. Mile: a concept that is a subconcept of item 16
8. Former baseball player: a concept
9. Mount Olympus: a constant that is an example of the concepts listed in items 2 and 6
10. Line segment: a concept
11. The line segment determined by the following two points: (a) the most extreme top corner of the textbook page you are now reading, and (b) the most extreme point at the right top corner of the same textbook page: a constant that is an example of item 10
12. Limit of a function: a concept
13. Baseball Hall of Fame celebrity: a concept that is a subconcept of item 8
14. $7(x + 4)/(3x)$, where $x \in$ {real numbers}: a concept that is a subconcept of item 22
15. Degree: a concept that is a subconcept of item 16
16. Standard unit of measure: a concept
17. Rectangle: a concept
18. Jackie Robinson: a constant that is an example of items 8 and 13
19. Real number: a concept that is a subconcept of item 1
20. Square (geometric): a concept that is a subconcept of item 17
21. Derivation of a function: a concept that is a subconcept of item 12
22. Polynomial: a concept that is a subconcept of item 1
23. Meter: a concept that is a subconcept of item 16

Concept Attributes

Whether or not a specific is an example of a particular concept depends on whether that specific possesses the defining *attributes* of the concept. For example, are you an example of the concept *preservice mathematics teacher?* By definition, a preservice mathematics teacher is a human being who is currently enrolled in a professional teacher-preparation program for the purpose of becoming qualified and certified as a mathematics teacher. Once a person completes such a program and takes a position as a mathematics teacher, the person is no longer classified as *preservice* but rather as an *inservice mathematics teacher.* Thus the attributes of a preservice mathematics teacher are: (a) human being, (b) enrolled in a professional program to prepare mathematics teachers, and (c) not an inservice mathematics teacher. If you possess all three of these characteristics, you are an example of the concept *preservice mathematics teacher.* By definition:

> A *concept attribute* is a characteristic common to all examples of a particular concept; a concept attribute is a necessary requirement for a specific to be subsumed within a concept.

The attributes define the concept. An even number, for example, is an integer that is a multiple of 2. Thus, the attributes of the concept even number are: (a) integer, and (b) multiple of 2. Any specific that meets these two requirements, for example, 10, $-8^{1/3}$, 0, 33 +47, −3.3 −2.7, or 196, is an even number. Any specific that does not—11, $\sqrt{8}$, 3/4, −0.001, you, or the book you are now reading—is not an even number.

Psychological Noise

Although you may be a preservice mathematics teacher, you possess a myriad of other characteristics that are not attributes of a preservice mathematics teacher. Not all preservice mathematics teachers have the same color eyes as you, nor are they your age, nor do they have the same likes and dislikes. Similarly, 10 ∈ {even numbers}, but all even numbers are not multiples of 5, less than 34, positive, and the principal square root of 100, as is 10.

Engage in Activity 4.3.

—————————— **ACTIVITY 4.3**——————————

Purpose: To enhance your concepts of *concept attribute* and *psychological noise.*

Procedure: With a colleague, examine the following two examples:

1. Until it's won, the amount of money each hour in a radio giveaway jackpot that begins with $100 and increases by $20 for each additional hourly unit.

2. The number of bricks in the first, second, third, . . . eighth row are arranged as follows:

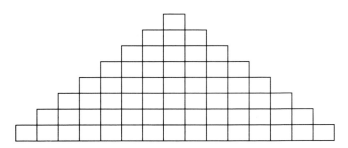

Given that a finite arithmetic sequence is an ordered subset of real numbers $a_1, a_2, a_3, \ldots a_n$ such that there exists $d \in$ {reals} such that $a_{i+1} - a_i = d$ for each integer $i < n$ (that is, the difference between any two consecutive numbers of an arithmetic sequence is the same), do you and your colleague agree that both examples are finite arithmetic sequences? If so, complete the following tasks:

1. List what you observed about the two examples that lead you to believe that both are finite arithmetic sequences.
2. List characteristics of example 1 that make it different from example 2.
3. List characteristics of example 2 that make it different from example 1.

———————————————————————

In Case 4.2 two mathematics teachers discuss their analyses of Activity 4.3.

CASE 4.2 ——————————————————

Tina: Practically all we did in our discrete mathematics course is work with sequences. An arithmetic sequence always looked like *a, a + d, a + 2d, a + 3d,* and so on until *a + kd* if it's finite.

Jermain: Yeah, like 4, 7, 10, 13, 16, 19. But this radio jackpot thing and this stack of bricks don't look like any sequences of numbers we ever studied. The bricks are in a sequence alright, but the elements are bricks, not numbers. The definition of an arithmetic sequence requires the elements to be real numbers.

Tina: That's what I thought when I first looked at them. Arithmetic sequences are usually expressed in textbooks as strings of numerals separated by commas. But when I reread these examples, I focused on the "*amount* of money" in the first and "*number* of bricks" in the second.

Jermain: Oh! So, it's not the dollars or bricks; it's amount or number as elements of the sequence. Okay, the elements really are real numbers and obviously each progresses by a common difference.

Tina: Let's express that in the more familiar textbook way. That'll make them easier to analyze.

Jermain: Example one is 100, 120, 140, 160, and so on until the jackpot is won. So let *h* be the number of hours before it's won and you get 100, 120, 140, 160, . . . , 100 + 20h.

Tina: And the brick-related one is 1, 3, 5, 7, . . . , 15.

Jermain: Or you could start counting from the bottom and write 15, 13, 11, . . . , 1. Either way, we have a finite arithmetic sequence.

Tina: Okay we've convinced ourselves that both are examples of finite arithmetic sequences. That brings us to the three "list tasks at the bottom.

Jermain: We've really already done the first one.

Tina: I agree; we matched characteristics of the examples to the definition of arithmetic sequence. We've just got to write them down now. The first attribute we talked about is that the elements are real numbers.

Jermain: Then we expressed them in the standard textbook form for finite arithmetic sequences, a, $a + d$, $a + 2d$, $a + 3d$, . . . , $a + kd$. Being able to do that shows the other attributes of the concept.

Tina: So let's go to the second "list" task, the characteristics of example 1 that make it different from example 2.

Jermain: For one thing the numbers for the sequence in example 1 are generated by dollars in a radio jackpot, in example 2 it was by the bricks in the rows of a stack.

Tina: For example 1, the a of a, $a + d$, $a + 2d$, $a + 3d$, . . . , $a + kd$ is 100 as opposed to 1 or 15, depending on which direction we start for example 2.

Jermain: And the d for example 1 is 100 instead of 2 or −2 for example 2. The k in example 1 is unknown, but for example 2 it's the number of rows of bricks, which is . . . 8.

Tina: Actually, since the number of rows of bricks is 8, $k = 7$. k is the number of rows less 1.

Jermain: What? . . . Oh, I see. Thanks.

Tina: Now for the third "list" task . . . We already did it when we did the second.

When you, like Tina and Jermain, listed characteristics of the two examples that verified that both are finite arithmetic sequences, you were, of course, listing attributes with respect to the concept. When you listed other characteristics of those two examples—characteristics distinguishing one example of a finite arithmetic sequence from others—you were identifying *psychological noise*. By definition:

Psychological noise is any characteristic of an example of a concept that is not an attribute of that concept.

All finite arithmetic sequences have a first element—that's an attribute of the concept. But to be finite arithmetic sequence the first element doesn't have to be 100 (as it is in example 1). Thus $a_1 = 100$ is a bit of psychological noise for example 1. The fact that you're reading this book right now is a bit of psychological noise with regard to your being an example of a mathematics teacher. All mathematics teachers are not reading this book right now.

The psychological noise in the examples which you give your students when you're leading them to construct mathematical concepts plays a key role in how well they conceptualize. The psychological noise in the examples you choose for your lessons will influence whether or not your students construct misconcepts. Subsequent sections of this chapter suggest how you should design lessons so that psychological noise helps rather than hinders learning.

Quickly revisit Case 1.2. The trash barrel at least roughly possesses the attributes of the concept *right cylinder*. Which of its characteristics are psychological noise for the concept? Unless Ms. Lowe's students are exposed to other examples of right cylinders—examples with other psychological noise (for example, used to move water, as in the case of a section of gardening hose, as opposed to used to hold trash)—she runs the risk of students misconstructing the concept of right cylinder to mistaken bits of psychological noise for attributes. This, of course, limits the concept in their minds (e.g., they may not recognize a figure to be a right cylinder unless it's also a trash barrel).

Concepts in Mathematics Curricula

Constructing concepts in our minds enables us to extend what we understand beyond the specific situations we've experienced in the past. Concepts are the building blocks of mathematical knowledge, but concepts are not the only type of mathematical content included in curricula. There are also discoverable relationships, conventions, and algorithms. Exhibit 4.2 lists some of the concepts typically included in secondary and middle school mathematics curricula.

Exhibit 4.2
A minute proper subset of the concepts typically included in secondary and middle school mathematics curricula

number	variable	point
natural number	set	line
whole number	intersection	line segment
prime number	union	plane
integer	finite	space
rational number	infinite	ray
irrational number	sequence	angle
real number	relation	polygon
complex number	function	distance
root	1:1 function	area
factor	permutation	volume
polynomial	limit	weight
interval	continuity	measurement
tangent line	derivative	perimeter
rate	integral	circle
vector	countable	fractal

INDUCTIVE REASONING

To conceptualize, that is, to construct-a-concept, students use *inductive reasoning* to distinguish examples from nonexamples of a particular concept. By definition:

> *Inductive reasoning* is generalizing from encounters with specifics. It is the cognitive process by which people discover commonalities among specific examples, thus leading them to formulate abstract categories or discover general relationships.

Students use inductive reasoning in Cases 4.3, 4.4, and 4.5.

CASE 4.3 _____

Over the past month, Rubin has encountered variables in his psychology, chemistry, and mathematics courses. During that time, he noticed differences and similarities among those variables. Although he never made a conscious effort to do so, he has begun to create a dichotomy between two types:

1. The first type includes variables such as (a) aptitudes people have for learning, (b) temperature fluctuations, and (c) {real numbers x such that $-2 \le 5x + 3 \le 10$}.

2. The second type includes variables such as (a) different types of emotional disorders, (b) atomic numbers of chemical elements, and (c) {integers x such that $x^2 - 25 \le 99$}.

Rubin thinks the first type is more difficult to deal with because, as he says, "It's too packed in to list two things that are next to one another." Rubin has apparently begun to form the concept of *continuous data* and the concept of *discrete data*. He does not, however, know the concepts by those names.

CASE 4.4 _____

After completing a homework assignment in which she used a protractor to measure the angles of six triangles her teacher drew on a task sheet, Robin looks at the resulting six triples: (100°, 45°, 35°); (80°, 61°, 415°); (30°, 60°, 90°); (142°, 15°, 23°); (60°, 60°, 60°); and (30°, 30°, 118°).

She thinks, "Anytime there's a big angle, the other two are small." She then attempts to draw a triangle with two "big" angles and finds it is impossible. Experimenting with triangles that are nearly equiangular, she finds all their angles are near 60°. Curious about the phenomenon, she measures the angles of 16 different triangles determined by concrete objects, such as two edges of a mirror. She then thinks, "Adding up the degrees of the three angles of *any* triangle will be about 180."

CASE 4.5 _____

While exploring different functions with the aid of a computer program, Christi notices that $f(i)$ for $i = 0, 1, 2, \ldots, 25$ is always a prime number when $f(i) = i^2 - i + 41$. Christi concludes she has discovered a function from {integers} into {primes}.

_____

In Case 4.3, Rubin organized specific variables into two categories, thus abstracting two concepts. Robin formed a conjecture from her experiences with specific triangles, thus abstracting a relationship. As illustrated by Case 4.5, inductive reasoning can sometimes lead to a conjecture that can be disproven with a counterexample (let $i = 41$). But disproving the conclusion does not discredit the reasoning.

CONSTRUCT-A-CONCEPT OBJECTIVES
The Construct-a-Concept Learning Level

Review the definition of construct-a-concept learning level and the examples of construct-a-concept learning objectives in Exhibit 3.10.

Stating Construct-a-Concept Objectives

How a teacher states objectives is a matter of individual style and preference. The mathematical content of a construct-a-concept objective is necessarily a concept. As long as your statement clearly specifies the mathematical concept you intend and you label it "construct-a-concept," the statement should sufficiently convey the intent of the lesson.

To continue refining your own concept of construct-a-concept objectives, here is an additional sample of such objectives taken from a variety of teachers' unit plans:

- Sort examples of a wide variety of geometric figures into the following categories (but not necessarily in association with these conventional names): (a) one dimensional, (b) convex polygon, (c) non-convex polygon, (d) two-dimensional non-polygon, (e) prism, (f) non-prism polyhedron, and (g) three-dimensional non-polyhedron. (*construct-a-concept*)
- Develop their own definition of absolute value of a real number. (*construct-a-concept*)
- Distinguish between examples of geometric sequences and examples of sequences that are not geometric. (*construct-a-concept*)
- Discover how countably infinite sets are like one another but different from other infinite sets. (*construct-a-concept*)

LESSONS FOR CONSTRUCT-A-CONCEPT OBJECTIVES
Challenging but Critical to Teach

Designing inquiry lessons for construct-a-concept objectives will tax your understanding of your students, pedagogical principles, and mathematics. Coming up with choice examples, nonexamples, problems, and leading questions that will stimulate students to use inductive reasoning to form concepts is challenging to say the least. However, students' conceptualizations provide the basis for subsequent meaningful learning of mathematics. For example, students who have themselves constructed the concept of limit of a function will more easily remember and comprehend the ϵ, δ definition of limit of a function than students who don't understand the interplay among ϵ, δ, and other variables used in the wording of the definition.

The failure of many students to develop healthy attitudes towards mathematics, mathematical skills, comprehension-level abilities to communicate about mathematics, and application-level abilities to do mathematics to solve problems is well publicized (Dossey, Mullis, Lindquist, & Chambers, 1988; "U.S. Students again Rank near Bottom in Math and Sciences," 1989; "U.S. Teens Lag Behind in Math, Science," 1989). Many of these failures can be traced to conceptual gaps in their learning (Ball, 1988b; Garner, 1990; Hiebert & Carpenter, 1992; Shuell, 1990). Such gaps are hardly surprising in light of the fact that many teachers never even consider conducting lessons for construct-a-concept objectives (Jesunathadas, 1990; NCTM, 1991.)

Designing Lessons for Construct-a-Concept Objectives

An *inductive learning activity* is one that stimulates students to reason inductively. Such inquiry activities are used in a four-stage lesson for construct-a-concept learning.

Stage 1: Sorting and Categorizing. In Stage 1 you present students with a task requiring them to sort and categorize specifics. While orchestrating the activity, managing the environment, and providing guidance, you allow students to complete the task themselves.

Stage 2: Reflecting and Explaining. In Stage 2 students explain their rationales for categorizing the specifics as they did. You raise leading questions, stimulate thought, and clarify students' expressions.

Stage 3: Generalizing and Articulating. In Stage 3 students describe the concept in terms of attributes (that is, what sets examples of the concept apart from nonexamples). They may also develop a definition for the concept; however, it isn't necessary for the conventional name of the concept to be used.

Stage 4: Verifying and Refining. In Stage 4 the description or definition is tested with additional specifics that the students already know to be exam-

ples and thus should fit, and with additional nonexamples which students know shouldn't fit. Further verification is pursued depending on your judgment of the situation. The description or definition of the concept is modified in light of the outcome of the tests. Prior stages are revisited as you judge necessary.

Selecting Examples and Nonexamples

One aspect of designing lessons for construct-a-concept objectives that you may find particularly trying is producing appropriate examples and nonexamples for students to categorize. As you determine examples and nonexamples of a concept to present to students, your attention to *concept attributes* and *psychological noise* is critical. Case 4.6 illustrates the point with a kindergarten teacher attempting to lead students to develop their concepts of number or set cardinality.

CASE 4.6

Mr. Edwards is using questioning strategies with individual kindergarten students to stimulate them to reason inductively to conceptualize set cardinality or "number of."

He displays Exhibit 4.3 to Stacy and asks her, "Which two groups are alike?" Stacy points to sets A and B and replies, "these."

Mr. Edwards: Why?
Stacy: Because they're not round like the other.
Mr. Edwards: Thank you. Now, can you see a way that this group of round things is like one of the other groups?
Stacy: No, it's different.

Mr. Edwards shows Stacy Exhibit 4.4. "Which of these two groups are alike?" Stacy points to A and C and says, "Because they have the same amount." Mr. Edwards says, "Thank you. Now, let's go back and look at this one again." He displays Exhibit 4.3 again and the activity continues.

Note how Mr. Edwards manipulated examples to control for psychological noise. Had Stacy readily categorized by cardinality upon seeing Exhibit 4.3, Mr. Edwards would have moved to a noisier situa-

Exhibit 4.3
Which two sets are alike?

A   B   C

Exhibit 4.4
Examples used by Mr. Edwards with less variability of psychological noise than Exhibit 4.3.

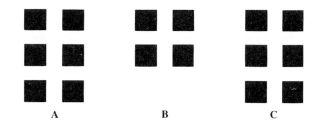

Exhibit 4.5
Examples with greater variability of psychological noise than Exhibit 4.3.

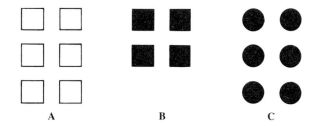

tion (for example, Exhibit 4.5) where the noise varies more. But since Stacy experienced difficulty with Exhibit 4.3, he reduced the noise by moving to Exhibit 4.4. In any case, Stacy eventually needs to recognize similarities and differences in cardinality even in high-noise situations because the real world is quite noisy.

In general, how well students construct-a-concept is dependent on how well they learn to distinguish psychological noise and concept attributes when sorting through examples and nonexamples. Distinguishing between examples and nonexamples in high-noise situations is indicative of a higher conceptual achievement level than when the distinction is made in low-noise situations.

Incorporating the Four Stages into a Construct-a-Concept Lesson

In Case 4.7 note how the teacher plans for Stage 1 of a construct-a-concept lesson, making use of his understanding of concept attributes and psychological noise.

CASE 4.7 _____

Working from a unit plan that includes the goal and objectives listed in Exhibit 4.6, Mr. Citerelli designs the initial lesson for the unit as he plans to conduct it for his intermediate algebra class. He thinks, "This first objective is the key to the whole unit. All the others depend on it. It says:

Distinguish between examples of arithmetic sequences and examples of other types of sequences, explain the defining attributes, and develop a definition.   (*construct-a-concept*)

"So the learning level is construct-a-concept and the mathematical content is the concept arithmetic sequence. That means inductive learning activities, beginning with a sorting and categorizing task with examples and nonexamples. The first thing I've got to do is come up with just the right set of arithmetic and nonarithmetic sequences for them to ponder.

"If I start with a list of arithmetic sequences, I can match each with a nonarithmetic sequence that has similar psychological noise. I don't want them to abstract the noise as part of the concept. . . ."

With the help of the course textbook and further thought, he develops the following two lists:

Examploc

3, 3.1, 3.2, 3.3, 3.4, 3.5, 3.6

$-13, -2, 9, \ldots, 130, 141, 152$

$15, 10, 5, 0, -5, -10, \ldots$

22.6, 22.6, 22.6, 22.6, 22.6, 22.6

Nonexamples

7, 0.7, 0.07, 0.007, 0.0007, 0.00007

46, 6.78, 2.60, 1.61, . . . , 1.02, 1.00, 1.00, 1.00

. . . , 16, 9, 4, 1, 0, 1, 4, 16, . . .

1, 2, 4, 8, 16, . . . , 1,048,576

1, 1, 2, 3, 5, 8, 13, 21, . . .

He thinks: "Not bad. The psychological noise in the examples varies, so they're unlikely to develop too narrow a concept. The characteristics of the nonexamples match the noise in the examples, so they should be able to sort out the attributes from the noise. Oh! I should also toss in a few real-life sequences just so they'll maintain the connection between the mathematics and the real world. That's going to complicate things. I'll just think of a few."

Six minutes later, he adds the following to the list:

Examples

Until it's won, the amount of money each hour in a radio giveaway jackpot that begins with $100 and increases by $20 every hour until there is a winner.

The amount of money in Betty's jar each Saturday if she starts with $60 and puts in exactly $7.50 each Friday night. (She never removes money or puts any in at any other time.)

The number of bricks in the first, second, third, fourth, . . . row that are stacked in a pyramid arrangement with 15 on the bottom and 1 on the top.

Nonexamples

The monthly savings account balance of a person who deposits $750 in the first month and leaves it there,

Exhibit 4.6
Goal and objectives for Mr. Citerelli's unit on arithmetic and geometric sequences.

Unit: Arithmetic and Geometric Sequences   (Intermediate Algebra)

Goal: The students explore arithmetic and geometric sequences, discovering and applying some fundamental theorems and algorithms about these types of sequences.

A. Distinguish between examples and nonexamples of arithmetic sequences, explain the defining attributes, and develop a definition.   (*construct a concept*)

B. Explain why the following relationship holds:

$$a_n = a_1 + (n - 1)(a_2 - a_1)$$

where a_n is the nth of an arithmetic sequence $(a_1, a_2, a_3, \ldots)$.   (*discover a relationship*)

C. State the definition of "arithmetic sequence," and the formula for finding the nth term of an arithmetic sequence. (*simple knowledge*)

D. Interpret and use fundamental shorthand notations conventionally used with sequences and series: "$a_i, a_2, \ldots, a_n$" or "(a_i) for $i = 1, 2, \ldots, n$" and "Σ".   (*comprehension*)

E. Explain why the following relationship holds:

$$\sum_{i=1}^{n} a_1 = (n / 2)(a_1 + a_n)$$

where $(a_1, a_2, a_3, \ldots)$ is an arithmetic sequence.   (*discover a relationship*)

F. Execute algorithms based on the two relationships listed in objectives B and E to find an unknown term of an arithmetic sequence and to find the sum of the first n terms of an arithmetic sequence.   (*algorithmic skills*)

G. Given a real-life problem, determines how, if at all, a solution to that problem is facilitated by using relationships and algorithms involving arithmetic sequences. (*application*)

H. Distinguish between examples and nonexamples of geometric sequences, explain the defining attributes, and develop a definition.   (*construct a concept*)

I. Explain why the following relationship holds:

$$a_n = a_1(a_2/a_1)^{n-1}$$

where a_n is the nth of a geometric sequence $(a_1, a_2, a_3, \ldots)$. (*discover a relationship*)

J. State the definition of "geometric sequence," and the formula for finding the nth term of a geometric sequence. (*simple knowledge*)

K. Explain why each of the following relationships hold:

1. $\displaystyle\sum_{i=1}^{n} a_i = [a_1^2(1 - (a_2 / a_1)^n] / [1 - (a_2 / a_1)]$

   where $(a_1, a_2, a_3, \ldots)$ is a geometric sequence.

2. $\displaystyle\sum_{i=1}^{\infty} a_i = [a_1(1 - (a_2 / a_1)^n]$

where $(a_1, a_2, a_3, \ldots)$ is a geometric sequence. (*discover a relationship*)

L. Execute algorithms based on the three relationships listed in Objectives I and K to find an unknown term of an geometric sequence and to find the sum of a geometric series.   (*algorithmic skills*)

M. Given a real-life problem, determine how, if at all, a solution to that problem is facilitated by using relationships and algorithms involving geometric sequences.   (*application*)

allowing it to collect interest at the rate of 4% compounded monthly.

The ages of all the people in our class, listed in alphabetical order.

He thinks: "I'll try starting the lesson off with the whole class in one large group. I'll present them with a task sheet with a single list of examples and nonexamples mixed up and have them try to pull one group out according to some common attributes. . . . But I'm afraid that would take a really long time and might get us into some other concepts I don't want to take time for. That's likely with this list; it;s pretty complex for them. Of course, they already know what a sequence is; that won't be a problem. But having them all see uniform differences between consecutive elements is problematic unless I use a simple list—limiting the examples to sequences like 5, 10, 15, 20, . . . and the nonexamples to ones like 5, 6, 8, 2, 0, 10. But I hate to simplify it and have them develop an overly limited concept of arithmetic sequences. . . .

"I know! Instead of making the list so that it's easier to distinguish examples from nonexamples, I'll give them a head start on the task by having them already grouped. Then it'll be their job to decide and explain how the examples are like one another but different from the nonexamples. That way I can keep the same variety of psychological noise without the danger of the activity being drawn out and heading out on a tangent. This'll give me more control over the situation."

Mr. Citerelli rearranges the list and adds the work space at the bottom as shown in Exhibit 4.7. He makes a copy for each student, one for him to use in class, and one for his file for use with subsequent classes.

He plans the rest of the learning activities for the final three stages of the lesson. The lesson plan is shown in Exhibit 4.8.

_____

In Case 4.8, Mr. Citerelli conducts Stage 1 (sorting and categorizing) and Stage 2 (reflecting and explaining) of the lesson he planned in Case 4.7.

CASE 4.8 _____

On the first day of the unit, Mr. Citerelli distributes copies of the tasksheet shown in Exhibit 4.7. He directs the students to take 13 minutes to examine the two lists silently and then write out a conjecture as to how the examples are like one another and how they are different from the nonexamples.

After each student has something written in the first blank, he engages the class in a question and discussion session. From engaging in such sessions before, the students have learned that whenever Mr. Citerelli calls on someone and says, "Keep it going," the following procedure is in effect until Mr. Citerelli interrupts: One student at a time has the floor. Anyone wanting to speak raises her or his hand to request the floor from the student who is speaking.

Mr. Citerelli: Bill, read your first conjecture.

Bill: The examples are alike because they're all in the same column. The nonexamples are in a different column.

Mr. Citerelli: That surely can't be contradicted. Now, let's hear an idea that might explain what I had in mind when I grouped the examples on the left and the nonexamples on the right. Okay, Mavis, you start: keep it going.

Mavis: The first thing I noticed is that both columns contain sequences. But those on the left have more of a pattern to them. Jeannie.

Jeannie: The ones on the right have patterns also. So, just having a pattern can't be it. Okay, Mark.

Mark: Not all of them. Look at the second one.

Jeannie: Sure it does —

Mr. Citerelli: Excuse me. Let's allow these two to hash this out in a two-way discussion while the rest of us listen.

Jeannie: The numbers on the second one are getting smaller; that's a pattern.

Mark: Not the last two numbers.

Jeannie: They might if we saw more decimal places. I think it has something to do with taking square roots. I played around with roots on my calculator and there's something related to roots of 46 with those numbers.

Mr. Citerelli: Excuse me. Mark, do you agree that at least some of the nonexamples sequences have predictable patterns?

Mark: Sure.

Mr. Citerelli: Those that agree, raise your hands. . . . It looks like that's one thing we agree on. Bill, would you please come up to the board and help us keep track of the points on which we all agree?

As the discussion continues, Bill takes notes on the board.

_____

In Case 4.9, Mr. Citerelli leads the class through Stage 3 of the lesson, Generalizing and Articulating.

CASE 4.9 _____

Mr. Citerelli: Mavis, do you want to modify your conjecture?

Mavis: No, but I'll withdraw it since we agree that some nonexamples have patterns also.

Mr. Citerelli: Thank you. Inez, read yours, and then keep it going.

Inez: You get the next number by adding something to the one before. Okay, Chico.

Chico: That's not right because look at the last nonexample. You add something to get to the next one. $1 + 1 = 2$, $1 + 2 = 3$, $2 + 3 = 5$, $3 + 5 = 8$, and so on. So, if Inez is right, then that one should be on the left side. Okay, Luis.

Luis: Besides, if Inez is right that you just added something, then the numbers should all be going up, but two of 'em do down and one stays the same!

Mr. Citerelli: Excuse me. Let's hear from Inez since it's her conjecture we're discussing.

Exhibit 4.7
Task sheet Mr. Citerelli uses on the first day of his construct a concept lesson on arithmetic sequences

EXAMPLES	NONEXAMPLES
3, 3.1, 3.2, 3.3, 3.4, 3.5, 3.6	7, 0.7, 0.07, 0.007. 0.0007, 0.00007
−13, −2, 9 ... 130, 141, 152	46, 6.78, 2.60, 1.61, ..., 1.02, 1.00, 1.00, 1.00
Until it's won, the amount of money each hour in a radio giveaway jackpot that begins with $100 and increases by $20 every hour until there is a winner.	The monthly savings account balance of a person who puts in $750 the first month and leaves it there, allowing it to collect interest at the rate of 4% compounded monthly.
15, 10, 5, 0, −5, −10, ...	The ages of all the people in our class, listed in alphabetical order.
The amount of money in Betty's jar each Saturday if she starts with $60 and puts in exactly $7.50 each Friday night. (She never removes money or puts any in at any other time.)	...16, 9, 4, 1, 0, 1, 4, 16, ...
22.6, 22.6, 22.6, 22.6, 22.6, 22.6	1, 2, 4, 8, 16, ..., 1,048,576
The number of bricks in the first, second, third, fourth, etc. row, arranged as follows:	1, 1, 2, 3, 5, 8, 13, 21, ...

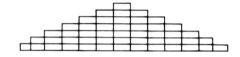

HOW ARE THE EXAMPLES ALIKE? HOW DO THEY DIFFER FROM THE NONEXAMPLES?

Write your first conjecture here: _____

_____

_____

Write your second conjecture here: _____

_____

_____

Write your third conjecture here:_____

_____

_____

Write your fourth conjecture here:_____

_____

_____

Inez: First of all, Luis, if you add negatives, they go down. Also, I'm changing my conjecture so that it's this: You get the next number by adding the *same* amount to each one.

Mr. Citerelli: I see Bill has written down Inez' revised conjecture. Bill, would you please write the first example under that. (Bill writes, "3, 3.1, 3.2, 3.3, 3.4, 3.5, 3.6.")

Mr. Citerelli: Thanks. Now write the first nonexample over here. (Bill writes, "7, 0.7, 0.07, 0.007, 0.0007, 0.00007.")

Mr. Citerelli: Now, if Inez' conjecture holds, what should be true about the two sequences Bill just wrote? . . . Okay, Bill.

Bill: You should be able to add the same thing to each of these to get the next one and you shouldn't be able to do it over here.

Exhibit 4.8
Mr. Citerelli's lesson plan for Objective A of Exhibit 4.6.

Objective: Distinguish between examples and nonexamples of arithmetic sequences, explain the defining attributes, and develop a definition.   (*construct a concept*)

The Four-Stage Lesson Plan

1. *Sorting and categorizing:* With the class organized in a single large group, I'll direct them to take 13 minutes to analyze the examples and nonexamples on the first-day's task sheet (Exhibit 4.7) and individually develop a first conjecture.
2. *Reflecting and explaining:* After everyone has written something for a first conjecture, I'll conduct a large-group question and discussion session in which they'll share and discuss a sample of their conjectures. I'll raise questions that lead them to verbalize their rationales.
3. *Generalizing and articulating:* Continuing with the large-group question and discussion session, I'll lead them to compare their conjectures with each other, emphasizing similarities and differences in intent as well as in wording. We'll work toward developing a commonly worded generalization. To do this we'll need to develop a test for concept attributes.

4. *Verifying and refining:* At the end of the question and discussion session, I'll assign the homework task sheet (Exhibit 4.10). On the second day, I'll direct several students to display their responses to item I of the homework on the board. We'll then engage in a question and discussion session in which we'll scrutinize those definitions, as well as others that surface during the session, for validity. The intent is to lead everyone to refine their own definitions until we converge on one that's consistent with the conventional meaning of "arithmetic sequence" and which they both comprehend and have ownership of.

Following our routine for making transitions from large-group to cooperative group sessions, I'll direct them into six cooperative task groups (Reggie's, Huey-Li's, Kathleen's, Choime's, Tabby's and James') with the individual roles that were established on Monday. Within each group, they will review one another's responses to items II, III, and IV of the homework task sheet.

The transition will then be made into the lesson for Objective B.

Mr. Citerelli: I need a volunteer to use Bill's test. Okay, Habebe. Now, if Habebe shows that Inez' conjecture fails Bill's test, what will we know? Mavis?

Mavis: That the conjecture is wrong.

Mr. Citerelli: And what if it passes? James?

James: I don't know. What's the question?

Mr. Citerelli: What was the question, Bill?

Bill: Here, I wrote it down.

James: Then the conjecture is right.

Mr. Citerelli: Do you agree, Anita? Keep it going.

Anita: Well, the conjecture is right. I agree with it. Chico.

Chico: But that's not what Mr. Citerelli asked. He asked *if* passing the test proves it's true and the answer to *that* question is no. Luis.

Luis: It's got to work for all of them and I see one it doesn't work for —

Mr. Citerelli: Let's have Habebe perform Bill's test. (See Exhibit 4.9.)

Habebe writes down the following:

$$3 + 0.1 = 3.1$$
$$3.1 + 0.1 = 3.2$$
$$3.2 + 0.1 = 3.3$$
$$3.3 + 0.1 = 3.4$$
$$3.4 + 0.1 = 3.5$$

$$3.5 + 0.1 = 3.6$$

Habebe: But it doesn't work for this other sequence because to get from 7 to 0.7 you have to add some negative number that's different than the one you add to get from 0.7 to 0.07.

Mr. Citerelli: While Bill and Habebe do the same at the board, I'd like the rest of you to find the difference for each of these at your places. Bill, you may use the calculator on my desk. Habebe, I'll get yours for you.

A few minutes after the following list appears on the board, everyone agrees that Inez' conjecture passes the first test:

$$7 + (-6.3) = 0.7$$
$$0.7 + (-0.63) = 0.07$$
$$0.07 + (-0.063) = 0.07$$
$$0.007 + (-0.0063) = 0.0007$$
$$0.0007 + (-0.00063) = 0.00007$$

Mr. Citerelli then directs the students to quietly perform the test on the remainder of the examples and nonexamples. During the activity, he circulates among them, looking at their work and occasionally whispering a probing question to individuals.

Exhibit 4.9
Habebe uses Bill's test on Inez' conjecture.

Twelve minutes later, the class returns to a question and discussion activity and the group agrees to Inez' conjecture. Then Mr. Citerelli directs each of them to formulate two more example sequences.

Mr. Citerelli: Mavis, Luis, and J. J., please write yours on the board.

Mavis writes: "5, 10, 15, 20, . . ."
Luis writes: "0, 0, 0, 0, 0, 0, 0, 0"
J. J. writes: "$\frac{1}{2}$, 0, $-\frac{1}{2}$, -1, $-1\frac{1}{2}$, -2

Mr. Citerelli: (Gesturing toward the three examples to illustrate his question) Think about what just went through your mind when you determined the third number of your sequence. . . . What told you what it should be, when you went from here to here? . . . J. J.

J. J.: Just make up a number; it doesn't make any different what you add until after the second.

Mr. Citerelli: How did you pick the first number, Alysia?

Alysia: I don't know.

Mr. Citerelli: Read your sequence.

Alysia: 9, 10, 11, 12, 13.

Mr. Citerelli: Why 9?

Alysia: I just like 9. My birthday is on the ninth.

Mr. Citerelli: And why 1?

Alysia: What do you mean?

Mr. Citerelli: Mavis chose a difference of 5, Luis chose 0, and J. J. picked $-\frac{1}{2}$. Why did you choose to create differences of 1?

Alysia: I don't know; it just seemed simple.

Mr. Citerelli: So Alysia is telling us that you get to pick anything you want for your first number and anything you want for the difference, but then after that everything else is determined for you. Is that right, Mark?

Mark: Yes.

Mr. Citerelli: Is that right, Jeannie?

Jeannie: Yes.

Mr. Citerelli: Is that right, Gomer?

Gomer: No.

Mr. Citerelli: Any why not?

Gomer: Because you wouldn't keep asking the question over and over if you agreed with the answers.

Mr. Citerelli: What have you got to say about all this, Inez? Keep it going.

Inez: Once you've got the first number and the difference between them, the pattern is set. Jacelyn.

Jacelyn: But how do you determine when to cut off the sequence?

Mr. Citerelli: Eureka! Thank you! That's what I was waiting to hear. Write down the three variables that determine any example sequence. Quickly, right now, on the paper in front of you! . . . Okay, what have you got Gomer? Keep it going.

Gomer: The first number, the second number, and how many numbers. Inez.

Inez: Instead of the second number, it should be the difference between the numbers. Mavis.

Mavis: But if you know the first and second, you know the difference. So, it's the same thing.

Inez: Oh, okay.

Mr. Citerelli: But you don't have the floor. Summarize what Gomer, Inez, and Mavis concluded about sequences that fit our example, Linda.

Linda: All you need is the first number, the difference that's the same between numbers, and how many numbers.

Mr. Citerelli: And what was Mavis' point, Linda?

Linda: Oh, yeah! You can figure the difference from the first two numbers.

Mr. Citerelli: Yes, Jeannie.

Jeannie: Shouldn't we give these sequences a name?

Mr. Citerelli: Pick somebody to make up one for us.

Jeannie: I think Bill should; he did all the writing on the board.

Mr. Citerelli: Bill?

Bill: How about "addition sequence," since you add the same thing to go from one to the other.

Mr. Citerelli: I like that. So, for now, let's call them "addition sequence." Yes, what is it, Gomer?

Gomer: You said "for now." That usually means there's already a name. What's the real name?

Mr. Citerelli: The real name is whatever we decide. But you'll find out there's a conventional name when you do your homework assignment from the text. Not now, don't get your books out yet! Let's get back to defining an addition sequence. As Linda said, we've got three determining variables: The first number, the difference between numbers, and the number of numbers.

Mr. Citerelli turns on the overhead projector; the students take the cue that they should be ready to take notes carefully. Mr. Citerelli uses the overhead projector to highlight what is said.

Mr. Citerelli: If we let a be the first number of an addition sequence, what will the second one be? Okay, J. J.

J. J.: a plus whatever the difference is.

Mr. Citerelli: Name that difference for us, Helen.

Helen: d

Mr. Citerelli: So the second number is what, Mavis?

Mavis: a plus d.

Mr. Citerelli: And the third, Habebe?

Habebe: $a + d + d$.

Mr. Citerelli: Simplify Habebe's expression for us, Helen.

Helen: $a + 2d$.

Mr. Citerelli: And the fourth number, Inez?

Inez: $a + 3d$.

Mr. Citerelli: And the fifth number, Allan?

Allan: $a + 4d$.

Mr. Citerelli: And the nth number Jacelyn?

Jacelyn: $a + 5d$.

Mr. Citerelli: And the $(n + 1)$th number, Linda?

Linda: Wait a minute! Jacelyn said "$a + 5d$," but you didn't ask her for the sixth number. You asked her for the nth. So it's not necessarily $a + 5d$, because n could be anything.

Mr. Citerelli: Oh, that's my fault. I didn't define n, did I? Now, I can't remember what I wanted it to be.

Quite a few students raise their hands to be recognized but Mr. Citerelli says, "Just a moment, let me reconstruct my thoughts before I forget what I was doing. Let's see. . . ." The following is now displayed on the overhead projector screen:

1st	a
2nd	$a + d$
3rd	$a + 2d$
4th	$a + 3d$
5th	$a + 4d$
.	.
.	.
.	.
6th	$a + ??$

Mr. Citerelli: Oh, I remember now. I was getting tired of listing each of these one at time, so I thought maybe we could just come up with a general nth term. So what is n now? Okay, Gomer.

Gomer: n is the one you want.

Mr. Citerelli: Okay. Do you want to put that another way, Linda?

Linda: n is the position of any number in the sequence. So the nth term is a plus n times d.

As Mr. Citerelli writes down "$a + nd$" in place of "$a + ??$," 15 hands are raised as students are eager to correct the error.

Mr. Citerelli: Okay, what's wrong now? Jacelyn.

Jacelyn: It's not nd. It should be n minus 1 times d.

Mr. Citerelli: Is this what you mean?

The line on the screen now reads: nth $a + (n - 1)d$

Jacelyn: Right.

Mr. Citerelli: By why?

Jacelyn: Look at the others. What you multiply d by is always 1 less than the position of the number.

Mr. Citerelli: Who agrees with Jacelyn? Everybody! Okay, we're about out of time. Here's the assignment that's due at the start of class tomorrow. Please use the rest of today's period to get started.

He distributes the task sheet that appears in Exhibit 4.10.

In Case 4.10, Mr. Citerelli leads the class through Stage 4 of the lesson, Verifying and Refining.

CASE 4.10

On the second day of the lesson, Mr. Citerelli has Leon, Jeannie, James, Luis, and Candice write their definitions from item I of the homework on the chalkboard:

Exhibit 4.10
Mr. Citerelli's homework assignment after the first day of his construct a concept lesson on arithmetic sequences.

I. Using a to represent the first term, d for the common difference between consecutive members, and n for the number of terms, define what we called in class today an addition sequence, and which your textbook calls an arithmetic sequence.

II. Carefully read Section 13.2 on pages 474–475 of your textbook. Be sure to familiarize yourself with the meanings of the following terms: arithmetic sequence, progression, common difference, and arithmetic means of two numbers. Add those terms and their definitions to the glossary in your notebook.

III. Determine whether each of the following sequences is or is not arithmetic. If it is, then solve for a, d, and n, according to your definition in I. If the sequence is not arithmetic, then prove that by illustrating that the difference between one pair of consecutive members does not equal the difference between some other pair of consecutive members.
   A. $\sqrt{3}, -\sqrt{3}, -3\sqrt{3}, -5\sqrt{3}, -7\sqrt{3}$
   B. $-1, 0, -1, 0, -1, 0, -1, 0, -1, 0, -1, 0$
   C. $7.1 + \pi, 7.1 + 2\pi, 7.1 + 3\pi, \ldots, 7.1 + 1000\pi$
   D. All whole numbers arranged in ascending order
   E. All integers arranged in ascending order
   F. The sequence of digits in the numeral π (i.e., 3, 1, 4, 1, 5, 9, 2, 6, 5, . . .)
   G. The amount of money you spend each month, beginning with January of last year
   H. $f(1), f(2), f(3), f(4), \ldots$, where $f(x) = x^2 - 5$
   I. $f(1), f(2), f(3), f(4), \ldots$, where $f(x) = x - 5$
   J. The accumulated total, by inning, of outs the visiting team makes in one regular nine-inning baseball game
   K. The accumulated total, by inning, of outs both teams make in a regular nine-inning baseball game

IV. Work the following exercises from page 476 of your text: 1, 7, 8, 9, 15, 19, 22.

Leon: An arithmetic sequence is one that has the same difference between any two numbers. The first number is a, the difference is d, and the last one is n.

Jeannie: A sequence is an addition sequence if and only if the first number is a, the next is $a + d$, the next $a + 2d$, the next $a + 3d$, and so on until the nth number, which is $a + (n - 1)d$. (d can be positive, negative, or zero.)

James: An arithmetic sequence, or arithmetic progression, is a sequence in which each term after the first is obtained by adding a constant, d, to the preceding term. In the sequence above the common difference is 5.

Luis: An addition sequence is one that has the same difference, d, between any terms, like a, all the way to n.

Candice: Addition, or arithmetic, sequences or progressions are ones in which the nth term is $a + (n - 1)d$.

Mr. Citerelli: Please spend the next 12 minutes comparing your definition to the ones on the board. Decide which ones, if any, are equivalent to yours. Which define an addition, or arithmetic, sequence as we described it yesterday? How about your own definition? Okay, you've got 11.5 minutes. . . . Okay, time is up. Let's look at Leon's first. Read it for us, Eldon.

Eldon: An arithmetic sequence is one that has the same difference between any two numbers. The first number is a, the difference is d, and the last one is n.

Mr. Citerelli: What do you think about that one, Eldon? Keep it going.

Eldon: Well, it's not the same as mine, but it's the same idea. I think it's right. Okay, Jeannie.

Jeannie: But he's got n as a member of the sequence. n isn't in the sequence. It's —

Mark: Sure it is, it's the —

Jeannie: Hey, you don't have the floor; I didn't call on you! As I was saying, n is the place of any one member of the sequence itself. Okay, Mark.

Mark: It's the same thing. The place is part of the sequence. Jeannie.

Jeannie: I'm going to ask you a question, Mark, but you've got to give me the floor right back. Okay? Which seat in this row are you in right now? Mark.

Mark: You can see I'm in the fourth, Jeannie.

Jeannie: Okay. Fourth is your place, but it's not you! Mark.

Mark: Okay, I see what you're saying. Uhh, Habebe.

Habebe: There's something wrong with Leon's definition. It says d is the difference between *any* two numbers. Leon.

Leon: That's the whole idea of an arithmetic sequence; they've got the same difference between the members. Habebe.

Habebe: Here let me show you. (Habebe writes the following on the board: 5, 10, 15, 20, 25, 30.)

Habebe: Is this an arithmetic sequence? . . . You agree, but the difference between 25 and 10 is 15 and the difference between 25 and 20 is 5. See, it's not the same between every two members. Leon.

Leon: You know what I mean. By "the difference between two numbers" I mean numbers next to each other.

Mr. Citerelli: Excuse me. What adjective might Leon add to clear up this matter. Mavis, keep it going.

Mavis: "Next to?" Linda

Linda: "Neighboring." J. J.

J. J.: That's what I was going to say. Okay, Habebe.

Habebe: I like "consecutive." Leon.

Leon: So, if I said, "an arithmetic sequence is one that has the same difference between *consecutive* numbers," it would be all right?

Mr. Citerelli: Excuse me. Everybody locate their work for sequence B in item II on the homework. Take 45 seconds to examine that and then think about Leon's questions. Is "same difference between consecutive numbers" adequate for the definition? . . . Okay, Inez, keep it going.

Inez: I said B wasn't arithmetic because to get from the first to the second, *d* must be 1, but from the second to the third, *d* must be −1. It makes a difference which way you're going. I think it's easier to write the definition kind of like Jeannie's. Leon.

Leon: I'm going to change mine. Let's talk about somebody else's definition.

Mr. Citerelli: Okay, what about Jeannie's? Read it, Bill, and keep it going.

Bill: A sequence is an addition sequence if and only if the first number is *a*, the next is *a* + *d*, the next *a* + 2*d*, the next *a* + 3*d*, and so on until the *n*th number, which is *a* + (*n* − 1)*d*. *d* can be positive, negative, or zero. Gomer.

Gomer: Do you have to say that last part? Isn't that understood as long as we know *d* is a number? Jeannie.

Jeannie: You're right. Just scratch that. Anybody else?

Mr. Citerelli: Nobody wants the floor to argue with Jeannie's definition? Okay, let's look at James'. Gomer.

Gomer: He didn't use the *a, d,* and *n* like we were supposed to. Mark.

Mark: And what's that part about the common difference being 5? James.

James: I don't know. That's just what the book said.

Mr. Citerelli: Excuse me. If you're going to copy straight from the book, it would be a good idea to credit the authors. Jeannie?

Jeannie: (looking in the textbook) I see where the difference-of-five business comes from; it's referring to an example that's not part of the definition.

Mr. Citerelli: I suggest we accept Jeannie's revised definition for an arithmetic sequence and move on. Yes, Mavis.

Mavis: Why "revised"?

Mr. Citerelli: Oh! She deleted this part about *d* being positive, negative or zero. Okay? Fine. Let's take a look at item III on the homework. Yes, Inez.

Inez: I was really confused by E.

Mr. Citerelli: Read it please.

Inez: "All integers arranged in ascending order."

Mr. Citerelli: List all integers in ascending order on the board for us, Candice. (Candice writes: . . . , −2, −1, 0, 1, 2, . . .)

Mr. Citerelli: How many of you said that's arithmetic? . . . Now, those of you who said it wasn't, raise your hands. Interesting! Why did you call it arithmetic, Chico?

Chico: Because there's the same difference between any two consecutive numbers.

Mr. Citerelli: Why did you say it wasn't Sydna?

Sydna: Because there's no *a*. I couldn't solve for *a*. If it's an addition sequence, it's got to have an *a*.

Mr. Citerelli: Inez, you didn't raise your hand either way. Why not?

Inez: I agree with Sydna. Our definition says you've got to have a first member. The book's definition says "first term." But I also agree with Chico. You can't disprove it's arithmetic by the way you told us. Any two consecutive numbers have the same difference. So what are we supposed to do?

Mr. Citerelli: Helen?

Helen: Let's just throw out that one; it's a bad item.

Mr. Citerelli: It may be a bad item, but I don't want to throw out that sequence. We have a decision to make. We must decide if we want to keep our current definition and restrict arithmetic sequences to those with a first member. Or, we can modify the definition to include sequences that are *open* on the left side. Gomer?

Gomer: What one is right?

Mr. Citerelli: Which one is right according to our textbook, Jacelyn?

Jacelyn: You've got to have a first member. And if that's the case, we've got to include that when we show a sequence isn't arithmetic.

Mr. Citerelli: Okay, keep that in mind. But before we decide, let me read you a definition from this book, the *CRC Standard Mathematical Tables* (Beyer, 1987, p. 8): "An arithmetic progression is a sequence of numbers such that each number differs from the previous number by a constant amount, called the common difference." Now, it goes on to mention a first term, but it's not part of the definition. What do you think, Alysia?

Alysia: Let's stick with our textbook and Jeannie's definition and have a first member.

Mr. Citerelli: Raise your hand if you vote in favor of Alysia's motion. . . . So be it. But remember that in another place, time, and textbook, it may be defined to include sequences without a first member.

Mr. Citerelli organizes the class into cooperative groups and continues with the plan outlined in Exhibit 4.8.

Engage in Activity 4.4.

_____ **ACTIVITY 4.4** _____

Purpose: To expand your insight regarding how to design lessons for construct-a-concept objectives.

Procedure: Select a concept from the following list:

Geometric sequence	Isomorphism
Rational number	Prime number
Prism	Derivative
Sample space	Integral

Variable   Area
Function   Volume

Design and teach a lesson for one or two students that lead the student or students to construct the concept you chose.

Discuss your experiences designing and teaching this lesson with colleagues who also engaged in Activity 4.4. Share with one another what you learned from your experiences.

INDICATORS OF ACHIEVEMENT OF CONSTRUCT-A-CONCEPT OBJECTIVES

In Case 4.10, Mr. Citerelli listened to the students' comments, the questions they raised, and the answers they gave; he observed how students completed tasks from Exhibit 4.7's task sheet. Such activities provided formative feedback to gauge how students were progressing toward Objective A and regulate the pace and design of the lesson. To make these formative evaluations as well as the summative evaluations near the end the unit, Mr. Citerelli *measures* student achievement relative to each objective. By definition:

> A *measurement* is a process by which data or information are gathered via empirical observation and are noted or recorded.

The results of your measurements of student achievement influence your formative and summative evaluations. Measurements are composed of *measurement items*. By definition:

> A *measurement item* is a component of a measurement by which students are confronted with a task and their responses to that task are observed (e.g., a single question on a test and the scoring key the teacher uses to quantify the student's response to that question).

Designing measurement items for evaluating achievement of construct-a-concept objectives usually requires more creative thought on your part than measurements for achievement of most other types of objectives. Engage in Activity 4.5.

_____ ACTIVITY 4.5 _____

Purpose: To stimulate your thoughts about how objectives' learning levels influence measurement item design and to stimulate you to begin thinking about how to design measurement items for construct-a-concept objectives.

Procedure: In collaboration with a colleague, design two measurement items for student achievement of Objective C in Exhibit 4.6. Then design two more items for Objective A.

In Case 4.11, two mathematics teachers respond to Activity 4.5.

CASE 4.11_____

Jermain: Why are we starting with Objective C instead of A?

Tina: My guess is because it should be easier to come up with items for C than for A since C is simple knowledge.

Jermain: And A is a construct-a-concept objective. We haven't gotten into simple-knowledge objectives yet, but they seem to just be memory-level learning.

Tina: So the measurement items for a simple-knowledge objective should only require students to remember content.

Jermain: Like for Objective C, to remember the definition of "arithmetic sequence."

Tina: Let's look up the definition of "arithmetic sequence."

Jermain: The students' final, or at least their most recent, version of the definition should be stated somewhere in the verifying and refining stage of the lesson—that would be Case 4.10.

Tina: The class decided on a modified version of Jeannie's definition. It's equivalent to something like this: A sequence is arithmetic iff there exist real numbers a and d such that the first term is a, the second is $a + d$, the third is $a + 2d$, and so on, with the nth term being $a + (n - 1)d$.

Jermain: So one of our items for Objective C could present them with the task of showing that they remember that definition or one that's equivalent to it. Why not just ask the student, "What's the definition of arithmetic sequence?" And then just see if they include all the attributes—nothing more, nothing less in the answer.

Tina: We could give them one point for each attribute and maybe subtract a point for anything they include that's not an attribute—like "the numbers increase from the first to the second to the third and so on by the same amount."

Jermain: For that they'd get a point for knowing the numbers changed by the same amount, but lose a point for saying it had to be an increasing sequence.

Tina: I can see that even simple-knowledge items might be a little more difficult to design than one might first imagine—that is, if you want valid ones.

Jermain: Okay for a second item on Objective C, we could ask them to list the attributes of any arithmetic sequence.

Tina: Just to toss in some variety, why don't we make this one a multiple-choice.

Exhibit 4.11 displays the two items Tina and Jermain designed to be relevant to students' achievement of Objective C.

Tina: Okay, now for the really tough one, Objective A. . . . . I really don't have a clue as to how to even start!

Jermain: Objective A says, "Distinguish between examples and nonexamples of arithmetic sequences, explain the defining attributes, and develop a definition—construct-a-concept." That's what they did in Citerelli's class.

Exhibit 4.11
Two measurement items Tina and Jermain designed for Objective B of Exhibit 4.6.

One Item

Task presented to the student: Use the area below to write the definition of arithmetic sequence:

Teacher's scoring key: 6 points maximum distributed as follows:

+1 if the response is written as a definition.

+1 for each of the following attributes included in the definition:

- sequence of numbers

- has a first element

- the difference between any two consecutive elements is the same

+1 if the definition does not include any errors (for example, indicates a characteristic that is not an attribute as an attribute).

+1 if the definition does not include any extraneous information, that is, something that is not erroneous but also is not relevant to defining arithmetic sequence (for example, "arithmetic sequences are important in problem solving").

Another Item

Task presented to the student: (Multiple-choice)   One and only one of the following is true for all arithmetic sequences. Which one is it? Show your answer by circling the letter in front of your choice:

A. The numbers in the sequence increase from first to second, from second to third, and so forth.
B. The numbers in the sequence decrease from first to second, from second to third, and so forth.
C. The sequence is finite.
D. The sequence has a first element.
E. The difference between any two numbers in the sequence is the same.

Teacher's scoring key: +1 for circling "D" only; otherwise score is 0.

Don't we know that at least the students who participated in the development of the definition achieved the objective?

Tina: Making observations during the lesson would seem to be the most efficient way of measuring a construct-a-concept objective.

Jermain: Like reading what they write on Mr. Citerelli's task sheets and just listening to them in class.

Tina: I agree. But what about trying to measure achievement of this objective for summative evaluation purposes at the end of the unit? Is there any way to do that?

Jermain: Let's just take a piece of Objective A. The first part of the objective says "distinguish between examples and nonexamples of arithmetic sequences." What if one of our items presented them with a list of sequences—some arithmetic, some not? Then we direct the students to circle the arithmetic ones.

Tina: That seems like the obvious thing to do until you realize that by the time the students are through this unit they should be able to execute an algorithm to test if a sequence is arithmetic or not. And maybe they could do the test without ever having conceptualized arithmetic sequences.

Jermain: So if we gave them sequences like −3, −3.2, −3.3, −3.4, and like −3, −3.1, −3.12, −3.123, −3.1234, and asked them to label each as being an example or not, you're saying they might get the item correct from just remembering to see if the differences between each pair of consecutive members is the same.

Tina: Exactly.

Jermain: But suppose we ask them to explain why that test works. Wouldn't that be getting at conceptualization?

Tina: Maybe so. Or would that just be showing that they comprehend the definition—not that they've actually constructed the concept in their heads? Sure is complicated!

Jermain: If we asked them to explain why my example is arithmetic and my nonexample isn't, that begins to measure conceptualization.

Tina: Depending on whether they were formulating their own explanation or just recalling one they had heard in class.

Jermain: Speaking of complicated, I think we're more likely to get at conceptualization instead of just comprehension or remembering an explanation from class if we choose examples and nonexamples that are complicated. Ones with psychological noise that are really different from what they are exposed to in class.

Tina: Like what?

Jermain: Like . . . remember Mr. Citerelli's thinking when he came up with those two real-world examples for the task sheet in Exhibit 4.7?

Tina: The examples about the radio giveaway and the stack of bricks.

Jermain: Right! If we came up with some sequences described in ways that sort of veil their algebraic characteristics—you know, really noisy—wouldn't that get closer to testing how well they constructed the concept of arithmetic sequence in their heads?

Tina: You may have hit on something! You also gave me another thought. What about getting the students to come up with their own examples and nonexamples—complicated, noisy ones. Oh, I've got it! What if we put them in teams and one team tries to stump the other team by developing examples and nonexamples where it is difficult to determine whether or not they're arithmetic?

Jermain: That's not exactly the kind of item you see on the typical math test, but let's try it.

Tina and Jermain developed three items for Objective A; they are displayed in Exhibit 4.12.

Note the two parts of a measurement item. In Exhibits 4.11 and 4.12, Tina and Jermain labeled them "Task presented to the student" and "Scoring key." That convention will be followed throughout the remainder of this text.

Continue to think of strategies for designing items for measuring achievement of construct-a-concept objectives in other content areas besides arithmetic sequences. Chapter 10 will deal in greater detail with questions about how to design construct-a-concept measurement items, as well as items for other learning levels.

DISCOVERABLE RELATIONSHIPS

Discoverable Relationships in Mathematics Curricula

A *relationship* is a particular association between either (a) concepts (for example, {irrationals} $\subseteq$ {reals}), (b) a concept and a specific (for example, $x^2 > -4 \; \forall \, x \in$ {reals}), (c) a specific and a concept (for example, 13 is prime), or (d) specifics (for example, $\sqrt{3} \geq 1.1$). Unlike concepts which are expressed by a word or phrase (for example, "rational number"), a relationship is expressed as a complete statement ("$a^2 + b^2 = c^2$").

A relationship is *discoverable* if one can use reasoning or experimentation to find out that the relationship exists. Examples of discoverable relationships are listed in Exhibit 4.13.

All relationships specified as mathematical content by learning objectives are not discoverable. There are also relationships that are a matter of *convention,* having been established through tradition or agreement. For example, the use of the numeral "$\sqrt{3}$" to mean "the positive number which when squared equals 3" is a matter of convention. Logic does not dictate that the symbol for "principal square root of three" should look like that. By reading Miller (1989) you'll learn something about the history of how the radical symbol evolved into common usage. However, the fact that the relationship $\sqrt{3}$ means "the positive number which when squared equals 3" is not one you would be expected to discover for yourself by using reasoning.

How to use direct instruction to inform students about conventional relationships is addressed in Chapter 5. The chapter you are now reading focuses on inquiry instruction, where you lead students to construct concepts and discover discoverable relationships.

Discovering Discoverable Relationships for Oneself

As with constructing concepts, students need to reason inductively to discover relationships. Review Cases 4.4 and 4.5 for examples of students discovering a relationship via inductive reasoning. Note that in both cases, students formed hypotheses or formulated a proposition from their experiments with specifics.

DISCOVER-A-RELATIONSHIP OBJECTIVES

The Discover-a-Relationship Learning Level

Review the definition of discover-a-relationship learning levels and the examples of discover-a-relationship objectives in Exhibit 3.10.

The mathematical content of a discover-a-relationship objective is necessarily a discoverable relationship. Some discover-a-relationship objectives only target students' discovering that the relationship does in fact exist. For example:

> From experimenting with various circles, conclude that the ratio of the circumference of any circle to its diameter is about 3.1. *(discover-a-relationship)*

Exhibit 4.12
Three measurement items Tina and Jermain designed for Objective A of Exhibit 4.6.

One Item

Task presented to the student: Is *S* an arithmetic sequence, given the following information about *S*?   (Circle Yes or No)

Bonnie eats exactly two bananas a day for a week beginning on a Sunday. S is the following sequence: The bananas she ate that week by the end of the day on Sunday, the bananas she ate that week by the end of the day on Monday, the bananas she ate that week by the end of the day on Tuesday, . . , the bananas she ate that week by the end of the day on Saturday.

Yes   No

If you circled "Yes," write a paragraph explaining exactly why it is. If you circled "No," write a paragraph explaining exactly why it is not.

Teacher's scoring key: 3 points maximum distributed as follows:

+1 for circling No and indicating that the reason is that members of the *S* are not real numbers but rather bananas.

+1 if the explanation does not include any errors.

+1 if the definition does not include any extraneous information.

A Second Item

Task presented to the student: Is *T* an arithmetic sequence, given the following information about *T*?   (Circle Yes or No)

Bonnie eats exactly two bananas a day for a week beginning on a Sunday. T is the following sequence: The number of grams of banana she consumed that week by the end of the day on Sunday, the number of grams of banana she consumed that week by the end of the day on Monday, the number of grams of banana she consumed that week by the end of day on Tuesday, . . . , the number of grams of banana she consumed that week by the end of day on Saturday.

Yes   No

If you circled "Yes," write a paragraph explaining exactly why it is. If you circled "No," write a paragraph explaining exactly why it is not.

Teacher's scoring key: 3 points maximum distributed as follows:

+1 for circling No and indicating that the reason is that it's unlikely that all 14 bananas had the same weight.

+1 if the explanation does not include any errors.

+1 if the definition does not include any extraneous information.

Third Item

Task presented to the student: Students will be paired off into two-person teams to play the "Is It an Arithmetic Sequence Game?" The directions for the game are as follows:

One team (call it "Team A" will make up four examples of sequences. Team A should design the sequences so that it is not easy to determine if it is or isn't arithmetic.

A second team (call it "Team B") then examines Team A's sequences and decides which are arithmetic and which are not. Team B must explain its rationale for the decision.

A third team (call it "Team C") serves as the referees for the game. Team C manages the game, hears the explanations, and awards points as follows:

+1 to Team A for each incorrect explanation given by Team B.

+1 to Team B for each correct explanation.

−1 to Team A for each sequence which Team B demonstrates Team A has mislabeled.

Teacher's scoring key: See Team C's role in rules for the game.

Exhibit 4.13
Examples of discoverable relationships typically included in mathematics curricula.

Rate $\times$ time = distance

Area of a rectangle = length $\times$ width

Sum of the three degree measurements of any triangle is 180

The ratio of the circumference of any circle to its diameter is π

The graph of a linear function is a line

The graph of $y = x^2$ is a parabola

$$\binom{n}{q} = \frac{n!}{q!(n-q)!}$$

$$\sum_{i=1}^{n} (2i - 1) = n^2$$

If $\triangle ABC$ and $\triangle DEF$ are such that $AB = DE$, $\angle B \cong \angle E$, and $BC = EF$, then $\triangle ABC \cong \triangle DEF$

The law of sines: The ratio of the sines of any two angles of a triangle equals the ratio of the lengths of the sides opposite them

The binomial expansion theorem

Cramer's rule for using determinants for solving a system of two linear equations

Others target students discovering why relationships exist. For example:

> Develop their own explanation as to why the ratio of the circumference of any circle to its diameter is about 3.1. (*discover-a-relationship*)

The Importance of Discover-a-Relationship Objectives

Consider the following four objectives:

A. Explain why the Pythagorean relationship exists. (*discover-a-relationship*)
B. State the Pythagorean theorem. (*simple knowledge*)
C. Given the length of two sides of a right triangle, solve for the third side using the relationship $a^2 + b^2 = c^2$, where c is the length of the hypotenuse and a and b are the lengths of the other two sides. (*algorithmic skill*)
D. Confronted with a real-life problem, determine how, if at all, the Pythagorean relationship can be used in solving the problem. (*application*)

By first discovering the relationship themselves (achieving Objective A), students are more likely to remember it (Objective B) and make sense out of the algorithm specified by Objective C. Furthermore, they can hardly achieve Objective D, which is to deduce when and how the relationship is applicable to solve real-life problems they've never before confronted, without having first achieved Objective A (Davis, Maher, & Noddings, 1990; Hiebert & Carpenter, 1992).

LESSONS FOR DISCOVER-A-RELATIONSHIP OBJECTIVES

Designing Discover-a-Relationship Lessons

To lead students to achieve a discover-a-relationship objective, you need to incorporate inductive learning activities in a four-stage lesson.

Stage 1: Experimenting. In Stage 1 students collect facts by experimenting with various specific situations, for example, they measure the three angles of a variety of triangles with a protractor or complete the first six steps of the activity described in Exhibit 4.14. You orchestrate the activity, manage the environment, and provide guidance.

Stage 2: Reflecting and Explaining. In Stage 2 students analyze outcomes of their experiments as you raise questions leading them to explain their analyses and begin to suggest possible general relationships.

Stage 3: Hypothesizing and Articulating. During Stage 3 students articulate propositions about possible relationships. With your guidance, they test, analyze further, and massage their stated hypotheses, conjectures, or propositions.

Stage 4: Verifying and Refining: In Stage 4 the students attempt to verify or disprove their statements about the relationship. The level of verification or proof may range from "seems intuitively clear," to a failure to produce a counterexample, to a formal deductive proof. If "holes" are found in the stated proposition, then the statement is modified

Exhibit 4.14
From *Connecting Mathematics* (Froelich, 1991).

The process of representing real-world situations mathematically is known as mathematical modeling. We will try to find a mathematical model for the total number of toothpicks required to construct a square of any size that is subdivided into 1 × 1 squares of toothpicks. A 1 × 1 square and a 2 × 2 square are shown below.

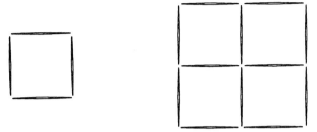

1. a. How many toothpicks does the 1 × 1 square require? _____

   b. The 2 × 2 square? _____

2. Make a 3 × 3 square and count the toothpicks. How many are there? _____

3. A trivial, but sometimes useful piece of information is the number that corresponds to the case of 0. How many toothpicks are required for a 0 × 0 square? _____

4. Complete this table:

Number of toothpicks on one side of the square	Total number of toothpicks in the square
0	
1	
2	
3	

To attack the general problem of finding a formula for the total number of toothpicks in any size square, we need more data. On the next sheet you will extend your table by analyzing the way the total number of toothpicks changes.

Exhibit 4.14
Continued

TOOTHPICKS AND MATHEMATICAL MODELS (CONTINUED)   SHEET 2

5. A good way to count the toothpicks for a given square is to count only the new ones added to the previous square, then add these to the previous square's total. The figure to the right shows how to do this for the 3 × 3 square.

The single tick marks represent the toothpicks counted first, the double tick marks those counted second, the triple tick marks those counted third, and the quadruple tick marks those counted fourth. Note that there are three toothpicks in every set and that there are four sets. This means that the 3 × 3 square requires twelve more toothpicks than the 2 × 2 square. Now try adding toothpicks in the same way to the 3 × 3 square to obtain a 4 × 4 square.

   a. How many toothpicks are there in each set? _____

   b. How many of these sets are there? _____

   c. What is the number of new toothpicks? _____

   d. What is the total number of toothpicks in a 4 × 4 square? _____
      Place the data in your table.

6. Suppose you have a $k \times k$ square and want to add enough toothpicks to make a $(k + 1) \times (k + 1)$ square. Use the same counting scheme as in part 5. The figure at the right may help you.

   a. How many toothpicks are there in each set?

      _____

   b. How many of these sets are there? _____

   c. What is the number of new toothpicks? _____

7. Use your formula for the number of new toothpicks in part 6 to predict the number of new toothpicks needed to build a 4 × 4 square into a 5 × 5 square. _____

8. How many new toothpicks does your formula predict are necessary to go from a 0 × 0 square to a 1 × 1 square? _____
   Does your table confirm this? _____

9. Mathematical models often can be extended beyond what is reasonable in a given problem situation. Consider the case $k = -1$.

   Extend your table to permit negative numbers. How many new toothpicks does your formula predict would be necessary to go from a (–1) × (–1) square to a 0 × 0 square? _____ Use this to find a number to place opposite –1 in your table. _____

10. Repeat what you did in part 9 for $k = -2$. _____

Exhibit 4.14
Continued

TOOTHPICKS AND MATHEMATICAL MODELS (CONTINUED) SHEET 3

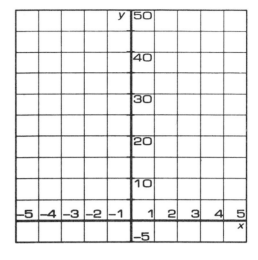

11. As a first step in finding a formula for the total number of toothpicks, graph all the pairs in your table on the coordinate axes at the right.

12. Does the graph have the shape of a parabola? Compare it to the graph of $f(x) = x^2$ by estimating each of the following:

The vertical shift _____

The horizontal shift _____

The vertical stretch _____

(Helpful hint: Because a parabola has a vertical line of symmetry, you can estimate the horizontal shift by locating a point halfway between the places the graph crosses the x-axis, also called the zeros of the function.)

13. Write the equation of the parabola given by your answers to part 12. _____

14. Use your calculator to test your equation. Substitute each value from the first column of the table below and record the predicted number of toothpicks. Also record the amount, if any, by which your prediction misses the actual number.

One side of the square	Total number of toothpicks	Predicted number of toothpicks	Amount of miss
–2	4		
–1	0		
0	0		
1	4		
2	12		
3	24		
4	40		

15. If your function does not predict the actual number of toothpicks, adjust the function until it does. For example, is the amount of miss the same each time? If so, adjusting the vertical shift will remedy this. Adjust your function and repeat the calculations.

until students agree to an acceptable proposition about the relationship.

Incorporating the Four Stages into Discover-a-Relationship Lessons

In Case 4.12, a teacher plans a discover-a-relationship lesson.

CASE 4.12

Ms. Gaudchaux's Algebra I students have already learned to plot points by hand for the graphs of simple algebraic functions. They also have experience using graphing calculators (like the *TI-82* or *Sharp EL-9300C),* not only as calculating tools but also from experimenting with relationships. As part of a unit on linear functions, she develops the lesson plan shown in Exhibit 4.15 for the following objective:

> Explain how the values of *a* and *b* affect the graph of the linear function *f(x) = ax + b.   (discover a relationship)*

In Case 4.13, Ms. Smith plans for her students to discover-a-relationship in a lesson where the students experiment with problem-solving strategies during Stage 1.

CASE 4.13

In the nine years that Ms. Smith has been teaching mathematics, she's noticed that most students who learn about rate relationships in one context (such as simple interest on savings = *prt*) do not recognize rate relationships in other contexts (such as distance = *rt).* Thus, when she planned the seventh-grade mathematics course she's currently teaching, she decided to attempt a general unit on rate relationships rather than treating interest rates on savings, rates of motion, interest rates on loans, discount rates, and other types of rate problems separately.

Now, she's in the process of designing the learning activities for the first objective of that unit; the objective is as follows:

> Explains why the accumulative effect of the application of rate per unit over an observed frequency of that unit is given by the product of the rate and the frequency. *(discover-a-relationship)*

She thinks, "It was really tough for me to put the relationship that's the content of this objective into words. But I know what I mean. It's the general relationship that is the foundation for distance formulas, interest rate formulas, pricing rate formulas, and anything else that's so much per unit. The learning level is discover-a-relationship, so I need inductive learning activities beginning with the class experimenting with sample problems without benefit of knowing the relationship ahead of time."

"I think I'll begin with students in small cooperative task groups, each working on a different problem in different real-world contexts. Maybe I can assign the problems according to their own personal interest. After seven weeks with this class, I know most of them pretty well. Okay, I'll begin with a list of different types of problems to which rate relationships are applicable. Let's see, there's distance when traveling, and bank interest . . . for savings and for loans. Then there are markups and discounts at stores. Oh, yeah! Sales commission is another. But except for distance ones, these all have something to do with money. I need more variety, or else they'll always think of rates as either money or distance. I also need to make these germane to their own lives. The savings interest is more relevant to them today than bank loans. What kinds of problems does the text have? They're scattered throughout the book, but not many of them will tease my students' interests. . . . Some of these I can modify to make them more like real life.

I should do this systematically and start with a list of areas from which to draw problems. Distance is one for sure and one on interest on savings. How about one for sports fans in the class—commissions for sports agents would be good. Oh, that reminds me! Rachael was discussing greeting cards for one of those mail-order firms. How does that work? They get so many prizes for selling so many dollars' worth of cards. That's like a commission. Maybe that could produce a problem for Rachael and a couple of others to work on."

With further thought, Ms. Smith develops the following list of problem areas:

Distance in traveling

Interest on savings

Interest on borrowing

Commissions received by celebrities' agents

Prizes for selling (e.g., mail-order greeting cards)

Discounts at stores

Cooking and diet-related rates

Prize-winning rates on radio giveaway games

Bonus-gift rates for purchases (e.g., number of free music CDs based on the number of purchases)

Physical fitness or growth (e.g., percent body fat, rate of improvement in weight lifting, growth rates, etc.)

Sports performance rates (e.g., percent of foul shots, batting averages, etc.)

Looking over the list she thinks, "How many problems do I actually need? Each task group should have at least three people and no more than five. With 31 in the class, that means eight groups, so eight problems. Well, I'm expected to cover motion, as well as interest, problems since they'll be on standardized tests. So, . . ."

After formulating a travel problem and two interest problems, she thinks: "Five more to go. Some of the students might remember distance and bank interest formulas from

Exhibit 4.15
Ms. Gaudchaux's lesson plan for a discover a relationship objective.

Objective: Explain how the values of *a* and *b* affect the graph of the linear function $f(x) = ax + b$.   (*discover a relationship*)

Note 1: During Stage 1, the class will be organized in cooperative groups as follows:

Group I
Student - Role

Lawanda - mgr/org
Juan L. - calmat sup
Chen - comm
Pauline - rec/timer
James - reporter

Group II
Student - Role

Angel - mgr/org
Haeja - calmat sup
Willard - comm
Eiko - rec/timer
Cynthia - reporter

Group III
Student - Role

Olando - mgr/org
Al - calmat sup
Brenda - comm
Fred -rec/timer
Bryce - report

Group IV
Student - Role

Ellen - mgr/org
Edgardo - calmat sup
Juan T. - comm
Paige - rec/timer
Kimberleigh - reporter

Group V
Student - Role

Wanda - mgr/org & comm
Suzanne - calmat sup
Salinda - rec/timer
Brookelle - reporter

Roles are defined as follows:

mgr/org	Designates the *manager and organizer* who chairs the meeting for the group and is responsible for maintaining group focus and reminding people to stay on-task.
calmat sup	Designates the *calculator and materials supervisor* who takes custodial care of, distributes, collects, and returns the group's calculators and other materials.
comm	Designates the *communicator* who communicates and clarifies the directions for the group.
rec/timer	Designates the *recorder/timer* who keeps track of time, making sure the group keeps to its schedule. He or she also maintains a record of the data collected by the group.
reporter	Designates the *reporter* who summarizes the group's findings and conclusions in writing and presents them to the rest of the class.

Note 2: The groups' recorder/timers will use the following task sheets during Stage 1:

Group I's Recorder/Timer's Task Sheet

i	$f_i(x)$	Picture of graph on calculator screen	Description of how this graph compares to the one just above
1	x		(Leave this cell blank.)
2	$x + 1$		
3	$x + 2$		
4	$x + 5$		
5	$x + 10$		
6	$x + 13$		

Exhibit 4.15
Continued

Group II's Recorder/Timer's Task Sheet

i	$g_i(x)$	Picture of graph on calculator screen	Description of how this graph compares to the one just above
1	x		(Leave this cell blank.)
2	$2x$		
3	$3x$		
4	$6x$		
5	$10x$		
6	$100x$		

Group III's Recorder/Timer's Task Sheet

i	$h_i(x)$	Picture of graph on calculator screen	Description of how this graph compares to the one just above
1	x		(Leave this cell blank.)
2	$x - 1$		
3	$x - 2$		
4	$x - 5$		
5	$x - 10$		
6	$x + 15$		

fifth and sixth grades. It'd be too bad if they just recall the formulas rather than discover them for themselves. But none of them will have pat formulas for any of the other areas. So, I'll make sure to assign students who are likely to recall the formulas to the other areas. Oh! Now that I think about it, it wouldn't be so bad if one or two of the groups recalled a formula, then we could compare it to how the other problems are solved. That way we could illustrate that all the solutions are based on the same relationship. . . . Oh, another idea!

When I direct them into the experimenting stage, I'll require each group to develop a visual diagram of what's happening in the problems. That way, it'll be easier for them to pick up a common pattern when we get into subsequent stages of the lesson. I'd better try that out myself for one of these I've already developed. The distance problems says:

Ron misses his bus one morning and has 25 minutes to walk the 4 miles to school. Will he make it on time if he covers .15 miles each minute?

Exhibit 4.15
Continued

Group IV's Recorder/Timer's Task Sheet

i	$t_i(x)$	Picture of graph on calculator screen	Description of how this graph compares to the one just above
1	x		(Leave this cell blank.)
2	$-x$		
3	$-2x$		
4	$-6x$		
5	$-10x$		
6	$-.5x$		

Group V's Recorder/Timer's Task Sheet

i	$u_i(x)$	Picture of graph on calculator screen	Description of how this graph compares to the one just above
1	x		(Leave this cell blank.)
2	$.1x$		
3	$.4x$		
4	$.01x$		
5	$.9x$		
6	$-.5x$		

The Four-Stage Lesson Plan

1. *Experimenting:* I'll direct the class to organize into the five cooperative groups with the calculator and materials supervisors making sure everyone in their respective groups has a graphing calculator ready to run and each recorder/timer has a copy of the task sheet. In the meantime, I'll briefly meet with the five communicators and explain the following directions to them:

   Use the calculators to graph the function listed on the first row of your task sheet. Make sure everyone gets the same graph; quickly sketch it in the indicated cell of the task sheet.

   Do the same for the function listed in the second row. Also, in the indicated cell, describe how the second graph compares to the first.

   Repeat what you did for the second function for the third, fourth, fifth, and sixth functions.

Exhibit 4.15
Continued

After all six graphs are simultaneously displayed on each calculator, discuss how all the graphs are affected by what operations are used with x. The discussion should take about 10 minutes, with another 4 minutes allowed to pull the report together and summarize the group's findings.

2. *Reflecting and Explaining:* After making the transition into a single group, I'll direct the reporters to spend five minutes explaining each group's findings. As the reporter speaks, I'll use the graphing calculator overhead display to exhibit the graphs (see Exhibit 4.16) from the reporting group.

   Next, I'll engage the class in a question and discussion session in which we'll tie the five reports together. This should lead them to begin to make conjectures about how *a* and *b* influence the graph of $y = ax + b$.

3. *Hypothesizing and Articulating:* For homework, I'll direct the students to individually propose a hypothesis describing how the location and angle (what we'll later refer to as the slope) of the line is influenced by *a* and *b*. The following day, we'll return to the same five cooperative groups and have them share their conjectures and come to a group consensus on an all-encompassing general conjecture. I'll encourage them to experiment further with various functions and the graphing calculators as they articulate their statements.

Each group will report its conjecture to the whole class and we'll compare the five conjectures in a question and discussion session. We'll attempt to agree on a single conjecture.

4. *Verifying and Refining:* I'll engage them in an independent-work session with Exercises 3, 4, 12, 17, 18, 22, 25, and 33 from pp. 231–232 of the textbook, completing the task as homework.

The following day, I'll engage them in a question and discussion session in which they'll reflect on their homework. This should lead them to either accept (for now) their conjecture as a theorem or refine it so that we're convinced the new conjecture is a theorem.

"How could they possibly diagram that? Let's see. . . ." She illustrates a solution with the diagram in Exhibit 4.17.

She then develops the following problem for the prizes-for-selling-greeting-cards category and draws the diagram appearing in Exhibit 4.18 as she would expect Rachael and others to illustrate their solution:

> For every $25 worth of greeting cards that Mary sells for a mail-order company, she receives 10 points toward prizes from their catalog. For example, it takes 30 points to get a pen and pencil set and 150 points to get an audiocassette player/recorder. How many points would Mary get for selling $200 worth of greeting cards?

Convinced that students will be able to produce comparable diagrams, Ms. Smith continues working until her list of problems for the initial learning activities is as follows:

1. Ron misses his bus one morning and has 25 minutes to walk the 4 miles to school. Will he make it on time if he covers .15 miles each minute?
2. City Bank is now paying 4¢ for each dollar that remains in a savings account for a whole year. How much interest will Lois make by leaving $60 in a City Bank savings account for a year?
3. Ernie asks Sally, "Would you lend me $15"

   Sally: Why should I?
   Ernie: Because I need to pick up my bike that's being fixed.

   Sally: No, I mean what's in it for me?
   Ernie: I'll pay you back in a month when I get paid for my paper route. But until I get my bike I can't work.
   Sally: You still haven't given me a good reason for lending you the money.
   Ernie: Okay! I'll give you a nickel more on the dollar.
   Sally: Make that a dime on the dollar for each week until you pay me back, and you've got a deal.

   If Ernie accepts the deal, how much more than $15 will he own Sally if he waits 4 weeks to pay her back?

4. For every $25 worth of greeting cards that Mary sells for a mail-order company, she receives 10 points toward prizes from their catalog. For example, it takes 30 points to get a pen and pencil set and 150 points to get an audiocassette player/recorder. How many points would Mary get for selling $200 worth of greeting cards?
5. Mau-Lin wants to buy clothes at a store that will cost her $45 today. However, she knows that in a week the store will have a sale marking everything down by 20 percent. How much will she save by waiting a week to purchase the clothes?
6. Lucy Davis is an agent for professional athletes. For negotiating their contracts, she is paid 5¢ out of every dollar the athletes earn from those contracts. How much will Lucy earn from a $125,000 contract?
7. A mail-order company that sells compact discs advertises that for every 12 discs purchased, a customer may select

Exhibit 4.16
What Ms. Gaudchaux expects
the calculators in the cooperative
groups to display upon
completion of Stage 1 of the
lesson outlined in Exhibit 4.15.

(a) Group I's graphs of $f_1(x) = x$,
$f_2(x) = x + 1$, $f_3(x) = x + 2$,
$f_4(x) = x + 5$, $f_5(x) = x + 10$,
$f_6(x) = x + 13$

(b) Group II's graphs of $g_1(x) = x$,
$g_2(x) = 2x$, $g_3(x) = 3x$,
$g_4(x) = 6x$, $g_5(x) = 10x$,
$g_6(x) = 100x$

(c) Group III's graphs of $h_1(x) = x$,
$h_2(x) = x - 1$, $h_3(x) = x - 2$,
$h_4(x) = x - 5$, $h_5(x) = x - 10$,
$h_6(x) = x - 13$

(d) Group IV's graphs of $t_1(x) = x$,
$t_2(x) = -x$, $t_3(x) = -2x$,
$t_4(x) = -6x$, $t_5(x) = -10x$,
$t_6(x) = -.5x$

(e) Group V's graphs of $u_1(x) = x$,
$u_2(x) = .1x$, $u_3(x) = .4x$,
$u_4(x) = .01x$, $u_5(x) = .9x$,
$u_6(x) = -.5x$

Exhibit 4.17
Diagram illustrating Ms. Smith's students' solution to Ron's walking to school problem.

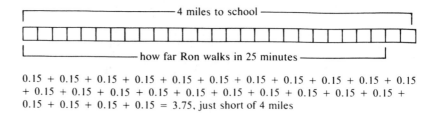

$$0.15 + 0.15 + 0.15 + 0.15 + 0.15 + 0.15 + 0.15 + 0.15 + 0.15 + 0.15 + 0.15$$
$$+ 0.15 + 0.15 + 0.15 + 0.15 + 0.15 + 0.15 + 0.15 + 0.15 + 0.15 + 0.15 +$$
$$0.15 + 0.15 + 0.15 + 0.15 = 3.75, \text{ just short of 4 miles}$$

Exhibit 4.18
Diagram illustrating Ms. Smith's students' solution to Mary's selling-greeting-cards problem.

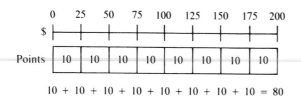

$$10 + 10 + 10 + 10 + 10 + 10 + 10 + 10 = 80$$

a free disc. How many discs would a customer need to purchase to receive 7 free discs?

8. Every school day, Woody eats a Whiz-O candy bar at lunch. Each Whiz-O contains 312 calories. How many calories does this habit add to Woody's diet during 9 weeks of school?

Pleased with the eight problems, Ms. Smith thinks: "That takes care of the most difficult part of designing this lesson. Now, to match students to the problems—I'd better see that the less-motivated ones are assigned something with which they can identify. Also, there should be at least one energetic thinker in each group. Okay, Rachael goes to the group with problem 4; I'll call that Group 4. She's bound to be interested in the greeting cards. Bart and Pete should be in separate groups; they get goofy together. Bart to Group 1 and Pete to 2. Let's see, Patrice should . . ."

With the groups of three or four assigned, Ms. Smith prepares to organize and manage the small-group activity efficiently by preparing a direction card that contains the following for each of the 31 students:

• Instructions on how to locate the other members of the task group using a mathematical expression on the card.
• The mathematical expression (e.g., the sum of the multiplicative inverses of 1, of 2, of 3, and of 4).
• The number of people in the task group which the student is to join (three or four).
• Instructions on what the task group is to do (one of the eight problems is stated, along with what the group is to accomplish relative to the problem).

Exhibit 4.19 displays one of the 31 direction cards.

Just before the students enter the classroom for the period during which she plans to begin the unit for the discover-a-relationship objective on rates, Ms. Smith tapes each student's card to the underside of her or his desktop. Initially, the students are not aware the cards are there.

The students are seated at their regular places when Ms. Smith begins the activity with these directions: "For the next 15 minutes or so we will be working in three- or four-person task groups. Cards with directions for locating your partners and the task your group is to accomplish are attached to the underside of your desktop. Please find the cards now and begin following the directions."

As Ms. Smith walks about the room monitoring behavior, the students quickly locate their partners and within minutes are on-task working out solutions to the problems. At 11:13, Ms. Smith calls for the first of the eight reports to the class.

Explanations of solutions for the first four problems (those involving Ron's rate of walking, City Bank's interest rate, Sally's interest rate, and the point rate for selling greeting cards) produce diagrams and repeated addition procedures similar to Exhibits 4.17 and 4.19. Group 5 (the ones solving Mau-Lin's discount rate problem) simply multiplies 45 by .20 for their answer, but Ms. Smith directs them to illustrate the multiplication with a diagram.

Group 6 fails to solve the sports-agent rate problem. They complain that they "couldn't add something 125,000 times." Other students ask, "Why didn't you just multiply?" Group 7 simply multiplies 12 by 7, but also illustrates their logic with a diagram similar to Exhibit 4.18. Similar to the first four groups, Group 8 uses repeated addition and a diagram in its solution.

In the ensuing discussion, similarities among the solutions to the eight problems are pointed out by different students responding to Ms. Smith's probing questions ("Why did Group 6 want to add five 125,000 times instead of 125,000 five times?"). However, before a general relationship is articulated by the class, Ms. Smith halts the activity and directs everyone to make a copy of each group's illustration and computations. As part of the homework assignment, each student is to develop a formula for solving these types of rate problems.

The following day, the students' formulas are reported and discussed and the class agrees to a multiplication rule for computing the accumulative effects of a rate applied to a frequency. Ms. Smith engages the class in a verification activity in which students apply their formula to additional problems and then develop a proof based on multiplication to accomplish the same result as repeated addition.

Engage in Activity 4.6

Directions for _Patrice Melville_

HOW TO FIND THE OTHER MEMBERS OF YOUR WORK GROUP

1. Simplify the following expression:

   $5^2 \div \sqrt{144}$

2. Get up and move about the room until you locate the __3__ other people with expressions on their cards that equal yours.

WHAT TO DO ONCE YOU'VE LOCATED YOUR PARTNERS

1. Find a convenient work area without disturbing other groups.

2. As a group, agree to a solution to the following problem:

   Mau-Lin wants to go to a store to buy clothes that will cost her $45 today. However, she knows that in a week the store will have a sale marking everything down by 20%. How much will she save by waiting a week to purchase the clothes?

3. Illustrate your solution with a diagram.

4. At about 11:15, select someone from the group to explain to the whole class your problem and how you solved it.

5. Return to your regular desk when Ms. Smith gives the signal around 11:15.

Exhibit 4.19
Direction card for one of Ms. Smith's students.

_____ **ACTIVITY 4.6** _____

Purpose: To expand your insights regarding how to design lessons for discover-a-relationship objectives.

Procedure: Select a discoverable relationship from the following list:

- If A is the lateral surface area of a right cylinder with radius r and height h, then $A = 2\pi rh$.
- The relationship that explains how the graph of $f(x) = ax^2 + c$ is determined by the values of a and b (e.g., if $a < 0$, then the parabola opens downward).
- The Pythagorean relationship
- The complex roots of the quadratic equation $ax^2 + bx + c = 0$ where a, b, and c are real constants can be found via the following relationship:
- $x = (-b \pm (b^2 - 4ac)^{1/2})/(2a)$
- The area of the interior of a rectangle is the product of the rectangle's length times its width.
- If C is the circumference of a circle and d is its diameter, then $3.1 < C/d < 3.2$.
- Rate × time = distance.
- $_nC_r = n!/(r!(n - r)!)$
- $x^a \cdot x^b = x^{a+b} \ \forall \ x \in \{\text{reals}\}$ and $a, b \in \{\text{whole numbers}\}$
- $(\sin \alpha)/(\cos \alpha) = \tan \alpha$
- If $x \in \{\text{reals}\}$ and n is rational constant $\ni f(x) = x^n$, then $f'(x) = nx^{n-1}$ (i.e., the power rule).

- If $x \in \{\text{reals}\}$ and a and b are real constants, then the graph of $f(x) = ax + b$ is a line.
- If E and F are mutually exclusive events, P(E) is the probability of E and P(F) is the probability of F, then P(E) + P(F) = P(E or F).
- $\sum_{i=1}^{n} a_i = (n/2)(a_1 + a_n)$ where $a_1, a_2, a_3, \ldots$) is an arithmetic sequence.

Design and teach a lesson for one or two students that lead the student or students to discover the relationship you chose.

Discuss your experiences designing and teaching this lesson with colleagues who also engaged in Activity 4.6. Share with one another what you learned from your experiences.

INDICATORS OF ACHIEVEMENT OF DISCOVER-A-RELATIONSHIP OBJECTIVES

Measuring students' achievement of a discover-a-relationship objective after they've experienced a four-stage lesson for that objective can be challenging responsibility. Ms. Gaudchaux's students in Case 4.12, for example, will have thoroughly discussed statements of the relationships indicated by the objective by the end of the lesson outlined in Exhibit 4.15. Thus, even those who really didn't discover the relationships for themselves may have had enough exposure to what their classmates discovered to simply remember statements such as: If $b < 0$, then the line intersects the y axis below the origin. Consequently, it is especially important to monitor student achievement *during* lessons for a discover-a-relationship objectives. Observe them experimenting and listen to their conjectures and their discussions.

One strategy for gaining some indication of discover-a-relationship level learning after a lesson is to confront students with items requiring them to describe the experiences that led them to discovery. Here's an example of such an item:

> *Task presented to the student:* You know that a in the function $f(x) = ax + b$ determines how the line graph of the function is inclined (or angled). Explain to me how experiments you and your classmates performed with calculators helped you to figure that out.
>
> *Teacher's scoring key:* Examine the student's response to determine how well the following criteria are met:
>
> A. The response displays comprehension of the task posed by the item.
> B. The response includes references to examining specific linear functions, comparing characteristics of the graph to values of a or b.
> C. The response displays the use of inductive reasoning from specific values of a in particular graphs to a statement of the general relationship.
> D. Nothing erroneous or extraneous is included in the response.

For each of the four criteria, award points as follows:

+2 if the criterion in question is clearly met.
+1 if it is unclear as to whether or not the criterion is met.
+0 if the criterion is clearly not met.

Engage in Activity 4.7.

_____ **ACTIVITY 4.7** _____

Purpose: To stimulate your thoughts about how objectives' learning levels influence measurement-item design and to stimulate you to being thinking about how to design measurement items for discover-a-relationship objectives.

Procedure: Design two measurement items for student achievement of the objective of the lesson you taught for Activity 4.6. Exchange your items with those designed by a colleague. Provide one another with feedback on the items. After refining your two items in light of your colleague's feedback, administer them to one or two students. Discuss what you learned from this experience with two or more colleagues.

In Case 4.14, two mathematics teachers discuss the two items one of them designed for Activity 4.7.

CASE 4.14 _____

Jermain: Since I selected the first relationship in Activity 4.6, the lesson objective to which my items are supposed to be relevant is:

Explain why the lateral surface area of a right cylinder equals $2\pi rh$.. (*discover-a-relationship*)

Tina: So, let's see your two items.
Jermain: Rather than design items only for formative feedback during the lesson, I decided to try my hand at trying to design them for summative evaluation near the end of the unit. I decided to give students a problem with the computation already set up and laid out for them. Then I would see if they can explain why the computation will give them the lateral surface area. Here it is.

Tina examines the item shown in Exhibit 4.20.

Tina: I like that the item directs the student to analyze why the computation works, not to set up or do the computation. It definitely taps a cognitive process that's not the usual focus on the solution. I'm not sure if by itself it tells us if the student actually discovered the relationship.
Jermain: I don't think any one item does that by itself. One measurement item is just one part of a measurement that, at best, gives us some indicator or evidence of student achievement. We as teachers have to make a judgment based on that evidence. The evidence isn't the answer, it's just something on which to base an answer.
Tina: I agree. We need to keep reminding ourselves that one item is only one small piece of a big puzzle. What about your second item?
Jermain: Well I began to worry that this first item may put too much of a premium on students' being able to comprehend the directions and also on their writing skills. So, instead of coming up with an entirely new idea for a second item, I concentrated on modifying this first one so that students' abilities to figure out what I wanted and to organize their thoughts in an essay weren't so critical. I wanted to allow them to concentrate more on the mathematics and less on the writing. So, I —
Tina: Show me the item.

Tina examines the item shown in Exhibit 4.21.

Tina: This version should be easier for most students. You've done some of the cognitive work for them.
Jermain: Which one do you like better?
Tina: It depends on whether you want them to organize their explanations themselves or you want to do some of the structuring for them. The first probably is a more sophisticated achievement of the objective. But the second one will be easier for you to score.
Jermain: Yeah. If this were only one of many items on a test and I had 30 students, I'd be happier with the second when I was up late at night scoring the test.

_____

Exhibit 4.20
The first item Jermain designed to be relevant to how well students discovered the formula for lateral surface area of a right cylinder.

Which of the following two items do you think would be easier for students?

1. Task Presented to the Student: Suppose you wanted to find how much paint would be needed to cover the outside of the tube pictured (it's open at both ends). Use from one-half to one page to explain why the size of the surface to be painted can be found by the following computation:

$$2 \times 3.14 \times 3.98 \times 15$$

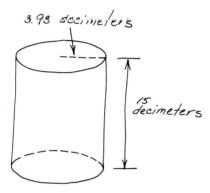

3.98 decimeters

15 decimeters

Scoring Key: 8 points maximum, distributed according to four 2-point scales, each with +2 for clearly explaining the point, +1 if there is some doubt that the point is explained, and +0 if the point is not explained. The four points are:

- The cylinder can be reformed into a rectangle without changing the lateral surface area.
- The circumference of the right cylinder is associated with one side of the rectangle.
- The height of the right cylinder is associated with the other side of the rectangle.
- The computation is associated with $2\pi rh$.

TRANSITIONAL ACTIVITIES FROM CHAPTER 4 TO CHAPTER 5 _____

1. Select the *one* response to each of the following multiple-choice items that either completes the statement so that it is true or accurately answers the question:

A. Which of the following is a concept?
   (a) December 10, 1968
   (b) 10 hours, 14 minutes, 19 seconds
   (c) A point in time

B. Which of the following is a specific?
   (a) 14 meters
   (b) The distance between two points
   (c) Perimeter

C. Which of the following is a relationship from a specific to a concept?
   (a) Paul Hoffman wrote *Archimedes' Revenge: The Joys and Perils of Mathematics*
   (b) Paul Hoffman wrote a book
   (c) People write books

D. Which of the following relationships is discoverable?
   (a) Among professional mathematicians, a proposition is not accepted to be a theorem until a proof of the proposition has been reviewed and judged as valid by a panel of referees.
   (b) The relation $\{(\sqrt{4}, 3), (3, -4), (2, \sqrt{9}), (0, -4)\}$ is a function from $\{0, 2, 3\}$ into {reals}.
   (c) NCTM stands for National Council of Teachers of Mathematics.

E. Which of the following relationships is conventional rather than discoverable?
   (a) A positive integer n is a friendly number iff n equals the sum of its proper divisors—that is, the sum of all the positive integers that factor n except for n itself.
   (b) $6, 28, 496, 2^{60}(2^{61} - 1) \in$ {perfect numbers}.
   (c) $60 \notin$ {perfect number}.
   (d) $\{1, 2, 3, 4, 5, 6, 10, 12, 15, 20, 30\} =$ {proper divisors of 60}.

F. A concept is a _____.
   (a) relationship
   (b) constant
   (c) variable

G. Students conceptualize when they _____.
   (a) comprehend the definition of a concept.
   (b) construct-a-concept in their own minds
   (c) explain the conventional meaning of a word naming a concept

H. Direct instruction is an appropriate strategy for designing lessons for which of the following types of learning objectives?
   (a) Construct-a-concept
   (b) Discover-a-relationship
   (c) Algorithmic skill

I. Inquiry instruction is an appropriate strategy for designing lessons for which of the following types of learning objectives?
   (a) Simple knowledge
   (b) Discover-a-relationship
   (c) Algorithmic skill

J. Students are stimulated to formulate generalizations from specifics during _____.
   (a) inductive learning activities
   (b) deductive learning activities

Exhibit 4.21
An item similar to exhibit 4.20's but with some of the cognitive work done for the student.

2. Task Presented to the Student: Suppose you wanted to find how much paint would be needed to cover the outside of the tube pictured (it's open at both ends). You can find the size of the surface to be painted with the following computation:

$$2 \times 3.14 \times 3.98 \times 15$$

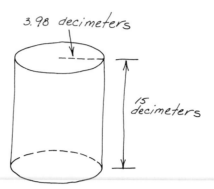

3.98 decimeters

15 decimeters

State the formula on which that computation is based.

_____

Why does that formula work for the tube in this problem? Explain why in a paragraph. Include a drawing showing how the tube has the same surface size as another, more familiar figure

Paragraph	Drawing
_____	
_____	
_____	
_____	
_____	
_____	
_____	
_____	
_____	

In the computation we calculate, 2 × 3.14 × 3.98 × 15? Why is there a 2?

In the computation, why is there a 3.14?

In the computation, why is there a 3.98?

In the computation, why is there a 15?

Scoring Key: 8 points maximum, distributed according to four 2-point scales, each with +2 for clearly explaining the point, +1 if there is some doubt about the explanation, and +0 if the point is not explained. The four points are:

• The cylinder can be reformed into a rectangle without changing the lateral surface area.
• The circumference of the right cylinder is associated with one side of the rectangle.
• The height of the right cylinder is associated with the other side of the rectangle.
• The computation is associated with 2πrh.

(c) direct instruction

(d) drill and practice activities

Compare your responses to the following; A-c; B-a; C-b; D-b; E-a, F-c; G-b; H-c; I-b; J-a.

2. Reexamine the objectives listed in Exhibit 3.9. Although the wording of the objectives does not totally communicate exactly what the teachers had in mind (the learning levels aren't labeled), infer the teachers' intentions by analyzing each objective to determine if the learning level is (a) construct-a-concept, (b) discover-a-relationship, or (c) neither (a) nor (b).

After completing this task, compare your responses to the following; keep in mind, however, that differences may be due to ambiguities in the phrasing of the objectives: A, B, C, D, and E of Unit I, A and E of Unit II, B and E of Unit III, B of Unit IV, D of Unit V, and A and E of Unit VI, appear to be discover-a-relationship objectives. Only Objective A of Unit V appears to be a construct-a-concept objective.

3. Discuss the following questions with two or more of your colleagues:

a. What mathematical information should students commit to memory?

b. What strategies should teachers employ to lead their students to achieve simple-knowledge objectives?

c. What mathematical expressions (for example, shorthand notations) should students comprehend and use?

d. How should lessons be designed to improve students abilities to communicate about mathematics?

e. In this age of computers and sophisticated calculators, with what algorithms do students need to become proficient?

f. What strategies should teachers employ to lead their students to achieve algorithmic-skill objectives?

5

Leading Students to Develop Knowledge, Comprehension, and Algorithmic Skills

This chapter explains how to design lessons that lead students to acquire and remember mathematical information, comprehend mathematical expressions, and develop algorithmic skills. In particular, Chapter 5 is designed to help you:

1. Distinguish among examples of (a) mathematical information students need to remember, (b) mathematical expressions and messages students need to comprehend, (c) algorithmic skills students need to develop, and (d) other types of mathematics content specified by learning objectives. (*construct a concept*)
2. Describe the reception-overlearning process by which students acquire and retain information. (*comprehension*)
3. Formulate simple-knowledge objectives that, for a given group of middle or secondary school students, are consistent with the NCTM *Standards*. (*application*)
4. Design lessons for simple-knowledge objectives. (*application*)
5. Design measurement items that are relevant to student achievement of simple-knowledge objectives. (*application*)
6. Describe the literal and interpretive understanding process by which students comprehend technical mathematical expressions and messages about mathematics. (*comprehension*)
7. Formulate comprehension objectives that, for a given group of middle or secondary school students, are consistent with the NCTM *Standards*. (*application*)
8. Design lessons for comprehension objectives. (*application*)
9. Design measurement items that are relevant to student achievement of comprehension objectives. (*application*)
10. Describe the follow directions, practice, error-analysis correction, overlearn process by which students develop algorithmic skills for arithmetic computations, reforming expressions, translating statements of relationships, and measuring. (*comprehension*)
11. Formulate algorithmic-skill objectives that, for a given group of middle or secondary school students, are consistent with the NCTM *Standards*. (*application*)
12. Design lessons for algorithmic-skill objectives. (*application*)
13. Design measurement items that are relevant to student achievement of algorithmic-skill objectives. (*application*)

MATHEMATICAL INFORMATION TO BE REMEMBERED

In Case 4.7, Mr. Citerelli began a unit targeting the 13 objectives listed in Exhibit 4.6. The "simple-knowledge" labels on Objectives C and J indicate students should *remember* certain information, namely the definition of "arithmetic sequence," and the formula for finding the nth term of an arithmetic sequence, the definition of "geometric sequence," and the formula for finding the nth term of a geometric sequence. Whereas constructing concepts and discovering relationships form the basis for learning meaningful mathematics, it is also practical for students to remember conventional names for concepts they've constructed and the statements of relationships they've discovered. Furthermore, they should be informed about and remember certain mathematical conventions and historical names and events, such as Nikolai Ivanovich Lobachevsky and Janos Bolyai inventing non-Euclidean geometries in the nineteenth century (Jones, 1989).

Of course, only a minute subset of mathematical information to which you expose your students can be or should be realistically committed to memory. You, like Mr. Citerelli in Case 4.7, need to decide what information your students need to know to enable them to do meaningful mathematics. Engage in Activity 5.1.

ACTIVITY 5.1

Purpose: To reflect on types of mathematical information you as a teacher should consider leading your students to remember.

Procedure: Suppose you were planning a unit for an Algebra II course to introduce (or review for some students) trigonometry. The content for that unit might include some of the following information items:

- Given $\triangle ABC$ such that $\angle C$ is a right angle, and the measure of $\angle A = \theta$, the following six definitions:

$$\sin \theta = \frac{\text{side opposite } A}{\text{hypotenuse}}$$

$$\cos \theta = \frac{\text{side adjacent to } A}{\text{hypotenuse}}$$

$$\tan \theta = \frac{\text{side opposite } A}{\text{side adjacent to } A}$$

$$\cot \theta = \frac{\text{side adjacent to } A}{\text{side opposite } A}$$

$$\sec \theta = \frac{\text{hypotenuse}}{\text{side adjacent to } A}$$

$$\csc \theta = \frac{\text{hypotenuse}}{\text{side opposite to } A}$$

- The cotangent, secant, and cosecant functions are the respective reciprocals for the tangent, cosine, and sine functions.
- Claudius Ptolemy (Egyptian who lived during the first century A.D.) contributed to the development of trigonometry in his attempts to solve astronomy and geography problems such as estimating the size of the earth and mapping the heavens.
- $\sin 30° = 1/2$; $\cos 30° = \sqrt{3}/2$; $\tan 30° = \sqrt{3}/3$; $\sin 45° = \sqrt{2}/2$; $\cos 45° = \sqrt{2}/2$; $\tan 45° = 1$; $\sin 60° = \sqrt{3}/2$; $\cos 60° = 1/2$; $\tan 60° = \sqrt{3}$
- $\sin \theta = \cos (90° - \theta)$; $\cos \theta = \sin (90° - \theta)$; $\tan \theta = \cot (90° - \theta)$; $\cot \theta = \tan (90° - \theta)$; $\sec \theta = \csc (90° - \theta)$; $\csc \theta = \sec (90° - \theta)$.
- The following quotient identities:

$$\tan \theta \equiv \frac{\sin \theta}{\cos \theta} \text{ for } \cos \theta \neq 0$$

$$\cot \theta \equiv \frac{\cos \theta}{\sin \theta} \text{ for } \sin \theta \neq 0$$

- The following identities based on the Pythagorean relationship:

$$\sin^2 \theta + \cos^2 \equiv 1$$

$$1 + \cot^2 \theta \equiv \csc^2 \theta$$

$$1 + \tan^2 \theta \equiv \sec^2 \theta$$

For each item of information listed, discuss with a colleague the advantages and disadvantages of having students remember it. Determine which, if any, information items from the list you would likely include among the things for students to remember as part of the unit.

In Case 5.1, two mathematics teachers engage in Activity 5.1.

CASE 5.1

Tina: The first one is the basic definition of the six trigonometric functions—the right triangle versions. They are conventional relationships not discoverable ones, so you would not have a discover a relationship objective for them. It's really vocabulary that's basic to doing trigonometry.

Jermain: It seems to me you have to have a simple-knowledge objective for students to remember those six ratios with their names. You don't want them having to look up the meanings of sine and so forth every time they come across it.

Tina: I agree, but I've got two questions about building this unit. Should these definitions be at the comprehension level rather than just at the simple-knowledge level? Since they're so critical to everything we do in trig, students need to be able to interpret the words, not just memorize them.

Jermain: I'm not sure. They seem so simple. Assuming that by the time students are taking trig, they have already constructed the concept of a ratio, what's there to comprehend? Anyway, whether we have a comprehension objective or not, students still have to commit the definitions to memory, so for now let's just say that unless students know these meanings off the tops of their heads, they're not going to be able to communicate about trigonometry. What's your other question?

Tina: When the objectives are listed for the unit, do we want students to memorize all six at once? Or should we only bother remembering "sine," "cosine," and "tangent," since you can do all the trig you want with just those three?

Jermain: Good point! And if you look at the next item on this Activity 5.1 list, the one about the reciprocals, you really don't need separate definitions for cotangent, secant, and cosecant. I guess you could do it either way.

Tina: It'd be really nice to cut the number of definitions to be memorized in half before you begin teaching them to do some actual trigonometry.

Jermain: Well, we do agree that at some point in time students need to remember which ratios are associated with which six words. Let's move on to the one about Ptolemy.

Tina: That one is interesting to me because, although I've taken a whole course on trig in high school, plus another in college, and have had units on trig in high school geometry as well as algebra, I never understood the convenience of using trig for astronomy and geography until last year when I took this math history course. We had to estimate the size of the earth using angle sightings from the moon like Ptolemy did. I gained an appreciation for the value of trig that I never had before!

Jermain: So you're saying that historical events like Ptlomey's contribution to the development of trig should be included. But do historical facts like this need to be committed to memory?

Tina: By remembering just a few such events, students gain a sense of how mathematics developed and its usefulness.

Jermain: But can't you accomplish that through exposure to historical accounts without making it a miserable chore, worrying about what they have to remember for a test? You can hardly enjoy and comprehend historical accounts if you're trying to memorize dates like the time frame between 125 A.D. and 151 A.D. when Ptlomey recorded his astronomical observations and trigonometric inventions in the *Almagest*.

Tina: Wow! I'm impressed the way you just spit out that trivia.

Jermain: You should be. Actually, when I read this Activity 5.1 assignment, the name "Ptolemy" seemed vaguely familiar, but I didn't really remember from where. So I just looked up some stuff in a couple of math history books. Ask me again tomorrow and I won't know "125 to 151 A.D."

Tina: But you will still have a better feel for the history of trigonometry and you'll still have an idea of mathematical discovery and invention in the Mediterranean during the first century A.D.

Jermain: I hear us agreeing that students need to comprehend a sample of historical accounts; there's not much advantage to getting them to memorize them.

Tina: Next on the list are these specific values for the so-called special angles—30°, 60°, and 45°. Obviously, those are all discoverable relationships.

Jermain: Clearly, you'd want students to discover each of those for themselves, but then what's the advantage of committing them to memory?

Tina: Because I've used them so much, I remember some of them myself. But not from when my teachers made me memorize them. Back then, I'd memorize them for the tests and then have to re-memorize them the next time. It's convenient to know some of these when you're working on some problems, but now we always have our calculators handy. I don't think there's a need to write a simple-knowledge objective for those relationships.

Jermain: I agree, but what about these quotient identities?

Tina: They're so easily discoverable from the definitions of the six basic trig functions. I see no advantage at all in memorizing those. The same is true for the last group of identities on our list. If you understand the six functions and the Pythagorean theorem, you can create these three relationships on the spot as you need them.

Jermain: I guess so, but what about some of the less obvious, but useful, identities like. . . . Let's see, let me look one up in the inside cover of my calculus book. Here, one of them is "$\sin u \sin v = \frac{1}{2} [\cos (u - v) - \cos (u + v)]$." It'd be pretty inconvenient and time consuming to have to rediscover one that complicated every time you needed it.

Tina: I noticed you didn't have it right off the top of your head.

Jermain: But I remembered it existed.

Tina: Good point. What we should do is have students discover these identities for themselves so they'll make sense out of them and be aware of their existence. Then we just teach them how to look them up when they need them rather than expect them to remember them by heart—like you, they'll forget anyway!

Jermain: Maybe you're right, but that's not how I was taught.

THE ACQUISITION AND RETENTION OF INFORMATION

Engage in Activity 5.2.

ACTIVITY 5.2

Purpose: To reflect on the process by which people acquire and remember information.

Procedure: Think of an item of information, like your own name, that you remember well but don't specifically recall the event in which you first acquired this knowledge. Speculate on how you first learned this information and explain why you think you'll never forget it.

Think of another item of information you also remember well, but this time the information should be something you discovered by yourself. Reflect on the events leading you to discover this information and explain why you think you easily remember the information today.

Think of a third item of information that you remember well, but this time it should be information about which you recall being informed (you didn't discover it for yourself; you read or heard of it). Explain why you think you easily remember the information today.

Now think of a final item of information that you have difficulty remembering, such as a formula you once learned for a test in school, but can't recall right now. Explain why you think you have difficulty remembering this information today.

Share with a colleague who is also working on this activity your examples and explanations. In collaboration, formulate a description of a process by which people acquire and retain information. Exchange and discuss your descriptions with other pairs of colleagues who engaged in Activity 5.2.

In Case 5.2, two mathematics teachers engage in Activity 5.2.

CASE 5.2

Jermain: Here, would you read mine (see Exhibit 5.1), while I read yours (see Exhibit 5.2)?

Tina: I have no quarrel with what you've done, especially the part about never forgetting my name.

Jermain: I follow what you've done also, but I have a question about the first one. "Most people enjoy [your] company more when [you] talk about them than when [you] talk about yourself." Is that a form of information or is a matter of opinion?

Tina: Good question! It's surely something I believe to be true, but it is a matter of opinion. Does that keep it from being information?

Jermain: I think it's information; it's just difficult to prove. Anyway, it's information that you believe is true. Let's not get hung up on the semantics and get on with the next part of this task.

Tina: To formulate a description of a process by which we acquire and retain information.

Jermain: In our examples, the acquisition of the information part varies. For some we found out from an outside

Exhibit 5.1
The written portion of Jermain's response to Activity 5.2.

Information I'll never forget, but don't remember learning

My name is Jermain Jones. Barring a traumatic event or a disease that robs me of my memory, I don't think I'll ever forget my name. I imagine that my mother, aunt, brother, and others who were around me continually in my first few years of life repeatedly referred to me by my name. Gradually, I must have made the association between my name and myself. I easily remember it because nearly every day of my life I have cause to say, write, hear, and read my name repeatedly. The ongoing repetition makes it stick in my memory.

Information I discovered myself and am not likely to forget

Rainbows typically appear when the sun shines shortly after a rain storm or during a light rain. I discovered that relationship myself from direct and repeated observations. I don't think I'll ever forget it because I discovered it myself and the belief is reinforced every time I see a rainbow.

Information about which I remember being informed and am unlikely to forget

My friend Tina's name is Tina Huerta. I learned Tina's name when she first introduced herself in class. However, even after I began working with her in cooperative group activities, I had trouble remembering Huerta. Then I made this silly association: Tina reminds me of "tiny." And something that's tiny is hard to find, so you're always saying "where to" find it; Huerta is pronounced "where-ta." Thus, I used a mnemonic device initially to remember her name.

Information I've forgotten but once knew

I've heard of the fundamental theorem of algebra. I'm sure I learned what it is for a number of mathematics courses I aced. However, I no longer have any idea as to how to state the fundamental theorem of algebra. It's probably something I use a lot, but I don't know which of the algebraic theorems I've learned over the years is called by that name.

Exhibit 5.2
The written portion of Tina's response to activity 5.2.

Something I'll always remember, but don't remember when I learned it

Most people enjoy my company more when I talk about them rather than when I talk about myself. That's something that I discovered to be true sometime between my preadolescent years and as a young adult. But I can't specifically put my finger on when I learned the relationship to be true. I won't forget it because the belief is reinforced again and again in my contact with people.

Note: It just dawned on me that this is all very mathematical in that I've discovered through my experience the following probability relationship: The probability that others will enjoy my company is greater when I focus the conversation on them than it is when I focus it on me.

Something I discovered on my own and will always remember

What I just wrote fits this category, but since I don't recall the events leading to the realization, I'll select another. It's that the sum of two odd integers is even. I distinctly remember doodling in middle school during a lesson on multiplying signed numbers. "A positive times a positive is positive," Mr. Heap said. That didn't seem surprising, but then I started looking at the sums of odd-integer pairs and I was surprised. I quit paying attention in class and started breaking up odd integers, like $17 = 16 + 1$ and $5 = 4 + 1$. I kept thinking about it and figured out why it's true. It wasn't until I became comfortable with algebraic notation that I expressed odd integers as $2i + 1$ for some integer i, and then proved my conjecture to be a theorem. Although my theorem seems awfully simple and trivial today, it

played a significant role in my mathematical development. Whenever, I'm struggling with a difficult proof or problem, I think back to how I worked out the explanation for that relationship when I was about 13 years old. It gives me confidence to keep trying and no matter how nontrivial the proof or problem seems, my strategies from age 13 still work.

Something about which I was informed and won't forget

"Direct instruction is used to inform students and help them remember; inquiry instruction is used to stimulate them to reason and draw conclusions for themselves." That's something about which I was informed during this mathematics teaching methods course. I won't forget it because we've repeated the idea again and again. Now that I think about it, it's probably an idea I discovered for myself as I recall my own learning experiences. However, it never before stuck with me to use the terms direct instruction and inquiry instruction in just those ways—although I'm pretty sure I was exposed to them before.

Something I no longer remember but once did

I memorized a massive amount of verbiage dealing with group theory during an abstract algebra course I recently took. *Homomorphism, ideal, rings, kernels, vector spaces,* and on and on and on. I even did well on tests regurgitating them. But right know I don't remember what's "ideal" and I still think of a "kernel" as having to do more with corn than with algebra. Although I don't really understand how to apply any of that material from abstract algebra, I do know how to look it up if I ever need it.

---

source, like hearing or reading about it. Others we figured out for ourselves.

Tina: The ones we figured out for ourselves tend to stay with us longer.

Jermain: But look at the two lists. The information that stuck also tended to be what we continued to use repeatedly. Repetition over time seems to make it indelible.

Tina: Right. Also, your use of a mnemonic device helps hold things in short-term memory.

Jermain: So let's list the process.

Tina: First, we are either informed of the information or figure it out for ourselves. To get an initial grip on some hard to remember things—ones we didn't figure out on our own—we might need to visualize a connection between something already familiar to us and the new, unfamiliar information.

Jermain: That's the mnemonic device.

Tina: To retain the information in long-term memory we need to refer to it repeatedly, be exposed to it, or use it over a period of time.

Jermain: That's what we called "*overlearning*" in our educational psychology course.

SIMPLE-KNOWLEDGE OBJECTIVES

Review the definition of simple-knowledge learning level and the examples of simple-knowledge objectives in Exhibit 3.10. The three simple-knowledge objectives in Exhibit 3.10, as well as Objectives C and J in Exhibit 4.6, indicate responses for students to remember when presented with certain stimuli. The intent of Objective C is for students to (a) respond to the stimulus "arithmetic sequence" with the definition they developed when they achieved Objective A, and (b) respond to the stimulus "*n*th term of an arithmetic sequence" with the equivalent of "$a_n = a_1 + (n - 1)(a_2 - a_1)$."

LESSONS FOR SIMPLE-KNOWLEDGE OBJECTIVES

Facilitating Reception and Retention Through Direct Instruction

Students achieve construct a concept and discover a relationship objectives by making decisions based on information they have acquired, such as examples and nonexamples of a concept or data collected in an experiment. On the other hand, students achieve simple-knowledge objectives by accurately *receiving* and *retaining* information. Reception and retention are accomplished through a five-stage *direct instruction process*:

Stage 1: Exposition. Students are exposed to the information they are to remember. Case 5.3 is an example.

CASE 5.3

Ms. Corbridge's students have already conceptualized Fibonacci sequences. Now she wants them to achieve the following objective:

State the definition of "Fibonacci number." (*simple knowledge*)

As part of a homework assignment she directs the students to copy the definition of Fibonacci numbers from page 301 of their texts and into the glossary they maintain in their notebooks. The next day she displays the definition on the overhead screen, reads it, and asks them to check the accuracy of the copies in their glossaries.

Stage 2: Explication. The students are provided with an explanation as to how they are to respond to the content's stimulus. For example, Ms. Corbridge tells her students, "Anytime you see or hear the words Fibonacci numbers, you are to think, 'a member of the infinite sequence whose first two terms are both 1 and whose subsequent terms are the sum of the previous two (i.e., 1, 1, 2, 3, 5, 8, . . .).' Also, anytime you see that sequence, think 'Fibonacci.' "

Stage 3: Mnemonics. "*Mnemonics*" is a word derived from Mnemosyne, the name of the ancient Greek goddess of memory. The word means *aiding the memory*.

For some, but not all, simple-knowledge objectives, you might consider providing students with mnemonic devices to enhance retention. Mnemonic devices have proven to be effective in helping stu-

dents remember new information (Joyce, Weil, & Showers, 1992, pp. 159–179; Woolfolk, 1993, pp. 267–274). I, for example, informed you about the derivation of "mnemonics" to help you remember its meaning. Thus, that was a mnemonic aid. However, unless you are already familiar with the goddess Mnemosyne, my mnemonic device isn't likely to be effective. The most effective mnemonic devices link new information to be remembered to something already familiar to the student. For example:

- To help students remember that "whole numbers" refer to {0, 1, 2, . . .}, whereas "counting numbers" refer to {1, 2, 3, . . .}, a teacher says, "The set of whole numbers is the one with the *hole* in it. The hole is the zero."
- If Ms. Corbridge in Case 5.3 related the history of Fibonacci numbers in a construct a concept lesson on Fibonacci sequences, she probably needs no mnemonic devices to help her students to remember the meaning of Fibonacci numbers. However, if the students have yet to associate the sequences with Leonardo Fibonacci, then she might consider a mnemonic gimmick to help them remember. For example, she could tell her students, "The word Fibonacci reminds me of *fibbed on arithmetic* because Fibonacci sequences are sort of like arithmetic sequences, since you have to add to find the next member. But they're not arithmetic because you don't keep adding the same number."

Usually, it isn't necessary to use mnemonics to help students remember definitions of concepts they have already constructed or statements of relationships they've already discovered. Mnemonic devices are more helpful for recalling conventions that are not logically connected to content students have already learned.

Stage 4: Monitoring and Feedback. The accuracy with which students recall what they are supposed to have memorized is monitored. Correct responses are positively reinforced and errors corrected. Case 5.4 is an example.

CASE 5.4

Matt: Ms. Corbridge, is 300 one of those kind of numbers?
Ms. Corbridge: What kind of numbers?
Matt: You know, the kind you were talking about.
Ms. Corbridge: What's the name?
Matt: You know, Fibba-something.
Ms. Corbridge: What's Matt talking about, Riley?
Riley: Fibonacci numbers.
Ms. Corbridge: Oh! Thank you, Riley. Fibonacci numbers! Repeat your question using the words "Fibonacci numbers," Matt.

Stage 5: Overlearning. Students *overlearn* by continuing to practice recalling content even after they have memorized it. Overlearning increases resistance to forgetting and facilitates long-term retention of information (Chance, 1988, pp. 221–222; Woolfolk, 1992, pp. 317–318). For example, even after the completion of the unit in which she introduced the Fibonacci sequence, Ms. Corbridge continues to confront students with tasks requiring them to use their knowledge of the meaning of "Fibonacci numbers."

A Five-Stage Lesson for a Simple-Knowledge Objective

In Case 5.5, a teacher plans a lesson to include the five stages leading to simple-knowledge-level learning.

CASE 5.5 _____

Ms. Ray designs the lesson for the following objective:

> State the definitions of the six trigonometric functions. (*simple knowledge*)

She thinks: "This lesson follows the discover a relationship one on the association between the size of one of the acute angles of a right triangle and the relative lengths of the triangle's legs. So, I hope they'll already understand how the value of θ affects the ratio of one side to another." She draws and muses over the picture in Exhibit 5.3.

"All we really need to do here is to get them to associate these six names with the right ratios. How can I help them keep the names straight? They're familiar with tangents and secants relative to circles, so maybe I could show them these ratios and show how y/x is associated with tangent and r/x with secant. . . . Hmm, then I'd have to get into circular functions and they're not ready for that yet. Besides it would take more time than I care to spend just so they'll see some logic behind the names. On the other hand, if we took the trouble to do that, I bet they'd never forget the

Exhibit 5.3
Ms. Ray's drawing and notes as she begins designing a simple-knowledge lesson.

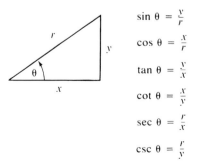

$$\sin \theta = \frac{y}{r}$$
$$\cos \theta = \frac{x}{r}$$
$$\tan \theta = \frac{y}{x}$$
$$\cot \theta = \frac{x}{y}$$
$$\sec \theta = \frac{r}{x}$$
$$\csc \theta = \frac{r}{y}$$

Exhibit 5.4
Ms. Ray modified the notes shown in Exhibit 5.3.

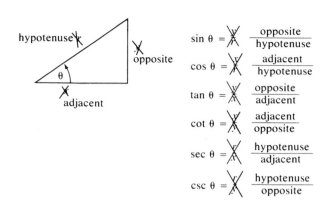

names that go with the ratios. No, I need to remember that this is a simple-knowledge lesson and just give them straightforward, direct instruction. I'll just tell them the names, sine θ is y over r, cos θ is x over r, and so forth. Oh, no! that's not the terminology they need to know at this point. We've worked only with right triangles independent of coordinate planes and circles to this point. So I'd better use these." She modifies the notes to read like Exhibit 5.4.

She continues: "That's better, and I think that's the way the book starts off too. Better check that. . . . Yep, that's good; I'm in line with the book.

"Okay, the first thing I'll do is write each function on the overhead and . . . No, here's a better idea! I'll start by having them list all six possible ratios. That way they'll automatically know that the right side of all six equations are permutations of three sides taken two at a time. It'll serve as a mnemonic. Then, after they've listed them, I'll start naming them—getting them to write each one out and saying it aloud. Might as well expose this stuff to as many of their senses as we can. I'd get them to smell these functions if I could. Hmm, actually I could appeal to their sense of touch with some concrete models of each function. . . . Not a bad idea! I'm not going to that trouble this time, but maybe I'll try that with another class.

"Oh! I've also got to make sure they get the abbreviations down. Better include those right from the start. Okay, so I get all the functions listed and names and abbreviations for them. Then to explain just what they're to remember—they're to respond with the right name to a given ratio and with the ratio to a given name. I'll explain that to them and test them both ways.

"I wish I could think of some good mnemonics for these. I ought to check with Frank; he's taught trig for years. I'll bet he's come up with some effective gimmicks. Hmm, how did I ever remember these? My teachers never used mnemonics, but I never forgot. Let's see . . . I remember! The sine and cosine have the hypotenuse in the denominator, and the sine has opposite for the numerator, so there's nothing left but adjacent for cosine's numerator. Tangent and cotangent are the ones without the hypotenuse and the numerators follow the same order as sine and cosine—opposite for the function and adjacent for the cofunction. I used to remember the cosecant is the reciprocal of sine and the secant is the reciprocal of cosine. I wonder if sharing that with them would work as a mnemonic? Maybe it would be better to leave them to their own devices. . . . I don't know. . . . Think I won't tell this class and see what they come up with. In fourth period I'll tell them and see if they have an easier time remembering—a little action-research project!

"Memorization and practice of homework, along with some computational practice, and then a quick quiz first thing the next day. We'll go over the quiz right away and correct errors. Overlearning shouldn't be difficult; they'll be using the names with these ratios for the rest of this unit, as well as for the next three units. If they get these correct now, there's no way I'll let them forget them before summer."

Engage in Activity 5.3.

─────────────── **ACTIVITY 5.3** ───────────────

Purpose: To expand your insights regarding how to design lessons for simple-knowledge objectives.

Procedure: Select one of the items of information from the following list:

- An integer a is a divisor of integer b iff there exists an integer i such that $b = ai$ (i.e., $a|b \Leftrightarrow \exists i \in$ {integers} $\ni b = ai$).
- The standard deviation of a sequence of rational numbers, $(x_1, x_2, x_3, \ldots, x_n)$, is σ where $\sigma = (1/N)\sum_{i=1}^{N}(x_i - \mu)^2$ and μ is the arithmetic mean of the sequence.
- The distance between two coordinate points, (x_1, y_1) and (x_2, y_2), in a Cartesian plane is $((y_1 - y_2)^2 + (x_1 - x_2)^2)^{1/2}$.
- {complex numbers} = {reals} $\cup$ {imaginaries}.
- Binomial expansion: $(x + y)^n = x^n + nx^{n-1}y + n(n-1)x^{n-2}y^2/2! + \ldots + nxy^{n-1} + y^n$.
- Volume of a sphere with radius $r = (4/3)\pi r^3$.

Design and teach a lesson for one or two students that leads the student or students to remember the information.

Discuss your experiences designing and teaching the lesson with colleagues who are also engaging in Activity 5.3. Share with one another what you learned from your experiences.

INDICATORS OF ACHIEVEMENT OF SIMPLE-KNOWLEDGE OBJECTIVES

Stimulus-Response

A measurement relevant to students' achievement of a simple-knowledge objective presents them with the task of exhibiting that when exposed to the stimulus specified by the objective, they respond with the word, image, symbol, name, definition, statement, or other content the objective specifies. Designing items for simple-knowledge typically won't tax your creative talents to the same degree as designing items for construct a concept or discover a relationship objectives. However, there are pitfalls to avoid. Consider the following objective:

State the Pythagorean theorem.   (*simple knowledge*)

When presented with the stimulus "Pythagorean theorem," students who achieve this objective remember a response equivalent to: "For any right triangle, the square of the length of the hypotenuse equals the sum of the squares of the lengths of the two legs." Now, examine the four measurement items in Exhibit 5.5 and judge how relevant each is to the aforementioned objective.

All four of Exhibit 5.5's items appear to have reasonable relevance for the stated objective. However, if your principal purpose for including this objective is to have students remember the Pythagorean theorem so that they can comprehend messages that use the expression Pythagorean theorem, then measurement items for the objective should maintain the stimulus-response order. Items 1 and 2 do that, but items 3 and 4 don't. Unlike items 1 and 2, items 3 and 4 require students to remember the name "Pythagorean theorem" in response to the statement of the relationship. Thus, those items require a task that is different from the one students confront when reading or hearing the expression Pythagorean theorem.

On the other hand, if you also want students to refer to the relationship as the Pythagorean theorem in communications they send, then items such as 3 and 4 of Exhibit 5.5 that reverse the stimulus-response order of the objective should also be used. The critical point here is for you to understand the objective well enough so that you design items that present students with tasks remembering appropriate responses to appropriate stimuli.

Avoiding Responses Beyond Simple Knowledge

Students' responses to simple-knowledge items should depend only on how well they remember information. Items are not relevant to simple-knowledge objectives if students have to use reasoning or higher-order cognitive processes to respond. But, the fact that an item is intended to measure simple-knowledge behavior does not guarantee that students will respond at the simple-knowledge level. In Case 5.6 a student responds to what was supposed to be a simple-knowledge item with reasoning because of an ambiguity in the wording of the item.

Exhibit 5.5
Four items *intended* to be relevant to how well students can state the Pythagorean theorem.

---

1. Task Presented to the Student
State the Pythagorean theorem. _____
_____
_____

Scoring Key. 2 points maximum, with +1 for indicating that the theorem is about right triangles and +1 if the relation $h^2 = a^2 + b^2$ is clearly implied.

2. Task Presented to the Student
Multiple Choice. Given $\triangle ABC$ with $m\angle B = 90°$, the Pythagorean theorem states that:
A. $(AB + BC)^2 = AC^2$
B. $AB = BC^2 + AC^2$
C. $AB^2 + C^2 = AC^2$
D. $AC^2 + AB^2 = BC^2$
E. $(AC + AB)^2 = BC^2$

Scoring Key. +1 for C only; otherwise + 0.

3. Task Presented to the Student
What is the name of the following theorem?

For any right triangle, the square of the length of the hypotenuse equals the sum of the squares of the lengths of the two legs.

Scoring Key. +1 for Pythagorean (spelling need not be exact as long as it is clear what the student meant); otherwise, +0.

4. Task Presented to the Student
Multiple Choice. If $\angle B$ of $\triangle ABC$ is a right angle, then $AB^2 + BC^2 = AC^2$. The name of this statement is
_____.
A. Euclid's fifth postulate
B. The fundamental theorem of geometry
C. Archimedes' principle of right triangles
D. Fermat's last theorem
E. The Pythagorean theorem

Scoring Key. +1 for E only; otherwise +0.

CASE 5.6 _____

Early in Mr. Garon's geometry course, Amy engaged in some of the learning activities that experience led her to discover for herself that the sum of the degree measures of the three angles of any triangle is 180. Six weeks later, as part of a unit on parallel lines in a plane, Amy proves that relationship to be a theorem using Euclid's parallel postulate. Now, Amy is taking the end-of-the-unit test, which includes the following item intended to measure how well students remember (at the simple-knowledge level) statements of the unit's theorems:

Task Presented to the Student: Circle T if the following statement is true; circle F if it is false:

T F   The sum of the degree measures of the three angles of any triangle is 180.
Scoring Key: +1 for circling T only, otherwise 0.

When Amy gets to that item on the test, she thinks to herself, "We proved that to be true, but we had to assume the parallel postulate. So, like Garon said, it's true in Euclidean geometry. But it's not always true because I heard that without the parallel postulate there might not be 180° in a triangle. I think it's less in some geometries. I guess Garon wants us to circle F since the statement isn't always true."

_____

Mr. Garon might argue that Amy should know better since they've been doing Euclidean geometry for the entire course. However, a simple-knowledge item doesn't and shouldn't contain a warning label for students "not to reason on this one." The difficulty is best avoided by wording items so that there is little or no room for misinterpretation.

THE LANGUAGE OF MATHEMATICS
Messages about Mathematics

Engage in Activity 5.4.

_____ **ACTIVITY 5.4** _____

Purpose: To reflect on the language of mathematics and the types of mathematical content students need to comprehend.

Procedure: Read the chapter from *Beyond Numeracy: Ruminations of a Numbers Man* (Paulos, 1991, pp. 82–86) reproduced in Exhibit 5.6. Discuss the following questions with a colleague who also read the selection:

1. What message does Paulos convey to the reader in this chapter?
2. Is the message of this chapter important for mathematics students to understand at some point in their school careers?
3. How does the language of this chapter compare to the language used in other books students read?

Exhibit 5.7 is a section from the first chapter of a high school geometry textbook (Burrill, Cummins, Kanold, & Yunker, 1993, pp. 56–61). With a colleague, read the section and discuss the following questions:

1. How does the language of this textbook section compare to the language of the selection in Exhibit 5.6?
2. What message do the authors of this section convey to the reader?
3. Is the message of this section important for mathematics students to understand at some point in their school careers?
4. To comprehend the messages of this section, with what shorthand symbols and technical expressions do students need to be familiar?

Exhibit 5.6
A chapter from *Beyond Numeracy: Ruminations of a Numbers Man* (Paulos, 1991, pp. 82–86).

FRACTALS

8

Imagine you're at the base of a barren mountain. If you were to walk up and down the mountain, you might estimate that the distance you'd walked was approximately 10 miles. Now, what if a 200-foot-tall giant were to take the same path to the summit and back. He might walk only 5 miles. He would be so tall that he would step right over small hillocks without having to go up and down them the way you would. By contrast, imagine an insect crawling up and down the same route. It might walk 15 miles since it would have to go up, over, and down rocks and small boulders that we would merely step over.

Likewise, suppose a tiny amoeba-sized animal were to wriggle its way along the same trail and back. It might travel 20 miles since it would have to go up and down tiny crevices and bumps in rocks and pebbles that even an insect would just step right over. Thus we come to the somewhat odd conclusion that the distance up and down the mountain depends to a large extent on who's doing the traveling. So too does the surface area of the mountain, the amoeba-sized animal finding it a considerably more spacious domain to roam around in than does the giant, who strides right past the smaller minutiae of the surface. The bigger the climber, the shorter the distance. The bigger the climber, the smaller the surface area. This is a characteristic of a fractal, to which the side of a mountain is a good approximation.

A tree's trunk, to cite another standard example of a fractal,

branches into a characteristic number of branches which, in turn, each branch into the same number of smaller branches which likewise each break up into the same number of yet smaller branches until we arrive at the twig level. What does this have in common with the surface of a mountain?

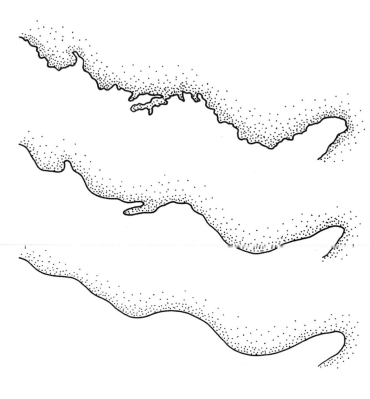

Increasingly fine views of the eastern coast of the United States.

Before we get to a definition, consider a coastal shoreline, yet another example due to mathematician Benoit Mandelbrot, the discoverer of fractal geometry. If we estimate the length of the eastern shoreline of the United States from a satellite, for example, we might come up with a figure of 2,500 miles or so. If, instead, we use detailed maps of the United States, which show the many capes and inlets along the shore, we may increase our estimate of the length of the shoreline to 7,500 miles. If we had nothing to do for a year and decided to walk

Source: From *Beyond Numeracy* by John Allen Paulos. Copyright © 1991 by John Allen Paulos. Reprinted by permission of Alfred A. Knopf Inc.

Exhibit 5.6
Continued

from Maine to Miami always staying within a yard or two of the Atlantic, the distance we would walk might be closer to 15,000 miles. We would trace not only the capes and inlets on the standard maps but the even smaller juttings and indentations which don't appear on the maps. Finally, if we can convince an insect to walk along the coast (maybe our mountain-climbing friend prefers to stay at sea level) and instruct it to remain always within a pebble's width of the water, we may find the length of the shoreline to be almost 25,000 miles. The shoreline is a fractal.

So too is a famous curve discovered in 1906 by Swedish mathematician Helge von Koch. Koch started with an equilateral triangle and replaced each line segment in it by one with an equilateral-triangle-shaped bump on its middle third. He repeated this procedure over and over and in the limit achieved a strange infinitely fuzzy snowflakelike curve.

sketch the whole coast or the considerably more detailed information obtained by a person walking along some small section of it. The surface of the mountain looks roughly the same, whether seen from a height of 200 feet by the giant or close up by the insect. The branching of the tree appears the same to us as it does to birds, or even to worms or fungi in the idealized limiting case of infinite branching. Likewise for the Koch curve.

Blowup of a part of a fractal, due to Benoit Mandelbrot

Moreover, as Mandelbrot has stressed, clouds are not circular or elliptical, tree bark is not smooth, lightning does not travel in a straight line, and snowflakes are most certainly not hexagons (neither do they resemble Koch curves). Rather, these and many other shapes in nature are near fractals and have characteristic zigzags, push-pulls, bump-dents at almost every size scale, greater magnification yielding similar but ever more complicated convolutions. There is even a natural way to assign a

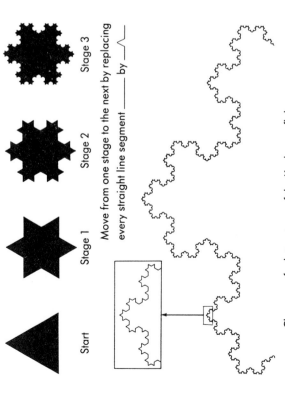

Start   Stage 1   Stage 2   Stage 3

Move from one stage to the next by replacing every straight line segment ____ by ⌃

Close-up of a later stage of the Koch snowflake curve

And what is a fractal? It's a curve or surface (or a solid or higher-dimensional object) that contains more but similar complexity the closer one looks. The shoreline, for example, has a typical jagged shape at whatever scale we draw it; i.e., whether we use satellite photos to

Exhibit 5.6
Continued

fractional dimension to these shapes, the fractals used to model coast-lines having dimensions between 1 and 2 (more than a straight line but less than a plane), while those used to model mountain surfaces having dimensions between 2 and 3 (more than a plane, but less than a solid). NASA photos indicate that the fractal dimension of the earth's surface is 2.1, compared with 2.4 for that of Mars's "woollier," more convoluted topography. Coined by Mandelbrot in 1975, the term "fractal" is an apt expression for *frag*mented, *fract*ured self-similar shapes of *fract*ional dimension.

Besides being a boon to computer graphics, where they are used to depict realistic-looking landscapes and natural forms, fractal-like structures are turning up frequently whenever fine structure is analyzed—on the surfaces of battery electrodes, in the spongy interior of intestines and lung tissue, in the variation of commodities prices over time, or in the diffusion of a liquid through semi-porous clays. With their beautiful and intricate complexity at all levels and scales of magnification, fractals are playing an increasingly important role in chaos theory (see the entry on *chaos*), where they can be used to describe a system's collection of possible trajectories. Their grotesque elegance is also apparent in purely mathematical contexts. A plane, for example, is partitioned into regions according to whether one or another root of an equation will eventually be obtained via a standard Newtonian method. The borders between these sections are staggeringly complex fractals.

Novelists too may someday find that fractal analogues in "psychic space" are helpful in capturing the fractured yet nevertheless coherent structure of human consciousness, whose focus can shift instantaneously from the moment's trivia to timeless verities and then back again, somehow preserving the same persona at the various levels. (See the entry on *human consciousness, its fractal nature.*) In this regard, the verbatim transcripts of ordinary conversations are quite revealing. The stops, starts, ellipses, bizarre syntax, vague references, unmotivated digressions, and sudden changes of direction are nothing like the sanitized "linear" version which usually emerges in print. There may be ways in which the above notions could be useful in cognitive psychology as well. The difficulty of a field of study, for example, might be looked upon as a fractal with brighter and/or more knowledgeable people taking larger cognitive steps over the tiny difficulties that others must patiently climb up and over.

Tina and Jermain respond to Activity 5.4 in Case 5.7.

CASE 5.7

Tina: Paulos' message is about the basic concept of a fractal and the uses of fractals.

Jermain: But what *is* the message?

Tina: The message is that a fractal is a curve or surface that contains more but similar complexity the closer you look—like a shoreline, the side of a mountain, or a cognitive process.

Jermain: Yes, but he doesn't only tell us that, he starts us off with examples that put us through vicarious experiences, almost like a construct a concept lesson.

Tina: Reading this gave me the idea that a teacher can sometimes lead students through an inductive learning activity by describing examples and nonexamples. So when it isn't convenient, you don't always have to have hands-on experiences for construct a concept lessons.

Jermain: Right. So, the chapter informs us about some examples that set us up for the definition of fractals, gives us the definition, and then polishes us off with some information about the utility or application of fractal theory.

Tina: Is the message important for mathematics students to understand at some point?

Jermain: Fractals have become a hot topic in recent years. Students shouldn't get out of high school without understanding at least what we just read—a conceptual, nontechnical understanding.

1-9 Right Angles and Perpendicular Lines

Objectives

After studying this lesson, you should be able to:

- identify and use right angles and perpendicular lines, and
- determine what information can and cannot be assumed from a figure.

Application

When carpenters put up the studs for the wall in a new home, they must be sure that each stud is at a *right angle* to the floor of the home. To check this, they can use a device called a carpenter's square. When the right angle of the carpenter's square is placed against the angle formed by a stud and the floor, its edges should lie flush against both the stud and the floor.

The figure at the right can be used as a model for the proper positioning of the studs in a wall relative to the floor. In this figure, each of the studs is *perpendicular* to the floor.

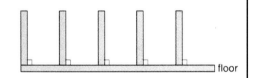

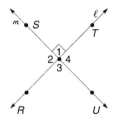

Perpendicular lines are two lines that intersect to form a right angle. In the figure at the left, lines ℓ and m are perpendicular. To indicate this, we write $\ell \perp m$, which is read "ℓ is perpendicular to m." Similarly, line segments and rays can be perpendicular to lines or other line segments and rays if they intersect to form a right angle. For example, in the figure, $\overrightarrow{RT} \perp \overline{SU}$, $\overrightarrow{US} \perp \overrightarrow{RT}$, and $\overline{TR} \perp \overrightarrow{US}$.

In the figure, $\angle 1$ is a right angle. Since $\angle 1$ and $\angle 3$ are vertical angles, what can you conclude about $\angle 3$? *It is also a right angle.*

Now, consider $\angle 2$ and $\angle 4$. Since $\angle 1$ forms a linear pair with $\angle 2$ and with $\angle 4$, what can you conclude about $\angle 2$ and $\angle 4$? *They are both right angles.*

If you draw two different lines, n and p, that are perpendicular, do you think the relationships between the four angles formed will be the same? *yes*

Based on this example, we could make the following conclusion, which will be proved in Chapter 2.

Perpendicular lines intersect to form four right angles.

Exhibit 5.7
Continued

Example 1

CONNECTION

Algebra

If $\overrightarrow{EB} \perp \overrightarrow{EC}$ and $\angle AEC$ and $\angle DEC$ form a linear pair, find $m\angle AEB$ and $m\angle DEC$.

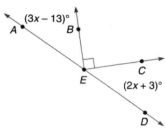

Since $\overrightarrow{EB} \perp \overrightarrow{EC}$, $\angle BEC$ is a right angle. Thus, $m\angle BEC = 90$. Since $\angle AEC$ and $\angle DEC$ form a linear pair, we know from our work in Lesson 1-8 that $m\angle AEC + m\angle DEC = 180$.

We can use the given information and the angle addition postulate to find the value of x.

$$m\angle AEC + m\angle DEC = 180$$
$$(m\angle BEC + m\angle AEB) + m\angle DEC = 180 \quad \text{Angle addition postulate}$$
$$[90 + (3x - 13)] + (2x + 3) = 180 \quad \text{Substitute 90 for } m\angle BEC,$$
$$5x + 80 = 180 \qquad 3x - 13 \text{ for } m\angle AEB, \text{ and}$$
$$5x = 100 \qquad 2x + 3 \text{ for } m\angle DEC.$$
$$x = 20$$

$$
\begin{aligned}
m\angle AEB &= 3x - 13 & m\angle DEC &= 2x + 3 \\
&= 3(20) - 13 & &= 2(20) + 3 \\
&= 47 & &= 43
\end{aligned}
$$

A compass and straightedge can be used to construct a line perpendicular to a given line through a point on the line, *or* through a point not on the line.

CONSTRUCTION

Construct a line perpendicular to line ℓ and passing through point T on ℓ.

1. Place the compass at point T. Using the same compass setting, draw arcs to the right and left of T, intersecting line ℓ. Label the points of intersection D and K.

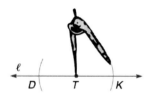

2. Open the compass to a setting greater than DT. Put the compass at point D and draw an arc above line ℓ.

3. Using the same compass setting as in Step 2, place the compass at point K and draw an arc intersecting the arc previously drawn. Label the point of intersection S.

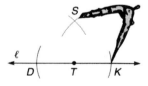

4. Use a straightedge to draw $\overleftrightarrow{ST}$.

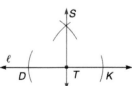

$\overleftrightarrow{ST}$ is perpendicular to ℓ at T.

Exhibit 5.7
Continued

CONSTRUCTION

Construct a line perpendicular to line ℓ and passing through point Q _not_ on ℓ.

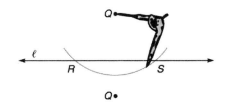

1. Place the compass at point Q. Draw an arc that intersects line ℓ in two different places. Label the points of intersection R and S.

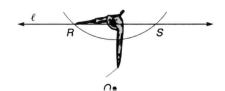

2. Open the compass to a setting greater than $\frac{1}{2}RS$. Put the compass at point R and draw an arc below line ℓ.

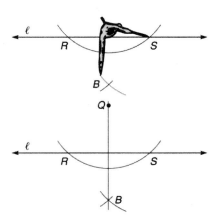

3. Using the same compass setting, place the compass at point S and draw an arc intersecting the arc drawn in Step 2. Label the point of intersection B.

4. Use a straightedge to draw $\overleftrightarrow{QB}$.

$\overleftrightarrow{QB}$ is perpendicular to ℓ.

In the application at the beginning of the lesson, we could have modeled the floor of the home using a plane instead of a line segment, as in the figure at the right. In this case, how could we determine whether the stud is perpendicular to the floor?

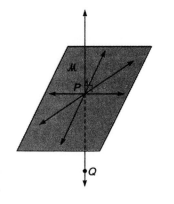

If a stud is perpendicular to the floor, then each side of the stud must be perpendicular to the portion of the floor that it intersects. Similarly, if _a line is perpendicular to a plane_, then the line must be perpendicular to every line in the plane that intersects it. Thus, $\overleftrightarrow{PQ} \perp \mathcal{M}$ and $\overleftrightarrow{PQ}$ must be perpendicular to every line in $\mathcal{M}$ that intersects it.

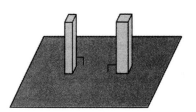

We can also talk about line segments and rays being perpendicular to planes. For example, in the figure, $\overline{PQ} \perp \mathcal{M}$ and $\overrightarrow{PQ} \perp \mathcal{M}$.

In this chapter, figures have been used to help describe or demonstrate different relationships among points, segments, lines, rays, and angles. Whenever you draw a figure, there are certain relationships that can be assumed from the figure and others that cannot be assumed.

Can be Assumed from Figure 1

All points shown are coplanar.

$\overleftrightarrow{CE}$, $\overrightarrow{DA}$, and $\overrightarrow{DB}$ intersect at D.

C, D, and E are collinear.

D is between C and E.

B is in the interior of $\angle ADE$.

$\angle CDE$ is a straight angle.

$\angle CDA$ and $\angle ADB$ are adjacent angles.

$\angle CDB$ and $\angle BDE$ are a linear pair.

$\angle CDA$ and $\angle ADE$ are supplementary.

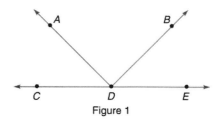

Figure 1

Cannot be Assumed from Figure 1

$\overline{CD} \cong \overline{DE}$

$\angle CDA \cong \angle EDB$

$\overrightarrow{DA} \perp \overrightarrow{DB}$

Figure 2, shown at the right, is marked so that these additional relationships are true.

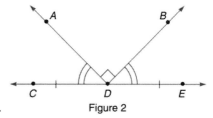

Figure 2

CHECKING FOR UNDERSTANDING

Communicating Mathematics

Read and study the lesson to answer each question.

1. What symbol do we use to indicate that two lines are perpendicular?

2. Two lines are perpendicular if they intersect to form a linear pair of angles that are also __?__.

3. If line ℓ intersects plane $\mathcal{P}$ at point T and $\ell \perp \mathcal{P}$, what must be true about any line, m, in $\mathcal{P}$ that passes through T?

4. From the figure at the right, can you assume that B is between A and C? that B is the midpoint of $\overline{AC}$? that $AB + BC = AC$?

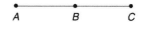

Guided Practice

Refer to the figure at the right to answer each question.

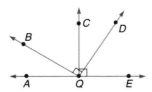

5. Which segment is perpendicular to $\overline{QA}$?

6. Which angles are complementary to $\angle BQC$?

7. Is $\angle BQC \cong \angle DQE$? Explain.

8. If $m\angle AQB = 4x - 15$ and $m\angle BQC = 2x + 9$, what is the value of x and $m\angle CQD$?

Exhibit 5.7
Continued

Determine whether each relationship can be assumed from the figure.

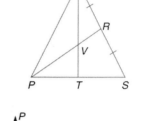

9. V is between Q and T.

10. $\overrightarrow{PR}$ bisects $\angle QPS$.

11. $PT = TS$

12. $\overrightarrow{PR}$ bisects $\overline{QS}$.

13. $\overline{QT} \perp \overline{PS}$

14. $\angle QRV$ is a right angle.

15. $\angle QVP$ and $\angle QVR$ form a linear pair.

16. In the figure at the right, $\overrightarrow{OP} \perp \mathcal{M}$ and $\overleftrightarrow{AB} \perp \overleftrightarrow{XY}$. How many right angles are in this figure?

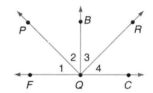

EXERCISES

Practice **Determine if the given information is enough to conclude that $\overrightarrow{QP} \perp \overrightarrow{QR}$.**

17. $\angle 1$ and $\angle 3$ are complementary.

18. $\angle 1$ and $\angle 4$ are complementary.

19. $\angle 2 \cong \angle 3$

20. $\angle 1 \cong \angle 4$

21. $m\angle 1 + m\angle 4 = m\angle 2 + m\angle 3$

22. $m\angle 1 + m\angle 2 = m\angle 3 + m\angle 4$

23. $\angle 1 \cong \angle 2$ and $\angle 3 \cong \angle 4$

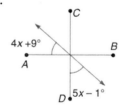

For each figure, find the value of x and determine if $\overline{AB} \perp \overline{CD}$.

24.

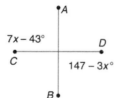

$7x - 43°$

$147 - 3x°$

25.

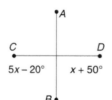

$5x - 20°$ $x + 50°$

26.

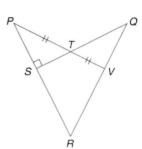

$4x + 9°$

$5x - 1°$

Determine whether each relationship can be assumed from the figure.

27. $\angle QVT$ is a right angle.

28. $\overline{QR} \perp \overline{PV}$

29. T is the midpoint of $\overline{PV}$.

30. $\overline{PV}$ bisects $\overline{QS}$.

31. $\angle SPT$ and $\angle VQT$ are congruent.

32. $PS = QV$

33. $PV = TV + PT$

34. $\angle STP \cong \angle VTQ$

Exhibit 5.7
Continued

35. Draw $\overleftrightarrow{PR}$. Construct line ℓ perpendicular to $\overleftrightarrow{PR}$ through P and line m perpendicular to $\overleftrightarrow{PR}$ through R. Now, locate point S on line m so that $RS = RP$. Finally, construct line k perpendicular to ℓ through S. What figure have you constructed?

36. $\overleftrightarrow{AB}$ and $\overleftrightarrow{CD}$ intersect at E. F lies in the interior of $\angle CEA$ and G lies in the interior of $\angle AED$. Also, $\angle CEA$ and $\angle FEG$ are right angles. Find $m\angle FEA$ if $m\angle CEF = 3x - 24$ and $m\angle AEG = 2x + 10$.

37. $\overleftrightarrow{AB}$ and $\overleftrightarrow{CD}$ intersect at Q and R is in the interior of $\angle AQC$. If $m\angle DQA = 2x - y$, $m\angle AQR = x$ and $m\angle RQC = y$, find the values of x and y so that $\overleftrightarrow{AB} \perp \overleftrightarrow{CD}$.

38. Find $m\angle BPC$ in the figure if $\overline{AC} \perp \overline{BC}$, $m\angle APC = 7x + 3$, $m\angle BPC = 16y$, $m\angle ACP = 3x + 2y$, and $m\angle BCP = 3x + 4y$.

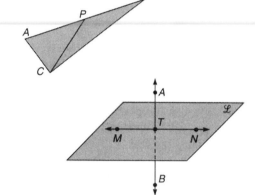

39. Find the values of x and y if $\overleftrightarrow{AB} \perp \overleftrightarrow{MN}$ and $\mathcal{L}$ contains $\overleftrightarrow{MN}$, $m\angle MTB = 2x + 6y$, $m\angle ATN = 4x + 3y$, and $m\angle BTN = \frac{8}{3}x + 5y$.

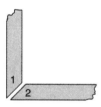

Critical Thinking

40. Given a line in a plane and a point on that line, explain why there is exactly one line in the plane perpendicular to the given line through the given point.

Application

41. Framing The corner of a frame for a painting is made by joining two pieces of wood so that they are perpendicular, as shown at the right. If $\angle 1$ is a 45° angle, what must be the measure of $\angle 2$?

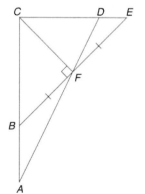

Mixed Review

Refer to the figure to answer each question.

42. If $AB = 2x - 3$, $BC = 3x + 13$, and $AC = 30$, find the value of x. **(Lesson 1-4)**

43. Name all the bisectors of $\overline{BE}$. **(Lesson 1-5)**

44. What angles have $\overline{CE}$ as a side? **(Lesson 1-6)**

45. If $m\angle BCF = 5x + 11$, $m\angle FCD = 3x + 23$, for what value of x does $\overrightarrow{CF}$ bisect $\angle ACE$? **(Lesson 1-7)**

46. If $m\angle AFB = d + 10$ and $m\angle CFD = 6d - 11$, find $m\angle DFE$. **(Lesson 1-8)**

Wrap-Up

47. Based on your homework and classroom discussions, what concepts from this lesson do you think should appear on a chapter test?

Tina: I agree. You know, I was just thinking how you could take the basic ideas from this chapter and build it into a really neat unit on fractals. Start off with some computer simulations, or at least some videotapes, where students visualize traveling over a surface repeatedly—each time with a more detailed eye. Starting off like the giant, then to a regular person, and so on until you were viewing it from an amoeba's perspective.

Jermain: Okay, we've got to get going with this activity. How does the language of this chapter compare to the language used in other books students read?

Tina: This chapter reads more like an essay for English class or even a novel than a typical mathematics text.

Jermain: It's a book about mathematics, but not a how-to-do-math textbook. You can read it straight through without stopping to compute or figure out symbols. It's not all that different from "normal" books—but maybe a bit more sophisticated than what high schoolers like to read.

Tina: Let's go to Exhibit 5.7.

Jermain: . . . Wow! Other than both being about mathematics there wasn't much similarity between working your way through these textbook pages and reading Paulos' chapter.

Tina: You said "working through" the textbook passages and "reading" Paulos' chapter. I think that captures the fundamental difference between the two. The textbook section dealt with much easier to understand content, but, like you said, I had to work my way through it rather than just read it.

Jermain: Exactly! Although I already understood the textbook's message about right angles and perpendicular lines, I had to go back and look at prior sections to understand how they worked through some of their examples. Like Example 1, I couldn't figure out where in the world they got $3x - 13$ for the measure of $\angle AEB$ and $2x + 3$ for the measure of $\angle DEC$.

Tina: Oh, I had the same trouble! When they referred to the angle addition postulate, I thought I knew what they meant until I was stumped about where the "$(3x - 13)°$" and "$(2x + 3)°$" came from. I thought maybe there was more to the postulate than I always thought. Then after going back through the earlier sections, I finally realized that $m\angle AEB = 3x - 13$ and $m\angle DEC = 2x + 3$ are just givens that the students are supposed to pick up from the picture. That really frustrated me.

Jermain: So, how would we answer this first question? How does the language of the textbook section compare to the language of Paulos' chapter?

Tina: For one thing the textbook section can't be read straight through; you've got to stop and work things out. Also, you have to go back and look things up in prior sections.

Jermain: And what about all the shorthand notations in the text, "$\overline{AB}$," "$\overrightarrow{AB}$," "AB," "$\angle ABC$," "$m\angle ABC$," and so on and so on?

Tina: That's a major factor in students' comprehension.

Jermain: Just think, this is only Chapter 1 of this textbook! Some kids will be seeing those symbols for the first time in this chapter and look how many are used in this section already.

Tina: They can't be expected to understand them like you and I do. We've been dealing with them for years. One thing I do like about this textbook section though is how the authors are really careful to distinguish between things like a set of points such as $\angle ABC$ and a number like $m\angle ABC$. It's really important for students to start out being precise when using mathematical language. Precision of its language is one of the great assets of doing math.

Jermain: I think being picky about saying two angles are equal or saying they are congruent or saying that you can't add angles, you can only add their measures, can really get confusing for students. A lot of textbooks aren't as precise as this one. They say things like "$\angle ABC = \angle DEF$" when they really mean "$\angle ABC \cong \angle DEF$."

Tina: It is confusing. But confusion is better than inaccuracies that lead to misconceptions down the road. Precise notation and language is an integral part of mathematics that should be attended to in curricula.

Jermain: I'm not completely convinced, but let's go on. There are a lot of other differences in the way these two selections are written and need to be read. Look how the textbook section requires the reader to use pictures and diagrams. There are three-dimensional sketches and little compass markings and all other kinds of symbolic subtleties for students to pick up on. Regular reading passages don't have all that.

Tina: Most people think of mathematics as being presented as this textbook does, not as in Paulos' chapter. That's why most people think math is so hard.

Jermain: Let's go on to the second question or we'll never get through Activity 5.4.

Tina: What message does the textbook section convey to students?

Jermain: It tells us the two objectives of the section, then sort of ties perpendicular lines to carpentry.

Tina: Then there's a definition for "perpendicular," followed by an example of perpendicularity in an algebra exercise and then it shows us how to construct a line perpendicular to a given line with a compass and straightedge.

Jermain: First from a point on the given line and secondly from an external point. Then there's more practice exercises. So what's the message?

Tina: The message is the meaning of perpendicularity and that it is used in carpentry and here's how to use it to solve for unknown angle sizes.

Jermain: That does it for me on the second question. Is the message important for students?

Tina: Of course they'll need this again and again as they continue to study mathematics.

Jermain: I agree, but I'm not sure that the applications in this section are all that useful. I keep wondering how anyone would know that an angle measure is $(3x - 13)°$ without first identifying x or knowing—I don't know—I guess they're building up to some algorithms in subsequent chapters.

Tina: I can see it's time to finish off the last question. With what shorthand symbols and technical expressions do students need to be familiar in order to comprehend this section?

Jermain: The section includes symbols for line segment, ray, congruent, line, angle, measure of an angle, perpendicular, right angle, being able to read all those diagrams . . .

Tina: Look at the diagram at the bottom of page 59—under Guided Practice for items 5 through 8. Look how perpendicularity is communicated. Students have to be taught to read that. That's not easy for students. It seems like comprehending the given and what they're supposed to do—the directions—is what will give students difficulty, not the mathematics itself.

Jermain: I'm still amazed at how much trouble and time I took to work through this section even though it included nothing with which I wasn't already thoroughly familiar and nothing that is mathematically difficult for even a ninth or tenth grader.

Tina: We have to consciously and systematically teach students to comprehend material in this form and show them how to draw pictures for themselves as they read. At least that's what I had to do to make sense out of Exhibit 5.7.

As Tina and Jermain discussed, everything students need to understand about mathematics can't be discovered first hand. We depend on what others say and write to help us fill in the gaps in our empirical experiences and what we construct and discover for ourselves. Thus, passages from mathematics books as well as other media presentations (videotape programs and CD-ROM disks) on mathematics are an integral part of mathematics curricula content. Questions and issues regarding the selection and use of mathematics textbooks, trade books, media, and technology are addressed in Chapter 7.

Technical Expressions

The language of mathematics, like any other language, depends on people agreeing to certain conventions about what is accepted usage for the meanings of (a) common English words with special definitions peculiar to mathematics (b) technical mathematical words, (c) numerals, (d) shorthand symbols, and (e) language and communication structures (expressing a relationship in graphical form).

Common English Words with Special Definitions. The meanings of some general-usage words, expressions, and statements vary depending on the mathematical contexts within which they are used. For example:

The general-usage word "*power*" ordinarily denotes "a capability of doing something." In an algebraic context (for example, x to the nth power), "power" refers to "the number of times a number is used as a factor." In the world of inferential statistics, the "power of a statistical test" refers to "the probability of rejecting a false null hypothesis."

Technical Mathematical Words. Some words, expressions, and statements have meanings only within a mathematical structure; "cosine," "Cauchy sequence," and "$\triangle ABC \cong \triangle DEF$".

Numerals. A *numeral* is a name for a number. Distinguishing between a number and its names (for example, 2 is a number with an endless list of names, including "2," "$12 \div 6$," and "$\sqrt{4}$") is critical to students' understanding of mathematics; how well students comprehend the meaning of "$x = y$" depends on how well they can discriminate between the concept of *number* and the concept of *numeral*.

Shorthand Symbols. Shorthand symbols like "$\sqrt{\ }$," "$\forall$," "$\int$," and "$\subseteq$" contribute to the mystery of mathematics for those who have not learned to translate them. On the other hand, such symbols serve two valuable purposes:

- Shorthand symbols save time and space in mathematical communications.
- By compacting communications, shorthand symbols facilitate the analysis and comprehension of statements of relationships. For example, is comprehension of the definition of "standard deviation" easier when it's stated in ordinary English or when using shorthand symbols? Compare the two:

Ordinary English Version: The standard deviation of a sequence of rational numbers is equal to the principal square root of the number derived by adding the squared differences between each member of the sequence (i.e., each data point) and the arithmetic mean of the sequence, and then dividing that sum by the number of data points.

Compact Version:

$$\sigma = \sqrt{\frac{\sum_{i=1}^{N}(x_i - \mu)^2}{N}}$$

where σ is the standard deviation of and μ is the arithmetic mean of $(x_1, x_2, x_3, \ldots, x_N)$.

As long as a person has been taught the meanings of the symbols and has become accustomed to using them, the compact form with the shorthand notations makes it easier to recognize critical relationships (for example, in the definition of "σ," it is clear that each difference is squared before the differences are summed).

Communication or Language Structure. Mathematical language includes technical structures such as Cartesian plane, vector space, group, field, geometry, or matrix that are used to organize and express ideas and relationships. As with other conventions, students need to be taught to comprehend and utilize such structures.

COMPREHENSION OBJECTIVES

Review the definition of "comprehension learning level" and the examples of comprehension objectives in Exhibit 3.10. The mathematical content of a comprehension objective can be either a *message about mathematics* (for example, the ϵ, δ definition of the limit of a sequence or the textbook's proof of the Pythagorean theorem), or a *type of technical mathematical expression* (for example, the summation notation). Comprehension objectives specifying a message about mathematics are concerned with students being able to interpret the meaning of that message. Comprehension objectives specifying a type of technical expression are concerned with students being able to make sense out of messages employing that type of expression and also using such expression in their own communications about mathematics.

LESSONS FOR COMPREHENSION OBJECTIVES
Language Arts Lessons

Lessons for comprehension objectives should be designed following principles suggested by the research-based literature on reading and language arts instruction (see, for example, Langer & Allington, 1992; and Santa & Alverman, 1991). By engaging students in learning activities that lead them to comprehend mathematical communications, you obviate one of the more mystifying aspects of formalized mathematics, namely negotiating its language.

Comprehension of a Message

Literal and Interpretive Understanding. Lessons for comprehension of particular messages should be concerned with two levels of understanding, *literal* and *interpretive*. Students *literally* understand a

message if they can accurately translate its explicit meaning, as Cathy demonstrates in Case 5.8.

CASE 5.8

Cathy examines the following definition of the absolute value of a real number:

$$|x| = |x| \text{ iff } x \geq 0 \text{ and } |x| = -x \text{ iff } x \leq 0$$

She then displays literal understanding of the definition by formulating the following explanation:

The absolute value of a number is the number itself, if and only if, the number is positive or zero. The absolute value of a number is its opposite, if and only if, the number is negative or zero.

Students understand a message at an interpretive level if they can infer implicit meaning and explain how aspects of the communications are used to convey the message, as is demonstrated by Cathy in Case 5.9.

CASE 5.9

Cathy examines the following definition of the absolute value of a real number:

$$|x| = |x| \text{ iff } x \geq 0 \text{ and } |x| = -x \text{ iff } x \leq 0$$

She then displays interpretive understanding of the definition by extending her previous explanation in Case 5.8 with the following:

"This means that the absolute value of any number is nonnegative. The absolute value of 10, for instance, is just 10 because, as the definition says, the absolute value of a positive number is the number itself. But for -10, the absolute value is its negative and the negative of a negative is positive, so the absolute value of -10 is 10. Zero is its own opposite, so when they wrote the definition, they included it in both cases."

Designing Learning Activities for Literal Understanding. Interpretive understanding depends on literal understanding. Thus, the initial phase of a comprehension lesson should promote literal understanding. To design the learning activities, you will need to analyze the message to be comprehended and identify the following prerequisites:

- *Vocabulary*. What common English as well as technical mathematical words will students need to understand in order to translate the message? Meanings for words, expressions, and symbols are learned through simple-knowledge lessons. Are there any prerequisite simple-knowledge objectives that should be achieved before students are ready for the comprehension-level learning activities?

- *Technical Expressions.* What shorthand symbols, communications or language structures, and other technical expressions are used to convey the message that the students need to comprehend? Cathy's explanation in Case 5.8 suggested that she understands how to read mathematical definitions. She seems to understand that "if and only if" serves as a two-way implication. Comprehending a definition requires specialized skills, as does comprehending proofs, word problems, graphs, and other types of communication structures.
- *Concepts.* What concepts does the author of the message assume the students have constructed prior to receiving the communications? In Case 5.8 Cathy's understanding of the definition depended on her prior construction of the concept nonnegative numbers.
- *Relationships.* What relationships does the author of the message assume the students have discovered prior to receiving the communications? In Case 5.8 Cathy's understanding of the definition depended on her prior discovery of the relationship: A real number and its opposite are equidistant from zero.

Once these four prerequisites are achieved, literal understanding of a message is effected through a four-stage *direct instructional* lesson.

Stage 1: The Message Is Sent to the Students.   For example, the definition of absolute value is stated orally and in writing.

Stage 2: The Message Is Rephrased and Explained. For example, "In other words, the absolute value of a number is the difference between the number and zero, but without concern for whether the number itself is greater than or less than zero."

Stage 3: Students Are Questioned about Specifics in the Message.   For example, "Is negative *x* in the second case a positive or negative number?"

Stage 4: Students Are Provided with Feedback on Their Responses to the Questions Raised in Stage 3.   For example, "I agree that the absolute value of a number can never be negative, but for this case negative *x* is a positive number."

Designing Activities for Interpretive Understanding. Interpretive understanding of a message is achieved with learning activities that utilize more inquiry and open-ended questions and discussions than the direct instruction for literal understanding. Students are stimulated to examine the message and extract its main idea, data base or facts, assumptions, and conclusions.

A Lesson for Comprehension of a Particular Message.   In Case 5.10, note how Mr. Matsumoto shifts from direct instructional activities during the literal understanding phase to activities in which students generate ideas during the phase for interpretive understanding.

CASE 5.10

As part of a unit on aspects of number theory, Mr. Matsumoto would like his students to discover the following relationship:

$$\sqrt{2} \notin \{rationals\}$$

However, he realizes that such an objective is a bit ambitious for this class, so he settles for helping them comprehend a classic proof for why $\sqrt{2}$ is not rational. Thus, his unit includes this objective:

Explains the classic proof by contradiction [using the supposition of $\sqrt{2} = p/q$ where $(p, q) = 1$] of the following theorem: $\sqrt{2} \notin \{rationals\}$.   (*comprehension*)

He thinks, as he designs the lesson for the objective, "I'd better recreate this proof for myself to make sure I thoroughly understand it." He writes out the proof as shown in Exhibit 5.8.

Looking over his work, he thinks, "That's a nice proof; there's a lot going on for them to understand. It's really too gimmicky for them to discover the theorem from it, but they'll gain a lot just from comprehending the argument.

"I've got to present this to them. I'll write it on the overhead as I explain the logic behind each step. But first, I'd better decide on the form of the presentation. This version (Exhibit 5.8) is too full of symbols for them. I'll go through my checklist of prerequisites for literal understanding first. Okay, vocabulary: They already know rationals, integers, irrationals, relatively prime—but not that expression for relatively prime ["$(p, q) = 1$"]; I'll write it out for them. Okay, they also know the definitions for even and odd; there's no new vocabulary here.

"Now, for symbols: I already said I should write out 'p and q are relatively prime' for '$(p, q) = 1$.' Let's see . . . all the set symbols are familiar to them and so is the implies symbol ["$\Rightarrow$"]; I can leave those. Such that ["$\ni$"] and there exist ["$\exists$"] have to go. And I'd better write out the names of the sets or else Jim and Blaine will be distracted.

"Concepts: Let's see . . . the only concept here that they lack is the big one, irrational numbers. They know the definition, but most haven't conceptualized the set. This lesson won't lead to conceptualization, but it's a step in that direction. There's no lesson for prerequisite concepts needed.

"Relationships: Oh, oh! They comprehend the definition of rational numbers, but the fact that a rational number can be expressed as the ratio of relatively prime integers is something that most of them haven't really internalized. So, I need to precede this lesson with a discover a relationship one on the following:

Exhibit 5.8
Mr. Matsumoto's proof as he initially wrote it.

$$\text{To prove } \sqrt{2} \notin \{\text{rationals}\}:$$

$$\text{Suppose } \sqrt{2} \in \{\text{rational}\}$$

$$\sqrt{2} \in \{\text{rationals}\} \implies \exists\, p, q \in \{\text{integers}\} \ni (p,q) = 1 \text{ and } \sqrt{2} = \frac{p}{q}.$$

$$\sqrt{2} = \frac{p}{q} \implies 2 = \frac{p^2}{q^2} \implies 2q^2 = p^2. \text{ Thus, } p^2 \in \{\text{evens}\}.$$

$$\underline{\text{Lemma:}}$$
$$\text{To prove } a^2 \in \{\text{evens}\} \implies a \in \{\text{evens}\}.$$
$$\text{Proof: Suppose } a \notin \{\text{evens}\}$$
$$a \notin \{\text{evens}\} \implies a \in \{\text{odds}\} \implies \exists\, i \in \{\text{integers}\} \ni a = 2i + 1.$$
$$a = 2i + 1 \implies a^2 = 4i^2 + 4i + 1 \implies a^2 = 2(2i^2 + 2i) + 1 \implies a^2 \in \{\text{odds}\}$$
$$\text{But } a^2 \in \{\text{evens}\} \;\otimes$$
$$\therefore a \notin \{\text{odds}\} \implies a \in \{\text{evens}\}.$$

$$\text{Thus, } p^2 \in \{\text{evens}\} \implies p \in \{\text{evens}\}.$$

$$p \in \{\text{evens}\} \implies \exists\, j \in \{\text{integers}\} \ni p = 2j.$$

$$\therefore 2q^2 = p^2 \implies 2q^2 = (2j)^2 \implies 2q^2 = 4j^2 \implies q^2 = 2j^2 \implies q^2 \in \{\text{evens}\}.$$

$$q^2 \in \{\text{evens}\} \implies q \in \{\text{evens}\}$$

$$\therefore q, p \in \{\text{evens}\}$$

$$\text{But } (p, q) = 1 \;\otimes$$

$$\therefore \sqrt{2} \notin \{\text{rationals}\}.$$

$$x \in \{\text{rationals}\} \implies \exists\, p, q \in \{\text{integers}\} \ni (p, q)$$

$$= 1 \text{ and } x = p/q$$

"That shouldn't be very difficult because it's just a matter of combining two relationships they've already discovered. . . . Okay, the other relationship they need is the one proved by the lemma. I'd better do a construct a concept lesson on that also. In fact, I ought to prove the lemma ahead of time, to cut down on the length of the proof. So, I've got two construct a concept lessons and one comprehension of a proof of a lemma lesson to conduct before the main one.

"Communication structures: We're okay here. They're already familiar with paragraph-type formats for proofs, as well as proof by contradiction."

After planning and conducting lessons for the following three prerequisite objectives, Mr. Matsumoto is ready for the comprehension lesson:

- Explain why any rational number can be expressed as the ratio of two relatively prime integers. (*discover a relationship*)
- Explain why if the square of an integer is even, then so is the integer. (*discover a relationship*)
- Explain a proof of the following theorem: $k^2 \in \{\text{evens}\} \implies k \in \{\text{evens}\}$. (*comprehension*)

He begins the literal-understanding phase of the lesson by telling students they will be examining a classic proof and that their job is to understand it well enough to explain why it's a valid proof. Having informed them of that objective, he directs them to copy the proof as he presents it step-by-step and to raise any questions to clarify the meaning of any step.

After presenting the proof and responding to students' questions, Mr. Matsumoto summarizes the argument and then queries students with exchanges such as the following:

Mr. Matsumoto: How could the author of this proof make this statement right here that $\sqrt{2} = p/q$, Wendy?

Wendy: There's a p and a q like that for any rational number. We showed that yesterday.

Mr. Matsumoto: Thank you. How did we get from $a = 2i + 1$ to $a^2 = 4i^2 + 4i + 1$, Nadine?

Nadine: You just square both sides of the equation, and that's what you get.

Mr. Matsumoto: What does this circled X mean right here, Jake?

Jake: That means you did something wrong?

Mr. Matsumoto: What do you mean by "wrong," Jake?

Jake: There's a mistake you've got to do over.

Mr. Matsumoto: Actually, this indicates a point where we made a statement that contradicts an earlier statement. That's different from being wrong; it's . . .

Exhibit 5.9
Adam's outline of the proof that
$\sqrt{2} \notin$ {rationals}.

Want: To show that $\sqrt{2}$ is not rational

I. Assume $\sqrt{2}$ is rational

II. So $\sqrt{2} = \frac{p}{q}$ so that p and q are relatively prime

III. p is even

IV. q is even

V. III and IV contradict II

VI. So I is false

VII. Conclusion: $\sqrt{2}$ is not rational

After completing this activity in which students are given feedback on their responses to Mr. Matsumoto's questions about the meaning of different aspects of the proof, Mr. Matsumoto begins raising more questions to elicit more in-depth ideas students might have about the proof. He begins this interpretive phase of the lesson with the following:

Mr. Matsumoto: I'd like for everyone to silently take six minutes to outline on a sheet of paper the main ideas of this proof. Use brief phrases for headings and subheadings that illustrate the logic of the argument. Okay, go.

He walks around the room, monitoring the work and selecting papers for the class to discuss. At the end of the six minutes he asks several students to put their outlines on the board. Included is Adam's, which appears in Exhibit 5.9.

Mr. Matsumoto: I really like the way Adam listed each climactic point in the proof, I through VII. Yes, Chen?

Chen: What does cli-whatever mean?

Mr. Matsumoto: "Climactic." Look at what Adam has pulled from the proof. He didn't list, for example, this step here where we go from $\sqrt{2} = p/q$ to $2 = p^2/q^2$. But he did list that p is even. Why, Chen, do you think he listed one but not the other?

Chen: Because squaring both sides of that equation is just a step leading to something. But p is even is something we are trying to show.

Mr. Matsumoto: I agree. What do we call a part of a story when something comes together at the end? It sounds sort of like "climactic," Grace?

Grace: Climax.

Mr. Matsumoto: The things Adam listed are climax points of the proof leading to the big conclusion he labels VII. Okay, Julio.

Julio: Proofs aren't stories.

Mr. Matsumoto: Anybody want to debate Julio's point? Okay, Grace.

Grace: Sure proofs are stories. They tell us the story of why something is true. Like showing that the square of 2 is irrational.

Julio: You mean the square root of 2 is irrational!

Grace: Right. What did I say?

Mr. Matsumoto: You said "square," even though you meant to say "square root." But there's something else I want to pick up that Grace said. She said we proved that the square root of 2 is *irrational.* Is that what we proved, Johnny?

Johnny: Yep, that's right.

Mr. Matsumoto: Irrational, or just not rational? Nettie.

Nettie: It's the same thing. If a number is not rational, then it's irrational.

Mr. Matsumoto: Adam?

Adam: That's true if we know the number is real. We never proved that $\sqrt{2}$ is real, so we didn't prove it's irrational, we just proved it is not rational.

The discussion about the proof continues for another 12 minutes and then Mr. Matsumoto moves on to another objective.

Comprehension of Technical Expressions

Students need to comprehend some technical expressions embedded in the language of mathematics in order to receive and send messages about mathematics. For example:

- Ruth understands the common logic structure of mathematical definitions. Thus, when she confronts the definition of "convex set" for the first time, she knows to look for features common to all convex sets that other sets do not have. Her understanding of mathematical definitions in general serves as an advanced organizer for comprehending unfamiliar ones.

Exhibit 5.10
Graphs of history test scores from two classes

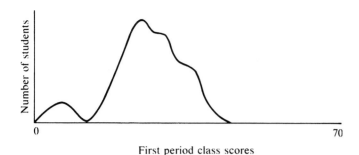

First period class scores

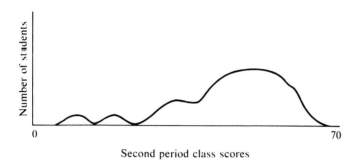

Second period class scores

• Exhibit 5.10 contains the graphs of the scores of two classes of students who took the same history test. By just glancing at it, Edwin reads graphs of real functions in Cartesian planes well enough to note the following:

(a) As a group the second-period class scored higher on the test than the first-period class because points on the second-period's graph tend to be farther to the right.

(b) The two classes contain approximately the same number of students because the areas under the curves are about the same.

(c) The first-period scores are more homogeneous than the second period scores because the scores for the first period are "piled up" and clustered together, whereas the second period scores are spread farther out.

A lesson for comprehension of a technical expression should include learning activities that (a) use direct instruction to inform students about the special conventions of the particular expression specified by the objective, and (b) use inquiry methods to help students develop strategies for using that type of expression. Case 5.11 is an example.

CASE 5.11 _____

Ms. McGiver has planned her prealgebra course so that students confront textbook word problems in every unit. However, after the first two units, she realizes that students are experiencing difficulty solving word problems, not neces-

sarily because they don't understand the particular mathematics applicable to the problem but because they have never developed strategies for solving word problems in general. Thus, she decides to insert a special unit designed to teach general strategies for solving word problems. Her first objective is to get students to *comprehend* problems as typically presented in textbooks. She states the objective as follows:

> After reading a textbook word problem, (a) identify the question posed by the problem, (b) clarify the question in student's own words, (c) specify the variable to be solved, and (d) list facts or data provided in the statement of the problem. *(comprehension)*

Ms. McGiver begins her lesson by displaying the following word problem with the instructions, "Just read this carefully without trying to solve it."

> Tom is on a television quiz show. He scores 5 points by correctly answering his first quiz-show question. He then misses the second question and loses 10 points. What is his score after the two questions?

Ms. McGiver knows that everyone in the class can readily solve that problem. So she's not surprised to hear some students blurt, "Aw, that's easy! It's −5." But rather than accept their solutions she insists they follow her directions:

Ms. McGiver: Now that you've read the problem, I want you to copy down and answer these questions.
She displays the following:

1. Solving this problem answers what question?
2. What variable does answering the question require you to find?
3. What information are you given with which to work?

After several minutes, she begins a discussion.

Ms. McGiver: How did you answer the first question, Stephanie?
Stephanie: What is his score after the two questions?
Ms. McGiver: Did anyone answer that question in a way that's essentially different from Stephanie's? Okay, Michelle.
Michelle: I put −5. Isn't that right?

A number of students interrupt, saying, "That's what I got, −5!" But Ms. McGiver gives them an icy stare, then turns back to Michelle.

Ms. McGiver: What is the question you were to answer?
Michelle: What was the score after the two questions?
Ms. McGiver: No, read the first question from your paper.
Michelle: Solving this problem answers what question?
Ms. McGiver: Now answer that question, Warren?
Warren: What is the score after two questions?
Ms. McGiver: If your answer to the first question doesn't essentially agree with what Stephanie and Warren read, then change it right now so it does. Okay, how did you answer the second question, Bonita?

Bonita: How many points Bill is behind.

Ms. McGiver: Behind! Why behind, Bonita?

Bonita: Because he lost more points than he gained.

Ms. McGiver: Angelo?

Angelo: The variable is how many points he has left. You don't know if he's behind or not until you solve for it.

Rita: But 10 is bigger than 5.

Ms. McGiver: You didn't listen to what Angelo said. Repeat what you said, Angelo.

Angelo: Just that you've got to know the variable before you solve for it. They're naming the variable after they solve it, so it's no longer a variable.

Ms. McGiver: Angelo, you're getting into some pretty sophisticated ideas. Thank you. I think Angelo has hit on the reason we're confused. We need to try this on problems that you won't solve so easily and then answer these questions before you—quote—know the solution. Here's the problem. Answer the same questions for it.

She displays the following:

An airplane travels 250 miles per hour for 2 hours in a direction of 138° from Albion, NY. At the end of this time, how far west of Albion is the plane?

Some students grumble that the problem is too hard, but Ms. McGiver simply uses a stern look and a gesture to tell them to just answer the three questions. After four minutes, she begins.

Ms. McGiver: Read your answer to the first question, Hartense?

Hartense: How far west of Albion is the plane?

Ms. McGiver: Anybody disagree? Okay, what do you have for the second question, Wil?

Wil: How far west the plane is.

Ms. McGiver: Far west from where, Joan?

Joan: From that place in New York.

Ms. McGiver: What kind of variable is it? . . . Anybody? Okay, Stephanie.

Stephanie: What do you mean?

Ms. McGiver: I mean is it an angle size, distance, weight, or what?

Stephanie: It's a distance.

Ms. McGiver: So what's the variable, Mike?

Mike: The distance from the town.

Ms. McGiver: Okay, what did you put for the third question, Zeke?

Zeke: I made a list: airplane going 250 miles an hour, 2 hours, at 138°.

Ms. McGiver: Does anyone have more to add? Okay, Joe.

Joe: It's by Albion, New York.

Ms. McGiver: Now, let's go back and answer the questions again for the first problem.

After they go through the first problem again, Ms. McGiver explains that they are to answer those three questions for every word problem they work for this class until she notifies them differently. She plans to continue going

over this process for comprehending word problems until they appear to do it automatically.

Engage in Activity 5.5.

_____ **ACTIVITY 5.5** _____

Purpose: To expand your insights regarding how to design lessons for comprehension objectives.

Procedure: Select either a message or a technical expression from the following list:

Messages

- The reading selection by Paulos in Exhibit 5.6.
- A passage of your choice from a middle or secondary school mathematics textbook.
- The proof of a theorem of your choice from a mathematics textbook.
- The definition of a technical mathematical word or expression of your choice from a mathematics textbook.

Technical Expressions

- Histograms
- Box and whisker plots
- Proofs presented in the two-column, statement-reason format
- Summation notation (for example, $\sum_{i=a}^{n} f(i)$)

Design and teach a lesson for one or two students that leads the student or students to comprehend the message or technical expression you chose.

Discuss your experiences designing and teaching the lesson with colleagues who are also engaging in Activity 5.5. Share with one another what you learned from your experiences.

INDICATORS OF ACHIEVEMENT OF COMPREHENSION OBJECTIVES

Comprehension of a Message Item

A measurement item relevant to students' achievement of a comprehension objective specifying a particular message as content presents students with the task of translating or interpreting meanings from the message. What, for example, might be an item relevant to the following objective?

Explain the following definition of "rational number": r is a rational number if and only if there exist two integers p and q such that $p/q = r$.   (*comprehension*)

Exhibit 5.11 displays one possibility.

Comprehension of a Technical Expression

A measurement item relevant to a comprehension objective specifying a type of technical expression as

Exhibit 5.11
Example of a measurement item designed to be relevant to how well students comprehend a definition of rational number.

Task Presented to the Student

Write *Yes* in the blank for each one of the following statements that can be implied from the definition of rational number as given in the textbook's glossary; write *No* in front of each of the other statements:

— **A.** If a number cannot be expressed as a fraction with an integer for the denominator and an integer for the numerator, then the number is *not* rational.

— **B.** A whole number is not rational unless it is in the form of a fraction.

— **C.** If $z = x/y$, and x and y are real numbers such that $y \neq 0$, then z is rational.

— **D.** The quotient of two counting numbers is rational.

— **E.** If a number is rational, then it is positive.

Scoring Key. 5 points maximum, with +1 for each answer as follows: A, yes; B, no; C, no; D, yes; and E, no.

---

content presents students with the task of translating messages using such technical expressions. What, for example, might be an item relevant to the following objective?

> Explain the meaning of expressions using the summation notation. (*comprehension*)

Exhibit 5.12 displays one possibility.

Novelty

Comprehension is a cognitive-learning level involving reasoning and judgment extending beyond what is simply remembered. Similar to construct a concept and discover a relationship items but dissimilar to simple-knowledge items, comprehension items present students with tasks that are not identical to ones they've previously encountered. The item's task needs to have at least some aspect that is novel for the students. The five statements (A through E) used in Exhibit 5.11 should be statements to which students have had no prior exposure. The questions used in Exhibit 5.12 should not have been previously answered in class. Of course, during learning activities for the objectives, it's expected that students will analyze similar but different statements about the mathematical content to be comprehended.

Engage in Activity 5.6.

Exhibit 5.12
Example of a measurement item designed to be relevant to how well students comprehend the summation notation.

Task Presented to the Student

Answer each of the following questions using the space provided:

A. Why is the following statement false?

$$\sum_{i=1}^{3} (i^2 - 1) = (1 - 1) + (4 - 2) + (9 - 3)$$

_____

_____

B. Why can't the following expression be translated?

$$\sum_{j=1/2}^{5} 3j$$

_____

_____

C. Why is the following statement false?

$$\sum_{n=2}^{3} 3^n = 3^2 + 3^3 + 3^4$$

_____

_____

Scoring Key. 6 points maximum, distributed as follows:
For A, +1 for clearly indicating that consecutive integers 1, 2, and 3 should be substituted for the index variable only, not for constants; +1 if the answer includes nothing false or irrelevant to the question.

For B, +1 for clearly indicating that the function is defined only for integer values for the index variable; +1 if the answer includes nothing false or irrelevant to the question.

For C, +1 for clearly indicating that the index variable should go from 2 to 3, not 2 to 4; +1 if the answer includes nothing false or irrelevant to the question.

—————— **ACTIVITY 5.6** ——————

Purpose: To extend your insights about how to design measurement items for comprehension objectives.

Procedure: Design a measurement item that you would use as an indicator of students' achievement relative to the objective for which you designed and taught a lesson when you engaged in Activity 5.5.

Exchange your item with that of colleagues who are also engaging in this activity. Critique and discuss one another's items.

ALGORITHMS

An *algorithm* is a multistep procedure for obtaining a result. Algorithms are based on relationships. For example, the algorithm used to find the distance between the two coordinate points $A(8, 7)$ and $B(3, -5)$ in the following computation is based on the Pythagorean theorem:

$$\begin{aligned} AB &= \sqrt{(8-3)^2 + (7-(-5))^2} \\ &= \sqrt{25 + 144} \\ &= \sqrt{169} \\ &= 13 \end{aligned}$$

Most people with a relatively unsophisticated understanding of the world of mathematics think of mathematics as nothing more than algorithms to be memorized (Cangelosi, 1990c). Unfortunately, traditional "schoolmath" (Fowler, 1994; Stewart, 1992) tends to focus almost exclusively on developing algorithmic skills while neglecting construct a concept, discover a relationship, comprehension, application, and creativity learning levels. In an effort to focus attention on aspects of doing mathematics other than executing algorithms, the shapers of curriculum reform movements may have left some teachers with the impression that developing students' algorithmic skills is no longer important. This, of course, was never the intent of those responsible for the NCTM *Standards* (NCTM, 1989, 1991), for calculus reform (Ferrini-Mundy & Graham, 1991), or any other widely accepted programs. Even when students use calculators and computers instead of paper and pencil calculations, they are using an algorithm to operate the technology. Furthermore, they need to understand the steps that the machine is helping them execute.

Algorithms include the following:

- *Arithmetic Computations.* Two examples are: (a) A long-division process using paper and pencil is used to find the quotient of two rational number expressed in decimal form; (b) a calculator is used to find the standard deviation of a data sequence.
- *Re-forming Symbolic Expressions.* Two examples are: (a) A completing-the-square process is used to change a quadratic function from standard form to the form $f(x) = a(x - h)^2 + k$ in order to determine the graphical characteristics of f; (b) an algebraic polynomial is factored
- *Translating Statements of Relationships.* Two examples are: (a) An equation of one unknown is solved (that is, the equation is manipulated so that the unknown comprises the left side and a constant in simplified form comprises the right side); (b) the formula $\sum_{i=0}^{n-1}(a + id) = (n/2)(2a + (n - 1)d)$ is used to find the sum of an arithmetic series.
- *Measuring.* Two examples are: (a) Protractor is used to estimate the degree measure of an angle; (b) the frequencies of Yes and No responses on a survey are tallied.

ALGORITHMIC-SKILL OBJECTIVES

Review the definition of "algorithmic-skill learning level" and the examples of algorithmic-skill objectives in Exhibit 3.10. Algorithmic-skill objectives are concerned with students knowing how to execute the steps in an algorithm. Because you know the answer to the question "What is 9 + 3?" without figuring it out, you have achieved a simple-knowledge objective dealing with arithmetic facts. However, unless you are quite unusual in this regard, you don't know the answer to the question, "What is 168 + 73?" What you do know is how to execute the steps in an algorithm for finding the sum of any two whole numbers such as 168 and 73. This latter skill is indicative of your achievement of an algorithmic-skill objective. Unlike simple-knowledge objectives, the process, not the final outcome, is the target of strategies for helping students achieve algorithmic-skill objectives.

LESSONS FOR ALGORITHMIC-SKILL OBJECTIVES

Facilitating Algorithmic Skills Through Direct Instruction

Gaining proficiency with an algorithm usually means that students must be engaged in learning activities which are more tedious and less interesting than learning activities for other types of objectives, such as discover a relationship. Sometimes games like the one integrated into Ms. Saucony's lesson in Case 9.8 can be used to relieve tedium and boredom during drill and practice activities. In any case, algorithmic skill is effected through *direct instruction* in a nine-stage lesson.

Before you can design learning activities that will take students through the nine stages of the lesson you must analyze the algorithm, delineating the steps for students to execute.

Analyzing the Algorithm

Engage in Activity 5.7.

_____ **ACTIVITY 5.7** _____

Purpose: To develop your abilities to delineate the steps students must learn when acquiring an algorithmic skill and to become aware of the number of cognitive steps seemingly simple algorithms involve.

Procedure: Select one of the following to analyze.

- An algorithm for factoring a trinomial in the form $ax^2 + bx + c$, where a, b, and c are real-valued constants and x is a real variable
- An algorithm for finding the complex roots of a quadratic equation
- An algorithm for graphing a quadratic function
- An algorithm for adding two fractions
- An algorithm for bisecting an angle with a straightedge and compass
- An algorithm for using a graphing calculator to concurrently display the graphs of the following three functions: $f(x) = \sqrt{x}$; $g(x) = x^2$; and $t(x) = x^3$
- An algorithm for using trigonometric functions to determine the unknown length of one leg of a right triangle, given the length of the other leg and the measure of one of the acute angles
- An algorithm for measuring the circumference of a circle

Exchange your list of steps with that of a colleague. Critique one another's analyses, assessing how well each of you identified all the steps students must learn in order to become proficient with the one or two algorithms you examined.

With your colleague address and discuss the following questions:
How is an algorithm like a fractal? Is not the process by which one mentally executes an algorithm a fractal?

The first few times you analyze the process, you may be quite surprised to discover that algorithms with which you are already proficient involve more steps than you had imagined. Schoenfeld (1985, p. 61) points out, "It is easy to underestimate the complexity of ostensibly simple procedures, especially after one has long since mastered them." Consider Case 5.12.

CASE 5.12 _____

Mr. Champagne proficiently factors quadratic trinomials with one variable and integer coefficients without much con-

scious effort. Thus, he doesn't consider the algorithm to be very complex until he thinks about each step his students will need to remember when they learn it for the first time. To factor $x^2 + 10x + 21$, they will need to:

1. Recognize that this is a quadratic trinomial in standard form.
2. Look for the greatest factor that is common to all three terms.
3. Attempt to factor the trinomial into two first-degree binomials because, in this case, there is nothing to "take out" (i.e., no $FAx^2 + FBx + FC$ which becomes $F(Ax^2 + Bx + C)$.
4. Write down: "$(x \quad\ )(x \quad\ )$"
5. Note that all coefficients are positive, so insert a "+" sign as follows: "$(x + \ )(x + \ )$"
6. Note that the constant term is 21
7. List each whole number pair whose product is 21
8. Note that the coefficient for the middle term is 10
9. Determine which of the pairs listed in Step 7 has a sum of 10
10. Note that $7 + 3 = 10$
11. Note that "7" and "3" should be inserted in the blanks in step 5 (in either order)
12. Insert "7" and "3" as follows: "$(x + 7)(x + 3)$"

_____

You may think that enumerating 12 steps for the algorithm Mr. Champagne plans to teach is making the simple complicated. However, please keep in mind that Mr. Champagne's students are just being introduced to this algorithm; consequently, each step represents a potential hurdle that he may have to help them negotiate.

After he examines the process, Mr. Champagne needs to make sure that his students are skilled at factoring integers before attempting to teach the algorithm in Case 5.12.

Nine Stages

Once you have the steps in the algorithm clearly delineated in your mind and students have achieved the prerequisite objectives, you're ready to design an algorithmic-skill lesson in nine stages.

Stage 1: Explanation of the Purpose of the Algorithm. Algorithms are based on relationships. If your students have experienced a discover a relationship lesson relevant to the algorithm, then explaining the purpose of the algorithm is a trivial task. The first stage generally involves nothing more than making an announcement such as, "This algorithm provides us with an efficient way of using our calculators to determine whether a quadratic equation has two, one, or no real roots."

Stage 2: Explanation and Practice Estimating Outcomes. Although algorithmic skills are acquired through direct instruction, students need to get into the habit of estimating or anticipating outcomes before executing the algorithm. This (a) tends to add a little interest to the task as students may be motivated to check their predictions, (b) provides an informal check on the accuracy of the process, and (c) maintains some connection between the algorithm and problem solving. Consider Case 5.13.

CASE 5.13 _____

Jenny works through the textbook exercises that are shown in Exhibit 5.13.

She thinks for the first, "Okay, that's just 9 times 4, which is 36 square meters. No, this is volume, so the answer should come out in cubic, not square, meters. What'd I do wrong? What's the formula again? . . . Oh, yeah, here it is; it's $\pi r^2 h$. Glad I caught that! So the answer is . . . punch up π on my calculator times 16 times 9 equals . . . 452.389 and so on. Okay, 452.39 m^3.

"Now, for the next one. This is a cone, but the dimensions are the same as for the last one. Let's see, this answer should be less than my last one because the top is squeezed together. I bet about 200 m^3. Okay, what's the formula? . . . 0.333 times π times 16 times 9 is . . . 150.645, and so on. So, 150.65 m^3. Why so much smaller? Oh, yeah, this formula is one-third of that one, not one-half."

Stage 3: General Overview of the Process. In this stage, students are provided with an outline of the algorithm they'll be executing. This is particularly important for algorithms with so many steps that students are likely to get involved in detail to the extent that they lose sight of the overall process.

Exhibit 5.13
Two textbook exercises Jenny worked.

Find the volume of the right cylinder:

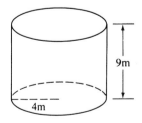

Find the volume of the cone:

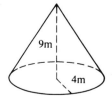

Imagine how confusing it would be to learn each step in the process of shooting a jump shot in basketball if you had never before seen anyone shoot a jump shot. Students need to visualize the overall process before they are ready to follow the detailed steps. the teacher in Case 5.14 conducts Stage 3.

CASE 5.14 _____

Using the overhead projector to illustrate his words, Mr. Anselmo tells his student: "To use this formula to solve quadratic equations, you will first put the equation in standard form so that you can identify *a, b,* and *c* of the formula. Then plug in the values for *a, b,* and *c* and work through the computations with your calculator, making sure to follow your order of operations. The computation will eventually get down to two cases, one for this plus and one for this minus. From there, you'll be working them out as two separate computations. Each result is a potential root."

Stage 4: Step-by-Step Explanation of the Algorithm. This is the paramount stage of the lesson. You begin by explaining the first step of the algorithm and then having the students try it themselves. You then explain how the result of that first step triggers the second. The second step is then explained and tried. Movement to subsequent steps and the steps themselves are each explained and tried in turn.

Consider teaching students three additional steps to be followed after the result or answer from the algorithm is obtained: (a) Compare the result to the previous estimate of the result, as Jenny did in Case 5.13; (b) check the results; (c) if an error is detected, redo previous steps that might have caused the error.

Stage 5: Trial Test Execution of the Algorithm. Students are assigned exercises selected to demonstrate any error patterns they may have learned. The purpose of this stage is to obtain formative feedback on which aspects of the algorithm students execute correctly and which they do not. This includes how they go about (a) estimating or anticipating outcomes, (b) executing each step in the process itself, and (c) checking for and correcting errors. Exhibit 5.14 illustrates sample exercises, including the teachers' annotations to a student's responses.

Stage 6: Error-Pattern Analysis. Students' responses to the trial exercises are analyzed to diagnose how students are executing the algorithm (for example, as indicated by the teacher's annotations in Exhibit 5.14).

Stage 7: Correction. Students are provided with additional explanations as warranted by the error-pattern analysis.

Exhibit 5.14
Sample exercise completed by a
student with teacher's error-
pattern analysis.

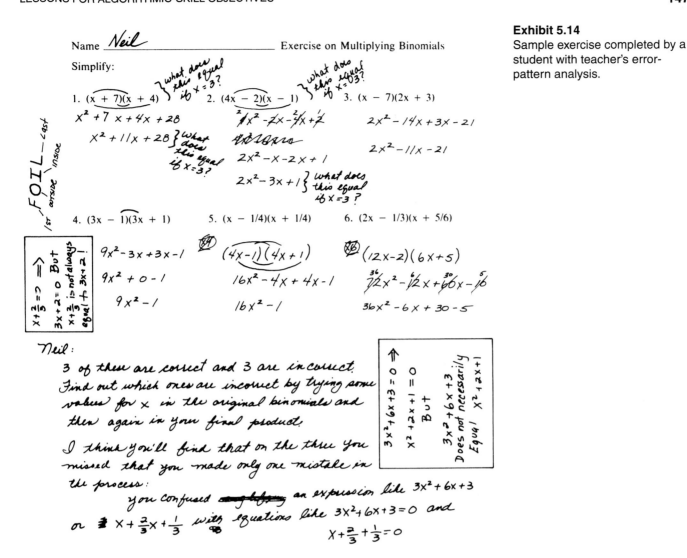

Stage 8: Practice. Students polish their skills and *overlearn* the algorithm through practice exercises.

Stage 9: Recycle Prior Stages as Warranted by Formative Feedback. Students' work continues to be monitored as they use the algorithm during subsequent lessons for other objectives.

A Nine-Stage Lesson for an Algorithmic-Skill Objective

A teacher engages students in a lesson for an algorithmic-skill objective in Case 5.15.

CASE 5.15

Ms. Allen is about two-thirds through a unit on derivatives of algebraic functions with her calculus class. The previous unit was on limits of functions; in this unit she has already completed lessons designed to lead students to (a) construct the concept of derivatives, (b) discover some relevant relationships involving continuity and tangent lines, (c) know some relevant vocab-

ulary and shorthand notations, and (d) comprehend the proofs of some relevant theorems such as the power rule.

Having already delineated the steps in the algorithm and feeling confident that the students have achieved the prerequisites, Ms. Allen begins a lesson for the following objective:

Given a continuous function $f: A{\rightarrow}B$, where $A, B \subseteq \{\text{reals}\}$ and $f(x) = a_0x^n + a_1x^{n-1} + a_2x^{n-2} + \ldots + a_{n-2}x^2 + a_{n-1}x + a_n$, computer $f'(x)$ using the algorithm based on the following relationship:

$$f'(x) = na_0x^{n-1} + (n-1)a_1x^{n-2} + (n-2)a_2x^{n-3} + \ldots 3a_{n-3}x^2 + 2a_{n-2}x + a_{n-1} + 0$$

(*algorithmic skill*)

Tying into the previous lesson, she tells the class: "Recall our definition of derivative of *f* at *x*." She displays the following on the overhead:

$$f'(x) = \lim_{h \to 0} \frac{f(x + h) - f(x)}{h}$$

Ms. Allen: From Theorems 4-1 and 4-3, we know two things. She displays and reads the following:

$$f(x) = a_0x^n + a_1x^{n-1} + a_2x^{n-2} + \dots$$
$$+ a_{n-2}x^2 + a_{n-1}x + a_n$$

Ms. Allen: If f has a derivative at x, then . . .
She displays and reads the following:

$$f'(x) = D_x(a_0x^n) + D_x(a_1x^{n-1}) + D_x(a_2x^{n-2}) + \dots +$$
$$D_x(a_{n-2}x^2) + D_x(a_{n-1}x) + D_x(a_n)$$

and

$$D_x(bx^m) = mbx^{m-1}$$

Ms. Allen: Those two relationships provide the basis for the algorithm you're about to learn. We'll use this algorithm to find the derivative of f at x. From Theorem 4-1 we get this first relationship that allows us to differentiate each term of f one at a time. This second relationship from Theorem 4-3 will be used to find each term's derivative. After the algorithm has been executed completely, what do you think we'll have? Jena.

Jena: f prime of x.

Ms. Allen: I agree, but what will f prime of x look like, Michael?

Michael: It'll be the derivative of f at x.

Ms. Allen: True, but . . . I'm sorry I didn't word my question clearly. Let me try again. Since $f(x)$ is a polynomial, will $f'(x)$ also be a polynomial, and if so, how will the two differ? Let me give everyone a chance to formulate his or her own answer. Okay, Dean.

Dean: f' will be a polynomial of one less degree than f.

Ms. Allen: Okay, let me write that down and you get it in your notes. Anything else we can predict about f', Kayleen?

Kayleen: The constant will go to 0, so you'll have one less term.

Ms. Allen: Okay, I'll get that down. . . .

Ms. Allen is now ready to shift into the fourth stage of the lesson, in which she'll enumerate, display, explain, and use an example to illustrate each step of the algorithm. See Exhibit 5.15.

She has Randy serve as chalkboard scribe. He is to follow her directions, working through an example at the board as she uses the overhead to list each step. The students know from previous sessions that she expects them to record the steps and work the example in their notebooks.

Ms. Allen: Akeem, when we're done today, would you mind if I duplicate your notes for Randy—at least the ones he'll miss while he's at the board?

Akeem: No problem.

Ms. Allen: Thank you. Okay, get this function down as Randy writes it on the board:

$$g(x) = 2x + 9x^4 - 17.4 - x^2 + 3/x + 5/x^2 - 2x^4 - 1/x$$

Our first step is to write the function in standard form, with all variables expressed in numerators with integer coefficients.

She displays the following general form under the rule on the overhead:

$$f(x) = a_0x^n + a_1x^{n-1} + a_2x^{n-2} + \dots$$
$$+ a_{n-2}x^2 + a_{n-1}x + a_n$$

Exhibit 5.15
Ms. Allen lists rules for the algorithm on the overhead projector as Randy differentiates $g(x)$ at the chalkboard.

Ms. Allen: Let's do that for Randy's example.

Randy writes the following on the board as the students try the task at their places:

$$g(x) = 7x^4 - x^2 + 2x - 17.4 + 2/x + 5/x^2$$

$$g(x) = 7x^4 - x^2 + 2x - 17.4 + 2x^{-1} + 5x^{-2}$$

Ms. Allen: If your g in standard form doesn't look like Randy's, then change it if you see what you did wrong. If yours doesn't agree and you don't know why, then ask me about it now. . . . Okay. Next we think about what the derivative of the function should be like. In Randy's example, g is what degree, Ruth?

Ruth: Fourth.

Ms. Allen: So g′ will have what degree, Ross?

Ross: Third.

Ms. Allen: And how many terms does g have, Jena?

Jena: I don't know.

Ms. Allen: Count them.

Jena: Oh, okay. Six.

Ms. Allen: So how many terms should we expect for g′ to have, Humula?

Humula: Six.

Ms. Allen: What's the derivative of a constant, Humula?

Humula: Zero.

Ms. Allen: Is one of the six terms of g a constant, Humula?

Humula: Yes, so g′ will have five terms.

Ms. Allen: So, now that we have the function in standard form with no variables in denominators, the next step is to apply Theorems 4-1 and 4-3 to find the derivative of each term individually. Let's do it for the first term of g. The rule is to multiply the coefficient by the exponent, reduce the exponent by 1, and then simplify. In general, bx to the mth becomes mbx to the m − 1 degree. Work it for the first term for Randy's example. . . . Does anyone disagree with $28x^3$? Okay, repeat the process for each of the other terms one at a time.

Several minutes later the explanation of the steps is completed and Ms. Allen has them differentiate a variety of algebraic functions on a task sheet. She circulates about the room monitoring work and providing help as needed. Rather than re-explaining the algorithm to individual students, she provides very specific directions. Here is one case in point:

Estes: How do you do this one?

Ms. Allen: What does this rule here in your notebook say?

Estes: Find the derivative of each term one at a time.

Ms. Allen: Then do it.

Estes: But this one's funny. What do I do with these negatives?

Ms. Allen: Follow the rule from your notebook.

Estes: You mean you can do that even for the negative of a negative?

Ms. Allen: Yes. Try it and I'll check with you after you've had a chance to complete this one and the next three.

From such exchanges and monitoring their work, Ms. Allen is convinced that students generally know the algorithm, but about a third of them tend to get careless in manipulating expressions with negative exponents and negative coefficients, especially when the coefficient is −1. Thus, she decides to include a larger share of functions with such expressions than she originally planned in the practice exercises for homework.

She plans to continue to check on their skill with this algorithm as students use it during the next lesson, which begins the next day and targets the following objective:

> Given a real-life problem, determines how, if at all, a solution to that problem is facilitated by finding the derivative of an algebraic function.   (*application*)

Engage in Activity 5.8.

─────────────── **ACTIVITY 5.8** ───────────────

Purpose: To expand your insights regarding how to design lessons for algorithmic-skill objectives.

Procedure: Select one of the algorithms listed for Activity 5.7.

Design and teach a lesson for one or two students that leads the student or students to develop their skills with that algorithm.

Discuss your experiences designing and teaching the lesson with colleagues who are also engaging in Activity 5.8. Share with one another what you learned from your experiences.

INDICATORS OF ACHIEVEMENT OF ALGORITHMIC-SKILL OBJECTIVES

Emphasis on the Process, Not the Outcome

Students achieve an algorithmic-skill objective by remembering how to carry out a procedure. Thus, an algorithmic-skill measurement item should present students with the task of recalling or effecting the algorithm step-by-step. The nature of algorithms is such that they are remembered via a *sequence* of responses. The first step is triggered by the initial stimulus. The first step serves as the stimulus for the second step, the second for the third, and so on. Thus, the accuracy of subsequent steps in the process depends on the accuracy of previous steps. Because of this phenomenon, algorithmic-skill items should be designed to identify which steps in the process are accurately remembered or executed and which are not. Unlike, simple-knowledge items, more than the final outcome to the initial stimulus needs to be detected. Consider Case 5.16.

Exhibit 5.16
Angel's responses to an exercise on simplifying polynomials.

Simplify:

$$8(3(x + 5) - (x^2 + 2))$$

$$8(3x + 15) - x^2 + 2$$

$$24x + 120 - x^2 + 2$$

$$-x^2 + 24x + 122$$

CASE 5.16

Ms. Comaneci's students complete a set of exercises to practice and provide formative feedback relative to the following objective:

Simplify algebraic polynomials with nested parentheses. (*algorithmic skill*)

She examines Angel's work on one exercise as it appears in Exhibit 5.16 and thinks to herself: Let's see, . . . his answer is off. It should be $-8x^2 + 24x + 104$. What did he do? He's working inside out; he remembered that. Good! Okay, here's his misstep. He missed distributing the negative sign to the 2. But if that's the only mistake then he'd have $+16$ there, not $+2$. . . . Oh, I see what else he did. He dropped the outside right parenthesis. That was just careless. Okay, I need to remind him of those two things."

Just as Ms. Comaneci analyzes Angel's work to identify which steps in the algorithm were remembered and which were not, algorithmic-skill items need to be designed so that the following occur:

- *The items' tasks are selected so that what students are remembering about the algorithm becomes apparent by their responses.* Had Ms. Comaneci looked only at Angel's answer rather than a display of his work, she would not have detected what he did right and what he did wrong—only that he did something wrong. Furthermore, had the exercise not included an example in which the negative sign was to be distributed, Angel's lack of attention to that task would not have surfaced. That particular error, in which a negative sign to be distributed, is far more common than one in which a negative coefficient other than 1 is to be distributed (Cangelosi, 1984c). Angel may not have made that mistake with this polynomial:

$$8(3(x + 5) - 4(x^2 + 2))$$

The point is that items need to sample a variety of situations to which the process is evoked.

Exhibit 5.17
Measurement item designed to be relevant to Ms. Comaneci's objective in Case 5.16.

> **Task Presented to the Student**
> Simplify (display your work):
>
> $$\frac{1}{3}(c - (c - 3c) - 6(2c + c))$$
>
> **Scoring Key.** 12 points maximum, distributed according to six 2-point scales, with a criterion for each scale so that $+2$ is awarded if the criterion is met in all phases of the work, $+1$ if it is met only some of the time, and $+0$ if it is never met. The six criteria are as follows:
>
> - Computations proceed from inside out relative to parentheses
> - Associative properties are properly applied
> - Distributive properties are properly applied
> - Numerical computations are accurate
> - Final answer is simplified completely
> - Final answer is equivalent to $-5c$

- *The items' scoring keys reflect the degree to which the process is remembered, not simply whether or not the final outcome is right or wrong.* Reread Case 5.12. Note that Mr. Champagne analyzed the algorithm and broke it down into specific steps for students to remember. Such an analysis provides the basis for scoring keys for items relevant to algorithmic-skill objectives. Exhibit 5.17 displays a measurement item relevant to Ms. Comaneci's objective in Case 5.16.

Error-Pattern Analysis

Some mistakes students make in executing algorithms are careless oversights that occur inconsistently in their work. Angel's failure to distribute the -1 and to attend to the outside right parenthesis in Case 5.16 may not be recurring types of errors. To determine if each was an isolated incidence of carelessness or evidence of a learned-error pattern, Ms. Comaneci needs to examine his work on additional exercises. It is not at all uncommon for students to develop consistent error patterns while attempting to learn an algorithm (Ashlock, 1990, p. 3–9; Schoenfeld, 1985, pp. 61–67). Unless these patterns are identified and corrected soon after they are learned, they may become solidified through practice and overlearning. Thus, it is critical for you to devise algorithmic-skill measurement items that help identify possible error patterns students might be learning during lessons on algorithms.

Exhibit 5.18
Cindy's responses to an exercise on simplifying polynomials.

Simplify:

$$8(3(x + 5) - (x^2 + 2))$$
$$8(3x + 15 - x^2 - 2)$$
$$8(3x + 13 - x^2)$$
$$24x + 104 - 8x^2$$
$$-8x^2 + 24x + 104$$
$$x^2 - 3x - 13$$

In Case 5.17, Ms. Comaneci takes advantage of her experiences observing students' work to devise a measurement item.

CASE 5.17

As she did for Angel, Ms. Comaneci's looks at Cindy's work, shown in Exhibit 5.18, and engages Cindy in the following conversation:

Ms. Comaneci: How did you get from $-8x^2 + 24x + 104$ to $x^2 - 3x - 13$?
Cindy: We're supposed to simplify these all the way—right?
Ms. Comaneci: Right.
Cindy: So I divided both sides by -8 to get rid of it in front of the x^2.
Ms. Comaneci: But I only see one side.
Cindy: Can't you just factor the -8 out of the equation?
Ms. Comaneci: What equation?
Cindy: (pointing to the polynomial expression "$-8x^2 + 24x + 104$") This one.
Ms. Comaneci: That's not an equation.
Cindy: It isn't?
Ms. Comaneci: Read this and tell me if . . .

From numerous exchanges similar to this one with Cindy, Ms. Comaneci has developed a wealth of knowledge about incorrect variants of algorithms students accidentally acquire. Her experiences with debugging students' error patterns have taught her to quickly identify some of the recurring ways students attempt algorithms. She uses this knowledge to devise measurement items for algorithmic-skill objectives that cause some of the more common error patterns to surface. Here she designs one such item to test students' proficiency with an algorithm for finding the distance between two points in a Cartesian plane. She thinks to herself, "Okay, this item is to help me see how they use the distance formula:

$$AB = \sqrt{(x_1 - x_2)^2 + (y_1 - y_2)^2}$$

where (x_1, y_1) and (x_2, y_2) are the coordinates for A and B respectively

"I'll make this one multiple choice with alternatives being answers resulting from commonly made errors. First, I'd better come up with a stem for the item. . . . "

She develops the following stem:

What is the distance between $A(7, -2)$ and $B(0, 3)$?

Next, she computes the correct alternative, writing out the work and examining it:

$$AB = \sqrt{(x_1 - x_2)^2 + (y_1 - y_2)^2}$$
$$= \sqrt{(7 - 0)^2 + (-2 - 3)^2}$$
$$= \sqrt{7^2 + (-5)^2}$$
$$= \sqrt{49 + 25}$$
$$= \sqrt{74}$$
$$\approx 8.60$$

Seeing her answer leads her to rethink the stem, saying to herself, "Should the answer be exact or in decimal form? Since they'll be using calculators, I'll use the decimal form and indicate to the nearest one-hundredth in the directions."

Reexamining the computation, she thinks about error patterns students have made in the past, including the following:

- Computing AB as $\sqrt{(x_1 - y_1)^2 + (x_2 - y_2)^2}$ which, if other errors aren't made, leads to an answer of 9.49.
- Computing AB as $\sqrt{(x_1 + x_2)^2 - (y_1 + y_2)^2}$ which, if other errors aren't made, leads to an answer of 6.93.
- Computing AB as $\sqrt{(x_1 + x_2^2) - (y_1 + y_2^2)}$ which, if other errors aren't made, leads to an answer of 0 or other possibilities, depending on which values are substituted for (x_1, y_1) and (x_2, y_2), respectively.
- The correct formula is remembered but computed as if it were $\sqrt{(x_1^2 - x_2^2) + (y_1^2 - y_2^2)}$, yielding 6.63 as the answer.
- $\sqrt{(7 - 0)^2 + (-2 - 3)^2}$ is simplified as $\sqrt{7^2 + (-5)^2} = 7 - 5 = 2$.
- $\sqrt{(7 - 0)^2 + (-2 - 3)^2}$ is simplified as $\sqrt{7^2} + \sqrt{(-5)^2} = 7 + 5 = 12$.

She enters the following item into her computerized file of measurement items:

Task Presented to the Student: To the nearest hundredth, what is the length AB for $A(7, -2)$ and $B(0, 3)$? Circle one of the following:

9.49	8.60	6.63	2.00
12.00	6.93	0.00	10.07

Scoring Key: 8.60 is the correct response. Note any other response the student makes as evidence of a possible error pattern.

Engage in Activity 5.9.

————————— **ACTIVITY 5.9** —————————

Purpose: To help you begin gaining the kind of experiences Ms. Comaneci used to design her item in Case 5.17.

Procedure: Examine the work with algorithms students displayed in Exhibit 5.19. For each, describe an error pattern the student might have displayed.

Compare your analyses with those of colleagues who are engaging in this activity. Also compare your and your colleagues' descriptions to the following ones:

- John's work suggests he's skillful in factoring but doesn't seem to discriminate between $ab = 0$ and $ab = c$, where $c \neq 0$. He seems to blindly use the algorithm without paying attention to the underlying relationship upon which it is based.
- Jane doesn't seem to discriminate among $a^n a^m$, $a^n b^m$, and $(a^n)^m$.

Exhibit 5.19
A sample of students' misexecuting algorithms.

Name ___John___

Solve for all real values of x:

1. $x^2 - 6x - 7 = 0$

$(x-7)(x+1) = 0$

$x - 7 = 0$ or $x + 1 = 0$

$x = 7$ or $x = -1$

2. $x^2 - 4x - 5 = 16$

$(x-5)(x+1) = 16$

$x - 5 = 16$ or $x + 1 = 16$

$x = 21$ or $x = 15$

3. $2x^2 - 9x + 7 = 25$

$(2x-7)(x-1) = 25$

$2x - 7 = 25$ or $x - 1 = 25$

$2x = 32$ or $x = 26$

$x = 16$ or $x = 26$

4. $3x^2 - 23x - 36 = 0$

$(3x+4)(x-9) = 0$

$3x + 4 = 0$ or $x - 9 = 0$

$3x = -4$ or $x = 9$

$x = -\frac{4}{3}$

Name ___Jane___

Simplify:

1. $(c^2)^2 = $ ___c^4___

2. $a^2 a^4 = $ ___a^6___

3. $(b^3)^2 = $ ___b^5___

4. $(x^3 y^5)^0 = $ ___$x^8 y^8$___

5. $b^5 b^6 = $ ___b^{11}___

6. $(w^1 q^2)r^4 = $ ___$w^3 q^7 r^7$___

Name ___Pat___

Add:

1. $\dfrac{x+3}{7x} + \dfrac{2x-8}{7x} = \dfrac{x+3+2x-0}{7x} = \dfrac{3x-5}{7x}$

2. $\dfrac{2x+1}{x-1} + \dfrac{5}{\sqrt{x-1}} = \dfrac{2x+1}{x-1} + \dfrac{25}{x-1} = \dfrac{2x+26}{x-1}$

• Pat's work displays two error patterns. First, he seems to think that the value of a fraction is unchanged if both the numerator and the denominator are raised to the same power. Second, he has some notion of some sort of cross-multiplication process for finding common denominators. He may be confusing the following relationships, the first used in adding fractions, the second in re-forming equations:

$$\frac{a}{c} + \frac{b}{d} = \frac{ad + bc}{cd}$$

$$\frac{a}{c} = \frac{b}{d} \Rightarrow ad = bc$$

• Pete appears to add virtually everything in sight to compute perimeters.

Exhibit 5.19
Continued

3. $\dfrac{\sqrt{x+4}}{x} + \dfrac{\sqrt{3x^2}}{6} = \dfrac{x+4}{x^2} + \dfrac{x\sqrt{3}}{6} = \dfrac{x+4}{x^2} \nearrow \dfrac{x^2(3)}{36} = 12(x+4) + x^4$

$\qquad\qquad\qquad\qquad\qquad\qquad\qquad\qquad\qquad \dfrac{}{12} \qquad\qquad\qquad ?$

4. $\dfrac{8-x}{9x} - \dfrac{1}{x^2} = \dfrac{8-x}{9x} \times \dfrac{1}{x} = \dfrac{x(8-x) - 9x}{9x} = \dfrac{8-x-9}{9} = \dfrac{-x-1}{9}$

– –

Name _Pete_

For each of the following figures find the perimeter:

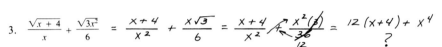

A: 22m 7m 23.1m

B: 5m 15m

C: 14m 4.3m 9.5m 5.6m 7m

D: 5m 20m 12m 7m

E: 26m 26m 11m

ANSWERS:

A's perimeter = _52.1m_   B's perimeter = _20 m_

C's perimeter = _40.4m_   D's perimeter = _44 m_

E's perimeter = _63 m_

Engage in Activity 5.10.

—————————— **ACTIVITY 5.10** ——————————

Purpose: To extend your insights about how to design measurement items for algorithmic-skill objectives.

Procedure: Design a measurement item that you would use as an indicator of students' achievement relative to the objective for which you designed and taught a lesson when you engaged in Activity 5.8.

Exchange your item with that of colleagues who are also engaging in this activity. Critique and discuss one another's items.

TRANSITIONAL ACTIVITIES FROM CHAPTER 5 TO CHAPTER 6 ——————————

1. Select the one response to each of the following multiple-choice items that either completes the statement so that it is true or accurately answers the question:
   A. Which one of the following would *not* be the type of mathematical content specified by a comprehension objective?
      (a) Statement of a relationship
      (b) Definition of a concept
      (c) Relationship
      (d) Technical expression
   B. Students learn the meaning of shorthand symbols by _____.
      (a) inductive reasoning
      (b) deductive reasoning
      (c) being informed
   C. Acceptable form for presenting the proof of a theorem is an example of a _____.
      (a) convention
      (b) discovery
      (c) constant
   D. Student perplexity is *not* a critical ingredient in lessons for which one of the following types of learning objectives?
      (a) Construct a concept
      (b) Discover a relationship
      (c) Simple knowledge
   E. Lessons for simple-knowledge objectives require _____.
      (a) direct instruction
      (b) inquiry instruction
      (c) error-pattern analysis
      (d) students to develop interpretive understanding

   F. Lessons for algorithmic-skill objectives require _____.
      (a) direct instruction
      (b) inquiry instruction
      (c) use of mnemonics
   G. Literal and interpretive understanding are associated with what level of learning?
      (a) Construct a concept
      (b) Discover a relationship
      (c) Simple knowledge
      (d) Comprehension
      (e) Algorithmic skill
   H. Overlearning is associated with what levels of learning?
      (a) Construct a concept and discover a relationship
      (b) Algorithmic skill and simple knowledge
      (c) Construct a concept and simple knowledge
      (d) Creativity and comprehension
   I. Error-pattern analysis is used in learning activities for what type of objective?
      (a) Simple knowledge
      (b) Discover a relationship
      (c) Comprehension
      (d) Algorithmic skill
   Compare your responses to the following: A-c; B-c; C-a; D-c; E-a; F-a; G-d; H-b; I-d.
2. Reexamine the objectives listed in Exhibit 3.9. Although the wording of the objectives do not totally communicate exactly what the teachers had in mind (the learning levels aren't labeled), infer the teachers' intentions by analyzing each to determine if the learning level is (a) simple knowledge, (b) comprehension, (c) algorithmic skill, or (d) none of the three.

   After completing this task, compare your responses to the following; keep in mind, however, that differences may be due to ambiguities in the phrasing of the objectives: The following appear to be simple-knowledge objectives: F of Unit I, D of Unit II, A of Unit III, A of Unit IV, B and C of Unit V, and B and F of Unit VI. Only Objective C of Unit IV appears to be a comprehension objective. The following appear to be algorithmic-skill objectives: G of Unit I, F and G of Unit II, C and F of Unit III, H of Unit IV, E of Unit V, and C and G of Unit VI.
3. Discuss the following questions with two or more of your colleagues:
   a. What types of problems do students need to learn to solve if they are to engage in meaningful mathematics?

b. How should lessons be designed so that students apply their concepts, discoveries, communication skills, algorithmic skills, and knowledge about mathematics to solve real-life problems? In other words, what strategies should teachers employ to lead their students to achieve application-level objectives?

c. How should lessons be designed to foster students' mathematical creativity?

d. What strategies should teachers employ to lead their students to appreciate and enjoy mathematics?

e. What strategies should teachers employ to lead their students to willingly choose to do meaningful mathematics?

6

Leading Students to Solve Problems, Be Creative with Mathematics, and Willingly Do Mathematics

This chapter explains how to design lessons that lead students to apply mathematics to real-life situations, foster their creativity with mathematics, and develop an appreciation for and willingness to do mathematics. In particular, Chapter 6 is designed to help you:

1. Distinguish between examples of deductive reasoning and examples of other forms of cognitive behavior. (*construct a concept*)
2. Explain how deductive reasoning is used to solve problems. (*comprehension*)
3. Formulate application-level objectives that, for a given group of middle or secondary school students, are consistent with the NCTM *Standards.* (*application*)
4. Design lessons for application objectives. (*application*)
5. Design measurement items that are relevant to student achievement of application objectives. (*application*)
6. Distinguish between examples of divergent thinking and examples of convergent thinking. (*construct a concept*)
7. Explain strategies for preserving and fostering students' creativity with mathematics. (*comprehension*)
8. Formulate creativity-level objectives that, for a given group of middle or secondary school students, are consistent with the NCTM *Standards.* (*application*)
9. Design lessons for creativity objectives. (*application*)
10. Design measurement items that are relevant to student achievement of creativity objectives. (*application*)
11. Describe how students develop their beliefs about mathematics and acquire confidence in doing mathematics themselves. (*comprehension*)
12. Formulate affective objectives that, for a given group of middle or secondary school students, are consistent with the NCTM *Standards.* (*application*)
13. Design lessons for affective objectives. (*application*)
14. Design measurement items that are relevant to student achievement of affective objectives. (*application*)

DEDUCTIVE REASONING FOR PROBLEM SOLVING

Review Case 3.1

In Case 3.1 Brenda *applied* certain concepts, relationships, algorithms, and information in an attempt to solve a real-life problem. Problem solving depends on deductive reasoning. When confronted with a question about a specific case, one *reasons deductively* by deciding how, if at all, a previously learned generality like a concept or relationship is relevant to that case. By definition:

Deductive reasoning is deciding that a specific or particular problem is subsumed by a generality. In other words, it is the cognitive process by which people determine whether what they know about a concept or abstract relationship is applicable to some unique situation.

The use of syllogisms is inherent in deductive reasoning. A *syllogism* is a scheme for inferring problem solutions, in which a *conclusion* is drawn from a *major premise* and a *minor premise*. The major premise is a general rule or abstraction. The minor premise is the relationship of a specific to the general rule or abstraction. The conclusion is a logical consequence of the combined premises. For example:

> *Major premise:* If the discriminant ($b^2 - 4ac$) of a quadratic equation is positive and not a perfect square, the equation has two irrational roots.
> *Minor premise:* The discriminant of $x^2 - x - 18 = 0$ (i.e., 73) is positive but not a perfect square.
> *Conclusion:* $x^2 - x - 18 = 0$ has two irrational roots.

Deductive reasoning is the logical foundation of formal proofs of theorems. Although they do not normally express the ideas formally, people use the same syllogistic, deductive logic in real-life problem solving. Consider Case 6.1.

CASE 6.1

Anna is building a playhouse with her children. She has the problem of figuring out how to precut the rafter ends so that they will be vertical to the ground when in place. She sketches a diagram with her planned dimensions of the rafters as shown in Exhibit 6.1.

Looking at her diagram, she thinks, "What should α and β be? $\alpha = \beta$ because they're opposite angles of a parallelogram. Okay, so now do I solve for one of them? β has got to be the same as this angle right here; I'll call it θ." She inserts "θ" as shown in Exhibit 6.2.

Anna begins to doubt that $\beta = \theta$, thinking, "Or does it? Let's see, these two lines are parallel, so we have . . . Okay, that's right, $\beta = \theta$! Alright, I should be able to find θ, since it's part of this triangle . . . in fact, it is a right triangle! A right triangle with two known sides, that means I can use a little trig here. Okay, I know θ's opposite side and its adjacent side. So, tangent is the operable function here. Tangent θ is 8 over 1½ so . . . get this calculator working, arctan, open parenthesis, 8, divide by 1.5, close parenthesis, equals . . . 1.38544. That's not right! Oh, no wonder, the calculator is set for radians. Okay, switch to degrees and try again. Ahh,

Exhibit 6.1
Anna's initial diagram.

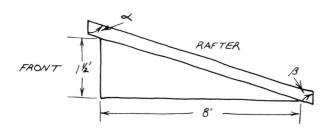

Exhibit 6.2
Anna inserts θ.

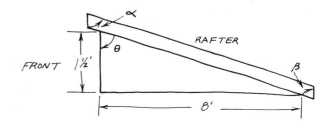

79.38—that's more like it! Okay, so I cut these two angles at almost 80°."

Anna used several syllogisms in formulating a solution to her problem; here are two of them:

> *Major premise:* Opposite angles of a parallelogram are congruent.
> *Minor premise:* The angle with α degrees and the one with β degrees are opposite angles of a parallelogram.
> *Conclusion:* $\alpha = \beta$.

> *Major premise:* The tangent of an acute angle of a right triangle is the ratio of the length of the side opposite to the angle to the length of the side adjacent to the angle.
> *Minor premise:* The angle with θ degrees belongs to a right triangle whose opposite side measures 8 feet and adjacent side measures 1.5 feet.
> *Conclusion:* $\theta = \tan^{-1}(8/1.5)$.

APPLICATION OBJECTIVES

Review the definition of "application learning level" and the examples of application objectives in Exhibit 3.10.

When confronted with a problem, a student who has achieved an application-level objective can determine how, if at all, the mathematical content of that objective can be used in a solution to that problem. During application-level lessons, students put into practice previously developed or acquired concepts, relationships, information, and algorithms.

Sometimes teachers confuse algorithmic-skill objectives with application objectives. Compare the following two objectives:

- Given the velocity of a moving object, determine how long it will take to travel a specified distance. (*algorithmic skill*)
- Given a real-life problem, determine how, if at all, using the relationship $rt = d$ (where r = the rate of travel, t = time of travel, and d = the distance traveled) will help solve the problem. (*application*)

Both objectives deal with the same relationship. But the application objective requires students to *determine when and how* to use the relationship, whereas the algorithmic-skill objective requires student to *remember how to execute the algorithm* based on the relationship. Lessons for application objectives should be designed quite differently from those for algorithmic-skill objectives.

LESSONS FOR APPLICATION OBJECTIVES

Deductive Learning Activities

A deductive learning activity is one that stimulates students to reason deductively. An application level objective is achieved through a four-stage lesson: (1) initial problem confrontation and analysis, (2) subsequent problem confrontation and analysis, (3) rule articulation, and (4) extension into subsequent lessons.

Stage 1: Initial Problem Confrontation and Analysis.
In the initial activity of this stage of the lesson, you confront students with a pair of problems. The pair is chosen so that the problems are very similar except that the content of the application objective applies to the solution of one of the problems but not the other. Suppose, for example, that the following objective is to be achieved:

> Given a real-life problem, decide if the solution requires computing the area of a polygonal region, and, if so, determine how to find that area. (*application*)

The content of the objective applies to the solution of the first of the following pair of problems, but not the second:

A. The front wall surrounding the chalkboard is quite drab. Students suggest that they make decorative posters on standard sheets of cardboard and use them to cover the wall completely, as begun in Exhibit 6.3. How many posters will be needed to complete the task?

B. There is a nasty-looking crack just above the chalkboard on one side of the wall of the classroom. Students suggest that they make decorative posters and use them to hide the crack, as begun in Exhibit 6.4. How many sheets will be needed to complete the task?

You then engage students in a deductive questioning/discussion session in which students describe how they would go about solving each problem and then explain why the objective's content was used in one problem but not the other, as in Case 6.2.

Exhibit 6.3
Classroom wall partially covered with decorative posters.

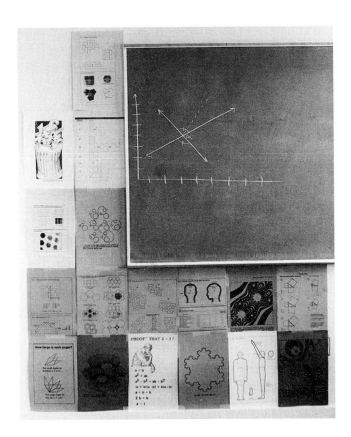

CASE 6.2 _____

Mr. Cummings uses the two sample problems above (A and B) for the application objective on polygonal area. He and one student engage in the following dialogue:

Mr. Cummings: How would you go about solving problem A?

Patsy: I'd divide the wall around the board into rectangles and then find out how many sheets would fit into each rectangle.

Mr. Cummings: But how would you go about finding out the number of sheets to use?

Patsy: I'd have to puzzle the sheets in.

Mr. Cummings: But how would you know how many puzzle pieces to use?

Patsy: By trying it.

Mr. Cummings: But suppose you wanted to find out how many sheets you needed without wasting a bunch of sheets? Is there an easier way?

Patsy: Oh! You mean by computing the area of the wall. Yeah, I could add up the rectangles' areas and divide that by the area of one sheet. Then I'd have it.

Mr. Cummings: Now, what about problem B? How would you solve that one?

Patsy: Just measure the length of the crack and divide that by the height of the sheet and that would give you the number of posters.

Exhibit 6.4
Side wall of classroom with crack partially covered by decorative sheets.

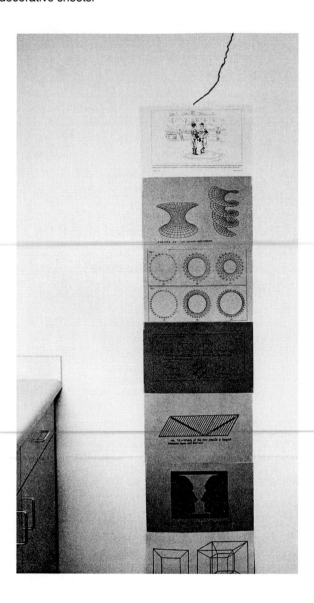

Mr. Cummings: Why didn't you compute areas for problem B like you did for problem A?

Patsy: B isn't an area problem.

Mr. Cummings: Why not? How is it different from A? They seem pretty similar to me.

Patsy: With A, we had to spread the posters all out. In B, the posters are lined up in just one column.

Stage 2: Subsequent Problem Confrontation and Analysis. Learning activities for the second stage are similar to those for the first, except students analyze solutions to additional pairs of problems. The pairs are selected so that the students are exposed to a variety of problem situations in which to determine if the mathematical content is applicable. For the ob-

jective on areas of polygonal regions, subsequent problems would include situations other than covering a wall with posters.

How many pairs of problems to include and how difficult each should be depend on how easily students are distinguishing between problems in which the content applies and those to which it doesn't. If they readily explain why the content works for one problem but not another, then you should engage them in more difficult problems. On the other hand, select easier problems and delay the start of the third stage if they are experiencing serious difficulties.

Stage 3: Rule Articulation. In this stage, students formulate rules for when the content of the objective applies to the solution of a problem. If relevant construct a concept and discover a relationship lessons preceded this one, then this often involves no more than rephrasing rules previously constructed or discovered. In cases in which students began the application level with some conceptual learning gaps relative to the content, this stage may require some inductive learning activities to help them reconceptualize or rediscover rules.

Stage 4: Extension into Subsequent Lessons. As suggested in Chapter 1, teaching functions are messy; one lesson does not always end before another begins. Achievement of one application objective is enhanced during the first two stages of lessons for subsequent application objectives. In Case 6.2 Mr. Cummings' questions stimulated Patsy to reason deductively about lengths (a topic from a prior unit) for the problem to which area computation does not apply. In a subsequent unit on volume Mr. Cummings will probably pair a problem that can be solved via a volume relationship with one that can be solved via an area relationship. Thus, application lessons on one content extend into those for subsequent content.

A Four-Stage Lesson for an Application Objective

Case 6.3 is an example of an application lesson.

CASE 6.3 _____

Exhibit 6.5 depicts what Mr. Wilson calls his "solution blueprint form." He got the idea for the form while attending an NCTM meeting (Cangelosi, 1989b), and it has proven successful enough for him to incorporate it into most application lessons he now teaches.

Mr. Wilson is beginning a lesson for the following objective:

Given a real-life problem, decide if use of either the multiplication principle for independent events, permutation formula, or combination formula will help solve the problem. (*application*)

Exhibit 6.5
Solution blueprint form Mr. Wilson has his students use during application-level lessons.

Solution Blueprint

Question(s) posed by the problem:

_____

Principal variable(s):

_____

Other variables affecting results:

_____

Possible approaches to consider:

_____

Delimited principal variable(s):

_____

Solution plan:

    Overall design

_____

    Measurements to make

_____

    Relations to establish

_____

    Algorithms

_____

Results:

_____

Conclusions:

_____

How you would solve this type of problem in the future?

_____

He directs his students, "Please take out one copy of our solution blueprint form. Now label it Jill and Jack's Locker Security Problem. Read Jill and Jack's locker security problem as I display it on the overhead." He displays:

Jill and Jack are debating whether it would be better if their school lockers were secured with combination locks or with key locks. Jill says, "Combination locks are better because you don't have to worry about keeping up with your key; you just carry your combination around in your head." Jack says, "Key locks are more secure because a thief could just keep trying your combination until she or he gets the right one." Jill counters, "The thief would have to try over a hundred combinations before finding yours and, besides, out of hundreds of locks, one key will be able to open more than one."

Mr. Wilson: Let's help settle the debate by finding out whether combination locks or key locks are more vulnerable to being opened by a thief. Everyone, write the question posed by the problem on the form. Read yours, Gene.

Gene: Which type of lock is more secure from a thief, combination or key?

Mr. Wilson: Does anyone disagree with Gene's answer? Okay, great! Now, what variables do we have to address, Larry?

Larry: Uhh, wait a minute . . . Just how secure the combination lock is and how secure the key lock is.

Mr. Wilson: Everybody write that down. What other variables are going to affect our results besides the two principal variables, Rembert?

Rembert: Oh, stuff like . . . ahh . . . how many thieves there are and a bunch of others.

Mr. Wilson: Good! Let's have Devon, Marilyn, Lynae, and Wanda each list one. Start, Devon.

Devon: How many keys the thief has.

Marilyn: How many numbers on the combination locks.

Lynae: How many locks out of so many one key will fit.

Wanda: I was going to say the same thing as Marilyn.

Mr. Wilson: Any other variables anybody wants to list? Brent.

Brent: How about the number of numbers in each combination?

Mr. Wilson: Yes, Winnie.

Winnie: All our locks use three-number combinations. Can't we just stick with that?

Mr. Wilson: If it's okay with you, Brent, let's make 3 the constant number in any one combination. Okay, considering this list of other variables, I'm going to move us along a little faster by telling you that I did a little research before class. I got Coach Bailey to loan me 100 locks and one randomly selected key. The key opened 5 of the 100 locks. Also, I noted that most locks used in school have 50 numbers on them. So, I suggest that for purposes of the Jill and Jack locker security problem, we control for some of these other variables by delimiting our two principal variables. We solve the problem for one thief operating with one key that'll open 5 percent of the locks, and that each combination lock has 50 numbers. Assuming you agree to that, what are our two principal variables after they've been delimited, Hank?

Hank: What's delimited mean again?

Mr. Wilson: Read the two general principal variables from the second line on your blueprint form.

Hank: How secure is the combination lock is one. The other is how secure the key lock is.

Mr. Wilson: Those are two great variables, but there's one difficulty with them if we're going to solve this problem. . . . What is it, Rembert?

Rembert: They're so general that we can't measure them. We need some mathematical variables.

Mr. Wilson: The delimited variables should be narrower, and—we hope—quantifiable. So, what are the delimited variables, Hank?

Hank: I want to pass. Would you ask somebody else?

Mr. Wilson: Sure, Reed?

Reed: One is the chance that the thief with the one key that opens 5 percent of the locks will open your key lock. The other one is the chance that the thief who's willing to try a lot of combinations will open your combination lock.

Mr. Wilson: I'll buy that. Everybody get that down. . . . Could we use a shorthand symbol for those so we can refer to them easily while we work on solutions for each? What do you want to call them, Hank?

Hank: "K" and "C."

Mr. Wilson: Let's take Hank's suggestion and call the event that the thief opens your key lock "K" and opens your combination lock "C." And since it's the probability of

those events we're interested in, let's use our conventional notation and call our delimited variables as "$P(K)$" and "$P(C)$," respectively.

At this point, the solution blueprint form has been filled in down to the "solution plan."

Mr. Wilson: After we solve for $P(K)$ and $P(C)$, what would we do next, Winnie?

Winnie: We compare them to see which is greater. If C is a more likely event, then Jack is right and key locks should be used. If K is more likely, then Jill is right and combinations are better.

Mr. Wilson: Okay, then let's split Jill and Jack's locker security problem into two subproblems: One is to figure $P(K)$ and the other to figure $P(C)$. Let's do $P(C)$ first. How do we go about solving $P(C)$? . . . Ilone.

Ilone: You've got to figure how many possible combinations there are on the lock.

Mr. Wilson: How many numbers on the lock, Hank?

Hank: 50.

Mr. Wilson: How many numbers in one combination, Tracy?

Tracy: 3.

Mr. Wilson: So, each of you silently figure how many possible lock combinations there are. You have three minutes. . . . What did you get, Rembert?

Rembert: 19,600.

Mr. Wilson: What did you do to get 19,600, and why did you decide to do it that way?

Rembert: It's a combination of 50 things taken 3 at a time, so I just used the combination function on my calculator.

Mr. Wilson: By the number of hands raised, it looks like a few people want to debate your method. Okay, Kabul, you and Rembert stand up and debate the differences in your approaches.

Kabul: I don't know why they call them "combinations," but I do know the order of the 3 numbers makes a difference. If the lock's combination is 20-30-40, then 40-30-20 won't open it. So it's a permutation, not a combination.

Rembert: So, what's the answer?

Kabul: 117,600.

Mr. Wilson: I see some other folks are anxious to speak. Yes. Marilyn.

Marilyn: But it's not a permutation either. A number can be repeated in a lock combination. What about 20-20-30?

Mr. Wilson: What's the rule for when permutations apply to a situation, Cassandra?

Cassandra: When you want to know how many ways so many things can happen out of so many. But there can't be any repeats in any one way. That's what we said the other day.

Mr. Wilson: And can a lock combination have repeats as 23-14-23, Nancy?

Nancy: Sure, and that's why Marilyn is right.

Mr. Wilson: So if permutations don't apply, what does? . . . Okay, Devon.

Devon: It'd be however many numbers times itself times it-self.

Mr. Wilson: Therefore, what? Finish the syllogism for the combination lock problem, Rembert.

Rembert: Therefore, the possible number of lock combinations is 50 × 50 × 50.

Mr. Wilson: So, what's $P(C)$, Kabul?

Kabul: Almost 0; it's $1 \div 50^3$. That's 0.000008 on my calculator.

Mr. Wilson: Let's move to the other subproblem in Jill and Jack's overall problem. . . . What's the other variable we need to solve for, Anson?

Anson: $P(K)$.

Mr. Wilson: How do we solve for $P(K)$, Nancy?

Nancy: You said it's 5 percent. A thief with a key can open 5 out of every 100 key locks. That means key locks are not nearly as secure as combination locks.

Mr. Wilson: Before you compare $P(K)$ to $P(C)$, explain how you got $P(K) = 0.05$, Nancy.

Nancy: You did it by experimenting.

Mr. Wilson: You mean we couldn't have just used either the permutation formula, the combination formula, or the multiplication principle for $P(K)$ like we did for $P(C)$? . . . Marie.

Marie: No, it's just one key that fits 5 out of 100 locks. If the thief tries your lock, there's a 5 percent chance he or she'll get in. There's not so many things to group out of so many—repeating or not repeating.

Mr. Wilson: Oh, grouping! Are you saying if there is no *grouping* or *arrangements,* then we don't have a case for permutations, combinations, or the multiplication rule? I understand. Let's go ahead and complete the solution blueprint form for Jill and Jack's overall problem.

Without further discussion, the students complete their forms.

Mr. Wilson continues the lesson by presenting another pair of problems that he considers more difficult than the ones involving $P(C)$ and $P(K)$. However, the students solve them efficiently and appear to distinguish clearly among problems to which combinations apply, permutations apply, the multiplication principle applies, and none of those applies. He thus decides against confronting them with additional problems in class. For homework, he assigns eight more problems. Permutations are applicable to two of them, combinations to two, and the multiplication principle to one other. The other three can be solved by applying prior content. He checks the homework to assess if additional learning activities are needed.

Also, in the next application on binomial distributions, combinations are needed for binomial distribution problems and permutations are needed for some of the problems that don't involve binomial distributions.

Engage in Activity 6.1.

───── **ACTIVITY 6.1** ─────

Purpose: To expand your insights regarding how to design lessons for application objectives.

Procedure: Select one of the following objectives.

- Given a real-life problem, determine how, if at all, a solution to that problem is facilitated by setting up and solving for a quadratic equation.   (*application*)
- Given a real-life problem, determine how, if at all, a solution to that problem is facilitated by setting up and solving for a system fo linear equations.   (*application*)
- Given a real-life problem, determine how, if at all, a solution to that problem is facilitated by using probability principles and methods of compound events.   (*application*)
- Given a real-life problem, determine how, if at all, a solution to that problem is facilitated by using relationships derived from triangle congruence postulates and theorems.   (*application*)
- Given a real-life problem, determine how, if at all, a solution to that problem is facilitated by using the following formula for compound interest where $A =$ the accumulated amount, $P =$ the principal, $r =$ the annual rate, $K =$ the number of times per year the interest is compounded, and $n =$ the number of years:

$$A = P(1 + r/k)^{kn}$$

(*application*)

- Given a real-life problem, determine how, if at all, a solution to that problem is facilitated by using the relationship that the ratio of the circumference of any circle to its diameter is π.   (*application*)

Design and teach a lesson for one or two students that leads the student or students to achieve that objective.

Discuss your experiences designing and teaching the lesson with colleagues who are also engaging in Activity 6.1. Share with one another what you learned from your experiences.

INDICATORS OF ACHIEVEMENT OF APPLICATION OBJECTIVES

Deciding How to Solve Problems

A measurement item for achievement of an application objective presents students with a problem and the task of deducing how, if at all, the mathematical content specified by the objective is useful in solving the problem.

Avoiding "Giveaway" Words

Contrast Case 6.4 to Case 6.5.

CASE 6.4 ─────────────────

The following is one of Ms. Kennedy's objectives for a unit involving discrete mathematics:

Given a real-life problem, decide if the solution requires determining a combination of *n* things taken *r* at a time and, if so, determine how to find that combination (*application*)

As part of a test to measure how well students have achieved the goal of the unit, Ms. Kennedy includes the following item she designed to be relevant to the aforementioned objective:

Task presented to the student: A group of three musicians has six instruments that they all can play (a synthesizer, a piano, two different acoustical guitars, and an electric guitar). How many different instrument combinations can the group play together? Display your work.
Scoring key: 2 points maximum, distributed as follows:

+ 1 for using $_nC_r = (n!)[(n - r)!r!]$ with $n = 6$ and $r = 3$.
+ 1 for answering 20.

Duane, a student, obtained a full two point score on this item with the following thought: "How many different instrument *combinations* can . . . Oh, so this a combination problem. Let's see, what are the numbers to plug in, ahh . . . there's a 3 and a 6. The rule is the bigger one is *n*, the smaller one *r*—so it's 6! over . . . which give me 20."

CASE 6.5

Like Ms. Kennedy, Mr. Koebbe targets the same objective stated in Case 6.4 in one of his units. But he included the following item to measure it on the unit test:

Task presented to the student: Aaron, Art, Mindy, and Van have a musical group with seven instruments available to them (a synthesizer, a piano, two different acoustical guitars, a base guitar, electric guitar, and a drum set). Aaron, Art, and Mindy can play any of the instruments except the drums. Van can play only drums.

The group refers to any set of four instruments they can be playing together as an "instrument arrangement." How many different instruments can the group play during a concert? Display your work.
Scoring key: 2 points maximum, distributed as follows:

+ 1 for using $_nC_r = (n!)[(n - r)!r!]$ with $n = 6$ and $r = 3$.
+ 1 for answering 20.

Luanda, a student, obtained a full 2-point score on this item with the following thoughts: "How many different instrument arrangements can the group play? . . . So, what's this instrument arrangement thing? Let's see, it says any set of four instruments they can be playing at once. So, that's like bass guitar, two acoustic guitars, and the piano—that's an instrument arrangement. How may of those are possible? . . . Aaron is playing piano and Art a guitar, and they switch, does that change the instrument arrangement? No. It's what is being played that counts. So, this isn't a permutation problem. It's a combination. So, okay, how many instruments can they play at once? 7? No, it's the number of people that count—that's Aaron, Art, Mindy, and Van—4 possible out of 7 instruments. So, it's a combination of 7 instruments taken 4 at a

time, which is . . . 35. Okay, is that right? Oh, no! Van is the only one that plays the drums. So, drums are in every arrangement of 4. I can just ignore drums, so it's really a combination of 6 instruments taken 3 at a time, which is . . . 20."

In Case 6.4 Duane keyed in on the word "combination," remembered the formula, and simply substituted the only data available. He demonstrated algorithmic skill relative to combinations, but he did not have to think deductively to respond correctly to the item. Thus, the item doesn't appear relevant to the application-level objective for which it was designed.

On the other hand, Mr. Koebbe in Case 6.5 avoided the word "combination" to increase the chances that in order to respond correctly, students would have to reason deductively, as Luanda did. Note, however, that Mr. Koebbe's item also taxes students' reading-comprehension skills to a greater degree than Ms. Kennedy's. Because of this unfortunate necessity, it's important to include comprehension-level objectives in units and test for achievement of them separately from application-level objectives.

Extraneous Data

Regarding the two items, note that the improved version of the item in Case 6.5 is not only void of giveaway words like "combination," but also includes extraneous information. Having 4 members and 7 instruments in a problem that requires a combination of 6 things taken 3 at a time taxes students' abilities to deduce what data are to be used in the formula. If the wording of the problem is such that only exactly what is needed is given, then the item is less likely to be at the application level. After all, with a real-world problem, a person is inundated with information, most of which is irrelevant to solving the problem. Revisit Exhibit 3.7.

Missing Data

Another strategy for designing application items is to confront students with problems without supplying them with all the information needed for the solution. Such items help test how well they can deduce what data needs to be collected. Keep in mind that in the real world, one must decide what data to collect to solve problems; data aren't always conveniently presented as numerals on a printed page.

Engage in Activity 6.2.

ACTIVITY 6.2

Purpose: To expand your insights regarding how to design missing-data, application-level measurement items.

Procedure: Design a missing-data item for the following objective:

Given a real-life problem, determine how, if at all, a solution to that problem is facilitated by using the following formula for compound interest, where A = the accumulated amount, P = the principal, r = the annual rate, k = the number of times per year the interest is compounded, and n = the number of years: $A = P(1 + r/k)^{kn}$. (*application*)

Compare your item to that of colleagues who are also engaging in Activity 6.2. Also compare your and your colleagues' work to the item shown in Exhibit 6.6.

Mixing Example and Nonexample Problems

To measure students' abilities to discriminate between problems to which an objective's content applies and

Exhibit 6.6
Example of a missing-data item designed to be relevant to students' achievement of the objective stated in Activity 6.2.

Task Presented to the Student

Several years ago Riley was shopping for a bicycle. There were two that interested him, one for $350 and the other for $150. His dad advised him at the time to buy the one for $150 and put the difference into a savings account. He liked the more expensive one so much more that he bought it anyway. Now, he wonders how much he would have in the bank if he had taken his dad's advice.

   Write a half-page letter to Riley explaining how to figure out how much he would have in the bank today if he had bought the less expensive bicycle and left the difference in a savings account. Be as detailed as reasonably possible.

Scoring Key. 18 points maximum, distributed according to nine 2-point scales, with a criterion for each scale so that + 2 is awarded if the criterion is clearly met, + 1 if it is unclear whether or not it is met, and + 0 if it is clearly not met. The nine criteria are as follows:
- The principal is set at $200.
- The question of whether the interest is simple or compound is raised.
- The question of the number of times per year interest is compounded is raised.
- The process for finding out how often the interest is compounded is explained (e.g., calling the bank or reading bank documentation).
- The question of how long it has been since the bicycle was purchased is raised.
- The process for finding out when the bicycle was purchased is explained (e.g., by looking up the receipt).
- The question of what is the rate of interest is raised.
- The process for finding out the interest rate is explained.
- A formula equivalent to the one stated in the objective is suggested.

---

problems to which it doesn't, both example and nonexample problems need to be included in the same measurement. As a nonexample problem relative to the application objective on combinations stated in Case 3.4, the following problem might be used.

Robbie can play the piano and harmonica, Amanda can play the piano, bass guitar, and lead guitar. The only two instruments that can be played by one person simultaneously are the harmonica and guitar. If the three musicians are to play four different kinds of instruments at the same time, what instrument must Amanda play?

Nonmathematical Topics for Problems

Application items confront students with problems to solve. If the nonmathematical aspects of the problem are familiar, students tend to find that item easier than one relevant to the same application objective but involving a less familiar subject. For example, students familiar with football will have an easier time visualizing the following problems than students who rarely watch or participate in football:

At the rate of 9 yards per second, how long will take a football player to run 10 yards straight downfield? At that rate how long would it take the same player to run from the team's 5-yard line to its 15-yard line if the player runs a straight route that makes a 20° angle with the sidelines?

Because you want your application-level items to discriminate on the basis of how well students achieved the mathematical learning objective, not how familiar they are with topics such as football, you need to choose nonmathematical topics carefully so that most students are familiar with the topic and a wide range of interests are included.

Engage in Activity 6.3.

_____ **ACTIVITY 6.3** _____

Purpose: To expand your insights regarding how to design items for application objectives.

Procedure: Design a measurement item that you would use as an indicator of students' achievement relative to the objective for which you designed and taught a lesson when you engaged in Activity 6.1.

   Exchange your item with colleagues who are also engaging in this activity. Critique and discuss one another's items.

DOING MATHEMATICS CREATIVELY
Some Thoughts on Creativity

Students do mathematics creatively by *thinking divergently* to originate ideas, conjectures, algorithms, or problem solutions. By definition:

Divergent thinking is atypical reasoning that deviates from the normal way of thinking. It is thought that produces unanticipated and unusual responses.

The antithesis of divergent thinking is *convergent thinking*. By definition:

Convergent thinking is typical reasoning producing predictable responses for most people.

People tend to produce creative ideas in response to dissatisfaction with available resources for dealing with perplexing problems. Contrary to popular belief that aptitude for creative production is found only in rare, exceptional individuals, virtually everyone possesses creative talents (Torrance, 1986). What is rare is for that talent to be recognized and rewarded. Historically, society and its institutions like schools and churches have frowned upon and generally discouraged creative thinking (Strom, 1969, pp. 222–236; Woolfolk, 1993, pp. 305–310). Divergent reasoning threatens common beliefs. Irrational thought and emotional behaviors are often associated with mental instability. However, Gordon (1961, p. 6) suggests that irrational, emotionally charged thought tends to produce an environment more conducive to creative production than rational, controlled thought. Joyce, Weil, & Showers (1992, p. 220) state, "Nonrational interplay leaves room for open-ended thoughts that can lead to a mental state in which new ideas are possible. The basis for decisions, however, is always rational; the irrational state is the best mental state for exploring and expanding ideas, but it is not the decision-making stage."

Creativity thrives in an environment in which ideas are valued on their own merit, not on the basis of how they were produced nor who produced them (Strom, 1969, pp. 258–267). In such an environment, irrationally produced ideas are evaluated with the same regard as those resulting from a rational process. The attention afforded an idea should not depend on the eminence of the originator.

Gordon's (1961) studies challenge typical views about creativity with four ideas:

- Creativity is important in everyday circumstances; it should not be associated only with the development of great works.
- Creativity is utilized in all fields, not just the arts.
- Creative thoughts can be generated by groups as well as by individuals alone via similar processes. This is contrary to the common view that creativity must be an intensely personal experience.
- The creative process is not mysterious; it can be described and people can be taught to use it.

Gordon's points are critical to justifying the inclusion of creativity-level lessons in mathematics curricula. However, how best to teach for creativity

is still not well understood. One difficulty is resolving the phenomenon that creative thought seems to rise unpredictably (Bourne, Dominowski, Loftus, & Healy, 1986, pp. 9–10).

Preserving Creativity

Studies indicate a steady decline in most students' curiosity and creative activity during their school years (Strom, 1969, pp. 259–260):

Given the great number of children with creative prospect and the fact that it represents a natural evolving process, the first concern among educators ought to be one of preservation. Creativity will develop if allowed to grow, if teachers permit and encourage a course already begun (see Gowan, et al., 1967). A primary clue comes from the process itself—allowing inquiry, manipulation, questioning, guessing, and the combination of remote thought elements. Generally, however, the preferred cognitive style of learning creatively is discouraged (in typical classrooms). Studies indicate that discontinuities in creative development occur at several grade levels and that the losses are accompanied by a decline in pupil curiosity and interest in learning. At the same grade levels at which creative loss occurs, increases are noted in the incidence of emotional disturbances and egregious behavior. Among Anglo-American cultures, the greatest slump in creative development seems to coincide with the fourth grade; smaller drops take place at kindergarten and seventh grade. Children at each of these grades perform less well than they did one year earlier and less well than children in the grade below them on measures of divergent thinking, imagination, and originality. This problem was ignored, since it was judged to be a developmental phenomena instead of man-made or culture-related (Torrance, 1962). Not long ago it was first recognized that in certain cultures the development of creative thinking abilities are continuous. And, even in our own country, under selective teachers who encourage creative boys and girls and reward creative behavior, no slump occurs at grade four.

As a teacher, you can choose not to include creativity-level objectives in your mathematics curriculum. However, simply managing to preserve students' creativity and allowing it to grow requires some conscious effort on your part.

Fostering Creativity

Consistent with the NCTM (1989) *Standards,* you may choose not only to preserve your students' creativity but also to conduct lessons that help them achieve creativity-level objectives. Creativity lessons can be efficiently interwoven with those for other types of objectives, especially construct a concept and discover a relationship. The strategy is to conduct these other lessons so that students feel free to question, make mistakes, and disagree with ideas, even yours. Particularly important is for them to be positively reinforced (Cangelosi, 1993, pp. 39–41) for depending on themselves and on their own devices for decision making and problem solving.

Although the creative process is not well understood, some promising methods for teaching for creativity have been tried and studied (Bourne, Dominowski, Loftus, & Healy, 1986, p. 9). Strom (1969, p. 261) recommends students be exposed to examples of creative production (for example, through historical accounts of mathematical inventions and discoveries, and through teachers' modeling divergent thinking in think-aloud sessions). Beyer (1987, pp. 35–37) points out the importance of heuristic activities such as brainstorming, open-ended question sessions, and discussions in which ideas for consideration are examined regarding purpose, structure, advantages, and disadvantages.

CREATIVITY OBJECTIVES

What is the fifth term in the infinite sequence (0, 5, 10, 15, . . .)? Most people who comprehend the question reason that the fifth term should be 20. They recognize the arithmetic of uniformly increasing multiples of 5 beginning with 0. Such a response requires *convergent* thinking because such thinking produces the expected answer. But suppose a student's thinking *diverges* from the usual pattern, as in Case 6.6.

CASE 6.6 _____

Ms. Strong: What is the fifth term in the infinite sequence 0, 5, 10, 15, and so forth?
Willie: 26.
Ms. Strong: Why 26?
Willie: Because each number is different from a perfect square by exactly 1, following a pattern. Willie writes:

$$0 = 1^2 - 1$$
$$5 = 2^2 + 1$$
$$10 = 3^2 + 1$$
$$15 = 4^2 - 1$$

Willie: So, the pattern repeats with $n^2 - 1$ once followed by $n^2 + 1$ twice, then another $n^2 - 1$, and so on.
_____

Willie's divergent reasoning justifies 26 for the fifth term just as well as convergent reasoning justifies 20. Do not confuse divergent thinking with the thinking of the student is Case 6.7.

CASE 6.7 _____

Ms. Strong: What is the fifth term in the infinite sequence 0, 5, 10, 15, and so forth?
Bonnie: 17.
Ms. Strong: Why 17?
Bonnie: I don't know. Did I guess right?
_____

Bonnie's unanticipated answer does not appear to be the result of divergent thinking.

Review the definition of "creativity learning level" and the examples of creativity objectives in Exhibit 3.10.

The condition of originality is met as long as the concept, conjecture, algorithm, or solution strategy is novel to the student. A student, for example, displays achievement at the creativity level by originating a method for proving a theorem, even if that method has been previously developed . However, the student must design the method without knowledge of the earlier work.

LESSONS FOR CREATIVITY OBJECTIVES
Synectics

One of the more systematic and researched methods for fostering creativity is referred to by its designer, William J. J. Gordon (1961), as "synectics." *Synectics* is a means by which *metaphors* and *analogies* are used to lead students into an illogic state for situations where rational logic fails. The intent is for students to free themselves of convergent thinking and to develop empathy with ideas that conflict with their own. Three types of analogies are used in learning activities based on synectics:

1. *Direct Analogies.* Students raise and analyze comparisons between the mathematical content and some familiar specific or concept. For example:
   • How is a function like a tossed salad?
   • What's the difference between a continuous sequence and frozen yogurt?
   • Which is rounder, a hexagon or a television show?

2. *Personal Analogies.* Students empathize with mathematical content, losing themselves in some imaginary world. For example:
   • Be f where $f: (-1, 6) \rightarrow \{reals\}$ such that $f(x) = 3/(6 - x)$. Describe how you feel as x moves from -1 to about 5.75. Describe how you feel as x moves from 5.75 nearer and nearer to 6.
   • You're the set of rational numbers, and you must give up one of your infinite subsets to the set of irrational numbers. You get to choose which one to give away. Which one is it and why?

- You have just invented a way of constructing an equilateral right triangle. How do you feel about your invention? How will this accomplishment change your life?

3. *Compressed Conflicts.* Compressed conflicts usually involve metaphors containing conflicting ideas. For example:

   - Draw a continuously discrete graph.
   - How would mathematics be different if only parallel lines could be perpendicular?
   - Show how an infinite set is small.

The metaphors and analogies are used to stimulate students to reconstruct old ideas, thus promoting divergent thinking.

A Lesson Designed to Foster Creativity

Synectics are used Case 6.8.

CASE 6.8

Ms. Ferney routinely mixes learning activities for creativity with lessons for other types of objectives. Her algebra class has recently engaged in construct a concept lessons on functions and continuity, as well as comprehension lessons on the language associated with those concepts. They have not, however, been introduced to the idea of limit of a function. At this point, she intends to help them achieve the following objective:

Generate a variety of novel functions and describe their features, including some suggesting the idea of limits. (*creativity*)

She directs the students to begin writing down functions of their own design. She insists that at least one of the functions have a domain that is not a set of numbers. After six minutes, she calls a halt to the activity and asks Brook to write one of his on the board; he writes the following and then returns to his place:

$$q(a) = -\sqrt{|9 - a|}$$

Ms. Ferney directs the class, "Please take a blank sheet of paper and number it from −3 to 2. Leave about three lines between numerals to write answers in response to items I'm about to give you." She lists the following items, giving them about two minutes for a response between each:

−3. How is Brook's function like a light?
−2. If you were Brook's function, why do you suppose you'd be accused of being fickle? How would you answer your critics?
−1. Why would anyone call Brook's function a variable constant?
0. Write out a question about Brook's function for the class to discuss.

1. Write out another question about Brook's function for the class to discuss.
2. Write out yet another question about Brook's function for the class to discuss.

Ms. Ferney: How did you answer item −3., Katrina?
Katrina: A night light is for security and the function is very secure because you can't take the root of a negative number, and by putting in the absolute value, that protects you from having a negative inside the radical.

Additional responses to each of the six items are reported and discussed in detail. Other functions are put on the board; similar questions are raised, and the responses are discussed. _____

Engage in Activity 6.4.

ACTIVITY 6.4

Purpose: To expand your insights regarding how to design lessons for creativity objectives.

Procedure: Select one of the following objectives:

- Describe a novel paradigm illustrating the following relationship: $x^a x^b = x^{a+b}$, where $x \in$ {reals} and $a, b \in$ {integers}. (*creativity*)
- Generate novel conjectures about constructions with a straightedge and compass and either prove or disprove them. (*creativity*)
- Invent patterns for novel sequences of numbers. (*creativity*)
- Invent novel structures for illustrating cause-and-effect relationships (e.g., unconventional graphical representations). (*creativity*)
- Describe a novel arithmetic in which at least some of the conventional algebraic field axioms do not hold. (*creativity*)
- Describe a novel non-Euclidean geometry in which at least some of the fundamental Euclidean postulates are not assumed. (*creativity*)

Design and teach a lesson for one or two students that leads the student or students to achieve that objective.

Discuss your experiences designing and teaching the lesson with colleagues who are also engaging in Activity 6.4. Share with one another what you learned from your experiences.

INDICATORS OF ACHIEVEMENT OF CREATIVITY OBJECTIVES

Unless you devise very unusual curricula for students, relatively few of your objectives specify creativity for the learning level. Lessons fostering mathematical creativity tend to be integrated with other lessons and extend beyond the confines of a single teaching unit. You may, for example, include short learning activities based on synectics within most teaching units, but you will detect an increase in students' creative mathematical pursuits only over the course of several units. Consequently, assessing achievement at the creativity level may be more of a long-range endeavor than assessing achievement of other types of cognitive objectives.

Measurement items for creativity objectives consist primarily of the following:

1. Presenting students with tasks relative to the specified content that can be accomplished via divergent thinking
2. Scoring students' responses in ways that reflect divergent rather than convergent thinking.

Note that the scoring keys for simple-knowledge, algorithmic-skill, comprehension, construct a concept, discover a relationship, and application objectives tend to reward convergent thinking (responses that match previously conceived responses).

Exhibits 6.7 and 6.8 provide examples of creativity objectives, each accompanied by an item designed to be relevant to it.

Engage in Activity 6.5

——————— **ACTIVITY 6.5** ———————

Purpose: To expand your insights regarding how to design items for creativity objectives.

Procedure: Design a measurement item that you would use as an indicator of students' achievement relative to the objective for which you designed and taught a lesson when you engaged in Activity 6.4.

Exchange your item with colleagues who are also engaging in this activity. Critique and discuss one another's items.

Exhibit 6.7
Example of a creativity objective on number patterns and an item designed to be relevant to it.

Objective. Categorize numbers in unconventional ways and formulates a rule for each category. (*creativity*)
Task Presented to the Student

Given $A = \{-\sqrt{3}, \sqrt{-3}, 27, 3, 3.333, \ldots\}$, compose five *distinct* (no two are equal) subsets of A such that each subset contains exactly three elements. For each of the five subsets, write a rule that defines set membership.

Write the rule without actually naming any of the three elements.
1st subset: _____
1st rule._____
_____
_____

2nd subset: _____
2nd rule: _____
_____
_____

3rd subset: _____
3rd rule: _____
_____
_____

4th subset: _____
4th rule: _____
_____
_____

5th subset: _____
5th rule: _____
_____
_____

Scoring Key. 5 points maximum, with + 1 for each subset-rule pair that fits the criterion established in the directions.

INFLUENCING STUDENTS' ATTITUDES ABOUT MATHEMATICS

Affective Objectives

Unlike cognitive objectives, *affective* objectives are not concerned with students' abilities with mathematical content but rather their attitudes about mathematical content. As indicated in Chapter 3, the affective domain includes two learning levels: *appreciation* and *willingness to try*.

Appreciation Objectives. Review the definition of appreciation learning level and the examples of appreciation objectives in Exhibit 3.10.

Achievement of an appreciation-level objective requires students to hold certain beliefs but does not require them to act upon those beliefs.

Willingness to Try Objectives. Review the definition of willingness to try learning level and the examples of willingness to try objectives in Exhibit 3.10.

By believing that an understanding of systems of linear equations can help solve problems they care about, students have achieved at the appreciation level. But to learn content at the willingness to act level, the student has to act upon that belief, for example, by trying to learn about system of linear equations.

Lessons for Appreciation Objectives

When you teach for an appreciation objective, you are attempting to influence students' preferences, opinions, or desires regarding mathematical content specified by the objective. Students who learn to value mathematical content are intrinsically motivated to

Exhibit 6.8
Example of a creativity objective on number theory and an item designed to be relevant to it.

Objective. Formulate and prove theorems about subsets of whole numbers. (*creativity*)

Task Presented to the Student
The number of dots in each of the following arrays is called a *triangular number:*

The set of triangular numbers is infinite. Take at least 15 minutes to examine triangular numbers. Then, make three different statements you think are true about all triangular numbers. These statements should be hypotheses that are not immediately apparent (e.g., all triangular numbers are positive integers) from just glancing at the numbers. Try to prove one of your statements. Display your work on the proof or attempt at a proof.

1st statement: _____
_____
_____

2nd statement:_____
_____
_____

3rd statement: _____
_____
_____

Proof of work toward a proof:

Scoring Key. The rules are based on comparing responses to those of others. First of all, any blatantly obvious statement, such as no triangular number is imaginary, is eliminated. Then each of the remaining statements is compared to a list of statements compiled from other students who have responded to this item. Comparison statements are sequenced from the most frequently occurring to the least frequently occurring. The statement from this student is then ranked in the sequence and given a number of points equal to its rank.

Thus, if there are 50 comparison statements and 20 of them have been made more than once, then if the statement is equivalent to one of the 20, it receives a score from 1 to 20, inclusive. If the statement is equivalent to one of the 30 unique comparison statements, it receives a score of 21. If the statement is not equivalent to any of the 50 statements, it receives a score of 36 (i.e., a three-way tie for 21st place). If the display of the work on the proof demonstrates a discernible line of thought, the statement score is multiplied by 4. If the statement is actually proved, that score is then doubled.

increase their skills and abilities with it, and thus achieve cognitive objectives you establish for the unit.

Telling students about the importance and value of certain mathematics is generally ineffectual as a learning activity for an appreciation objective. Consider Case 6.9.

CASE 6.9 _____

Mr. Shaver realizes that if his algebra students appreciate the value of being able to use permutation and combination formulas efficiently, they will be more receptive to achieving the cognitive objectives of his unit on those topics. Thus, his initial objective for the unit is the following:

Recognize the advantage of being able to use the following formulas in problem-solving situations:

$$_nP_r = (n!)/((n - r)!)$$

$$_nC_r = (n!)/((n - r)!r!$$

(*appreciation*)
In an attempt to achieve the objective, he tells the class: "Today, people, we're going to begin studying about

permutations and combinations. We need to learn about permutations and combinations so that we can extend our abilities to solve probability problems. Now, I know you enjoy working with probabilities because solving probability problems helps us make critical decisions in our lives.

"Well, once you understand how to use permutations and combinations, you'll be able to solve some really neat probability problems that'll actually make a difference in your own lives. You're going to enjoy this first activity. First, think about how many ways you can arrange . . . "

In general, students do not learn to appreciate something by being told what they enjoy and will find important (Cangelosi, 1993, pp. 94–98, 144–149). Rather than wasting time with lip service for his appreciation-level objective, Mr. Shaver should integrate learning activities for the appreciation objective into lessons for his cognitive objectives so that the following occur:

1. *The first few examples used to introduce the content involve situations in which most students have already demonstrated an interest.* Questions such as those listed in Exhibit 2.2 can get students' attention and entice them into the study of mathematics.
2. *Initially, tasks to which the mathematical content is applied are selected so that the value of the new concept, relationship, information, expression, message, or algorithm is readily demonstrated.* For example, if the content is the formula for computing rectangular areas ($A = l \times w$), then which one of the following tasks would better demonstrate the advantage of having such a formula?

- Find the area of the following rectangle:

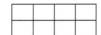

- Find the area of the following rectangle:

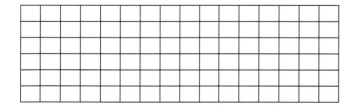

It is just as easy to count the unit squares to find the area of a 4-by-2 rectangle as it is to use the area formula. The value of the formula is apparent for the task of finding the area of the 16-by-6 rectangle, since, with the formula, students need to count only the number of unit squares on two edges rather than all 96 cells.

Similarly, the value of the quadratic formula is demonstrated with the second rather than the first of the following two tasks; the first equation is more easily solved via factoring:

- Find the real roots of the following equation:

$$x^2 - 4x = 21$$

- Find the real roots of the following equation:

$$15x^2 - 7x = 2$$

3. *Whenever the unit's learning goal requires the introduction of a new concept or relationship, students construct the concept or discover the relationship for themselves.* These levels of learning have the added benefit of developing in students a feeling of ownership in the mathematical content. Ms. Citorolli's students in Cases 1.7 1.10 are more likely to appreciate arithmetic sequences than students who were simply told about them. Similarly, when Ms. Smith's students work with rate relationships, they'll be working with mathematics they discovered themselves.

Note how learning activities for an appreciation objective are integrated with lessons for a cognitive objective in Case 6.10.

CASE 6.10

The first few lessons of Mr. Polonia's unit on permutations and combinations include learning activities designed to help his algebra students achieve three objectives:

1. Recognize the advantage of being able to use the following formulas in problem-solving situations:

$$_nP_r = (n!)/((n-r)!)$$
$$_nC_r = (n!)/((n-r)!r!)$$

(*appreciation*)
2. Discriminate between examples and nonexamples of each of the following two concepts: permutations and combinations.   (*construct a concept*)
3. Explain why each of the following relationships hold:

$$_nP_r = (n!)/((n-r)!)$$
$$_nC_r = (n!)/((n-r)!r!)$$

(*discover a relationship*)

Mr. Polonia begins the first learning activity by telling the class: "Over the past two weeks, I've kept notes on comments I've overheard students make. Here, I'll show you five of them. I won't tell you who said what, but you may recognize your own words in one."

He reads each as he displays the following on the board:

- Did you notice that at the [school] dances, they never play two slow songs in a row? I think they're afraid of too much close dancing.
- One of us is bound to win the drawing; they pick five winners!
- Almost every time a teacher picks a group to do something, there are more nonblacks than blacks—like Johnson today, he picked me and two whites to supervise the drawing.
- Ms. Simmons has never chosen one of my poems for the newspaper.
- You ought to try the lunch room; there'll always be at least one thing you like.

Mr. Polonia continues: "Tomorrow, we will divide up into small collaborative groups with each group assigned to analyze one of these statements for implications and causes. Let's take one now to show you what you'll be doing." He displays the following:

> Almost every time a teacher picks a group to do something, there are more nonblacks than blacks—like Johnson today, he picked me and two whites to supervise the drawing.

Mr. Polonia: This statement hints at the possibility of racial bias influencing teachers' selection of student groups and committees. How might we examine the validity of that suggestion?

Theresa: We could keep a record of groups that teachers select over the next month or so and see how often blacks are in the minority.

Tracy: And if blacks are in the minority most of the time, then that would show bias.

Eva: I don't think so.

Tracy: Why not?

Eva: We African Americans are a minority in the school, so you expect most of the groups would have more nonblacks.

Milton: I think it's because the teachers always want to have one black in a group, so they have to spread us out in all the groups.

Mr. Polonia: How often would groups have blacks students in the majority if the teachers never considered color when they picked groups?

Don: That's impossible. A few teachers are out-and-out prejudiced, but the others bend over backwards to show they're not.

Mr. Polonia: Maybe so, but if we figured what the numbers would be if the choices were never biased, then we'd have something to compare with the actual choices. Theresa suggests we keep a record.

Tracy: Well, if there were no bias, then the percentage of groups with a majority of African-American students should equal the percentage of African-American students in school.

Mr. Polonia: Okay, in this class we have 9 black students and 15 nonblack students. That's . . .

Eva: Nine out of 24 is 37.5 percent.

Tracy: So, 37.5 percent of the groups in this class ought to have an African-American majority and the other . . .

Eva: 62.5 percent . . .

Tracy: The other 62.5 percent should have an African-American minority.

Estelle: I don't think it's that simple because . . .

After a few more minutes, Mr. Polonia calls a halt to the discussion and directs the students as follows: "I would like for us to continue to work on this problem, but to move us toward developing a model, let's limit the situation for now to selecting groups of three people each from this class. Remember 9 of us are black and 15 are nonblack. The question is, if there is no bias in the selection of a group of three, what are the chances that either two or three of the three will be black? What's the first thing we need to do to figure that chance?

Eva: Make a sample space.

Mr. Polonia: The sample space for this problem might be quite long. So, for homework let's divide up the work by having each of you list all possible groups of three from the class of which you yourself are a member. Tomorrow, we'll eliminate the duplications, combine the rest, and voilá! We'll have our sample space.

After further clarification of the assignment, the students begin the task, returning the next day to learn that there are many more possible groups of three than they had expected—2,024 in all. In class they complete the arduous task of counting the number of groups for each relevant category and to the surprise of most, discover the following:

> Four percent of the groups are all black, 27 percent contain 2 blacks and 1 nonblack, 47 percent contain 2 nonblacks and 1 black, and 22 percent contain all nonblacks.

Thus, they conclude that under the no-bias supposition, 31 percent of the time a group of three would have a black majority. After further discussion regarding the implication of their findings—that is, how much above or below the 31 percent figure should be tolerated before the figures are indicative of bias, Mr. Polonia directs their attention to the process by which they obtained the 31 percent figure. All agree that the process was quite tedious and that they should search for easier ways.

From work with other examples, Mr. Polonia leads the students over the next few days to construct the concepts of permutations and combinations, and to discover relationships on which they base algorithms they invent for computing them.

Because Mr. Polonia was concerned with the appreciation objective as well as his cognitive objectives, he carefully chose initial examples that would get students' attention. Once he had them working on a problem, the mathematical content to be taught (permutation and combination formulas) came as a welcome tool for making their work easier and more efficient.

Lessons for Willingness to Try Objectives

Even though students have learned to appreciate certain mathematical content, they still may not attempt to work vigorously with it because they lack confidence that they will use it successfully in situations they find meaningful. Until they have accumulated successful experiences in using mathematics, they tend to be reluctant to pursue problem solutions, as did Mr. Polonia's students in Case 6.10 and Brenda in Case 3.1.

Willingness to try objectives, such as the following one, require learning activities similar to appreciation objectives:

> Attempt to (a) solve problems involving permutations and combinations, and (b) discover models that facilitate efficient solutions to such problems. (*willingness to try*)

But to take students that one extra affective level from appreciation to willingness to try, you must select problem tasks that are interesting enough to maintain their attention and yet easy enough for them to experience success. Keep the following in mind:

- *Until students gain confidence in their problem-solving abilities and in the benefits of working on perplexing mathematical tasks, most of the mathematical tasks you assign them should be such that they will feel successful before becoming frustrated.* As their confidence builds, you gradually work in more perplexing and challenging tasks.
- *The more a task relates to what already interests students, the more students tend to tolerate perplexity before giving up.* It is quite a challenge for you to have to judge that fine line between interest and frustration.
- *Achievement of willingness to try objectives requires a learning environment in which students feel free to experiment, question, hypothesize, and make errors without fear of ridicule, embarrassment, or loss of status.* Chapter 8 includes suggestions to help you create such an environment in your classroom.
- *By presenting students with problems requiring application of previously acquired mathematical skills and abilities, students not only maintain and improve earlier achievements, they are also provided with additional opportunities to succeed with mathematics.* The four-stage application lessons ensure that students are confronted with problems to which the content of the objective applies, as well as problems to which content from previously achieved objectives is applicable. Thus, application lessons afford students experiences

with success by including activities in which they apply previously learned mathematics.

Engage in Activity 6.6.

_____ **ACTIVITY 6.6** _____

Purpose: To expand your insights regarding how to design lessons for affective objectives.

Procedure: When you engaged in Activities 4.4 and 4.6, you designed a lesson for a construct a concept objective and a lesson for a discover a concept lesson. Retrieve your plan for one of those lessons. Now, design a lesson for an affective objective that you can integrate into the lesson for that construct a concept or discover a relationship lesson.

Exchange your integrated lesson plans with a colleague who is also engaging in Activity 6.6. Critique one another's work.

INDICATORS OF ACHIEVEMENT OF AFFECTIVE OBJECTIVES

A Matter of Choice, Not Ability or Skill

An item is relevant to achievement of a cognitive objective when students who have achieved that objective can perform the task presented by the item with a higher success rate than those who have not achieved the objective. On the other hand, affective objectives are not concerned with students being able to do anything. Achievement of an appreciation objective is the acquisition of a belief in the value of something. Achievement of a willingness to act objective is the acquisition of a tendency to attempt something.

The scoring key for an affective item does not address whether or not students' responses indicate that they *can* perform the task presented, but rather how they *choose* to respond to the task. Consider the problem of designing an item for the following objective:

> Attempt to formulate algebraic open sentences themselves when solving word problems before turning to others for help to set up the sentence for them. (*willingness to try*)

To be relevant to this objective, an item must present students not with the task of formulating an open sentence for a word problem, but instead with the task of choosing between attempting to formulate open sentences themselves or having it done for them.

The Self-Report Approach

One option is to use the *self-report* approach and simply ask students what they would do. Here's an example of an item for the aforementioned objective based on that approach:

Task Presented to the Student

Multiple choice: Suppose that while thumbing through a magazine, you came across one of those brain-teaser type sections in which there was a mathematical word problem to solve. You read the problem and think that with some effort you might be able to solve it by setting up an algebraic equation. You are not sure if you can solve it, but there is a note telling you that a solution is worked out on another page of the magazine. Which one of the following actions are you most likely to take?

A. Work on the problems yourself until you come up with a solution. Only after you come up with the solution do you check with the one given on the other page.
B. You go directly to the solution on the other page rather than try to solve the problem yourself.
C. You neither try to solve the problem yourself nor look at the solution on the other page.
D. You see if it is a kind of problem you already know how to solve; if it is, you solve it yourself before checking with the other page. If it isn't one you know how to solve, you don't pay any more attention to the problem.
E. You see if it is a kind of problem you know how to solve; if it is, you solve it yourself before checking with the other page. If it isn't one you know how to solve, you don't try to solve it but check with the other page to learn how.
F. You attempt to solve it yourself before checking with the other page. However, if after about five minutes you don't make much progress, you find out how to solve it from the other page.

    Scoring Key: 3 points maximum scored according to the following: +3 for selecting A; +2 for selecting F; +1 for selecting D or E; +0 for B or C.

The value of the self-report approach is limited to situations in which students are confident that they risk nothing by answering honestly. Fortunately, you may want to measure your students' achievement of affective objectives only for formative feedback, not for summative evaluations. Assessments of both their progress relative to appreciating mathematics and willingness to do mathematics provides you with critical formative feedback for regulating lessons. However, you may be well advised to base grades only on evaluation of their cognitive mathematical achievements.

The Direct Observational Approach

An alternative to self-reporting is directly observing students' behaviors in situations where they are free to make choices that reflect appreciation or willingness to try. Here, for example, is an item designed to measure the same willingness to try objective as the previous multiple-choice item:

Description of the Task Presented to One Student at a Time

Computer-Administered Item: From a bank of word problems, the teacher selects one that she or he believes the student is capable of solving with some degree of effort (where the equation to formulate isn't immediately obvious). The word problem is presented on the computer screen to the student with the following instructions:

    Enter an algebraic equation for solving the given problem. First label the variable. You may request help in setting up the equation anytime in the process by typing HELP to access HELP MODE. After you've received help, the computer will automatically return you to SOLUTION MODE, but you can return to HELP MODE by again typing HELP. Good luck!

    Scoring Key: The teacher observes the student at work, recording the number of seconds spent in SOLUTION MODE and the number of seconds spent in HELP MODE (Exhibit 6.9). The score for the item is $S \div H$, where S = the number of seconds in SOLUTION MODE and H = the number of seconds in HELP MODE.

Engage in Activity 6.7.

─────────────── **ACTIVITY 6.7** ───────────────

Purpose: To expand your insights regarding how to design items for affective objectives.

Procedure: Design a measurement item that you would use as an indicator of students' achievement relative to the objective for which you design a lesson when you engaged in Activity 6.6.

    Exchange your item with colleagues who are also engaging in this activity. Critique and discuss one another's items.

TRANSITIONAL ACTIVITIES FROM CHAPTER 6 TO CHAPTER 7

1. Select the response to each of the following multiple-choice items that either completes the statement so that it is true or accurately answers the question:
   A. With which one of the following do students usually have to deal when solving real-life problems, but not when solving textbook word problems?
      (a) Identify variables and solve for variables
      (b) Identify relationships
      (c) Remember and execute algorithms
      (d) Distinguish between relevant and irrelevant data

Exhibit 6.9
Measuring affective objectives via computer-administered items.

B. Which one of the following do students usually have to determine in order to solve textbook word problems?
   (a) The variable to be solved as indicated by the question given in the problem
   (b) The implications of the solution outcome
   (c) What measurements to make
   (d) Whether or not mathematics should be used to solve the problem

C. Learning activities for which one of the following types of objectives are *least* likely to be effectively integrated into lessons for other types of objectives?
   (a) Willingness to try
   (b) Creativity
   (c) Algorithmic skill
   (d) Appreciation

D. Which one of the following strategies is *least* likely to enhance students' achievement of an appreciation objective?
   (a) Students use the objective's content to solve problems that concern them.
   (b) The teacher tells students how important understanding the content will be to them.
   (c) The teacher demonstrates that use of the content can save time.
   (d) Students discover and invent mathematics for themselves.

E. Student perplexity is a critical ingredient in lessons for all *but* which one of the following types of objectives?

   (a) Creativity
   (b) Application
   (c) Algorithmic skill
   (d) Discover a relationship
   (e) Construct a concept

F. Lessons for application objectives require _____.
   (a) direct instruction
   (b) deductive learning activities
   (c) inductive learning activities
   (d) use of mnemonics

G. Synectics is used in learning activities for what type of objective?
   (a) Simple knowledge
   (b) Algorithmic skill
   (c) Application
   (d) Creativity
   (e) Appreciation

H. Students utilize syllogisms during _____ lessons.
   (a) construct a concept
   (b) application
   (c) direct instructional
   (d) creativity

Compare your responses to the following: A-d; B-a; C-c; D-b; E-c; F-b; G-d; H-b.

2. Reexamine the objectives listed in Exhibit 3.9. Although the wording of the objectives does not totally communicate exactly what the teachers had in mind (the learning levels aren't labeled), infer the teachers' intentions by analyzing each objective

to determine if the learning level is (a) application, (b) creativity, (c) appreciation, (d) willingness to try, or (e) other than one of those four.

After completing this task, compare your responses to the following; however, keep in mind that differences may be due to ambiguities in the phrasing of the objectives: The following appear to be application objectives: H of Unit I; H of Unit II; D and G of Unit III; I of Unit IV; F of Unit V; and H of Unit VI. Objective I of Unit I and Objectives F and G of Unit IV appear to be creativity objectives. Objectives D of Unit IV and I of Unit VI appear to be at the appreciation learning level. Objectives B of Unit II and E of Unit VI appear to be at the willingness to try level.

3. Discuss the following questions with two or more of your colleagues:

   a. In Case 1.2, Case 2.2, Case 2.4, Case 3.3, Case 3.5, Case 3.6, Case 4.7, Case 4.12, Case 4.13, Case 5.10, Case 6.2, Case 6.3, Case 6.8, and Case 6.10, students are led to do meaningful mathematics with learning activities the teachers designed themselves and which extend beyond what's available in typical school mathematics textbooks. What do teachers like these use for sources of ideas on teaching mathematics?

   b. Quite a few teachers in the above cases depended on overhead projectors during large group presentations and during question and discussion sessions. Isn't there technology available that generates higher quality displays than what is possible with overhead projectors?

   c. What technologies are available to help teachers produce lesson plans and accompanying task sheets?

   d. What materials and supplies do teachers need to have on hand for learning activities that lead students to do meaningful mathematics?

   e. What about graphing calculators, computer software, video and laser technology, and various types of networks? How available are they and how should they be incorporated into mathematics curricula?

   f. What should teachers think about when arranging and organizing their classrooms? How does the use of technology and cooperative learning affect how classrooms should be organized and laid out?

   g. How can teachers take advantage of professional associations like NCTM to improve mathematics curricula and their own teaching performance?

Resources and Technology for Teaching Mathematics

This chapter provides an overview of resources and technologies to help you lead students to do meaningful mathematics as suggested in Chapters 4 through 6. In particular, Chapter 7 is designed to help you:

1. Describe a variety of resources (including professional organizations, inservice educational opportunities, and literature) for stimulating ideas on teaching mathematics and learning about mathematics and its historical origins. (*comprehension*)
2. Describe a variety of mathematics curriculum materials typically available for use in secondary and middle schools. (*comprehension*)

3. Develop your own strategies for incorporating various technologies (eg., computer, calculator, video and audio, multimedia, and network) and curriculum materials (eg., textbooks) into your teaching so as to enhance learning activities and the efficiency with which you organize and prepare for instruction. (*application*)
4. Explain the relative advantages and disadvantages of different ways of organizing and arranging your classroom. (*comprehension*)

SELECTION AND USE OF TEXTBOOKS

You, of course, are the person ultimately responsible for designing, developing, and organizing the mathematics curricula for the students assigned to you. Plan to draw your ideas from many sources including other teachers, instructional supervisors, professional journals such as *Mathematics Teacher* and *Mathematics Teaching in the Middle School,* inservice conferences and workshops, college or university courses, teacher resource manuals, trade books, magazines, television and video programs, computer networks and technology-based information systems, reference books, textbooks and accompanying supplements for teachers, and personal experiences. The availability, dependability, quality, and sophistication of these sources vary considerably depending on where you teach and how assertive and resourceful you are in seeking them out and taking advantage of them. Not necessarily the most useful, but

surely the one that is standard virtually anywhere you teach is an adopted mathematics textbook.

In some school districts a single publisher's textbook series, with a volume for each course, may be adopted either school-wide or district-wide. In other school districts, textbook-adoption policies may allow textbooks to be considered on a course-by-course basis so that texts for different mathematics courses might be drawn from a variety of publishers.

For each set of student textbooks for a course, there is typically a special edition of the book for teachers that includes margin notes, answers to exercises, and addenda as an aid in the designing and planning of instruction (see Exhibit 7.1). A variety of ancillary materials for teachers is also available from most publishers; these include such items as bulletin board displays, overhead transparencies, black-line masters for making transparencies, chapter tests, test-item pools (sometimes on computer disks), scope and sequence charts for planning a course using the textbook, and lists of instructional materials for use with the texts including audiovisuals, concrete manipulatives and models, and computer software packages.

The degree of control you can exercise regarding the selection of textbooks for your courses varies considerably depending on your school situation. Typically, selections are from a state-adopted list of approved textbooks. Some districts depend on panels of mathematics teachers and school administrators to select mathematics textbooks for all the schools in the district. In other districts, the selections are done at the school level, usually by Mathematics Department faculty members. Of course, options for new texts are hardly available until existing texts are worn out or clearly out of date. In many situations, teachers are required to live with whatever textbooks that have been adopted for them.

When selecting a mathematics textbook, the following questions should be raised:

- *How well do the book's topics match those specified by relevant curriculum guidelines—including the ones you're supposed to follow at your school—and the ones you have listed for your teaching units?* It is not a drawback for the text to include topics you do not plan to include in your teaching units as long as the text's treatment of topics you do include is not dependent on book topics you exclude. Including topics in your units that are not dealt with in the text can be inconvenient.

- *Does the text provide high-quality exercises relevant to the learning objectives you want your students to achieve?* More than anything else, textbooks provide teachers with an abundance of exercises for students to practice. Traditionally, the preponderance of textbook exercises are of the skill-level variety. Even most textbook word problems require only algorithmic skills once the wording is deciphered and comprehended.

- *How accurate is the mathematics presented in the text?* Virtually all textbooks contain a few misprints and report a few incorrect computational results. Sometimes such mistakes provoke healthy discussions that enhance rather than detract from learning. However, conceptual errors or mathematical treatises that conflict with what you want your students to learn can hinder your lessons. For example, many algebra books define a *variable* as "a letter that stands for a number." If you take that definition literally—and I assume you want your students to take mathematical definitions literally—then interest rates, age, speed, time, shape, set, location, length, number of, angle, angle measure, and all the other variables we deal with in problem solving are not variables. These texts say a variable is a *letter*—not what the letter stands for, but the letter itself! Such a restrictive definition precludes connections of mathematics with real-life situations. Furthermore, in the language of a rigorous mathematical system, arithmetic and

Exhibit 7.1
A variety of ancillary instructional materials are available from most textbook publishers.

algebraic operations such as addition ($+$) are defined on numbers, not letters. Set theory operations such as intersection ($\cap$) are defined for sets, not letters. Consequently, you need to consider the conceptual treatment of key topics such as variables, functions, and measurement before adopting a textbook.

- *How readily can the textbook be used with the technology of your choice, especially graphing calculators and computers?* Most textbooks published since the NCTM *Standards* provide some attention to calculator-based and computer-based activities. Unfortunately, in many texts the technology-based activities are clearly token inserts presented in addition to the "real mathematical" topics of the chapter. Fortunately, there's a trend to publish textbooks that actually integrate the use of technology in the treatise of mathematical topics, not just have them as an extra add-on. Exhibit 7.2 displays an example of a "Graphic Calculator Exploration" exercise from a textbook chapter on systems of equations and inequalities. Exhibit 7.3 is a computer-based exercise from that same chapter.

- *How consistent are the book's organization and presentations with research-based teaching and learning principles like those suggested by the NCTM Standards?* Few if any mathematics textbooks are written in accordance with research-based teaching and learning principles like those suggested in Chapters 4 through 6. Thus, you can expect to have to organize your lessons somewhat differently from your textbook's presentations. However, it would be convenient to use a text that is in harmony with teaching strategies you employ. In the supplemental materials accompanying textbooks, most publishers now include a cross-reference list of entries in the texts to the NCTM *Standards*. In further response to the *Standards,* suggestions for attending to cooperative learning, problem solving, connections among mathematical subdisciplines (for example, algebra and geometry), use of calculators, use of computers, alternative assessments, multicultural considerations, and use in "gifted and talented" programs are also commonly inserted into teacher supplements.

- *How readable is the textbook for your students? Will they understand the explanations?* Typically, students do not read explanations in mathematics textbooks. Generally, they read only examples and exercises (Cangelosi, 1985). However the need for students to read about mathematics is well publicized (NCTM, 1989).

- *How practical and helpful are the supplements for teachers?* Will they really provide a high-quality service to professional mathematics teachers like yourself, or are they just gimmicks to make the textbooks more appealing to school administrators and textbook adoption boards?

- *How much does the textbook cost?* Cost factors may or may not be critical, depending on the particular textbook-acquisition arrangement under which your school administrators work.

- *How attractively packaged is the text?* The text's aesthetic appeal (such as, colorful pictures and clever use of white space) may influence the amount of time your students spend with the book. Be careful, however, that you don't let an appealing package obscure substantive factors (such as accuracy of the mathematics).

Engage in Activity 7.1.

_____ **ACTIVITY 7.1** _____

Purpose: To increase your familiarity with current secondary and middle school mathematics textbooks and to develop your ability to critique texts.

Procedure: Obtain two mathematics textbooks currently being used in secondary or middle schools. If reasonably possible, select two competing texts from different publishers that are intended to be used for the same course. Current school textbooks are available for checkout at many college and university curriculum libraries for teaching majors. Also, you may be able to borrow texts from local schools.

Compare the two textbooks with regard to each of the questions raised above.

Exchange your comparative critiques of the textbooks with those of colleagues who are engaging in Activity 7.1. Discuss the features of the textbooks and how you might incorporate them in your teaching.

When choosing a school in which to practice your profession, you should assess the availability of resources and the degree to which you and other teachers exercise control over those resources, as well as the selection of textbooks and other learning materials.

SOURCES OF IDEAS ON MATHEMATICS AND TEACHING MATHEMATICS

Colleagues

Preservice teacher preparation programs provide beginning teachers with necessary, but insufficient, competencies to be successful inservice teachers. Your effectiveness as a mathematics teacher depends on how well you develop those competencies on the job as a professional inservice teacher (Duke, Cangelosi, & Knight, 1988). To be consistently effective, especially in the first few years of your career, you need support, guidance, and feedback as you

Exhibit 7.2
A calculator-based exercise from an Algebra II textbook.

Graphing Calculator Exploration: Graphing Systems of Equations

You can use a graphing calculator to graph and solve systems of equations, since several equations can be graphed on the screen at the same time. If the system of equations has a solution, it is located where the graphs intersect. The coordinates of this intersection point, (x, y), can be determined by using the trace function.

Graph the system of equations $y = -5.01x + 3.12$ and $y = 3.78x - 2.56$ on the standard viewing window.

Casio

ENTER: [GRAPH] [(-)] 5.01 [ALPHA] [X] [+] 3.12 [:] [GRAPH] 3.78 [ALPHA]
[X] [−] 2.56 [EXE]

TI-81

ENTER: [Y=] [(-)] 5.01 [X|T] [+] 3.12 [ENTER] 3.78 [X|T] [−] 2.56 [GRAPH]

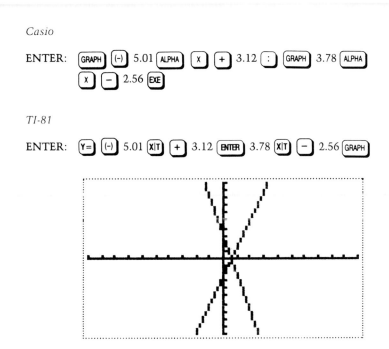

Now use the trace function to determine the coordinates of the intersection point.

Casio   *TI-81*

ENTER: [SHIFT] [TRACE]   ENTER: [TRACE]

The trace function on the Casio accesses the last function graphed, while the TI-81 allows you to access any of the functions by pressing the up or down arrow keys. Use the arrow keys to move the cursor along one of the functions to the intersection point and determine the coordinates of the point.

Exhibit 7.2
Continued

The "zoom-in" feature of the calculator is very useful for determining the coordinates of the intersection point with greater accuracy. Begin by setting the cursor on the intersection point and observing the coordinates of this point. Then zoom-in and place the cursor on the intersection point again. Any digits that are unchanged since the last trace are accurate. Repeat this process of zooming-in and checking digits until you have the number of accurate digits that you desire.

To zoom-in on the Casio, return to the text screen and insert a factor command before the original function. This will reduce each range value by the factor entered.

Casio

ENTER: [G↔T] [⇒] [SHIFT] [INS] [SHIFT] [Factor] 10 [:] [EXE]

Once the lines have been replotted, trace to the intersection point again and check the coordinates. If you need to zoom-in again, simply press [G↔T] and [EXE] .

To zoom-in on the TI-81, use the [ZOOM] key and set the factors to 10. This will reduce the values in the range setting by a factor of 10.

TI-81

ENTER: [ZOOM] 4 10 [ENTER] 10 [ZOOM] 2 [ENTER]

Now, trace to the point of intersection again and check the coordinates. If you need to zoom-in again, press [ZOOM] 2 and [ENTER] .

This process determines that the x- and y-coordinates of the intersection point of the system $y = -5.01x + 3.12$ and $y = 3.78x - 2.56$ are (0.646188, -0.117406), accurate to six digits. You will need to zoom-in about six times to obtain this degree of accuracy.

You can also graph systems of inequalities on a TI-81 graphing calculator. Prepare to graph by resetting the range values to the standard viewing window. Then clear any functions from the Y= list. Do this by pressing [Y=] and then using the arrow keys and the CLEAR key to select and clear all functions. Next, return to the home screen by pressing [2nd] and then [QUIT] .

Let's graph the system of inequalities $y \geq x + 3$ and $y \leq -2x - 1$.

Exhibit 7.2
Continued

We will graph the system of inequalities with the **Shade** function. It graphs functions and shades above the first function entered and below the second function entered. The "greater than or equal to" symbol in $y \geq x + 3$, indicates that values on the line and above the line $y = x + 3$ will satisfy the inequality. Similarly, the "less than or equal to" in $y \leq -2x - 1$ indicates that values on the line and below the line $y = -2x - 1$ will satisfy the inequality. Therefore, the function $y = x + 3$ will be entered first and $y = -2x - 1$ will be entered second.

TI-81

ENTER: 2nd DRAW 7 X|T + 3 ALPHA , (-) 2 X|T - 1) ENTER

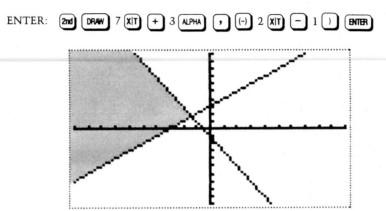

The shaded area indicates points which will satisfy the system of inequalities $y \geq x + 3$ and $y \leq -2x - 1$.

Before you graph another system of inequalities, you must clear the graphics screen.

TI-81

ENTER: 2nd DRAW 1 ENTER   *Clears the graphics screen.*

Example

Graph the system of inequalities $\begin{cases} y \leq 0.5x - 2 \\ y \geq -4x + 1 \end{cases}$.

Values below the line $y = 0.5x - 2$ will satisfy the inequality $y \leq 0.5x - 2$.

Values above the line $y = -4x + 1$ will satisfy the inequality $y \geq -4x + 1$.

So, we will enter the function $y = -4x + 1$ first and the function $y = 0.5x - 2$ second.

Exhibit 7.2
Continued

ENTER:  7 (-) 4  + 1 ALPHA , 0.5

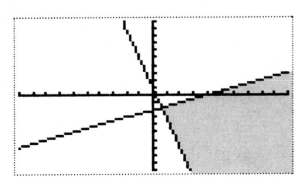

The points in the shaded area satisfy both $y \leq 0.5x - 2$ and $y \geq -4x + 1$.

EXERCISES

Use your graphing calculator to solve the following systems of equations by graphing. Determine the x- and y-coordinates accurate to six decimal places.

1. $y = 1.236x - 1.0825$
   $y = 0.7896x + 5.1783$

2. $y = 2.5x - 3$
   $y = -1.8x + 2$

3. $2.1x + 3.2y = 4.3$
   $1.4x - 1.8y = 1.6$

4. $3.12x + 4.68y = 5$
   $-4.38x + 9.21y = 1.6$

5. $y = 8x + 1.27$
   $y = -5x - 3.61$

6. $y = 2.345x + 1$
   $y = 0.8765x - 3$

If you have a TI-81 graphing calculator, graph each system of inequalities and sketch the graph.

7. $y \geq x$
   $y \leq 3$

8. $y \geq 5x$
   $y \leq 8x$

9. $y \leq 4x - 2$
   $y \geq 0.5x$

10. $y \leq -0.1x - 5$
    $y \geq 0.2x - 5$

11. $y \geq 5 - x$
    $y \leq 0.8x - 7$

12. $y \geq 12 - 4x$
    $y \leq -3x + 9$

13. $y \geq 3x + 0.5$
    $y \leq -6x - 2.8$

14. $12x + 6y \geq 12$
    $y \leq x$

Exhibit 7.3
A Computer-based exercise from an Algebra II textbook.

Technology

▶ BASIC
Spreadsheets
Software

Solving Systems of Equations

You have studied several ways to solve a system of equations. You can also use the BASIC program below to solve a system of two equations. It gives one of three outputs: the ordered pair solution, a message saying there are infinitely many solutions, or a message saying there is no solution. The ordered pair solution is the ordered pair that satisfies both equations. The second response tells you that the two equations are equivalent and there are an infinite number of solutions that satisfy both equations. The third response states that there are no ordered pairs that satisfy both equations.

The BASIC program requires you to first write each equation of the system in standard form. The first equation will be named $Ax + By = C$ and the second equation will be named $Dx + Ey = F$. The program will ask you to enter the values for A, B, and C and then for D, E, and F.

```
100  PRINT "ENTER A, B, AND C FOR THE EQUATION AX + BY = C."
110  INPUT A,B,C
120  PRINT "ENTER D, E, AND F FOR THE EQUATION DX + EY = F."
130  INPUT D,E,F
140  IF A*E = B*D GOTO 190
150  X = (C*E-F*B)/(A*E-B*D)
160  Y = (A*F-D*C)/(A*E-B*D)
170  PRINT "(";X;",";Y;")"
180  GOTO 230
190  IF A*F=C*D GOTO 220
200  PRINT "THERE IS NO SOLUTION."
210  GOTO 230
220  PRINT "THERE ARE INFINITELY MANY SOLUTIONS."
230  END
```

To run the program, type RUN and then hit the enter key. Enter each value requested when a question mark appears.

EXERCISES

Use the BASIC program to determine what type of solution each system of equations has. If it has a unique solution, state it.

1. $x + 3y = 6$	**2.** $3x - y = 1$	**3.** $x - 5y = 2$
$2x + 6y = 24$	$-6x + 2y = -2$	$-2x + 10y = 4$
4. $x + 4y = 2$	**5.** $3x - 6y = 12$	**6.** $9x + 3y = 9$
$-x + y = -7$	$2x + 3y = 1$	$3x + y = 3$

develop curricula, design and conduct lessons, manage students, and assess achievement (Cangelosi, 1991, pp. xi–xii, 121–173; Evans, 1989).

Research findings in the area of instructional supervision suggest that the most useful means of stimulating ideas on teaching involve interactions among teachers. Visiting one another's classrooms (Allen, Davidson, Hering, & Jesunathadas, 1984), peer coaching (Chase & Wolfe, 1989; Chrisco, 1989; Raney & Robbins, 1989), colleague mentoring (Duke, Cangelosi, & Knight, 1988), sharing responsibilities for students (Cangelosi, 1993, pp. 131–135, 211–215), and think sessions are invaluable ways for you to learn from other teachers as they learn from you (as you'll note Casey Rudd does when you read Chapter 11).

Some schools have established systems whereby the school week is structured so that teachers have time to work with one another, engage in joint planning, collaborate on developing integrated curricula, and participate in workshops. In other schools such collegial efforts occur only when individual teachers initiate their own informal networks. Unfortunately, teaching becomes a solitary art in some schools with climates that discourage collegiality.

In many geographic areas, collaborative networks of mathematics teachers have been established with support of funding agencies (e.g., through Eisenhower projects and the National Science Foundation); the networks provide a means for mathematics teachers from different schools and school districts to interact, share ideas, and provide assistance to one another. The *Mathematics Teacher Network* in northern Utah (Wilford, 1993) is one such network.

The National Council of Teachers of Mathematics and Other Professional Organizations

Besides supporting teachers' causes, professional organizations such as, NCTM; National Education Association (NEA); Mathematical Association of America (MAA); and American Federation of Teachers (AFT), provide forums for idea sharing and resource materials in the form of journals, books, pamphlets, video programs, and computer software. If you are not already a member, you should make a copy of Exhibit 7.4 and join NCTM. Membership benefits include:

1. A subscription to your choice of *one* of the following journals:

   Mathematics Teacher. Published nine times a year, it contains articles (see Appendix B and Exhibits 3.5 and 3.6) specifically for the purpose of providing secondary school mathematics teachers with practical ideas they can implement in their classrooms.

Exhibit 7.4
NCTM membership application.

NCTM Membership Invitation

❏ Yes! I want to enjoy the benefits of NCTM membership. Please send my Welcome Kit and the journal I've indicated right away.

Name _____
School _____
Address _____
City _____
State/Province _____ Zip/Postal Code _____
Work Phone [___] _____ Home Phone [___] _____

1. Type of membership:
   ❏ Individual $45.00   ❏ Student $22.50

2. Choice of journal(s): One subscription comes with NCTM membership, additional subscriptions are $15 each for individual members and $7.50 for students. Please check one or more choices.
   ❏ *Teaching Children Mathematics* (9 issues)
   ❏ *Mathematics Teacher* (9 issues)
   ❏ *Mathematics Teaching in the Middle School* (4 issues)
   ❏ *Journal for Research in Mathematics Education* (5 issues)

3. Payment:
   NCTM membership $_____
   + Add'l. subscriptions $_____
   + Foreign postage* $_____
   = Total enclosed $_____

*Outside the U.S., add $8.00 for first journal and $4.00 for each additional journal. Canadians enter "U.S." after the amount in your personal checks.

I've enclosed:
   ❏ Check/money order payable to NCTM
   ❏ Mastercard ❏ Visa
Credit card # _____
Card expires _____ Signature _____

Mail with payment to:
   NCTM
   1906 Association Drive
   Reston, VA 22091-1593
Or fax credit card orders to: (703) 476-2970
For faster service, call toll-free 1 (800) 235-7566

Source: Reprinted by permission from the National Council of Teachers of Mathematics.

Mathematics Teaching in the Middle School. Published four times a year, this is similar to *Mathematics Teacher* but focuses on the middle school level. Appendix D contains an example of one of its articles.

Teaching Children Mathematics. Published nine times a year, this is similar to the prior two journals but focuses on the elementary and pre-K school levels. Appendix E contains an example of one of its articles.

Journal for Research in Mathematics Education. Published five times a year, it reports research studies relevant to questions about teaching and learning mathematics.

Besides suggestions and ideas to implement in your classroom, the first three journals listed include newsworthy items and information relevant to professional mathematics teachers: (a) reviews of publications, software, manipulatives, and technology, (b) notices of professional conferences, and workshops, and (c) information on how to obtain instructional materials).

2. A subscription to *NCTM News Bulletin* (published six times a year) which reports on current events relevant to the mathematics teaching profession.
3. A discount on subscriptions to the three journals you did not select as part of your regular membership fee, as well as other publications such as NCTM *Yearbooks* and NCTM *Addenda Series*.
4. Opportunities to participate in national and regional NCTM conferences consisting of lectures, workshops, seminars, displays, business meetings, and exchanges of ideas among an international group of colleagues.
5. Ready means for acquiring and obtaining discounts on books, monographs, display materials, videotape programs, tests, manipulatives, computer software, and calculators relevant to professional development and your work with students.

Each state has an affiliate of the NCTM in which you should actively participate. Local district-, county-, or city-wide affiliates can also be of service to you and your colleagues. If one doesn't exist in your area, then organize one. To do so, contact your statewide affiliate or the NCTM headquarters in Reston, VA.

Other organizations, especially the MAA, coordinate many of their activities with NCTM's. MAA is particularly valuable to you if you teach at the college or university level.

Engage in Activity 7.2.

_____ **ACTIVITY 7.2** _____

Purpose: To increase your familiarity with *Mathematics Teacher* and *Mathematics Teaching in the Middle School,* to stimulate your ideas for designing lessons for your students, and to increase your understanding of what to expect from an NCTM conference.

Procedure: Examine at least three recent issues of *Mathematics Teacher* or *Mathematics Teaching in the Middle School.* Familiarize yourself with some of the journal's regular features such as the "Calendar" and "Technology Reviews". Read two articles and discuss them with colleagues.

Interview an inservice mathematics teacher or professor who attended a recent NCTM conference. Assess their impressions regarding what they gained from it. Compare your assessments to those of colleagues who interviewed others.

School-District Sponsored Resource Centers and Workshops

Most, but not all, public school district offices sponsor periodic inservice workshops for teachers. Outside consultants—a mathematics education specialist from a university or a mathematics teacher from another district—or teaching or district office professionals from within the district may present ideas about classroom management, alternative assessment, introduction of a new computer software package that the district has just made available to mathematics teachers, or integrating mathematics curricula with those of physical education and social studies. Many districts also maintain resource centers where teachers can borrow instructional materials, professional enrichment literature, computer software, equipment for classroom use, audiovisual materials, and mathematical manipulatives. School mathematics departments typically maintain their own collections of such materials for their teachers.

Colleges, Universities, Foundations, Research and Development Centers, and Government Agencies

Colleges and universities through regular on-campus programs, evening schools, summer schools, extension and outreach programs, and distance-education networks offer inservice and graduate-level courses for teachers. Mathematics courses and advanced mathematics teaching methods courses are typically included among the offerings.

Both government agencies and research and development centers such as the National Center for Research on Teacher Education in East Lansing, Michigan and Far West Laboratory in San Francisco are sources of professional enrichment materials. Foundations, including the National Science Foundation in Washington, DC, distribute reports and announcements on funded projects for inservice teacher education programs as well as curriculum and professional enhancement materials [see, *Mathematics Instructional Materials: Preschool - High School* (National Science Foundation, 1993)]. There are also opportunities for you to obtain funding for your own curriculum development, inservice education, or action-research projects through some of these agencies [*Eisenhower National Clearinghouse for Mathematics and Science Education: Guidebooks to Excellence: A Directory of Federal Resources for Mathematics and Science Education Improvement for the Far West Region* (U.S. Department of Education, 1994)]. NCTM journals and the *NCTM News Bulletin* keep their readers apprised of some of these opportunities.

Trade Books

Besides textbooks, commercial publishers also produce *trade books* on mathematics and the history of mathematics. Trade books, which are not specifically intended for use as textbooks, are particularly valuable to have on hand; they are generally more appealing than typical textbooks for students who want to read about mathematics. Compare, for example, the appeal of reading the chapter from *Beyond Numeracy: Ruminations of a Numbers Man* in Exhibit 5.6 to that of a typical chapter of a school mathematics textbook. Exhibit 7.5 includes a list of a minute subset of trade books currently available.

Engage in Activity 7.3.

_____ **ACTIVITY 7.3** _____

Purpose: To increase your understanding and appreciation of mathematical trade books and to stimulate your ideas for incorporating them in your teaching.

Procedure: Obtain copies of two of the books listed in Exhibit 7.5. Look over each book without reading it from cover to cover just to acquaint yourself with its contents and presentation of mathematics. Reading the preface may be a helpful way of starting to accomplish this. Select and read a chapter from each book.

Share what you learned from the books with colleagues and let them share what they learned from their selections with you. Discuss how you might incorporate such trade books in your mathematics curricula.

Books on Mathematics Teaching

Besides the book you are now reading, there are numerous publications addressing the complex question of how to teach mathematics. Furthermore, there are books filled with activities, exercises, and problems for you to consider when developing curricula, designing units, and planning lessons. Exhibit 7.6 includes a sample of such books.

Engage in Activity 7.4.

_____ **ACTIVITY 7.4** _____

Purpose: To further acquaint you with books that contain suggestions for teaching mathematics and that provide

sources for learning activities, problems, and exercises that you can incorporate in the lessons you design and conduct for your students.

Procedure: Obtain a copy of one of the books listed in Exhibit 7.6. Look it over without reading it from cover to cover just to acquaint yourself with its contents and how it might serve as a resource as you develop curricula and design units and lessons.

Share what you have learned from the book with colleagues and let them share what they learned from their selections with you.

HANDS-ON MANIPULATIVES AND CONCRETE MODELS

Learning activities in which students work with hands-on, concrete objects and models are common in mathematics lessons in the primary grades, but in the past they have been relatively rare at the secondary and middle school levels. Fortunately, the NCTM *Standards* have influenced secondary and middle school mathematics teachers to incorporate them in their lessons also. All students, even those in college and high school, need experience working with manipulatives and concrete models such as those pictured in Exhibit 7.7, particularly during construct-a-concept lessons and discover-a-relationship lessons. For virtually all mathematics concepts and relationships, students should work from hands-on concrete examples, to numerical examples, to pictorial representations, and finally to symbolic representations.

Once middle school, secondary school, college, and university teachers begin involving their students in hands-on activities with concrete objects, they tend to continue doing so. Students prefer these activities to more passive paper and pencil exercises, and consequently are more cooperative, appreciative, and easier to manage. However, manipulatives should not be selected only for the purpose of keeping students busy and entertained, as in Case 7.1.

CASE 7.1 _____

In the faculty lounge at the end of the school day, mathematics teachers Lottie Walker and Fred King have the following conversation:

Fred: How'd your day go?
Lottie: Fantastic! We worked with Möbius strips (Hoffman, 1988, pp. 108–121) in all my classes today. They had a ball, got some great discussions going! They were fascinated.
Fred: What's a Möbius strip?
Lottie: Here, I'll show you. See this strip of paper. I'll mark it

Exhibit 7.5
A small sample of available trade books on mathematics and the history of mathematics.

Barnsley, M. (1988). *Fractals everywhere.* Boston: Academic Press.

Barrow, J. D. (1992). *Pi in the sky: Counting thinking being.* Boston: Little, Brown.

Bell, E. T. (1965). *Men of mathematics.* New York: Simon and Schuster.

Beltrami, E. (1993). *Mathematical models in the social and biological sciences.* Boston: Jones and Bartlett.

Benjamin, A., & Shermer, M. B. (1993). *Mathemagics: How to look like a genius without really trying.* Los Angeles: Lowell House.

Bolt, B. (1992). *Mathematical calvacade.* New York: Cambridge University Press.

Bowers, J. (1988). *Invitation to mathematics.* New York: Basil Blackwell.

Boyer, C. G. (1991). *A history of mathematics* (2nd ed.). New York: John Wiley.

Cajori, F. (1985). *A history of mathematics* (4th ed.). New York: Chelsea Publishing.

Devaney, R. L. (1990). *Chaos, fractals, and dynamics: Computer experiments in mathematics.* Menlo Park, CA: Addison-Wesley.

Dunham, W. (1994). *The mathematical universe: An alphabetical journey through the great proofs, problems, and personalities.* New York: John Wiley.

Eves, H. (1983). *Great moments in mathematics before 1650.* Washington, D.C.: Mathematical Association of America.

Eves, H. (1983). *Great moments in mathematics after 1650.* Washington, D.C.: Mathematical Association of America.

Flato, M. (1990). *The power of mathematics.* New York: McGraw-Hill.

Gardner, M. (1969). *The unexpected hanging: And other mathematical diversions.* New York: Simon & Schuster.

Gibilisco, S. (1990). *Optical illusions: Puzzles, paradoxes, and brain teasers, #4.* Blue Ridge Summit, PA: Tab Books.

Hall, N. (Ed.). (1991). *Exploring chaos: A guide to the new science of disorder.* New York: W. W. Norton.

Hall, R. S. (1973). *About mathematics.* Englewood Cliffs, NJ: Prentice-Hall.

Hardy, G. H. (1992). *A mathematician's apology.* New York: Cambridge University Press.

Hoffman, P. (1988). *Archimedes' revenge: The joys and perils of mathematics.* New York: Fawcett Crest.

Hogben, L. (1983). *Mathematics for the millions.* New York: W. W. Norton.

Kasner, E., & Newman, J. R. (1989). *Mathematics and the imagination.* Redman, WA: Tempus Books.

King, J. P. (1992). *The art of mathematics.* New York: Fawcett Columbine.

McLeish, J. (1991). *Number: The history of numbers and how they shape our lives.* New York: Fawcett Columbine.

Müller, R. (1989). *The great book of math teasers.* New York: Sterling Publishing.

National Council of Teachers of Mathematics. (1989). *Historical topics for the mathematics classroom.* Reston, VA.

Pauloo, J. A. (1001). *Beyond numeracy: Ruminations of a numbers man.* New York: Knopf.

Peterson, I. (1988). *The mathematical tourist: Snapshots of modern mathematics.* New York: Freeman.

Pólya, G. (1977). *Mathematical methods in science.* Washington, D.C.: Mathematical Association of America.

Pólya, G. (1985). *How to solve it: A new aspect of mathematical method* (2nd ed.). Princeton, NJ: Princeton University Press.

Poundstone, W. (1992). *Prisoner's dilemma.* New York: Doubleday.

Russell, B. (1993). *Introduction to mathematical philosophy* (revised edition). London, England: Routledge.

Salem, L., Testard, F., & Salem, C. (1992). *The most beautiful mathematical formulas.* New York: Wiley.

Schiffer, M. M., & Bowden, L. (1984). *The role of mathematics in science.* Washington, D.C.: Mathematical Association of America.

Stevenson, F. W. (1992). *Exploratory problems in mathematics.* Reston, VA: National Council of Teachers of Mathematics.

Stewart, I. (1992). *Another fine math you've got me into. . . .* New York: Freeman.

Stewart, I. (1992). *The problems of mathematics* (2nd ed.). Oxford, England: Oxford University Press.

Stewart, I., & Golubitsky, M. (1992). *Fearful symmetry: Is God a geometer?* Oxford, England: Blackwell.

Tymoczko, T. (1986). *New directions in the philosophy of mathematics.* Boston: Birkhäuser.

Wickelgren, W. A. (1974). *How to solve problems: Elements of a theory of problems and problem solving.* New York: Freeman.

A and B like this. . . . Now, I'll twist it and attach A to B with tape. Now, use your pencil to draw a line from A to B. (See Exhibit 7.8.)

Fred: There, but I never crossed an edge!

Lottie: Use these scissors to cut down the middle on the line.

Fred: Oh, wow! How can that be? It's still only one large band! Why did that happen?

Lottie: That's what the lively discussions in my classes were all about today. I told them if they cooperate during the next unit on polynomial operations, we'll do more of these fun sorts of things afterwards.

Exhibit 7.6
A sampling of available books on teaching mathematics.

Brown, S. I., & Walter, M. I. (1990). *The art of problem posing* (2nd ed.). Hillsdale, NJ: Lawrence Erlbaum Associates.

Cobb, P. (Ed.). (1994). *Learning mathematics: Constructivist and interactionists theories of mathematical development.* Hingham, MA: Kluwer.

Connolly, P., & Vilardi, T., Eds. (1989). *Writing to learn mathematics and science.* New York: Teachers College Press.

Fey, J. G., Ed. (1992). *Calculators in mathematics education: 1992 yearbook.* Reston, VA: National Council of Teachers of Mathematics.

Froelich, G. W. (1991). *Connecting mathematics.* Reston, VA: National Council of Teachers of Mathematics.

Geddes, D. (1992). *Geometry in the middle grades.* Reston, VA: National Council of Teachers of Mathematics.

Geddes, D. (1994). *Measurement in the middle grades.* Reston, VA: National Council of Teachers of Mathematics.

Hirsch, C. R., Ed. (1986). *Activities for implementing curricular themes from the agenda in action: Selections from the Mathematics Teacher.* Reston, VA: National Council of Teachers of Mathematics.

Kapaddia, R., & Borovcnik, M., Eds. (1991). *Chance encounters: Probability education.* Hingham, MA: Kluwer.

Kellough, D., Ed. (in press) *Integrating mathematics and science for intermediate and middle school students.* Columbus, OH: Prentice-Hall.

Krantz, S. G. (1993). *How to teach mathematics: A personal perspective.* Providence, RI: American Mathematical Society.

Lerman, S., Ed. (1994). *Cultural perspectives on the mathematics classroom.* Hingham, MA: Kluwer.

Mathematical Association of America and the National Council of Teachers of Mathematics. (1980). *A sourcebook of applications of school mathematics.* Reston, VA, and Washington, D.C.

National Council of Teachers of Mathematics. (1989). *Curriculum and evaluation standards for school mathematics.* Reston, VA.

National Council of Teachers of Mathematics. (1991). *Professional standards for teaching mathematics.* Reston, VA.

National Council of Teachers of Mathematics. (1992a). *A core curriculum.* Reston, VA.

National Council of Teachers of Mathematics. (1992b). *Data analysis and statistics.* Reston, VA.

National Council of Teachers of Mathematics. (1993). *Assessment standards for school mathematics: Working draft.* Reston, VA.

Peitgen, H., Jürgens, H., & Saupe, D. (1992). *Fractals for the classroom: Part One: introduction to fractals and chaos.* Reston, VA: National Council of Teachers of Mathematics.

Phillips, E. (1991). *Patterns and functions.* Reston, VA: National Council of Teachers of Mathematics.

Posamentier, A. S., & Stepelman, J. (1990). *Teaching secondary school mathematics: Techniques and enrichment units* (3rd ed.). Columbus, OH: Merrill.

Reys, B. J. (1991). *Developing number sense in the middle grades.* Reston, VA: National Council of Teachers of Mathematics.

Romberg, T. A., Ed. (1992). *Mathematics assessment and evaluation: Imperatives for mathematics educators.* Albany, NY: State University of New York Press.

Schoenfeld, A. H. (1985). *Mathematical problem solving.* San Diego, CA: Academic Press.

Skemp, R. R. (1971). *The psychology of learning mathematics.* Middlesex, England: Penguin.

Skovsmose, O. (1994). *Philosophy of critical mathematics education.* Hingham, MA: Kluwer.

Sobel, M. A., & Maletsky, E. M. (1988). *Teaching mathematics: A sourcebook of aids, activities, and strategies* (2nd ed.). Englewood Cliffs, NJ: Prentice Hall.

Swetz, F., & Hartzler, J. S., Eds. (1991). *Mathematical modeling in the secondary school curriculum.* Reston, VA: National Council of Teachers of Mathematics.

Webb, N. L., & Coxford, A. F., Eds. *Assessment in the mathematics classroom: 1993 yearbook.* Reston, VA: National Council of Teachers of Mathematics.

Zawojewski, J. S. (1991). *Dealing with data and chance.* Reston, VA: National Council of Teachers of Mathematics.

Ms. Walker seems to think of her Möbius-strip activity as an aside from her regular lessons, solely for the purpose of entertaining and fascinating students. Such fascinations can lead some students to appreciate mathematical phenomena and motivate them to pursue other mathematical relationships. But more is gained from experiences with concrete objects when those experiences are an integral part of lessons that target the learning goal of the unit. In Chapter 11, for example, Mr. Rudd uses the manipulative activity shown in Exhibit 11.22 to help students discover that $a^2 - b^2 = (a + b)(a - b)$. In Case 3.4, Mr. Pitkin incorporates learning activities with manipulatives and concrete models into a unit on Platonic solids. When he first read about the activities in the *Mathematics Teacher* article in Exhibit 3.5, he was not involved in teaching a unit to which the activities would be relevant. But he filed the article for later reference when he might be teaching the unit alluded to in Case 3.4.

Exhibit 7.7
Examples of concrete manipulatives and concrete models.

Exhibit 7.8
Möbius strip.

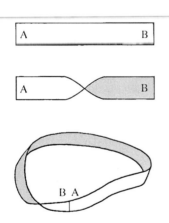

Concrete materials collected from students' everyday environments usually make manipulatives and mathematical models that are more meaningful to students than prepared instructional materials available from commercial outlets. Such "natural" objects help associate mathematics with real life. However, the commercial products—attribute blocks, pattern blocks, fraction bars, pentominoes, geoboards, base-ten blocks, geometric solid models, conic section models, algebra tiles, tangrams, and measuring devices and scales—are quite convenient for lessons focusing on contrived problems. In other words, you need to use both natural and contrived

objects. The commercial products are advertised in catalogs such as: *Hands-On Math* (Delta Education, 1994); *Middle Grades Mathematics Catalog* (Creative Publications, 1994); *1994 Secondary Mathematics* (Dale Seymour Publications, 1994); *Materials for Learning Mathematics and Science* (Cuisenaire Company, 1994); and *A Universe of Math Manipulatives* (ETA, 1994), and displayed and demonstrated at NCTM conferences and other professional meetings for mathematics teachers. As an NCTM member you can expect to receive copies of these catalogs and notices of workshops demonstrating their use.

Engage in Activity 7.5.

ACTIVITY 7.5

Purpose: To stimulate your ideas on incorporating manipulatives and concrete models in lessons you design.

Procedure: Study the descriptions of the learning activities in Exhibit 7.9 [an excerpt from *Patterns and Functions* (Phillips, 1991, pp. 60–65)]. Select some subset of those activities that you can conduct with two or three students. After obtaining the necessary materials, plan and conduct the activities you selected with the students.

Share with colleagues what you learned from having conducted the activities and let them share what they learned from experiences conducting activities with other students.

CALCULATORS

Considering the wealth of research supporting the use of calculators in mathematics curricula at all grade levels and for all courses (Hembree & Dessart, 1986; Kaput, 1992) and the relatively low cost of powerful hand-held calculators, it seems just as critical for all students to have ready access to a calculator as it is for them to have paper and pencils.

Once students understand how and why an algorithm works, calculators can relieve them from the tedium of having to work out each step during learning activities in which their energies should be directed toward more sophisticated cognitive processes (e.g., inductive reasoning, deductive reasoning, comprehension, or divergent thinking). Calculators free both you and your students to work on problems requiring manipulation of real world, realistic data; whereas, paper and pencil calculations are simply too time consuming unless the problem is contrived so that numbers are easy to work with and result in pat answers. Because Mr. Citerelli's students in Cases 4.7 through 4.10 had their calculators in hand as he led them to construct the concept of arithmetic sequence, they were able to find the difference between consecutive numbers in complicated-looking sequences as easily as they could for simple-looking sequences. In Case 6.3, Mr. Wilson and his students were able to try out various algorithms with realistic data in their quest for a solution to the combination lock versus key lock problem.

Besides relieving you and your students from time consuming, boring algorithms, calculators also serve as valuable tools for exploring mathematics. Revisit Case 4.12, for example, and note how Ms. Gaudchaux's students use graphing calculators in cooperative groups to discover the effects of a and b on the graph of $f(x) = ax + b$. Case 7.2 is another example of the calculator as an exploratory tool during stage 1 (experimenting) of a discover a relationship lesson.

CASE 7.2 _____

For her algebra II class, Ms. Long is conducting the experimenting stage of a lesson targeting the following objective:

> Explain how the values of t, f, and g affect y, where t is a real number variable, $f(t) = x$, and $g(x) = y$. (*discover a relationship*)

Exhibit 7.9
Examples of Learning activities.

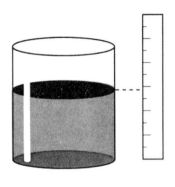

Fig. 5.6

Fig. 5.7

INVESTIGATION 2. THE BOTTLE FUNCTION

Problem: Investigate the relationship between the volume and the height of a bottle.

Teacher Notes

Materials. Supply each group with a straight-sided transparent container (different sizes for different groups); some sand, rice, or water; and a measuring cup, a ruler, and some graph paper. For this first experiment, you may wish to provide some axes already drawn. You will also want to try out the size of the measuring cup to be sure it does not fill up the container too quickly or too slowly.

Launch. Demonstrate how to add the same amount of water to a straight-sided transparent container. After each addition of water, measure the height of the water in the container (fig. 5.6). Record the data on a graph. Divide the class into small groups.

Explore. Allow students to work in groups of two or three. One student puts a measure of water into the container; the second student measures the height (in centimeters is simplest); and the third records the data in a table and a graph. If the students are careful about their measurements, they should produce a straight-line graph (fig. 5.7). You will want them to have to use enough measures in filling the bottle to make the "straightness" of the line, the constant slope, clear and convincing.

Summarize. What pattern do you notice in the table and in the graph? You can expect students to say something about the increases in height being the same for every measure added—or the slope of the graph being the same—in words appropriate to the age group.

Will this pattern go on forever? [Until the container overflows!]

Source: Reprinted with permission from E. Phillips, in *Patterns and Functions,* pp. 60–67. Copyright 1991 National Council of Teachers of Mathematics.

Exhibit 7.9
Continued

◆   ◆   ◆   ◆   ◆   ◆   ◆   ◆

What would the graph look like if we keep on dumping in measures? [See fig. 5.8.] [The height keeps on increasing, up to a limit.]

What does it depend on? [The number of measures]

What would happen if we used a different measure? The different groups could compare their experiences. Smaller measures produce smaller increases in height. But the rate of growth is still a constant.

What is the slope of the line? What does this mean? [It is the change in height per unit measure, or the change in height per unit of volume.]

You may ask each group to repeat the experiment using a larger or smaller measure. For additional related activities, see Stewart et al. (1000).

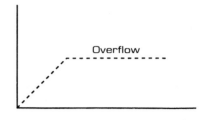

Fig. 5.8

Extension 2.1. *Different-shaped containers*

Use two different straight-sided containers, one wider than the other. *What will the graph look like?*

Discussion. Give each group two or three different cylindrical bottles. Each group should add measures (*m*), record heights (*h*), and make graphs for each container (fig. 5.9).

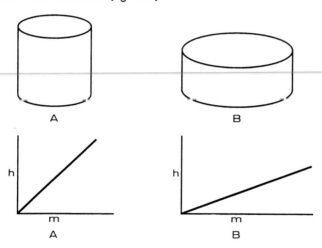

Fig. 5.9

What happens after you add a measure to bottle A? [The height increases.] *Does the same thing happen when you add the same measure to bottle B?* [Yes, but B's height grows more slowly.]

How are the graphs the same? How are they different? In each case the information graphed shows that height depends on the number of measures added. *The graphs are different, so what else does height depend on? What makes it grow quickly? Slowly?* Students will talk about the containers being wide or narrow. Discuss the "cross section" of each bottle. Using the cross sections of containers is a good way to describe the shape or the volume of the containers. The cross sections of a cylinder are congruent circles.

Reasoning

Extension 2.2. *Irregular-shaped containers*

Repeat the preceding bottle experiments with irregular-shaped transparent containers (fig. 5.10).

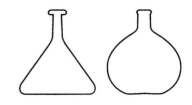

Fig. 5.10

Exhibit 7.9
Continued

♦　　♦　　♦　　♦　　♦　　♦　　♦　　♦

Discussion. Before beginning, ask students to *think about what will happen as each measure is added. Will this container fill at the same rate as the containers in figure 5.9?*

After the data are graphed, ask questions that focus on the relationship between the growth in the height of the water and the cross section of the containers.

How did your data and graphs differ from those in the experiment you did with the straight-sided containers? [The curved containers sometimes filled quickly, sometimes slowly.]

What is increasing in your experiment? [Height]

When is the height increasing most rapidly? Most slowly? Students should be able to point to the narrow parts of the bottles as the places that filled most rapidly. They may also relate this to the steepest parts of the graph.

Could the graph in figure 5.11 go with the bottle in figure 5.11? [No. The bottle starts out wide and so the height should grow slowly.]

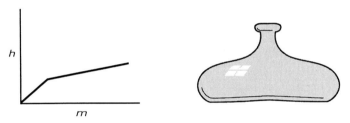

Fig. 5.11

Summarize. The height, the number of measures, and the cross section all relate to each other. Height depends on the number of measures added. The graph is a record of how fast the height of the water grows compared to the cross section of the bottle.

Extension 2.3. Determining the shape of a bottle

Sketch the shape of the bottle if the graph of the water height and the number of measures is given.

Discussion. Give the students graphs (fig. 5.12) and ask them to sketch the shape of the corresponding bottles (fig. 5.13).

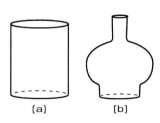

Fig. 5.13

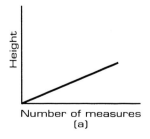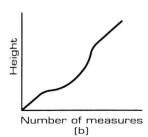

Fig. 5.12

Exhibit 7.9
Continued

♦   ♦   ♦   ♦   ♦   ♦   ♦   ♦

Discuss the rate of change. Where is the rate, height/cross section, the greatest? A constant? Let students make up a graph. Have students explain the shapes that go with each graph.

Extension 2.4. Decreasing rates of change

Discussion. From the chemistry lab borrow a bottle that allows water to be drawn off the bottom; attach it to a ring stand (fig. 5.14).

Draw off measures of water and record the height of the water in the bottle. Focus on the height of the bottle. Ignore the distance from the bottle to the table. This will produce a graph similar to figure 5.15. The graph is decreasing from left to right.

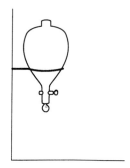

Fig. 5.14

Extension 2.5. More experiments

The following experiments can be conducted in class. For each experiment, allow the groups time to carry out the experiment; collect and organize the data; draw an appropriate graph; answer the questions; and, if possible, determine a rule for the functional relationship between the varying quantities.

Experiment 1. Circumference and pi

Collect several circular lids or cans in different sizes . Older students can measure the circumference (using a string) and the diameter and then plot each point (diameter, circumference) on a graph. Younger students can use a string or colored tape to determine the length of the circumference. They can attach the tape or place the string on the graph at the appropriate diameter (fig. 5.16a). The diameter can be determined by placing the circular lid on the horizontal axis so that the horizontal axis divides the circle into two congruent halves (for younger students). Alternatively, the diameter can be determined by tracing the lid on a piece of paper, cutting out the circle, and folding it in half. The crease line is the diameter.

Fig. 5.15

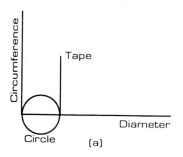

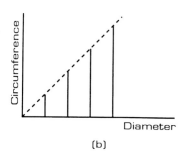

Fig. 5.16

After each circumference has been determined and plotted on a graph with its corresponding diameter, draw a line through the points (fig. 5.16b). Ask the students to *calculate the vertical and horizontal distances between two points on the line.* This is the process used to find slope (Extension 1.1 in this chapter). *Calculate the ratio of vertical distance to horizontal distance or circumference to diameter.* The ratios come very close to 3.14, which is an approximation for π. This would be an appropriate time to discuss some of the history of π. (See *The Story of Pi* by Tom Apostol [1989].)

What does the graph of the circumference to the diameter look like? [A straight line] *What is the slope of the line?* [Approximately 3.14] We call

Calculator

Connections

Exhibit 7.9
Continued

◆   ◆   ◆   ◆   ◆   ◆   ◆   ◆   ◆

Calculator

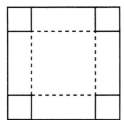

Fig. 5.17

this number π. *Determine a rule that relates the circumference of a circle to its diameter.* [Circumference = diameter × π] The equation $c = \pi d$ is a linear equation, and π is the slope of the line. *Use both your graph and the rule for circumference to find the circumference of a circle with a diameter of 6 centimeters. What is the diameter of a circle whose circumference is 54 centimeters?*

Experiment 2. The open box

Give each student a square piece of centimeter paper. Describe how an open box can be made by cutting an identical square from each corner of the large square and folding the edges to form a box (fig. 5.17). This problem is from the *Curriculum and Evaluation Standards for School Mathematics* (NCTM 1989, p. 80).

Let students guess which box will have the greatest volume. *If we cut out different-sized squares, which box will have the greatest volume? What is the smallest square we can cut? The largest square?* Review volume for younger students. Centimeter cubes can be stacked in the box to illustrate the concept of volume (Beaumont, Curtis, and Smart 1986). Have each group cut out various-sized squares with a whole-number length and calculate the volume. Organize the data in a table (fig. 5.18). Graph the data (fig. 5.19).

Length of the side of cutout square (in units)	Dimensions of the open box	Volume (in cubic units)
1	1 × 16 × 16	256
2	2 × 14 × 14	392
3	3 × 12 × 12	432 (greatest volume)
4	4 × 10 × 10	400
5	5 × 8 × 8	320
6	6 × 6 × 6	216
7	7 × 4 × 4	112
8	8 × 2 × 2	32
9	9 × 0 × 0	0

Fig. 5.18. Data for original 18-by-18-centimeter square

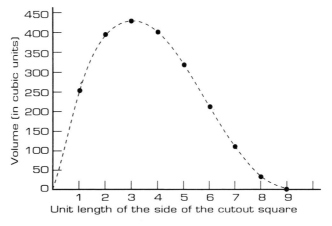

Fig. 5.19

Exhibit 7.9
Continued

◆　　◆　　◆　　◆　　◆　　◆　　◆　　◆

If we allow the length of the side of the cutout square to be a rational number, can we obtain a larger volume? Try some values very close to 3. [They produce a box with a smaller volume.] *Is the graph a parabola?* [No, it is not symmetric.]

———————————————

Looking toward Algebra: The pattern for volume can be generalized into an equation that relates the volume, *V*, and the length, *x*, of the side of the cutout square (fig. 5.20).

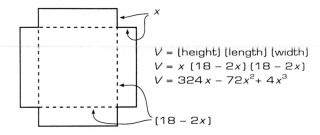

$V = (\text{height}) (\text{length}) (\text{width})$
$V = x (18 - 2x) (18 - 2x)$
$V = 324x - 72x^2 + 4x^3$

Fig. 5.20

Since the greatest exponent of the variable is 3, this equation is called a *cubic equation*. Older students can extend this problem to an $m \times n$ rectangle.

———————————————

Experiment 3. Bouncing ball

Drop a ball from a specified height and record the maximum height after each bounce. This will take some practice to read the maximum height between bounces (fig. 5.21a).

The height is approximately half the previous height. The graph is an exponential decay (see decreasing exponential function in chapter 1). See figure 5.21b.

Connections

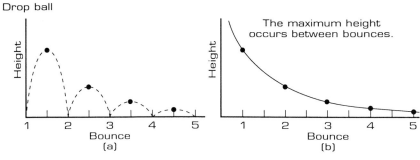

Fig. 5.21

For younger students the relationship between the drop height and the height of the first bounce can be determined for various drop heights. This relationship is linear. *What will happen if we try different balls and different starting heights?*

Exhibit 7.9
Continued

♦   ♦   ♦   ♦   ♦   ♦   ♦   ♦

Experiment 4. The Ferris wheel

Suppose a person is riding on a Ferris wheel. Record the height of the person from the ground after a specified time interval (fig. 5.22a). Measure the height from the bottom of the chair to the ground. The distance is a vertical distance. As an interval of time, use the time between chairs as they pass through the loading position. A Ferris wheel can be made from a paper circle notched at regular intervals to indicate the seats. Use a tack to position the wheel on a piece of cardboard.

Collect data through two or three complete turns of the Ferris wheel. Graph the data (fig. 5.22b).

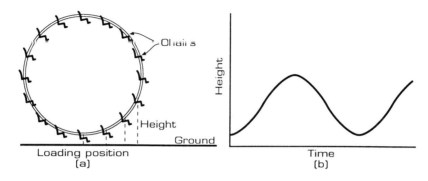

Fig. 5.22

Why does the graph not start at zero? What is the maximum height? When does it occur? Why does the shape of the graph repeat? When does it repeat?

Looking toward Trigonometry: This graph, which looks like a wave, is the graph of the *trigonometric function* $h = \sin x + b$. The variable h is the height of the seat from the ground, and the variable b is the height of the seat in a loading position from the ground.

Experiment 5. The distribution of the sum of two dice

In this experiment we will toss a pair of dice and calculate the sum of the numbers. Ask students, *Guess which sum will occur most often? Least often?* Throw a pair of dice thirty-six times and record the sum of the numbers of the two dice. The sum 7 should occur most often, the sums 2 and 12 least often. The more trials that occur, the more likely it is that these distributions will occur. Collect the data and graph the sum and the number of times each sum occurs (fig. 5.23). For younger students a bar graph can be used.

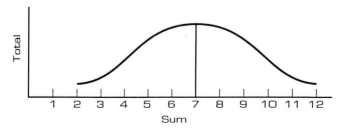

Fig. 5.23. Sum of two dice when rolled a large number of times

Exhibit 7.9
Continued

♦   ♦   ♦   ♦   ♦   ♦   ♦   ♦   ♦

Looking toward Probability and Statistics: The resulting graph is called a *bell-shaped curve,* a normal curve, or the binomial distribution. If the students have studied probability, this problem can be posed as, *Which sum is most likely to occur?* The data can be analyzed theoretically by arranging all the sums in a chart (fig. 5.24). The *probability* of a sum occurring is the number of times the sum occurs divided by the total possible sums.

Die 1

Sum		1	2	3	4	5	6
	1	2	3	4	5	6	7
	2	3	4	5	6	7	8
Die 2	3	4	5	6	7	8	9
	4	5	6	7	8	9	10
	5	6	7	8	9	10	11
	6	7	8	9	10	11	12

The sum 7 occurs 6 times out of 36 total sums.

Probability (sum of 7 occurs) = $^6/_{36}$

Fig. 5.24

Additional sources of experiments that relate mathematics to science can be found in TIMS (Teaching Integrated Mathematics and Science project, University of Illinois, Chicago, IL 60680).

As shown in Exhibit 7.10, she uses the TI-81 display calculator with an overhead projector to demonstrate what she explains as students work along with their calculators.

Using ideas gained from an inservice workshop (Edwards, 1994), a book (Demana, Waits, & Clemens, 1992), and a journal article (Cieply, 1993), Ms. Long had designed the lesson so that she initially presents students with a physics problem involving motion they could simulate on their graphing calculators:

Frank Thomas of the Chicago White Sox is at the plate in a game against the Baltimore Orioles. The pitcher throws a fast ball at the waist about 3 feet high. Thomas hits the ball at a velocity of 150 feet per second at a vertical angle of 20° straightaway toward center field. The center field fence is 20 feet high and 400 feet from home plate. At the moment he hits the ball there is a 6 mph wind blowing straight in from center field. Is this hit a home run? Is the ball catchable?

Using the parametric graphing utility mode of the TI-81 (Texas Instruments, 1990), Ms. Long explains the following as she defines the functions on her display calculator and the students follow along on theirs:

The problem will be analyzed in terms of vectors so that the horizontal component of motion is a distance problem. The distance the ball travels equals the rate multiplied by the time of travel. For the purposes of this problem, the ball is assumed to maintain a constant speed during its flight. The horizontal speed is 150 cos 20°, so the horizontal component of motion is (150 cos 20°)t. The effect of the wind is −8.8 feet per second, so the net horizontal component of motion is $x_{1t} = (150 \cos 20°)t - 8.8t$. The vertical component of motion is related to gravity, with an initial velocity of 150 sin 20° and an initial starting height of 3 feet. Then $y_{1t} = -16t^2 + (150 \sin 20°)t + 3$. The graph produced by this set of parametric equations represents the flight path of the ball as it travels toward the center field wall. Use the following RANGE values: $T_{min} = 0$; $T_{max} = 5$; $T_{step} = .05$; $X_{min} = 0$; $X_{max} = 420$; $X_{scl} = 50$; $Y_{min} = -25$; $Y_{max} = 100$; $Y_{scl} = 10$.

She draws the outfield wall on the screen as shown in Exhibit 7.11a by returning to the home screen (2nd QUIT) and choosing the "Line ("command from the DRAW menu and entering the endpoints of the wall, "Line (400, 20, 400, 0)", and pressing ENTER.

Exhibit 7.10
Ms. Long uses the display
version of her graphing
calculator as her students use
theirs at their desks.

She executes the function and the students follow the flight of the ball as it moves from Thomas' bat toward the wall (see Exhibit 7.11b). They use the TRACE function to track the flight of the ball and determine if it's catchable (see Exhibit 7.11c).

Having exposed them to a model for the basic problem, Ms. Long uses cooperative group sessions to lead the students in using the calculators to address the following questions and tasks:

1. What would happen to the ball if the wind suddenly died? What if the wind increased to 12 mph? Graph three possibilities at the same time. (See Exhibit 7.11d.)
2. What would happen if the ball is hit at an angle of 25°? Compare this hit with the original hit at 20° with a 6 mph wind. (See Exhibit 7.11e.)
3. A line drive is a ball hit on what appears to be a straight line. If a line drive is hit at a 10° angle, what velocity would it take for it to clear the fence and be a home run?
4. Compare the time of flight of a high fly ball to a line drive using the TRACE function. Graph both simulations at the same time.
5. What is the optimal angle to hit the ball for a home run?
6. What variable is more important to hitting a home run, the angle of the hit or the initial velocity?
7. Change the problem situation to a punter on a football field. What should the punter do to produce the optimal "hang time" for a punt?
8. Change the problem situation to a golfer hitting a golf ball with different types of clubs. For example, a driver has a

head angle between 9.5° and 11°. Simulate several different iron shots at the same time.
9. Develop a problem using the same mathematics as in the baseball problem, but make the problem something other than sports.

_____

In Case 7.3, a teacher has his students use calculators with a fraction display feature to compare different ways of expressing numbers.

CASE 7.3 _____

After completing a unit on rational numbers, Mr. Clair-Tresia is determined to reinforce the association among the various types of numerals used to express rational numbers (that is, fractions, mixed numbers, decimals, and percents). So until he is convinced that his seventh graders thoroughly grasp the connections among these forms of expressions and comfortably communicate with one form as well as the others, he incorporates the following strategy in units subsequent to the one on rational numbers:

He assigns problems and exercises and presents students with tasks so that some students will be doing the mathematics using one form of expression while others do the same mathematics using another form of expression. Then he has them use their TI-*Explorer* calculators (one of several brands and models with fraction and mixed-number displays and operations in addition to the usual decimal expressions) to compare the different forms.

Exhibit 7.11
Ms. Long's students use the Parametric Mode on their graphing calculators.

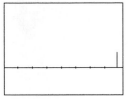 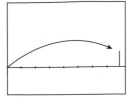 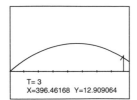 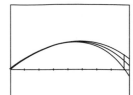 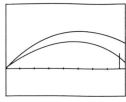

(a) The center field wall appears on the screen

(b) Students watch the ball's flight on their calculator screens

(c) The TRACE function is used to determine how high up the ball strikes the fence

(d) The graphs of three different wind conditions

(e) Graphs for hits at 20° and 25°

For example, during a unit on perimeter and area, he directs one group of students to complete task sheet I, another group to complete task sheet II, and a third group to complete task sheet III, as shown in Exhibit 7.12.

For I, the first group answers "$22\frac{47}{140}$ meters. "The second group gets 22.08 m, and the third group gets 1329/60. After each group reports their answers, Mr. Clair-Tresia asks the class, "Which field has the least amount of fencing on it? Which has the most?" Using the display version of the TI-

Explorer that he simply sets on the overhead projector (see Exhibit 7.13), he uses the Ab/c key to convert "1329/60" to "22 U49/60" and the F$\leftrightarrows$D key to convert it to "22.816667. "As the students follow along with their own calculators, he also converts "47/140" (the fractional part from task sheet I) to ".0016667." The students then discuss and answer his two questions.

In Case 7.4, the convenience of students having their calculators at hand is demonstrated.

Exhibit 7.12
Three task sheets assigned by Mr. Clair-Tresia.
Tasksheet I
How many meters of fencing is needed to enclose th property diagrammed below?

Tasksheet II
How many meters of fencing is needed to enclose the property diagrammed below?

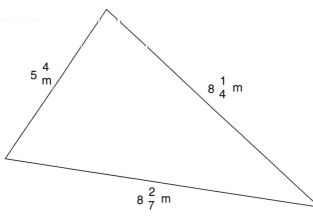

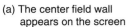

Tasksheet III
How many meters long is the fence that is built along the edge of the stream diagrammed below?

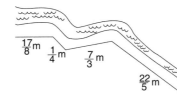

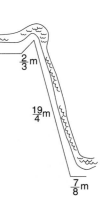

Exhibit 7.13
Examples of display calculators for use with overhead projectors.

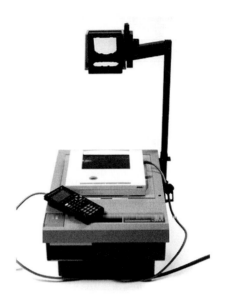

Nate: How?

Ms. Van Dusen: Get into graph mode. Let Y1 = $2x^2 - 17x + 21$. . . . Now, let Y2 = $(2x - 7)(x - 3)$. Okay. Now, graph them both on the same screen.

Nate obtains the results displayed in Exhibit 7.14a.

Ms. Van Dusen: If $2x^2 - 17x + 21 = (2x - 7)(x - 3)$, what would you expect about the graphs of Y1 and Y2?

Nate: I don't know.

Ms. Van Dusen: Would Y1 = Y2?

Nate: Sure.

Ms. Van Dusen: Look at the two curves on your calculator. Are they the same?

Nate: No. Oh, then $2x^2 - 17x + 21$ isn't the same as $(2x - 7)(x - 3)$ or else they'd only be one curve!

Ms. Van Dusen: You've just invented a test for factoring accuracy.

Seconds later, Nate enters $2x^2 - 17x + 21$ for Y1 and $(2x - 3)(x - 7)$ for Y2 on his graphics calculator resulting in the display in Exhibit 7.14b.

CASE 7.4 _____

Nate works an exercise assigned by his algebra teacher, Ms. Van Dusen, as follows:

Factor $2x^2 - 17x + 21$
$(2x-7)(x-3)$

He then engages Ms. Van Dusen in the following conversation:

Nate: Is this right?

Ms. Van Dusen: I don't know. Check it out on your graphics calculator.

Read the article by Dunham and Dick (1994) from *Mathematics Teacher* reprinted in Exhibit 7.15.

COMPUTER TECHNOLOGY

The Role of Computers in Teaching Mathematics

Computers can be used in mathematics curricula to perform the same functions as calculators. Calculators have the advantages of being compact and portable and they are also considerably less expensive. Because

Exhibit 7.14
Displays on Nate's Sharp *EL-9300C* calculator.

a. $Y1 = 2x^2 - 17x + 21$
$Y2 = (2n - 3)(x - 7)$

b. $Y1 = 2x^2 - 7x + 21$
$Y2 = (2x - 3)(x - 7)$

computers have more memory, process information faster, and provide much more vivid, elaborate, and flexible displays, they can perform a wider range of functions than calculators. Both calculator and computer technologies need to be thoroughly integrated into mathematics curricula in all courses and at all grade levels (Kaput, 1992; Lacampagne, 1993; NCTM, 1989).

The many ways you and your students can and should use computers increases as the technology continues to be advanced.

Teacher Uses

As a teacher you need exclusive access to your own computer to produce documents, create illustrations, conduct computer-enhanced learning activities, personally do mathematics, retrieve information, maintain measurement-item pool files and generate tests, and keep records.

Producing Documents. Word processing makes it possible for you to efficiently produce lesson plans (see eg., Exhibits 4.8, 4.15, and 11.10); task sheets (Exhibits 4.7 and 11.12); advanced organizers and presentation outlines (Exhibits 6.5, 9.4, and 9.5); class meeting agendas (Exhibit 11.18); tests (Exhibit 11.30); and correspondence to parents and others (Exhibit 8.17).

Creating Illustrations. The combination of word processing, art programs, graphics programs, and desktop publishing software provides you with a user-friendly way to produce eye-catching professional displays. Relatively few teachers have the time or artistic talent to produce illustrations by hand with chalk, overhead transparency pens, or marking pens that can compete with those generated with a computer. Which of the two illustrations in Exhibit 7.16 do you think students find more engaging?

Conducting Computer-Enhanced Learning Activities. In Case 7.2, Ms. Long projected the image on her calculator screen for her entire class to see as she explained and demonstrated the solution to a problem. Likewise, you can work at a computer station and project the image from your computer screen onto a television monitor or through an overhead projector with the aid of an LCD (liquid crystal display) panel. See Exhibit 7.17. However, for students to be able to work along with you on their own computers they must be able to attend to your presentation while at their own computer terminals or PCs. However, in most classrooms, students usually have to leave their seats and move to a computer station or lab to do work on computers themselves. Due to the availability of project funds for educational technology, more and more classrooms around the country are being equipped with networked computer terminals built into students

Exhibit 7.15
"Research on Graphing Calculators" (Dunham & Dick, 1994).

Penelope H. Dunham and Thomas P. Dick

Research on Graphing Calculators

The National Council of Teachers of Mathematics has long advocated the use of calculators at all levels of mathematics instruction, and graphing calculators are no exception. Indeed, the *Curriculum and Evaluation Standards for School Mathematics* (NCTM 1989) makes the following underlying assumption for grades 9–12 (p. 124):

Scientific calculators with graphing capabilities will be available to all students at all times.

Evidently, the call has been heeded. Commenting on changes in undergraduate mathematics education for the Mathematical Association of America, Leitzel (1993) noted the "explosive growth in the use of graphing calculators in secondary schools" and urged college mathematics faculty to take advantage of students' facility with this technology. Curriculum reformers at both the secondary school and collegiate levels have used technology as a catalyst for change. The availability of graphing calculators has motivated us to reexamine what and how we teach mathematics. The multiple-representation approach to function (tabular, graphical, symbolic) advocated by the *Curriculum and Evaluation Standards* has appeared as a central feature in many calculus reform projects. In turn, the assessment of student achievement is reflecting these changes. For example, on the 1995 Advanced Placement calculus examination, the College Board will require the use of a graphing calculator capable of *at least* numeric differentiation, numeric integration, and root finding.

Is the use of graphing calculators really a good thing for mathematics education? Graphing calculators have their share of detractors, and we can hear the echo of the "crutch" premise (see Usiskin [1978]) now applied to algebraic-manipulation skills and curve sketching. Both advocates and skeptics are keenly interested in what mathematics education research has to say about the impact of this technology on teaching and learning mathematics.

The graphing-calculator phenomenon is new enough that relatively little research has found its way into the journal literature. Conference proceedings—in particular, the annual International Con-

Technology is used as a catalyst for change

ference on Technology in Collegiate Mathematics—and doctoral dissertations are the most fruitful sources of research on graphing calculators at this time. This article presents an overview and discussion of some of the results.

GRAPHING CALCULATORS AND ACHIEVEMENT STUDIES

Comparing common test scores of students receiving graphing calculator–based instruction to those of students receiving traditional instruction yields some information, but this process is much like comparing apples and oranges if the course goals are different. Several studies of precalculus students at both the secondary school and collegiate levels have attempted to compare overall achievement between experimental groups—for whom the "treatment" is the use of computers or graphing calculators in instruction—and control groups taught in a traditional way. The results have been mixed but encouraging.

Ruthven (1990), Quesada and Maxwell (1992), and Harvey (1993) found significant differences in favor of the experimental groups. Harvey analyzed data from the 1988–89 field test of a graphing-intensive curriculum, the Computer and Calculator in PreCalculus Project (C^2PC). In this study, noteworthy because of its size, Harvey compared school mean scores on a "calculus readiness" (CR) test for fifty-five schools using both graphing technology and the C^2PC materials in precalculus with the scores of twenty-two control schools with traditional precalculus courses. He found statistically significant differences favoring the C^2PC schools on the CR test.

Edited by **J. Michael Shaughnessy**
Portland State University
Portland, OR 97207

Penny Dunham teaches at Muhlenberg College, Allentown, PA 18104. She is interested in gender issues and teaching mathematics with technology. Thomas Dick is director of the Calculus Connections Project at Oregon State University, Corvallis, OR 97331, and his interests include professional and curriculum development involving the use of technology.

Exhibit 7.15
Continued

Using the same data, Alan Osborne (personal communication reported in Dunham [1992]) analyzed individual scores on the CR pretest and posttest and examined the effects of instruction for those students in the experimental and control schools who did not achieve CR pretest scores sufficient for calculus placement. Those students receiving the calculator instruction subsequently attained calculus placement on the CR posttest at nearly twice the rate of those receiving traditional instruction.

In other studies, Rich (1991), Shoaf-Grubbs (1992), and Army (1992) found no difference in overall precalculus achievement between the experimental and control groups, whereas Giamati (1991) found significant differences in favor of the control group.

Van Cleave (1993) has noted that graphing calculators were allowed on the tests administered in the studies of Ruthven and Harvey but not in the other studies mentioned. Therein lies a catch-22 situation in attempting to perform an experimental group–control group study of achievement and graphing-calculator use. On the one hand, those critics who worry specifically that students will rely on the calculator as a crutch will certainly cry foul if the experimental group has the advantage of graphing calculators. On the other hand, Ruthven (1990) argues that not allowing students to use graphing technology when they have become accustomed to it forces them to do mathematics "under unduly artificial conditions" (p. 438).

A true experimental study that attempts to isolate the effects of the availability of graphing calculators on students would be so constrictive in its controls that the results would be of little practical use. No one believes that simply carting a set of graphing calculators into a classroom will have some magical effect on students. However, some researcher will attempt to compare two classes in which the content, instruction, and testing are identical, and the presence of graphing calculators is the only difference. Such studies can offer us little insight. Even if the researcher were able to match exactly the content and instruction between an experimental and a control group of randomly selected students—a difficult task indeed—attributing any significant differences in achievement between the two groups to the mere presence of graphing calculators would be irresponsible. One would immediately want to know *how* students used the graphing calculator and investigate *why* the differences appeared.

For example, is the quantity of graphs that can be generated by means of the calculator the essential variable? Or is the *dynamic* generation of a graph crucial and an important factor in the effectiveness of graphing calculators in mathematics instruction? What is the more important role the calculator plays for the student—to confirm results

obtained by paper-and-pencil computation or to encourage exploration and investigation?

In all the studies mentioned, the experimental groups also received different instruction and used different curriculum materials than the control groups. Proponents of graphing-calculator use generally have a whole package of curricular and instructional goals in mind, and the corresponding changes in content and activities made possible by the graphing calculators are what really excite them. For example, the vision of making a "multiple representation approach" a central tenet in the philosophy of a mathematics curriculum rings hollow unless students and instructors actually have the tools to use numeric and graphic strategies in addition to the traditional paper-and-pencil algebraic techniques. Graphing calculators furnish those tools. As another example, mathematical modeling using real data is also made more feasible by the availability of graphing calculators.

GRAPHING CALCULATORS AND CONCEPTUAL UNDERSTANDING

By analyzing the specific content of assessment items and students' responses, and by probing students' conceptual understanding through interviews, researchers can paint a more detailed picture of the effects of graphing calculator–based instruction on students' learning. A natural area of inquiry is that of students' understanding of graphs and the function concept. Dunham's review of research (1993) reports that many students who use graphing technology—

Mathematical modeling is feasible with graphing calculators

Find a function *f* whose graph passes through all four points. (Note: this item could stipulate a particular type of function, such as a *polynomial* function.)

Fig. 1

Exhibit 7.15
Continued

Time Elapsed	Cell Population
60	4500
90	5200
120	6100
150	7300
180	8600

What kind of model best fits the bacterial growth data above—linear, quadratic, or exponential?

Fig. 2

- place at higher levels in a hierarchy of graphical understanding (Browning 1989);
- are better able to relate graphs to their equations (Rich 1991; Ruthven 1990);
- can better read and interpret graphical information (Boers-van Oosterum 1990);
- obtain more information from graphs (Beckmann 1989);
- have greater overall achievement on graphing items (Flores and McLeod 1990);
- are better at "symbolizing," that is, finding an algebraic representation for a graph (Shoaf-Grubbs 1992; Rich 1991; Ruthven 1990);
- better understand global features of functions (Rich 1991; Beckmann 1989);
- increase their "example base" for functions by examining a greater variety of representations (Wolfe 1990); and
- better understand connections among graphical, numerical, and algebraic representations (Beckmann 1989; Browning 1989; Hart 1992).

Each problem can be approached in more than one way

Again, the mere presence of graphing technology cannot account for these results. Rather, the combination of technology and changes in curriculum and instruction must be examined. **Figures** 1 through 4 illustrate some types of questions that exemplify the multiple-representation shift in curricular emphasis. Note how each problem can be approached in more than one way and how the graphing calculator could be used as either an exploratory or a confirmatory tool in the solution. Certainly one can argue that graphing calculators are not *necessary* to adopt some of these changes, but the technology has clearly served as a catalyst.

Although these research results are extremely encouraging, not all results have been positive. Becker (1992) found that graphing-calculator use did not improve students' understanding of the concept of function in a college precalculus course, and

Giamati (1991) reported that a control group of students better understood graphical transformations and curve sketching. Interested readers should closely examine details of these studies.

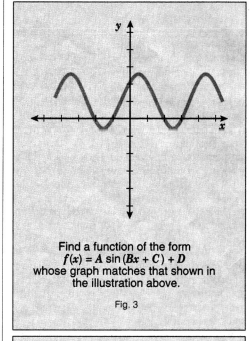

Find a function of the form
$f(x) = A \sin(Bx + C) + D$
whose graph matches that shown in the illustration above.

Fig. 3

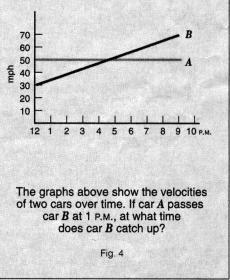

The graphs above show the velocities of two cars over time. If car *A* passes car *B* at 1 P.M., at what time does car *B* catch up?

Fig. 4

GRAPHING CALCULATORS AND PROBLEM SOLVING

Dick (1992) cites three ways that graphing calculators can lead to improved problem solving: (1) calculators free more time for instruction by reducing

Exhibit 7.15
Continued

attention to algebraic manipulation; (2) calculators supply more tools for problem solving, especially for students who have weaker algebraic skills, and can serve as a monitoring aid during the problem-solving process; and (3) students perceive problem solving differently when they are freed from the burden of numerical and algebraic computation to concentrate on setting up the problem and analyzing the solution.

Dunham's review of the research (1993) supports these claims. Not only were the students who used graphing technology more successful on problem-solving tests (McClendon 1992), they also—

had more flexible approaches to problem solving (Boers-van Oosterum 1990);

were more willing to engage in problem solving and stayed with a problem longer (Farrell 1990; Rich 1991);

concentrated on the mathematics of the problems and not on the algebraic manipulation (Rizzuti 1992);

solved nonroutine problems inaccessible by algebraic techniques (Rich 1991); and

believed calculators improved their ability to solve problems (McClendon 1992).

This last observation suggests that graphing calculators can also affect attitudes. Some research suggests an interesting interplay between confidence and gender, with female students benefiting more from graphing calculators. See Dunham (1992, 1993) for a discussion.

GRAPHING CALCULATORS AND CLASSROOM DYNAMICS

Classroom observations and interviews with both students and teachers suggest that graphing calculators have significantly changed the climate of the classroom.

Farrell (1990) noted that students became more active in classrooms in which graphing technology was being used, with more group work, investigations and explorations, and problem solving being observed. Simonsen (1992), Beckmann (1989), Davis (1990), Rich (1991), and Dick and Shaughnessy (1988) report a shift to fewer lectures by teachers and more investigations by students in graphing-calculator classrooms. Graphing calculators become a third agent in the classroom, and students consult with both the technology and the teacher (Farrell 1990).

A teacher initially may feel uncomfortable with a perceived loss of control over the classroom environment, which is part of the price paid for new excitement. Indeed, the rejuvenation that many teachers report may prove to be the most important impact of graphing calculators. The "what if" and "why

does this happen?" questions—from *students*, not teachers—are almost unavoidable in the course of graphing-calculator use. An unexpected calculator "event" may not be readily explainable by the teacher, and dealing with that uncertainty can be unsettling. However, these instances can afford new opportunities for engaging students in mathematical discussion. Teachers will need more flexibility and more willingness to ad lib when such moments arise. They can no longer only follow a script of the day's lesson.

FUTURE RESEARCH NEEDED ON GRAPHING CALCULATORS

Most studies mentioned in this article have been descriptive; they tell us *what* happens in classrooms equipped with graphing calculators. For research effectively to guide curriculum development and instruction, we need to find out *why*. The following questions are not a comprehensive research agenda but a starting point for researchers interested in this area of inquiry. (Thanks go to Jim Fey and members of the audience at the NCTM Research Presession at the annual meeting in Nashville for articulating some of these issues.)

What aspect of graphing calculators brings about improved understanding?

Is it the presence of a graph, the dynamic creation of the graph, the ability to manipulate graphs, or the ability to generate many graphs quickly and easily?

What role do multiple representations play in learning with graphing calculators?

The NCTM's *Curriculum and Evaluation Standards* (1989) and many of the current calculus reform efforts are based on a multiple-representation approach to the function concept. How important is the linkage among numerical, graphical, and symbolic representations in understanding functions and graphs? What preferences do students show for different representations of functions?

What paper-and-pencil skills retain their importance?

Few would suggest that graphing calculators make paper-and-pencil skills obsolete, and research can help us find the proper balance. What paper-and-pencil skills must be developed before students are introduced to graphing technology? Do students need extensive experience with point plotting or scaling before using graphing calculators? How important is practice in algebraic manipulation to continued success in mathematics?

Can technology use impede understanding?

Does it take a while to learn a graphical way of

Graphing calculators become a third agent in the classroom

Exhibit 7.15
Continued

*Graphing
calculators
can empower
students*

thinking before benefits emerge? As graphing
technology gets easier to use, will we see more
positive effects of its use? Does graphing technology promote any new errors or misconceptions?

*What accounts for the difference between success
and failure in implementing the use of graphing
calculators?*

Several factors that may play a role are the "user
friendliness" of the machines, the availability of
course materials designed to take full advantage
of technology, the adequacy of in-service education for teachers, and the attitudes of both teachers and students toward the technology.

CONCLUSIONS

The early reports from research indicate that
graphing calculators have the potential dramatically to affect teaching and learning mathematics,
particularly in the fundamental areas of functions
and graphs. Graphing calculators can empower students to be better problem solvers. Graphing calculators can facilitate changes in students' and teachers' classroom roles, resulting in more interactive
and exploratory learning environments.

Hembree and Dessart's meta-analyses (1986,
1992) looked at twenty years of studies of non-
graphing calculators and confirmed their value in
mathematics teaching. The research cited in the
foregoing indicates that reason also exists for optimism about the value of teaching with graphing
calculators, but it is far too early in the game to
draw final conclusions. Many more studies are
needed before the research community can formulate answers to the questions raised in the last section of this article. The evidence supporting the use
of graphing calculators, particularly with regard to
students' understanding of function and graphing
concepts, problem solving, and classroom dynamics,
certainly suggests that this technology can be a catalyst for, and not an obstacle to, mathematics
learning.

REFERENCES

Army, Patricia D. "An Approach to Teaching a College
Course in Trigonometry Using Applications and a
Graphing Calculator." Ph.D. diss., Illinois State University. *Dissertation Abstracts International* 52
(1992):2850A.

Becker, Barbara A. "The Concept of Function: Miscon-
ceptions and Remediation at the Collegiate Level."
Ph.D. diss., Illinois State University. *Dissertation
Abstracts International* 52 (1992):2850A.

Beckmann, Charlene E. "Effects of Computer Graphics Use on Student Understanding of Calculus Concepts." Ph.D. diss., Western Michigan University.
Dissertation Abstracts International 50
(1989):1974B.

Boers-van Oosterum, Monique A. M. "Understanding
of Variables and Their Uses Acquired by Students in

Traditional and Computer-Intensive Algebra." Ph.D.
diss., University of Maryland College Park. *Dissertation Abstracts International* 51 (1990):1538A.

Browning, Christine A. "Characterizing Levels of
Understanding of Functions and their Graphs."
Ph.D. diss., Ohio State University. *Dissertation
Abstracts International* 49 (1989):2957A.

Davis, Marsha. "Calculating Women: Precalculus in
Context." Paper presented at Third Annual Confer-
ence on Technology in Collegiate Mathematics,
Columbus, Ohio, 9–11 November 1990.

Dick, Thomas. "Super Calculators: Implications for
Calculus Curriculum, Instruction, and Assessment."
In *Calculators in Mathematics Education*, 1992
Yearbook of the National Council of Teachers of
Mathematics, edited by James T. Fey, 145–57.
Reston, Va.: The Council, 1992.

Dick, Thomas, and J. Michael Shaughnessy. "The
Influence of Symbolic/Graphic Calculators on the
Perceptions of Students and Teachers toward Math-
ematics." In *Proceedings of the Tenth Annual Meet-
ing of PME-NA,* edited by Merlyn Behr, Carole
Lacampagne, and Margariete Wheeler, 327–33,
DeKalb, Ill.: Northern Illinois University, 1988.

Dunham, Penelope H. "Teaching with Graphing Calculators: A Survey of Research on Graphing Technology." In *Proceedings of the Fourth International Conference on Technology in Collegiate Mathematics,*
edited by Lewis Lum, 89–101. Reading, Mass.:
Addison-Wesley Publishing Co., 1992.

———. "Does Using Calculators Work? The Jury Is
Almost In." *UME Trends* 5 (May 1993):8–9.

Farrell, Ann M. "Teaching and Learning Behaviors in
Technology-Oriented Precalculus Cassrooms." Ph.D.
diss., Ohio State University. *Dissertation Abstracts
International* 51 (1990):100A.

Flores, Alfinio, and Douglas McLeod. "Calculus for
Middle School Teachers Using Computers and
Graphing Calculators." Paper presented at Third
Annual Conference on Technology in Collegiate
Mathematics, Columbus, Ohio, 9–11 November
1990.

Giamati, Claudia M. "The Effect of Graphing Calculator Use on Students' Understanding of Variations on
a Family of Equations and the Transformations of
Their Graphs." Ph.D. diss., University of Michigan.
Dissertation Abstracts International 52 (1991):103A.

Hart, Dianne K. "Building Concept Images: Super-
calculators and Students' Use of Multiple Representations in Calculus." Ph.D diss., Oregon State University. *Dissertation Abstracts International* 52
(1992):4254A.

Harvey, John G. "Effectiveness of Graphing Technologies in a Precalculus Course: The 1988–89 Field Test
of the C^2PC Materials." Paper presented at the Technology in Mathematics Teaching Conference, Birm-
ingham, England, September 1993.

Hembree, Ray, and Donald J. Dessart. "Effects of
Hand-Held Calculators in Precollege Mathematics
Education: A Meta-analysis." *Journal for Research
in Mathematics Education* 17 (1986):83–99.

——— "Research on Calculators in Mathematics Education." In *Calculators in Mathematics Education,*
1992 Yearbook of the National Council of Teachers
of Mathematics, edited by James T. Fey, 22–31.

Exhibit 7.15
Continued

Reston, Va.: The Council, 1992.

Leitzel, James R. C. "Changing Undergraduate Programs in Mathematics." *UME Trends* 5 (May 1993):6.

McClendon, Mickey A. "The Development of a Graphics Calculator Study Guide for Calculus Students." Ph.D. diss., University of Oregon. *Dissertation Abstracts International* 52 (1992):2450A.

National Council of Teachers of Mathematics. *Curriculum and Evaluation Standards for School Mathematics*. Reston, Va.: The Council, 1989.

Quesada, Antonio R., and Mary E. Maxwell. "The Effect of Using a Graphing Calculator on Students' Performance in Precalculus: A Preliminary Report." In *Proceedings of the Fourth International Conference on Technology in Collegiate Mathematics*, edited by Lewis Lum, 380–84. Reading, Mass.: Addison-Wesley Publishing Co., 1992.

Rich, Beverly. "The Effect of the Use of Graphing Calculators on the Learning of Function Concepts in Precalculus Mathematics." Ph.D. diss., University of Iowa. *Dissertation Abstracts International* 52 (1991):835A.

Rizzuti, Jan M. "Students' Conceptualizations of Mathematical Functions: The Effects of a Pedagogical Approach Involving Multiple Representations." Ph.D. diss., Cornell University. *Dissertation Abstracts International* 52 (1992):3549A.

Ruthven, Kenneth. "The Influence of Graphic Calculator Use on Translation from Graphic to Symbolic Forms." *Educational Studies in Mathematics* 21 (1990):431–50.

Shoaf-Grubbs, Mary Margaret. "The Effect of the Graphics Calculator on Female Students' Cognitive Levels and Visual Thinking." In *Proceedings of the Fourth International Conference on Technology in Collegiate Mathematics*, edited by Lewis Lum, 394–98. Reading, Mass.: Addison-Wesley Publishing Co., 1992.

Simonsen, Linda. "Perceptions of Teachers on the Impact of Super Calculators." Paper presented at the meeting of the Oregon Educational Research Association, Portland, Oregon, 1992.

Usiskin, Zalman. "Are Calculators a Crutch?" *Mathematics Teacher* 71 (May 1978):412–13.

Van Cleave, Martha D. "The Effects of Using Graphing Technology on Student Performance in High School and College Precalculus Mathematics." Unpublished paper, 1993.

Wolfe, Mary D. "Design and Development of an Interactive Computer Graphics Tool to Aid in the Understanding of the General Function Concept." Ph.D. diss., Georgia State University. *Dissertation Abstracts International* 51 (1990):1945A.

desks. Not many teachers are likely to inherit such a technology-enhanced classroom, but by assertively pursuing grant money, a classroom so equipped may not be as improbable as you might think.

There is a fast-growing number of powerful, engaging, practical to use in your classroom, commercially available computer software systems for doing mathematics that you can incorporate into your teaching. Among others, they include *DERIVE, Function Analyzer, Function Supposer, GeoExplorer, Geometer's Sketchpad, GEOMETRIC SuperSUPPOSER, Graph Explorer, LOGO Math Tools and Games, MathCAD, and Mathematica*. What are the right software systems for you? After questioning scores of mathematics teachers, mathematics education specialists, and mathematicians regarding their preferences, I'm convinced teachers prefer whatever they are used to. Once people become acquainted with and use any particular software version, they tend to be sold on it and resist switching to another.

The software systems make it possible for you and your students to easily and quickly (a) generate example after example with parameters you've defined, (b) execute algorithms, (c) create illustrations, and (d) explore relationships. For example, once students have learned to construct an angle with a ruler and straightedge, there's not much gained by having them repeat that process time and time again.

However, if you want them to discover relationships involving angles, they may need to construct many angles. The computer software makes it possible for them to experiment with scores of angles of whatever size they choose, move them around, stack them, rotate them, close them, open them, build figures from them, and so forth, nearly as fast as they can decide what they want done. Thus, they spend time doing mathematics rather than trying to draw and manipulate pictures.

You can engage students in contrived problem solving learning activities with computer-simulated manipulatives and models in much the same way that biology students use computers to simulate animal dissection. For example, in Case 1.2, Ms. Lowe used a trash barrel to lead students to discover a formula for surface area of a right cylinder. As an alternative to getting her students to imagine the barrel being cut and unrolled in the large-group questioning session, she might have had students work with a computer-simulation program that allowed them to experiment with a variety of figures emanating from the reshaping of a right cylinder.

Exhibit 7.18 describes an example of a learning activity using *Geometer's Sketchpad* (Bennett, 1993, pp. 243–250), which is quite easy to learn and to build your sophistication with (especially the Windows version). Once you and your students are acquainted with *Geometer's Sketchpad*, each com-

Exhibit 7.16
Which will be more engaging to
students?

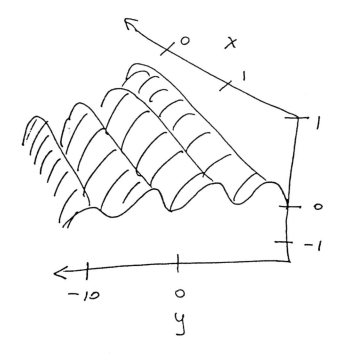

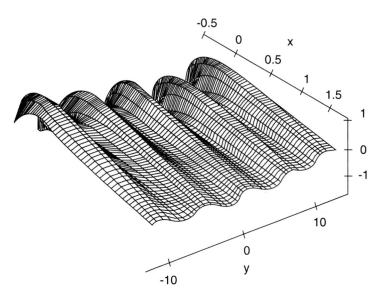

puterized step in the activity, such as "Construct ray *AB* and perpendicular lines through *A* and *B*", can be executed in only a few seconds.

Case 7.5 is an example of a teacher conducting computer-enhanced learning activities.

CASE 7.5 _____

Mr. Fernandez's classroom has a computer station for presentation and a cluster of six PCs for student use. To accommodate the 29 students in his seventh grade mathematics class, he frequently organizes the class into five activity groups. While one group takes a turn on the computers the other four are busy with other work.

As part of a unit entitled "Collecting, Analyzing, Interpreting, and Presenting Data," Mr. Fernandez conducts a lesson for the following objective:

> Use measures of central tendency and measures of variability to describe characteristics of data sets. (*comprehension*)

Building on ideas he picked up at an NCTM conference (Puhlmann & Petersen, 1992) and making use of a software package, *Mathematics Exploration Toolkit,* Mr. Fernandez explains and demonstrates the following assignment:

Part 1 - Measurements. At home, record the height and age of each member of your household, including yourself.

Exhibit 7.17
Displaying computer screens'
images during large group
presentations.

Part 2 - Computer.

1. From the keyboard, enter the title of your graph in the title box of the chart on the screen.
2. Enter the headings: NAME   HEIGHT   AGE(yrs)
3. Enter the name, height, and age of each member of your household as prompted on the screen.
4. When the chart is complete, click on the double-bar graph icon in the lower right-hand part of the screen.
5. You should see a bar graph. Now, click on "Average" (lower right of screen). Make sure the average height and age are shown at the bottom.
6. You are ready to print. Make sure the printer is switched to match the letter on your computer (A, B, C, D, E, or F). Push the "Print Screen" key.
7. When the graph is printed, check to see that it looks correct. (It's okay if the last few letters of longer names are chopped off.) If you are satisfied, go back to the screen.
8. Click on "Average" again. Click on the picture of the chart (lower right) to bring back the chart.
9. Click on the picture of the computer. Select "Clear Screen." Do not save your chart. When your screen is cleared, return to your seat.

Part 3 - Interpreting and Writing. The third part of the assignment is to compute a few more statistics, interpret the data, and write an article about them. Do the following:

1. Compute the mode, median, and range of the heights and of the ages.
2. Think about the following questions before you write your article.

(a) How will your means compare to your classmates? Will they be higher or lower? Why?

(b) How do your medians compare to your means? Can you explain why they may be different, close, or far apart?

(c) Are there modes in heights or ages? Why or why not?

(d) How do you expect your ranges to differ from those of your classmates? Why?

Exhibit 7.19 is one student's finished product from the assignment.

In a subsequent activity, students work in pairs measuring each other's heights and arm spans to address the question, "Am I square?" Mr. Fernandez collects their data and uses the same software to summarize and display it from his computerized teaching station. The display for 10 of the students is shown in Exhibit 7.20.

Engage in Activity 7.6.

—————————— **ACTIVITY 7.6** ——————————

Purpose: To stimulate your ideas on incorporating computer software packages in lessons you design.

Procedure: With a colleague, select and study an article from a recent issue of *Mathematics Teacher* or *Mathematics Teaching in the Middle School* that describes learning activities using computer software packages (eg., "Using Technology to Understand the Jury-Decision-Making Process" Goldberg 1994).

Exhibit 7.18
Using the Geometer's SketchPAD (Bennett, pp. 243–250) to investigate the Pythagorean theorem.

Investigation: The Pythagorean Theorem

In this investigation you'll create a script for constructing a square, then construct squares on the sides of a right triangle. The areas of these squares illustrate perhaps the most famous relationship in mathematics—the Pythagorean Theorem.

Sketch

Record a script for constructing a square:

Step 1: Construct ray AB and perpendicular lines through A and B.

Step 2: Construct circle AB.

Step 3: Construct C, the intersection of the circle and perpendicular line.

Step 4: Construct a line through C, perpendicular to $\overleftrightarrow{AC}$.

Step 5: Construct D, the fourth vertex of the square, at the intersection of perpendicular lines.

Step 6: Hide the ray, lines, and circle and construct segments as needed. Construct the polygon interior of the square.

Start with a blank sketch and construct a right triangle:

Step 7: Construct $\overline{AB}$.

Step 8: Construct a line perpendicular to $\overline{AB}$, through A.

Step 9: Construct $\overline{AC}$ with C any point on the perpendicular.

Step 10: Construct $\overline{BC}$. Hide the line.

Investigate

Play your square script on the two endpoints of each side of your right triangle. If your script constructs the square to fall into the triangle, undo and select the points in the opposite order.

Measure the areas of the squares and look for a relationship among these areas. Can you translate this discovery into a relationship among the sides of the right triangle?

Use Calculate to confirm your findings.

Drag the vertices of the triangle to confirm that this relationship holds for all right triangles.

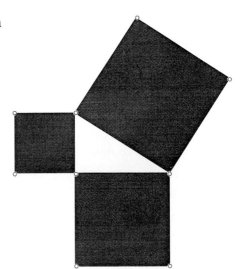

Source: *Exploring Goemetry with Geometer's SketchPAD* by Dan Bennett (1993), pp. 243-250. © 1993 by Key Curriculum Press, P.O. Box 2304, Berkeley, CA 94704.

Exhibit 7.18
Continued

Investigation: The Pythagorean Theorem

Student Audience: High School

Prerequisites: Students should know what a **right triangle** and a **square** are and should know terms like **hypotenuse** and **leg**. Students should know how to find the **area of a square**.

Sketchpad Proficiency: Experienced User

Class Time: 30-45 minutes

Example Script/Sketch: 4/Square (By Edge) (Mac Script) and **Pythagorean Theorem** (Mac Sketch) or **regpoly\4byedge.gss** and **8pythag\pytheorm.gsp** (Windows)

Construction Tips: This construction involves recording a script for constructing a square and playing this script on the sides of a right triangle. You can speed things up by having students use a pre-made script such as **4/square (By Edge)** (Mac) or **regpoly\4byedge.gss** (Windows). This script starts with a ray so that it will be reversible; that is, selecting given points in different order yields different squares. This is important—if students use an irreversible script they'll have one or more squares falling inside the triangle. If a student's script constructs the square the "wrong way," have them undo and try again, selecting the givens in the opposite order. But don't spend half the period trying to help students get their squares going the "right" way. the investigation can still be carried out (the Pythagorean Theorem still works) if squares fall inside the triangle.

Investigate/Conjecture: If areas are displayed with precision greater than tenths place, students may not do the mental math to notice that the areas of the squares on the legs add up to the area of the square on the hypotenuse. Guide them to this conjecture by suggesting they try to get one or two of the sides to be an integer length. When they perform some calculations with the measures, they'll discover:

The sum of the areas of the squares constructed on the legs of a right triangle is equal to the area of the square constructed on the hypotenuse.

Some students already familiar with the Pythagorean Theorem are likely to write: $a^2 + b^2 = c^2$ as their conjecture. Have them express the theorem in words. You may want to have students label their diagrams to correspond to this familiar formula.

Explore More

1. Some other similar shapes can be tried on the sides of the right triangle with the construction students already have. For example, select the vertices of the square in the "wrong" order when you construct the Polygon Interior to get an X shape instead of a square. The sum of the areas of these shapes on the legs will equal the area of the shape on the hypotenuse. Students can play scripts for other regular polygons on the sides of a right triangle. See the sketch **Unsquare Pythagoras** (Mac) or **8pythag\unsquare.gsp** (Windows) to see how the Pythagorean Theorem can be generalized to other similar shapes.

2. Students should play their square script on a scalene triangle to show that the Pythagorean Theorem applies only to right triangles, thus demonstrating the converse of the theorem.

3. This is a variation on 1 above. The triangles constructed are similar, thus, the sum of the areas of the small triangles is equal to the area of the triangle on the hypotenuse.

One visual proof of the Pythagorean Theorem is demonstrated by the sketch **Shear Pythagoras** (Mac) or **8pythag\shear.gsp** (Windows) and is further explained in the demonstration activity of the same name. The **8-Pythagorean Theorem** folder (Mac) or **8pythag** directory (Windows) contains several demonstrations of the theorem.

Exhibit 7.18
Continued

Investigation: The Pythagorean Theorem (Continued)

Conjecture: Write the Pythagorean Theorem in your own words in the space below.

_____

_____

Present Your Findings

Discuss your results with your partner or group. To present your findings you could:

1. Print a captioned sketch that shows a right triangle with squares on the sides. Show measures that illustrate the Pythagorean Theorem.

2. Create and add comments to a script that constructs a right triangle with squares on the sides.

Explore More

1. Try constructing other similar shapes on the sides of a right triangle to see if the Pythagorean Theorem can be generalized to shapes other than squares. Try equilateral triangles, regular pentagons, or hexagons. (Use scripts that create these shapes "by edge.")

2. See if the Pythagorean Theorem works for any triangles besides right triangles. Make more conjectures.

3. Construct a line through the right angle vertex, perpendicular to the hypotenuse. Construct the point of intersection of this line and the hypotenuse. Reflect this point across each of the legs. Reflect the right triangle vertex across the hypotenuse. Use these points and the vertices of the original right triangle to construct triangles on the sides of your right triangle. What can you say about these triangles? Does the Pythagorean Theorem apply?

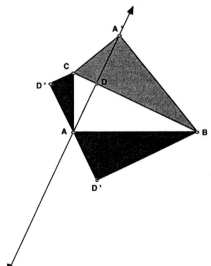

Exhibit 7.18
Continued

Demonstration: Visual Proof of the Pythagorean Theorem

In this activity you'll do a visual demonstration of the Pythagorean Theorem based on Euclid's proof. By **shearing** the squares on the sides of a right triangle you'll create congruent shapes without changing the areas of your original squares.

Sketch

Step 1: Open the sketch **Shear Pythagoras** (Mac) or **8pythag\shear.gsp** (Windows). You'll see a right triangle with squares on the sides.

Step 2: Measure the areas of the squares.

Step 3: Drag point *A*, then point *B*, onto the line that's perpendicular to the hypotenuse. Note that as the squares become parallelograms their areas don't change.

Step 4: Drag point *C* so that the large square deforms to fill in the triangle. The area of this shape doesn't change either. It should appear congruent to the shape you made with the two smaller parallelograms.

Step 5: Change the shape of the triangle and try the experiment again.

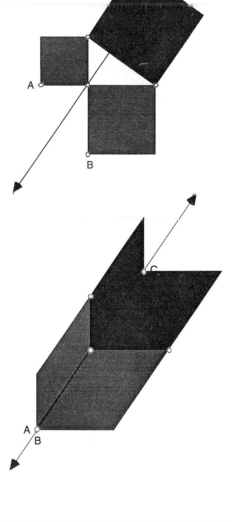

Investigate

You should now have two shapes. One shape was formed from the two squares on the legs of the right triangle. The other shape was formed from the square on the hypotenuse. What can you say about these shapes?

Conjecture: Write your conjectures below.

_____

_____

_____

_____

_____

_____

_____

_____

_____

Explore More

Once you've manipulated the squares so that you have congruent shapes, you can Copy and Paste the shape that's on the hypotenuse. Drag the copy over the shape on the legs and see that it fits perfectly.

Exhibit 7.18
Continued

Demonstration: Visual Proof of the Pythagorean Theorem

Student Audience: High School/College/Teacher Education

Prerequisites: Students will appreciate this more if they already have some experience with the Pythagorean Theorem.

Sketchpad Proficiency: Beginner

Class Time: 20-30 minutes

Sketch Needed: **Shear Pythagoras** (Mac) or **8pythag\shear.gsp** (Windows)

Demonstration Tips

You can demonstrate and talk about this sketch in a whole class presentation using an overhead projector, or students can play with the sketch independently, in which case you may want to reproduce the activity sheet for them. If students aren't familiar with the Pythagorean Theorem, this demonstration is unlikely to lead to new insights, but it does offer a nice visual proof along the lines of Euclid's proof of the theorem and is intriguing to play with or watch.

Because neither the squares' heights nor bases (the sides of the triangle) change as the squares are sheared into parallelograms, their areas remain constant (*bh* is a formula students should be familiar with; it works for any parallelogram, including squares). Showing all hiddens may help you figure out how the figure is constructed. (Shearing is technically defined as translating each point on a figure in a direction parallel to an axis by a distance proportional to the point's distance from the axis. This is an example of Cavelieri's principle applied in two dimensions, which states that if you distort a figure without changing the lengths of any of its cross sections parallel to a given axis, you won't change the figure's area. Cavalieri's principle applies to volumes and cross sectional areas in three dimensions.)

Use keyboard commands for undo and redo to rapidly repeat the demonstration.

Step 2: You may want students to calculate the sum of the areas on the legs to confirm that it's equal to the area on the hypotenuse.

Investigate/Conjecture

Assuming students already know the Pythagorean Theorem, they can restate it here in terms relevant to the demonstration:

The sum of the areas of the squares on the legs of a right triangle is equal to the area of the square on the hypotenuse.

The squares on the sides of a right triangle can be sheared, without changing their areas, so that a shape on the legs is congruent to a shape on the the hypotenuse.

Explore More

There are a variety of investigations students can do in relation to the Pythagorean Theorem. Have students experiment with the sketch **Unsquare Pythagoras** (Mac) or **8pythag\unsquare.gsp** (Windows), or have them try circles, equilateral triangles, or other similar figures on the sides of right triangles. The folder **8-Pythagorean Theorem** (Mac) or directory **8pythag** (Windows) has several demonstrations related to the Pythagorean Theorem.

Exhibit 7.18
Continued

Investigation: Dissection Proof of the Pythagorean Theorem

A dissection proof is done by cutting a figure into pieces and rearranging the pieces to demonstrate some property. Many proofs of the Pythagorean Theorem involve cutting up the squares on the sides and rearranging them to fit in the square on the hypotenuse.

Sketch

Step 1: Construct a right triangle *ABC*.

Step 2: Use a script to construct squares on the sides.

Step 3: Find the center of the square on the large leg by constructing the diagonals. Hide the diagonals.

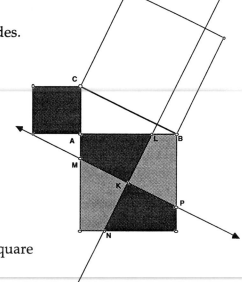

Step 4: Construct a line through this center, parallel to the hypotenuse.

Step 5: Construct another line through the center, this time perpendicular to the hypotenuse.

Step 6: Construct points where these lines intersect the sides of the square.

Step 7: Construct four polygon interiors in this square as shown, using the center as one vertex.

Step 8: Construct the polygon interior of the square on the small leg of the triangle.

Investigate

You now have five pieces: four in the large square plus the one small square. Can these five pieces be rearranged to fit in the square on the hypotenuse? Select these polygon interiors and choose Cut in the Edit menu. Now choose Paste. The pieces will now be free, and you can move them around. Drag them into the square on the hypotenuse and arrange them so they fill this square without gaps or overlapping. What does this demonstrate? Will this work for any size or shape of right triangle? Use Undo to go back to before you cut the pieces. Change the triangle and repeat the experiment.

Conjecture: In the space below, state the Pythagorean Theorem in terms of the dissection you did.

_____

_____

_____

Present Your Findings: Compare and discuss your results with your partner or group. To present your findings, print a captioned sketch showing the dissection proof.

Explore More: Do some research into other dissection proofs of the Pythagorean Theorem. Many cultures had dissection proofs of the theorem long before Pythagoras' time. U. S. President Garfield even came up with an original dissection proof.

Exhibit 7.18
Continued

Investigation: Dissection Proof of the Pythagorean Theorem

Student Audience: High School/College/Teacher Education

Prerequisites: This investigation could be used to introduce the Pythagorean Theorem.

Sketchpad Proficiency: Experienced User

Class Time: 20-30 minutes

Example Sketch: Dissected Pythagoras (Mac) or **8pythag\dissect.gsp** (Windows)

Construction Tips: Students are given minimal construction instructions in this activity. They should be familiar enough with Sketchpad to construct, for example, a right triangle with no instructions.

Step 1: Construct a segment, construct a line perpendicular to one endpoint. Construct a segment on this line and hide the line. Construct the hypotenuse of the triangle.

Step 2: Students need a script that constructs a square given the endpoints of a side. The script **4/Square (By Edge)** (Mac) or **regpoly\4byedge.gss** (Windows) will do the job.

Step 3: The diagonals are not shown in the figure. The large side in the figure here is $\overline{AB}$. Students should not make their initial triangle isosceles, though they can later investigate that case.

Step 4: In the figure, this is the line through K, parallel to $\overline{BC}$.

Investigate/Conjecture: Students must make sure they select only the interiors before cutting. The pieces can be arranged in the square on the hypotenuse as shown:

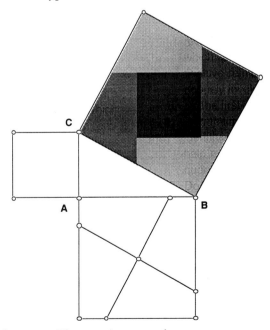

Students should state the Pythagorean Theorem in terms of square areas:

The sum of the areas of the squares on the legs of a right triangle is equal to the area of the square on the hypotenuse.

Exhibit 7.19
Kevin James' response to Mr. Fernandez's family-statistics Assignment.

Kevin Janes

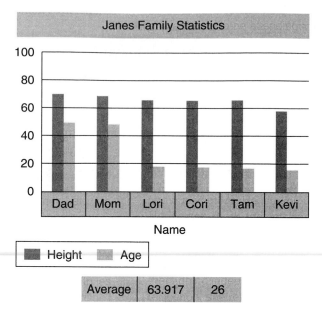

| Average | 63.917 | 26 |

My family consists of mostly teenagers and adults. Therefore our mean (average) height is higher than most of my classmates, because they have younger people in their family. The median age in our family is not very close to the mean because all of the adult kids in our family have moved out. There is a height mode in our family. This is different because most people don't have two people in their family that are the same height. We have a big age range in my family, it is 37 years. We have this range because my parents are a little older than usual parents of seventh graders. The range in my family for age is 37 yrs., and for height 10". There is no age mode, but there is a height mode- 64". The median height is 64" and for age is 17 yrs. The mean age for my family is 26 yrs., and for the height 63.917".

Assuming you had access to the computer software for you and your students, discuss where, if at all, you'd incorporate these activities in a mathematics curricula. Discuss what mathematical objectives would lessons using these activities be likely to accomplish with students.

Some teachers are reluctant to apply computer and graphing calculator technology in their teaching because they are not comfortable with the software systems or the more sophisticated features of the calculators. If you find yourself in this position or know colleagues who are, note the abundance of comprehensible, intelligible literature available for learning how to use this technology to do mathematics and integrate it with instruction. Generally, both the hard copy and computerized technical manuals for the software systems are easy to follow and readers can start to use the system immediately, gradually moving toward sophisticated applications as they're needed. In other words, you can do mathematics with these systems almost immediately and learn the systems as you do more mathematics. Besides the technical documentation, there are books for teachers, students, and mathematicians that demonstrate the technology. For example:

Calculus and the DERIVE Program: Experiments with the Computer (Gilligan & Marquardt, 1991)

A Guided Tour of the TI-85 Graphics Programmable Calculator with Emphasis on Calculus (Lucas & Lucas, 1992)

Mathematica in Action (Wagon, 1991)

Professional journals are filled with ideas for enhancing your teaching with technology see Exhibit 7.21; inservice workshops, presentations at NCTM regional and national conferences, and university courses provide additional sources.

Personally Doing Mathematics. You can hardly teach students to discover and invent mathematics unless you do mathematics and remain an active

Exhibit 7.20
Part of the summarized data
Mr. Fernandez displayed for
the class.

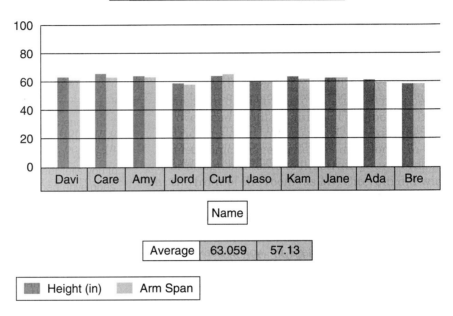

Am I Square?

	Name	Height (in)	Arm Span
1	David M.	64	62
2	Carey L.	67	64
3	Amy S.	66	65
4	Jordan W.	60	59
5	Curtis F.	66	67
6	Jason C.	60	60
7	Kameron E.	64	62
8	Janelle A.	63	63
9	Adam Mac.	63	62
10	Bret A.	61	61

Average	63.059	57.13

Height (in)   Arm Span

student of mathematics yourself. Your computer can serve as a tool in your personal quest to do mathematics and update and advance your mathematical talents. Consider Case 7.6.

CASE 7.6

Ms. Groves uses her computer to work out mathematics problems and exercises in preparation for designing lessons for her classes; she tries out mathematical routines to see what will and won't work as examples and nonexamples for construct a concept lessons. During the summer months she needs her computer for the graduate-level mathematics courses she takes. During the school year, it is difficult for her to find time to do mathematics for her personal professional development that is not directly related to what she teaches. To assure herself that she'll not neglect this need to grow as a mathematician, she decides to always be involved in a self-help project requiring her to do mathematics. For example, to improve her skills with mathematical software systems while actively doing mathematics, she schedules

one hour a week to use DERIVE software to perform the 22 experiments laid out in *Calculus and the DERIVE Program: Experiments with the Computer* (Gilligan & Marquardt, 1991). Exhibit 7.22 shows one of the experiments.

Engage in Activity 7.7.

ACTIVITY 7.7

Purpose: To broaden your experiences with computer software systems for doing mathematics.

Procedure: From a colleague, classroom teacher, professor, technology resource center, computer store, or other available source, access a computer software program (e.g., *Geometric Supposer* or *Mathematica*) that you have never before used. Learn just enough about it to try it out, playing and doing mathematics with it.

In discussions with colleagues, compare the software you tried to those they tried.

Exhibit 7.21
"Hidden Behaviors in Graphs," (Donley & George, pp. 466–468).

H. Edward Donley and Elizabeth Ann George

Hidden Behaviors in Graphs

Through the use of graphing calculators or computers, instructors can expose students to richer examples in algebra and exploit the relationship between algebraic analysis and graphical analysis. The NCTM's Commission on Standards for School Mathematics (NCTM 1989) recommends incorporating this technology into the curriculum, thereby supplying students with new approaches in the investigation of mathematical ideas. Changes in both our curriculum and instructional methods are necessary to create an environment wherein students can develop the new problem-solving strategies that this technology makes possible.

One topic that should receive more emphasis is the concept of scale in graphs. The scale at which one views a problem can radically change the characteristics of the problem. For example, at a large scale the diffusion of a dye in still, clear water is smooth and orderly, but at a molecular scale it is random and erratic. Models of diffusion at a large scale are deterministic, involving differential equations, whereas models of diffusion at a small scale involve statistics. As a second example, consider the Dow Jones Industrial Average. It appears to change erratically from day to day, influenced by the national and international events of the day. Yet when it is viewed on a longer scale, clear economic trends emerge. This article demonstrates how to construct functions that appear "normal" at one scale but have interesting hidden behaviors at smaller scales. As students work with these examples and "zoom in" on the small-scale anomalies, they will—

discover the importance of scale in graphs,

understand the effects of changing the windows for a graph, and

realize resolution problems in computer and calculator graphing.

All graphs in this article were generated on a Casio fx-8000G graphing calculator, which has the same resolution as the TI-81 graphing calculator. Graphing devices with other resolutions may give different results. Although the Casio does not display axis labels, the figures in this paper include labels for clarity.

GRAPHING RESOLUTION IN AN AREA PROBLEM

A common problem in calculus is to find the area between $y = x^2$ and $y = x^3$. Students can easily draw incorrect conclusions if they plot the graph with an inappropriate scale. With a window of $[-5, 5] \times [-5, 5]$ on a graphing calculator, it appears that the graphs of $y = x^2$ and $y = x^3$ coincide for x between 0 and 1. See **figure 1.** The existence of an interval of coincidence indicates that one must resolve the points of intersection. Zooming in reveals the existence of a region between the graphs of the two functions.

Alternatively, one can use analytical methods to find this region without encountering the foregoing

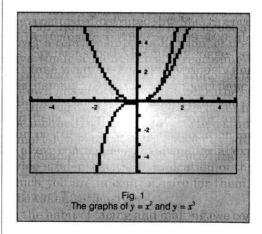

Fig. 1
The graphs of $y = x^2$ and $y = x^3$

Ed Donley is an applied mathematician at Indiana University of Pennsylvania, Indiana, PA 15705. He is interested in numerical analysis, supercomputing, and incorporating technology into the classroom. Elizabeth George teaches mathematics at the Ellis School, Pittsburgh, PA 15206. She is interested in learning styles, fractals and chaos, and incorporating technology into the curriculum.

Exhibit 7.21
Continued

difficulties. This example can be used to contrast graphical and analytical methods.

AN EXAMPLE OF A RATIONAL FUNCTION

Graphical methods are preferable to analytical methods for the function

$$f(x) = \frac{x^7 - 4x^5 - 3x^4 + 4x^3 + 12x^2 - 12}{x^7}.$$

Its graph, shown in **figure 2a,** does not appear to exhibit any unusual behavior. However, zooming in on the positive root reveals that this function actually has a simple root and a double root that almost coincide, as shown in **figure 2b.** The flatness of the graph near these roots—due to the function's nearly having a triple root there—presents a problem in zooming. If one were just to zoom in, keeping the vertical and horizontal scales identical, the graph would eventually disappear into the horizontal axis. To recover the display, one must decrease the vertical scale while leaving the horizontal scale unchanged; hence the large difference in scales in **figure 2b.**

The reason for the hidden behavior in this example becomes apparent if the function is written in factored form,

$$f(x) = \frac{(x^2 - 2)^2 (x^3 - 3)}{x^7}.$$

Its roots are $-2^{1/2}$, $2^{1/2}$, and $3^{1/3}$. Two of the roots almost coincide because $2^{1/2} \approx 3^{1/3}$.

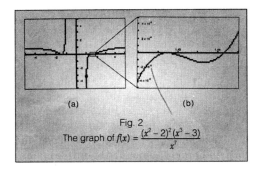

(a)   (b)

Fig. 2
The graph of $f(x) = \frac{(x^2 - 2)^2 (x^3 - 3)}{x^7}$

OTHER EXAMPLES OF RATIONAL FUNCTIONS

Rearranging the two factors, $x^2 - 2$ and $x^3 - 3$, can create other rational functions with interesting behaviors. Placing one of the factors in the numerator and one in the denominator of a rational function gives a root and a vertical asymptote at nearly the same value of x. Algebraically, this result indicates the presence of a factor in the numerator that nearly cancels a factor in the denominator. For example, the graph of

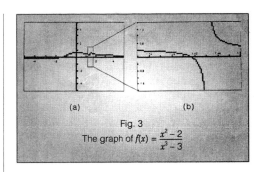

(a)   (b)

Fig. 3
The graph of $f(x) = \frac{x^2 - 2}{x^3 - 3}$

$$f(x) = \frac{x^2 - 2}{x^3 - 3}$$

is shown in **figure 3a.** The vertical asymptote at $x = \sqrt[3]{3}$ is not visible at this resolution. However, once the root of the denominator is found and one zooms in on the graph of f near this root, the vertical asymptote becomes visible (see **fig. 3b**). Finding the roots of the denominator of more complicated rational functions may require a numerical root-finding method or an examination of the graph of the denominator.

Two nearly coincident vertical asymptotes can be obtained by placing both factors, $x^2 - 2$ and $x^3 - 3$, in the denominator. The graph of

$$f(x) = \frac{1}{x^5 - 2x^3 - 3x^2 + 6} = \frac{1}{(x^2 - 2)(x^3 - 3)},$$

shown in **figure 4a,** reveals only one of the two positive vertical asymptotes. Zooming in and drastically extending the range of y-values (**fig. 4b**) shows the asymptotes at both $x = 2^{1/2}$ and $x = 3^{1/3}$.

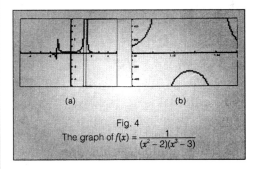

(a)   (b)

Fig. 4
The graph of $f(x) = \frac{1}{(x^2 - 2)(x^3 - 3)}$

Functions with hidden relative extrema can be derived from functions with nearly coincident roots. Vertically shifting the graph may yield approximately equal relative extrema at the translated roots. Alternatively, integrating the function produces a new function whose derivative has nearly coincident roots. These roots may correspond to relative extrema of the new function.

More examples of rational functions with hidden behaviors can be generated with other integers

Graphs may have interesting hidden characteristics depending on the scale

Exhibit 7.21
Continued

TABLE 1			
Nearly Equal Numbers			
$2^{1/3}$	$3^{1/4}$		
3	$8^{1/2}$		
$3^{1/2}$	$4^{1/3}$		
2	$5^{1/4}$	$9^{1/3}$	
$3^{1/2}$	$8^{1/4}$	$5^{1/3}$	$6^{1/3}$
$2^{1/2}$	$5^{1/4}$	$4^{1/3}$	$8^{1/5}$ $9^{1/5}$

*Try
comparing
$2^{1/3}$ with
$3^{1/4}$*

raised to rational powers. (See **table 1.**) The pair $2^{1/2}$ and $3^{1/3}$ is not unique; in fact, comparing $i^{j/k}$ for $i, j,$ and k varying from 1 to 12 gives 417 distinct pairs whose relative differences are less than 0.005. (The relative difference between two numbers is the absolute difference between the two numbers divided by the magnitude of one of the numbers.)

HIDDEN BEHAVIORS IN OTHER ELEMENTARY FUNCTIONS

Rational functions are not the only elementary functions that can exhibit hidden behaviors. The graph of

$$f(t) = \sin t + 0.05 \sin(50t)$$

is shown in **figures 5a** and **5b.** This function might represent a sound wave emitted from a speaker, in which the first term represents the desired sound and the second term represents static—high-frequency, low-volume noise. The static is only noticeable if one listens closely, corresponding to zooming in on the graph.

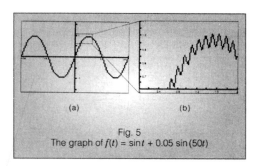

Fig. 5
The graph of $f(t) = \sin t + 0.05 \sin(50t)$

Functions involving exponents can also have hidden behaviors. If an aerosol droplet with diameter 5.00×10^{-4} cm is initially at rest and then allowed to fall through air under the influence of gravity, its velocity is

$$(1) \qquad v(t) = 0.0750e^{-13100t} - 0.0750 \text{ cm/s}.$$

This function is derived from Newton's laws of motion, using calculus (Donley 1991). At a large scale (see **fig. 6a**), the function appears to be constant for $t > 0$. However, it is obvious from (1) that $v(t)$ is not constant. Furthermore, the graph seems to indicate that $v(0) \neq 0$, contradicting the asser-

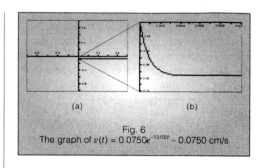

Fig. 6
The graph of $v(t) = 0.0750e^{-13100t} - 0.0750$ cm/s

tion that the particle starts at rest. Zooming in on the origin (see **fig. 6b**) resolves both of these seeming contradictions. The particle starts at rest and then quickly approaches its terminal velocity,

$$v_{\text{terminal}} = -0.0750 \text{ cm/s}.$$

Students who have mastered rates of exponential decay would be able to deduce this outcome from (1). But for those who have not yet mastered exponential decay, examining the graph and then comparing it with (1) may help them discover the concept themselves.

CONCLUSION

A variety of behaviors in graphs can be hidden when the graphs are viewed at only one scale. Thoroughly to understand a graph's behavior, important regions must be viewed at different scales. Students learn the importance of varying scales in graphs from exploring examples. Graphing calculators and computers enable us explicitly to emphasize in our curriculum the concept of scales in graphs.

REFERENCES

Donley, H. Edward. "The Drag Force on a Sphere." *UMAP Modules in Undergraduate Mathematics and its Applications.* Module 712. Arlington, Mass.: Consortium for Mathematics and Its Applications, 1991.
National Council of Teachers of Mathematics. *Curriculum and Evaluation Standards for School Mathematics.* Reston, Va.: The Council, 1989.

Exhibit 7.22
An experiment from *Calculus and the DERIVE Program: Experiments with the Computer*
(Gilligan & Marquardt, 1991, pp. 145–148).

OBJECTIVES

1. To use *DERIVE* to find the critical points of a function of two variables.

2. To use *DERIVE* to determine whether a critical point is a relative maximum, a relative minimum or a saddle point of the original function.

BACKGROUND INFORMATION

A *value* (a, b) is a critical value of the function $z = f(x, y)$ if $\frac{\partial}{\partial x} f(a, b) = f_x(a, b) = 0$ and $\frac{\partial}{\partial y} f(a, b) = f_y(a, b) = 0$. The associated triple, (a, b, c) where $c = f(a, b)$ is called a *critical point* of the function.

The *Second Partial Derivative Test* states that we calculate a number K as follows:

$$K = f_{xx}(a, b) \cdot f_{yy}(a, b) - \left[f_{xy}(a, b) \right]^2$$

and then the function f has :

a relative minimum at (a, b, c) if $K > 0$ and $f_{xx}(a, b) > 0$;

a relative maximum at (a, b, c) if $K > 0$ and $f_{xx}(a, b) < 0$;

a saddle point at (a, b, c) if $K < 0$.

PROCEDURES

1. Consider the function $f(x, y) = 3x^2 + y^3 - 6xy - 9y + 2$. We first define the function in an algebra window (see window #2 of Figure 1) and then calculate the first partials of f and display the $\boxed{\text{S}}$implified forms in lines 3 and 5. Note, $f_x = 6x - 6y$ and $f_y = -6x + 3y^2 - 9$.

2. Next, we set $f_x = 0$ (in line #6) and sol$\boxed{\text{L}}$ve for y in line #7 to determine that $x = y$. In line #8 we set $f_y = 0$. In this case, it is an easy substitution of y for x in line #8 to obtain line #9.

3. sol$\boxed{\text{L}}$ve line #9 for y to obtain, in lines #10 and #11 the values −1 and 3. Since we previously determined that $x = y$, the critical values are $(-1, -1)$ and $(3, 3)$.

4. Now, we need to calculate the second partials, f_{xx} and f_{yy}. We do this in lines #12 and #14 with the simplified results in lines #13 and #15. Also, f_{xy} is authored in line 16 and the simplified form is in line #17. To find the value of K, we define it (as above) in line #18 and $\boxed{\text{S}}$implify it to obtain $36y - 36$ in line 19. Substituting 3 for y, yields the value of 72 for K in line #21 and we deduce that since $K > 0$ and $f_{xx} > 0$, that the point $(3, 3, -25)$ is a relative minimum.

The reader should verify the results in Figure 1 as described in Procedures 1 through 4 above.

Source: Reprinted with permission from L.G. Gilligan & J.F. Marquardt, Sr., in *Calculus and the DERIVE Program: Experiments with the Computer,* 2nd ed., pp. 145–148. Copyright 1991 Gilmar Publishing Company.

Exhibit 7.22
Continued

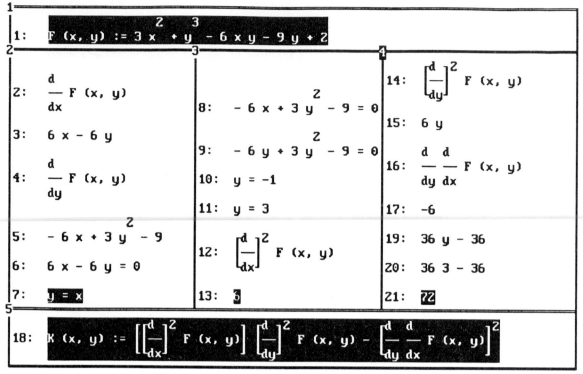

1: $F(x, y) := 3x^2 + y^3 - 6xy - 9y + 2$

2: $\dfrac{d}{dx} F(x, y)$

3: $6x - 6y$

4: $\dfrac{d}{dy} F(x, y)$

5: $-6x + 3y^2 - 9$

6: $6x - 6y = 0$

7: $y = x$

8: $-6x + 3y^2 - 9 = 0$

9: $-6y + 3y^2 - 9 = 0$

10: $y = -1$

11: $y = 3$

12: $\left[\dfrac{d}{dx}\right]^2 F(x, y)$

13: 6

14: $\left[\dfrac{d}{dy}\right]^2 F(x, y)$

15: $6y$

16: $\dfrac{d}{dy}\dfrac{d}{dx} F(x, y)$

17: -6

19: $36y - 36$

20: $36 \cdot 3 - 36$

21: 72

18: $K(x, y) := \left[\left[\dfrac{d}{dx}\right]^2 F(x, y)\right]\left[\dfrac{d}{dy}\right]^2 F(x, y) - \left[\dfrac{d}{dy}\dfrac{d}{dx} F(x, y)\right]^2$

FIGURE 1.

5.   The reader should verify that when K is evaluated at the critical value $(-1, -1)$, we obtain $K = -72$ and thus $(-1, -1, 7)$ is a saddle point.

Finally, we conclude with several graphs of the function. The only difference in the graphs represented in the windows of Figure 2 is the view point of "EYE". Can you "see" the relative minimum at $(3, 3, -25)$?

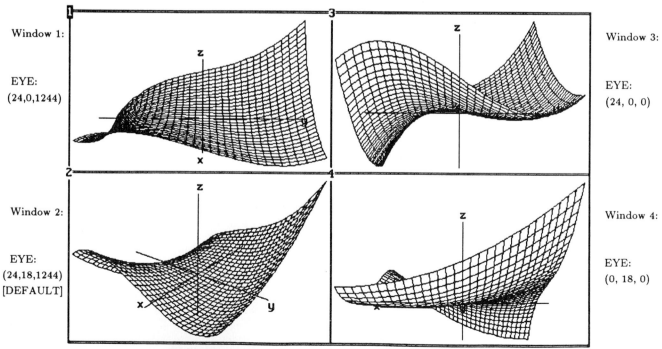

Window 1:

EYE:
(24,0,1244)

Window 2:

EYE:
(24,18,1244)
[DEFAULT]

Window 3:

EYE:
(24, 0, 0)

Window 4:

EYE:
(0, 18, 0)

FIGURE 2. In each case, the X and Y lengths are 12.

Exhibit 7.22
Continued

Experiment #22 Data Sheet

Name _____   **Date** _____

Lab Partner _____

1. Verify that $(-1, -1, 7)$ is a saddle point. (See Procedure 5.)

For each of the functions listed in questions 2 and 3, find all the critical values using *DERIVE*.

2. $f(x, y) = x^2 + y^2 - 12x + 6y - 7$ 3. $f(x, y) = 3x^2 + 3y^2 - 2xy - 12x + 4y - 10$

_____   _____

_____   _____

In questions 4 through 7, use *DERIVE* to determine relative extrema and saddle points.

4. $f(x, y) = 3x^2 + 3y^2 - 2xy - 12x + 4y - 10$

_____

_____

5. $f(x, y) = 3x^2 + 3y^2 - 2xy - 20x - 4y + 48$

_____

_____

6. $f(x, y) = -12x^2 - 3y^2 + 4xy + 16x - 8y + 60$

_____

_____

7. $f(x, y) = \frac{4}{x} - \frac{32}{y} + \frac{xy}{8}$

_____

_____

Exhibit 7.22
Continued.

8. The point $(6,-3,-52)$ in exercise 2 is a relative minimum. Try to graph the function with *DERIVE* to verify that.

9. Consider the function $f(x,\ y) = \frac{1}{3}x^3y + x^3 + \frac{1}{2}x^2y^2 + \frac{3}{2}x^2y - xy^2 - 4xy - 3x + y^2 + 6y.$

a) Find f_x and $f_y.$ $f_x = $ _____

   $f_y = $ _____

b) Find the critical points of f. [HINT: Factor f_x into three factors and solve each factor for x. Then substitute each of the three values (two are numerical and one is algebraic) into $f_y = 0$. You should end up with three critical values one of which is the solution of a cubic and should be approximated to six digit precision.]

_____

_____

c) Determine whether each of the critical points represent relative maxima, relative minima, or saddle points.[15]

_____

_____

_____

---

[15]Adapted from *Uses of Technology in the Mathematics Curriculum: A Manual of Laboratory Exercises and Resources for College Teachers* by Benny Evans and Jerry Johnson, Oklahoma State University and The National Science Foundation [USE-8950044], 1990, pp. 102-105.

Retrieving Information and Communicating. Through your computer you can gain access to information about mathematics and the teaching of mathematics. Diskettes, CD-ROMs, and especially computer networks allow you to access libraries directly from your computer. For example, the CD-ROM disc *MathFINDER* (available from The Learning Team) contains a collection of 1,100 lessons from 30 mathematics curricula projects that are keyed to the NCTM *Standards*. In seconds, you can call up a lesson plan, problem, or exercise from material on a single disk that would take about 1,600 pages if printed in a book. Advertisements for previewing and purchasing such software can be found in professional journals and at professional conferences.

You can interact with and exchange information and materials with colleagues from all over the world through electronic mail systems.

Maintaining Measurement-Item Pool Files and Generating Tests. As explained in Chapter 10, you will find your computer to be an invaluable aid in the development, organization, and management of measurements for assessing your students' progress and achievement of learning goals. Wait until you study Chapter 10 before concerning yourself with item pool files and this particular use of computers.

Recordkeeping. Maintaining data on 125 students (an average four- or five-section load for mathematics teachers) requires a computer. Exhibit 11.31 illustrates the kind of detailed student test data that can be efficiently managed with a computer. Consider Case 7.7.

CASE 7.7

In preparation for a scheduled conference with Dustin, one of his students, and Dustin's father, Mr. Saunders calls up Dustin's file on his computer screen. He makes notes regarding Dustin's progress relative to specific goals and objectives to be discussed at the conference. He also prints a copy of the selected information from the file to give to Dustin and his father.

Student Uses

Engaging in Computer-Assisted Learning Activities.
To take full advantage of the computer-enhanced learning activities you conduct, your students need to perform corresponding computer tasks. Networked student computer stations with site licenses for software systems make it convenient for students to complete individual assignments and engage in cooperative group activities using the same software systems for doing mathematics that you use.

Prior to the proliferation of software for doing mathematics, the principal use of computers in mathematics classroom was *computer-assisted instruction*

(CAI). CAI is programmed instruction in which students are confronted with exercises (usually at the algorithmic-skill level) and are given feedback on their responses. Programs branch, so that a sequence of correct student responses triggers more difficult exercises, whereas incorrect responses trigger easier tasks for students. CAI allows you a degree of flexibility in individualizing lessons according to student achievement levels, especially in accommodating variability in proficiency with algorithms. It affords you more time to conduct construct a concept, discover a relationship, and application learning activities. Much of the burden of practice-feedback-practice aspects of algorithmic-skills lessons is facilitated with computers, especially during stages 5, 6, and 7 of algorithmic-skills lessons. Consider Case 7.8.

CASE 7.8

To help him deal with the variable achievement levels among his prealgebra students, Mr. Hornacek uses intra-class grouping that allows each subgroup to progress at its own rate. He often conducts a lecture, discussion, or questioning session with one group of about 10 students while a second group is working independently on textbook exercises and the third group polishes algorithmic skills with the help of CAI programs.

Periodically, the three groups rotate, so Mr. Hornacek spends about the same amount of time with each while monitoring the other two. He finds this arrangement to be especially important for accommodating the needs of special students who are mainstreamed into his classes. Because he depends on CAI for a major share of direct instructional activities, he's able to devote more personally involved time to the more interesting aspects of teaching, namely inquiry lessons.

Doing Mathematics. Just as language arts students are far more likely to engage in creative writing and editing when they have access to word processing, mathematics students are more likely to experiment with data and test hypotheses creatively when they have a computer to relieve them of mindless work (Kaput, 1992). Consider Case 7.9.

CASE 7.9

During an algebra II unit utilizing the Pythagorean theorem, Amanda becomes intrigued by the puzzle of identifying Pythagorean triples (three integers a, b, and c such that $a^2 + b^2 = c^2$). She engages her teacher, Mr. Johnson, in a conversation:

Amanda: There should be a way of finding three lengths for sides of right triangles that's easier than trial and error and more trial and error!

Mr. Johnson: Why don't you see if you can find a pattern by looking at a number of Pythagorean triples and comparing them to one another and also to integer triples that aren't Pythagorean?

Amanda: That would take me all year to come up with enough to pick out a pattern!

Mr. Johnson: Not if we use a computer to do the work for us. We can easily write a program to generate scores of both kinds of triples for you to analyze.

Within 15 minutes Amanda has two lists of triples to analyze. Not having to generate the examples and nonexamples of Pythagorean triples by hand, she has the time and energy to devote to the sophisticated analytical task of exploring patterns.

Over the next several weeks, with some prodding and guidance from Mr. Johnson, Amanda not only develops and tests propositions about Pythagorean triples, she also involves some of her classmates in the effort. Eventually, she becomes convinced—but does not deductively prove—the following:

(a, b, c) is a Pythagorean triple iff $a = v^2 - u^2$, $b = 2uv$, and $c = u^2 + v^2$ for any positive integers u and v such that $v > u$, u and v are relatively prime, and either u or v is even.

Mr. Johnson has Amanda report her conjecture to the class, and although she has no formal proof prepared, she challenges anyone to find a Pythagorean triple that doesn't fol-low her pattern or to find a non-Pythagorean triple that does. Attempts at counterexamples are quickly dispensed with using a computer program that indicates whether or not a given triple is Pythagorean and whether or not it fits Amanda's pattern.

Computers, like calculators, relieve students of the burdens of working out algorithms during lessons in which their energies and time should be directed toward more sophisticated cognitive processes like doing application-level lessons.

Computer Programming. By writing computer programs to execute algorithms, students enhance their understanding of the algorithms themselves. Posamentier and Stepelman (1990, pp. 148–149), for example, suggest that a lesson for learning an algorithm for solving systems of linear equations might include activities in which students devise a flow chart and write a program for executing that algorithm. To construct the flowchart and BASIC program shown in Exhibit 7.23, students must analyze the algorithm, examining it one step at a time.

Exhibit 7.23
Student generated flowchart and BASIC program for solving $\{ax + by = c, dx + ey = f\}$.

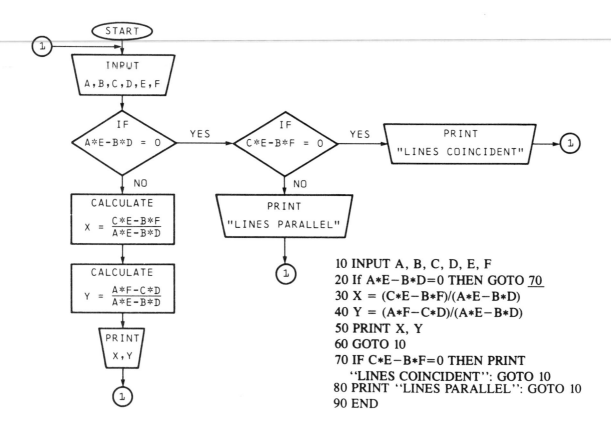

```
10 INPUT A, B, C, D, E, F
20 If A*E−B*D=0 THEN GOTO 70
30 X = (C*E−B*F)/(A*E−B*D)
40 Y = (A*F−C*D)/(A*E−B*D)
50 PRINT X, Y
60 GOTO 10
70 IF C*E−B*F=0 THEN PRINT
     "LINES COINCIDENT": GOTO 10
80 PRINT "LINES PARALLEL": GOTO 10
90 END
```

Taking Tests. Some types of tests, especially those using multiple-choice items and error-pattern analyses, are more efficiently administered to students via computers than in the more traditional paper and pencil format (Cangelosi, 1990b, pp. 131–133). Chapter 10 further addresses this issue.

VIDEO AND AUDIO EQUIPMENT
Overhead Projector

An overhead projector is a standard classroom feature. Making presentations with an overhead projector is usually preferable to using a chalkboard or dry-erase surfaces because, with the overhead, you can (a) maintain eye contact with students and monitor their behavior, (b) prepare professional-looking illustrations, (c) review and reuse illustrations, (d) focus students' attention on one aspect of your illustrations at a time, and (e) save transition or "dead" time in class by not having to erase, rewrite, or prepare material while students are waiting. Compare Case 7.10 to Case 7.11.

CASE 7.10

Mr. Barkin wants to explain the development of a formula for approximating the area of a circular region that's depicted in Exhibit 7.24.

His geometry students are poised with pencils and notebooks as he announces, "Let's develop a formula for approximating the area of any circular region." He turns toward the chalkboard and draws a circle as shown in Exhibit 7.25. Looking over his shoulder he says, "Does everyone have a circle in their notes? Okay, let's call the radius of the circle *r*," as he draws on the board. "And circumscribe the circle in a square like this," he continues. Some students, especially those having difficulty seeing his illustrations until he turns around and moves away, entertain themselves with off-task conversations. Mr. Barkin is slightly annoyed with the noise, but because his back is turned, he's not sure who is talking, so for now, he ignores it.

Facing the class, he asks, "What is the area of the large rectangle?" Some students don't pay attention to the question because they are now busy copying the figure that they couldn't see while Mr. Barkin was drawing it. Others are cued to stop talking by Mr. Barkin facing the class. Leona answers, "$4r^2$." Mr. Barkin: "Why $4r^2$." Leona: "Because . . ."

The lecture/discussion continues, with Mr. Barkin eventually constructing the octagon whose area approximates that of the circle and concluding that the circle's area is approximately $(3.111 \ldots)r^2$.

The session was marred by some students' failing to pay attention whenever he turned his back to write on the board. They were restless as he blocked their view of the board, so they entertained themselves in off-task ways. Some of the other students tried to remain on-task but always

Exhibit 7.24
Development of a formula for approximating the area of a circular region.

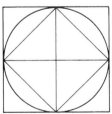

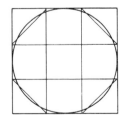

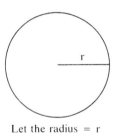

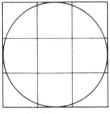

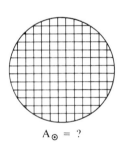

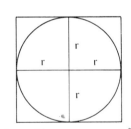

$A_\odot = ?$

Let the radius = r

Area of large square = $4r^2$, thus $A_\odot < 4r^2$

Area of interior square = $2r^2$, so $2r^2 < A_\odot < 4r^2$

each of 9 squares has an area = $\frac{4}{9}r^2$

The area of the octagon ≈ $A_\odot$
And the area of the octagon = $\frac{7}{9}$ of the area of the large square.

Thus, the area of the octagon = $\frac{7}{9}(4r^2) = \frac{28}{9}r^2 = (3.111\ldots)r^2$.
∴ $A_\odot ≈ (3.111\ldots)r^2$

seemed to be a step behind trying to copy what was on the board as Mr. Barkin went on to the next phase of his explanation.

CASE 7.11

Like Mr. Barkin, Ms. Ramos conducts a lecture/discussion session in her geometry class to develop an approximation of a circular region that's depicted in Exhibit 7.24. However, instead of turning her back to the class to illustrate points on the chalkboard, she uses an overhead projector and transparencies she prepared prior to meeting with the class (see Exhibit 7.26). Thus, she is able to monitor the students' behavior throughout the session and all students are able to see and copy the figures and make notes at the same time.

There is much less off-task behavior than in Case 7.10. Before moving on, Ms. Ramos is able to see when students are finished writing and whose attention is drifting. Students who appear disengaged are immediately asked a question or hear their name used during the presentation. For exam-

Exhibit 7.25
Mr. Barkin explains the development of the formula from Exhibit 7.24 with his back to the class.

Exhibit 7.26
Ms. Ramos faces the class to explain the development of the formula from Exhibit 7.24 with the aid of an overhead projector.

ple, "How many small squares do we have now, Nancy?" or "Okay, everyone quietly count the number of squares there are inside the circle—you too, Scott."

In contrast to Case 7.10 in which students were looking at or copying from the board while Mr. Barkin talked about something else, Ms. Ramos' students see only what she wants them to see since she controls illustrations with a flip of a switch, placement of a transparency, or exposure of only part of a transparency.

——————————

The overhead projector is more versatile than simply serving as a superior substitute for a chalkboard or a white board:

- An *LCD panel* allows you to project images from a computer screen through the overhead projector.
- *Display calculators* allow you to project images from a calculator screen through the overhead projector.
- You can use *colorful, translucent versions of manipulatives and mathematical models* (see Exhibit

Exhibit 7.27
Colorful, translucent versions of commercially available manipulatives and mathematical models can be used with an overhead projector.

7.27) to illustrate and demonstrate points with the overhead projector.

- An *electronic image writer* (Exhibit 7.28) allows you to display on the overhead screen what you write and draw, but without being confined to the area near the overhead projector. Thus, you can move about the room (as far as the cable of the electronic image writer will stretch) while illustrating points for all the class to see. Furthermore, the electronic image writer makes it possible for you to control as well as write on projected images from your computer screen as you move about the room.

Visual Presenter

Like the overhead projector, the *visual presenter* (Exhibit 7.29) displays images. However, instead of projecting light through transparencies, the visual presenter uses a small video camera to display the image on its platform onto a television monitor. Unlike an overhead projector, a visual presenter can project images of objects that are not translucent. Thus, you can use a visual presenter to display (in color) documents directly from the original sources without having to convert them to transparencies, as well as solid, concrete manipulatives and models. Imagine how convenient it is for displaying work students produce independently or in cooperative groups. For example, instead of having students copy their homework onto the board, they simply place it on the platform of the visual presenter for all to see.

Videotape Player-Recorders and Camcorders

There are available an impressive variety of professionally produced videotape programs which can be incorporated in some of your teaching units. For example, the *NCTM Educational Materials Catalog* (NCTM, 1994) lists programs such as "Similarity," "Sines and Cosines," "The Story of Pi," and "The Theorem of Pythagoras". Many can be purchased or rented from commercial outlets and others can be borrowed from media libraries or instructional resource centers. Public and cable television provides a ready source of mathematical presentations such as *PBS* specials and the *Discovery Channel,* some of which can be recorded with permission for classroom use. Besides showing existing programs, you may want to make your own videotape presentations or use a camcorder to tape students' demonstrations or for collecting data to solve problems.

Consider Case 7.12.

Exhibit 7.28
Electronic image writers allow you to use your overhead projector while moving about the classroom.

Exhibit 7.29
The visual presenter uses a miniature television camera display.

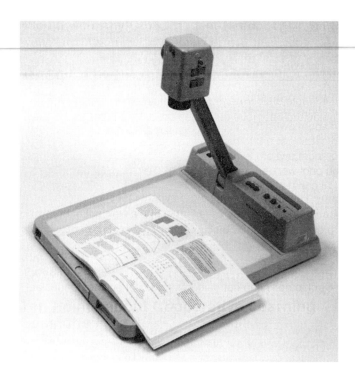

CASE 7.12 _____

Similar to Mr. Barkin in Case 7.10 and Ms. Ramos in Case 7.11, Mr. Pettis conducts a lecture/discussion session in his geometry class to develop an approximation for the area of a circular region, as depicted in Exhibit 7.24. However, prior

to the session, he videotaped his presentation, along with computer-generated graphics. As pictured in Exhibit 7.30, he shows the tape on a television monitor in front of the room as he walks about the room with a wireless remote control, monitoring students' note taking. At points he judges appropriate, he pauses the tape, raises questions for discussion, and inserts explanations as needed.

Optical Laser Discs and CD-ROM

Optical laser discs or videodiscs are shaped like records, but they have video and audio information etched on their metallic surfaces. Discs can contain a variety of media, including still photographs, animated computer graphics, video programs, and multilingual audio tracks. They are played on laser disc players and viewed via a video monitor or television set. For lists of available titles see educational technology catalogs such as *Business & Technologies Technology Catalog for Mathematics* (1994).

Regarding CD-ROMs, Lamb (1993, p. 709) states:

> Compact discs are an exciting emerging technology. Like a printer or a scanner, a CD-ROM player is a peripheral device. The player allows you to access information stored on CD-ROM discs. For example, you could access the entire contents of an encyclopedia on a compact disc. You can also play music and sounds from a standard audio compact disc. Audio CDs are exclusively designed for storage and reproduction of music, while CD-ROM discs give you access to data and graphics, as well as sounds and music. The [CD-ROM discs] are ROM or read-only-memory discs. As a result, you can read the information from the discs, but

Exhibit 7.30
Mr. Pettis monitors students as they watch a videotape of him explaining how to approximate areas of circular regions.

you can't write to the disc. Although similar in some ways to videodiscs, compact discs store information in digital form rather than analog form.

Compact discs have many uses. For example, you can access public domain programs. Or, you could listen to speeches or music. Because compact discs are a random-access storage medium, they can be repurposed like laserdiscs to suit your individual, instructional needs.

The biggest advantage of compact discs is their storage capacity. Compact discs can store an enormous amount of information. A single CD-ROM disc can store up to 656 megabytes of information.

Multimedia Networks

By perusing recent issues of various professional journals that focus on instructional technology (e.g., *Technology and Learning* and *The Technological Horizons in Education Journal*), you'll note one word cropping up again and again: "multimedia." Both articles and advertisements suggest that the learning activities in some classrooms today and in many more classrooms of the future will be supported by multimedia networks. With multimedia networking, you and your students will interface print media, hands-on manipulatives, computers, video and audio equipment, and telecommunications for accessing information; experimenting; sharing ideas; and interacting with students, teachers, professionals in mathematically oriented occupations, and mathematicians across the globe. Thus you will extend your classroom far beyond the walls of the school.

Engage in Activity 7.8.

_____ **ACTIVITY 7.8** _____

Purpose: To stimulate your ideas regarding how to enhance lessons via educational technology.

Procedure: With a colleague, reexamine the lesson delivered by the teacher in one of the following cases: Cases 4.7–4.10, Cases 4.12 and 4.13, Case 5.5, Case 5.15, Cases 6.2 and 6.3, or Case 6.8. Discuss ways additional technology might have been incorporated in the lesson.

Share you work on this activity with those of other pairs of colleagues who reexamined other lessons.

MEASURING INSTRUMENTS

Because leading students to do meaningful mathematics requires you to teach them to address real-life problems, your students will need to experience working with numbers they obtain from their real-life environments. As previously defined, *measurement* is the process by which we make empirical observations, by which we see, hear, feel, taste, smell, or touch, and then record what is observed in the form of data. Measuring instruments such as the following provide a conventional means for systematically gathering data during problem solving:

- Clocks, stopwatches, and timers (for measuring the variable time)

- Rulers, tape measures, calipers, trundle wheels, and odometers (for measuring the variables *distance* or *length*)

- Thermometers (for measuring the variable *heat*)
- Barometers (for measuring the variable *atmospheric pressure*)
- Scales and balances (for measuring the variable *weight*)
- Protractors (for measuring the variable *angle size*)
- Unit cubes and containers (for measuring the variable *volume*)
- Counters (for measuring the variable *cardinality*)

Such instruments should be standard fare in every mathematics classroom. Measuring instruments that are more specific to certain types of problems should be available as needed (e.g., a sphygmomanometer for measuring *blood pressure* and a docimeter for measuring *sound levels*).

THE CLASSROOM ARRANGEMENT

Consider Case 7.13.

CASE 7.13 _____

Prior to the opening of the school year, Ms. Haimowitz examines the classroom depicted in Exhibit 7.31 to which she is assigned to spend nearly 10 months conducting five mathematics classes each school day.

She thinks, "This just won't do. First, if I'm at one point in the room, I can't easily get to any one student's desk without negotiating an obstacle course and disturbing other students. If I'm up here explaining something in front of the class and a student in the middle of the fifth row gets off-

task, I can't readily walk over to him or her without being a disturbance myself."

Ms. Haimowitz sits down and makes the following wish list of classroom features that will facilitate her classroom management style and the type of learning activities she plans to conduct:

- Quick and easy access between any two points in the room.
- An area for large-group lecture, discussion, questioning, and individual-work sessions where students are seated at desks from which they can view the whiteboard, overhead screen, and video display while listening to whomever has the floor.
- Areas in which students engage in small-group cooperative learning activities, working on tasks, discussing mathematics, or tutoring one another.
- Computer stations where students work either independently or in pairs.
- Tables where students can work alone, in pairs, or in triples on mathematical laboratory activities.
- A traffic area for people entering and exiting the room that is easily monitored.
- A room where Ms. Haimowitz can meet with individuals privately (for example, to deal with a student's misbehavior away from the rest of the class).
- A mini-library and quiet reading room for a few students at a time.
- Cabinets and closets for securely storing equipment and supplies out of sight.
- A secure teacher's desk at a favorable vantage point.
- A for-the-teacher-only computer station interlinked with the overhead projector, video monitor, students, computers, and printers.

Exhibit 7.31
Ms. Haimowitz's classroom initially.

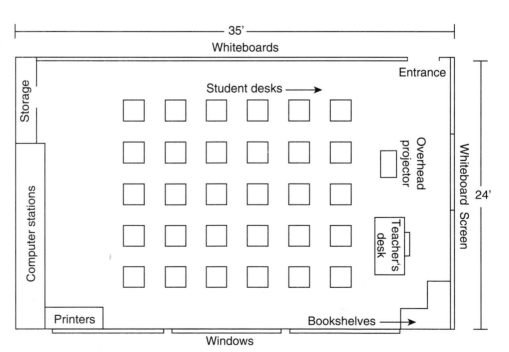

Ms. Haimowitz looks at her room in its present state (Exhibit 7.31) and her list and realizes that all 11 features are impossible. But she determines to get the most from what she's been handed. She takes measurements of the room and its equipment, makes some scale drawings, and designs a workable arrangement. Following a few visits to the school-district storehouse, a little trading with colleagues, and some help from a custodian, Ms. Haimowitz begins the school year with the room arranged as indicated by Exhibit 7.32. To accommodate small-group sessions, students rearrange their desks as shown in Exhibit 7.33.

Engage in Activity 7.9.

───────────── **ACTIVITY 7.9** ─────────────

Purpose: To stimulate your ideas regarding how to design and organize your classroom in light of your needs as a teacher.

Procedure: With a colleague, review the 11 features on Ms. Haimowitz's wish list. Discuss each and assess its importance relative to the smooth operation of the classroom and your needs as a teacher. Modify the list as you see fit.

Visit a mathematics teacher's classroom in a middle or secondary school. Make a diagram of the room and how it is arranged. Assess how well the classroom matches the features on your wish list. Rework the diagram so that the classroom arrangement is a better match with your list.

Exchange your work with that of colleagues who are also engaged in this activity.

EXTENDING THE CLASSROOM BEYOND THE WALLS OF THE SCHOOL

While it is true that multimedia networking helps bring a global environment into your classroom, you still need to lead your students to mathematics outside the classroom, making real-world measurements and integrating their mathematics with what they learn in other academic areas. Assignments in which they gather data at banks, real estate offices, engineering firms, sporting events, industrial sites, construction sites, concerts, home, social events, agricultural sites, museums, science laboratories, business firms, hospitals, criminal and civil courts, prisons, churches and temples, parks, nurseries, and just about anywhere else you can imagine are critical to your efforts to maintain the association between mathematics and the real world.

Traditionally, people are more likely to associate field trips with a science or social studies class than with a mathematics class. But wherever there is science, social studies, physical education, art, language, or music, there is mathematics. Consider taking your mathematics class on a joint field trip with a social studies, science, or English class and use the trip as part of an effort to integrate curricula across academic areas. Involving students in mathematics clubs may help stimulate these types of outside-of-school activities.

Exhibit 7.32
Ms. Haimowitz's classroom set-up for large-group sessions.

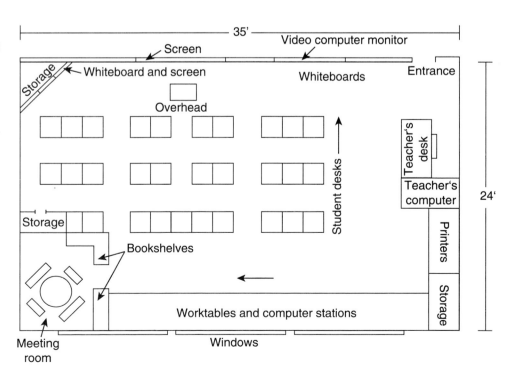

Exhibit 7.33
Ms. Haimowitz's classroom set-up for small-group sessions.

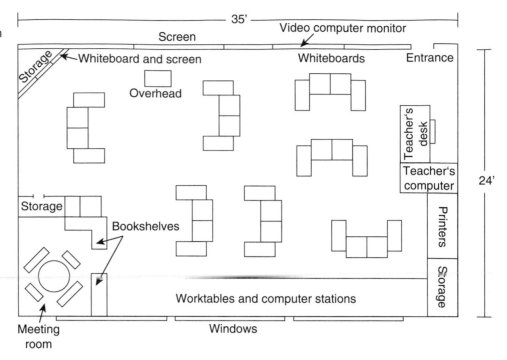

TRANSITIONAL ACTIVITIES FROM CHAPTER 7 TO CHAPTER 8

1. In Activities 4.4, 4.6, 5.3, 5.5, 5.8, 6.1, 6.4, and 6.6 you developed lesson plans. Go back through those lesson plans and think about how you might be able to improve them by incorporating additional concrete manipulatives, technology, and measuring instruments.

2. No matter how well you design lessons, incorporating attention-getting technology and stimulating field trips, your efforts may still fail if you do not effectively accomplish the most worrisome task faced by teachers, especially beginning teachers (Cangelosi, Stryuk, Grimes, & Duke, 1988; Doyle, 1986; Ryan & Cooper, 1992, p. 485; Weber, 1994). The task is to obtain and maintain your students' cooperation so that they willingly engage in your well-planned learning activities. Developing sound strategies for gaining and maintaining your students' cooperation is the focus of Chapter 8. Prepare for Chapter 8 by discussing the following questions with two or more colleagues:

   a. Some teachers orchestrate smoothly operating classrooms where students cooperatively go about the business of learning mathematics with hardly any disruptions. Other teachers spend more time ineffectively dealing with student misbehaviors than conducting worthwhile learning activities. The suggestions in Chapters 4–6 for designing meaningful mathematics lessons would not work for the latter group of teachers because the students wouldn't cooperate. What do the teachers in the former group do to gain and maintain students' cooperation?

   b. What are some of the strategies employed by teachers to build and maintain a classroom climate that is conducive to cooperation and engagement in doing meaningful mathematics?

   c. What impact does the manner and style in which a teacher communicates with students and parents—how assertively the teacher speaks, the teacher's body language, and whether the teacher uses descriptive or judgmental language—have on how well students cooperate in the classroom?

   d. What classroom rules of conduct and procedures for safe, efficient classroom operations should a teacher establish? How should those rules and procedures be enforced?

   e. What are some effective strategies for dealing with students who are being uncooperative and are off-task?

8

Gaining Students' Cooperation in an Environment Conducive to Doing Mathematics

This chapter suggests ways for you to gain and maintain your students' cooperation; it is designed to help you:

1. Differentiate between examples and nonexamples of each of the following: (a) allocated time, (b) transition time, (c) on-task behavior, (d) engaged behavior, (e) off-task behavior, (f) disruptive behavior, (g) isolated behavior, (h) behavior pattern, (i) businesslike classroom environment, (j) descriptive communication, (k) judgmental communication, (l) supportive reply, (m) assertive communication, (n) hostile communication, and (o) passive communication. (*construct a concept*)

2. Explain why the success of teachers' lessons depends on how well they plan and implement ways to teach students to be on-task. (*discover a relationship*)

3. Explain fundamental principles for (a) communicating with students in a way that increases the likelihood that they will choose on-task instead of off-task behaviors, (b) establishing a favorable climate for learning meaningful mathematics, (c) establishing and enforcing rules for conduct and routine procedures, and (d) dealing with off-task behaviors. (*comprehension*)

4. Describe a plan for managing student behavior for a given mathematics lesson with a given group of students. (*application*)

A WELL-DESIGNED LESSON GONE AWRY

Chapters 4 to 6 provided suggestions for designing lessons to enable students to do meaningful mathematics. However, even when you design a lesson that is appropriate for your objective, learning activities are unlikely to succeed unless you include measures for gaining and maintaining students' cooperation. Although the teacher in Case 8.1 develops a sound lesson plan for her objective, the lesson goes awry because she fails to practice sound classroom and behavior management principles.

CASE 8.1 _____

As part of an algebra I unit on graphs and linear functions, Ms. Lewis planned a lesson intended to help students achieve the following objective:

Explain why the graph of $y = ax + b$, where x and y are real variables and a and b are real constants, is a line. (*discover a relationship*)

At the end of Monday's class, she makes the following homework assignment: Solve each of the following for x and plot the solution on a number line:

$$-4 = 3x - 1 \qquad -2 = 3x - 1$$
$$0 = 3x - 1 \qquad 3 = 3x - 1$$
$$4 = 3x - 1 \qquad 10 = 3x - 1$$

For Tuesday, she plans to have the students transfer the six number lines from their homework onto a Cartesian plane as indicated in Exhibit 8.1. Then she plans to ask them leading questions to get them to discover that when the number lines are located where $y = -4$, $y = -2$, $y = 0$, $y = 3$, $y = 4$, and $y = 10$, respectively, the solution points are contained by a single line.

Exhibit 8.1
A diagram of the Cartesian plane that Ms. Lewis expects her students to plot from their homework points.

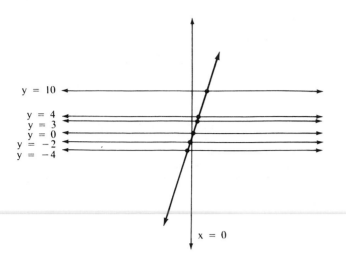

She plans a few more examples along with a few nonexamples (e.g., a set of equations that include $3 = x - 7$, and $-4 = x + 5$, and another set of the form $y = 3x^2 - 1$) on which the students are to repeat the homework task and then discuss the outcomes to discover the relationship specified by the objective.

It's now Tuesday and the bell to begin the class rings. Ms. Lewis moves to the front of the room as some students stream into the room while others sit at their desks passing time in various ways. Joyce and Junie are talking about their plans for that night, while Randall feverishly works on his history assignment. Ms. Lewis attempts to speak above the rising noise level in the room as she yells, "Okay, people, settle down. . . . Hey, Patrick, did you hear me?" Patrick: "No, ma'am. What'd you say?" Ms. Lewis: "If you weren't so involved with Cindy over there, maybe you'd hear something!" Laughter erupts from the class, as comments are made like, "Wooo, Patrick is involved with Cindy!" Feeling embarrassed that once again she's having trouble getting the class's attention, Ms. Lewis give a half-hearted laugh at the joke on Patrick, but she realizes her that comment was counterproductive with respect to getting the lesson started.

Raising her voice above the din, Ms. Lewis calls roll:

Ms. Lewis: Genan?
Genan: Here.
Ms. Lewis: Paulette?
Paulette: Here.
Ms. Lewis: James? . . . James, aren't you here? James, answer the roll!
James: Oh! Yes, I'm here.
Ms. Lewis: Answer me right away next time. Okay, Jeannie? . . . Has anyone seen Jeannie?
Davilon: Oh, yeah, she's still in orchestra.
Ms. Lewis: Why doesn't anyone ever tell me these things? . . . Okay, Winston?

Exhibit 8.2
Melissa copies her homework onto the board.

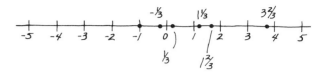

Seventeen minutes after the bell, the roll has been taken, the absentee list is posted on the door to be picked up by the office staff, and the students are finally settled well enough for Ms. Lewis to begin putting her lesson plan into effect. She announces, "Take out your homework." This leads to another eruption of student comments and quips such as Shauna's: "What homework? I didn't know you were going to pick this up!" Ms. Lewis responds, "If you had listened yesterday, you'd know about the homework. Melissa, do you have yours? . . . Great, you're such of a dependable student! Write it up on the board for me."

Some students pay attention while others entertain themselves in other ways as Melissa writes what appears in Exhibit 8.2 on the board.

Ms. Lewis says to Melissa: "That's not how you were supposed to do it. Did anybody do this the way I told you to?" Remembering that Ms. Lewis had just praised her for being dependable, Melissa feels embarrassed. Hearing another round of remarks and quips from the class, Ms. Lewis is clearly annoyed. She says, "Okay, settle down. Let me show you how you were supposed to do this assignment." As Melissa sheepishly returns to her place, Ms. Lewis begins writing on the board, using a separate number line to plot each of the six points (Exhibit 8.3). As Ms. Lewis writes on the board with her back to the class, a number of students pass the time by talking and doing things unrelated to the learning activity. As she writes, Ms. Lewis worries that the noise in her room is distracting neighboring classes, so she yells out without turning to face the class, "Pipe down!" In a moment she tries, "That's enough noise already!" and then, "If you don't get this now, you won't know it for the test!"

With each of the six points plotted on separate number lines on the board, Ms. Lewis directs the class, "Now, take out a sheet of graph paper and draw this first number line on the line where $y = -4$. Then do the second one on the horizontal line where $y = 0$, and . . ." As she continues with the directions, some students are searching for graph paper while others are trying to borrow some. Only a few are actually listening to the directions.

Six minutes later, everyone has graph paper and is ready to follow Ms. Lewis' fourth repeat of the directions. She starts again, "Now this time *listen!* Here, I'll show you on the chalkboard graph." Midway through the explanation, Andrew enters the room and walks up to Ms. Lewis with an admit slip for being late. "Would you sign this for me, Mrs. Lewis?" Ms. Lewis: "Why are you late?"

Exhibit 8.3
Ms. Lewis steps in for Melissa.

Eight minutes later, some of the students are quietly working on the task, some are waiting for Ms. Lewis to provide them with individual help, and some have completed the task and have begun to think about other things. Ms. Lewis tries to get to each students requesting help, but time doesn't permit.

Finally, she calls for their attention and tells the class, "This is what you should have done on your graph paper." She then produces the drawing in Exhibit 8.4 on the chalkboard graph.

To lead the students to discover the relationship specified by the objective, she asks, "What can you say about these six points?" A number of students shout out replies.

Ms. Lewis: Pipe down! We talk one at a time in here. . . . That's better. Okay, Eileen.

Eileen: They're all lined up in a row.
Ms. Lewis: That's right. Now, what does that tell us?

The discussion continues, but the students don't appear to be relating the six equations to $y = 3x - 1$ and the bell to end the period is about to ring. Frustrated, Ms. Lewis aborts her plan to use inductive questioning leading students to discover the relationship for themselves. She says, "Okay, this is what you're supposed to understand. We could express these six equations as one by writing $y = 3x - 1$ and then plot the coordination points (x, y) like . . ."

The bell rings and the students rush for the door before Ms. Lewis finishes the explanation and before she assigns homework.

Exhibit 8.4
Ms. Lewis' work on the chalkboard graph.

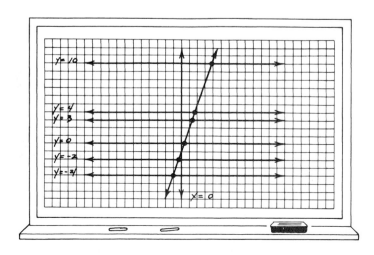

Exhibit 8.5
Example of an agenda for one class period.

Unit: #6, Graphs and Linear Equations / *Day:* 2nd /
Date: Tues., 10/18
Objectives: #3. Explain why the graph of $y = ax + b$
(where x and y are real variables and a
and b are real constants) is a line (*dis-cover-a-relationship*)

#4. States that the graph of $y = ax + b$
(where x and y are real variables and a
and b are real constants) is a line (*sim-ple knowledge*)

Agenda for the class session:

1. As students enter the room, direct them to begin immediately the following assignment appearing on the board.
   A. Take out your homework and place it on your desk.
   B. Work exercise items 13, 14, 18, 21, and 23 from page 124 of the text.
2. As they work on the assignment, move from student to student silently taking roll and checking homework. Note whose homework you want to use as examples for explanations to the class.
3. Call a halt to the individual work. Have someone put her or his homework on the board as everyone else takes out a sheet of graph paper.
4. Direct the person at the board to transfer the six number lines, each with a plotted solution for x, onto the board graph where $y = -4, -2, 0, 3, 4,$ and 10, respectively. Direct those at their places to do the same on their graph papers.
5. Use leading questions to lead them to discover that the six points are collinear as follows:

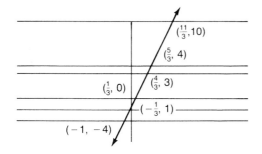

6. Use leading questions to get them to associate the six equations with $y = 3x - 1$.
7. Have the person at the board return to his or her place and assign everyone to repeat the procedure completed for homework and in item 4 above on each of the following sets of equations:

$$-9 = 5x + 4 \qquad 4 = -2x \qquad 3 = x - 7 \qquad -1 = 3x^2 - 1$$
$$-5 = 5x + 4 \qquad 1 = -2x \qquad -4 = x + 5 \qquad 1 = 3x^2 - 1$$
$$0.9 = 5x + 4 \qquad 0 = -2x \qquad 0 = 7x - 1 \qquad 8 = 3x^2 - 1$$
$$3 = 5x + 4 \qquad -12 = -2x \qquad 13 = x - 7 \qquad 9 = 3x^2 - 1$$

Keep the previous work on the board, so as they are working you can provide efficient help as you circulate about the room working with individuals.

8. When at least 75% of the class have completed the first three sets and five have completed all four sets, call a halt to the work and engage them in an inductive questioning session to get them to discover the relation specified by Objective #3.
9. After they've articulated the relation, have them enter it into their notes and have at least five people repeat it aloud.
10. Assign: (a) Complete the exercise begun at the beginning of class, (b) study pp. 126–127, working through the examples, and (c) work exercise items 1, 5, 7, 9, 15, 17, 21, and 22 from pp. 127–128.
11. As time permits, have them begin their homework.

A TEACHER'S MOST PERPLEXING PROBLEM

Why do some teachers orchestrate smoothly operating classrooms in which students cooperatively and efficiently go about the business of learning with relatively few disruptions (e.g., Mr. Citerelli in Cases 4.7–4.10) whereas others like Ms. Lewis struggle ineffectively with student misbehaviors while trying to involve them in planned learning activities? Whether your teaching experiences are satisfying, or are marked by on-going, frustrating struggles in which you attempt to get your students to cooperate, depends largely on how well you apply fundamental, research-based classroom management principles (something Ms. Lewis failed to do to do in Case 8.1). Overwhelmingly, teachers indicate that classroom management and discipline problems are the source of their greatest difficulties, leading to feelings of inadequacy in their first few years of teaching (Cangelosi, Struyk, Grimes, & Duke, 1988). Studies conducted over the past 75 years suggest that improper management of student behavior is the leading cause of teacher failure (Bridges, 1986, p. 5).

ALLOCATED AND TRANSITION TIMES

Examine the class meeting agenda shown in Exhibit 8.5. Note that five learning activities are planned:

1. Item 1 of the agenda indicates that the students are to work on exercises from page 124 of their text at the very beginning of the period.
2. Items 4–6 indicate that the students are to transfer results from their previous homework onto a single Cartesian plane and then engage in a question/discussion session intended to culminate with two discoveries.
3. Item 7 indicates that students are to work individually at their places as the teacher provides one-to-one help.
4. Items 8–9 indicates the students are to engage in a question/discussion session intended to culminate in a discovery.
5. Items 10–11 indicate that the students are to engage in a homework assignment.

The time periods during which you plan to have your students involved in learning activities are referred to as *"allocated time."* Thus, the lesson plan in Exhibit 8.5 provides five different allocated time periods. The time students spend between learning activities is referred to as *"transition time."* If the lesson plan of Exhibit 8.5 is followed, transition time should occur during the following periods:

1. While students are entering the room, obtaining the directions for the initial assignment, taking out their homework, and locating the materials to begin the exercise from page 124.
2. As indicated by item 3, when they have just stopped the first learning activity and are receiving directions for the second.
3. Just after the learning activity in item 6, as they receive directions for and prepare to work on the exercises indicated by item 7.
4. When the teacher calls a halt to the individual work exercises and directs the students into the question/discussion session indicated by items 7–8.
5. While the teacher assigns homework.
6. As the class session ends and the students exit the classroom or wait for their next class.

STUDENT BEHAVIORS
On-Task Behavior

A student's behavior is *on-task* whenever the student is attempting to follow the teacher's directions during either transition or allocated time. Students' behaviors in the following examples are on-task:

- As Joe enters the classroom for his algebra I class, he sees his teacher point to the assignment on the board. He immediately goes to his desk and begins the assignment.

- During a question/discussion session, Jolene listens to what her teacher and classmates are saying, occasionally volunteering her own questions, comments, and responses to others' questions.

Engaged Behavior

A student exhibits *engaged* behavior by being on-task during allocated time. In other words, whenever students are attempting to participate in a learning activity as planned by a teacher, the students are *engaged in the learning activity*. The students in the following examples display engaged behaviors:

- During a question/discussion session, Jolene listens to what her teacher and classmates are saying, occasionally volunteering her own questions, comments, and responses to others' questions.
- Carol works on the textbook exercises assigned by her teacher.

Off-Task Behavior

A student's behavior is *off-task* whenever the student fails to be on-task during either transition or allocated time. The behaviors of students in the following examples are off-task:

- As Marlene enters the classroom for algebra I class, she ignores her teacher's directions to begin the assigned exercises; instead, she grabs Justin and begins arguing with him over a disagreement they had earlier.
- During a question/discussion session about graphs of linear equations, Steven quietly daydreams about the car he plans to buy.

Disruptive Behavior

A student's behavior is *disruptive* if it is off-task in such a way that it interferes with other students being on-task. Thus, a student who is being disruptive not only fails to cooperate during transition or allocated time but also prevents or discourages others from behaving in accordance with the teacher's plans. The students in the following examples are being disruptive:

- As Marlene enters the classroom for algebra I class, she ignores her teacher's directions to begin the assigned exercises; instead, she grabs Justin and begins arguing with him over a disagreement they had earlier.
- During a question/discussion session about graphs of linear functions, Rudolph interrupts others while they are talking and makes jokes that distract others from concentrating on the planned mathematical topic.

Exhibit 8.6 provides examples of student behaviors classified as *on-task, engaged, off-task,* and *disruptive.*

Exhibit 8.6
Examples of student behaviors.

On-Task

Engaged in Learning Activities

- Responding to questions during a question/discussion session in a manner consistent with the procedures established by the teacher.
- Attempting to solve a problem posed in class.
- Making suggestions, raising questions, and posing problems as directed by the teacher for group discussion session.

On-Task During Transition Time

- Listening to the teacher's directions for the next learning activity.
- Moving from a small-group to a large-group class arrangement as directed by the teacher.
- After completing a test, patiently and quietly waiting for other students to finish theirs.

Off-Task

Disruptive

- Throwing paper across the room while the teacher is explaining an algorithm at the chalkboard.
- Fighting with another student as the two are about to leave the classroom.
- Making a rude remark in response to the teacher's question.

Nondisruptive

- Daydreaming during an explanation of an algorithm.
- Working on a writing assignment for English class during time allocated for individualized work on a mathematics exercise.
- Discreetly using unauthorized notes to cheat on a test.

Isolated Behavior

An incident in which a student exhibits a particular behavior is considered *isolated* if that behavior is not habitual for that student. In the following examples, Debbie's off-task behavior during a lecture and Frank's on-task behavior during an exercise are *isolated:*

- Ordinarily, Debbie diligently listens to and takes notes during her teacher's lectures. However, today she is excited about being offered a job and she thinks about the job rather than concentrating on her teacher's explanations about the graphs of linear equations.
- Ordinarily, Frank puts hardly any effort into his mathematics assignments, completing only mindless, one-step exercises and skipping others. However, because an unusual aspect of today's assignment intrigues him, he assiduously works through every exercise.

Behavior Pattern

A student displays a *behavior pattern* by habitually repeating a particular type of behavior. For example:

- Debbie almost always listens diligently to her teacher's lectures and carefully takes notes.
- Christine and Walt frequently talk to one another in mathematics class, but the conversations are rarely about mathematics.

TEACHING STUDENTS TO BE ON-TASK

Learned Behaviors

Socializing with friends, eating, sleeping, partying, watching television, and playing games are the kinds of behaviors that people, including your students, are ordinarily inclined to exhibit. Entering a classroom in an orderly manner, working collaboratively on a mathematics project, waiting one's turn to speak during an inductive questioning session, quietly waiting for directions, taking tests, raising a hand before speaking, and doing homework are the kinds of behaviors we expect from our students. Such on-task behaviors tend to conflict with those that people are naturally inclined to perform; they are *learned* by students. Thus, you should plan to *teach* your students to choose on-task behaviors instead of off-task behaviors, making sure that their efforts to cooperate with you are positively reinforced.

Communicating Expectations

You are responsible for helping your students achieve learning objectives by leading them to engage in learning activities. This requires motivating them to be on-task and preventing them from disrupting the learning opportunities of their classmates. But because of experiences they may have had with other teachers and adults who were not as conscientious or as able as you in obtaining and maintaining their cooperation, they may initially come to your class failing to grasp just how serious you are regarding these responsibilities. Thus, one of your first challenges will be to communicate exactly how you expect them to conduct themselves in your classroom. The teacher in Case 8.2 fails to heed that advice.

CASE 8.2

Mr. Boone is conducting the third day's session in an algebra I course. He asks, "Who can tell me what a *variable* is?" Four students raise their hands, but before Mr. Boone calls on one of them, Mike yells out, "A variable is a letter that stands for a number."

Mr. Boone: Where did you learn that?
Robin: That's what we had in preal . . .
Mr. Boone: We are supposed to raise our hands and wait our turn to talk.
Robin: Mike didn't!
Mr. Boone: Then Mike was rude. Anyway, this is really important; get it down.

Mr. Boone writes the statement shown in Exhibit 8.7 on the overhead projector. Most of the students have difficulty reading what's on the overhead screen; some don't bother trying. Carney whispers to Mai-Lin, "What's that say?" Mr. Boone sees them and snaps, "Apparently you two don't need to understand this or else you wouldn't be wasting your time talking!"

Near the end of the period, Mr. Boone assigns homework and warns, "I'll be checking to see that it's done first thing tomorrow. If you don't have it, you'll lose points on your grade."

The next day he has students place their homework papers on their desks, and he quickly walks by each desk, checking the names of the those who don't have anything written down for the assignment. No further reference is made to the homework.

Although Mr. Boone said, "We are supposed to raise our hands and wait our turn to talk," he tolerated Mike speaking ahead of those who raised their

Exhibit 8.7
Mr. Boone's display of the definition of *Variable*.

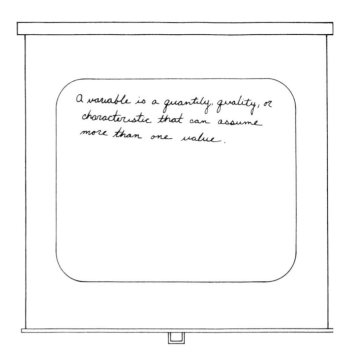

A variable is a quantity, quality, or characteristic that can assume more than one value.

hands and tried to speak in turn. Thus, he unwittingly communicated to the class that he does not take his own dictates very seriously and does not expect them to either. By presenting the important definition on the overhead so that it was difficult for most of the class to read, he unwittingly hinted that the mathematical content isn't important enough for him to take the trouble to express it clearly. Mr. Boone also played down the importance of the mathematical topic of the moment by raising the irrelevant question, "Where did you learn that!" Calling Mike "rude" and being sarcastic with Carney and Mai-Lin encourages antagonistic relationships. Students learn that they are expected to compete with Mr. Boone in a game of put-downs. The way in which homework was assigned and checked suggested that the experience of doing it is not as important as having something down on paper to avoid a loss of points.

By contrast, the messages students receive in Case 8.3 are the messages the teacher intends for them to receive.

CASE 8.3

Ms. Strong is conducting the third class session of an algebra I course. She says, "I'm going to ask you a question. You are to take 30 seconds to formulate an answer silently in your mind. Then, if you want to share your answer with the class, please raise your hand to be recognized. The question is, What is a variable?" Sybil says, "It's a . . ." Ms. Strong

Exhibit 8.8
Ms. Strong's display of the definition of *Variable*.

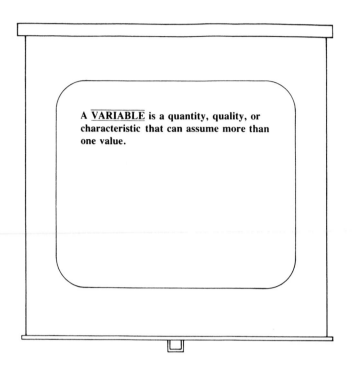

A <u>VARIABLE</u> is a quantity, quality, or characteristic that can assume more than one value.

immediately faces Sybil, interrupting her with a stern look and a gesture silently indicating silence. Thirty seconds later, Ms. Strong calls on John, who says, "A variable is a letter that stands for a number." "That's a definition that appears in some books. I'm glad you remembered it. However, you need to understand a different definition for variable for the work we'll be doing in here. Here's our definition," she replies as she displays the overhead transparency slide shown in Exhibit 8.8.

Near the end of the period, Ms. Strong makes a homework assignment that's clearly related to the day's activities about variables. The next day, she begins the period with a short test. Students who worked diligently on the homework assignment have no trouble with the test, but others find it too difficult.

Reinforcing On-Task Behaviors

Besides directly communicating your expectations for student behavior, you need to make sure that their cooperative, on-task behaviors are *positively reinforced*. A positive reinforcer is a stimulus occurring after a behavior that increases the probability of that behavior being repeated in the future.

In Case 8.3 Ms. Strong positively reinforced students' doing homework by following up the assignment with a short test that was rewarding only for those who had done the homework. She also avoided positively reinforcing Sybil's speaking out of turn behavior by not allowing her to have the floor.

Consistent positive reinforcement of isolated behaviors results in the formation of behavior patterns; furthermore, students will extinguish a behavior that proves unrewarding (Cangelosi, 1993, pp. 36–44, 228–230). Thus, it is critical that you make sure that your students' on-task behaviors, not their off-task behaviors, are positively reinforced.

Planning for Students to Be On-Task

Students' understanding of your expectations, positive reinforcement of on-task behaviors, and discouragement of off-task behaviors are such critical factors to your teaching success that you cannot afford to allow them to be left to chance. You need to deliberately design strategies for teaching students to be on task as an integral part of your plans to teach them mathematics. Such plans should include methods for (a) establishing a favorable climate for learning mathematics, (b) effectively communicating with students and their parents, (c) establishing and enforcing rules of conduct and classroom procedures, (d) conducting engaging learning activities, and (e) effectively dealing with off-task behaviors. These topics are addressed in the remainder of this chapter as well as in Chapters 9 and 11.

ESTABLISHING A FAVORABLE CLIMATE FOR LEARNING MATHEMATICS

Priority on the Business of Learning Mathematics

Your students are in the *business of learning;* you are in the *business of teaching,* of helping them learn. In Case 8.1 Ms. Lewis struggles unsuccessfully to engage her students in learning activities. Her students did not seem to consider learning mathematics as serious business. As is true in many classrooms, a major portion of the time students spent in Ms. Lewis' class was wasted with matters unrelated to learning mathematics such as taking roll, inefficient transitions, and off-task verbal exchanges. Whether your teaching experiences are dominated by exhausting, frustrating struggles with off-task student behaviors or by satisfying efforts to engage students in smoothly run learning activities depends largely on whether your students consider your classroom a place for killing time or a place for conducting the business of learning mathematics.

Students learn that learning mathematics is serious business in your classroom, not from you telling them so, but from the attitude you display from the first day they meet you. First of all, *you* must sincerely believe that the lessons you plan for your students are vital to their achievement of worthwhile learning goals. Then you demonstrate that belief by (a) getting the class off to a businesslike start, (b) being prepared and organized, (c) modeling professional, purposeful behavior, (d) orchestrating efficient transitions, and (e) maintaining a comfortable, nonthreatening environment.

A Businesslike Beginning

Students arrive in your class on the first day of school with some preconceived notions about what to expect and what is expected of them. The vast majority anticipate being required to follow teachers' directions and know that antisocial behaviors like fighting, blatant rudeness, and highly disruptive conduct like screaming in class are not generally tolerated. But experience has taught them that teachers vary considerably when it comes to dedication to their work; what they tolerate; what they expect; how aware they are of what students are doing; how assertive, decisive, and predictable they are; how much respect they have for their students and themselves. In their initial encounters with you they will not yet know the following:

- How seriously you take your responsibility for helping them learn.
- Which specific student behaviors you expect, which you demand, which you tolerate, which you appreciate, which you detect, which you ignore, which you reward, and which you punish.
- How predictably you react to their behaviors.

Thus, your students are initially filled with uncertainties about you. During this period of uncertainty, they will be observing your reactions, assessing your attitudes, assessing their place in the social order of the class and their relationship with you, and determining how they will behave in your classroom. Because students tend to be more attentive to your words, actions, and reactions during this feeling out period, it is an opportune time for you to communicate some definitive messages that establish the classroom climate and set the standards of behavior for the rest of the course. Thus, it is critical for you to begin each course in a very businesslike fashion, tending to the work at hand: learning and teaching mathematics.

Being businesslike does not require you to be somber, stiff, or formal. The business of learning and teaching mathematics is best conducted in a friendly, relaxed atmosphere where hearty laughter is appreciated. Being businesslike does require that learning activities, whether enjoyable or tedious, be considered important and that matters unrelated to achievement of learning goals be dispatched efficiently.

To effect a businesslike beginning to your course, immediately involve students in a learning activity with the following features:

- *Directions for the activity are simple and unlikely to confuse anyone.* This allows your students to get to the business of learning mathematics without experiencing bewilderment over what they are supposed to be doing. This initial experience teaches students to expect to understand your directions and enhances the chances that they will attend to them in the future. If students are confused by your initial directions, they may not be as willing to try to understand subsequent ones. Later, after they have developed a pattern of attending to your directions, you can begin introducing more complicated procedures to be followed.
- *The activity involves them in a mathematical task that is novel for them, but one in which they are likely to succeed and experience satisfaction.* Leaving them with the impression that they successfully learned by doing mathematics should serve to positively reinforce engaged behaviors.
- *All students are concurrently engaged in the same activity.* Later in the course it will be advantageous to have students working on differentiated learning activities. But, initially, having all students working on the same task allows you to keep directions simple, monitor the class as a whole, and compare how different students approach a common task. Besides, until you become better acquainted with students, you hardly have a basis for deciding how to individualize.
- *The activity is structured so that you are free to monitor student conduct and immediately stem any displays of off-task behaviors.* Jacob Kounin (1977) demonstrated that students are more likely to cooperate with a teacher they believe is on top of things and in control of classroom activities. He coined the term *"withitness"* to refer to teacher's awareness of what students are doing. You are in a better position to be *with-it* during activities in which you are free to move about the classroom and position yourself near students, than at times when your movements are restricted, for example when you are stationed at a chalkboard, standing behind a lectern, or sitting at your desk. Surely you want to be especially with-it during the early phases of a course. Case 8.4 illustrates an ideally designed beginning to a course.

CASE 8.4

It is opening day of a new term at Enterprise High School. The bell ending the third period rings; there are five minutes before the bell for the fourth period. Mr. Krebs, in preparation for the arrival of his fourth-period geometry class, turns on a video player with a prominently displayed monitor and the volume control set rather loud. As required by school policy, Mr. Krebs stations himself just outside his classroom during the change in periods. As students enter the room, they hear Mr. Krebs' voice emanating from the video monitor and repeating the following message, which appears in print on the screen (see Exhibit 8.9): "Please sit at the desk displaying a card with your name. If no desk has your name card on it, please sit at one of the desks with a blank card. There you will find a marking pen for you to print and display your first name. Once seated at your desk, please remove the questionnaire from inside your desk. Clear the top of your desk except for the questionnaire, a pen or pencil, and your name card. Answer items 1 through 4 on the questionnaire and wait at your desk for further instructions. Thank you. This message will be repeated until the beginning of the fourth period. After the bell the directions for today's first lesson will appear on the screen." The questionnaire is shown in Exhibit 8.10

Five seconds after the bell, the message stops repeating and Mr. Krebs is circulating among the students. He gently taps the desktop of one inattentive student and points toward the monitor. The student takes the cue. Several times students attempt to speak to him, but he responds with a gesture indicating to them to watch the screen. Mr. Krebs' image appears on the video screen with the following message, as Mr. Krebs himself continues to move about the room supervising the students. "I'm about to show you two objects. One we'll call object A, the other object B. Here they are." The objects in Exhibit 8.11 appear on the screen.

The voice continues: "Both objects are trees. *Describe* how they look different in the blanks for item 5 on your ques-

tionnaire. . . . If you wrote that object B is larger, then I can't argue with you. But if so, take about 25 seconds more to describe in what way object B is larger than object A. Thank you. Now, I'll show you objects C and D." The objects in Exhibit 8.12 appear on the screen.

The video presentation continues in a similar vein with students describing differences between each of the pairs for items 6–10 as they appear on the screen as shown in Exhibit 8.13.

As this continues, Mr. Krebs is circulating about the room reading over students' shoulders as they write. After item 10, the video program signs off and Mr. Krebs engages the students in a question/discussion session in which they share responses to items 5–10. Mr. Krebs highlights descriptions such as *taller, wider, pointier, rounder, boxier, smoother,* and *rougher.* He plays upon these descriptors to explain what geometry is about.

Mr. Krebs collects completed questionnaires; he will use their responses to the first four items to assess students' attitudes and perceptions about geometry. He then distributes copies of the course syllabus and uses it to preview the course for the students. Textbooks are distributed and some administrative matters taken care of just before the bell sounds.

Mr. Krebs had checked the roll and posted the attendance report outside the classroom door for the office personnel while the students were in the midst of the video presentation.

Preparation and Organization

Mr. Krebs left his students with the impression that he expects directions to be followed and that the business of learning is to be afforded the highest pri-

Exhibit 8.9
Opening day in Mr. Krebs' fourth-period geometry class.

Exhibit 8.10
Questionnaire Mr. Krebs used on the first day of class.

1. What is your name? _____
2. Name two things that are more fun for you than filling out this questionnaire?
   _____
   _____
3. Name two things that are less fun for you than filling out this questionnaire.
   _____
   _____
4. What do you think geometry is? _____
   _____
   _____

WAIT FOR FURTHER DIRECTIONS FROM
THE VIDEO SCREEN
BEFORE FILLING OUT THE REST OF
THIS QUESTIONNAIRE

5. How does object A look different from object B?
   _____
   _____
6. How does object C look different from object D?
   _____
   _____
7. How does object E look different from object F?
   _____
   _____
8. How does object G look different from object H?
   _____
   _____
9. How does object I look different from object J?
   _____
   _____
10. How does object K look different from object L?
    _____
    _____

Exhibit 8.11
Objects A and B appear on the television screen.

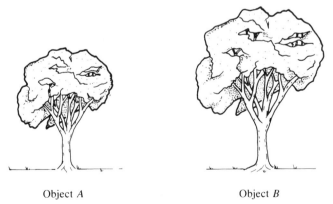

Object *A*   Object *B*

Exhibit 8.12
Objects C and D appear on the television screen.

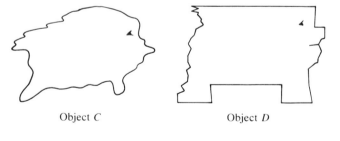

Object *C*   Object *D*

ority in his classroom. Specific steps Mr. Krebs took to convey that message included the following:

- *Prepared the videotape presentation.* This use of technology managed to grab students' attention, freed Mr. Krebs to remain near the students to monitor their behaviors, and gave the students the impression that he has his classroom organized and under control.

- *Prepared name cards and placed them on desks.* Mr. Krebs used the class list to make the name cards and assign seats. The fact that these arrangements were made ahead of time gives students still another hint that this classroom is an orderly place. Because of the name cards, Mr. Krebs can call each student by name on the very first day of

Exhibit 8.13
Objects E and F, G and H, I and J, and K and L appear in sequence on the television screen.

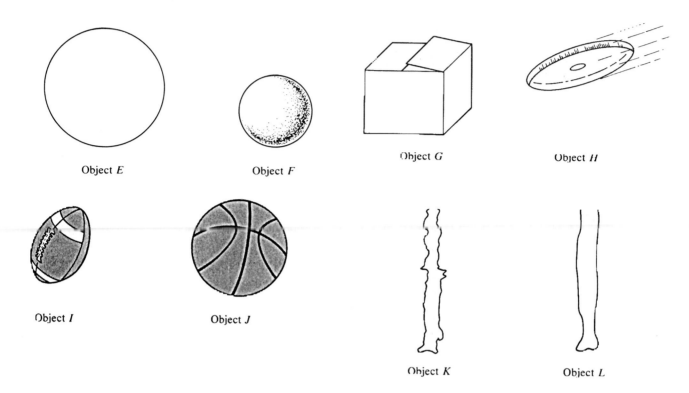

Object *E*

Object *F*

Object *G*

Object *H*

Object *I*

Object *J*

Object *K*

Object *L*

class, although he has approximately 150 students per term in his five sections of mathematics. This allows Mr. Krebs, for example, to use the name of a student whose attention appears to be drifting in the midst of the question/discussion session. A student is more likely to be efficiently cued back on task when called by name than when being addressed as "the person in the pink shirt."

The name cards also facilitate roll-taking.

• *Prepared a questionnaire and specific directions.* Students were kept busy from the moment they entered the room. The specificity of the directions and the structure of the questionnaire reduced transition time, leaving more time for the business of learning.

• *Prepared a learning activity that rapidly moved students' attention from the familiar (trees, balls, boxes, and sticks) to an overview of geometry.* Students experienced success in an activity that for them was novel.

• *Prepared a course syllabus.* A course syllabus, especially if it is well organized and professional looking, provides a businesslike touch to the beginning of a course and serves as an advanced organizer as the course progresses. Exhibit 11.4 provides an example of a course syllabus.

• *Organized supplies and materials ahead of time so that administrative matters like distributing textbooks could be efficiently completed.* Transition time was reduced, thus allowing more allocated time for students to get to the business of learning mathematics.

Your preparation and organization for the first day's lesson sends students a message that helps set the tone for the rest of the course. Being prepared and organized—not only for the first day but for the entire school year in all your courses—requires planning that begins weeks prior to the opening day of school.

Before the start of the school year, spend some time in your classroom visualizing exactly what you want to be going on there throughout the upcoming school session. Picture yourself conducting different learning activities and managing transition times. What traffic patterns for student movement do you want followed? How will you control the sounds in your classroom? For example, do you want only one person speaking at a time during large-group sessions and several speaking in hushed tones during small-group activities? What procedures do you want students to follow for such matters as using computers, sharpening pencils, going to the rest room, and obtaining and returning supplies? How do you plan to make time for completing work that does not involve your interacting with students? Anticipate problems that might arise, like students refusing to follow directions or supplies that don't arrive on time, and simulate alternative ways of responding to these problems.

Consider Case 8.5 (adapted from Cangelosi, 1993, pp. 62–63).

CASE 8.5

Mr. Martin made a checklist that included the following questions for him to answer before planning to meet his class for the first time:

I. Classroom Organization and Ongoing Routines
   A. What different types of learning activities (video presentations, computer-assisted instruction, large-group question/discussion sessions, small-group cooperative learning sessions, and independent project work) do I expect to conduct this term?
   B. How should the room be organized (placement of furniture, screens, and displays) to accommodate the different types of learning activities and the corresponding transition times?
   C. What rules of conduct and routine procedures will be needed to maximize engagement during the different types of learning activities and maximize on-task behavior during transition times?
   D. What rules of conduct and routine procedures will be needed to discourage disruptions to other classes or persons located in or near the school?
   E. What rules of conduct and routine procedures are needed to provide a safe, secure environment in which students and other persons need not fear harm, embarrassment, or harassment?
   F. How will rules and procedures be determined (strictly by me, by me with input from the students, democratically, or some combination of these)?
   G. When will rules be determined (from the very beginning, as needs arise, or both)?
   H. How will rules be taught to students?
   I. How will rules be enforced?
   J. What other parts of the building (detention room or other classrooms) can be utilized for separating students from the rest of the class?
   K. Whom, among building personnel, can I depend on to help handle short-range discipline problems and whom for long-range problems?
   L. How do I want to utilize the help of parents?
   M. What ongoing routine tasks (reporting daily attendance) will I be expected to carry out for the school administration?
   N. What events on the school calendar will need to be considered as I schedule teaching units, lessons, and learning activities?
   O. What possible emergencies (fire, student suffering physical trauma) might be anticipated and, considering school policies, how should I handle them?
II. One Time Only Tasks
   A. How should I communicate the general school policies to my students?
   B. What special administrative tasks will I be required to complete (identifying the number of students on the reduced-payment lunch program, checking health records)?
   C. What supplies (textbooks) have to be distributed?
   D. Are supplies available and ready for distribution in adequate quantities?
   E. How should I distribute and account for supplies?
   F. Are display cards with students' names ready?
   G. How should I handle students who appear in class on the first day but are not on the roll?
   H. What procedures will be used to initially direct students into the classroom and to assigned places?
   I. For whom on the student roster might special provisions or assistance be needed for certain types of activities (students with hearing loses, students using wheelchairs)?
   J. For whom on the student roster will I need to schedule IEP conferences and, for each, who is the relevant special education resource person?
III. Reminders for the First-Week's Activities
   A. Do lesson plans for the first week call primarily for learning activities that each have (a) uncomplicated directions that are easy to follow, (b) challenge, but with which all students will experience success, (c) built-in positive reinforcers for engagement, and (d) simultaneously involve all students?
   B. Do the first-week's lesson plans allow me to spend adequate time observing students, getting to know them, identifying needs, and collecting information that will help me make curricula decisions and design subsequent lessons?
   C. Do plans allow me to be free during the first week to closely monitor student activities and be in a particularly advantageous position to discourage off-task behaviors before off-task patterns emerge, and positively reinforce on-task behaviors so that on-task patterns emerge?

Modeling Businesslike, Purposeful Behavior

You teach your students the importance of learning mathematics and being on-task in your classroom more by the attitudes you consistently demonstrate than by telling them, "Learning mathematics is important," and "Pay attention." Your classroom behavior serves as a model for students to imitate. Which of the teachers, the one in Case 8.6 or the one in 8.7, demonstrates to her class that she affords the business of learning and teaching mathematics highest priority? Which one allows herself to be easily distracted from that business?

CASE 8.6

Just as the third-period bell rings, signaling the beginning of prealgebra class, one of Ms. Simmons' students, Cole, begins telling her about a movie he saw last night. Not wanting to seem uninterested, Ms. Simmons continues to talk with Cole, delaying the start of the learning activity by six minutes.

Later during the period, while explaining to the class the differences between prime and composite numbers, Ms. Simmons notices Doris staring off into space, seemingly oblivious to the explanation. Without moving from her position in front of the room, Ms. Simmons stops her presentation to the class and says to Doris, "Earth to Doris, Earth to Doris—come in Doris; return to this planet for your math lesson!" Doris glares back at Ms. Simmons, who retorts, "Don't glare at me, young lady! You're the one in outer space instead of where you should be!" Embarrassed in front of her classmates, Doris half smiles and appears to pay attention. Ms. Simmons says, "That's better, now keep paying attention." But Doris isn't thinking about the prime and composite numbers which Ms. Simmons is covering. As she pretends to attend to mathematics, Doris' mind is focused on her embarrassment. She feels Ms. Simmons insulted her. Furthermore, some of the other students who were engaged in the learning activity prior to the incident are no longer concentrating on mathematics.

A few more minutes into the explanation, Ms. Simmons notices Mr. Thibodeaux, the principal, beckoning her to the door. She abruptly stops the lesson with, "Just a minute class. I have some business to take care of with Mr. Thibodeaux." In a few minutes, the class gets noisy and Ms. Simmons turns from her conversation in the doorway to yell, "Knock it off in here ! I can't hear what Mr. Thibodeaux is saying; it's important!" Eight minutes later, Ms. Simmons is ready to reengage the students in the lesson, but it takes a while for most of them to shift their thoughts back to mathematics.

CASE 8.7

Just as the third-period bell rings, signaling the beginning of prealgebra class, one of Ms. VonBrock's students, Emerald, begins telling her about a movie she saw last night. Not wanting to seem uninterested but recognizing that it's time for the initial learning activity to begin, Ms. VonBrock says, "I really want to hear about that movie, but I'm afraid it's time to start class. Please tell me about it when we have time."

Later, while explaining to the class the difference between prime and composite numbers, Ms. Von Brock notices Jefferson staring off into space, seemingly oblivious to the explanation. Without missing a word in her presentation to the class, Ms. VonBrock moves over to Jefferson and gently taps his desktop. Jefferson wakes up from his daydream and appears to be attending to the explanation, which continues without interruption as she moves about the room.

A few minutes later, Ms. VonBrock notices Ms. Henderson-Clark, the principal, beckoning her to the door. Rather than stop in mid-explanation, she acknowledges Ms. Henderson-Clark with a hand signal indicating "just a moment, I can't stop now." In two minutes, with Ms. Henderson-Clark still waiting in the doorway, Ms. VonBrock reaches a stopping point and tells the class, "Keep that last thought in mind—all composite numbers can be expressed as the product of factors, each of which is prime—while I quickly find out what Ms. Henderson-Clark needs." At the door, Ms. Henderson-Clark attempts to engage Ms. VonBrock in a conversation about a meeting to be held that night. However, Ms. VonBrock responds with, "I can't stop my lesson right now. Please come back in 25 minutes, I'll have them doing independent work then." After that 22-second interruption, she returns to the explanation, by asking, "Now, what was that last thought I asked you to keep in mind? . . . Okay, Maxine." Maxine: "You said that all . . . "

Efficient Transitions

Unlike Ms. Simmons, Ms. VonBrock indicated to her students that the time allocated for learning is too precious to be wasted. By efficiently using the transition times between learning activities, you not only save allocated time, you also communicate to your students the importance of getting down to business. The efficiency of your transitions is dependent, at least partially, on how you manage to take care of administrative chores, direct students into learning activities, distribute learning materials, and prepare illustrations and audiovisual aids.

Taking Care of Administrative Chores. Administrative chores, like checking the roll and completing accident reports, are a necessary aspect of your responsibilities as a teacher. However, it is not necessary to spend over a third of your class time, as do many teachers, with such noninstructional matters (Cangelosi, 1992, p. 138; Jones 1979). As Ms. Krebs demonstrated in Case 8.4, you can check attendance, homework, and other things while students are busing working on assignments or a test. A seating chart and prepared forms with students' names and grids for checking off such things as whether or not an assignment has been completed facilitates recordkeeping and other routine matters with minimal infringement on class time.

Directing Students into Learning Activities. The directions for a learning activity are delivered during the preceding transition period. That transition period is efficient only if those directions are delivered concisely and clearly enough for students to be properly engaged in the learning activity with only minimal delays. Suggestions for giving directions are provided in Chapter 9. For now, keep in mind how Mr. Krebs in Case 8.4 managed to communicate very specific directions to students while remaining free to monitor student behavior closely during the transition period.

Distributing Learning Materials. Having materials laid out for students ahead of time helps streamline transition periods. Mr. Krebs in Case 8.4, for example, had the questionnaires tucked away in students' desks before they arrived. However, materials in students' hands before they are needed can be a distraction. The teacher in Case 8.8 manages to distribute materials ahead of time in a way that heightens students' curiosity without being a distraction.

CASE 8.8

With the help of his student aide, Mr. Deer seals enough seven-piece tangram sets in envelopes for each student in this fifth-period geometry class (see Exhibit 8.14). Written on each envelope is "Do not open until Mr. Deer tells you to." Prior to fifth period, Mr. Deer and the aide taped envelopes out of sight to the underside of students' desktops.

Mr. Deer spends the first 30 minutes of fifth period reviewing homework and conducting a lecture/discussion session. After that, he places his hands on his head and directs the students into small task groups and says, "Everyone put their hands on their heads like this. . . . Thank you. Please keep them there until you see me take mine down. On the underside of your desktop is an envelope containing some tangrams we're about to use. Tangrams are—" Two students start to reach for their envelopes. Mr. Deer responds, "My hands are still on my head." The two students put their hands back on their heads and he continues to explain what they are to do with the tangrams. He removes his hands from his head says, "Now, locate the envelopes. Open them and go to work."

Preparing Illustrations and Audiovisual Aids. Contrast the efficiency of the transition in Case 8.9 to that in Case 8.10.

CASE 8.9

Mr. Burson's class has just completed a learning activity in which several students illustrated problem solutions on the chalkboard. The class is now in transition as Mr. Burson prepares to present a proof he wants the class to comprehend. As the students sit and wait, Mr. Burson erases the students' work from the board and then takes six more minutes to copy the proof onto the board. In the meantime, students find ways to kill the time.

CASE 8.10

Mr. Bretan's class has just completed a learning activity in which several students illustrated problem solutions on the chalkboard. Now, Mr. Bretan shifts to the next learning activity by turning on the overhead projector to display a

Exhibit 8.14
Tangrams Mr. Deer attached to the underside of students' desktops.

proof he had previously copied onto a transparency slide. He begins explaining the proof.

Whenever feasible, consider preparing visual and even audio presentations before they are needed for class. This initially infringes on your out-of-class time, but remember that these materials will also be available for use in subsequent classes. Thus, the net savings in time works in your favor. Because he did not use students' time to write on the chalkboard with his back to the class, Mr. Bretan minimized transition time and facilitated keeping students on-task. As suggested in Chapter 7, overhead projectors, visual presenters, videocassette recorders, computers (especially with word processing, desktop publishing, and graphics capabilities), LCD panels, and videodisc players are some of the widely available cost-effective devices that make it easier for you to conduct high-quality professional demonstrations that streamline transitions and enhance the businesslike atmosphere of your classroom.

A Comfortable Nonthreatening Environment

Unless students feel that it is safe for them to participate in learning activities, doing mathematics without being ridiculed, embarrassed, or harmed, the classroom climate will not be conducive to on-task, engaged behaviors. Why would a student ever be fearful of putting forth a concerted effort in a learning activity (i.e., of becoming highly engaged)? The reasons are complex and varied. Some students may fear that their efforts to achieve learning goals will be ridiculed by peers who do not value academic achievement. Achieving the goal of acceptance by a peer group is typically more important in the mind of an adolescent than is achieving a learning goal determined by a teacher. Often, mathematical learning appears to be a long-range goal, whereas peer acceptance is immediate and urgent. Consequently, when a student feels that peers do not value school achievement, the student may fear separation from peers as a consequence of engagement in learning activities.

If students feel that a teacher has challenged or embarrassed them in front of their peers, they may consider engagement in learning activities to be tantamount to collaborating with a resented authority figure. Fears related to labeling compound the problems. Some students believe that if they put an effort into learning activities and still fail to achieve learning goals, they will either be labeled "stupid" or fail to live up to a previously acquired label of "smart." Consequently, they are afraid to risk failure, so they do not try.

Due to threats by school yard bullies or outbursts of antisocial conduct or gang-related violence, school may be such a frightening place for some students that they worry more about protecting themselves than they do about learning. One can hardly be concerned with mathematics when in fear for one's life.

These sources of fear do not excuse misbehavior or disengagement from learning activities. However, to establish a climate in your classroom that is favorable to learning, you must see to it that students' fear and discomfort are overcome and they learn that your classroom is a safe haven for intellectual pursuits like doing mathematics. You teach students that attitude by the manner in which you communicate with them and by establishing and consistently enforcing sensible rules of conduct.

COMMUNICATING EFFECTIVELY
Proximity and Body Language

Put yourself in the place of a student sitting in Ms. Spencer's class. As pictured in Exhibit 8.15, she's telling you and your classmates something. Now visualize yourself in Ms. Castillo's class. As pictured in Exhibit 8.16, she's telling you and your classmates something.

To which of the two teachers do you think you might listen more carefully? Research suggests that students are more likely to listen to a teacher who is facing them, making eye contact, and is nearby than one in the posture illustrated by Ms. Spencer in Exhibit 8.15 (Cangelosi, 1993, pp. 99–100; Jones, 1979). Ms. Spencer's body language suggests that she doesn't take what she's saying seriously enough to face her listeners. Ms. Castillo's body language clearly tells her students, "I'm talking to you and I expect you to be listening to this important message!" Your posture, body position, location in the room, use of eye contact, gestures, and facial expressions provide students with an indication of the degree to which you are in control, care for them, and expect to be taken seriously.

Get in the habit of facing and making eye contact with students to whom you are speaking. When addressing an entire class, move your eyes about the room, making eye contact with one student after another. Managing to focus your eyes on each student regularly during the course of classroom activities, and occasionally making positive expressions and gestures (a smile, a wink, a thumbs up) when you've caught the student's eye, helps establish an atmosphere of mutual respect. When addressing only one or two students at a time, body position can be used to clearly indicate to whom your message is in-

Exhibit 8.15
Ms. Spencer speaking to you.

Exhibit 8.16
Ms. Castillo speaking to you.

tended. Which teacher displays the more effective use of body language, the one in Case 8.11 or the one is Case 8.12?

CASE 8.11 _____

Mr. Adam's students are at their desks individually working on an assignment as he moves about the room answering questions and providing one-to-one help. While reviewing an algorithm with Bernice, he hears Charlie and Leona talking from their desks across the room. Without turning from Bernice, he yells, "No more talking you two!" Others in the class stop their work to find out to whom he's speaking.

CASE 8.12 _____

Ms. Petrovich's students are at their desks individually working on an assignment as she moves about the room answering questions and providing one-to-one help. While reviewing an algorithm with Terry, she hears Moe and Bernie talking from their desks across the room. She softly tells Terry, "Excuse me, I'll be back within 35 seconds." Ms. Petrovich pivots and faces Moe and Bernie, calmly walks directly toward them, and squats down so they are on the same eye level. With her shoulders parallel to Moe's, she looks Moe in the eyes and softly says, "I would like for you two to work on these exercises without further talk." She immediately turns to Bernie, achieves eye contact, and repeats the message. Standing up, she pivots and returns to Terry.

_____

Ms. Petrovich's manner made it clear that what she had to say was meant only for Moe and Bernie. Other students didn't need to stop their work to find out that her message didn't apply to them. It is to your advantage to speak so the entire class can hear you *only* when you expect all students to focus attention on your words. Having had the experience of stopping their work to listen to you, only find out that you are speaking to someone else, conditions students to turn you off.

Descriptive versus Judgmental Language

Students feel less threatened, less defensive, and more willing to engage in learning activities when working with teachers who consistently use *descriptive language* than those who use *judgmental language* (Van Horn, 1982). *Descriptive language verbally portrays a situation, behavior, achievement, or feeling. Judgmental language verbally summarizes an evaluation of a person, achievement, or behavior with a characterization or label.* Judgmental language that focuses on personalities is especially detrimental to a climate of cooperation in the classroom (Ginott, 1972).

The teacher, Mr. Farr, in Case 8.13 uses descriptive language.

CASE 8.13 _____

Ken and Oral begin talking to one another while Belinda is addressing the class and explaining how to solve a problem. Mr. Farr says, "Excuse me, Belinda." Turning to Ken and Oral, he says, "Your talking is preventing me from concentrating on what Belinda is explaining to us."

After Belinda's explanation of how she solved the problem, Mr. Farr exclaims, "By multiplying the expression by $(x - 3)/(x - 3)$, you made it obvious that the limit had to be 14. I'm glad you thought of doing that!"

Later in the class period, Mr. Farr returns Robin's test paper with the following comment written next to one of the items: "You completed the steps in the algorithm without a single error. However, your answer doesn't take into account that the denominator cannot be zero."

_____

The teacher, Mr. Wilcox, in Case 8.14 uses judgmental language.

CASE 8.14 _____

Amber and Abu begin talking to one another while Gail is addressing the class and explaining how she solved a prob-

lem. Ms. Wilcox says, "Excuse me, Gail, but there are a couple of rude people in here!"

After Gail's explanation of how she solved the problem, Ms. Wilcox exclaims, "Gail, you are quite a mathematician; that was ingenious!"

Later in the period, Ms. Wilcox returns Jorge's test paper with the following comment written next to one of the items: "You're too mechanical; you've got to be more of a thinker."

_____

The extra thought required for using descriptive rather than judgmental language will be well worth the benefits in terms of student attitudes and classroom climate. You should consistently make descriptive instead of judgmental comments to your students for the following reasons:

- *Descriptive language is far richer in information than is judgmental language.* Students gain specific information about their work, behavior, or situation from your descriptive comments. Judgmental comments provide only broad labels (such as, "good"-"bad") that students would be better off determining for themselves in light of specific information. Once your students learn that your comments tend to be filled with helpful information, they are likely to be more attentive to your words.

- *Descriptive language focuses on the business at hand, not on personalities.* Communicating about work to be performed, rather than judgments about those performing the work, enhances the businesslike atmosphere of the classroom. Comments such as "You're rude!" or "You're smart!" detract from the business of engaging in learning activities.

- *Unlike judgmental language, descriptive language avoids the labeling of students and the dangerous practice of confounding mathematical and other academic achievement with self-worth.* The delicate and complex relationship among students' self-concepts, desires to be loved and accepted, and experiences with successes and failures is a topic for extensive study (Cangelosi, 1993, pp. 26–33, 91–119). It is a common mistake to think that students will be motivated to cooperate and study diligently because their teachers praise them for appropriate behaviors and achievements and withhold praise or criticize them for misbehaving and failing to achieve. To the contrary, such tactics are more likely to backfire than to motivate desirable behaviors and efforts.

In Case 8.14 for example, Ms. Wilcox's reference to Amber and Abu as "rude people" may lead them to believe she no longer respects them and their only course is to try to live down to their reputations as rude people. Also, overhearing Ms. Wilcox label Gail "quite a mathematician" might trigger the following thought in the mind of another student: "I didn't solve the problem, so I must not be much of a mathematician!" The praise may also have a detrimental effect on Gail's attitude as she feels pressure to live up to Ms. Wilcox's label. In time, she might protect her reputation as "quite a mathematician" simply by avoiding attempts at mathematical tasks at which she could fail.

Supportive versus Nonsupportive Replies

The teacher in Case 8.15 tries to encourage a student to pursue a mathematical task confidently, only to reap the opposite effect.

CASE 8.15

Mr. DeCarlo is moving about his classroom as students work individually on factoring polynomials. As he passes Rosalie, she says, "I can't figure these out; they're too hard for me!" Mr. DeCarlo responds, "Rosalie, these should be easy for a smart girl like you! Here, I'll show you how simple they are."

What impact do you think Mr. DeCarlo's well-intentioned response had on Rosalie's thinking about doing mathematics and working with him? She said the exercises are hard. He said they should be easy for a smart girl. Besides denying her feelings, Mr. DeCarlo has indicated that if she thinks the exercises are hard, she's not smart. Rosalie is less inclined to work with Mr. DeCarlo because in her mind, he doesn't listen to what she says (he contradicted what she said) and he thinks she's stupid.

Because his response to Rosalie's expression of frustration failed to demonstrate that he understood that she was experiencing difficulty, Mr. DeCarlo's reply was *nonsupportive*. A reply to an expression of feelings (usually frustration) is considered *supportive* if the response clearly indicates that the feelings have been recognized and not judged to be right or wrong. Case 8.16 provides an example of a teacher making a supportive reply.

CASE 8.16

Mr. Marciano is moving about his classroom as students work individually on factoring polynomials. As he passes Seritta, she says, "I can't figure these out; they're too hard for me!" Mr. Marciano responds, "You're having difficulty identifying the common terms. That can be a real struggle."

Mr. Marciano demonstrated that he heard and understood what Seritta said. Once he lets her know he recognizes her frustration and she doesn't have to feel uncomfortable about it, Seritta is ready to work with him on the exercise. He listened to her and now she's prepared to listen to him.

Assertive versus Hostile or Passive Communications

Studies examining traits of teachers whose students display high levels of on-task behaviors suggest that your students are more likely to cooperate with you if you consistently communicate with them in an *assertive* manner rather than either a *hostile* or *passive* manner (Canter & Canter, 1976). Your *communications are assertive when you send exactly the message that you want to send, being neither intimidating nor intimidated.* Consider Case 8.17.

CASE 8.17

"Ms. Fisher, you know those problem solutions you wanted us to give you Friday?" says Paulette, a student in Ms. Fisher's statistics class. Ms. Fisher: "Yes, Paulette. What about them?" Paulette: "Could we wait 'til Monday to turn them in?" Others in the class chime in with comments such as, "Oh, please Ms. Fisher, be nice just this once!" Paulette: "We've got a game Thursday night and I know you want to support the team!" Chen: "You wouldn't want us to miss the game, would you?"

Ms. Fisher is tempted to "be nice" and to show support for the team, and enjoy the students' cheers by giving in to their wishes. However, she also realizes the consequences of delaying the assignment. Some students will fall behind in their work. If she doesn't get their work until Monday, she won't be able to examine and annotate them over the weekend, disrupting her own schedule. Furthermore, she knows that by adjusting their own schedules, the students could complete their work on time without missing the game.

Ms. Fisher announces to the class, "I understand that you are worried about making it to this important game and still finishing your work on time. You have cause for concern. But changing the due date will mess up our schedule. Because I need the weekend to go over your work and provide you with feedback, the work is still due on Friday." "That's not fair!" cries Porter. Ms. Fisher: "Yes, I know it seems unfair to you. Now let's turn our books to page 101."

A less-assertive teacher in Ms. Fisher's situation might have feared jeopardizing a friendly relationship with students by not agreeing to their request. Actually, her assertive communication enhances her relationship with students because students learn that she takes their work very seriously and her plans for them are well enough thought out and not changed whimsically. Furthermore, had she altered her plans, inconveniencing herself and causing the class to fall behind, she may have disappointed herself for failing to do what she thought best. Such disappointments often lead to feelings of resentment directed towards the students (Wolpe & Lazarus, 1966).

Rather than being assertive, your *communications are hostile when they are intimidating or include personal innuendoes and insults.* Ms. Fisher would have displayed hostile communications if she had responded to the students' request in Case 8.17 as follows:

> You people are always trying to get out of work! Do you think your game is more important than mathematics? Mathematics will take you a lot farther in life than games. Besides, if you weren't so lazy, you'd have these problems solved in plenty of time for your game!

Hostile communications encourage antagonistic feelings that detract from an atmosphere conducive to cooperation and learning.

Passive communications erode the teacher's control of classroom activities. Your *communications are passive when you fail to convey the message you want because you are intimidated or fearful of the reactions of the recipients of your message.* Ms. Fisher's communications would have been passive if she had responded to the students' request in Case 8.17 as follows:

> Well, we really need to have the problems solved by Friday; I really should be going over them this weekend. I wish you wouldn't ask me to do this because I. . . . Oh, okay, just this once—since this is an important game."

Being Responsible for One's Own Conduct

People who frequently communicate passively tend to feel that others control their lives. However, except for the relatively unusual cases where one person physically accosts another, one person cannot *make* another do something. Once students realize this and realize that you hold them responsible for their own conduct, they are disarmed of excuses for misbehavior. Eavesdrop on the otherwise private conversation between two teachers in Case 8.18.

CASE 8.18 ⎯⎯⎯⎯⎯⎯⎯⎯⎯⎯⎯⎯⎯⎯⎯⎯

Mr. Suarez: Didn't you have Carolyn Smith in prealgebra last year?
Mr. Michelli: Yes. How's she getting along in algebra I?

Mr. Suarez: Awful! Today, I asked her why she didn't have her homework and she told me she had better blinking things to do than my blinking homework.
Mr. Michelli: Except I bet she didn't say "blinking." Her vocabulary is more to the point.
Mr. Suarez: You've got that right. She used a very vulgar word out loud in front of the class.
Mr. Michelli: What did you do?
Mr. Suarez: I was dumbfounded; I didn't know what to do. So, I bought myself some time by telling her to meet me after school today.
Mr. Michelli: If she shows up, what do you plan to do?
Mr. Suarez: I had planned to take firm measures to prevent her from pulling this kind of thing again. But then, Bill, who has her for biology, told me she's an abused child and we need to give her every break. After he told me about the kinds of things she's suffered, I understand why she's so uncooperative. How do you think I should handle it?
Mr. Michelli: First of all, knowing about her unfortunate situation helps us understand why she misbehaves. But you don't do her a favor by ever excusing misbehavior. Sure, she has it rougher than most of us, but she's still capable of conducting herself in a civil, cooperative manner in your classroom. Our job is to hold her to the same standards of classroom conduct we expect of everybody else. Because we're aware of her background, it's easier for us to respond to her misbehaviors constructively rather than angrily.
Mr. Suarez: So, I should stick with my plan for being firm with her.
Mr. Michelli: Let's hear it, and you also need to come up with a strategy if she fails to show up this afternoon.
Mr. Suarez: Well, first, in no uncertain terms I plan to tell her that . . .

⎯⎯⎯⎯⎯⎯⎯⎯⎯⎯

To lead students to understand that they are in control of their own conduct, consistently use language that is free of suggestions that one person can determine how another chooses to behave. Purge utterances such as the following from your communications with students: "You made me lose control." "You hurt his feelings!" "Watch out or you'll get her into trouble." "Does he make you mad?" "If she can prove the theorem, so can you."

Replace such nonsense with remarks like these: "It's difficult for me to control myself when you do that." "He felt bad after you said that!" "Be careful not to influence her to do anything she'll regret." "Do you get mad when he does that?" "We know the theorem can be proved; she did it."

Remind students that they are in control and responsible for their own conduct whenever they say things such as, "Well, Sue made me do it!" or "Why blame me? I wasn't the only one!"

Communicating with Parents

A Cooperative Partnership.   Ideally, you, each student, and the student's parents form a cooperative team working together for the benefit of the student. Unfortunately, not all parents are able and willing to contribute to such a team. But whenever you do elicit parents' cooperation in support of your work with their children, you reap a significant advantage in managing student behavior and, thus, helping students achieve learning goals. Most, although not all, parents are in a position to (a) encourage their children to cooperate with you and to do mathematics, (b) provide time and space for their children to do homework and monitor their attention to homework assignments, (c) motivate their children to attend school regularly, and (d) work with you in addressing discipline problems their children might present in your classroom.

The key to gaining parents' cooperation is establishing and maintaining an active, two-way channel of communications. Such a channel for each student needs to be opened either before serious disruptive behavior patterns arise that call for immediate parental help, or summative evaluations of student achievement must be reported, especially ones involving low grades. You open communication channels before crises arise by keeping parents apprised as to what learning goals their children should be striving to achieve and your plan for helping them reach those goals. Parents need to be informed as to how they can help. Vehicles for keeping parents informed include teacher/parent conferences and written communications.

Teacher/Parent Conferences.   Except for formal back-to-school nights held several times a year in most middle, junior high, and senior high schools, parents typically expect to have conferences with teachers only to receive news about summative evaluations of their children's achievements or when serious discipline problems arise. To establish open channels of communications, however, you need to hold conferences with parents that focus on *formative* evaluations. Note in Case 8.19 how the teacher persists in steering the conversation away from the parent's obsession with Is he causing you trouble? and Is he going to pass? and toward Let's talk about what we're trying to accomplish and how we can get it accomplished.

CASE 8.19 ————————————————

Ms. Sloan teaches 148 students in five sections of mathematics. She does not have time to confer with her students' parents as frequently as she would like. However, by routinely calling three parents every school day and limiting each phone conference to a maximum of 10 minutes, she's able to speak with a parent of each student at least once every 10 weeks. Here's her initial conversation with Redfield Breaux's mother:

Ms. Sloan: Ms. Breaux, this is Nancy Sloan, Redfield's pre-algebra teacher. If you can manage the time right now, I'd like to spend five to ten minutes talking with you about Redfield's work in mathematics. Can you do that right now or should I call you back at a more convenient time?

Ms. Breaux: Oh, this is fine. Is Redfield giving you some kind of trouble? Isn't he doing his work?

Ms. Sloan: He's been very cooperative with me and seems to be working very hard. I just wanted to get acquainted with you and let you know some of the things we're trying to accomplish in mathematics class.

Ms. Breaux: Do you think he'll pass? I never could do math myself, so I can't help him with his homework.

Ms. Sloan: We're just beginning a lesson on rates and percents, and right now we're looking at ways to determine the best prices when shopping.

Ms. Breaux: That sounds more interesting than the math I had in school. Will he be able to learn it?

Ms. Sloan: Yes, he should improve both his skill with percentages and, more importantly, his ability to apply mathematics to his everyday life. Tomorrow, I'm going to ask the students to find newspaper ads that include things like interest rates at banks and discount sales at stores.

Ms. Breaux: It'd be good for him to look at newspapers instead of watching TV all the time.

Ms. Sloan: Oh, you've given me an idea! Let's capitalize on his taste for television to build his interest in using mathematics to solve shopping problems. I'll ask him to make a record of rate-related and percentage-related information from television commercials. Anytime he happens to be watching TV, he should take notes that we'll use in mathematics class.

Ms. Breaux: I can make sure he has a pad and pencil anytime he's in front of that television.

Ms. Sloan: That would really help. Thank you.

Ms. Breaux: Anything else?

Ms. Sloan: Does Redfield have a regular time set aside for homework?

Ms. Breaux: No, but I sure could make him do that. How much time does he need?

Ms. Sloan: He takes five subjects. The assignments vary a lot from subject to subject. For mathematics, he needs around 45 minutes a night. Would you please help him schedule a homework routine?

Ms. Breaux: That's a good idea. I'm working tonight, so I won't see him until late. If he's not up, I'll catch him in the morning.

Ms. Sloan: I really look forward to working with you. My time is up; I've got to phone some other parents. Please feel free to call me. I'll check back with you midway through the term, or sooner if necessary.

Ms. Breaux: Thank you for calling. Good-bye.

Ms. Sloan: Good-bye, Ms. Breaux.

————————————

Regularly scheduled face-to-face teacher/parent conferences are common in most elementary schools. Although not as common and more difficult to schedule, more and more secondary and middle schools are also setting aside days for such conferences, especially for reporting summative evaluations. School-sponsored teacher/parent conferences and, especially, individual teacher initiatives, such as Ms. Sloan's makes, make it easier to solicit parents' help in crisis situations. Consider Case 8.20.

CASE 8.20 ——————————

For two weeks, Theresa has displayed a pattern of disruptive talking in Mr. Boher's general mathematics class. The second time he stops today's lesson to deal with the problem, he asks her to meet with him after school for yet another discussion on how they can work on breaking the pattern. Today, after school, he informs Theresa that he will arrange a conference with her parents for the propose of devising a way to motivate her to terminate the disruptive talking pattern.

The next day, Mr. Boher, Theresa, and her father meet, and at Mr. Doher's insistence agree to the following plan.

> Beginning the next day, and continuing for the next two weeks, the first time Mr. Boher detects Theresa talking disruptively in mathematics class, he will issue her a warning. If she continues or disrupts the class a second time that day, he'll direct her to leave class and wait for the next period in the waiting room outside the office of Ms. Slezinger, one of the school counselors. Each day Theresa doesn't stay until the end of class, she reports to Mr. Boher to make up missed work. On those days, she'll miss her bus and her father will pick her up at 4:30, when Mr. Boher leaves the building. At the end of the two weeks, if Theresa has stayed to the end of at least seven of the ten class periods, she'll be declared "cured" and the "treatment" will be terminated. If she has to meet after school more than three of the ten days, then another three-way conference will be held to map out an alternative strategy.

————————————

Consider the following suggestions whenever you meet one of your student's parents for a scheduled conference (Cangelosi, 1993, p. 113):

- Prepare an agenda for the conference that specifies the purpose of the meeting for example, to increase the rate at which the student completes homework assignments), a sequence of topics to be

discussed, and a beginning and ending time for the conference.
- Except for special situations, invite the student to attend and participate in the conference. Healthier, more open attitudes are more likely to emerge when the student is included.
- Schedule the meeting in a small conference room or other setting where distractions like telephone calls are minimal and there is little chance for outsiders to overhear the conversation.
- Provide a copy of the agenda to each person in attendance. During the meeting, direct attention to the topic at hand by referring to the appropriate agenda item and by using other visuals (a portfolio with samples of the student's work, for example).
- During the conference, concentrate remarks on descriptions of events, behaviors, and circumstances. Focus on needs, goals, and plans for accomplishing goals. Completely avoid characterizations and personality judgments. Use descriptive rather than judgmental language.
- During the conference be an active listener so that you can facilitate two-way communications to get your planned message across and also gain ideas for working more effectively as a collaborative team.

Written Communiques. Besides conferences with parents, which out of necessity are infrequent, some teachers send home weekly or monthly newsletters that are designed to apprise parents of what is going on in courses their children are taking. Exhibit 8.17 shows an example of a weekly newsletter one teacher sends to parents.

By taking the time to write such form letters, you foster the goodwill and understanding of parents. Their understanding of what you are trying to accomplish with their children will serve you well when you want to call on them for help.

Professional Confidences

Violation of Trust. Does anything bother you about the teacher's conduct in Case 8.21?

CASE 8.21 ——————————

In a teacher/parent conference with Lamar Monson's father, Ms. Bangater says, "Lamar is one of my better mathematicians. If only all of my students caught on so fast! Like Lamar's friend Ward Anderson—no doubt a great kid, but he can't hold a candle to Lamar when it comes to doing mathematics."

Trust between a professional teacher and a student is a critical ingredient in establishing a class-

Exhibit 8.17
Sample of a weekly newsletter
one teacher sends to parents.

PARENTS' NEWSLETTER FOR GEOMETRY
2nd PERIOD
From Charog Berg, Teacher
Vol. 1, No. 13, Week of November 25

Looking Back
Our last letter mentioned that we had begun a unit on quadrilaterals and polygons. I
think most of the students were somewhat bored with the 1.5 days we spent reviewing and using definitions of the terms trapezoid, parallelogram, rectangle, rhombus,
square, perimeter, base, and height. I was pleasantly surprised that most already
possessed a working vocabulary of these terms from their work in previous mathematics courses.

Enthusiasm picked up when we delved into some hands-on problems that led
to some useful discoveries about quadrilaterals. Ultimately, the students developed
some shortcut algorithms based on relations and theorems they discovered. Toward
the end of the unit, we worked on applying our discoveries to real-life problem situations. This might explain why your daughter or son spent time gathering measurements from around your living space.

The results of the unit test given on November 22 proved interesting—to me
anyway. The scores were somewhat higher than I had anticipated; I felt pleased
about that. But what really surprised me was that according to my statistical analysis
of the results, the class did far better on the parts of the test that taxed their thinking
abilities than on the parts where they only had to remember something.

This Week
This week we will be working on more-sophisticated problems involving parallelograms and their relations in three-dimensional space. I hope that words such as
plane and half-plane will creep into your son's or daughter's vocabulary as we begin
examining the space about us in terms of sheets of points. One of the purposes is to
get the students to analyze spatial problems systematically, but in a way that does
not occur to most people.

Homework assignments will include: (a) Study and work selected exercises
from pages 264–269 for Tuesday's class; (b) watch the television program entitled
"Spatial Fractions" from 7:00 to 8:30 on Channel 7 Tuesday night and be prepared to
discuss its contents on Wednesday; (c) begin working on the worksheet to be distributed on Wednesday and have it completed for Friday's class; (d) study for a test
on Monday, December 2.

Looking Forward
After we review the test results on Tuesday, December 3, we'll tie together what we
learned from these last two units with some work with mosaics and mapping three-
dimensional space. This will lead us into the study of geometric similarities and proportions.

room climate conducive to cooperation and on-task behaviors. Teachers violate that trust by gossiping about students or sharing evaluations or information with unauthorized persons. Ms. Bangater's comments to Lamar's father should have been confined to Lamar's achievements, behaviors, and work; there is no need to talk about other students. Once students acquire the idea that a teacher gossips about them, they tend to be vary guarded around that teacher, failing either to share ideas or to attempt taxing tasks.

Privileged Information.   When and to whom should you communicate information and express your judgments about students' achievements and behav-

iors? According to one set of published guidelines only the following have a right and need to know (Cangelosi, 1993, p. 116):

• For most cases, the student needs to be kept apprised of her or his achievement of learning goals and evaluations of school conduct.

• The parents need to be aware of their child's level of achievement and behaviors because of the following: (a) Parents who are informed about their child's accomplishments in school are in an advantageous position to help their child cooperate and achieve. (b) Parents are legally responsible for their child's welfare; they have a right to know how the school is impacting upon their child.

- Professional personnel, like guidance counselors or another one of the student's teachers, who have a responsibility to that student sometimes need to know about the student's achievement and behaviors so they are in a better position to carry out that responsibility.
- Instructional and administrative supervisory personnel who evaluate the teacher's performance and work with the teacher to improve instruction sometimes need to be aware of an individual student's achievement and behaviors in order to meet their own responsibilities to the teacher.
- Instructional leaders (e.g., the principal, or the mathematics department head) whose judgments impact curricula and management of the school sometimes need to be aware of an individual student's achievement or behaviors so that they will be in an advantageous position to make school-level decisions.
- Because a school often acts as an agency that qualifies students for occupations, for entry into other institutions, or for other privileges such as scholarships, it may sometimes be necessary for a representative of an institution to which a student has applied to have knowledge of that student's achievements and behaviors. However, school personnel should seriously consider following a policy that they release information on an individual student's achievements or behaviors to such representatives only with student and parent authorization.

ESTABLISHING RULES OF CONDUCT AND CLASSROOM PROCEDURES

Necessary Rules of Conduct

Virtually all schools publish a set of *rules for student conduct* (e.g., fighting is prohibited on school property). Furthermore, teachers typically have their own sets of rules for how students are to conduct

themselves in the classroom. The *classroom rules of conduct* you establish should provide students with general guidelines for their behavior while under your supervision. There are four purposes for classroom rules of conduct:

1. To secure the safety and comfort of the learning environment.
2. To maximize on-task behaviors and minimize off-task behaviors.
3. To prevent activities of the class from disturbing other classes and others outside of the class.
4. To maintain acceptable standards of decorum among students, school personnel, and visitors to the school campus. (Cangelosi, 1990a, p. 29)

A few well-understood, broadly stated rules that clearly serve the aforementioned purposes are preferable to a great number of specific, difficult to remember rules (Evertson, 1989).For example, rules similar to those listed in Exhibit 8.18 may be all you need, providing you make sure your students clearly understand them and that they are consistently enforced.

Having such rules prominently displayed in the classroom reminds students of how you expect them to behave and helps you efficiently respond to students' disruptive behaviors. Case 8.22 is an example.

CASE 8.22 _____

Mr. Martinez has the rules listed in Exhibit 8.18 displayed on the front wall of his classroom. While explaining the algorithm for bisecting an angle with a straightedge and compass, he notices Don lightly pricking Justin's arm with the point of his compass. Justin jerks away, turns to Don, and whispers between gritted teach, "Cut it out!" With the class's attention to the explanation already disrupted, Mr. Martinez stops speaking to the class, walks directly to Don, looks him in the eye, and says, "Please meet me right after class today, so we can schedule time to discuss ways to prevent

Exhibit 8.18
The Rules of Conduct Mr. Martinez displays in his classroom.

Classroom Rules of Conduct

Rule 1:
Respect your own rights and those of others. (*Note:* All students in this class have the right to go about the business of learning mathematics free from fear of being harmed, intimidated, or embarrassed. Mr. Martinez has the right to go about the business of helping students learn mathematics in the manner in which he is professionally prepared without interference from others.)
Rule 2:
Follow directions and procedures as indicated by Mr. Martinez.
Rule 3:
Adhere to school rules.

you from violating Rule 1 again." Mr. Martinez continues the explanation.

While rules, like the four listed above, serve a necessary purpose, having *unnecessary rules* can be disruptive and detract from a businesslike atmosphere. Case 8.23 is an example.

CASE 8.23

Mr. Leggio grew up with the idea that it is rude for men to wear hats indoors. Without much thought, he instituted a "no hat wearing" rule for the male students in his classroom. His efforts to enforce the rule have caused a number of disruptions to learning activities. On most days Mr. Leggio stands by the doorway at the beginning of each period to check on students for such things as chewing gum and boys wearing hats. This often delays the start of learning activities by a few minutes.

Today, while Mr. Leggio is writing on the chalkboard, Mark slips on a baseball hat. Ten minutes later, Mr. Leggio notices it, stops the lesson and snaps, "I'll take that hat, young man!"

Mark: Why?
Mr. Leggio: You know you're not supposed to wear a hat in here!
Mark: Why?
Mr. Leggio: Because it's not polite.
Mark: Who does it hurt?
Mr. Leggio: I can't teach when you're wearing a hat!

Some class members laugh and Mr. Leggio begins to feel uncomfortable. Feeling the need to assert his authority, he yells, "Either you give me that hat right now, or you're out of this class for good!" Mark grins and slowly swaggers up to the front of the room and gives up his hat. Mark turns away from Mr. Leggio making a face mocking Mr. Leggio as he slowly returns to his desk. Students laugh, but Mr. Leggio is not sure why as he continues the lessons.

Mr. Leggio cannot use three of his four classroom rules of conduct to justify his no-hat rule: It does not (a) secure the safety and comfort of the learning environment; (b) maximize on-task behaviors and minimize off-task behaviors; or (c) prevent the activities of the class from disturbing other classes and others outside of class. He could argue that the rule helps maintain acceptable standards of decorum among students, school personnel, and visitors to the school campus. However, he should be careful to assure that any rule based on the latter clearly does help maintain an atmosphere of politeness and cooperation, and does not just impose his personal tastes upon the students.

The unpleasant consequences of having unnecessary rules of conduct include the following: (a) Teachers become responsible for enforcing rules that are difficult to defend. (b) When students find some rules to be unimportant, they generalize that others may be unimportant also. (c) Students who are penalized for resisting unnecessary rules are likely to become disenchanted with school and distracted from the business of learning.

Procedures for Smoothly Operating Classrooms

Whereas rules of conduct define general standards for behavior, *classroom procedures* are the specific operational routines that students must follow. How smoothly classroom operations proceed is typically dependent on how well procedures have been established for movement about the room, use of supplies, transitions between learning activities, large-group sessions, small-group sessions, individualized work, and administrative functions. For example, recall Mr. Citerelli's procedures for speaking during question/discussion sessions as explained in Case 4.8. Like Mr. Martin in Case 8.5, you need to determine such procedures when you organize your classroom and curricula for an upcoming school year. During the year, however, situations arise that lead you to either modify previous procedures or develop new ones. Consider Case 8.24.

CASE 8.24

Mr. Hood has organized his third-period consumer mathematics course so that large-group and collaborative learning activities are confined to Mondays, Tuesday, Thursdays, and Fridays. Wednesdays are saved for individual, make-up, and enrichment work. Every Wednesday, students are free to determine how they spend their time as long as they are in the classroom and independently working on mathematics in a way that does not disturb their classmates.

Mr. Hood's classroom is arranged similarly to the one diagrammed in Exhibit 7.32. There are 12 computers in the room to accommodate the 29 third-period students.

A month into the consumer mathematics course, Mr. Hood discovers that on Wednesdays the student demand for use of the computers exceeds the availability of computer time. Students regularly complain that they don't get to the machines because computer time is being monopolized by some of their classmates. Another complaint involves diskette abuse. The following procedure that Mr. Hood had been using for maintaining and using diskettes is apparently not working:

Storage space is provided for each student in the file boxes kept on the computer tables. To use a computer, a student retrieves a personal diskette from the file, inserts it in an available machine, completes the work, and returns the diskette to the file.

Students complain that other students are tampering with and misfiling their diskettes. On some Wednesdays, arguments have erupted over allegations of diskette-stealing and computer-hogging (see Exhibit 8.19).

Mr. Hood discusses ways to set up more efficient procedures for computer use on Wednesdays and for diskette use and maintenance. Based on input from the students, Mr. Hood establishes the following procedures:

The 12 computer stations are numbered 1 through 12. During the last 10 minutes of class each Tuesday, Mr. Hood will circulate among the students a clipboard containing the sign-up sheet for scheduling computer time on Wednesday. The sheet indicates five 10-minute blocks of time for each station. Each student schedules up to 20 minutes of computer time the first time the sheet is passed around the room. The clipboard is recirculated, in reverse order, until either all students' computer-time needs have been filled or all the 10-minute blocks are exhausted.

Regarding diskette use, the procedures are revised as follows:

The file boxes will be discarded. Students are responsible for the security of their own diskettes, which will be kept in a portable storage box that can be carried to and from the computer stations.

Teaching Rules and Procedures to Students

Formulating necessary rules and routine procedures will lead to a smoothly operating classroom only if students comprehend them, understand just how to follow them, are positively reinforced for following them, and suffer consequences for violating them. Thus, you need to apply sound pedagogical principles to deliberately teach students about rules and procedures just as you do to teach them mathematics. The time you spend explaining and demonstrating rules and routine procedures will result in time saved, because students will spend more time on-task and transitions will be more efficient.

DEALING WITH OFF-TASK BEHAVIORS
A Systematic Approach

By establishing a favorable classroom climate, communicating effectively, establishing necessary rules and procedures, and conducting engaging learning activities (the topic of Chapter 9), you avoid many of the off-task behaviors that are so pervasive in most of today's classrooms. However, with a group of 25 or 30 adolescents, you will still have to deal with some isolated off-task behaviors and off-task behavior patterns. The key to dealing effectively with off-task behaviors—including those that are disruptive, rude, or even antisocial—is to calmly utilize systematic teaching strategies for getting students to supplant off-task behaviors with on-task ones. It is quite natural for teachers to want to retaliate against and display power over students who are infringing on the rights of those about them. But such knee-jerk responses are virtually always counterproductive.

Exhibit 8.19
Mr. Hood needs to change procedures for students accessing computers.

Rather than allowing emotions to cloud her thinking, the teacher in Case 8.25 systematically and thoughtfully deals with a serious disruptive behavior pattern.

CASE 8.25

Matthew, one of Ms. Asgill's algebra I students, is working in a small-group activity with five others, playing a game called "Complete the Equation." The student conducting the game draws the next "rule" card and reads aloud, "the square root of an odd integer." The players hurriedly try out some ideas on their calculators, attempting to come up with the number that will complete the equation they've built to this point. . . . Suddenly Oliver exclaims, "I got it . . . equation!" Matthew stands up and yells, "Oliver, you cheat, I was about to get mine!" With that, Matthew shoves Oliver, toppling him backward and upsetting the game board and other materials. Having observed the incident from her position across the room where she was working with another group, Ms. Asgill walks unhesitatingly between Matthew and Oliver, looks Matthew in the eye, and in a calm voice says, "Step into the hallway with me." Indicating with a gesture that he is to go first, she follows him to a point just outside the classroom. She faces him directly looking into his eyes and says in a firm, calm voice, "You stay right here until I get back. I'm going to see if I can help Oliver; he may be hurt." She turns away before Matthew has a chance to reply. Actually, she had already noted that Oliver didn't appear to be hurt, but she immediately returns to the scene of the game, where an audience has gathered around Oliver who is announcing his plans for retaliation. Ms. Asgill interrupts him with, "I'm sorry this happened, but I'm pleased that you're not hurt." Cutting off a student starting to criticize Matthew, Ms. Asgill continues, "Eric and Beatrice, please pick up this mess and set up the game again. We'll start over with Oliver conducting for three players." Raising her voice, she announces, "Everyone return to work. Thank you."

Quickly returning to Matthew standing against the hallway wall, she says, "I do not have time to deal with the way you behaved during Complete the Equation. Right now, I have a class to teach and you need to continue practicing with equations. We'll have time to discuss how to prevent these disruptions before the first bell tomorrow morning. Within three minutes after your bus arrives tomorrow, meet me at my desk. Will you remember or shall I call your house tonight to remind you? Matthew replies, "I'll remember." Ms. Asgill responds, "Very well, it's up to you. We have only 13 more class minutes to work with equations. Go get your textbook and notebook and bring them with you to my desk." There, Ms. Asgill directs him to complete an exercise at a desk away from the other students. The exercise relates to the same skill that Complete the Equation is designed to develop.

Later in the day, when she finally has a chance to be alone, Ms. Asgill thinks, "I bought myself some time to decide what to do about Matthew's hostile outbursts. . . . I took a chance stepping in front of him while he was still angry. Suppose he had turned on me? Then I wouldn't have him in my class anymore, and I wouldn't have to be here trying to figure out a solution.

"This the third time he's had a disruptive outburst—but it's the first time he's gotten physically violent. Every time it's been during some type of group activity where there's a lot of student interaction. I don't know if he's been the instigator each time, but he's been right in the middle. But I'm not going to worry with who caused what, just with preventing this from happening again before somebody really gets hurt.

"Until he's learned that antisocial behavior isn't tolerated in my classroom, he'll have to be excluded from student-centered activities—nothing where he interacts with others, unless I'm right on top of things orchestrating every move.

"That takes care of the immediate goal of preventing recurrences. But if he doesn't learn to control that temper, at least in my class, another outburst will eventually occur, and besides—I don't want to have to keep him separated for the rest of the year. Tomorrow, maybe I should explain my dilemma to him and ask what he would do to solve the problem if he were in my place. That tactic worked well before with Janice. But no, Matthew isn't ready for that; he's far too defensive. He'd start trying to tell me how it's so unfair, that he's always picked on. Here's what I'll try:

1. Tomorrow, I will not even attempt to explain my reasons for what I'm doing. If I do, he will try to argue with those reasons and I don't need that. I will simply tell him what we're going to do and not try to defend the plan.
2. Whenever he would normally be in a group activity that I'm not personally directing, I will assign work for him to do by himself at a desk away from the others. As far as possible, his assignment will target the same objective as the group activity.
3. I'll watch for indicators that he is progressing toward willingness to cooperate in activities with other students.
4. As I see encouraging indications, I will gradually work him back in with the other students. But I will begin very slowly and only with brief, noncompetitive activities.

"Now to prepare for this. . . . I'd better come up with a contingency plan if he doesn't show up for our meeting tomorrow morning."

Note how Ms. Asgill addressed the problem of eliminating the undesirable behavior pattern as she would a problem of how to help a student achieve a learning objective. By applying teaching techniques to the job of teaching students to choose cooperative on-task rather than uncooperative off-task behaviors, she is able to focus her time, energy, and thought on the real issues at hand. In Case 8.25, she did not try to moralize to Matthew about the evils of fighting. She realized that such preaching would fall on deaf ears.

Teachers who do not systematically focus on the behavior to be altered tend to compound difficulties by dwelling on irrelevant issues. For example, in Case 8.1 Ms. Lewis called attention to Patrick's "involvement with Cindy" instead of focusing attention on the business at hand. Later, she asked Andrew, "Why are you late?" instead of quickly directing him to his seat and continuing with the lesson. In Case 8.6, Ms. Simmons dwelt on Doris' daydreaming to make a joke at Doris' expense.

Do not interpret your students' off-task behaviors as a personal attack on you. It's annoying to have your plans disrupted, your efforts ignored, and your authority questioned by adolescents. But they do it out of ignorance, boredom, or frustration, or for other reasons that do not threaten your personal worth. Keeping this in mind helps you maintain your wits well enough to take decisive, effective action that terminates the misbehavior and reduces the probability of it recurring in the future.

Eleven Suggestions for Confronting Off-Task Behaviors

Suggestion 1: Deal with Off-Task Behavior as You Would with Any Other Student Need.
How would you react if you were the teacher in Case 8.26?

CASE 8.26

You have just begun a unit with your intermediate algebra class on logarithms. With the help of an overhead projector, you explain the following definition:

$$\log_b x = y \Leftrightarrow b^y = x$$

Feeling confident that your presentation went well, you move on to the next stage of the lesson and distribute a task sheet with exercises shown in Exhibit 8.20.

Exhibit 8.20
Task sheet relative to comprehending the definition of $\log_b x$.

Fill in the blanks so the statements are true:

If $\log_3 9 = y$, then $y = $ _____.
$\log_{10} 1000 = 3$ because $10^- = $ _____.
If $\log_a 8 = 3$, then $a = $ _____.
Since $3^{-1} = \frac{1}{3}$, $\log_- \frac{1}{3} = $ _____.
If $\log_5 x = 1$, then $x = $ _____.

Directing the students to complete the sheet quickly, you walk around the room checking on how they are doing. You note Chuck staring intently at the first one, with the blank left unfilled. "What are you thinking about for this first one?" you softly ask him. Chuck replies, "I don't know how to do it." You respond, "What's the definition of a logarithm?" Chuck immediately writes:

$$\log_b x = y \Leftrightarrow b^y = x$$

You: In this first one, what's b in the definition?
Chuck: 3.
You: What's x?
Chuck: 9.
You: Then what's y?
Chuck: That's what I can't figure.
You: What does the definition say y should be?
Chuck: It's that little number at the top right here. He points to the exponent "y" in the definition.
You: What's that little number called in the equation?
Chuck: I don't know.
You: Have you heard of the word "exponent"?
Chuck: I guess so.
You: What's 3^2?
Chuck: I don't know.
You: What's 3×3?
Chuck: 9.
You: What's 3^2?
Chuck: I don't know.
You: What's $5 \times 5 \times 5$?
Chuck: Uhh, 5×5 is 25 times 5 is, ahh . . . 125.
You: What's 5^3?
Chuck: I don't know.

Although you know that Chuck has completed courses in beginning algebra and geometry and that you've covered exponents with this class earlier in the course, it appears that Chuck does not know enough about exponents to be ready for this current unit on logarithms.

Doesn't Case 8.26 present you with a frustrating situation? Chuck is unable to participate in the learning activities for the unit that you've planned. But are you angry with or threatened by Chuck not understanding what he should understand? My guess is that rather than reacting in anger to his lack of mathematical proficiency, you are thinking about strategies you should apply to help Chuck heal this learning gap. Either you need to do remedial work with him yourself or refer Chuck to some other source of help, such as a tutor or placement in a lower-level mathematics class.

Now imagine yourself in Case 8.27.

CASE 8.27

You have just begun a unit with your intermediate algebra class on logarithms. With the help of an overhead projector, you explain the definition of a logarithm.

Feeling confident that your presentation went well, you move to the next stage of the lesson and distribute a task sheet for the students to complete quietly at their desks. As you walk around the room checking on how students are doing, you notice Aretha and Armond engrossed in a conversation having nothing to do with your lesson. Neither has even attempted the first item on the task sheet.

Unless the students complete the task sheet as directed, the next phase of your lesson will be meaningless. Quickly, you go over to Aretha and Armond and say, "Let's go to work; you only have four more minutes to finish these." They look at you, smile, and say "Okay, we will." You walk away, only to look back and see that they are once again talking and have not begun the exercises.

Most of us are more likely to react in anger to students' lack of cooperative, on-task behaviors than to their lack of some prerequisite academic achievement. But being on-task is a prerequisite to successful participation in learning activities and needs to be *taught* to students. Students learn to supplant off-task behaviors with requisite on-task behaviors when we respond to their displays of off-task behaviors with sound, systematic pedagogical techniques, not when we react emotionally.

Suggestion 2: Deal Decisively with an Off-Task Behavior or Don't Deal with It at All. What are students learning about the need to follow Ms. Rockwell's directives from their experiences in Case 8.28?

CASE 8.28

Some of Ms. Rockwell's students are busy taking a test, while others are supposedly working with computers in the back of the room. As Ms. Rockwell is doing paper work at her desk, she becomes concerned that conversations among those at the computer stations are interfering with the thoughts of the test-takers. She yells from her desk, "No talking in the back!" Momentarily the students stop talking, but within a minute the conversations are again loud. "Didn't I say no talking?" Ms. Rockwell yells. This time, the noise level hardly drops at all. Five minutes later, Ms. Rockwell tries, "Hey, you back there, I've already told you to stop talking! This is your last warning." In another four minutes, she tries again, "How many times do I have to say no talking?" The talking continues.

Ms. Rockwell's test-takers should have been afforded the opportunity to work in undisturbed silence. Thus, the disruptive talking should have been dealt with—not ignored. However, ignoring the talking would have been preferable to Ms. Rockwell's indecisive approach. She allowed the talking to continue while at the same time telling them that no talking was allowed. She might as well have said, "See, you don't have to worry about what I tell you. There are no consequences." She should not give commands she doesn't plan to enforce. An example of a decisive intervention would be for her to walk to the back of the room, shut down the computers, direct the students in the back to wait in another location outside the classroom until after the test, and direct those students to complete the computer work after school.

Suggestion 3: Control the Time and Place for Dealing with Disruptions. In Case 8.25, Ms. Asgill focused her immediate efforts on getting the class reengaged in the learning activities after Matthew's outburst. She delayed developing a plan to deal with Matthew in a setting that she could readily control until she had adequate time to do so. Had she attempted to teach Matthew to change his disruptive behavior pattern at the scene of the incident right after it occurred, she would have had to contend with the following: (a) She would be burdened with supervising the rest of the students and thus could not focus her full attention on working out a solution to the problem with Matthew. (b) Matthew would have an audience of peers whose perceptions are more important to him than anything Ms. Asgill might be trying to tell him at the moment. (c) She would have little time to think through a plan. (d) Neither she nor Matthew would have time to cool down from the incident.

Don't feel obliged to demonstrate your authority by publicly dealing with a student who has been disruptive. It is usually more efficient to get everyone back on-task first and then work on preventing future occurrences at a time and place away from other students. It is easier to work with a student who has disrupted the class if the student is not on-stage in front of peers. You need not be concerned that other students will think the disruption went unpunished; word will get back that you handled the situation decisively (Cangelosi, 1990a, p. 53).

Suggestion 4: Leave Students Face-Saving Ways to Terminate Misbehaviors. You are asking for trouble by ever doing anything that leads students to feel embarrassed in front of their peers. If you expect dignified behaviors from your students, you need to avoid situations in which they feel their dignity is compromised. Thus, your strategies for dealing with off-task behaviors—even annoying, rude ones—should allow students face-saving ways of choosing to be on-task. This is often difficult to do. When students behave rudely, it is tempting to respond with clever comebacks or put-downs. Not only does this practice destroy a healthy climate, it can also backfire, as it does in Case 8.29 (adapted from Cangelosi, 1993, p. 209).

CASE 8.29

Mr. Sceroler is urging his eighth-grade class to get their homework in on time as he says, "There's nothing I can do if you don't have the work for me to see." Ronald, from the back of the room and in a barely audible tone, quips to the student next to him, "He could always go ——— off!" Having overheard the comment, Mr. Sceroler yells at Ronald, "What was that you said?" Ronald begins to grin and look around at his classmates. "You were trying to show off for us and now you can't say anything! What did you say?" Ronald, with his head down, whispers "Nothing." Seeing Ronald back down, Mr. Sceroler begins to feel confident as he persists, "What was that? Speak up. What did you say?" Now, facing Mr. Sceroler, Ronald says in a loud voice, "I said I didn't say nothin'!" Mr. Sceroler retorts, "You can't even use decent English. Of course you didn't say anything. You aren't capable of saying anything, are you?" Some class members laugh. Enjoying the audience, Mr. Sceroler smiles. Ronald, very concerned with what his classmates are thinking, suddenly stands up and shouts at Mr. Sceroler, "I said you could always go ——— off, but then I forgot you don't have a ———!"

By trying to outwit Ronald instead of providing him with a face-saving way of getting back on task, Mr. Sceroler escalated what would have been a self-terminating incident into a seriously unfortunate confrontation with unpleasant consequences. After overhearing Ronald's initial remark, what was Mr. Sceroler's purpose in asking, "What was that you said?" Ronald tried to end the incident by not replying, but Mr. Sceroler's persistence left Ronald with only two options—either lying or repeating what would surely be interpreted as an obscenity. Had Mr. Sceroler behaved professionally as a secure adult, instead of trying to demonstrate his superiority over an adolescent, he would have either ignored the remark or politely directed Ronald to meet with him at a more convenient time.

Suggestion 5: Terminate Disruptions without Playing the "Detective" Game. In Case 8.29, Mr. Sceroler knew that Ronald was the one who had made the rude comment. Often however, teachers are unable to detect the source of disruptions. Case 8.30 is an example.

CASE 8.30

Mr. Cambell's lectures, class discussions, and individual help sessions are habitually interrupted by a few students who covertly hoot, "Ooohh-ooooh-ooooh." Initially, he reacted to the disruptive noise by asking, "Okay, who is the owl in here?" His frequent attempts to identify the culprits are fruitless. Students are getting bolder with the hooting and more clever at concealing the source. Apparently, more students are joining in the game.

Frustrated, Mr. Cambell seeks the advice of another mathematics teacher, Ms. Les. She suggests that the students don't really intend to make his life miserable, which is what he's allowing to happen, but that they are simply enjoying a game of cat-and-mouse that he's unwittingly playing with them. She says he can terminate the game by no longer trying to catch the culprits. She advises him to devise a plan for getting the culprits to stop their discourteous disruptions without having to identify them.

Ms. Less advises, "Stop worrying about identifying the hooters. Confront the class with the fact that you do not appreciate the rudeness. Explain that you are responsible for teaching them mathematics, but that you cannot do so effectively when they are making that noise. Ask them to respect your rights and one another's rights to go about the business of teaching and learning. Follow up that speech with some action. Anytime you've got a lesson going in which you're lecturing, conducting a discussion, or explaining something, and you hear that noise, immediately initiate an alternative activity that doesn't require you to speak to students—one that is less pleasant and allows you to monitor their every move closely."

Taking Ms. Les' advice, Mr. Cambell explains his feelings to the class and there is no hooting for several days. Then, while explaining how to find the standard deviation of a distribution, Mr. Cambell hears the dreaded "Ooohh-ooohooooh." Abruptly, he stops the explanation and silently and calmly displays a transparency on the overhead with the following message: "Open your book to page 157. Study the explanation and examples on standard deviation and work exercises on pages 158–159. Most of what we planned to talk about today is covered on those pages. Do not forget we have a test on Thursday. It covers the unit objectives on means, variances, and standard deviations. Good luck."

Mr. Cambell watches them reluctantly work through the text material without his help. Some students start to ask him questions, but a stern look and signal for silence puts an end to that.

Suggestion 6: Utilize the Help of Colleagues, Parents, and Supervisors; Don't Be Fooled by the "Myth of the Good Teacher." In Case 8.30, Mr. Cambell sought the counsel of a trusted colleague. Unfortunately, some teachers are deluded by what Canter and Canter (1976, pp. 6–7) refer to as the "myth of the good teacher." According to the myth, really "good" teachers handle all their own discipline problems without outside help; seeking help is considered a sign of weakness. In reality, consulting with colleagues is a mark of professional behavior

(Bang-Jensen, 1988; Raney & Robbins, 1989). Furthermore, your supervisors are legally and ethically responsible for supporting your instructional efforts (Cangelosi, 1991; Stanley & Popham 1988a; Stiggins & Duke, 1988), and parents typically have greater influence over their children than do teachers (Canter & Canter, 1976).

Suggestion 7: Have Alternative Lesson Plans Available for Times when Students Do Not Cooperate as You Planned. Expect your students to cooperate with you and choose to engage in learning activities. Your confident expectations increase the chances that they will. Do not abort a well-designed learning activity as soon as it does not go as smoothly as you planned. However, by being prepared in the event that some students refuse to cooperate, you protect yourself from operating under the stress of having no alternative if the activity should be aborted. Ms. Asgill in Case 8.25 and Mr. Cambell in Case 8.30 demonstrated the advantage of having alternative and less-enjoyable activities ready for times when students' off-task behaviors rendered their original plans unworkable. Ideally, the alternative activities target the same objectives as the original ones.

Suggestion 8: Concern Yourself as Much with Decreasing the Incidence of Nondisruptive Off-Task Behaviors as You Do with Decreasing Disruptive Off-Task Behaviors. Nondisruptive off-task behaviors (mind-wandering, daydreaming, failing to attempt assignments, being under the influence of drugs during learning activities, sleeping in class) are easier to disregard than disruptive behaviors which infringe on the rights of the class as a whole. However, you should be concerned with all forms of off-task behavior because when students are off-task, they are failing to benefit from your planned lessons, and thus are diminishing their chances of achieving learning goals. Your responsibility for helping them achieve learning goals includes helping them supplant off-task with on-task behaviors. Furthermore, students who are not being disruptive but are off-task tend to fall behind in a lesson. Once students miss one part of a lesson, they are likely to fail to learn from subsequent parts even though they may re-engage in learning activities. Those unable to follow a lesson are likely candidates for boredom and disruptive behaviors.

Suggestion 9: Never Use Corporal Punishment. There may be times when you need to restrain students in order to prevent them from injuring themselves or others (including you). But do not confuse necessary physical constraint with the administration of corporal punishment. *Corporal punishment* is physical pain intentionally inflicted on a student for the purpose of leading the student to feel sorry for something the student did. For you, as a teacher, to inflict such a form of punishment is far more harmful than helpful (Curwin & Mendler, 1980; Rose, 1984, Welsh, 1985). Although numerous prominent professional organizations like the National Education Association, the American Federation of Teachers, and the American Psychological Association have issued statements adamantly opposing its use in school and its use has been banned in some states, corporal punishment continues to be widely, but inconsistently, practiced in schools (Cangelosi, 1993, pp. 215–220). The arguments against the use of corporal punishment and in favor of more-effective and less-destructive discipline practices are compelling (see, for example, Azrin, Hake, & Hutchinson, 1965; Azrin, Hutchinson & Sallery, 1964; Bandura, 1965; Bongiovanni, 1979; Cangelosi, 1993, pp. 215–220; Delgado, 1963; Hyman & Wise, 1979; Kohut & Range, 1979; Rust & Kinnard, 1983; Strike & Soltis, 1986; Sulzer-Azaroff & Mayer, 1977; Ulrich & Azrin, 1962; Welsh, 1985).

Suggestion 10: Maintain Your Options; Avoid "Playing Your Last Card." Understand the extent and limits of your authority. Never threaten a student with anything unless you know you can follow through. For example, if you tell a student, "Either start working now or you're out of this class for good!" what are you going to do if the student refuses? You have extended your authority as far as it reaches, exhausting your options. Obtain the help of supervisors well before you run out of ways deal with problems.

Suggestion 11: Know Yourself and Your Students. Continually examine your motives for your work with students. Be receptive to differences among your students. What works with one may be a disaster with another. New ideas should be tried out cautiously—first with individuals you know best and then extended to others as the ideas prove promising. The better you understand yourself and your students, the more likely you will be able to gain students' cooperation and respond sensitively, flexibly, decisively, and effectively to discipline problems whenever they do occur.

CONDUCTING ENGAGING LEARNING ACTIVITIES

"Math is so dumb!" "Class is boring!" "This stuff is so dry!" "Who cares about this secant line crap!" "I'm never going to use this; I'm going to be an artist, not an engineer!" "I can't do homework until my show is over!" "It's so boring just sitting in here with them jabbering about x's and y's!" "None of this has anything to do with me!"

Embedded in those familiar cries are the more common reasons why students get off-task during learning activities. To keep students on task, you must not only establish a favorable classroom climate, communicate effectively, establish necessary rules and procedures, and effectively deal with off-task behavior, you must also design, organize, and conduct learning activities that hold students' attention. Chapter 9 provides suggestions for doing that.

TRANSITIONAL ACTIVITIES FROM CHAPTER 8 TO CHAPTER 9 _____

1. Select the one response to each of the following multiple-choice items that either completes the statement so that it is true or accurately answers the question.
   A. Time for students to achieve learning objectives increases as _____.
      (a) more time is spent on simple-knowledge and algorithmic-skill activities instead of higher-cognitive-level activities such as construct a concept or application
      (b) more time is spent on higher-cognitive-level activities and less time is spent on simple-knowledge and algorithmic-skill activities
      (c) allocated time decreases
      (d) transition time decreases
   B. Which one of the following statements is true?
      (a) Students who are on-task are engaged in learning activities.
      (b) Students who are off-task are being disruptive.
      (c) Engaged behaviors are never off-task.
   C. Students develop on-task behavior patterns because _____.
      (a) isolated on-task behaviors are positively reinforced
      (b) isolated off-task behaviors are positively reinforced
      (c) of inherent instincts about right and wrong
   D. Students develop off-task behavior patterns because _____.
      (a) isolated on-task behaviors are positively reinforced
      (b) isolated off-task behaviors are positively reinforced
      (c) of instincts about right and wrong

   E. A classroom with a businesslike atmosphere is characterized by ———.
      (a) democratic decision making
      (b) authoritarian decision making
      (c) a highly formalized structure
      (d) purposeful activity
   F. Which of the following contributes to a businesslike classroom atmosphere?
      (a) Use of descriptive language.
      (b) Use of judgmental language.
      (c) Maximizing transition time.
      (d) Consistent use of corporal punishment for unbusinesslike behaviors.
   G. Students tend to be most receptive to signals about your expectations of them _____.
      (a) following tests
      (b) during the first few days of the school year
      (c) during the last few days of the school year
   H. A supportive reply to a student tends to communicate _____.
      (a) assertiveness
      (b) passiveness
      (c) acceptance of feelings
      (d) value judgments
   I. By "withitness," Kounin refers to how ____.
      (a) well a teacher maintains students on-task and engaged in learning activities
      (b) aware a teacher is of what's going on in the classroom
      (c) well a teacher displays enthusiasm for learning
      (d) assertively a teacher conducts herself or himself with students

   Compare your responses to the following: A-d; B-c; C-a; D-b; E-d; F-a; G-b; H-c; I-b.
2. Chapter 8 provided suggestions for managing student behavior—positively reinforcing on-task behaviors, organizing and preparing efficient transitions, focusing on the business of learning, and using descriptive instead of judgmental language. In Case 8.1 Ms. Lewis failed to heed a number of those suggestions. Reread Case 8.1 and identify behaviors Ms. Lewis exhibited that were inconsistent with the suggestions. Indicate what she might have done differently to improve her classroom climate and to encourage her students to be on-task. Compare your work on this activity to that of a colleague.
3. Apparently Mr. Krebs spent an extraordinary amount of time preparing for the class session described in Case 8.4. In what ways were his preparations for this class more elaborate than what you would expect from most mathematics teachers? How do you think those efforts will pay

off in practical dividends for him throughout the remainder of the geometry course? Compare your answers to those of a colleague.

4. Imagine having just accepted a position teaching at a middle or secondary school. You've just been assigned a classroom and received your teaching schedule for the upcoming school year (two algebra I sections, one geometry, one consumer mathematics, and one precalculus). Consider how you might answer the questions appearing in Case 8.5. Compare your responses to those of a colleague.

5. Imagine having just directed your students to devise proofs independently for a theorem you've just stated. Although you were quite clear that they were to work silently by themselves, you notice that Haywood and Howard are talking. You walk over to them and realize that they are discussing how to prove the theorem. State an example of a *descriptive* comment you could make to them. State an example of a *judgmental* comment you could make to them. What are the relative advantages and disadvantages of making the first instead of the second comment? Compare your work on this activity with that of a colleague.

6. After you've directed students to devise a proof for a theorem, Delcima exclaims to you, "I could never make up my own proof!" State an example of a *supportive* comment you could make to Delcima. State an example of a *nonsupportive* comment you could make. What are the relative advantages and disadvantages of making the first instead of the second comment? Compare your work on this activity to that of a colleague.

7. After you've directed students to devise a proof for a theorem, Billy exclaims to you, "We've already got too much work to do! Do we really have to prove this?" State an example of an *assertive* comment you could make to Billy. State an example of a *passive* comment you could make. State an example of a *hostile* comment you could make. What are the relative advantages and disadvantages of making the first instead of either the second or third comment? Compare your work on this activity to that of a colleague.

8. By their comments in Cases 8.31 and 8.32, teachers violate principles suggested in Chapter 8. What principles are they violating?

CASE 8.31 ⎯⎯⎯⎯⎯⎯⎯⎯⎯⎯

Mr. Zebart confronts Jackie, Fred, and Lamont with evidence that they cheated on a test. "What have you got to say for yourselves?" he asks. Lamont: "I didn't steal the test; Jackie already had it before I even knew about it!" Mr. Zebart: "So, Jackie, you not only cheated, but you got these other two to cheat also!"

CASE 8.32 ⎯⎯⎯⎯⎯⎯⎯⎯⎯⎯

Mr. Meyers, a school custodian, notices that one of the teachers, Ms. Orlando, appears a bit haggard. He says, "You seem a bit out of sorts. Are you okay?" Ms. Orlando: "Oh, thanks for asking. I'm okay—it's just Justin Thomas. He's so frustrating to work with! The next time he gives me trouble, I'm going to have to talk to one of the counselors about him."

⎯⎯⎯⎯⎯⎯⎯⎯⎯⎯

Compare your responses on this activity to that of a colleague and to the following:

> Mr. Zebart failed to convey that the students are responsible for their own behaviors. Ms. Orlando violated professional trust by sharing privileged information about a student.

9. Observe a mathematics class in a middle or secondary school. Distinguish the transition time from the allocated times in the class period. For each transition time and each allocated time, note one student who is on-task and one who is off-task. Describe the behaviors that led you to believe they were, respectively, on-task and off-task. If you were in the teacher's place, what might you do to positively reinforce the on-task behavior? What might you do to discourage recurrences of the off-task behaviors? Share your work on this activity with a colleague.

10. Discuss the following questions with two or more of your colleagues:
   a. Why are some students bored with the mathematics lessons of one teacher but enthusiastically engage in the mathematics lessons of another teacher?
   b. What strategies do teachers employ to help students understand and follow directions for learning activities?
   c. What strategies do teachers employ to keep students engaged in the following types of learning activities?
      • Large-group presentation
      • Cooperative learning
      • Question/discussion
      • Independent work
   d. What are the preferable methods of motivating students to do homework assignments?
   e. What are appropriate strategies for responding to questions raised by students during mathematics lessons?

Engaging Students in Learning Activities

This chapter suggests and illustrates strategies for conducting learning activities so that students willingly and enthusiastically engage in them. Chapter 9 is designed to help you:

1. Develop techniques that encourage students to be on-task when you are giving directions. (*application*)
2. Distinguish between reasoning-level and memory-level questions raised by students and develop strategies for responding to student-initiated questions appropriate for the lesson's objective. (*application*)
3. Develop techniques that encourage students to be engaged during the following types of learning activities: (a) large-group presentations; (b) cooperative learning sessions, (c) question/discussion sessions, (d) independent work sessions, and (e) homework assignments. (*application*)

IDEAS FOR GIVING DIRECTIONS

Explicitness, Specificity, and Directness

Indirect and inexplicit communications are appropriate for inquiry-learning activities to stimulate your students to reason, discover, or create. Case 9.1 is an example.

CASE 9.1

As part of a unit on the behavior of trigonometric functions, Mr. Koebbe is trying to lead students to discover certain relationships among various components of a function and its graph (for example, how b in $y = a \sin(b\phi + c) + d$ influences the period of the graph). At one point in the lesson, Maria shows him her calculator with the display shown in Exhibit 9.1 and says, "I see what happens to the period if you multiply the angle, but what if you divide it?" Mr. Koebbe responds, "Hmmm, I wonder. Let's think about it. Would that exaggerate the influence of the angle? Or maybe not . . . hmmm . . . before you try some examples on your calculator let's see if we can predict what will happen.

Mr. Koebbe knew the answer to Maria's question, but instead of answering it directly, he probed with another question. His indefinite, evasive communication was appropriate in Case 9.1 because Mr. Koebbe's objective was to stimulate Maria to reason, not simply to know the answer. However, when you are not trying to stimulate thinking, but are providing students with *directions* for an upcoming learning activity, your communications should be extremely *explicit, specific,* and *directly to the point.*

Ordinarily, you give directions during the transition period just before the start of a learning activity. Directions must be explicit, precise, and concise so that transition time is minimized and allocated time is not wasted as a result of students failing to follow the directions for the learning activity. Compare Case 9.2 to Case 9.3. In which one are the teacher's directions clear and to the point? In which will student engagement in the upcoming learning activity be impaired because the directions don't fully communicate exactly what is to be done?

Exhibit 9.1
Maria examines the behavior of trigonometric functions.

CASE 9.2

As part of a lesson on pattern recognition, Ms. Bey addresses her prealgebra class as follows: "I have three books here. This one is called *Mathematical Cavalcade* (Bolt, 1992), this one is *Puzzles, Paradoxes and Brain Teasers* (Gibilisco, 1990), and this one is *Mathemagics* (Benjamin & Shermer, 1993). These books are filled with fun ideas, games, experiments, and things you can do with mathematics. There are some real surprises in store in these pages! Anyway, I want each of you to read about one of these things in here and teach the rest of us about it. Any questions? Yes, Shelton."

Shelton: Can I do the one on magic? Magic is awesome!

Ms. Bey: Yes, you may choose something out of *Mathemagics*.

Eicho: Oh, we get to pick which one we want! Suppose I want the same one as —

Ms. Bey: Please, Eicho, don't interrupt. Everyone will get a chance to choose.

Eicho: But suppose . . .

Ms. Bey: I'll pass these books around and you can write down the project of your choice.

Ms. Bey continues to give directions for the activity, but students are more attentive to the books being passed around. Some are trying to read about the experiments, games, and demonstrations while others beckon them to hurry and pass the book to the next student. Only a few follow Ms. Bey's directions on what they are to do and pay attention to the schedule for completing the activity.

CASE 9.3

In preparation for an activity on pattern recognition, Ms. Culbertson selects 28 experiments or demonstrations (one for each student in her prealgebra class) from the same three trade books mentioned in Case 9.2. She duplicates the relevant pages for each (see Exhibit 9.2).

She then develops the guide sheet displayed in Exhibit 9.3 and duplicates one for each student. She also makes a transparency slide of the guide sheet as well as the two sample entries shown in Exhibit 9.2. Based on her prior assessments of students' interests and needs, she assigns selections one to each of the 28 students. For each student she makes up a packet consisting of the copy of the selection from the books and a guide sheet.

The next day Ms. Culbertson puts a packet in each student's desk just before the beginning of the prealgebra period. She addresses the class: "I placed a packet inside your desk—No, Rasheed, not yet. Leave it there until I tell you it's time. Thank you. Your individual packet contains a copy of a page or two out of one of those three books." She displays the three books and continues, "The pages in your packet are different from everyone else's. They explain either an experiment, a demonstration, or a game that you will teach yourself and then teach to the rest of us in the class. Here's an example." She turns on the overhead projector and quickly displays the two samples from Exhibit 9.2, keeping them on just long enough to give the students an idea of what they'll be reading, but not long enough for them to read any more than a word or two.

Ms. Culbertson then goes through the directions step-by-step, displaying each line from Exhibit 9.3 as she explains the step. Only after she's completed the instructions, does she direct them to examine their packets.

Eight Points about Directions

Ms. Culbertson's explicit directions more efficiently communicated exactly what students were to do during learning activities than did Ms. Bey's. Ms. Culbertson took advantage of the following:

1. Students in classes where teachers display *businesslike attitudes* are more likely to efficiently following directions than do those whose teachers seem lackadaisical and less organized. Ms. Culbertson appeared to know exactly what tasks students were expected to complete and had well-organized plans for accomplishing those tasks.

Exhibit 9.2
Two examples Ms. Culbertson chose from *Mathematical Cavalcade.*

76 Calculator golf

Hole A
Find a given
$56.7 < a^2 < 57.7$
Par 4
Hole B
Find b given
$181 < 17b < 183$
Par 3
Hole C
Find c given
$4.5 < \frac{269}{c} < 4.9$
Par 4
Hole F
Find f given
$21 < 1.3^f < 22$
Par 5
Hole E
Find e given
$128 < e\,(e + 9) < 130$
Par 4
Hole D
Find d given
$6.9 < d + \frac{1}{d} < 7.0$
Par 3
Hole G
Find g given
$0.7 < g^2 < 0.8$
Par 3
Hole H
Find h given
$0.90 < \frac{h - 10}{h + 10} < 0.91$
Hole I
Find i given
$8.4 < \sqrt{i} < 8.5$
Par 3

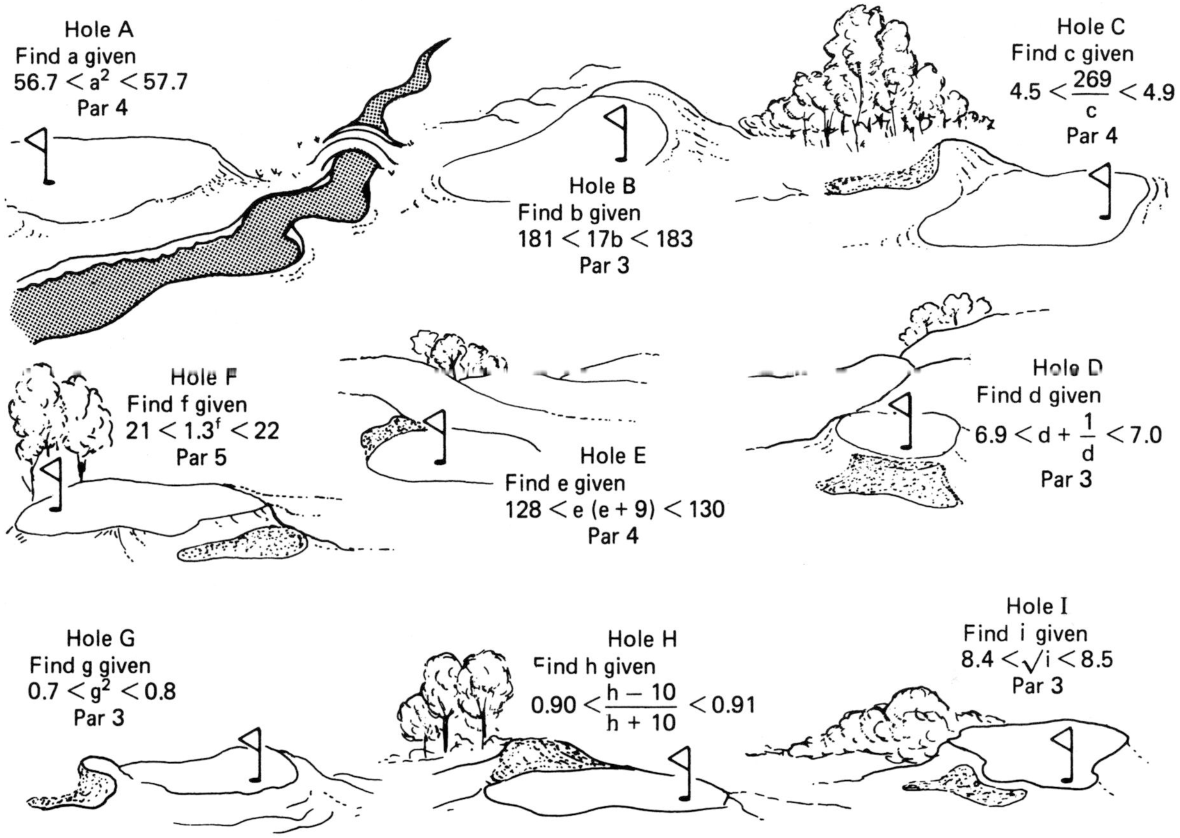

This is a game based on your ability to estimate. You will need a calculator and a means of recording your estimates. To play a hole, make an estimate of a number for the letter and use your calculator to work out the value of the calculation indicated. If this number lies between the limits indicated you will have 'holed in one'. This is unlikely, so record your estimate and the result of the calculation. From this you should be in a position to make a better estimate and get nearer to the hole.

Make further estimates and test their accuracy with your calculator until your estimate lands you in the hole between the limits. The number of estimates you require for a hole is your score.

Above is a nine-hole course with suggested pars for each hole. The par is the estimated standard score for the hole that a good player should make. Can you match par or better? Make up a similar course yourself and challenge your friends.

Exhibit 9.2
Continued

117   This tetraflexagon has six faces

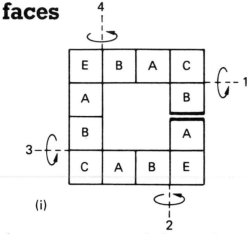

(i)

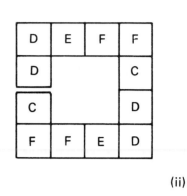

(ii)

Four-sided paper structures made from strips of paper which can be folded to expose different surfaces are known as tetraflexagons. The one discussed here can be folded to expose any one of six faces denoted here by A, B, C, D, E, F. Made with care it gives an intriguing object to manipulate. Instead of the same letter repeated four times on each exposed surface a message of four letter words can be sent, such as:

LILY WITH MUCH LOVE FROM JOHN

To make this flexagon carefully draw the band of twelve squares shown in figure (i) on plain paper. (A 3-cm edge to each square is appropriate.)

Letter the band as shown in (i), cut it out, turn it over and letter the underside as shown in (ii). Where the band has been cut between A and B the cut edges have been marked with a double line, for they will later be stuck together.

Carefully fold the band along each of the edges of the squares so that it flexes easily. (If card is used then score all the fold lines.) Return the band to the configuration shown in (i) and fold it along the dotted lines in the order indicated. In each case fold under. The result should look like (iii).

Now fold as indicated in (iii) where the first and third folds are up over, and the second fold is under. At the third fold tuck C behind A so the result looks like (iv) and the reverse side like (v).

Use a piece of sticky tape to join the top edge of the A to the edge of the B behind as shown. These should be the edges marked in (i). By folding along the horizontal mediator you will now be able to expose any of A, B, C, D and by folding along the vertical mediator find E and F.

Have fun!

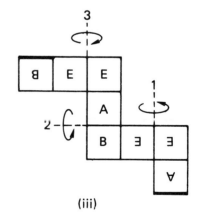

(iii)

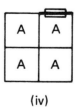

(iv)

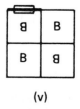

(v)

Exhibit 9.3
The guide sheet Ms. Culbertson uses to Communicate Directions.

You are responsible for teaching the class the experiment, demonstration, or game explained in your packet. Here's what you should do next to meet this responsibility:

1. Carefully read the page or pages in the packet. Teach yourself to do the experiment, perform the demonstration, or play the game. This will require you to do it yourself more than once. This task is to be completed by the following date: _____.

2. Ms. Culbertson has assigned the following partner for you: _____ _____.

   During the last five minutes of today's class, meet your partner to decide on a time when the two of you can get together outside of class. You will practice teaching your experiment, demonstration, or game to your partner and your partner will practice teaching you. The task of teaching one another is to be completed by the following date: _____.

   Your partner's name is _____.

   Here's a place to write down the date, time, and place you and your partner will meet:

   _____

3. Meet on the day and at the time you scheduled with your partner. Practice teaching one another as indicated above. Give one another suggestions on how each of you can teach your experiments, demonstrations, or games to the whole class.

4. Plan to teach our class about your experiment, demonstration, or game. The lesson should take between 10 and 15 minutes. Use some visuals or illustrations in your lesson. Also get the class involved in doing some mathematics themselves. Be ready to explain your plan to Ms. Culbertson on the following date: _____. You and Ms. Culbertson will schedule the date you'll teach your lesson to the class. Here's a place to write it down:

   _____

5. After discussing your plan with Ms. Culbertson, teach your experiment, demonstration, or game to the class on the scheduled date.

6. After your lesson, the class will discuss with you what they learned.

2. Because giving directions is a frequent, routine occurrence in a classroom, teachers can minimize transition time, streamline communication procedures, display a more businesslike attitude, and reduce the amount of teacher-talk in classrooms by establishing *signals* or *cues* that nearly instantaneously communicate certain recurring expectations to students. Ms. Culbertson's use of the overhead projector helped focus of students' attention.

3. Speaking to students who are not attentively listening is not only a waste of time and energy, it also encourages inattentive behavior patterns. By deliberately *gaining at least the appearance of everyone's attention before providing directions*, teachers communicate the seriousness of the directions and increases the chances that the directions will be followed. Ms. Culbertson planned her presentation so that students did not have potential distractions like the packets at hand and she achieved eye contact with students to check on whether or not they were ready to listen.

4. Students who have learned that their teacher tends to *say things only once* tend to listen the first time the teacher speaks. Sometimes teachers make the mistake of saying, "I'm only going to say this once," but then end up repeating themselves because their initial directions were vague.

5. Students are more likely to listen carefully to the directions of teachers who *restrict their remarks to exactly what students need to know* to successfully engage in the upcoming learning activity. Ms.

Culbertson didn't mix uninformative, inane words with directions. You don't need to say things, such as, "You're really going to like this!"

6. When teachers are providing directions, they are not conducting an inquiry lesson. Efficiently communicated directions in which transition time is minimized *do not normally allow time for students to debate the pros and cons of what is to be done.* Unlike Ms. Bey in Case 9.2, Ms. Culbertson never provided students with an opening for arguing about which experiment, demonstration, or game they would be assigned.

7. Students are far more likely to follow directions that *provide very specific guidelines for exactly what is to be done and when* than they are for ambiguously worded general directions.

8. The *more senses (seeing, hearing) through which directions are communicated,* the more likely students are to understand them. Besides telling her students what to do, Ms. Culbertson displayed the written guide sheet.

VARIETY OF LEARNING ACTIVITIES

In Cases 4.7 through 4.10, Mr. Citerelli conducted a construct a concept lesson on arithmetic sequences. As outlined in his lesson plan in Exhibit 4.8, the lesson consisted of a variety of learning activities. He began with a brief, large-group session in which students independently examined examples and nonexamples. Then he moved into the second stage of the lesson with a large-group question/discussion session. Continuing with the question/discussion session through the third stage, he had students engage in homework, another question/discussion session, and a cooperative learning activity in small task groups during the fourth stage.

If you incorporate too many types of learning activities into a single lesson, you'll find yourself spending an inordinate amount of time in transition periods giving directions. However, an optimal mix of different types of sessions guards against monotony and keeps students from getting bored. The rest of this chapter presents ideas for keeping students engaged during various types of sessions.

IDEAS FOR LARGE-GROUP PRESENTATIONS

Student Engagement During Large-Group Presentations

To be engaged in a large-group presentation, students must listen attentively to try to follow the teacher's thought pattern. Thus, they are expected to be cogni-

tively active but physically inactive. Note taking may also be necessary. Such behavior is not readily achieved for students of any age and is virtually impossible to sustain for younger students. Presentations that continue uninterrupted for more than ten minutes are ill-advised learning activities. In Case 9.4, the teacher's presentation style is not likely to maintain students' attention. In contrast, the teacher in Case 9.5 utilizes presentation techniques designed to obtain and maintain student engagement.

CASE 9.4 _____

Mr. Johnson's 26 students are sitting at their desks. Nine have paper and pencil poised to take notes, but others are involved with their own thoughts as he begins, "Today, class, we're going to study a measure of central tendency called the arithmetic mean. Some of you may have already heard of it." He turns to the chalkboard, and while writing, continues to speak, "The arithmetic mean of N numbers equals the sum of the numbers divided by N." Keeping his side to the class, he says, "For example, to compute the mean of these numbers—15, 15, 20, 0, 13, 12, 25, 40, 10, and 20—we would first add the numbers to find the sum. Right?" He looks at the class but doesn't notice whether students appear to respond to his question, turns back and adds the numbers on the board. Turning to the class, he says, "So the sum is 170. Now, since we have 10 numbers, N in the formula is 10 and we divide 170 by N, or 10. And what does that give us? It gives us 17.0. So, the arithmetic mean of these numbers is 17.0. Is that clear?"

Mr. Johnson stares at the class momentarily, notices Armond nodding and softly saying, "Yes." With a smile, Mr. Johnson quickly says, "Good! Okay, everybody, the arithmetic mean is an important and useful statistic. Suppose, for example, I wanted to compare the following group of numbers—from his notes he copies the following numbers on the board: 18, 35, 30, 7, 20—to these over here." He points to the previous data set.

Mr. Johnson: What could we do, Ramon?

Ramon: Compute that arithmetic thing you told us about.

Mr. Johnson: That's right! We could compute the arithmetic mean. $18 + 35 + 30 + 7 + 20 = 110$, and $110 \div N$—which in this case is 5, okay?—is 22.0. Okay? Now, that means this second data set has a higher average than the first, even though the first had more numbers. Any questions? . . . Good! . . . Oh, okay Angela?

Angela: Why do you write 17.0 and 22.0 instead of 17 and 22? Aren't they the same?

Mr. Johnson: Good question. Hmmm, can anybody help Angela out? . . . Well, you see in statistics the number of decimal places indicates something about the accuracy of the computations, and for that matter, the data-gathering device. So that one decimal point indicates that the statistics are more accurate than if we had just written 17 and 22 and not as accurate if we had written, say 17.00000 or 22.00000. Got it? That was a good question. Do you understand now?

Angela: I guess so.

Mr. Johnson: Good! Now, if there're no more questions, there's some time left to get a head start on your homework.

CASE 9.5

Ms. Erickson's 27 students are quietly sitting at their desks, each ready with paper and pencil or pen. She has previously taught them how to take notes during large-group presentations so that they record information during the session on paper and then, after the session, organize the notes and transfer them into their required notebooks.

After distributing a copy of the form in Exhibit 9.4 to each student, she faces the class from a position near the overhead projector and says, "I'm standing here looking at you people and I just can't get one question out of my mind." Very deliberately, she walks in front of the fourth row of students and quickly, but obviously, looks at their feet. Then she moves in front of the first row and repeats the odd behavior with those students. "I just don't know!" she says shaking her head as she returns to her position at the overhead.

She switches on the overhead, displaying the first line of Exhibit 9.4, and says, "In the first blank on your form please write: Do the people sitting in the fourth row have bigger feet than those in the first row?" She moves closer to the students, obviously monitoring how well her directions are followed. Back at the overhead as they complete the chore, she says, "Now, I've got to figure a way to gather data that will help me answer that question." Grabbing her head with a hand and closing her eyes, she appears to be in deep thought for a few seconds and then suddenly exclaims, "I've got it! We'll use shoe sizes as a measure. That'll be a lot easier than using a ruler on smelly feet!" Some students laugh, and one begins to speak while two others raise their hands. But Ms. Erickson quickly says, "Not now please, we need to collect some data." She flips an overlay away from the second line of the transparency, exposing "Data for row 4."

Ms. Erickson: "Those of you in the fourth and first rows, quickly jot down your shoe size on your paper. If you don't know it, either guess or read it off your shoe if you can do it quickly. Starting with Jasmine in the back and moving up to Lester in front, those of you in the fourth row call out your shoe sizes one at a time so we can write them down in this blank at our places." As the students call out the sizes, she fills in the blank on the transparency as follows: 6, 10.5, 8, 5.5, 6, 9. Exposing the next line, "Data for row 1," on the transparency she asks, "What do you suppose we're going to do now, Pauline?" Pauline: "Do the same for row 1." Ms. Erickson says, "Okay, you heard Pauline; row 1, give it to us from the back so we can fill in this blank." The numbers 8.5, 8, 7, 5.5, 6.5, 9, and 8 are recorded and displayed on the overhead.

Ms. Erickson: "Now, I've got to figure out what to do with these numbers to help me answer the question." Several students raise their hands, but she responds, "Thank you for offering to help, but I want to see what I come up with." Pointing to the appropriate numerals on the transparency, she seems to think aloud saying, "It's easy enough to compare one number to another. Jasmine's 6 from row 4 is less than Rolando's 8.5 from row 1. But I don't want to just compare one individual's number to another's. I want to compare this whole bunch of numbers (circling the set of numbers from row 4 with an overhead pen) to this bunch (circling the numbers from row 1). I guess we could add all the row 4 numbers together and all the row 1 numbers together and compare the two sums—the group with the greater sum would have the bigger feet."

A couple of students try to interrupt with "But that won't wor . . . " but Ms. Erickson motions them to stop speaking and asks, "What's the sum from row 4, Lau-chou?"

Lau-chou: 45.

Ms. Erickson: Thank you. And what is the sum for row 1, Stace?

Stace: 59.

"Thank you. So row 1 has bigger feet, since 59 is greater than 45," Ms. Erickson says as she writes, 59 > 45.

Ms. Erickson: I'll pause to hear what some of you with your hands up have to say. Evangeline?

Evangeline: That's not right; it doesn't work.

Ms. Erickson: You mean 59 isn't greater than 45, Evangeline?

Evangeline: 59 is greater than 45, but there are more feet in row 1.

Ms. Erickson: All the people in row 1 have only two feet, just like the ones in row 4. I carefully counted. [Students laugh.] Now that we've taken care of that concern, how about other comments or questions? Brook.

Brook: You know what Evangeline meant! She meant there're more people in row 1. So what you did isn't right.

Ms. Erickson: Alright, let me see if I now understand Evangeline's point. She said we don't want our indicator of how big the feet are to be affected by how many feet, just the size of the feet. So, I've got to figure out a way to compare the sizes of these two groups of numbers when one has more numbers than the other. I'm open for suggestions. . . . Kip?

Kip: You could drop the two extra numbers from row 1; then they'd both have 6.

Ms. Erickson: That seems like a reasonable approach. I like that. But first let's hear another idea—maybe one where we can use all the data. Myra?

Myra: Why not do an average?

Ms. Erickson: What do you mean?

Myra: You know, divide row 4's total by 6 and row 1's by 8.

Ms. Erickson: How will that dividing help? Seems like just an unnecessary step. Tom.

Tom: It evens up the two groups.

Ms. Erickson: Oh, I see what you people have been trying to tell me! Dividing row 4's sum of 45 by 6 counts each number 1/6. And dividing row 1's sum of 59 by 8 counts

Exhibit 9.4
Form Ms. Erickson uses during a large-group presentation.

An Experiment

Question to be answered: _____

_____

Data for Row 4: _____

Data for Row 1: _____

Treatment of data for row 4:

Treatment of data for row 1:

Treatment to compare the two sets of data:

Results: _____

_____

Conclusions: _____

_____

each number 1/8. And that's fair, since 6 one-sixths is a whole, just as 8 one-eighths is a whole. How am I doing, Jasmine?

Jasmine: A lot better than you were.

Flipping over another overlay, Ms. Erickson displays the next two lines from Exhibit 9.4 and continues.

Ms. Erickson: Let's write: "The sum of row 4's numbers is 45." 45 ÷ 6 is what, Lester?

Lester: 7.5.

Ms. Erickson: Thanks. And on the next line we write 59 ÷ 8. Which is what, Sandy?

Sandy: 7.375.

Ms. Erickson: Since 7.5 is greater than 7.375, I guess we should say that the feet in row 4 are larger than the feet in row 1. That is, of course, if you're willing to trust this particular statistic—which is known as the "MEB." Any questions? Yes, Evangeline.

Evangeline: Why the MEB?

Ms. Erickson: Because I just named it that after its three inventors, Myra, Evangeline, and Brook. They're the ones that came up with the idea of dividing the sum.

Ms. Erickson shifts to direct instruction to help students remember the formula, practice using it, and remember its more conventional name, "arithmetic mean," during the remainder of the session.

Thirteen Points about Large-Group Presentations

Consider the following thoughts when designing large-group presentations:

1. Students are more likely to be engaged during a presentation if the teacher has *provided clear directions for behavior.* Students need to have learned how to attend to a presentation. Questions about how to take notes, if at all, should be answered before the presentation begins.

2. Some sort of *advanced organizer to direct students' thinking helps them actively listen* to the speaker. Ms. Erickson used the form in Exhibit 9.4 to focus students' attention and structure the activity. Consider taking that idea a step further by having an outline of the presentation (see Exhibit 9.5) or a session agenda (see Exhibit 9.6) in the hands of students or displayed on an overhead transparency. You can then use it to direct attention and provide a context for topics and subtopics. Having such advanced organizers in students' hands facilitates their note taking and helps you monitor their engagement, for example, by sampling what they write on the form in Exhibit 9.7. By using transitional remarks such as "Let's Move on to item 4" in conjunction with an outline or agenda, you help students maintain their bearings during sessions.

3. *Signals, especially nonverbal ones, can efficiently focus students' attention* during a presentation. Ms. Erickson's curious behavior in Case 9.5, deliberately staring at feet, encouraged students to take notice and wonder, what is she going to do next? Her deliberate movements in the first part of the presentation established cues she took advantage of in the remainder of the session. For example:

   After distributing the form, she walked directly to a point near the overhead projector and faced the class. From that position she spoke to the students. Silently, she walked directly to a point in front of the fourth row, then to a point in front of the first row, and then back to the position near the overhead projector where she once again spoke to the class. When she wanted students to look at an illustration, she switched on the overhead projector. When she wanted them to stop looking at it, she turned the overhead projector off or controlled what they could see with transparency overlays.

   These movements cued students to associate her location and movements with what they should be doing throughout the session (e.g., listen attentively when she's by the overhead projector).

4. Presentations are useful learning activities when teachers want to have a group of students all following a common thought pattern. Lectures, such as Ms. Erickson's, that are designed to do more than just feed information to students, run the risk of become discussion or question sessions. Thus, *some means for staying on track should be considered* when planning the presentation. One method is to have signals worked out with students so that they clearly discriminate between times when you are only lecturing and other times when discussions or questions are welcomed. While standing by the overhead projector Ms. Erickson presented the task to be addressed, collected information, and focused thoughts on examining information. During this first part, she had students speak, but they did not enter into a discussion session. They simply provided information used in the presentation.

5. *Voice volume, inflection, pitch, rhythm, and pace should be strategically modulated according to the message you want to send and to the level of students.* Even when the message itself is important and exciting, monotone speech is a recipe for boredom. Punctuate key sentences with voice variations. Follow key statements and questions with strategic pauses. Pauses indicate points to ponder. Pace your speech so that sessions move briskly but still allow students enough time to absorb your messages and take notes. The type of lesson you're teaching should, of course, influence pace. A lecture for an inquiry-learning activity

Exhibit 9.5
Example of outline distributed to students for a large-group presentation.

Topic: Proof by induction
Date: 3/7

Presentation Outline

I. Review of familiar methods of proving theorem
    A. Direct
    B. By contradiction
II. Types of theorems to which proof by induction applies
III. Logic of a proof by induction
    A. Sequential cases
    B. Is it true for one case?
    C. If it's true for one case, will it be true for the next case?
IV. Some everyday examples of the induction principle
    A. Playing music
    B. On soccer field
    C. In the kitchen
    D. Eating food
    E. Computer programming
V. An example with an arithmetic series, $\sum_{i=1}^{n} i = n(n+1)/2$
VI. Formalizing the process
    A. Show the statement is true for $i = a$.
    B. Show that if the statement is true for some value of i, then it must also be true for $i + 1$.
    C. Draw a conclusion.
VII. Proof of the following theorem:

$$\sum_{i=1}^{n} i^2 = (n/6)(n+1)(2n+1)$$

VIII. Summary

Exhibit 9.6
Example of a class meeting agenda distributed to students.

Meeting Agenda for 10/18
Algebra II, 4th Period

1. Hello (0.50–0.75 minutes)
2. Formative quiz and roll (15–16 minutes)
3. Review quiz items and discuss some subset of the following questions, as needed according to the quiz review (10–20 minutes):
    a. What is a proportion?
    b. What types of problems does setting up proportions help solve?
    c. What is the so-called proportion rule?
    d. What are some efficient strategies for estimating solutions to problems involving proportions?
4. Lecture presentation on further applying our understanding of proportions to problems involving direct and indirect variations (10–15 minutes)
5. Homework assignment (2–4 minutes)
6. Head start on homework (7–21 minutes)
7. Prepare for dismissal (1–1.75 minutes)
8. Be kind to yourself (1310 minutes)

Exhibit 9.7

Example of a note taking form a teacher distributed to students for use during a large-group presentation.

Topic: Developing the quadratic formula Date: 1/23	
Main Ideas	**Margin Notes**
The need for a general method:	
Completing-the-square method:	
The need for an easier method:	
Completion-of-the-square example:	
Generalizing completing-the-square method:	

Exhibit 9.7
Continued

Main Ideas	Margin Notes
Reforming expressions to obtain the formula:	
Examples of equations solved with the formula: 1.	
2.	
3.	
Summary:	
What to do next:	

would ordinarily proceed at a slower pace than one using direct instruction. Quina (1989, p. 143) suggested that between 110 and 130 words per minute is optimal.

6. Students are more likely to follow presentations that *utilize professional quality media and technology.* Students can hardly be engaged when learning activities require them to read, see, or hear something that is unintelligible. As suggested in Chapter 7, technological advances make computerized multimedia presentations cost effective for everyday classroom use.

7. At least three advantages can be gained by videotaping presentations ahead of time and playing them for students in class:

   a. *Videotaped presentations avoid some of the interruptions in thought that occur when students make comments or ask questions.*

   b. *The teacher can more attentively monitor students' behavior and effectively respond to indications of disengagement.*

   c. *Kinks and mistakes in the presentation can be corrected and improvements made before the presentation is played for the class.*

      With videotape and other record-and-play devices, teachers can easily start, interrupt, replay, terminate, modify and repeat presentations.

8. Entertaining is not teaching. However, interjecting a bit of humor or other *attention-getting devices helps keep students more alert than does a straight monologue.* Make sure that the attention-getting devices don't attract attention away from the objective of the lesson.

9. *Students are more likely to follow a presentation in which the teacher maintains eye contact with them.* This, of course, was one of the advantages Ms. Erickson had in using the overhead projector rather than a chalkboard.

10. Mind-wandering and daydreaming are major causes of student disengagement during presentations. *Teachers can deal more effectively with mind-wandering and daydreaming behaviors when they move about the room as they speak.* Rather than standing behind a lectern, Quina (1989, pp. 141–142) suggested purposeful movements, with the room divided into quadrants:

Beginning teachers sometimes unconsciously pace the floor, moving from one side of the room to another. The observing students' heads move as though they are watching a tennis match. To avoid this, think where you want to be standing as you develop parts of your lecture. You can divide the room into quadrants and intentionally move into each quadrant at different stages of your lecture. For example, after introducing the question, "Why do we need to communicate?" the

teacher may move to the left side of the room, give some information on communicating in pantomime, provide a quick pantomime, then move to the right side of the room to discuss ways we designate things, illustrating by pointing to objects, and then ask a related question, "How is pointing and acting things out like using words?" The teacher may then walk to the back of the room and ask even more pointed questions: "What would happen if we did not have words? What would it be like if words were not available right now?"

The shift in position in the room corresponds to the development of the lecture, providing a spatial metaphor for organization. As the teacher walks back to the front of the room to sum up, the very return to the front of the room, to the beginning point, suggests a completion, a completed square, circle, or other shape. These movements are intentional. They can be planned in advance or they can be used spontaneously. Either way, they are intentional—not random pacing.

Typically, mathematics teachers feel confined to the front of the room to illustrate what they say on an overhead, whiteboard, or chalkboard. But such restrictions aren't necessary if, for example, you use an electronic image writer (as mentioned in Chapter 7) or assign students to illustrate your words for you at the front of the room (as Mr. Citerelli did with Bill in Case 4.9).

11. *Students who hear their names are usually alerted to listen to what is being said.* Thus, many teachers purposefully interject the names of individual students into their presentations.

12. During presentations, teachers should frequently monitor their students' comprehension of what is being said. *Planned breaks in a presentation, in which students are asked questions, can provide you with formative feedback that should guide subsequent stages of the presentation.*

13. Sometimes, students become disengaged during a presentation because the teacher uses an unfamiliar word, expression, formula, or symbol. The teacher continues, assuming that students understand. The students are no longer listening to what the teacher is saying because they are busy trying to figure out the unfamiliar word, expression, formula, or symbol. *Make sure that vocabulary and notations necessary for comprehension of your presentation are taught prior to the session.*

RESPONDING TO STUDENTS' QUESTIONS

Memory-Level and Reasoning-Level Questions

A question that can be answered by remembering a previously learned response is referred to as *memory-*

level question. A question that requires the respondent to use reasoning and make judgments to answer is referred to as a *reasoning-level question.*

Engage in Activity 9.1.

ACTIVITY 9.1

Purpose: To reflect on the difference between memory-level and reasoning-level questions.

Procedure: Analyze the cognitive processes a person would use to answer the following questions; classify each as either *memory level* or *reasoning level:*

A. According to Kennedy (1989), the supply and demand relationship between trigonometry and another field of study was so intimate prior to the thirteenth century that the two were indistinguishable. What is the other field?

B. What is a polyhedron?

C. Would it be better to weigh this box in kilograms or grams?

D. In Exhibit 4.7, how are the examples alike? How do they differ from the nonexamples?

E. How will sketching a graph of this bivariate data help us determine the relationship between the independent and dependent variables?

F. Have you ever written a computer program in BASIC?

G. How long would it take you to write a BASIC program for solving systems of n linear equations with n variables?

H. Does $x^2 + 4x = 18$ have rational roots?

I. Why are so few women mentioned in historical accounts of mathematics prior to the twentieth century?

J. Who was Maria Gaetana Agnesi?

Compare your classifications with those of a colleague. Resolve any differences in a discussion.

In Case 9.6, two mathematics teachers discuss their responses to Activity 9.1.

CASE 9.6 ─────────────────

Tina: I classified questions A, B, F, H, and J as memory level; the others as reasoning level.

Jermain: Yours agree with mine except for H. Why don't you think determining if a quadratic equation has rational roots involves reasoning? You don't just remember whether it does or not; you have to figure it out.

Tina: True, but I walked through the process I used to answer the question as, "No, it has two irrational roots." And what I did was to simply *remember* that one method for determining the nature of the roots of a quadratic equation is to compute the discriminant. I did that by remembering the expression $b^2 - 4ac$, and going through the algorithm for calculating its value for $a = 1$, $b = 4$, and $c = -18$. That gave me 88 which isn't a perfect square. And I remembered the rule: If the discriminant is positive, but not a perfect square, the equation has two irrational roots. I just used an algorithmic skill—not any reasoning.

Jermain: I guess it all depends on where you're coming from. I can see that for experienced people—like us—who have addressed the question for numerous quadratic equations time and time again, there's virtually no conscious reasoning. So maybe I classified question H as reasoning level because I was thinking of a less-experienced person who had to think through why the discriminant rule works. But even for us, who do this fairly mindlessly, didn't we use at least some deductive reasoning to determine the discriminant applied to this case—you know, the syllogism thing?

Tina: You've got a point, but it just seems so automatic. We can agree that for most people—surely the inexperienced algebra student—Question H is reasoning level.

Jermain: Some of these other questions might also be reclassified if you viewed them from different backgrounds.

Tina: Yeah, like I. If all one did was to remember an opinion expressed by a mathematical historian, there wouldn't be much reasoning.

Jermain: But even then, one reasons when choosing to agree with the historian's opinion.

───────────────

Your strategies for addressing students' reasoning-level questions should differ from those for answering their memory-level questions. If you're in the midst of an inquiry lesson for a construct a concept, discover a relationship, application, or creativity objective when students raise a reasoning-level question, you may want to lead the students to develop their own answers to the question rather than answering the question yourself. On the other hand, you may be inclined to be more direct when students raise memory-level questions, especially during lessons for simple-knowledge or procedural-skills objectives.

Student-Initiated Reasoning-Level Questions

Imagine yourself conducting a class session as part of an application-level lesson on compound probability. A student, Jennifer, asks you:

In biology class, we learned about this genetic thing—a defect where if the parents had it, there's a 25 percent chance that a kid they have will also have it. What if they have two kids, what are the chances that one or both will the defect? Is it 50 percent or does it stay 25 percent?"

Such a question is answerable via a cognitive process—namely deductive reasoning that involves more than just recalling a response. Being in the middle of an application-level lesson dealing with the content of the question compound probability, you want to respond in a way that will advance the cause of the lesson. You have at least four options: (a) *answer the question directly,* (b) *use a think-aloud strategy,* (c) *probe back to the student,* and (d) *probe and redirect the question to other students.*

Answer the Question Directly. Answering the question directly would be the easiest and quickest thing to do. Give the answer and, since it's a reasoning-level question, explain the rationale for it. For example, you might respond to Jennifer's question as follows:

Actually Jennifer, I think the probability would be somewhere between 25 percent and 50 percent. Think of the probability of neither of the two children inheriting the defect. The chances of the first not having it is 75 percent; the chances of the second is also 75 percent. It's a compound probability of two independent events, so you multiply .75 by .75. And that would about .56 according to my calculator. So, if there is a 56 percent chance of neither having it, there must be a 44 percent chance that one or both will get it. . . . Okay?

Use a Think-Aloud Strategy. Rather than explaining the answer directly, you may spend more time demonstrating what goes through one's mind when formulating a solution. For Jennifer's question, you would be modeling the application-level behavior you want the students to learn. For example:

Gracious, Jennifer, that's a challenging question. Let's see, how would I go about solving that one? You've got two kids, the first or older one, and then the second. The probability of the first having the defect is 25 percent, did you say? . . . Okay. And is the probability of the second one inheriting the defect affected by whether or not the first one has it? No. So, no matter what, the probability for the second is also 25 percent. So the first thing that comes to mind is to add the two and I get the 50 percent you got, Jennifer. Let me see, is that right? It couldn't be because if the parents had five children, for example, that would be .25 five times, and that would be a probability of 1.25 or 125 percent which is impossible. The probability has to be less than or equal to 1.

Oh, let's try it case by case. What's the probability of the first having the defect and the second not? The chances are .25 for the first and the .75 for the second not to have it. That's what? The multiplication rule applies since they're independent events. .25 × .75 is about .19. That takes care of one case. Now, what about the first not having it, but the second one does—that's another .19. What's left? Both of them having it. That's .25 × .25 which is about .06. That's all the pos-

sibilities. So we add them up since they're mutually exclusive events and we get 44 percent. Does that seem right?

Oh! I didn't have to spend all that time; I just thought of an easier way! Couldn't we have just looked at the complement? Then we'd have only one case to figure! The probability of neither child having the defect would by simply .75^2 and that's about .56. So our answer would be 100 percent − 56 percent = 44 percent—same thing as before, but we found it with less work.

Probe Back to the Student. Even more time-consuming but probably more beneficial for the student is to respond with a sequence of your own questions that stimulate students to engage in the type of reasoning demonstrated by the think-aloud example. If you responded as follows, you would be probing back to the student:

You: What makes you think it might be 50 percent?
Jennifer: There's 25 percent chance the first one has it, right?
You: Right.
Jennifer: And 25 percent for the second one. So, that's another 25 percent chance—giving you a total of 50 percent.
You: Then what would the probability be of having at least one child with the defect if the family had five children?
Jennifer: 5 × .25.
You: Which is?
Jennifer: . . . ahh, 1.25. . . . That's impossible!
You: Why don't you try a case-by-case strategy?
Jennifer: Like what?
You: Here come up to the overhead projector.

You would continue along those lines, leading Jennifer through the thought process.

Probe and Redirect the Question to Other Students. To involve more students in the activity, respond with leading questions, but direct them to other students as well as Jennifer. For example:

You: Which do you think is right, 50 percent or 25 percent, Wade?
Wade: It's got to be more than 25 percent because that's the probability if they had only one child.
You: So, does it make it 50 percent, Agnes?
Agnes: That's all that's left.
You: Okay class, assuming we agree with Agnes, compute the probability of at least one child having the defect if the family has five children instead of only two children. Quickly, now everyone. . . . Okay, what did you get, Jennifer?
Jennifer: 1.25, but that can't be because . . .

Student-Initiated Memory-Level Questions

Imagine yourself conducting a class session as part of a lesson on compound probability. A student, Janet, asks you: "What does mutually exclusive mean?"

Such a question is answerable by recalling a response, in this case, a definition. Your options, of which there are at least five, are simpler to implement than those for reasoning-level questions. They include: (a) *answer the question directly,* (b) *use a how-might-we-find-that-out strategy,* (c) *refer the student to a source to be used right away,* (d) *refer the student to a source to be used at a later time,* and (e) *redirect the question to another student.*

Answer the Question Directly. Here is an example

of answering Janet's memory-level question directly:

> Two events are mutually exclusive if they are so related that one cannot happen if the other does. For example, you cannot get both an A and D on Thursday's test. If you get an A, you can't get a D. If you get a D, you can't get an A. The two events are mutually exclusive.

Use a How-Might-We-Find-That-Out Strategy. Con-

sider choosing this alternative if you are interested in teaching students how to use reference sources for themselves. For example:

You: We really need to know what "mutually exclusive" means. Where should we go to look it up?
Janet: It's probably in the book, but I don't know where.
You: Why don't your try the index? That should give us some page numbers.

Refer the Student to a Source to Be Used Right Away. You might, for example, say:

> Quickly, get the mathematics dictionary off the shelf. Look up the definition and read it to the class.

Refer the Student to a Source to Be Used at a Later Time. For example, you might say:

> As soon as we finish this discussion, please look up the definition either in your textbook or in the mathematical dictionary on the shelf. We'll take a minute at the beginning of class tomorrow for you to report it to us.

Redirect the Question to Another Student. For example:

You: Who remembers the definition of "mutually exclusive"? . . . Okay, Salvador.

Salvadore: You said it's when two things can't happen at the same time.

ASKING STUDENTS QUESTIONS
Student Engagement During Questioning Sessions

For students to be engaged in a questioning session, they must attentively listen to each question asked by the teacher, attempt to formulate answers to that question, and either express their answers in a manner prescribed by the teacher or listen to others express their answers.

Recitation Sessions for Memory-Level Questions

Recitation is one type of questioning session in which teachers raise memory-level questions to help students review information (e.g., definitions) or practice remembering steps in algorithms. Case 9.7 is an example:

CASE 9.7 _____

Mr. Winn: What will the graph of $3x - 7 = 10y + 1$ look like, Deanna?
Deanna: It would be a line.
Mr. Winn: How do you know that?
Deanna: Because the highest power of the variable is 1.
Mr. Winn: That's right. Now, what does the graph of $y = x^2 - 16x + 5$ look like, Gail?
_____

Recitation sessions can be pretty dry and boring. Yet television quiz shows and board games such as Trivial Pursuit enjoy immense popularity although they are forms of recitations addressing memory-level questions. Thus, you might consider occasionally tailoring some of your recitation sessions along the lines of some of the popular quiz games. Consider Case 9.8.

CASE 9.8 _____

Ms. Saucony periodically has her algebra II students play a game with the following rules:

1. One student is selected as the game conductor, another as game scorekeeper.
2. The rest of the class is divided into two teams, A and B.
3. Six members of each team are selected to serve as that team's panel.

4. Panels A and B sit at separate tables in front of the room.
5. The game conductor randomly draws the name of a non-panelist member of one of the teams. That student then selects one of the following categories for the first question to the opposing team:

   • Geometric terms, symbols, and expressions
   • Algebraic terms, symbols, and expressions
   • Statistical terms, symbols, and expressions
   • Trigonometric terms, symbols, and expressions
   • Geometric relationships
   • Algebraic relationships
   • Statistical relationships
   • Trigonometric relationships
   • Mathematical history
   • Potpourri

6. The game conductor randomly draws a question card from the selected category and asks the question to the panel (panel A if the student selecting the category is from B and vice versa).
7. The panel members have 15 seconds to confer and answer the question. If they answer correctly, their team is awarded two points. If they fail, then the panel members call on a non-panelist from their team for the answer. If the team member correctly answers the question, the team gets one point. If that member doesn't, then the conductor asks the same question of the other panel, and that team goes through the same process. If no correct answer is forthcoming, then the conductor announces the correct answer and no points are awarded.
8. A second non-panelist is randomly chosen to select a category and steps 6 and 7 are repeated with the following expectations:
   • A new category has to be selected; no previously selected category can be chosen until all categories have been used once.
   • Each time a panel calls on one of its non-panelist team members to answer a question, they must select a student who has not been called on earlier in the game.
9. The game continues along these lines (repeating the cycle established in steps 6–8) until a prespecified number of questions have been asked.

Question/Discussion Sessions for Reasoning-Level Questions

Generally more interesting than recitation sessions are question/discussion sessions in which the teacher raises reasoning-level questions as part of a lesson for either a construct a concept, discover a relationship, comprehension, application, or creativity objective. Such questions are designed to stimulate students to think, discover, and reason. Case 9.9 is an example.

CASE 9.9

Mr. Grimes is conducting an inductive learning activity designed to help his 28 algebra students achieve the following objective: Distinguish between examples of *variables* and examples of *constants*. (construct a concept)

   With the overhead projector he displays the list in Exhibit 9.8.

Mr. Grimes: Notice that some of the elements in this set are marked with blocks and others with balls. Can anyone tell why the ones with blocks belong together and the ones with balls belong together?

Akeem, Jardine, and Sharon eagerly raise their hands. Immediately, Mr. Grimes calls on Jardine.

Jardine: The ones with blocks are all in this room. Gary is here, the screen is there, and most of us are 15 years old.

Akeem and Sharon are waving their hands trying to get Mr. Grimes' attention. Akeem cries, "No, no!" as three other students also raise their hands.

Mr. Grimes: Easy Akeem. What's the matter?

Akeem: That can't be right because I don't see any 13s in here. And besides, one of the ones with a ball is "people in this room." I think the ones with balls have something to do with numbers.

Mr. Grimes: Okay, Sharon, before you fall out of your desk.

Sharon: The ones with the blocks are exact and the—

Mr. Grimes: Excuse me, Sharon, but the procedure is that you must counter the previous hypothesis before you give your own.

Sharon: Oh, I'm sorry, what was it again?

Exhibit 9.8
Mr. Grimes' overhead transparency for his inductive learning activity on variables and constants.

■ GARY ABOUD
● RECTANGLE
● RATIONAL NUMBER
■ 13
■ THE OVERHEAD PROJECTOR SCREEN YOU SEE RIGHT NOW
● PEOPLE IN THIS ROOM
● AGE
■ 15 YEARS OLD

Akeem: I said the ones with balls have something to do with numbers, but I see that's not right because 13 is a ball. I thought it was a block at first.

Mr. Grimes: Okay, go on, Sharon.

Sharon: Like I was saying, the ones with the blocks are exact things—like Gary, not just people in the room; or 13, not just any rational number. Do you see what I'm saying?

Mr. Grimes: Do you understand what Sharon said, Vesna?

Vesna: Oh! Ahh, sure.

Mr. Grimes: Good! Yes, Jardine, what is it?

Jardine: I don't. Can you explain it more?

Sharon: Look at the ones with balls. There can be all different kinds of rectangles. A rational number can be 13, 15, or 100.75. People in this room can be any of us. And there's more than one age.

Jardine: Yea, but Gary is a person in this class and 13 is a rational number. So, why do they have blocks instead of balls?

Mr. Grimes: I'm glad you raised that question. Who wants to answer? Okay, Akeem.

Akeem: It's like Sharon said. They're just one of a kind. Gary is only one person in this . . .

The session continues toward closure, with Mr. Grimes defining a constant and then a variable with input from Akeem, Jardine, and Sharon.

———————————

What do you think of Mr. Grimes' use of questioning, or Socratic, methods for stimulating students to reason? The session was probably very valuable for Akeem, Jardine, and Sharon. But what about the other 25 students; what did they gain? Mr. Grimes seemed to know how to effectively utilize questioning strategies, but only a relatively small portion of his class seemed involved. For reasoning-level questioning sessions to be effective for all students, students must do more than passively listen to their classmates' responses. They don't necessarily have to be recognized and state their answers aloud for the group, but they do need to formulate and articulate their own answers for themselves.

Because Mr. Grimes allowed Jardine to answer aloud immediately after that initial question was raised, most students did not have time to formulate their own answers. They quit thinking about their own answers to listen to Jardine's. Only the outspoken, quick-to-respond students engaged in the learning activity as they should. Mr. Grimes did not allow enough time to elapse between questions being asked and when they were answered aloud for the class. The overall, average time that teachers wait for students to respond to in-class questions is less than two seconds (Arnold, Atwood, & Rogers, 1974;

Tobin, Tippins, & Gallard, 1994). After experiencing a few sessions such as Mr. Grimes', in which they are asked questions they don't have the opportunity to answer, most students will not even attempt to formulate their own responses. Some will politely listen to the responses of the few, others entertain themselves with off-task thoughts, and others, if allowed, entertain themselves with disruptive behaviors (Cangelosi, 1993, pp. 170–175).

Mr. Grimes should not discard Socratic methods, but he needs to reorganize his questioning sessions and apply techniques that lead all students to address all questions raised. What strategies might you employ to accomplish this? One alternative is to preface questions with directions for all students to answer each question in their minds without answering aloud or volunteering answers until you ask them to do so. In Case 9.10 the teacher applies that strategy to Mr. Grimes' situation.

CASE 9.10 ——————————————

Mr. Smart is conducting an inductive learning activity designed to help his 28 algebra students achieve the following objective: Distinguish between examples of *variables* and examples of *constants*.   (*construct a concept*)

With the overhead projector he displays the list in Exhibit 9.8.

Mr. Smart: I am going to ask you some questions, but I don't want anyone to answer aloud until I call on her or him. Just answer the question in your mind.

He then asks them to consider the differences and similarities between the items on the list marked with balls and those with blocks. Two students eagerly raise their hands and say, "Oh, Mr. Smart!" He is tempted to call on them to positively reinforce their enthusiasm, but he resists, instead cuing them to follow directions with a gesture and a stern look. He waits, watching students' faces. Convinced after three minutes that all have thought about the question and most have an answer ready, he asks, "Joyce, do you have answer?" Joyce nods.

Mr. Smart: Good! How about you, Curtis?

Curtis: Yes.

Mr. Smart: Fine! Are you ready, Melissa?

Melissa: Not yet.

Mr. Smart: Just think aloud for us. Let's hear your thoughts about the two kinds of elements on the list.

Melissa: I don't see how they're different. Some of the ones with the balls are about mathematics, but then so are some of those with blocks.

Mr. Smart: I think that's an important observation. Now, I'd like some volunteers to share their answers with us. Okay, Ruth?

Ruth: I was thinking like Melissa, and then I . . .

Another possibility is to direct students to write answers to questions on forms you supply or on their own paper as you circulate about the room quietly reading samples of their responses. Case 9.11 is an example of a teacher applying this option to Mr. Grimes's situation.

CASE 9.11

Mr. Cramer is conducting an inductive learning activity designed to help her 28 algebra students achieve the following objective: Distinguish between examples of *variables* and examples of *constants*.   (*construct a concept*)

She distributes the form appearing in Exhibit 9.9 and says, "At the bottom of this handout, please write one paragraph describing why you think the elements with the blocks in front go together and the ones with the balls go together. In what ways are all the ones with blocks alike but different from the ones with the balls? You have nine minutes for this task. I'll be around to read answers, but just keep working. Please don't talk to me during this time. Now, begin." She

demonstratively sets the timer on the chronograph she has on her wrist.

As students think and write, Ms. Cramer moves about the room, reading over shoulders. Some students are slow to start until she passes their desks and gently taps on their forms. As she samples their writing, she notes to herself the student answers she wants to use in the upcoming large-group discussion and answers she wants to avoid.

At the nine-minute mark, she moves to the front of the room and displays Exhibit 9.10 on the overhead.

Ms. Cramer: Please read yours, Simon.
Simon: Well, I didn't know exact—
Ms. Cramer: Just read it from your paper.
Simon: The blocks are alike because first of all they have the blocks. And then they are all things that you can see or that are numbers. The ball ones have balls in front. They have one geometry thing and two that are types of numbers and another that's a group of people. They both seem pretty mixed up, alike in some ways and different in others.

Exhibit 9.9
The form Ms. Cramer distributed during her inductive lesson on variables and constants.

■ WILSON McCARDLE
● RECTANGLE
● RATIONAL NUMBER
■ 13
■ THE OVERHEAD PROJECTOR SCREEN YOU SEE RIGHT NOW
● PEOPLE IN THIS ROOM
● AGE
■ 15 YEARS OLD

How are the ■'s alike but different from the ●'s?
How are the ●'s alike but different from the ■'s?

_____
_____
_____
_____
_____
_____
_____
_____
_____

COMPARISON

_____
_____
_____

Exhibit 9.10
Ms. Cramer's overhead transparency for her inductive learning activity on variables and constants.

Person	■	●

Ms. Cramer writes Simon: and then writes "can see or is a number" under the ■ on the transparency and "types of things" under the ● heading.

Ms. Cramer: Read yours, Megan.

Megan: Those with balls are kinds of things, not exact things. The ball ones are things you study about. The blocks are more exact. The blocks also have a weird thing, but I think he's cool anyway.

The class laughs as Ms. Cramer adds to the transparency. She writes Megan: in the Person column, "actual and exact" under the ■, and "kinds of things" under the ● heading.

Ms. Cramer: On two lines of your form under the heading Comparison, quickly write one or two sentences describing how Simon's and Megan's answers are similar. You've got one minute.

She quickly moves about the room glancing at their responses as the session continues toward closure.

You might also consider having students formulate and discuss answers in small task groups and then making group reports of their findings and conclusions to the large group. Engaging students in these types of cooperative group sessions is addressed in a subsequent section of this chapter.

Six Points about Question/Discussion Sessions

Here are some thoughts for you to keep in mind when designing learning activities in which you raise questions for your students to answer:

1. Unlike recitation sessions, student engagement during reason-level questioning sessions requires students to take time to ponder and think about questions posed by teachers before expressing an-

swers. Consequently, *students are unable to engage in reasoning-level questioning sessions unless their teachers provide for periods of silent thinking between the time when questions are asked and when answers expected.*

2. Having all students write out their responses to questions posed by a teacher has at least four advantages over having only students who are called on express their answers:

(a) *Students have to organize their thoughts to write out answers, and this provides an additional learning experience; (b) allowing time for students to write serves as a silent period for all students during which they can be thinking about how to respond to questions; (c) written responses make it possible for teachers to preview students' answers and decide which ones should be read to the class; (d) having written responses available to read to the class avoids some of the stammering and grasping for words that is typical of students answering aloud in front of their peers.*

3. *By directing a question to a particular student before articulating the question itself, a teacher may discourage other students from carefully listening to that question.* In most cases asking, "What has the Pythagorean relationship got to do with the distance formula? . . . Traci." is preferable to "Traci, what has the Pythagorean relationship got to do with the distance formula?" With the latter phrasing, students other than Traci may not bother to listen to or think about how to answer the question since they know it's not directed at them.

4. Teachers need to move quickly from one student to another so that as many students as possible express answers aloud. However, with reasoning-level questions, some students' answers are complex and need to be discussed in some detail; answers are not simply right or wrong. To involve more students, maintain a single focus, and yet have some particu-

lar answers fully discussed, *teachers should use the responses of some students to formulate subsequent questions for other students.* Ms. Cramer in Case 9.11, for example, directed the class to compare Simon's answer to Megan's.

5. Students are more likely to engage in question/discussion sessions in which (a) *questions relate to one another and focus on a central theme or problem rather than appear isolated or unrelated,* and (b) *questions are specific rather than vague.* Vague questions such as Do you understand? hardly focus thought as well as, How would reducing the denominator affect the value of y? If you want to assess students' understanding, confront them with a specific mathematical task and observe their responses.

6. Learning activities conducted prior to question/discussion sessions can serve to maintain the focus of the questioning session. Also, students learn the importance of engaging in question/discussion sessions when the sessions culminate in problem resolutions that are applied in subsequent learning activities. Note, for example, how Mr. Citerelli had students use what they gained from question/discussion sessions in other types of activities in Cases 4.7 to 4.10.

IDEAS FOR COOPERATIVE LEARNING SESSIONS

Students Learning from One Another

Cooperative learning activities in which students learn from one another have proved to be quite successful (Augustine, Gruber, & Hanson, 1990; Good, Mulryan, & McCaslin, 1992; Leighton, 1994; Lyman & Foyle, 1990; Slavin, 1991a, 1991b; Voorhies, 1989). Students can engage in cooperative learning activities in large group settings, but small task groups are particularly well-suited for students teaching one another.

Intraclass grouping arrangements provide greater opportunities than whole-class activities for students to interact with one another, for tasks to be tailored to special interests or needs, and for a variety of tasks to be addressed during class. A variety of intraclass task-group patterns are commonly used to facilitate cooperative learning. They include (a) *peer instruction groups,* (b) *practice groups,* (c) *interest or achievement-level groups,* and (d) *problem-solving groups.*

Peer Instruction Groups

In a peer instruction group one student, or a team of students, teaches others, either presenting a brief lesson, tutoring, or providing help with specified tasks. Traditionally, this type of activity involves a student, who is relatively advanced in the achievement of a particular objective, working with students who need special help in achieving that objective. Case 9.12 is an example.

CASE 9.12

Mr. Jackson notes the following from the results of a unit test he recently administered to the 21 students in his probability and statistics class:

- Regarding test items 3, 7, 8, and 16, all of which are relevant to students' comprehension of the central limit theorem, Anita responded correctly to all four, whereas none of the following students got more than two of the items correct: Bernie, Deborah, Amalya, Francine, and Jay.
- Regarding test items 5, 6, and 11, all of which are relevant to how well students construct the concept of a normal distribution, Benju responded correctly to all three items, but none of the following students got any of the three items correct: Bernie, Amalya, Don, Steve, and Malcom.

Mr. Jackson things that (a) Anita and Benju's insights into the content would be enhanced by experiences teaching their peers, (b) the other eight students will not succeed in the next unit until they better achieve certain objectives from the unit, and (c) Bernie and Amalya need to construct the concept of a normal distribution before they can comprehend the central limit theorem. Thus, he decides to conduct a session in which the class is subdivided into three groups:

- Group I—Anita will explain the central limit theorem and how she worked test items 3, 7, 8, and 16 to Deborah, Francine, and Jay.
- Group II—Benju will explain normal distributions and how he worked test items 5, 6, and 11 to Bernie, Amalya, Don, Steve, and Malcom.
- Group III—The other 11 students will work on an individual assignment.

But peer instruction does not have to involve mentor students who display more advanced achievement levels than their peers. Consider the ideas demonstrated by Case 9.13.

CASE 9.13

Ms. Harris integrates historical topics into most of the units for her algebra class of 25 students. As part of the unit on numbers and numeration, she subdivides the students into five groups of five, with groups assigned to historical topics as follows:

Group A

Topic: Origins of Hindu-Arabic numeration system

Students: Osprey, Byron, Bryce, Chris, and Nadine

Group B

Topic: Origins of our beliefs about prime numbers

Students: Marion, Joe, Charlene, Jennifer, Dominica

Group C

Topic: The discovery of π

Students: Patti, Scott, Jan, Chen-Pai, Garth

Group D

Topic: The history of perfect, deficient, and abundant numbers

Students: Crystal, Henry, Cinny, Jason A., Jason T.

Group E

Topic: Karl Friedrich Gauss and the theory of numbers

Students: Julie, Eian, John, Rich, Willie

She then conducts an hour-long task-group session, with each of the five groups studying and discussing its topic using references from Ms. Harris' resource library. For homework, each student prepares a 15-minute lesson on her or his group's topic to be presented to four students from the other groups.

Over the next two days, Ms. Harris conducts additional task-group sessions in which the five students from each group present their 15-minute lessons to groups of four students from other groups. For example, Osprey presents her lesson on the origins of Hindu-Arabic numbers to Marion, Patti, Crystal, and Julie. Marion presents his on the origins of our beliefs about prime numbers to Osprey, Patti, Crystal, and Julie. Patti presents hers on the discovery of π to Osprey, Marion, Crystal, and Julie. Crystal presents hers on the history of perfect, deficient, and abundant numbers to Osprey, Marion, Patti, and Julie. And Julie presents hers on Gauss and the theory of numbers to Osprey, Marion, Patti, and Crystal.

The other four groups for rounds of lesson are: Byron, Joe, Scott, Henry, and Eian; Bryce, Charlene, Jan, Cinny, and John; Chris, Jennifer, Chen-Pai, Jason A., Rich; Nadine, Dominica, Garth, Jason T., Willie.

Practice Groups

Large-group recitation sessions like those in Cases 9.7 and 9.8 do not always provide highly efficient ways for students to review, drill, and receive feedback for memory-level objectives. With small-group arrangements, several or more students can recite concurrently. Students, for example, could work in groups of three each. One student reads questions about vocabulary, symbols, and relationships from a

pack of cards. The other two answer and the questioner gives feedback. The role of questioner rotates. Another possibility is for students to play mathematics memory games as was done in Case 9.8. But to increase individual involvement and the number of trials per student, students play in groups of five rather than as a whole class.

Interest or Achievement Groups

Intraclass groups may be organized around interests as in Case 9.14 or around achievement levels as in Case 9.15.

CASE 9.14

Mr. Frank sometimes groups his geometry students according to their individual areas of interests. For a unit on similarity between geometric figures, he uses four different interest groups: sports, pets, partying, and music. For one of the unit's discover a relationship objectives, each of the four groups works within its interest area during the experimenting stage. Reports from the four groups are then used in subsequent stages in large-group sessions.

The arrangement of four subgroups is also used in other lessons, such as one for an application-level objective. In general, the small interest-group sessions are used for students to confront tasks in their respective areas of interest; these are followed by large-group sessions, in which the mathematics used by all four groups is discussed and analyzed.

CASE 9.15

To help her deal with the wide range of student achievement levels in her seventh-grade general mathematics class, Ms. Rosenberg conducts virtually the whole course with the 32 students partitioned into three groups:

- The green group—consisting of 8 students who average about 3.5 weeks per teaching unit
- The blue group—consisting of 15 students who average 2.5 weeks per teaching unit.
- The gray group—consisting of 9 students who average about 1 week per teaching unit.

For all practical purposes, she conducts three courses in one. She is able to manage such a configuration by staggering large-group, small-group, and individual sessions among the groups.

Problem-Solving Groups

Small task-group sessions can enable students to work concurrently on a variety of problems that will be subsequently used in large-group activities. Case 9.16 is an example of such a session being used within an application-level lesson.

CASE 9.16

Mr. Breland has 23 prealgebra students working in four groups—A, B, C, and D, in the arrangement illustrated in Exhibit 9.11—as part of a lesson for the following objective:

> When confronted with a real-life problem, determine whether or not computing a ratio will facilitate solution of the problem.   (application)

As directed by Mr. Breland, each group has 18 minutes to answer the questions listed on its task sheet and prepare a 6-minute oral report on its work to be presented to the class as a whole. The four task sheets are depicted in Exhibit 9.12.

As the groups complete their tasks, Mr. Breland circulates about the room, monitoring each group and cuing students to remain on-task as the need arises. After the session, a designated member of each group reports it findings. Mr. Breland then conducts a large-group question/discus-

Exhibit 9.11
Mr. Breland's arrangement for a small-task-group problem-solving session.

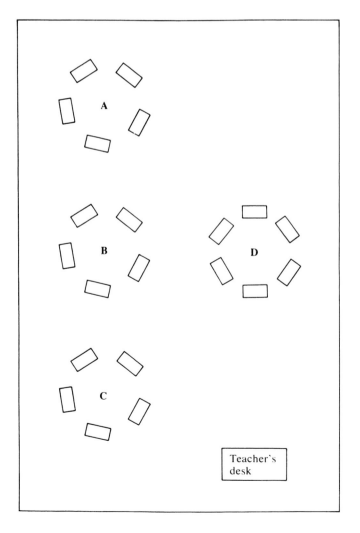

sion session for the rule-articulation stage of the lesson. Prompted by Mr. Breland's deductive questions, students examine and compare the four group reports to articulate the rules for applying ratios to real-life problems.

Guidance and Structure for Maintaining Engagement

Research studies that examine how students spend their time in classrooms indicate that they are likely to have poor engagement levels in small-group learning activities unless the teacher is actively involved in the session (Evertson, 1989; Fisher, Beliner, Filby, Marliave, Cahen, & Dishaw, 1980). But a teacher cannot be in the middle of several groups at once and often subgroups fail to address their tasks due to a lack of guidance. Consider Case 9.17 for example.

CASE 9.17

Ms. Clay has her prealgebra students organized into four subgroups similar to the arrangement in Exhibit 9.11. She directs them, "I want each group to discuss when we use ratios to solve real-life problems. Okay, go ahead and get started."

After six minutes discussing what they're supposed to be doing, the students in one group no longer bother with ratios and socialize with one another. Ms. Clay hardly notices that they're off-task because she is busy explaining to another group what she meant them to do. A third group becomes quite noisy, and Ms. clay raises her voice from her position with the second group and announces, "Better keep it down in here. You won't learn how to apply ratios unless you get on the stick and get your discussion going." In the fourth group, Magdalina dominates the first five minutes telling the others about ratios. She stimulates Ann's interest and the two of them engage in a conversation in which Magdalina reviews what Ms. Clay explained in a previous session about computing ratios. The other three members of the group are doing other things unrelated to the topic.

After managing to get the second group on track, Ms. Clay moves to the noisy third group, saying, "You people aren't following directions; you are supposed to be discussing problems that use ratios." She then tells the group what she had hoped they'd discover for themselves.

After spending nine minutes with the second group, Ms. Clay calls a halt to the activity and announces, "Okay, class let's rearrange our desks back. Now that you understand when to apply ratios, I want to move on to . . .

Ms. Clay failed to obtain satisfactory student engagement because her directions did not spell out what tasks each subgroup was to accomplish and just how to go about completing them. Without an advanced organizer (see Mr. Breland's in Exhibit 9.12) to focus students' attention, it was difficult for

Exhibit 9.12
Four task sheets for Groups A, B, C, and D in Mr. Breland's prealgebra class.

Group A

DIRECTIONS: Answer the questions based on the box score from Tuesday's Flyers-Tigers basketball game. Prepare a 5-minute oral report to the class that explains what problem-solving strategies you used to answer the questions.

Flyers 79, Tigers 75

Flyers	min.	fgm-fga	ftm-fta	reb.	ass.	pf	tp
Champagne	23	4–7	2–2	8	1	4	10
Noto	28	9–19	6–8	4	2	2	26
Kora	21	3–4	4–9	11	3	4	10
Guillory, K.	15	2–7	2–3	2	0	0	8
Demouy	32	4–6	0–0	3	10	3	8
Guillory, T.	11	0–3	0–0	0	2	1	0
Miller	20	7–13	1–1	1	1	0	15
Knight	5	0–0	0–0	0	0	2	0
Losavio	5	1–3	0–0	0	0	0	2
Totals	160	30–62	15–23	29	19	16	79

Tigers	min.	fgm-fga	ftm-fta	reb.	ass.	pf	tp
Cassano	32	11–19	0–0	4	3	4	22
Silva	30	2–9	5–8	7	0	4	9
Burke	14	0–6	1–2	2	1	2	1
Parino	32	12–27	5–5	9	7	3	29
Price	22	4–5	0–0	4	7	5	8
Weimer	19	3–6	0–4	6	2	1	6
Bowman	11	0–4	0–1	1	1	0	0
Totals	160	32–76	11–20	33	21	19	75

1. By how much did the Flyers win?
2. Which team made the most 3-point goals?
3. Who made more field goals, Noto or Parino?
4. Who was the more accurate field goals shooter, Noto or Parino?
5. Who scored more points for the amount of time he played in the game, Noto or Parino?
6. Since the Tigers made more field goals than the Flyers, how did the Flyers manage to score 4 more points than the Tigers?
7. If Kora had played the whole game, rebounding at the same rate as he did for the time he was in the game, what would his rebound total have been?
8. For which of the preceding seven questions did you use ratios to help determine your answers?

her to provide guidance efficiently to one group while monitoring the others. Furthermore, her students are less likely to engage diligently in her next intra-class group session because they failed to achieve closure on this one, and Ms. Clay did not follow up the work they did in the subgroups. Unlike Mr. Breland in Case 9.16, she did not take what the subgroups did and use it in a subsequent activity.

In Case 9.17, Ms. Clay also illustrated another common misapplication of cooperative learning by stepping in and doing the second group's work for it. Some teachers get so frustrated when subgroups fail to maintain their focus that they break into lectures when they should simply ask a leading question or two and let the students do their own work. Otherwise, a large-group session would be more efficient.

Exhibit 9.12
Continued

Group B

DIRECTIONS: Answer the questions based on the labels from the two soup cans. Prepare a 5-minute oral report to the class that explains what problem-solving strategies you used to answer the questions.

CHICKEN WITH LETTERS

Size: 10.6 oz (298 g)   *Price:* 58¢

Nutritional Information

Serving size (condensed) ....4 oz
Serving size (prepared) ....8 oz
Per serving:
    Calories..60
    Protein (grams) 3
    Simple sugars (grams) 1
    Complex carbohydrates (grams) 6
    Fat (grams)...2
    Cholesterol (mg) 10
    Sodium (mg) 870
Percentage of U.S. Recommended Daily Requirement:
    Protein..........................4   Riboflavin 2
    Vitamin A.......................8   Niacin...........................4
    Vitamin C ....*   Calcium ....*
    Thiamine 2   Iron..............................2
*Contains less than 2% of the US RDA of this nutrient.

NOODLES AND CHICKEN

Size: 10.6 oz (298 g)   *Price:* 61¢

Nutritional Information

Serving size (condensed) ....4 oz
Serving size (prepared) ....8 oz
Per serving:
    Calories..80
    Protein (grams) 3
    Simple sugars (grams) 1
    Complex carbohydrates (grams) 8
    Fat (grams)...3
    Cholesterol (mg) 15
    Sodium (mg) 960
Percentage of U.S. Recommended Daily Requirement:
    Protein..........................4   Riboflavin 2
    Vitamin A.......................25   Niacin...........................6
    Vitamin C ....*   Calcium ....*
    Thiamine 4   Iron..............................4
*Contains less than 2% of the US RDA of this nutrient.

1. With which soup do you get more grams for the money?
2. Which soup has more vitamins?
3. Which soup has more cholesterol?
4. Which soup has more vitamins per calorie?
5. Which soup is the best buy considering only the amount of iron it provides?
6. What appears to be more expensive, calories or complex carbohydrates?
7. How many grams of sodium are contained in the entire can of Noodles and Chicken?
8. For which of the seven preceding questions did you use ratios to help determine your answers?

Exhibit 9.12
Continued

Group C

DIRECTIONS: Answer the questions based on the lists of songs from audio tape albums. Prepare a 5-minute oral report to the class that explains what problem-solving strategies you used to answer the questions.

RABID DOG IN CONCERT

Price: $9.98

Side One	*Side Two*
Every Rose Ain't a Flower (2:55)	Feelin' Too Much Pain (3:06)
Three-Woman Dog (4:20)	Too Fine To Be Mine (2:30)
After the Pigs Come Home (3:01)	Too Young (3:11)
Smilin' 'stead of Cryin' (4:44)	Lucy the Lucky One (2:05)
My Kind of Party (3:15)	It Lasts Forever (8:09)
Allison (2:02)	

THE SENSATIONAL SCREAMERS ONE MORE TIME

Price: $8.79

Side One	*Side Two*
Who Likes to Kill Animals? (5:17)	Reasons to Live (3:11)
Help Is on the Way (2:10)	Not Much More to Say (5:12)
Casey the Drum-Man (2:14)	Not too Much Longer (2:09)
Momma Said It's Okay (3:29)	No-Mo-Dough (2:45)
Comfort (4:04)	Not Much Help (3:00)
One More Time (3:35)	Mindy, Mindy (1:55)

1. Which of the two tapes has more songs?
2. Which of the two tapes has more songs for the money?
3. Which of the two tapes has more minutes of music?
4. Which of the two tapes has more minutes of music for the money?
5. Which of the two tapes do you like better?
6. On average, how long does one side of these two tapes play?
7. What's the difference in the time between the longest and shortest songs on the two tapes?
8. For which of the seven preceding questions did you use ratios to help determine your answers?

Ten Points about Cooperative Learning Sessions

Consider the following when designing cooperative learning sessions:

1. Expect the sort of off-task behaviors Ms. Clay's students exhibit in Case 9.17 unless you *clearly define not only tasks for each cooperative task group, but also the individual responsibilities of each group member* (as indicated Ms. Gaudchaux' lesson plan in Exhibit 4.15).

2. *All group members should be jointly accountable for completing the shared task, with each member responsible for fulfilling an individual role.*

3. *Efficient procedures for making transitions into and out of small-group activities avoid the time-wasting chaos* following a teacher's directions such as, "Lets' move our desks so that we have four groups of six each." In Case 4.13, Ms. Smith used an especially efficient and attention-getting

Exhibit 9.12
Continued

Group D

DIRECTIONS: Answer the questions based on the data given about crime in our city during the years 1990 and 1991. Prepare a 5-minute oral report to the class that explains what problem-solving strategies you used to answer the questions.

	1995	1996
Population	320,000	323,000
Murders	34	37
Rapes	99	112
Robberies	704	691
Aggravated assaults	1,001	1,120
Burglaries	3,092	3,212
Thefts by larceny	7,344	7,360
Motor vehicle thefts	1,611	1,786

1. Did crime increase or decrease from 1995 to 1996?
2. Which type of crime is the most common?
3. Relative to the size of the population, did the rate of murders go up or down from 1995 to 1996?
4. Relative to the size of the population, did the rate of burglaries go up or down from 1995 to 1996?
5. The rate relative to population of which type of crime increased the least?
6. The rate relative to population of which type of crime increased the most?
7. By how much did the population grow over the course of one year?
8. For which of the preceding seven questions did you use ratios to help determine your answers?

method for getting students into an intraclass group session. Case 9.18 illustrates another idea.

CASE 9.18

Prominently displayed on the front wall of Ms. Bringhurst's classroom is a brightly colored 2 by 3.5-foot poster depicted in Exhibit 9.13. She moves the arrow to the symbol on the poster to indicate if students should be working alone (1), in pairs (2), . . . in groups of five (5), . . . or as a single large group (whole class).

4. *Task sheets and advanced organizers* (Exhibit 9.12) direct students' focus and provide them with an overall picture of what they are expected to accomplish in their groups.
5. You can avoid the need for interrupting cooperative-group work to clarify directions the whole class should hear by *specifying the task and directions for everyone before attentions are turned to individual group activities.*
6. You need to *monitor groups' activities, providing guidance as needed without usurping individual students' responsibilities for designated tasks.* You should move from one group to another, cu-

ing students to remain on-task without actually becoming a member of any one group. Mr. Breland applies this suggestion in Case 9.19.

CASE 9.19

Mr. Breland stops to sit with Group C as they struggle with question 4 from Exhibit 9.12. One student tells him, "I like the Sensational Screamers better. Doesn't that make a difference?" Mr. Breland turns to the group, "What does *more* minutes of music mean?" Noticing the discussion is on track, he moves over to Group B, continuing to keep an eye on all the groups.

7. *Formative feedback should be used to regulate activities.* Engaged behaviors during task-group sessions are observable—students should be involved in discussions and working on a specified task. Thus, formative feedback for regulating activities is relatively easy to obtain.
8. *Closure points are needed for lengthy sessions.* As with other types of sessions, students need to have engagement positively reinforced. Mr. Breland was able to achieve this by posing a sequence of questions on the task sheets of Exhibit 9.12 rather than just one question.

Exhibit 9.13
The poster Ms. Bringhurst displays to indicate grouping arrangements.

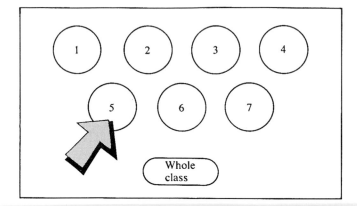

IDEAS FOR INDEPENDENT WORK SESSIONS

Student Engagement During Independent Work Sessions

The importance of having students interact with one another in cooperative group activities is emphasized in the NCTM *Standards* (NCTM, 1989, pp. 140–142; 1991, pp. 34–62). But a lesson's group activities need to be interspersed with some quiet think time during which students can engage in independent work. Note, for example, Ms. Gaudchaux's lesson plan in Exhibit 4.15. She integrated small task-group, question/discussion, independent work, and homework sessions in her lesson.

Engagement in independent work sessions requires a student to complete an assigned task without disturbing others also working on the task. Typically, students work individually, with the teacher available for help. Independent work sessions are appropriately used in a variety of ways:

9. *Individual group work should be followed up and utilized during subsequent learning activities.* Note that with Ms. Gaudchaux's lesson plan in Exhibit 4.15, the large-group activities depend on information gathered and descriptions formulated in the small task groups.

10. You should *model active listening techniques.* Students do not automatically know how to listen to one another without being shown. From classes they take with teachers other than you, they may unfortunately have learned that anything of academic importance is said by teachers, not peers. Thus, you should demonstrate that you listen intently to them and make use of what they say. Mr. Breland applies this suggestion in Case 9.20.

- *As an integral part of an inquiry lesson, students work independently on tasks that were defined previously during a large-group session. The work from the independent session is subsequently used in follow-up activities.* In Case 4.8, Mr. Citerelli began a construct a concept lesson with an independent work session in which students completed Exhibit 4.7's task sheet. The products of this activity were used in the lesson's reflecting and explaining stage during a large-group question/discussion session.

- *As an integral part of a direct instruction lesson, students independently practice in a large-group session what has just been explained to them. The teacher provides individual guidance during the independent work session. Students receive feedback on what they practiced, either in a subsequent large-group session, a cooperative group session, or by the teacher collecting and then annotating their work.* For example, after explaining an algorithm for differentiating algebraic functions, Ms. Allen in Case 5.15 directed her students to complete a related exercise as she circulated about the room monitoring work and providing help as needed. She used her observations of their work as formative feedback to regulate the remainder of the lesson.

- *Students use part of a class period to begin a homework assignment in an independent work session. This practice allows them to start the assignment while the teacher is still available to provide guidance.*

CASE 9.20

Mr. Breland stops to sit with Group B as they struggle with question 6 from Exhibit 9.12. As Emily is commenting, John attempts to engage Mr. Breland with his own private question, "Mr. Breland, this doesn't make . . . " But Mr. Breland uses a frown and a hand motion to cue John to be quiet and then says to the group, "Excuse me, Emily, would you repeat that last part about adding the two prices? I missed what you said about that." Emily repeats and finishes her comment. Mr. Breland says, "Thank you. That should shed some light on John's concern. John, raise your concern with the group." John: "To me, the question ought to be . . . "

Later in the large-group session, Mr. Breland uses the comments that different students made in their subgroups as a basis for discussion.

Independent work sessions are essential to most teaching units. However, they need to be integrated with other types of learning activities, monitored, and guided. Rosenshine (1987, p. 261) states:

> Studies have shown that when students are working alone during seatwork they are less engaged than when they are being given instruction by the teacher. Therefore, the question of how to manage students during seatwork, in order to maintain engagement, becomes of primary interest.

One consistent finding has been the importance of a teacher (or another adult) monitoring the students during seatwork. Fisher et al. (1980) found that the amount of substantive teacher interaction with students during seatwork was positively related to achievement and that when students have contacts with the teacher during seatwork their engagement rate increases by about 10 percent. Thus it seems important that teachers not only monitor seatwork, but that they also provide academic feedback and explanations to students during their independent practice. However, the research suggests that these contacts should be relatively short, averaging 30 seconds or less. Longer contacts would appear to pose two difficulties: the need for a long contact suggests that the initial explanation was not complete and the more time a teacher spends with one student, the less time there is to monitor and help other students.

Another finding of Fisher et al. was that teachers who had more questions and answers during group work had more engagement during seatwork. That is, another way to increase engagement during seatwork was to have more teacher-led practice during group work so that students could be more successful during seatwork.

A third finding (Fisher et al. 1980) was that when teachers had to give a good deal of explanation during seatwork, then student error rates were higher. Having to give a good deal of explanation during seatwork suggests that the initial explanation was not sufficient or that there was not sufficient practice and correction before seatwork.

Another effective procedure for increasing engagement during seatwork was to break the instruction into smaller segments and have two or three segments of instruction and seatwork during a single period.

Six Points about Independent Work Sessions

Here are some ideas to consider when designing and conducting independent work sessions:

1. *By providing explicit directions and clearly defining the task, you avoid many of the nagging questions about what to do.* The idea is to devote the time you spend conferring with individual students to guide and prompt them, not to reiterate directions in response to questions such as, "What are we supposed to be doing?"
2. *Having artifacts (for example, notes, a sample exercise, and a list of steps in an algorithm) from the pre-* *ceding group-learning activity still visible to students on the chalkboard or in their notebooks during an independent work session provides a reference that facilitates the efficiency with which students receive help.* For example, consider Case 9.21.

CASE 9.21

Ms. Towers has just conducted a large-group presentation that included an explanation of an algorithm for factoring algebraic polynomials, a demonstration of the algorithm with an example, and the class working through an example with Ms. Towers' guidance.

Leaving the two completed examples and the step-by-step outline of the algorithm on the chalkboard, Ms. Towers directs the students into an independent work session in which they are to practice the algorithm on six exercises from the textbook.

In a few minutes, Phyllis and Juaquin raise their hands. Silently acknowledging Juaquin with a wink and hand gesture, Ms. Towers moves to Phyllis' desk; Phyllis says, "I don't know where to start." Ms. Towers, seeing that Phyllis has nothing written on her paper, says "Read the first two steps from the board and then look at what we did first for the example on the right. I'll be back within 30 seconds." She moves directly to Juaquin's desk and Juaquin says, "Is this right?" Detecting that he's begun the first exercise by factoring out only 2 when he could have factored out 6, she responds, "It's not wrong, but you could make it easier on yourself if you repeat step 2 before continuing—see if there's still another factor that's common." She walks back to Phyllis as Juaquin blurts out, "Oh, yeah! The 3 . . ." Realizing that he's being disruptive, Juaquin grabs his mouth, muffling the rest of his sentence.

Back at Phyllis' desk, Ms. Towers sees that Phyllis is now started and softly tells her, "Just keep following the steps on the board and checking how that example is worked—one step at a time. I'll check with you every few minutes." By this time, three others have their hands up. By referring to the outline and examples and raising pointed questions, Ms. Towers has all three students back on track within a minute. She continues moving about the room, responding to students' requests for help and volunteering guidance as she sees fit from observing their work. At no time does she spend more than 20 seconds at a time with any one student.

3. *You can provide efficient individual guidance and help to students, but only if you organize for it prior to the session and communicate assertively during the session.*
4. *Cooperative learning activities can be incorporated into independent work sessions to increase opportunities for students to receive help.* Ms. Strickland in Case 9.22 manages to do this in an unusual way.

CASE 9.22

At the beginning of the school year Ms. Strickland constructs a flag-raising device. Each device is supplied with yellow, red, and green flags, which can be raised one at a time. She then produces enough such devices to install them on the corners of the students' desks in her classroom.

She then establishes a procedure for independent work sessions whereby students display (a) a yellow flag as long as they are progressing with the work and do not feel a need for help, (b) a red flag to indicate a request for help, and (c) a green flag to indicate that they've finished the work and are willing to help others. See Exhibit 9.14.

As Ms. Strickland monitors a session, she responds to a red flag either by conferring with the student herself or by signaling a student who has raised a green flag to provide the consultation.

Ms. Strickland believes her system has four distinct advantages over the conventional hand-raising procedure: (a) Cooperative learning among students is encouraged; (b) when waiting for help, students can continue doing some work without having to be burdened with holding a hand; (c) students who finish the task before others have something to do that will not only help their peers but will be learning experience for them also; and (d) the systematic air of the procedure enhances the businesslike environment of the classroom.

4. *To avoid having students who finish early idly waiting for others to complete a task, you can sequence independent work sessions so they are followed by individual activities with flexible beginning and ending times.* Students do not work at the same pace. Unless the task can be completed by all in less than ten minutes, you need to manage independent work sessions to accommodate the fact that they will be finishing at varying times. One solution is to schedule a subsequent activity that early finishers can start (e.g., begin a homework assignment) but which can be interrupted conveniently when you are ready to halt the independent work session after all or almost all the students have completed the task. Case 9.23 is an example.

CASE 9.23

Ms. Wharton has established a routine in which each teaching unit includes a long-range assignment that requires students to use computers to complete. The assignment is given at the beginning of the unit and is not due until the day of the summative unit test. Ordinarily it involves either completing some programmed exercises related to the unit's objectives or writing programs for executing algorithms learned during the unit. Ms. Wharton's classroom is equipped with nine microcomputers, but she has no fewer than 21 students in any one of her classes.

Exhibit 9.14
Flag raising during one of Ms. Strickland's independent work sessions.

For independent work sessions she has established a routine by which students who finish the task before the session is completed work on their computer assignment. Those who may have already completed the computer assignment have the option either of beginning their homework assignment or using the computers in other ways (e.g., to play games).

_____

5. *As with other types of learning activities, students need feedback to correct errors, reinforce correct responses, and positively reinforce engagement.* Formative feedback is facilitated during independent work sessions because each student's efforts are reflected by a product (written responses on a task sheet). Note how Ms. Allen utilized formative feedback during the independent work session she conducted near the end of Case 5.15.

IDEAS FOR HOMEWORK ASSIGNMENTS
Appropriate Uses of Homework

Homework provides students with opportunities to work alone at their own pace. The crowded social setting of a classroom is not particularly conducive to the concentrated, undisturbed thinking that is an essential ingredient in achieving construct a concept, discover a relationship, comprehension, application, and creativity objectives. Furthermore, school schedules often do not allocate adequate classroom time for practice exercises that are essential for achieve-

ment of simple-knowledge and algorithm-skill objectives. Posamentier and Stepelman (1990, p. 48) suggest that for many students, classroom instruction serves as a forum for exposure to new material, whereas the genuine learning experiences occur while they are engaged in homework. Learning activities via homework assignments are complementary classroom activities as: (a) preparations for classroom activities, (b) extensions of classroom activities, and (c) follow-ups to classroom activities.

Use of Homework as Preparation for Classroom Activities

One way you help students associate mathematics with their own real worlds is to engage them in learning activities using numbers and other mathematical variables from their outside of school environments. Rather than always working with numbers from textbooks or data that you bring to class, occasionally assign homework in which students collect data or other information for use in classroom activities. Mr. Fernandez did this in Case 7.5, as does Mr. Greene in Case 9.24.

CASE 9.24

Mr. Greene directs his students near the end of a class period, "As part of your homework assignment, locate three circles determined by objects in or near your home. Anything that determines a circle will be fine, such as, the base of a light, a bicycle wheel, a dinner plate, or the top of your little brother's head. After locating each of your three

Exhibit 9.15
The form Mr. Greene uses on an overhead transparency to record data students collected for homework

Person	Object	Circumference (C)	Diameter (D)	C/D

circles, measure its diameter and circumference. Write the measurements down and bring in the three pairs of numbers to class tomorrow."

The next day, Mr. Greene displays Exhibit 9.15 on the overhead projector and directs students, one at a time, to call out circumference/diameter pairs. Each student contributes one pair as Mr. Greene completes the form in Exhibit 9.16.

Mr. Greene then conducts an inductive question/discussion session leading students to discover that the ratio of the circumference of any circle to its diameter is a constant that is slightly greater than 3.

You may sometimes use a homework assignment to expose students to a problem or task that stimulates them to direct their thoughts toward a topic you plan to introduce during the next classroom session. Cases 9.25 and 9.26 are examples.

CASE 9.25

Ms. McKnight conducts an inquiry lesson on permutations, followed by a direct lesson on using the formula $_nP_r = n!/((n - r)!)$. For homework she assigns nine word problems. The first eight problems can be solved using the permutation formula; to solve the ninth, a combination formula is needed. Ms. McKnight doesn't plan a lesson on combinations until the next day, after the homework is due.

The homework is reviewed in class the following day. Some students automatically used the permutation formula for the ninth problem. Others realized that this problem was different from the others but didn't devise a solution. One student correctly solved the ninth problem via a tedious examination of all possible cases. Students complain to Ms. McKnight that the ninth problem was a "trick" problem. Acknowledging her "error," Ms. McKnight uses their discussion of that problem as a springboard into the day's lesson, which is about combinations.

CASE 9.26

Mr. Cooper's students know how to plot points on an algebraic function in a Cartesian plane. However, except for linear functions they are unaware of any methods for sketching a graph without plotting numerous points.

The day before he plans to introduce shortcuts for finding key features of graphs of quadratic functions (e.g., the vertex and line of symmetry), Mr. Cooper assigns three quadratic functions to be graphed for homework.

The next day students have the graphs for class, with varying degrees of accuracy. Some complain about how boring it was to plot so many points. Mr. Cooper jumps on the students' expressed need for some shortcuts and embarks on his planned inquiry lesson to discover some useful relationships.

Some skills or knowledge needed for participation in an upcoming classroom activity may be efficiently acquired during a homework assignment. For example, consider Cases 9.27 and 9.28.

CASE 9.27

Mr. Triche assigns some background reading on the Pythagoreans for homework. The next day he draws on that knowledge of mathematical history for a lesson on polyhedra.

CASE 9.28

Ms. Clarion distributes a list of words and symbols she plans to use in a large-group presentation the next day. For homework, the students are directed to look up and memorize the definitions of those words and symbols.

Traditionally, students depend on time allocated for homework to study for in-class tests. Assignments to study for tests need to be specific; students

---

Exhibit 9.16
Mr. Greene records one pair of measurements from each student.

Person	Object	Circumference C	Diameter D	C/D
Barbara	ring	6.8 cm	2.2 cm	3.09
Andrea	barrel bottom	32"	10"	3.20
Jerry	jar	19"	6"	3.17
Oral	base of light fixture	78.74 cm	25 cm	3.15
Glenn	wheel	81.5"	26"	3.13
Karel	top of head	7.75"	2.94"	2.94

do not naturally know how or what to study without specific instructions from you. Students can also be assigned take-home tests, which provide formative feedback that you use to regulate classroom activities. Case 9.29 is an example.

CASE 9.29

Unsure of just how ambitious objectives should be for an upcoming unit on systems of linear equations, Mr. Title assigns homework to test tentative unit objectives. The next day he reviews students' responses to the homework test items and has students do think-aloud exercises to give him an idea as to how they're approaching different mathematical tasks. He uses the information gained from this activity to determine what the unit's objectives should be.

Use of Homework as Extension of Classroom Activities

One of the disadvantages of independent work sessions is that students complete assigned tasks at different times. Often, there is inadequate class time allocated for all students to complete the tasks in class. Furthermore, practice exercises to polish algorithmic skills may be too time consuming to schedule during class. Homework assignments relieve at least some of the pressure of trying to squeeze necessary work into class periods.

Use of Homework as a Follow-Up to Classroom Activities

For some objectives, students need time alone to analyze content at their own pace. Case 9.30 is an example.

CASE 9.30

Ms. Hundley designs a lesson to help students use a problem-solving strategy in which they consciously and systematically move through the nine stages for solving real-life problems that Brenda negotiated in Case 3.1. She believes that students will learn to apply the strategy only by having experience trying it out on their own with numerous problems. Many students, she's noted, lack the confidence to depend on their own thinking; they would rather be told a solution than devise one. Consequently, she wants them to experience their initial success with this problem-solving strategy by themselves, not in a social setting.

Thus, she structures the lesson so that she spends nearly an entire class period in a large-group presentation explaining how to do a homework assignment. She begins by saying, "Your homework assignment for tonight will be to solve three problems that I will distribute on a task sheet at the end of to-

day's period. When you solve these problems, I want you to follow a procedure that is outlined on this solution blueprint form. I'll give you a copy of it now. (She distributes three copies of a form quite similar to the one appearing in Exhibit 6.5.)

She then spends the next 45 minutes explaining how to use the form and the nine-stage strategy for solving a problem. The day's classroom activities present the strategies to the students, but the homework is the activity leading them to apply the strategy.

A more common type of homework assignment that follows up classroom activities is homework that is used to provide formative feedback on what was learned in class. A lesson is presented in class and students are assigned exercises that serve as a formative test of the day's objectives. The results are used to reinforce what was learned and identify areas in need of remediation.

Four Points about Homework Assignments

Unlike most other types of learning activities, students typically must allocate their own time for engaging in homework assignments. Sometimes students doing homework have parents nearby encouraging them to be on-task. However, parental supervision of students' homework is extremely variable and depends on circumstances in homes, ages of students, and a myriad of other factors. Engagement in a homework assignment usually requires students to (a) understand the directions for the assignment, (b) schedule time away from school for the assignment, (c) resist outside of school distractions while completing the assigned task, and (d) deliver a report of the completed work in class by a specified deadline.

To motivate your students to engage in homework you assign, consider the following suggestions:

- *Every day for the first few weeks of a course, assign clearly defined, specific tasks for homework. Spend class time during that early part of the course teaching students to schedule time for homework and efficient ways of completing it. Follow up on every assignment.* Until you make a concerted effort to teach them, your students are unlikely to (a) know how to schedule time for homework, especially considering that they have assignments from other courses besides yours; (b) discriminate whether content relative to an assignment should be memorized, figured out by themselves, or found out from an outside source; (c) know how to study; and (d) know how you expect results of their homework to be reported. Your extra efforts along these lines during the first few weeks of a course will pay dividends in time saved and completed assignments once students learn your routine and expectations. Students will develop a behavior pattern of engaging in homework if initial efforts are positively reinforced.

- *Positively reinforce engagement in homework and punish failure to do homework by designing units so that success in classroom activities, especially tests, depends on homework efforts.* Students can be motivated to engage in homework faithfully without your having to resort to awarding points toward grades for turning in assignments. Consider the system Ms. Goldberg changed to in Case 9.31 (adapted from Cangelosi, 1990a, pp. 59–60).

CASE 9.31

Ms. Goldberg, a mathematics teacher, uses a procedure in which each student's grade is determined by the number of points accumulated during a semester. Her students have two ways to earn points: (a) Half the total possible points are based on their test scores; (b) the other half are awarded for homework that, when turned in on time, is scored according to the number of correct responses.

Ms. Goldberg discovers that a number of students receive high marks on their homework but low marks on their test papers. Under her system, such students are able to pass the course. After analyzing the situation she realizes that these students are either copying their homework from others or having others do it for them. Thus, she decides to change her grading procedures. She will annotate students' homework to provide them with feedback, but she will not grade their homework so that it influences their semester reports. Ms. Goldberg begins to make a concerted effort to assign homework and design tests so that completing homework will clearly be an effective way to prepare for tests.

To begin conditioning her students to the new system, she assigns homework one day and then on the next day administers a test that covers the same objectives as the homework.

————————

Beginning class periods with a short test that includes items similar to exercises from the previous homework assignment teaches students the importance of doing homework far better than preaching to them about the importance of homework or threatening to lower grades if they don't do it. In Case 9.32 a teacher demonstrates a businesslike attitude to motivate students to do homework.

CASE 9.32

Mr. Heidingsfelder carefully examines the 30 algebraic inequalities from the exercises in the class textbook. From the 30, he selects the 13 exercises he thinks will provide students with the most useful practice for the different problem-solving situations they'll encounter in a subsequent lesson.

The day after the assignment he collects the work and performs a quick error-pattern analysis (Ashlock, 1990). The papers are returned to the students with a clear indication of exactly which steps in the algorithm they did correctly and which they did incorrectly. Because he had carefully selected the exercises, he was able to do the analysis more efficiently than if they had been selected with less thought.

While the rest of the students are correcting their work and beginning an independent work session, he calls aside the five students, Angela, Donna, Pruitt, Pam, and Carl, who did not complete the homework and says, "I'm sorry you didn't give me an opportunity to provide you with the feedback on how to solve the inequalities we had for homework."

Pam: "I would have done it but—" Mr. Heidingsfelder interrupts, saying, "It doesn't make any difference why you didn't do it. I've just got to figure out when you can get this done so I can get my analysis back to you before you leave school today. You need that from me before you will be able to go on to our next lesson." Pruitt: "I forgot . . ." Mr. Heidingsfelder: "Please let me think how to help you. I've got it! Here's what we'll do. I'll meet you in here as soon as final announcements are completed this afternoon. As soon as you've finished the 13 exercises, I'll give you my analysis."

————————

- *Keep in mind that students have other assignments besides yours. Fewer, but well-chosen, exercises tend to be more productive than a lengthy assignment that is more time consuming for you and the students. Long-range assignments that are expected to take days for the students to complete should be broken out into a sequence of shorter assignments, with due dates that serve as progress points toward completion.* Consistently heeding this suggestion in the early stages of a course encourages students to get into a routine of doing homework. Otherwise, they tend to be overwhelmed by lengthy assignments until just before they are due.
- *To elicit parents' cooperation in encouraging and supervising homework, utilize ideas from the section "Communicating with Parents" beginning on page 257 of this book.* What you gain from taking this suggestion varies considerably, depending on students' home situations. Some students do not even live with responsible guardians. But when you do elicit parental support, students engagement in homework activities tends to increase remarkably.

TRANSITIONAL ACTIVITIES FROM CHAPTER 9 TO CHAPTER 10

1. Retrieve one of the lesson plans you developed when you completed Activities 4.4, 4.6, 5.3, 5.5, 5.8, 6.1, and 6.4. Identify the different types of learning activities you incorporated in the lesson.

Rethink your lesson plan in light of the suggestions from Chapters 8 and 9; revise it as you see fit. Explain to a colleague how and why you modified your original plan. Listen to a similar report from a colleague engaged in this activity. Discuss what you both gained from the experience.

2. Retrieve one of your lesson plans from Activities 4.4, 4.6, 5.3, 5.5, 5.8, 6.1, and 6.4 that does not include a heavy dose of cooperative learning activities. Redesign it so that cooperative learning is emphasized. Discuss with a colleague the relative advantages and disadvantages of the original plan as compared to the redesigned plan. Return the favor by discussing your colleague's work on this activity.

3. Compare Mr. Smart's method of engaging students in questioning sessions in Case 9.10 to that of Ms. Cramer in Case 9.11. Which one of the two methods do you expect to use more? Explain why. Exchange your work on this activity with a colleague and discuss similarities and differences between the two.

4. Observe a mathematics class in a middle, junior high, or high school. For each allocated time period, classify the type of learning activity as either (a) a large-group presentation; (b) a question/discussion session, (c) a cooperative group session, (d) an independent work session, or (e) other type of session. Select one of the sessions and design an alternative type of learning activity. Explain the relative advantages and disadvantages of the two approaches for the given circumstances. Compare your work on this activity to someone else's.

5. Relative to keeping students engaged, discuss with a colleague the relative advantages and disadvantages of a teacher using videotaped presentations instead of making the presentation entirely "live."

6. Relative to keeping students engaged, discuss with a colleague the advantages and disadvantages of a teacher using pre-prepared task sheets and advanced organizers for small-group cooperative learning sessions.

7. Swap stories with a colleague about homework assignments from mathematics teachers that include examples of efficient, productive assignments, as well as examples of useless or counterproductive assignments.

8. Discuss the following questions with two or more of your colleagues:
   a. What strategies should teachers employ to accurately monitor students' work for the purpose of guiding mathematics instruction?
   b. What strategies should teachers employ to make accurate summative evaluations of their students' mathematical achievements?
   c. How should grades be determined? How should students' progress in mathematics be reported to their parents and to the students themselves?
   d. How should student portfolios be used to reflect and stimulate mathematical achievement?

10

Monitoring Student Progress and Evaluating Achievement

This chapter introduces fundamental principles and strategies for monitoring your students' progress and assessing their achievement of mathematical learning goals. Chapter 10 is designed to help you:

1. Distinguish among examples of measurements, formative evaluations, and summative evaluations. (*construct a concept*)
2. Explain why a measurement's validity depends on its relevance and reliability and the value of a measurement depends on its validity and usability. (*comprehension*)
3. Describe the common uses of three types of measurements of student achievement: teacher-produced measurements, commercially produced tests, and standardized tests. (*comprehension*)
4. Explain the need for alternative assessments as a complement to more traditional approaches. (*discover a relationship*)
5. List and explain the following steps of the process for designing and constructing valid achievement measure-

ments: (a) clarify the learning goal, (b) develop a measurement blueprint, (c) obtain relevant item pools, and (d) synthesize the measurement. (*comprehension*)
6. Organize a system for maintaining item pools that enhances your capability of producing valid and usable measurements of student achievement. (*application*)
7. Explain strategies for designing measurements so that they tend to (a) be relevant to students' achievement of stated learning goals, (b) provide internally consistent results, and (c) have scorer consistency. (*comprehension*)
8. Describe the following methods for converting measurement scores to grades and explain the relative advantages and disadvantages of each: (a) traditional percentage, (b) visual inspection, and (c) compromise. (*comprehension*)
9. Develop strategies for building and using individualized student portfolios as a tool for communicating students' mathematical achievements. (*application*)

DIFFICULT DECISIONS

Formative Feedback

Consider a sample of the complex questions you face as you plan and conduct teaching units:

- Who in the class has discovered why the product of a negative and positive integer is negative, why the product of two natural numbers is positive, why the product of two negative integers is positive, and why

zero times any integer is zero? Is the class ready to move to algorithmic-skill and application lessons using those relationships or should this discover-a-relationship lesson be extended for another day?
- How well are these students following my explanation of this algorithm for computing compound interest? Should I go back and review the steps, push on, or stop and have them practice the steps up to this point?

- Unless these students have achieved the goal of this unit on limits of algebraic functions, they're not ready to begin the one on derivatives. Who is ready to move on and who isn't?

By answering such questions, you make formative evaluations that are necessary for designing and regulating your lessons. However, your empirical senses (sight, hearing, touch, smell, and taste) are incapable of directly observing what is in students' minds and how well they have achieved or are achieving learning objectives. Thus, you must set up situations that encourage students to make observable responses that provide you with indirect evidence of learning. Doing this so that the evidence, although indirect, reflects students' actual achievement of learning objectives is no trivial task. It requires you to apply a sophisticated understanding of your learning goals (including mathematical content and the learning levels specified by the objectives), how your students think, and fundamental principles for assessing student achievement.

The idea of using formative feedback on student achievement was introduced in Chapter 2 in the section Mechanisms for Monitoring Student Progress and Utilizing Feedback in the Design of Lessons. From Chapters 4 through 6, review the descriptions of the four stages of a construct a concept lesson, the four stages of a discover a relationship lesson, the five stages of a simple-knowledge lesson, the literal and interpretive understanding stages of a comprehension lesson, the nine stages of an algorithmic-skill lesson, the four stages of an application lesson, lessons for creativity, and lessons for affective objectives; note how formative feedback plays an integral role in each type of lesson.

Summative Evaluations

There are also complex questions that you must answer when you conclude a teaching unit. For example:

- What letter grade should I assign Louise for this unit?
- Rosita's father wants a report on her progress in mathematics. What should I tell him?
- Did Grayson achieve this goal well enough to receive at least a B?

You make summative evaluations of how well students achieved learning goals so that you can determine individual grades and periodically report on students' achievement to the students themselves, their parents, and to authorized professionals such as your school principal. As a teacher, though, formative feedback is more important because it influences your instructional behaviors. However, because students and parents tend to be grade conscious, you are likely to find them keenly interested in your periodic summative evaluations but barely aware of your ongoing formative evaluations. In any case, you are responsible for both types of evaluations, and summative, like formative, requires access to data that reflect how well your students have achieved learning goals and objectives.

COMMON MALPRACTICE

Observations and tests provide the basis for teachers' evaluations of student achievement. Unfortunately, studies examining the validity of tests commonly used in schools (both commercially produced and teacher prepared) and the evaluation of methods of many teachers suggest that common malpractice and inaccurate evaluations are widespread (Romberg, 1992a, pp. 1–3; Romberg, 1992b; Stiggins, Conklin, & Brideford, 1986). Too often, faith is placed in poorly designed tests that tax students' test-taking skills but don't reflect actual achievement of the teachers' learning goals (Cangelosi, 1990b, p. 3). Of particular concern are incongruences between learning levels specified by the objective and the actual learning levels measured by tests. It is quite common for teachers to include higher cognitive-level objectives (e.g., application or creativity) for their units, but to test only for achievement of lower cognitive levels (e.g., simple knowledge or algorithmic skill). The consequence of this practice is pointed out by Stiggins (1988, p. 365):

> Teacher developed paper-and-pencil tests and many tests and quizzes provided by textbook publishers are currently dominated by questions that ask students to recall facts and information. Although instructional objectives and even instructional activities may seek to develop thinking skills, classroom assessments often fail to match these aspirations. Students who use tests to try to understand the teachers' expectations can see the priority placed on memorizing, and they respond accordingly. Thus poor quality assessments that fail to tap and reward higher-order thinking skills will inhibit the development of those skills.

RESEARCH-BASED PRACTICE

Although testing is widely malpracticed, you can, as do many teachers, manage to collect valid data and accurately evaluate students' achievement of learning objectives—no matter what the learning level. To do this, you need to apply principles and strategies consistent with findings reported in the literature from the field of educational measurement and evaluation. Chapters 4, 5, and 6 included suggestions for designing measurement items relevant to student achievement at various learning levels. You extended your ability to apply research-based strategies of item design by engaging in Activities 4.5, 4.7, 5.6, 5.9, 5.10, 6.2, 6.3, 6.5, and 6.7.

Engage in Activity 10.1.

—————————— **ACTIVITY 10.1** ——————————

Purpose: To acquaint yourself with some of the available information on designing measurement items and other topics related to evaluating student achievement in the literature on educational measurement and evaluation.

You Need: Access to at least two of the following four books:

National Council of Teachers of Mathematics. (1989). *Curriculum and evaluation standards for school mathematics.* Reston, VA: Author.

National Council of Teachers of Mathematics. (1991). *Professional standards for teaching mathematics.* Reston, VA: Author.

National Council of Teachers of Mathematics. (1993). *Assessment standards for school mathematics: Working draft.* Reston, VA: Author.

Romberg, T. A. (1992). (Ed.). *Mathematics assessment and evaluation: Imperatives for mathematics educators.* Albany, NY: State University of New York Press.

In addition you need access to two textbooks on educational measurement and evaluation. The following is a sample list of such references:

References providing suggestions on measurement item design

Bergman, J. (1981). *Understanding educational measurement and evaluation.* Boston: Houghton-Mifflin, pp. 88–140.

Cangelosi, J. S. (1990). *Designing tests for evaluating student achievement.* New York: Longman, pp. 79–135.

Carey, L. M. (1994). *Measuring and evaluating school learning* (2nd ed.). Needham Heights, MA: Allyn and Bacon, pp. 113–400.

Cunningham, G. K. (1986). *Educational and psychological measurement.* New York: Macmillan, pp. 134–151.

Ebel, R. L., & Frisbie, D. A. (1986). *Essentials of educational measurement* (4th ed.). Englewood Cliffs, NJ: Prentice-Hall, pp. 126–200.

Marshall, J. C., & Hales, L. W. (1971). *Classroom test construction.* Reading, MA: Addison-Wesley, pp. 49–166.

Payne, D. A. (1992). *Measuring and evaluating educational outcomes.* New York: Macmillan, pp. 120–219.

Worthen, B. R., Borg, W. R., & White, K. R. (1993). *Measurement and evaluation in the schools.* New York: Longman, pp. 259–371.

References providing suggestions on using computerized item pool files

Cangelosi, J. S. (1990). *Designing tests for evaluating student achievement.* New York: Longman, pp. 41–61.

Carey, L. M. (1994). *Measuring and evaluating school learning.* (2nd ed.). Needham Heights, MA: Allyn and Bacon, pp. 58–67.

References providing information on interpreting the results of standardized tests

Airasian, P. W. (1991). *Classroom assessment.* New York: McGraw-Hill, pp. 357–406.

Cangelosi, J. S. (1990). *Designing tests for evaluating student achievement.* New York: Longman, pp. 178–195.

Cunningham, G. K. (1986). *Educational and psychological measurement.* New York: Macmillan, pp. 218–241.

Ebel, R. L., & Frisbie, D. A. (1986). *Essentials of educational measurement* (4th ed.). Englewood Cliffs, NJ: Prentice-Hall, pp. 288–300.

Oosteroff, A. (1994). *Classroom applications of educational measurement* (2nd ed.). New York: Macmillan, pp. 357–443.

Payne, D. A. (1992). *Measuring and evaluating educational outcomes.* New York: Macmillan, pp. 356–383.

References providing information on grading and reporting student achievement

Cangelosi, J. S. (1990). *Designing tests for evaluating student achievement.* New York: Longman, pp. 196–213.

Cunningham, G. K. (1986). *Educational and psychological measurement.* New York: Macmillan, pp. 171–186.

Ebel, R. L., & Frisbie, D. A. (1986). *Essentials of educational measurement* (4th ed.). Englewood Cliffs, NJ: Prentice-Hall, pp. 243–266.

Oosteroff, A. (1994). *Classroom applications of educational measurement* (2nd ed.). New York: Macmillan, pp. 329–256.

Payne, D. A. (1992). *Measuring and evaluating educational outcomes.* New York: Macmillan, pp. 464–489.

Procedure:

1. From the first set of four books (NCTM and Romberg), read at least two of the following selections: (a) *Curriculum and Evaluations Standards for School Mathematics,* pp. 189–248; (b) *Professional Standards for Teaching Mathematics,* pp. 71–119; (c) *Assessment Standards for School Mathematics: Working Draft,* pp. 27–56; and (d) *Mathematics Assessment and Evaluation: Imperatives for Mathematics Educators,* Chapter 7 (Senk, 1992) and Chapter 8 (Harvey, 1992).
2. Select and read at least one treatise on measurement item design, as referenced above. Then read selections from at least one of the other three areas listed above.

—————————————————————

MEASUREMENTS

As indicated in Chapter 4, *measurement* is a process by which data are gathered through empirical observations. Teachers measure students' achievements by seeing what students do, reading what they write, and hearing what they say. What you remember or record from those observations provides the data for your formative and summative evaluations. Typically, teachers depend on *tests* for the data they use in evaluations. By definition:

Tests are planned measurements by which teachers attempt to create opportunities for students to display their achievements relative to specified learning goals.

Tests are composed of measurement items. Each item of a test confronts students with a task and provides a means for observing and quantifying their responses to the task. Exhibit 10.1 provides a sample of four different items relevant to a variety of learning objectives.

Note that what is labeled Task Presented to the Student is the aspect of the item with which students are confronted on a test. The item's scoring key

Exhibit 10.1
Four examples of measurement items.

Task Presented to the Student
Express the following number of stars as a base three numeral:

$$* \quad * \quad * \quad * \quad * \quad * \quad * \quad * \quad * \quad *$$

Answer: _____
Scoring Key.   +1 for "102;" otherwise +0

Task Presented to the Student
Using only the space provided, prove that subtraction of integers is *not* commutative.

Scoring Key.   3 points maximum scored according to tho following:

- +3 for either a counterexample (e.g., $3 - 7 = -4$, but $7 - 3 = 4$) or for a tenable abstract argument (e.g., if $a, b \in$ {integers} such that $a > b$, then $a - b$ is positive, but $b - a$ is negative.)).
- +1 if the response indicates the student knows what "subtraction is not commutative" means but doesn't prove it (e.g., $a - b \neq b - a$ for some integers a and b).
- +0 otherwise

Task Presented to the Student
Multiple Choice.   Circle the letter in front of the response that either correctly answers the question or completes the given statement so that it is true.

A history test and a science test are given to the same class of students. Which one of the following statistics would be an indication of whether or not students who do better in history also tend to do better in science?

A. The difference in the arithmetic mean of the history test scores and the arithmetic mean of the science test scores.
B. The pooled variance from both the history and science test scores.
C. The standard deviation of the history test scores

minus the standard deviation of the science test scores.
D. A correlation coefficient computed from both the history and science tests scores.
Scoring Key.   + 1 for circling D only; +0 otherwise

Task Presented to the Student
While on a 55-kilometer journey, a car traveled along a 10-kilometer stretch where the road had a steady 8° angle of inclination. How much altitude did the car gain while traveling along that particular stretch of road? Express your answer in kilometers so that it is accurate to two decimal places. Please clearly display your work, including a diagram illustrating the problem.
Display of work

Answer: _____

Scoring Key.   5 points maximum scored according to the following:
- +5 for an answer of 1.39 with an appropriate equation and diagram displayed. For example,

$$\sin 8° = x/10 \Rightarrow x = (10)(0.1392) = 1.392$$

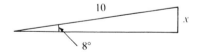

- If the response doesn't qualify for the full 5-point maximum, then distribute from 0 to 4 points as follows:
  +1 for correctly identifying the unknown to be solved.
  +1 for a correct diagram.
  +1 for a correct equation.
  +1 for an answer that is conceptually correct but is not expressed in kilometers accurate to two decimal places (e.g., 1.4 or 1392 m).

provides the rules the teacher uses to observe and quantify students' responses to the item. A student's *test score* is the sum of the scores received on the items that comprise the test.

EVALUATIONS

An *evaluation,* whether formative or summative, is a value judgment. You cannot solve for a *qualitative* variable, such as how well one of your students achieved a learning goal without making a value judgment—an evaluation. Such evaluations are necessarily dependent on measurement results (students' test scores or what you see a student do or hear the student say). However, do not make the mistake of equating measurement results with student achievement. An evaluation of a student's achievement of a unit's learning goal involves two distinct steps:

1. Measurement results are obtained relative to a *quantitative* variable, such as the number of points accumulated from a set of measurement items.
2. An evaluation is made relative to a *qualitative* variable, such as the student's achievement of the learning goal in light of the measurement results.

Measurement results provide only evidence, not a definitive reflection, of student achievement. How well the results or scores reflect actual achievement depends on the validity of the measurement. Thus, how much one of your evaluations is influenced by measurement results should be a function of the measurement's *validity.*

MEASUREMENT VALIDITY

A measurement is *valid* to the same degree that it is both *relevant* and *reliable.*

Measurement Relevance

Items Are Relevant to Stated Objectives.
For a measurement to be relevant, its items must pertain to the *mathematical content* and to the *learning level* specified by the objectives that define the learning goal. A measurement item pertains to the mathematical content and learning level specified by an objective if students must operate at the specified learning level (construct a concept, simple knowledge, or application) with the specified mathematical content (arithmetic sequences, ratios, or polygonal similarity) in order to successfully respond to the item.

How well do the three measurement items designed by the teacher in Case 10.1 (adapted from Cangelosi, 1990b, p. 28) pertain to the objective?

CASE 10.1 _____

To help her evaluate her seventh-graders' achievement of the learning goal for a unit on surface areas, Ms. Curry is designing a test. The unit has nine objectives. The following is the ninth objective:

> When confronted with a real-life problem, determines whether or not computing the area of a surface will help solve the problem.   (*application*)

Ms. Curry constructs the following three measurement items intended to be relevant to the ninth objective:

1. ***Task Presented to the Student:*** Answer the following multiple-choice question.

   Computing a surface area will help you solve one of these three problems. Which one is it?

   A We have a large bookcase we want to bring into our classroom. Our problem is to determine if the bookcase can fit through the doorway.
   B. As part of a project to fix up our classroom, we want to put stripping along the crack where the walls meet the floor. Our problem is to figure how much stripping to buy.
   C. As part of a project to fix up our classroom, we want to put carpet down on the floor. Our problem is to figure how much carpet to buy.

   Scoring Key: + 1 for C only; + 0 otherwise.

2. ***Task Presented to the Student:*** Answer the following multiple-choice question.

   What is the surface area of one side of the sheet of paper you are now reading? (Use your ruler to help make your choice.)

   A. 93.5 square inches
   B. 93.5 inches
   C. 20.5 square inches
   D. 20.5 inches
   E. 41.0 square inches
   F. 41.0 inches

   Scoring Key: + 1 for A only; + 0 otherwise.

3. ***Task Presented to the Student:*** Answer the following multiple-choice question.

   As part of our project for fixing up the classroom, we need to buy some paint for the walls. The paint we want comes in two different size cans. A 5-liter can costs $16.85 and a 2-liter can costs $6.55. Which one of the following would help us decide which can is the best buy?

   A. Compare 5 × $16.85 to 2 × $6.55
   B. Compare $16.85 ÷ 5 to $6.55 ÷ 2
   C. Compare $16.85 − $6.55 to 2/5

   Scoring Key: + 1 for B only; + 0 otherwise.

How well do Ms. Curry's items in Case 10.1 match the stated objective? The first one appears relevant because it requires students to *apply* (the objective's learning level) their understanding of *surface area* (the objective's content). Of course students might select C for item 1 just by guessing, but to increase one's chances from one-third based on random guessing, one must reason deductively about surface area.

Item 2 does not seem to match the objective very well. The correct response of A can be selected simply by remembering how to compute a surface area without having to decide when surface area should be computed. Thus, although item 2 appears to pertain to the content of the objective—surface area— its learning level is algorithmic skill rather than application. Item 2 is not relevant to the objective because it pertains to the wrong learning level.

Item 3 requires students to operate at the application learning level as specified by the objective. However, the item fails to match the objective because its content is not surface area.

Emphasis on Objectives According to Relative Importance. For a test to be relevant to a stated learning goal, not only must each of its items match one of the objectives, but various objectives must be represented on the test according to their importance to achievement of the goal. Suppose, for example, that you wanted to design a measurement relevant to your students' achievement of the following learning goal:

Understand that $\pi = C/d$ for any circle and makes use of that relationship in the solution of real-life problems.

Further suppose that you define this goal with the following objectives:

A. Provide an inductive argument for concluding that the ratio of the circumference of any circle to its diameter is π. (discover a relationship)

B. Display a willingness to attempt to develop a method for obtaining a rational approximation of π. (willingness to try)

C. Explain at least three methods for obtaining rational approximations of π: (a) a method for averaging measurements that the students themselves invent; (b) an ancient method (e.g., one listed by von Baravelle (1989); and (c) a computer-based method. (comprehension)

D. State the following: (a) π is the ratio of the circumference of any circle to its diameter, (b) π is an irrational number, and (c) $\pi \approx 3.1415929$. (simple knowledge)

E. Explain why $C = \pi d = 2\pi r$ for a circle with circumference C, diameter d, and radius r. (discover a relationship)

F. Solve for the circumference of a circle, given either its radius or its diameter. (algorithmic skill)

G. Solve for the diameter and radius of a circle given its circumference. (algorithmic skill)

H. Given a real-life problem, determine how, if at all, a solution to that problem is facilitated by using the relationship $\pi = C/d$.

There are eight objectives defining the goal. In your opinion, are some of the objectives more important to goal attainment than others? If not, then your test should reflect students' achievement of any one objective by one-eighth, or 12.5 percent. Thus, for the case in which you believe each objective is equally important, then 12.5 percent of the test points should match Objective A, 12.5 percent for Objective B, . . , and 12.5 percent for Objective H.

On the other hand, suppose you had these thoughts: "Objectives A and H are more important than the others. Objective A's importance stems from the fact that if students discover that ratio, they can always develop the related formulas for themselves. Objective H is the culminating objective of the unit. Objectives B and C, although important, are less important than the rest. I included those mainly as interest-builders. All the rest seem about equally important."

If you really thought like that, you might decide to design the test with relative weights for the objectives, as indicated in Exhibit 10.2.

Thus, to design a relevant test in this case you would select measurement items and distribute the points according to the values in Exhibit 10.2. If, for example, 50 is the maximum possible score a student could attain on the test, then approximately 10 of those points should pertain to Objective A, 3 to Objective B, 3 to Objective C, 6 to Objective D, 6 to

Exhibit 10.2
Hypothetical way to weight eight objectives.

Objective	Relative Weight
A	20%
B	6%
C	6%
D	12%
E	12%
F	12%
G	12%
H	20%

Objective E, 6 to Objective F, 6 to Objective G, and 10 to Objective H.

Measurement Reliability

For a measurement to produce valid results, it must not only be relevant to the intended learning goal, it must also be *reliable*. A measurement is reliable to the same degree that it can be depended on to yield consistent, noncontradictory results. To be reliable a measurement must have both *internal consistency* and *scorer consistency*.

Internal Consistency. Suppose a friend tells you, "Math is so boring; I don't know how you can bear studying it!" You respond, "You find mathematics pretty dry, eh?" Your friend: "Absolutely! Of course, I love using numbers to solve problems—and there's something beautiful about geometry." Does your friend like mathematics or not? Such comments are contradictory. Thus, the results of the informal measurement, based on what you heard the friend say, lack *internal consistency*. By definition:

> A measurement is *internally consistent* to the degree to which the results from various items comprising the measurement are in harmony.

Consider the internal consistency of partial test results Ms. Curry obtained in Case 10.2 (adapted from Cangelosi, 1990b, p. 30).

CASE 10.2

Ms. Curry administers a 22-item test to help her evaluate students' achievement of the learning goal for a unit on surface area. Two of the items, 7 and 19, are intended to measure the sixth of the unit's nine objectives, which is:

> Given the dimensions of a right triangle, compute its area.   (algorithmic skill)

Items 7 and 10 follow:

7. *Task Presented to the Student*
What is the area bounded by a right triangle with dimensions 5 cm, 4 cm, and 3 cm? (Display your computations and place your answers in the blank.)

Answer: _____
Scoring Key: 4 points maximum score distributed as follows:
+ 1 if A = 1/2 *bh* is used.
+ 1 if 4 and 3 are used in a computation but not 5.
+ 1 if 6 (irrespective of the units) is given as the area.
+ 1 if the answer is expressed in square centimeters.

19. *Task Presented to the Student*
What is the area of the interior of $\triangle ABC$ if $m \angle B = 90°$, $AB = 6$ cm, $BC = 8$ cm, and $AC = 10$ cm? (Display your computations and place your answer in the blank.)

Answer: _____
Scoring Key: 4 points maximum score distributed as follows:
+ 1 if A = 1/2 *bh* is used.
+ 1 if 6 and 8 are used in a computation but not 10.
+ 1 if 24 (irrespective of the units) is given as the area.
+ 1 if the answer is expressed in square centimeters.

Curious about how well her students achieved the sixth objective, Ms. Curry notes five students' performances on items 7 and 19 as displayed in Exhibit 10.3.

Relative to the sixth objective, the data suggest that Roxanne's level of achievement is high, Luanne's is low, and Mel's may be somewhere in between. However, Ms. Curry is perplexed by the performances of Izar and Jan on these two items. Does Izar know how to compute areas of right triangles? The results of item 7 suggest not, whereas item 19's results suggest yes.

Relative to the sixth objective, Ms. Curry's test yielded contradictory results, at least for Izar and Jan. If the test results are dominated by such inconsistencies, the test lacks internal consistency and is, therefore, unreliable. On the other hand, if there are few contradictions and the results are more in line with what Ms. Curry obtained for Roxanne, Luanne, and Mel, the test is internally consistent.

For a measurement to produce internally consistent results, it must be designed so that the tasks are presented clearly and unambiguously. For students to respond consistently to items, they must clearly understand the task required by each item. Directions need to be unambiguously communicated. In Case

Exhibit 10.3
Results from five Students on items 7 and 19 of Ms. Curry's test.

Student	Points on Item 7	Points on Item 19
Roxanne	4	4
Luanne	1	0
Izar	0	4
Mel	3	2
Jan	4	1

10.3 students are confronted with a vaguely defined task.

CASE 10.3

One of Mr. Cotrell's teaching units includes the following objective:

> Interpret the meaning of expressions using the language of sets.   (*comprehension*)

Among the items on his unit test both of the following two are designed to measure that objective:

9. *Task Presented to the Student*

How many elements in {8, −9, 0, 11.3, 77}?

_____

Scoring Key: + 1 if the answer is 5, otherwise +0.

11. *Task Presented to the Student*

How many elements in {*a, b, c, d*}?   _____

Scoring Key: +1 if the answer is 4, otherwise +0.

Confronted with the first item, one student, Robin, counts the five elements and writes 5 in the blank. For the next one she thinks, "1, 2, 3, 4, . . . the answer is 4. Oh! Maybe not. *a, b, c,* and *d* could be variables and maybe two or more are equal to one another. If *a* = *b*, that'd make no more than 3 in the set. . . . The answer could be 1, 2, 3, or 4. So, it's got to be 1, because I know there's at least 1 element, but I can't tell if there's more."

_____

To fix item 11, Mr. Cotrell needs to replace {*a, b, c, d*} with an unambiguous expression (e.g., {Jackie Robinson, Martin Luther King, Marie Curie, Robert Kennedy} or the roman letters {"a," "b," "c," "d"}). It's easy to understand how ambiguity crept into Mr. Cotrell's item. Ideally, when he reviews the test results with the class, Robin will explain her reasoning and Mr. Cotrell will turn his "mistake" into a productive learning experience.

To be internally consistent a measurement must also include an adequate number of items. In a test with a large number of items there is a greater likelihood that consistent student response patterns will emerge than in one with only a few items. If, for example, Mr. Cotrell's test in Case 10.3 included ten items similar to item 9 and ten ambiguous ones similar to item 11, then a consistent pattern to Robin's responses would likely surface. There would be a clear distinction between her responses to items with well-defined sets (e.g., {8, −9, 0, 11.3, 77} and {Jackie Robinson, Martin Luther King, Marie Curie, Robert Kennedy}) and those with ambiguously defined sets (e.g., {*a, b, c, d*} and {tall people in the classroom}). Furthermore, the more items on a test, the less affected are the test results by fortuitous factors.

Suppose, for example, that one of a test's objectives is measured by only two true/false items. By random guess, a student has a 25 percent chance of scoring 0, a 50 percent chance of scoring 1, and 25 percent chance of scoring 2. Results of the two items are unlikely to distinguish consistently between students who have and have not achieved the objective. However, if there were ten such true/false items, then random guessing is less of a factor, with a 0.1 percent chance of scoring 0, a 1.0 percent chance of scoring 1, a 4.4 percent chance of scoring 2, a 11.7 percent chance of scoring 3, a 20.5 percent chance of scoring 4, a 24.6 percent chance of scoring 5, a 20.5 percent chance of scoring 6, a 11.7 percent chance of scoring 7, a 4.4 percent chance of scoring 8, a 1.0 percent chance of scoring 9, and a 0.1 percent chance of scoring 10.

Tests need to be administered under controlled conditions. A scientific experiment is the application of systematic procedures for the purpose of uncovering evidence that helps answer a specified question. An achievement test is a type of scientific experiment in which the question to be answered is how well students have achieved a particular learning goal. The experimental conditions need to be controlled to minimize distractions to students and assure that directions are followed. Internal consistency is threatened whenever students' thoughts are interrupted during testing or student cheating is allowed. References are available that suggest how to prevent student cheating without threatening the businesslike environment of your classroom (see Cangelosi, 1982, pp. 237–238; 1990b, pp. 63–69; 1993a; 1993b, pp. 267–272).

Scorer Consistency.   Engage in Activity 10.2.

_____ **ACTIVITY 10.2** _____

Purpose: To gain an experience leading to discovery of critical relationships involving the measurement variable *scorer consistency.*

Procedure:

1. Examine Exhibit 10.4. Note that it contains two items as they appeared on a test that Eugene took. Eugene's responses are included. The maximum possible score on item 1 is 1 point; for item 2, it is 4 points. Without consulting with anyone score Eugene's responses to the two items.
2. Still working independently, compare Eugene's response to item 2 to those of Shirley and of Lydia, as displayed in Exhibit 10.5. Rank the three proofs from best to worst.
3. Now compare your scoring and rankings to those of a colleague who is also engaging in this activity.

_____

Obviously, Eugene's response to item 1 merits the full point. But how many points out of 4 did you

Exhibit 10.4
Eugene's responses to two test items.

Name *Eugene Ibavruri*

1. (1 pt.) Is the sum of any two odd integers odd or even?

even

2. (4 pts.) Either prove or disprove that the sum of any two odd integers is even.

$a+b$ is even for any $a, b, \in$ Odds because:
if a and b are odd, then they can be written as $2i+1$ for a and $2i-1$ for b so that $i \in$ Integers
Then $a+b =$
$(2i+1) + (2i-1) = 2i + 2i + 1 - 1$
$= 4i + 0 = 4i$
and $4i$ is even. QED

Exhibit 10.5
Shirley's and Lydia's responses to item 2 from Exhibit 10.4.

Shirley

2. (4pts.) Either prove or disprove that the sum of any two odd integers is even.

Two odds are EVEN bECauSE $7+7=14$, $3+1=4$, $9+1=10$, ...

Lydia

2. (4 pts.) Either prove or disprove that the sum of any two odd integers is even.

$a+b \in \{even\}$ for any $a, b \in \{odd\}$ because:
$a, b \in \{odd\} \Rightarrow$ There exist $i, j \in \{integers\}$
such that $a = 2i+1$ and $b = 2j+1$.
So, $a+b = (2i+1) + (2j+1) = 2i + 2j + 2$
Thus, $a+b = 2(i+j+1)$. And since integers are closed under addition $i + j + 1 \in \{integers\}$ and so $a+b$ is twice Sum integer which makes $a+b$ even by definition.

award for his response to item 2? Surely Eugene's response indicates he's captured the conceptual spirit of a proof, but his proof is flawed. For one thing, he's demonstrated the proposition to be true only for consecutive odd integers, not any two odd integers.

Shirley's proof seems to be the least complete. But her examples are relevant, so should not some of the 4 points be awarded? Since Eugene gave a general proof, but only for consecutive odd integers, do you think his work merits more points than Shirley's?

Lydia's response seems complete and clear. I assume you awarded the full complement of points for it. In step 3 of Activity 10.2, did you and your colleague have an easier time agreeing on the score for Eugene's response to item 1 than for his response to item 2? By definition:

> A measurement has *scorer consistency* to the same degree that (a) the teacher (or whomever scores the test) faithfully follows the items' scoring keys so that the measurement results are not influenced by *when* the measurement is scored; and (b) different teachers (or scorers) who are familiar with the measurement's content agree on the score warranted by each item response so that results are not influenced by *who* scores the measurement.

Scorer consistency of a measurement will be poor if the measurement is dominated by items that do not have clearly specified scoring keys. There is only one correct response to item 1 of Exhibit 10.4; consistent scoring here poses no difficulty. Item 2, on the other hand, requires the scorer to make judgments about responses. To build scorer consistency into such items, scoring keys must specifically indicate just how points are to be distributed. Formulating scoring keys is a major aspect of measurement item design.

Scoring keys for most of the items appearing throughout this book are specified. Of course, for an item to be relevant, both the *task to be presented to the student* component and the *scoring key* component must be developed in light of the objective the item is intended to measure.

MEASUREMENT USABILITY

No matter how valid a test might be for measuring student achievement, it is of no value if it is too time consuming to administer or score, costly to purchase, or threatens the well-being of your students. A measurement must be practical for your needs. Whenever designing or selecting a test to help you assess student achievement, you need to consider the measurement's *usability* as well as its validity. By definition:

> A measurement is usable to the degree that it is inexpensive, brief, easy to administer and score, and does not interfere with other activities.

Exhibit 10.6 depicts the variables you should be taking into consideration whenever selecting or designing a test.

TYPES OF TESTS
Commercially Produced Tests

Mathematical achievement tests can be purchased from commercial publishers. Ordinarily, each set of

Exhibit 10.6
Test quality variables.

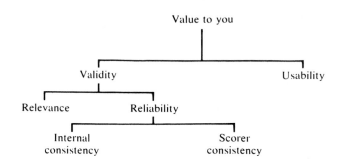

student textbooks is accompanied by a packet of materials for the teacher that includes tests—usually one test per chapter. Most such tests emphasize simple-knowledge and algorithmic skills. Because they don't tend to be relevant to higher cognitive learning levels (construct a concept, discover a relationship, and application), it's rarely advisable to use them for unit tests. However, tests from textbook publishers can be a source of individual items, especially at the algorithmic-skill level, for you to incorporate in tests you design yourself. Pools of individual items are available from some commercial outlets. Advertisements for such products are sent to practicing mathematics teachers and members of NCTM; they are also found in professional journals and displayed at meetings of professional societies.

Unlike tests packaged as part of a textbook series, some commercially produced tests are administered on a school-wide basis once or twice a year. These are the big-event tests that some people *naively* think of as true measures of students' intellectual achievements. Although capable of providing some evidence of the *average* achievement level of a *group* of students regarding some broad general areas, big–event, commercially produced tests do not yield data relative to the specific achievement of individual students (Cangelosi, 1990b, p. 26).

Standardized Tests

The more familiar big-event, commercially produced tests—such as, *Sequential Tests of Educational Progress End-of-Course Tests: Algebra / Geometry, Grades 9–12* (Floden, 1985); *Stanford Achievement Test: Mathematics Tests* (Aleamoni, 1985); and *Stanford Diagnostic Mathematics Test* (Rogers, 1985)—are standardized. A standardized test is one that has been field tested for the purpose of assessing its reliability and establishing normative standards to be used in interpreting scores.

Unfortunately, misuses and overuses of standardized tests are quite common, especially in school districts where evaluations of teaching success are untenably linked to students' scores on these tests (Archibald & Newman, 1988; Cangelosi, 1991, pp. 10–117). The five references on interpreting standardized tests that are listed in Activity 10.1 are a sample of the literature with which teachers should be familiar. Romberg, Wilson, Khaketla, and Chavarria (1992, p. 61) studied six of the more commonly used standardized mathematics tests and compared them to the NCTM *Standards*. They state:

> the six standardized tests most widely used at state and district levels in schools in the United States are examined to determine whether or not they are appropriate instruments for assessing the content, process, and levels of thinking called for in the *Standards*. The results show that the tests are not appropriate. They are found to be generally weak in five of the six content areas and in five of the six process areas. Furthermore, the tests place too much emphasis on procedures and not enough on concepts.

Regarding a follow-up study, they further reported (pp. 69–70):

> The aim of the follow-up study (Romberg, Wilson, & Chavarria, 1990) was to demonstrate the existence of test items that are more closely aligned with the *Standards* than are the items found in the six tests of the first study. The investigation drew upon items and tests from two sources: newly adopted state tests and foreign tests. The study looked at materials from California, Connecticut, South Carolina, Massachusetts, and Vermont; then it considered materials from several foreign countries—primarily Britain, but also Australia, France, Korea, the Netherlands, and Norway.
>
>   The conclusion of the investigation was that there are test items which are currently in use that are more closely aligned with the *Standards* than the six standardized tests that are most widely used now at the eighth-grade level in the United States. Several states are implementing reforms in their assessment practices and have developed tests to reflect the objectives described in the *Standards*. In addition, many tests and test items that are currently used in foreign countries, most notably Britain, surpass American standardized tests in their alignment with the *Standards*. The feature shared by all of these tests and test items is that they are open response, not multiple choice in format. The content and processes measured in these items are rich and varied. Many of the items are able to assess higher-order thinking with greater ease than do typical multiple-choice questions. Process areas such as Problem Solving, Reasoning, and Communication lend themselves to an open-response format, and this has been borne out in our investigations. In United States tests, only 1 percent of the items could be classified as Problem Solving, 20 percent as Communication (and that at the lowest levels of communication), and 1 percent Reasoning. In contrast, the open-response tests

being developed in several states and in Britain contained excellent examples of items in those three process areas.

The report includes six examples of test items from such state or foreign tests. Exhibit 10.7 displays those six items along with Romberg, Wilson, Khaketla, and Chavarria's (1992, pp. 70–73) comments about each.

Teacher-Produced Tests

Although occasionally useful for some purposes, standardized and other types of commercially produced tests can hardly be relevant to the learning goals you determine appropriate for each unique class of students you teach. Thus, it is imperative for you to design and develop most of the measures of your students' mathematical achievements. Teacher-produced tests are the most commonly used source of data for formative and summative evaluations.

DESIGNING TEACHER-PRODUCED TESTS

A Systematic Approach

The Haphazard Method. Case 10.4 is an example of how one teacher goes about designing and developing a unit test.

CASE 10.4 _____

Ms. Houlahan begins the task of developing a test she plans to administer to her geometry class tomorrow. She thinks, "Let's see, this unit was on π and using $\pi = C/d$ in problem solving. I'll start with an easy item—one about the value of π. . . . I could just ask, what is π? But that'd be ambiguous; they wouldn't know if I meant for them to put 3.14 something, or circumference ÷ diameter. Hmmm, okay, first two items." She writes:

1. π is between what two whole numbers? _____ and _____.
2. For any circle with diameter d and circumference C, $C/d =$ _____.

"Now what should I do for item 3?" she thinks, "I'd better grab some of these problems out of the book, and just change some of the numbers around. Anyone who has been paying attention and keeping up with the homework shouldn't have any trouble with them. Okay, page ahh . . ."

Ms. Houlahan continues in this vein until her unit test is ready. _____

Ms. Houlahan's haphazard method is unlikely to produce a very relevant measurement for her learning goal. For one thing, she didn't seem to pay attention to the objectives that define the goal (if she had even defined it at all.). This procedure of thinking up

Exhibit 10.7
Items from state or foreign tests with author comments.

1. *Connecticut Common Core of Learning Assessment Project:*
   Students are given an article from the newspaper entitled, "Survey Finds Many Below Town's Mean Income."
   They are then given the following questions: Use the article and your understanding of statistics to complete the following tasks:
   1. Write an expository paragraph that begins with either:
      — The headline is fine because . . . OR
      — The headline is absurd because . . .
   2. Write an expository paragraph that begins with either:
      — The article makes sense and has no statistical errors because . . . OR
      — The article is absurd and makes statistical errors because . . .
   3. How can more than half the people be below the mean income?

Source: Reprinted from T. A. Romberg, L. Wilson, M. Khaketla, and S. Chavarria, "Curriculum and Test Alignment," in T. A. Romberg, ed., *Mathematics Assessment and Evaluation: Imperatives for Mathematics Educators*, pp. 70–73, by permission of the State University of New York Press. Copyright 1992 State University of New York Press.

4. Create a data set to show how more than half the numbers are below the mean. Describe your reasoning.

SURVEY FINDS MANY BELOW TOWN'S MEAN INCOME*

OLD SAYBROOK - A recent survey shows more than half of the respondents earn well below the town's mean annual income of $37,500. Vicki McCourt, a member of the Old Saybrook Affordable Housing Task Force, said 65% of the 200 respondents reported earning less than $30,000 a year. "There are no houses in Old Saybrook that anyone can afford within the mean income—they just cannot do it," McCourt said.

This item is a good example of a problem in the content area of Statistics, the process area of Communication, and a conceptual level of knowledge.

2. *California Assessment Program*
   James knows that half of the students from his school are accepted at the public university nearby. Also, half are accepted at the local private college. James thinks that this adds up to 100 percent, so he will surely be accepted at one or the other institution. Explain why James may be wrong. If possible, use a diagram in your explanation.

   This item taps into the critical process areas of reasoning and communication.

   The following three items are taken from British tests:

3. *London & East Anglian Group for GCSE Examinations*
   An air-mail letter to India costs 34p. How can you pay correct postage using only 4p stamps and 11p stamps?

   This item, in the content area of Number Systems and Number Theory, is a computation problem, but at a conceptual rather than procedural level.

Source: Connecticut State Department of Education, Connecticut Common Core of Learning Performance Assessment Project. Used with permission. This item has been replaced by a revision pilot tested in Spring, 1991. The project was funded by a grant from the National Science Foundation.

Exhibit 10.7
Continued

4. "Beefo Cubes" are 2 cm × 2 cm × 2 cm.

They are sold in a thin cardboard sleeve 4 cm × 4 cm × 8 cm.

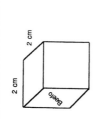
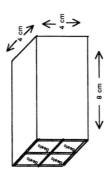

How many cubes are in one full sleeve?

This item could be classified into content areas of either Geometry or Measurement, and a process level of Connections or Problem Solving; it requires a conceptual level of knowledge.

5. *Northern Examining Association*
The picture shows a woman of average height standing next to a lamp post.
a) Estimate the height of the lamp post.
b) Explain how you got your answer.

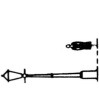

This item is a refreshingly different estimation problem, one that does not involve simply rounding numbers. The "b" part of the problem makes it a good communication problem also. It could be classified as either Measurement or Number Relations and again is at a conceptual level.

6. *The Netherlands*
The results of two classes of a math-test are presented in a stem-leaf-display:

CLASS A		CLASS B
7	1	
7	2	34
4	3	
55	4	
4	5	
1	6	5
1	7	12344668
9966555	8	114
97	9	1

Does this table suffice to judge which class performed best?

Source: de Lange, van Reeuwijk, Burrill, & Romberg (in press). Used with permission.

This open-ended item requires that the student have a conceptual understanding of the data represented in the display and be able to communicate those concepts by means of a valid mathematical argument.

These six items are a sample of the kinds of problems that are possible when one is not bound by the multiple-choice format. Each problem is rich, engaging, and interesting. Tests that are comprised of items such as these can provide a more valid means of assessing the content areas, processes, and levels of knowledge described in the *Standards*. Perhaps most important, a student who encounters test items such as these will come away from the test having *learned* some mathematics through the experience.

items in the same order they'll appear on the test typically results in tests that overemphasize easy to measure objectives and neglect the more difficult to measure objectives. Consequently, the tests stress lower-level cognitive learning (simple knowledge and algorithmic skills). Thus, students bother to learn only at the lower levels (Stiggins, 1988; Stiggins, Conklin, & Bridgeford, 1986).

The Research-Based Method. A more systematic approach is needed, one with the following advantages over the haphazard approach:

- You have a system for designing tests that reflects objectives according to your judgment of their relative importance to goal attainment. You consciously control the content and learning levels to which the test is relevant.
- You establish a system that facilitates both test validity and the ease with which you produce them.

There are four phases to the systematic, research-based method: (1) clarifying the learning goal, (2) developing a test blueprint, (3) obtaining relevant item pools, and (4) synthesizing the test.

Clarify the Learning Goal

Eavesdrop on the faculty room conversation in Case 10.5.

CASE 10.5 _____

Mr. Coco: Hey Eva, would you take a look at this test for me? Do you think it's any good?

Ms. Scott: Good for what?

Mr. Coco: For my algebra II class; it's the first draft of my midterm.

Ms. Scott: I can't judge the validity of this test without knowing what you want to evaluate.

Mr. Coco: What my students learned.

Ms. Scott: What did you intend for them to learn?

Mr. Coco: Algebra.

Ms. Scott: You've got to be more specific than that. A test's validity depends on how relevant it is to exactly what it's evaluating. Unless you have the learning goal you want to evaluate clearly spelled out, there's no way to judge how relevant a test is. If this test is reliable—and from the looks of it, I'll bet it is—then it's relevant to something. The question is whether or not that something is what you want.

_____

You can hardly be expected to create an achievement test until you've answered the question, Achievement of what? Thus, the first step in the test design and development process is to clarify the learning goal to which the test is supposed to be relevant. Fortunately, you initially defined your learning goal with a set of objectives when you developed the teaching unit. All that needs to be done for this step is to weight each objective according to its relative importance to goal achievement.

For example, suppose that the goal for the unit is the one on the relation $\pi = C/d$ given on page 74 and defined by Objectives A through H. Further suppose that you think those objectives should be weighted as indicated in Exhibit 10.2. Having weighted the objectives, the learning goal is clarified and you are prepared to move on to the second stage of test design and development.

Develop a Test Blueprint

After the learning goal is clarified with a list of *weighted* objectives, the next step is to develop a *blueprint* listing the features you want to build into the test. You need to make decisions regarding (a) the complexity of the test design, (b) how much class time you'll devote to administering it, (c) how much of your time you'll devote to scoring it, (d) types of items comprising the test, (e) types of technology students should use when taking the test (e.g., should they use graphing calculators), (f) types of references (e.g., notes or tables) students should be able to access during the test, (g) number of items, (h) difficulty of the items, (i) maximum number of points, (j) number of points for each objective, (k) method of determining cutoff scores, and (l) the outline for the test.

Complexity of the Test Design. Whether your test blueprint describes a complex or simple test design depends on how sophisticated your students are in taking tests and the nature of the learning goal. Test directions need to be simple enough so that students don't exert greater effort comprehending how to take the test than they do thinking about the relevant mathematics. Ordinarily tests emphasizing simple-knowledge and algorithmic-skill objectives can be designed to be much more simple than those emphasizing higher cognitive or affective objectives.

Administration Time. Generally speaking, students need more time to respond to items for higher cognitive objectives than to items involving primarily memory. Also, tests with many items tend to be more reliable than those with fewer items (Cangelosi, 1982, pp. 229–236). The Catch-22 is that the more items you include, the less time is available per item. Traditionally, the number of items and time allotted for mathematics tests are such that students must rush through each item without time for reasoning-level thinking.

By allotting adequate time for administering a reliable test that is relevant to higher cognitive objectives, you enhance validity while reducing usability. How you decide to resolve the conflict between validity and usability determines the length of the test and the administration time. Keep in mind that you don't necessarily have to restrict test-taking activities to the length of a class period. The administration of a test may be extended over several days. Parts of the test can be taken home by students or can be done in collaborative task groups. Students can bring artifacts or documents from work completed at home or in collaborative groups to the in-class part of a test. The in-class part of the test can include items requiring students to use work completed at home or as part of a group project. Reread Case 4.13; Case 10.6 is a follow up to that case.

CASE 10.6

Ms. Smith thinks to herself as she plans a test for the goal of the unit on general rate relationships presented in Case 4.13, "This is going to be a difficult test to design. We have discover a relationship, comprehension, simple-knowledge, algorithmic-skill, and application objectives. I really should include some nontraditional performance items, but those types of open-response questions where they have to explain answers are time consuming. And we really can't afford to use much more than one whole class period administering it. Furthermore, I'd like to positively reinforce the students who were diligent about their homework throughout the unit and those who really contributed to the cooperative group activities. But I don't want to just give them points for participation; this test should be relevant to their achievement of the unit's objectives—not to how cooperative they were."

After further thought, Ms. Smith decides on the following plan: Only one class period will be devoted to taking the test. However, several days prior to the test, Ms. Smith will give them a take-home part to complete. On test day they will bring this with them and attach it to the in-class part of the test. The take-home part includes the following:

- Directions to make copies of a specified subset of documents they completed for homework during the course of the unit.
- A half-page essay summarizing the discussion from the student's cooperative group activity in Case 4.13.
- A one-page essay describing the similarities and differences between the mathematics used to solve the problem from the student's cooperative group and the mathematics used to solve the problem from any other group chosen by the student.
- A three-quarter-page essay, including at least one illustration, explaining how any of the problems addressed in the cooperative groups could have been solved without ever multiplying two numbers.

Included among the items on the in-class part will be some that require students to refer to the documents from the take-home part and demonstrate comprehension of their essays; For example:

Task Presented to the Student: Briefly look at your work for exercise 4 from page 144. Suppose a friend of yours also tried that exercise, but got 50 meters for a final solution. In two sentences explain to your friend why 50 meters is not a reasonable solution to this particular problem.

_____

_____

_____

Scoring Key: 6 points maximum based on the following criteria:

- Evidence of an attempt at exercise 4 from page 144 is attached.
- Indicates comprehension of why 50 meters is unreasonable (e.g., the bike would have had to travel backwards to be no more than 50 meters from the bike rack).
- Nothing is included in the response that is erroneous or irrelevant to the question raised by the item.

Each criterion is scored on the following 2-point scale:

+2 iff it is clear that the criterion is clearly met.

+1 iff it is unclear whether or not the criterion is met.

+0 iff it is clear that the criterion is not met.

_____

Scoring Time. Just as you schedule class time to administer tests, so must you also schedule professional time to score tests. The amount of time you are willing and able to devote to this task influences the number and types of measurement items. Romberg, Wilson, Khaketla, and Chavarria (1992, pp. 69–70) laud the open-response, nontraditional items and criticize traditional multiple-choice or one-answer-only items. The nontraditional items, often referred to as *performance,* or *alternative,* items, are often more relevant to the objectives of a *Standards*-based curriculum, but they are typically less usable because they are more time consuming to score. They are also more difficult to score reliably. In Case 10.6, Ms. Smith mitigated both of these difficulties by developing specific criteria for the item's scoring key. Ms. Smith is able to score even essay items in a reasonable amount of time because her scoring keys delineate criteria with scoring scales. See, for example, the scoring form in Exhibit 10.9, which accompanies the test in Exhibit 10.8.

In scheduling time to score tests, keep in mind that your students' learning is enhanced if you provide them with feedback on their test responses sooner rather than later (Beyer, 1987, pp. 71–73, 148).

Exhibit 10.8
Example of a test document with one student's responses.

Algebra I * 4th Period
Opportunity to Demonstrate Some of What You Understand About the Behavior of Functions

I. What is your name? *Shawna Vaughn*

II. Using your graphing calculator, graph $f(x) = 2x$ and $g(x) = x^2$ on the same screen.

  A. In a paragraph, explain why the graph of f includes points below the horizontal axis, but the graph of g doesn't. *In f, x is all real numbers and if you times it by 2, its still all real numbers, so it goes both above + below the horizontal axis. In g, if you square any number, it is always a positive result. Thats why the graph of g is only positive (and zero) and stays above the horizontal axis.*

  B. Compute each of the following:

  $f(1) - f(.5) =$ ___1___ $g(1) - g(.5) =$ ___.75___
  2   -   1   = 1   *1 - .25 = .75*

  $f(2) - f(1) =$ ___2___ $g(2) - g(1) =$ ___3___
  4x - 2x   *4 - 1 = 3*

  C. Notice that for $x > 0$, f increases at the same rate along a straight line. But for $x > 0$, the rate of increase for g changes with the graph curving upward "faster and faster." Write a paragraph explaining why the rate of increase for f remains steady but for g the rate of increase changes as x gets larger. Use the results of your computations in Part B in your explanation.

  f remains steady, because if $x > 0$, then it means the range is 2 times every positive number x. This was included in the original graph where $x =$ all numbers, but now it's just limited to $x > 0$, so it only includes that part of the line. And that part increases at the same rate along a straight line. g curves up "faster + faster" as x increases because as the domain increases, the square of each element of the domain increases. The bigger the number, the bigger the square.

Types of Items. The variety of test items is literally limitless. Written response, computerized, oral response, or demonstration items can be multiple choice, essay, short answer, display (such as presentation of a proof), true/false, completion, matching, or a myriad of other types you invent yourself. The NCTM's (1989, pp. 189–243; 1993) evaluation standards emphasize the need for measuring student achievement in a variety of ways using innovative and unconventional test items. The following passage is from *Assessment Standards for School Mathematics: Working Draft* (NCTM, 1993, p. 51):

> To make valid assessments of student learning in a classroom that strives to match the vision of the NCTM's *Professional Standards for Teaching Mathematics,* the assessment activities must be aligned with instructional activities. Those activities that are designed to assess learning must be consistent with those that are instructional. For example, if students engage in writing, then their knowledge of

Exhibit 10.8
Continued

D. In comparing the two graphs on your calculator notice
that $g(x) < f(x)$ when $0 < x < 2$. But when x > 2, $g(x)$
> $f(x)$. Write a paragraph explaining why this happens.

This is because when $0 < x < 2$, if you take an example of an x value, 1, in $g(x)$, the y-coordinate would be 1^2 or 1, and in $f(x)$, the y-coordinate would be 2(1) or 2. So $f(x) > g(x)$. When $x > 2$, if you take an example of an x value, 3, in $g(x)$, the y-coordinate would be 3^2 or 9. In $f(x)$, the y-coordinate would be 2(3) or 6. So, $g(x) > f(x)$.

III. Smile, you've finished taking advantage of this opportunity.

---

mathematics should be assessed, in part, by having them write about their mathematical ideas. If technology is used in instruction, then technology should be used in assessment. The activities that are used to gather information about student learning should be consistent with, and sometimes the same as, the activities used in instruction.

The types of items you specify in a test blueprint are a function of six variables: (1) content of the objectives, (2) learning level of the objectives, (3) relative weights assigned to objectives, (4) time allotted for test administration, (5) time allotted for scoring, and (6) technology available for use on the test.

Technology Available for Student Use. The test shown in Exhibit 10.8 requires students to have access to graphing calculators. Harvey (1992) classifies three types of tests: (1) *calculator-passive tests* for which calculator use is not intended and students using calculators would be considered to have an unfair advantage over students without calculators, (2) *calculator-neutral tests* that have no calculator-sensitive items and on which calculator use is not required, and (3) *calculator-based tests* that contain items for which most students will need calculators. After reviewing research literature comparing these three types of tests, Harvey concludes (pp. 167–168):

. . . present testing practices hold today's students hostages to yesterday's mistakes. One reason for this is that "What is tested is what gets taught" (Mathematical Sciences Education Board, 1989, p. 69). Thus, as long as mathematics tests fail to incorporate the use of calculators, I am certain that mathematics instruction will fail to incorporate the use of calculators effectively, and so today's students will be prisoners to a mathematics curriculum that is failing to prepare them for the society in which they will live both now and in the twenty-first century.

Just permitting students to use calculators while taking mathematics tests will not be enough. Students will need to be taught how and when to use calculators while solving all kinds of mathematics problems. Equally important, tests will have to actively account for changes in the ways that mathematics problems are solved and the kinds of mathematics problems that can be solved when calculators are used. I conclude that calculator-passive and calculator-neutral tests do not satisfactorily account for these changes and that only calculator-based tests can. In addition, it seems clear that each time calculators become more capable and more responsive to mathematics instruction—and each is occurring—mathematics tests will have to be changed.

Besides calculators, students may need access to other technologies like computers and presentation devices for certain measurements of their achievements. Whatever technologies students use to do mathematics while engaging in your learning activities need to be incorporated in a subset of the items they encounter on your tests.

Exhibit 10.9
Scoring form for test shown in Exhibit 10.8

Algebra I * 4th Period
Opportunity to Demonstrate Some of What You Understand About the Behavior of Functions

Scoring form for ___Shawna Vaughn___

Note: For each criterion listed for Items II-A, II-C, & II-D, points are awarded as follows:

+2 if the criterion in question is clearly met
+1 if it is unclear as to whether or not the criterion is met
+0 if the criterion is clearly not met

Each encircled numeral (either 0, 1, or 2) indicates the number of points your response received for the given criterion.

II-A:
Writes a paragraph addressing the question   0   1   ②
Points out that $2x$ can be negative   0   1   ②
Points out that x^2 cannot be negative   0   1   ②
Nothing erroneous or extraneous included   ⓪   1   2   __6__ (08)

II-B:
Answers "1" for $f(1) - f(.5)$ 0   ①
Answers "2" for $f(2) - f(1)$ 0   ①
Answers ".75" for $g(1) - g(.5)$ 0   ①
Answers "3" for $g(2) - g(1)$ 0   ①   __4__ (04)

II-C:
Writes a paragraph addressing the question   0   1   ②
Points out that the constant effect
of f on x is to multiply x by the same
number, namely 2   0   ①   2
Points out that the effect of g on x
is to multiply x by itself and, unlike 2,
x varies, thus as x varies so does the
number by which it's being multiplied   0   ①   2
Uses work from "B" to illustrate points   ⓪   1   2
Nothing erroneous or extraneous included   0   1   ②   __6__ (10)

II-D:
Writes a paragraph addressing the question   0   1   ②
Uses the fact that $x^2 < x$ for $0 < x < 1$ ⓪   1   2
Uses that g "catches up" with g at $x = 2$ 0   1   ②
Uses the fact that $x^2 > x$ for $x > 1$ 0   1   ②
Nothing erroneous or extraneous included   0   1   ②   __8__ (10)

The score you earned for this Opportunity is __24__ out of a possible 32.

References for Student Use. When developing a test blueprint, you also need to consider what, if any, reference materials you will allow students to use during the test. Do you want them to be able to refer to their notes, a list of formulas, tables, artifacts from homework or cooperative group activities, or the textbook? After all, when we do mathematics and solve problems in the real world, we don't handicap ourselves by not using available tools and reference sources. Rather than simply *allowing* students to use references, you might consider having them *prepare* reference materials for use on an upcoming test. Consider Case 10.7

CASE 10.7 _____

On Monday, Mr. Manion speaks to his geometry class:

Mr. Manion: On Thursday you'll have an opportunity to display what you've learned to do using similarity relationships. Yes Ann, you want the floor.

Ann: Does that mean you're going to give us a test?

Mr. Manion: Yes, that's another way of saying it. To take full advantage of this opportunity, you'll not only need the usual things like your calculator, pencil, and eraser, you'll also need to make sure your notebook is well organized so you can efficiently refer to definitions, postulates, and theorems we've been accumulating over the last month. Make sure you've got those in the sequence we used to develop them because you'll need to look up and explain some proofs. You're aware that how we proved a theorem depends on prior theorems, postulates, and definitions. Yes, Tom.

Tom: Isn't it the same for definitions. Like we used the definition of "betweenness" to define "line segment," so it wouldn't be right to use "line segment" in the definition of "betweenness."

Mr. Manion: Thanks for bringing that up. Make sure we keep that in mind. Yes, Carolyn.

Carolyn: Why can't we just use our books? You always let us use our notes, but not our books.

Mr. Manion: I used to have my classes use their textbooks on tests. Obviously, when you do mathematics outside of class you can refer to textbooks or anything else you can find.

Carolyn: That's what I mean.

Mr. Manion: Hang on, Carolyn, I'm not finished. There are two reasons why I decided it's not in your best interest to have an open-book test. First of all, in the past my students would waste a lot of valuable test-taking time trying to read the book. Instead of just using the book to look up a formula or definition, they'd try to look up problems and answers. But the answers to the test items aren't in the book and it's too late to be trying to study the book. It hurt their chances of scoring high because to score high they needed to depend on their own reasoning abilities. Yes, Willard.

Willard: So you were sort of protecting them from themselves.

Mr. Manion: I guess you could say that. My second reason for requiring you to use your notes but not allowing you to use the text is that it encourages you to keep a well-organized notebook that you can use efficiently. You learn by taking the material from class and from the textbook and putting it in your own words for you to use as a reference. Yes, Carolyn.

Carolyn: Anything else we should have for the test; will we need out protractors?

Mr. Manion: You should always have your usual complement of measuring tools handy. But I'm glad you just reminded me of one more important item I almost forgot to tell you to bring. You know the cutouts you made in your collaborative groups last Wednesday? Bring those with you; I'm going to ask you to use them on the test in a way that is similar to what you did in your group, but with a different twist. Okay, let's go over the list of things you'll need to have ready for Thursday's opportunity. First, make sure you have . . .

_____

Number of Items. The test blueprint should include an estimate of the number of items you'll need. The estimate depends on time allotted for administration and scoring, the weighting of the objective, types of items, and learning levels of the item.

Difficulty of Items. A major concern of item-response theory is the relationship between how difficult various tests items are for students to answer and exactly what the test measures (Hambleton & Swaminathan, 1985; Millman & Greene, 1989; Wood, 1988). In designing a test, you should be concerned with the roles played by items relative to how difficult they are for students to answer. Items are classified according to their difficulty levels (Cangelosi, 1990b, pp. 53–54):

- *Easy Items.* An item is *easy* if at least 75 percent of the students for whom it is intended respond to it correctly. A test needs a number of easy items to measure relatively low levels of achievement. Such items provide information about what students with less-than-average achievement of the goal have learned.

- *Moderate Items.* An item is *moderately difficult* if between 25 percent and 75 percent of the students respond to it correctly. Moderate items are valuable for measuring the achievement levels of the majority of students for whom the test is designed.

- *Hard items.* An item is *hard* if no more than 25 percent of the students respond to it correctly. A test needs a number of hard items to measure relatively advanced levels of achievement. Unless a test has some hard items to challenge students with advanced goal attainment, the extent of those students' achievement levels is not detected.

Compare the three items in Case 10.8 (adapted from Cangelosi, 1990b, p. 53).

CASE 10.8

Objective 9 of Ms. Curry's sixth-grade mathematics unit on surface areas reads:

> When confronted with a real-life problem, determine whether or not computing the area of the surface will help solve the problem.   (*application*)

Three of the items Ms. Curry has constructed for that objective are as follows:

1. *Task Presented to the Student:* Answer the following multiple-choice question.

Carpet is to be bought for the rectangular-shaped floor of a room. The room is 8 feet high, 12 feet wide, and 15 feet long. Which one of the following computations would be the most helpful in deciding how much carpet to buy?

A. 12 feet + 8 feet + 15 feet
B. 2 × (12 feet + 15 feet)
C. 12 feet × 8 feet × 15 feet
D. 12 feet × 15 feet

Scoring Key: +1 for D only; otherwise +0.

2. *Task Presented to the Student:* Answer the following multiple-choice question.

Suppose we want to build bookshelves across one wall of our classroom. The shelves are to be 18 inches apart. Which one of the following computations would be the most helpful in figuring out how many shelves we can fit on the wall?

A. The area of the wall
B. The width of the wall
C. The height of the wall
D. The perimeter of the wall

Scoring Key: +1 for C only; otherwise +0.

3. *Task Presented to the Students:* Answer the following multiple-choice question.

The 13 steps of a staircase are to be painted. Each step is 36 inches wide, 12 inches deep, and 7 inches high. Which one of the following computations would be most helpful in determining how much paint will be needed?

A. [(12 inches × 13) × (7 inches × 13)] ÷ 2
B. 36 inches × [13 × (12 inches × 7 inches)]
C. (13 × 7 inches) × (36 inches + 12 inches)
D. 13 × [(36 inches × 7 inches) + (36 inches × 12 inches)]

Scoring Key: +1 for D only; otherwise +0.

Which of the three items in Case 10.8 do you think will be easiest for Ms. Curry's students? Which will be the hardest? She needs items like the first to help her detect the lower boundary of her students' achievement of the objective. The third should help her detect the upper boundary.

Commercially produced standardized tests are dominated by moderate items and designed so that the average student score is about 50 percent of the maximum possible score. Typical teacher-produced tests are dominated by easy items, with the average score about 80 to 85 percent of the maximum. Your tests will produce more detailed feedback on student achievement (especially for formative feedback) than typical teacher-produced tests if you include easy, moderate, and hard items and design the test so that the average score is about 50 percent of the maximum (Cangelosi, 1982, pp. 309–339; Hofmann, 1975). Of course, if you apply this suggestion to tests for summative grade evaluations, then you should not use traditional percentage grading, where 60 to 70 percent is typically required for passing and 90 to 94 percent is the cutoff for an A. A method for converting scores to grades that can tolerate unconventionally difficult tests is explained in a subsequent section of this chapter; it is referred to as the "*compromise method.*"

Estimate Maximum Number of Points on the Test. Many teachers arbitrarily set the total number of points for each test at 100. Educational measurement specialists tend to discourage this practice, arguing that a maximum point total should be a function of the number and complexity of the items (Cangelosi, 1990b, pp. 47–48). If all items have scoring keys stipulating either +1 or +0, as would be appropriate for a right or wrong type of item, the maximum number of points equals the number of items. However, some types of items (e.g., display of a proof, show your work, or essay) provide for responses that are not simply right or wrong. Such items have more complex scoring keys and cause the maximum points possible on a test to exceed the number of items.

While developing the test blueprint, you should estimate the maximum possible score by multiplying the number of items planned for the test by an estimate of the average maximum score per item. A more accurate estimate is unnecessary for purposes of the blueprint.

Number of Points for Each Objective. To distribute the maximum number of points on a test according to relative importance of objectives, multiply the weight of each objective by that maximum. This yields an estimate of the number of points that should be devoted to items relevant to that objective. For example, if you weighted Objectives A to H as indicated in Exhibit 10.2, and if you estimated the test to have 60 points, then use Exhibit 10.10 as the blueprint for a test of students' achievement of the goal those objectives define.

Method for Determining Cutoff Score. Suppose you plan to use the 60-point test to make summative evaluations of how well your students achieved the

Exhibit 10.10
Point distribution for a 60-point test based on weights of Exhibit 10.2.

Objective	Weight	Computation	Test Points
A	20%	0.20 × 60	12
B	6%	0.06 × 60	3 or 4
C	6%	0.06 × 60	3 or 4
D	12%	0.12 × 60	7 or 8
E	12%	0.12 × 60	7 or 8
F	12%	0.12 × 60	7 or 8
G	12%	0.12 × 60	7 or 8
H	20%	0.20 × 60	12
	100%		About 60

goal about the relationship $\pi = C/d$ given on page 74. You're faced with the decision of how to convert the test scores (44, 51, 44, 9, 39, . . . , 58) to letter grades (A, B, C, D, F). The need to make such a decision raises issues regarding how *cutoff scores* should be identified.

A subsequent section of this chapter deals with setting cutoff scores for determining grades. The task is mentioned here to indicate that the method of determining cutoff scores should be listed in the test blueprint.

Test Outline. Finally, the test blueprint should contain an outline indicating the sections and subsections of the test. Exhibit 10.11 is an example of a test blueprint.

Obtain and Maintain an Item Pool File

Relevant Item Pools. After clarifying the learning goal and developing a test blueprint, you need to have an item pool for each objective. An *item pool* is a collection of measurement items, each designed to be relevant to the same learning objective. A set of item pools is an *item pool file*.

Beginning an item pool for each objective that defines a learning goal is the most difficult phase of the test design and development process if you've never before measured students' achievement of that particular goal. However, once you have built a collection of items for each objective, you may need only to retrieve preexisting item pools.

Advantages of an Item Pool File. There are five reasons for developing and maintaining an item pool file:

1. Building item pools focuses your attention on one objective at a time, stimulating you to expand your ideas on how student achievement of each objective can be demonstrated.
2. Each item in a pool is designed to focus on the content and learning level specified by the objective. Thus, a test synthesized from items drawn from

item pools is more likely to be relevant than one with items designed as the test is being put together (as did Ms. Houlahan in Case 10.4).

3. Having access to an item pool for each objective before items are actually selected for a test makes it easier to construct the test according to the relative weights assigned to objectives.
4. Being able to associate each item with a particular objective provides a means for assessing how well *specific* objectives were achieved, not just general goal achievement. This facilitates access to *diagnostic* information needed for formative feedback.
5. It is much easier and efficient to create and refine tests once a system for maintaining and expanding an item pool file is in place.

Desirable Characteristics of Item Pools. To take full advantage of having item pools, build them so that the following occur:

- Each item contains both a task for students to confront and a scoring key.
- Each pool contains a variety of types of items (e.g., brief essay, demonstration, and display problem solution).
- Each pool contains easy, moderate, and hard items.
- Data relative to each item's performance (once it's used) are filed. Item analysis data indicates how difficult the item proved to be and how well students' performance on it correlates with their overall test scores (Cangelosi, 1982, pp. 309–340).
- The item pool file is organized and maintained so that retrieving existing items, constructing tests, creating new items, modifying existing items, and gaining access to information about items are executed efficiently.

Exhibit 10.12 outlines a convenient scheme for organizing an item pool file.

Computerized Item Pool File. Twenty years ago teachers organized and managed item pools on index cards in file boxes. Today, microcomputers allow you

Exhibit 10.11
Sample test blueprint.

Unit 16: Circumferences, Diameters, and π

Administration Time. Two sessions:
1. Parts I, II, III, and IV on Wed., Jan. 22, 1:10–2:00
2. Parts V and VI on Thurs., Jan. 23, 1:10–1:45

Scoring Time
1. Part I to be scored by aide on Wed. between 2:45–5:00
2. Part IV to be scored by me as administered
3. Parts II and III scored by me on Wed. between 3:15–5:00
4. Parts V and VI scored by me on Thurs. between 3:15–5:00

Item Formats

Objective	Format of Items
A	Essay
B	Interview
C	Brief essay and display computation
D	Multiple choice and completion
E	Multiple choice and brief essay
F	Multiple choice, display computation, and completion
G	Multiple choice, display computation, and completion
H	Multiple choice and display problem solution

Technology for Students to Use.
Calculator, caliper, ruler, and measuring tape

References for Students to Use.
Notebook only

Number of Items
About 60

Difficulty of Items
Average score should be slightly greater than half the maximum total, with approximately 30 percent of the items easy, 50 percent moderate, and 20 percent hard. These ratios should be nearly consistent across all eight objectives.

Maximum Number of Points.
60

---

to organize and manage item pools so efficiently that you can concentrate your energies on the creative aspect of the process—designing the items. Computer programs developed especially for setting up and utilizing item pools are readily available from both commercial and public-domain sources. Computer software catalogs, computer retail stores, computer magazines, professional journals for teachers, and school-district resource and media centers have information on how to obtain the software for such pro-

grams. Of course, you don't have to have special software to maintain and manage a computerized item pool file. Many teachers use standard word-processing programs with (a) each pool stored in a document file, (b) the pools for a single unit listed under a directory, and (c) the directories for each course on a single disk. Other teachers prefer to write their own program for an item pool file.

These programs free you from the time-consuming clerical aspects of expanding pools, modifying

Exhibit 10.11
Continued

Maximum Number of Points for Each Objective

Objective	Points
A	12
B	3 or 4
C	3 or 4
D	7 or 8
E	7 or 8
F	7 or 8
G	7 or 8
H	12

Method for Determining Cutoff Scores

The compromise method (Cangelosi, 1990b, 208–210) will be used to convert test scores to letter grades, with the following midpoints for criterion intervals:

25% (approx. 15 pts.) for F
40% (approx. 24 pts.) for D
55% (approx. 33 pts.) for C
70% (approx. 42 pts.) for B
85% (approx. 51 pts.) for A

Test Outline

First Session

Part I: 24 multiple-choice items, 1 point each. Directions given orally to the group as a whole. Items distributed among the eight objectives as follows:

D-7; E-5; F-5; G-5; H-2

Part II: Three display-computation items, distributed among the objectives as follows:

One 2-point item on C; one 3-point item on F; and one 3-point item on G

Part III: Two brief essay items, distributed among the objectives as follows:

One 2-point item on C and one 2-point item on E

Part IV: One 4-point interview item relevant to Objective B, individually administered one-to-one while group takes Parts I, II, and III.

Second Session

Part V: Two display-problem-solution items, with each item 5 points for Objective H.
Part VI: One 12-point essay item, relevant to Objective A.

---

items, retrieving items in accordance with test blueprints, synthesizing tests, and printing tests. You can then focus more on intellectual tasks.

The teacher in Case 10.9 is using a commercially produced program to add a new item she's just designed to one of her item pools.

CASE 10.9

Ms. Castillo accesses her item pool program and engages the computer in the following exchange:

Computer: What function do you want?

1. Review table of contents
2. Review existing pool
3. Modify existing pool
4. Begin new pool
? Help

Ms. Castillo: 3
Computer: What pool? Enter code for course/learning goal. If you need a list of codes, enter LIST instead.
Ms. Castillo: ALG1/12

Exhibit 10.12
Organizational scheme for an item pool file.

```
┌─────────────────────────────────────────┐
│  Course                                  │
│     Learning goal                        │
│        Objective                         │
│           Difficulty level               │
│              Type of item                │
│                                          │
└─────────────────────────────────────────┘
```

Computer: What subfunction do you want?

1. Review table of contents for AGL1/12
2. Add new item
3. Modify existing item
4. Delete item
5. Add or modify item analysis data
6. Modify existing ALG1/12 parameters
? Help

Ms. Castillo: 2
Computer: What objective? Enter code. If you need a listing of objectives and codes, enter LIST instead.
Ms. Castillo: 4
Computer: What is the difficulty level of the item (e, m, or h)? If you need a list of codes, enter LIST instead.
Ms. Castillo: m
Computer: What type of item?

1. multiple choice	5. essay	8 performance
2. matching	6. brief essay	observation
3. completion	7. display work	9 other
4. true/false		? help

Ms. Castillo: 7
Computer: Enter the task you want presented to the student.
Ms. Castillo: Simple interest on a certain amount of money for one year was $30. If the interest rate had been 1 percent lower, $250 more would have had to be invested to produce the same amount of interest. What was the amount invested? What was the rate of interest? Please clearly display your work on this problem.
Display of work:

Answer for amount invested: _____
Answer for interest rate: _____

Computer: Enter the scoring key. If you need a list of codes, enter LIST instead.
Ms. Castillo: 6 points possible, distributed as follows:

- +1 if there is some open sentence that includes principal and interest rate as variables.
- +1 if the relationship interest = rate × time × principal is used somewhere in the response.
- +1 if appropriate simultaneous equations with rate and principal as the only variable appear somewhere in the response. Example:

$$30 = RP$$
$$30 = (R - 0.01)(P + 250)$$

- +1 if 750 is given as a solution for the principal.
- +1 if 4 percent is given as a solution for the interest rate.
- +1 if no other solutions are included (e.g., −1000 for principal).

Computer: Do you have any notes to add about this item?
Ms. Castillo: n
Computer: Your new item has been stored in the AGL1/12 pool. Do you want to add another item to this pool?
Ms. Castillo: n

_____

Synthesize the Test

The final step in the test design and development process is to select, organize, and compile the items into a test, as specified by the test blueprint. The blueprint indicates the number of items to be selected from each pool, their formats, and the difficulty levels. This phase can be efficiently handled using a computer and printer.

DESIGNING ITEMS

Creating measurement items relevant to your objectives is no trivial task. Organizing and managing item pools with a computer relieves you from most of the tedious work associated with test construction. However, the quality (validity and usability) of your rests depends primarily on how creative you are in designing the individual items comprising the item pools. Your ability to create relevant items will flourish as you gain experience applying (a) Chapter 4's suggestions for designing items relevant to construct a concept objectives and discover a relationship objectives, (b) Chapter 5's suggestions for designing items relevant to simple-knowledge, comprehension, and algorithmic-skill objectives, and (c) Chapter 6's suggestions for designing items relevant to application, creativity, and affective objectives.

USING TEST RESULTS

Formative Feedback

Obviously, you and your students depend on achievement test results as indicators of how you should regulate your teaching and they should regulate their studying. Reviewing results from recently taken tests is a prime learning activity that provides students with formative feedback. Annotated and scored tests should be returned to students as soon as reasonably possible; ordinarily, students are primed for corrective feedback and reinforcement the day after a test. "Why didn't you teach us this before we took the test?" is an oft-heard question in sessions in which recently tested mathematical content is reviewed. The answer, of course, is, "The experience of working with the content under test conditions led you to be more receptive to my teaching."

Here is a routine some teachers successfully follow in the class period after a test has been administered and test documents are returned to students:

1. Test documents are returned with *descriptive* annotations. Descriptive comments provide students with specific information about their performance (e.g., "Your drawing made it easier for me to follow your logic" or "Squaring both the numerator and denominator changed the value of this function"), as opposed to judgmental comments like "good" or "poor".
2. In a brief large-group session, the teacher makes general comments about the test and, if necessary for the first few tests, explains how to interpret scores and annotations.
3. A small task-group session is held, with each group of about six students going through the test item by item and answering one another's questions.
4. A large-group question/discussion/presentation session is held in which the teacher (a) reviews matters that test results indicated need reviewing, and (b) responds to student questions that were either not answered in the small-group session or arose as a result of that session.

Such activities are particularly effective when students realize that subsequent tests will include items relevant to objectives from prior tests. Test review sessions should be conducted with the clear understanding that they are learning experiences; they are not intended to simply provide students with a summative evaluation of their performance.

Converting Test Scores to Grades

Grading. Test review sessions are used to provide students with formative feedback. Grades are the traditional means for communicating your summative evaluations of achievement of learning goals. Periodically assigning letter grades to students' achievements is a responsibility faced by practically all middle and secondary school mathematics teachers. Data from tests are the primary basis for grades.

Many methods for converting test scores to grades are used; none appears completely tenable (Cangelosi, 1990b, 196–212; Gronlund & Linn, 1990, pp. 427–452; NCTM, 1993, pp. 113–138; Oosterhof, 1994, pp. 329–356). How to establish suitable cutoff scores for grades is a question that has been addressed by evaluation specialists but never satisfactorily answered (Berk, 1986; Cangelosi, 1984a; Livingston & Zieky, 1982). Research studies of grading methods have been more successful in demonstrating the weaknesses of common practice than in providing practical and effective models.

Traditional Percentage Method. The most commonly practiced and familiar method of converting test scores to grades is *traditional percentage grading*. With the traditional percentage method, a percentage of the test's maximum possible score is associated with a cutoff score for each grade. For example, 94 to 100 percent for an A, 86 to 93 percent for a B, 78 to 85 percent for a C, 70 to 77 percent for a D, and 0 to 69 percent for an F. Traditional percentage grading has two major flaws:

1. The percentages are set so high that teachers must either give tests dominated by easy items or assign failing grades for achievement to the majority of their students. (As explained in the section Difficulty of Items, to measure a wide range of achievement levels in a class of students, tests should be designed so that the average score is about 50 percent of the maximum.)
2. Inflexible cutoff points lead teachers to associate different grades with scores that are not significantly different. Consider Case 10.10 (adapted from Cangelosi, 1990b, p. 206).

CASE 10.10

Mr. Nelson administers a test consisting of 25 four-point items. Joyce, Albin, and Winthrop score 93, 86, and 84, respectively. With Mr. Nelson's traditional percentage grading scale, Joyce receives a B for being correct on 23.25 items ($93 \div 4 = 23.25$). Albin also receives a B for being correct on 21.5 items ($86 \div 4 = 21.5$). But Winthrop receives a C for correctly answering only one-half item less than Albin ($84 \div 4 = 21$). See Exhibit 10.13.

Visual Inspection Method. Smith and Adams (1972, pp. 237–239) suggest that the flaws of the traditional

Exhibit 10.13
Comparison of three grades determined by the traditional percentage method.

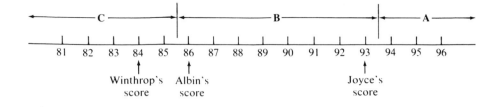

Exhibit 10.14
Number line for use with visual inspection grading.

Exhibit 10.15
Sample score distribution.

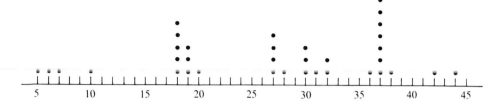

Exhibit 10.16
Example of grades assigned via visual inspection.

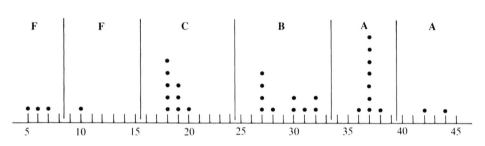

percentage method are avoided in the *visual inspection method*. With the visual inspection method, test scores are converted to letter grades as follows:

1. A number line is drawn that encompasses the range of the test scores. For example, if the lowest test score is 5 and the highest is 44, the number line given in Exhibit 10.14 would suffice.
2. The frequency distribution of the test scores is graphed onto the line. Exhibit 10.15 is an example.
3. Gaps or significant breaks in the distribution are identified.
4. A letter grade is assigned to each cluster of scores appearing between gaps.

For example, if C is defined as average, the cluster containing the middle score might be given the grade C. Or the teacher may choose to sample some of the test papers from a particular cluster based on the quality of the sample. Every score within the same cluster is assigned the same letter grade. Exhibit 10.16 depicts one possible assignment of grades for Exhibit 10.15's distribution.

Compromise Method. Cangelosi (1990b, pp. 208–210) raises concerns about the visual inspection method and suggests an alternative.

A Conflict Between Theory and Practice

Teachers who are introduced to the visual inspection method readily recognize the following advantages it has over the traditional percentage method:

- Tests can include appropriate proportions of easy, moderate, and hard items without fear that too many students will receive low grades. The difficulty of the test can be factored into the grading scheme.
- Scores that are not markedly different from one another are not assigned different grades; the error of the measurement is recognized.

However, teachers tend to reject the visual inspection method because of the following:

- Establishing criteria for A, B, C, D, and F *after* a test has been administered does not appear as objective as having predetermined cutoff scores (e.g., 70 percent for passing) of which students can be aware *prior* to taking the test.
- Norm-referenced methods (i.e., in which students' scores are compared to one another) encourage an unhealthy competition among students for grades more than do criterion-referenced methods [i.e., in which no score is interpreted in light of others'

Exhibit 10.17
Inconvenient score distribution for use with visual inspection grading.

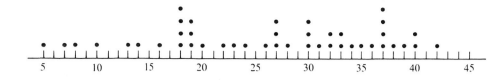

Exhibit 10.18
Sample letter grade cutoff scores.

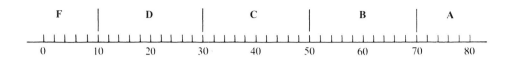

Exhibit 10.19
Sample letter grade cutoff scores with grey in-between scores.

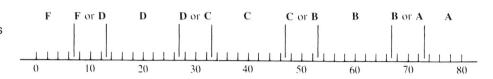

scores but only in relation to a set standard (e.g., 70 percent)].

- Test scores don't always fall into convenient clusters with significantly large enough gaps to distinguish between different grades according to the visual inspection method. The distribution of Exhibit 10.17 is possible.

A Resolution

The method suggested here realizes the principal advantages of visual inspection method while obviating the three weaknesses mentioned above. This method is a *compromise* between the traditional percentage and visual inspection method and is implemented as follows:

1. As with traditional percentage grading, establish cutoff scores for each grade before the administration of the test. However, there are two differences:

- To allow for the use of a test that includes hard and moderate as well as easy items, the percentage of points that a student must score to obtain a certain grade is set unconventionally low. Exhibit 10.18, for example, presents possible criteria for a test designed to produce an average score of 40 out of a possible 80.

- The cutoff score for each letter grade is established with the understanding that there be a buffer, or grey, zone between each letter grade category. In Exhibit 10.19, for example, to be assigned a *definite* B, a score would have to be at least three points above the B cutoff score of 50 and no greater than three points below the A cutoff score of 70. For those familiar with the *standard error of measurement statistic (SEM)*, a SEM would be an ideal determiner of the length of this buffer zone (Cangelosi, 1982, pp. 292–300). However, simply "backing off" several points in both directions around each cutoff point is sufficient.

2. Assign in-between grades to scores that fall within cutoff score intervals. For example, a score of 51 might convert to a grade of B or C. Final determination of whether or not the higher or lower grade prevails in any of these in-between cases depends on data collected from other sources (e.g., an abbreviated retest or an interview that requires the student to expatiate on his or her response). You also have the option of simply letting the grade for that test remain in limbo between two letter grades and then factoring in the in-between grade into your final determination of the specific report card grade.

Point and Counterpoint

The compromise method is likely to be criticized on two accounts:

- Some teachers are uncomfortable with scores falling within buffer zones. There *should* be clear lines of demarcation between grades.
- Unconventionally difficult tests, replete with moderate and hard items, may lead to greater student frustration, since the students will miss more items than on more commonly used easier tests.

There *should* be clear lines of demarcation between letter grades, and it isn't always convenient for a score to fall within a buffer zone. However, the state of the art of measuring student achievement is not advanced to the point that definite lines of demarcation, discriminating between levels of achievement, are tenable. The educational community needs to recognize this fact.

Regarding the second criticism, there are some distinct pedagogical disadvantages to using unconventionally difficult tests. However, once students become accustomed to struggling with challenging test items, a teacher can utilize such tests as tools to help students achieve higher cognitive learning objectives (e.g., application level) (Bloom, Madaus, & Hastings, 1981).

ALTERNATIVE AND AUTHENTIC ASSESSMENTS

Since the mid 1980s, arguments have been forwarded in professional education journals and conferences regarding the use of *alternative assessments*. Alternative to what? one might ask. Alternative assessment refers to evaluations that are dependent on measurements that use instruments and processes somewhat dissimilar from traditional paper and pencil tests, especially multiple-choice tests. The movement toward alternative assessments is a reaction against the tradition of reporting student achievement almost solely on the basis of results of tests that emphasize only simple knowledge and algorithmic skills. These traditional tests may afford some attention to comprehension but virtually ignore other higher, cognitive achievement learning levels such as construct a concept, discover a relationship, application, and creativity. The movement favors *performance-based measurements* or *authentic assessments* that closely reflect how well students can do meaningful mathematics, not simply regurgitate information about mathematics or execute algorithms (Costa, 1989; Gipps, 1993; NCTM, 1993; Haney, 1985; Webb & Romberg, 1992; Wiggins, 1989; Wolfe, 1989). In other words, evaluations should be based on measurements that are relevant to how well students perform relative to meaningful learning objectives—which is exactly what has been emphasized throughout this chapter as well as in Chapters 4, 5, and 6.

Specialists in educational measurement and evaluation urge teachers not to abandon validity and reliability considerations in using alternative assessments anymore than they should when using traditional approaches (Lane, 1993; Miller & Legg, 1993).

Another aspect of the achievement-assessment reform movement relates to how summative evaluations of student achievement are reported. Traditionally, teachers are expected to distill communications about what and how well each student learned mathematics to a single symbol, such as a letter grade. Learning mathematics, as with all learning in the classrooms, is far too complex to communicate on a simple report card or even a check list of "goals achieved." Parent/student/teacher conferences are a beneficial and necessary means for supplementing report cards. However, there is also a need for a record that can document in some detail what students accomplished as a result of their experiences in school. One mechanism gaining widespread popularity as either a supplement to or even a replacement for the traditional report card is *individual student portfolios*.

INDIVIDUALIZED STUDENT PORTFOLIOS

One point on which virtually everyone seems to agree is that meaningful evaluations of student achievement should be based on multiple lines of evidence (American Psychological Association, American Educational Research Association, & National Council on Measurement in Education, 1985; NCTM, 1993). In other words, no one type of test or performance observation provides sufficient relevant and reliable data to reflect what students have actually learned; a variety of measurements are needed. Furthermore, at least some of the measurements should be individually tailored to students' characteristics, tendencies, and learning styles. Case 10.11 demonstrates the dilemma teachers face in trying to report their assessments of students' achievements, and emphasizes the need for alternatives to traditional measurement, evaluation, and reporting practices.

CASE 10.11 _____

Their students having just departed for the day, Hadezza Robinson and Tyler Longley engage in the following conversation in the faculty workroom of Greystone High School:

Ms. Robinson: You don't look happy, Tyler. Did you have one of "those" days?

Mr. Longley: Actually, I'm really pleased with the way the day went; the kids really got into their work. But thanks for asking.

Ms. Robinson: Well, you don't appear very pleased, sitting there grimacing and moaning to yourself.

Mr. Longley: My students' had such a productive day that I feel worse about having to boil down all their accomplishments in mathematics to a grade and some check marks. It's distressing!

Ms. Robinson: So it's about one of those times of year again when we have to get grade reports out. I'm not looking forward to it either, but I'd think your students' successes would make grading a more pleasant chore. It's always easier to report successes than failures.

Mr. Longley: I would've thought so too, but that's not the way things are working. Let me give you an example of my dilemma. You know Rebecca Powell?

Ms. Robinson: Sure, I have her brother T. J. for precalculus.

Mr. Longley: Rebecca really got turned on to mathematics in our unit on probability. She began to see application of mathematics she's been exposed to for the past couple of years—something she's never recognized before. She demonstrated such creativity in that unit, coming up with all kinds of ways to apply the relationships and algorithms.

Ms. Robinson: I'm trying to figure out why all this is distressing you. I'd think you'd be jumping at the chance to report her successes!

Mr. Longley: I am, but the report card business has me hamstrung because the grade period covers four units. She got an A for the probability unit, and an A for a unit on sequences. But for the descriptive statistics unit and another on special functions, she didn't learn much of anything. When I average out her grades she'll end up with a B– at best. B– just doesn't reflect her enthusiasm for what she did with probabilities. If only I had made a more concerted effort to relate real-life situations in the statistics and special functions unit like I did for the other two units, she might have gotten turned on to those also!

Ms. Robinson: I understand what you're saying. You want to highlight her accomplishments without having them blended with and played down by her lack of success in other areas.

Mr. Longley: And that's only one example that's bothering me. Sawyer Bond's scores on my written-response tests are really low. But now and then when I catch him in a one-on-one situation and ask him to explain concepts, relationships, and algorithms, he shows sophisticated insights. I think his test performances in mathematics are affected by some major learning gaps relative to reading comprehension. And on top of that, he doesn't demonstrate his understanding in large-group class activities because he acts shy in large-group situations. But I think this kid has learned a lot about doing mathematics; it just doesn't show up on conventional tests and demonstrations. If I give him a mathematics achievement report based on the usual measures, it's going to send him and his parents the wrong message. On the other hand, I've got to grade equitably.

Ms. Robinson: To compound the problem, I bet you've got students whose test scores exceed their true levels of achievement.

Mr. Longley: You've got that right! I can think of several who are really test-wise, plus they have exceptional language arts skills.

Ms. Robinson: What we need is to keep an individualized file for each student—one that reflects their special accomplishments and interests as well as reports of more general achievement levels.

Mr. Longley: Which one of us is going to propose that at the next faculty meeting?

––––––––––

But how can you efficiently maintain and manage a file on each student? Some teachers do so with individualized portfolios. Similar to the way artists, models, craftspersons, architects, and researchers build a collection of their works as evidence of their accomplishments, teachers can guide their students to organize, develop, refine, and maintain samples of work reflecting what they've learned. Consider Case 10.12.

CASE 10.12

Just before the beginning of the school year, Ms. Dumars organizes some of the bookcases and utility shelves in her classroom to accommodate products from her students' work.

One set of shelves is set aside for student portfolios, with enough space to hold each student's hard-plastic portfolio file box. The portable file boxes, which students can purchase in the school bookstore, will house the individualized portfolios. A second set of shelves is reserved for print and written materials, concrete models, video presentations, and other artifacts from cooperative group activities in which students will be engaging during the year. The individualized portfolios will not contain these artifacts, but each student's portfolio will include references to those artifacts to which she or he contributed.

As the school year begins, the portfolios serve as a focus for much of the course work. For the geometry course, each student's portfolio is organized into the following sections, with the material for each section in a labeled file folder:

1. *A one- or two-page autobiographical sketch that the student fills out.* Ms. Dumars has students complete a questionnaire about themselves on the first day of class. Besides information about their families and background, they indicate their special interests, likes, and dislikes. Periodically she has them update the questionnaires as their situation and interests change. She believes that by opening the portfolio with something personal about the individual student, the student is more likely to think of the portfolio and the mathematical activities reflected in it to be uniquely hers or his. The portfolios might also help students warm up to mathematics as a personal activity that really can be tailored to an individual's interest.

2. *A table of contents for the portfolio.*

3. *Selected papers from the students ongoing, evolving writing project.* The first week of class Ms. Dumars directs the students to write a one to one and one-half page persuasive essay on topics they choose themselves. Throughout the course she refers to those essays and has them "operate" on them. For example, at one point she has them distinguish between statements they made that are propositions and statements that are not propositions. Later she has them identify arguments in the essays that were based on inductive reasoning and those that were based on deductive reasoning. Until then, none of the students had ever before realized that they were using deductive, and especially inductive, arguments daily. She even had them break down some of their deductive arguments into the components of a syllogism (major premise, minor premise, and conclusion). She used this to teach students strategies for formulating propositions and proving theorems. The essays, and subsequent versions of them, are used throughout the course, for example, to illustrate how the indirect proofs and counterexamples we use in mathematics are

simply formalizations of what they themselves do whenever they make valid arguments in everyday life. Another type of ongoing writing project involves students corresponding with pen pals from a sixth-grade class in one of the city's middle schools. Ms. Dumars worked out an arrangement with a colleague who teaches mathematics in the middle school. The colleague's sixth graders send letters to Ms. Dumars' students raising questions about how to use geometry to solve some of the problems they're working on in sixth-grade mathematics. Thus, over the year, Ms. Dumars' students keep copies of letters sent to them as well as their own replies. A subset of the correspondence is selected for the portfolios.

4. *Copies of reports and other documents resulting from work in the student's special area of expertise.* In December Ms. Dumars directs each student to select a topic (e.g., Pascal's triangle, three-dimensional similarities, compass and straightedge constructions, non-Euclidean geometries, Möbius strips, the golden section) about which the student would become the class expert and periodically teach to the class. Selected materials used by the student and records of presentations such as a videotape recording, are appropriate for this section of the portfolio.

5. *Selected documents reflective of the student's accomplishments while engaged in Unit 1 of the course.* The student chooses homework, concrete models constructed, computer programs written, theorems proved, tests completed, or other materials indicative of what was gained from the unit.

6.–20. *Selected documents reflective of the student's accomplishments while engaged in Units 2 through 16 of the course, respectively.*

21. *Five tests completed at any point during the course, selected as reflective of accomplishments by the student.* Copies of the first five tests the student takes are inserted in this section. With each subsequent test, the student has the option of supplanting one of the prior tests with the new one.

22. *The student's journal.* Each school day, Ms. Dumars requires the students to write a brief paragraph summarizing their class-related mathematical activities since their previous journal entry. The journal is stored in this section of the portfolio.

Throughout the course, in collaboration with Ms. Dumars each student selects material for the portfolio that's indicative of mathematical accomplishments. Not only are additions continually being made, but as the student refines ideas and supplants previously held conceptions (or misconceptions) with freshly constructed concepts and discoveries, the contents of the portfolio are altered and replaced. Exactly what's included in the portfolios varies considerably among students, as well as from unit to unit; they should be individualized.

Besides being a focal point of learning activities, the portfolios are used to communicate students' accomplishments to themselves, their parents, and school administra-

tors. Ms. Dumars is required by her school administrators to assign grades for periodic reports. She used to include these grade reports in students' portfolios. However, after discovering that some parents and school administrators tended to focus on the grades instead of the more information-rich materials, she sends the grades reports home, but no longer allows them to be part of the portfolios.

———————————

Engage in Activity 10.3.

—————————— **ACTIVITY 10.3** ——————————

Purpose: To gain an experience that will help you refine your strategies for using individualized student portfolios.

You Need: Copies of plans for lessons you've designed (see Activities 4.4, 4.6, 5.3, 5.5, 5.8, 6.1, and 6.4).

Procedure: With a colleague discuss (a) the advantages and disadvantages of using individualized student portfolios, and (b) Ms. Dumars' use of portfolios in Case 10.12. Which of her ideas would you tend to incorporate in your own teaching? Which would you not? Why?

Select a sample of lessons you previously designed. With your colleague discuss how you might incorporate individualized student portfolios in the lessons. Also discuss the use of portfolios as a mechanism for evaluating and communicating student achievement during units that include those lessons.

TRANSITIONAL ACTIVITIES FROM CHAPTER 10 TO CHAPTER 11 ——————

1. Select the one response to each of the following multiple-choice items that either completes the statement so that it is true or accurately answers the question:

   A. Anytime teachers evaluate student achievement, they _____.

      (a) make value judgments
      (b) use valid measurements
      (c) base the evaluation on unit test results
      (d) determine better ways of teaching

   B. Stiggins suggested which one of the following, according to the quote beginning on page 308?
      (a) All achievement measurements emphasize simple-knowledge achievement and procedural skills.

(b) The cognitive levels at which students are tested tend to limit the cognitive levels at which they learn.

(c) Commercially produced tests are superior to teacher-designed measurements.

(d) Valid and usable measures of student achievement are virtually impossible to design.

C. Which one of the following is NOT a measurement?

(a) Administering a unit test

(b) Seeing a student write on the board

(c) Hearing a student say, "Math is fun!"

(d) Seeing that a student is unable to bisect an angle with a compass and straightedge

(e) Seeing that a student is not bisecting an angle with a compass and a straightedge

D. Which one of the following is a *necessary* condition for measurement relevance?

(a) Internal consistency

(b) Pertinence to the stated learning levels

(c) Validity

(d) Usability

E. Which one of the following is a *sufficient* condition for measurement relevance?

(a) Internal consistency

(b) Pertinence to the stated learning levels

(c) Validity

(d) Usability

F. Which one of the following is a *necessary* condition for measurement reliability?

(a) Scorer consistency

(b) Usability

(c) Relevance

(d) Pertinence to the intended content

G. Which one of the following is a *sufficient* condition for measurement reliability?

(a) Usability or relevance

(b) Usability and relevance

(c) Internal or scorer consistency

(d) Internal and scorer consistency

H. Which one of the following is a *sufficient* condition for a measurement to be a valuable information-gathering tool?

(a) Usability, internal consistency, and pertinence to the intended content

(b) Relevance, reliability, and validity

(c) Relevance, reliability, and usability

I. Which one of the following modifications to an item is most likely to improve the item's scorer consistency?

(a) Raise the learning level to which the item is relevant from simple knowledge or algorithmic skill to one that requires reasoning (e.g., application).

(b) Make the rules in the scoring key more specific.

(c) Change the format from multiple choice to essay.

(d) Provide greater latitude for the scorer to use professional judgment.

J. Which one of the following measurement variables depends on the stated purpose of the measurement?

(a) Usability

(b) Relevance

(c) Scorer consistency

(d) Internal consistency

K. Which one of the following measurement variables depends on the time it takes to administer a test?

(a) Usability

(b) Relevance

(c) Scorer consistency

(d) Internal consistency

L. Out of concern for his students' abilities to read books and articles about mathematics, Mr. Kembloski includes an objective in most of his teaching units for his students to remember definitions of certain mathematical terms. During the course, he plans to build their reading vocabulary of mathematical words. One item he intends to be relevant to one of those objectives is to following.

Task Presented to the Students

Fill in the missing word:

A _____ is a curve or surface (or solid or higher-dimensional object) that contains more but similar complexity the closer one looks.

Scoring Key: +1 for "fractal" only; 0 otherwise.

Which one of the following is a weakness of the item?

(a) "Fractal" is not a mathematically well-defined word.

(b) The item reverses the stimulus-response order of the objective.

(c) The item requires only simple-knowledge cognition.

M. An item with a scoring key designed to reflect which steps in a process students do or do not remember is likely to be relevant to which one of the following types of objectives?

(a) Discover a relationship

(b) Creativity

(c) Construct a concept

(d) Application

(e) Algorithmic skill

(f) Simple knowledge

N. Why should at least some items that are designed to measure students' achievement of an application objective that specifies the Pythagorean relationship as content confront students with situations in which that relationship does not apply?

(a) The Pythagorean relationship is limited; student have broader concerns.

(b) Learning the Pythagorean relationship is a prerequisite to learning about other relationships (for example, the formula for finding the distance between two coordinate points in a Cartesian plane).

(c) Students need to learn about other relations involving triangles, not only $c^2 = a^2 + b^2$.

(d) Achievement of an application objective requires students to discriminate between problems to which the specific content does and doesn't apply.

O. For items to be relevant to a creativity objective, they must _____.

(a) provide students with opportunities to think convergently

(b) present students with tasks never previously accomplished by anyone

(c) require students to produce novel products

(d) have scoring keys that discriminate between atypical and typical reasoning

Compare your responses to the following: A-a; B-b; C-d; D-b; E-c; F-a; G-d; H-c; I-b; J-b; K-a; L-b; M-e; N-d; O-d.

2. Imagine yourself planning to teach a mathematics course in either a middle, junior high, or high school. Obtain a copy of a textbook appropriate for that course. Organize the course into units by identifying the titles for the first, second, third,

and so on, units (See Exhibit 2.14). Now select one of the units and write a goal and define it with a set of objectives. Make sure you label the learning level for each. Weight the objective according to relative importance.

3. For each objective in Transitional Activity 2, develop two measurement items.

4. Set up a computerized item pool file. For each objective in Transitional Activity 2, insert an item pool in your file along with the two measurement items developed for Transitional Activity 3.

5. Develop a test blueprint for a unit test that is relevant to the goal you stated for Transitional Activity 2.

6. Using the blueprint you developed for Transitional Activity 5, construct a unit test.

7. Exchange your work for Transitional Activities 2 through 6 with that of a colleague. Give one another feedback; discuss strengths and weaknesses of the two tests.

8. Prepare for your work with Chapter 11 by discussing the following questions with two or more colleagues:

(a) How realistic is it for teachers to try to implement the research-based strategies suggested in Chapters 4 through 10? Is there really enough time in the day to design, organize, and conduct units and lessons like some of the teachers do in the cases from those chapters?

(b) Should teachers in their very first year in the classroom try to use innovative instructional strategies, or should they stick with the more traditional approaches until they gain more experience and confidence?

(c) How can a beginning teacher actually apply the ideas from the previous chapters in a realistic classroom situation?

(d) Realistically, what should a conscientious, creative beginning teacher expect to face during the first year on the job? What strategies have or have not worked for others?

Theory into Practice: Casey Rudd, First-Year Mathematics Teacher

This chapter takes you through Casey Rudd's first year as a mathematics teacher as he learns to put research-based principles and techniques into practice. Chapter 11 is designed to help you:

1. Given a realistic role description for a mathematics teacher in a school, determine and explain alternative ways of fulfilling that role in a manner consistent with suggestions in Chapters 1 through 10 of this text. (*application*)

2. Explain how to integrate the various aspects of teaching mathematics, (that is, designing courses, organizing for a school year, developing teaching units, managing student behavior, engaging in students in learning activities, evaluating student achievement, and relating as a professional) into the role of a mathematics teacher during the course of a school year. (*application*)

3. Anticipate and describe examples of the types of events and problems you are likely to confront while meeting your responsibilities as a mathematics teacher in a school. (*construct a concept*)

CASEY RUDD AND HIS FIRST TEACHING POSITION

Preservice Preparation

Casey Rudd is embarking on his initial year as a professional mathematics teacher. Having recently graduated from college with a major in the teaching of mathematics at the secondary and middle school levels, he successfully completed more than a dozen college mathematics courses, including courses in calculus, analysis, abstract algebra, geometry, number theory, historical foundations of mathematics, discrete structures, and statistics. However, only a couple of his college mathematics instructors employed the kind of teaching strategies that were recommended by his methods of teaching mathematics course—a course that used the textbook you are reading now. Although confident in his ability to do mathematics, he worries that he lacks the conceptual and application levels of understanding necessary to generate the real-life examples and nonexamples that will engage his students in the kind of learning activities explained in Chapters 4, 5, and 6.

A semester-long student-teaching experience provided some opportunities to try out many of the ideas from the methods of teaching mathematics course—primarily those from Chapters 8 and 9. However, in student teaching Casey tailored his teaching style to the curriculum already established by his cooperating teacher. The cooperating teacher was very supportive of his efforts and immensely helpful in providing learning materials and suggestions on managing behavior and organizing lessons. But opportunities to design complete units were quite limited, since Casey had not been involved in planning the courses prior to the opening of the school year.

Although enthusiastic about embarking on his professional career, Casey is understandably nervous about succeeding with a full complement of mathematics classes for which he is solely responsible.

Selecting a Position at Malaker High School

Even before graduation, Casey discovered that a demand existed for people with his qualifications to teach mathematics. As long as he didn't restrict his choice of geographical location too much, opportunities were open to him for positions in many school systems of virtually every variety. After interviewing for nine positions and being offered four, he decided to accept an offer to join the faculty of Malaker High School. The decision was a function of variables such as salary, teaching assignment, location, reputation, philosophy, personnel, stability of the faculty, economic base of support for schools in the community, and administrative style. To assess these variables, he had carefully read literature provided by school district personnel offices, read curriculum guides, counseled with trusted faculty members from his college, carefully listened and raised questions at formal interviews with district personnel officials and school administrators, and had sought out and spoken with potential faculty colleagues.

Among his reasons for favoring Malaker High were the following:

- He was impressed by the apparent competence and dedication of some of the mathematics teachers he met, especially Vanessa Castillo, who appeared willing to work cooperatively with him.
- Mathematics Department Chairperson Armond Ziegler, Principal Harriet Adkins, and Associate Principal Jack Breaux all spoke as if the welfare of students was their first priority and the opinions of faculty were both sought after and utilized. They portrayed the attitude reflected in Ms. Adkins' words, "Teachers are here to help students. Administrators and supervisors are here to help teachers help students."
- His first-year assignment at Malaker High would include the teaching of a precalculus course each semester. At most of the other schools where he interviewed such choice courses were the exclusive domain of veteran teachers.

The Assignment

The Teaching Load. Exhibit 11.1 reflects Casey's year-long teaching load. Casey was somewhat concerned that his teaching assignment at Malaker included four different courses in a five-class load. The assignment at some of the other schools included multiple sections of the same course, so that he might have taught two sections of consumer mathematics and three sections of geometry. However, the precalculus assignment was especially appealing and he thought to himself, "It's unrealistic to expect to keep all the sections of the same course at the same level throughout the year. I still have to prepare differently for two different sections of the same course. Besides, it's the total number of students that influences workload far more than the number of courses."

Other Responsibilities. Besides teaching five classes per semester, Casey is expected to do the following:

- Serve as homeroom monitor and administrator for a group of 24 tenth graders.
- Serve as a general supervisor of students during school hours, enforcing school rules.
- Although free to eat lunch during the A lunch period, serve as a lunchroom monitor during that time.
- Assist in the governance of the school by responding to administrator's requests for input and participating in both general faculty and Mathematics Department meetings.
- Cooperate in the school's system for both administrative supervision and instructional supervision of his own teaching and that of other teachers (see Cangelosi (1991) for an extensive treatise on evaluating classroom) instruction for purposes of both administrative and instructional supervision.
- Participate in professional development activities, by attending inservice workshops, taking college courses, and being involved in organizations such as the local affiliate of NCTM.
- Represent Malaker High as a professional in the community.

In conversations with Armond Ziegler and Vanessa Castillo, Casey discussed the possibility of organizing a student mathematics club.

ORGANIZING FOR THE YEAR

The Situation as of July 15

With the opening of school about five weeks away, Casey is given keys for the building and his home-base classroom (Room 213), a faculty handbook, a copy of the State Education Office's *Curriculum Guide for Mathematics,* the schedule in Exhibit 11.1, and for each of the assigned courses, a teacher's edition of the textbook. As part of his preservice experi-

Exhibit 11.1
Casey Rudd's first-year teaching schedule.

First- and Second-Semester Schedule			
Class Period	**Assignment**	**Room**	**Course Credits Per Semester**
Homeroom 8:10–8:25	10th grade–B	213	—
1st 8:30–9:25	Algebra I*	213	0.5
2nd 9:30–10:25	Preparation	—	—
3rd 10:30–11:25	Geometry*	213	0.5
4th 11:30–12:25	Geometry*	108	0.5
Lunch A 12:30–12:55	Lunch supervision	Lunchroom	—
Lunch B 1:00–1:25	Free	—	—
5th 1:30–2:25	Consumer Math*	213	0.5
6th 2:30–3:25	Precalculus**	213	0.5
Announce-ments 3:25–3:30	—	213	—

*Two-semester course (one group of students both semesters)
**One-semester course (different group of students each semester)

ence in college, Casey had conducted numerous mathematics lessons, but never before has he been responsible for organizing and preparing entire courses and a classroom for conducting business. He begins by surveying Room 213, for which he will be responsible, and then Room 108, the home base for a biology teacher and the classroom for his fourth-period geometry class. He thinks: "Twelve computers available in my room; that leaves eleven for students if I reserve one exclusively for myself. But there are none in Room 108, and with those fixed lab tables, 108 is just too inflexible for me to operate in there! Why can't I use my own room for fourth period? I'll ask Armond if he can work something out and get that switched for me. For now, I should get my room arranged the way I want it. . . . But how do I want it arranged? I guess that depends on how I organize the courses—how much students need to use the computers, and so forth—and how many students each period. Harriet said we won't get class rolls until the first week of school but that my classes should run between 20 and 25.

"So I really need to get a better idea of how I want to organize the courses before worrying much more about the room. Of course, the room will also influence the courses—if there are no computers available for fourth period and I'm in a inflexible lab, that's going to limit what I can do for that geometry class.

"Armond said the textbooks are set for this year, but I'd have a say in the choice of some of the texts next year when there is supposed to be a turnover. Might as well start going through these four texts and see what I have to work with."

Over the next few days, Casey familiarizes himself with the textbooks and state curriculum guide, taking notes to be used in planning the courses. The curriculum guide simply lists goals to be covered in each course; the goals are quite consistent with the topics listed in the textbooks. He judges that the textbooks should be quite useful sources of exercises, examples, definitions, postulates, and theorems. But he notes that for most topics he won't be able to depend on them for construct a concept, discover a relationship, or application objectives. Overall, he's pleased that they seem to be more in line with the NCTM *Standards* than the texts he encountered as a student. His text for algebra I is *Merrill Algebra One* (Foster, Rath, & Winters, 1986); for geometry, it's *Merrill Geometry: Applications and Connections* (Burrill, Cummins, Kanold, & Yunker, 1993); for consumer mathematics, it's *Applying Mathematics: A Consumer/Career Approach* (Keedy, Smith & Anderson, 1986); and for precalculus, it's *Precalculus* (Cannon & Elich, 1994).

Variable Help from Colleagues

Discovering the Computer Lab. With Armond Ziegler, Casey raises the issue of scheduling his fourth-period geometry class in Room 213 instead of 108. Understanding of Casey's plight, Armond checks on the matter and finds out that 213 is the only room available during fourth period that is large enough to accommodate a health science class. It seems that due to a new state-mandated health science requirement, a double section of more than 40 students will be using Room 213, with extra desks brought in just for fourth period. Room 108 is too inflexible for extra desks to be brought in. Casey's panicky feelings over thoughts of this fourth-period onslaught on his home-base classroom are somewhat tempered during the following conversation with Armond:

Armond: Why don't you have your students use the computer lab for some of your activities?

Casey: What computer lab?

Armond: I didn't realize no one told you about it. We have a room with 35 computer stations and a dozen or so printer stations. It's available for student use from 7 to 8 in the mornings and from 3:30 in the afternoon to 8 at night. During the school day, you can schedule a whole class in there on a first-come, first-served basis. But no one class can use it more than one time in a week.

Casey: Really? I can't believe I missed it when I toured the school!

Armond: I should have made a point of showing it to you; it's in the basement. Most teachers don't even think about it, but a few—especially in business education—think of it as their exclusive domain.

Casey: What about the computer science classes; don't they tie it up all day?

Armond: No, there's a special computer science classroom for most of their classes, just like there's a computerized writing lab for the English department. You can arrange to hold a class in the lab with Mr. Tramonte in the library.

Casey: I'd better get my courses organized and decide what days I'll need it. You did say first come, first served, didn't you?

Armond: Yes, but he won't put you on the schedule before August 10, the day the faculty is officially supposed to arrive. But it would be a good idea to apprise him of your intentions to schedule classes periodically.

Casey: Thanks.

Discouraging Advice from Don Delaney. Buoyed by thoughts of how he might take advantage of the computer lab, Casey begins organizing his courses. He is sitting on the floor of Room 213 with a box of odds and ends (pipes, wheels, measuring devices, dice, playing cards, string, and a barrel) thinking about introducing various teaching units with inquiry lessons as Vanessa Castillo and Don Delaney enter (see Exhibit 11.2):

Vanessa: Casey, I'd like you to meet Don Delaney, another member of our Mathematics Department with whom you'll enjoy working.

Casey: Hello, Don, very nice to meet you.

Don: So, you're the new man on the block! Welcome to Malaker High—glad to have you.

Vanessa: Don teaches algebra II and trigonometry—

and, like you, has a section of algebra I this year.

Don: Right. But what's all this stuff you've got here? Looks more like you teach shop than mathematics, Casey.

Casey: These are things I've been collecting to use as manipulatives for my inquiry lessons.

Don: So you're another eager beaver, fresh out of college type who's going to try that discovery stuff! Look, take some advice from this veteran. I've been in this business for nine years and all that discovery stuff just wastes time and gets you in trouble.

Casey: What do you mean?

Don: Look, you don't need to know how a car works to be able to drive it. Mathematics works the same way. Students can learn mathematics correctly without knowing how it works. You spend all that time trying to get them to discover and you never get around to covering the material. Only the really smart kids are capable of understanding why, and they'll learn that when they get to college.

Casey: So that's why you think this discovery stuff wastes time. But how can it get me trouble?

Don: In two ways. One, ever try to manage a class of teenagers when they're all disorganized, running around measuring stuff? I've got perfect control of my classes; they stay in their seats with book, paper, pencil, and calculator—that's all they need!

Casey: And the second way?

Don: Look what you've got here—cards, dice, and a wine barrel. Bring that into a mathematics class and you'll have parents coming down on you for encouraging their children to gamble and drink. You might have gotten away with that 20 years ago when teachers had some respect and authority, but now everything you do is questioned, so it's best not to try anything radical. Remember, this is a litigious society; there's a lawyer out there waiting to pick your pocket!

Casey: Ouch! I didn't think about that!

Don: Hey, we've got a close-knit department here; we look out for one another. All of us love the students and we love mathematics.

Casey: Well, thanks for the advice.

Don: Hey, advice is cheap. Like I said, welcome aboard. You'll really like it here. Are you coming, Vanessa?

Vanessa: I'll meet you in the workroom in 15 minutes. I need to talk with Casey about a few things first.

Progressive and Pragmatic Advice from Vanessa Castillo. After Don leaves, Vanessa continues the conversation with Casey.

Vanessa: What'd you think about Don's advice to you?

Exhibit 11.2.
Casey about to hear some discouraging advice from Don.

Casey: He's a bit skeptical about how I think mathematics should be taught.

Vanessa: That's an understatement! Don's a super guy who loves to work with kids, but he's dead wrong about how to teach mathematics. I gave up trying to argue with him years ago—he'll never change because he lacks the conceptual basis for teaching any way other than to mimic his own teachers, some of whom he idolized. If I had said anything while he was giving you his standard line, we would have gotten into a useless debate, and I thought it was more important for you to hear what he had to say.

Casey: That I shouldn't use inquiry teaching strategies?

Vanessa: Of course you should teach inquiry strategies. It's the only way to lead students to higher learning levels like construct a concept. And that's not to say there isn't a place for direct teaching, such as for algorithmic skills. But Don does have a message we should heed.

Casey: Which is?

Vanessa: Which is to start off conservatively. You and I know that discovery, inductive, and deductive lessons, and all those other methods work—in fact, they're absolutely essential to students doing meaningful mathematics. But, as a beginning teacher, you should not try to deviate too quickly from what these students are used to, until you've had time to gain experience by trying out different strategies and seeing what works best for you and your students. In other words, don't try to teach every lesson with every class in the "right" way. For the first month or so of school, stick mostly to the textbooks, deviating from them and experimenting with your progressive ideas more and more as you build upon your experiences. Before you know it, you'll have built a growing arsenal of ideas and materials and be teaching confidently, as you know you should. Just give yourself time; don't expect too much of yourself too soon or you'll set yourself up for failure.

Casey: That's pretty heavy stuff you're laying on me!

Vanessa: Like Don said, advice is cheap.

Casey: Then, I'll ask for a bit more. I'm having a terrible time getting my courses planned and organized. I've gone through the textbooks, looked at the available materials and facilities, and all that, but I just can't get a handle on the courses from A to Z. I can put together individual lessons, but I have trouble fitting the pieces together.

Vanessa: I know just what you mean, and I have a very definitive suggestion. For each course, begin by writing a syllabus. Write it for the students to read. Being forced to describe the purposes and organization of the course for students will organize your thoughts into a coherent whole. Not only do syllabi lend a businesslike air to your courses and serve as guides for students, but trying to write them lends structure to the process of organizing and planning the courses.

Planning and Organizing the Courses by Writing Syllabi

First-Period Algebra I. Taking Vanessa's advice, Casey sits at his computer outlining the course syllabus for his algebra I course with the aid of a word-processing program. He thinks: "This syllabus needs to be designed so that it sends students the message that this class is serious business and I'm serious enough about it to have it well organized and planned out. The syllabi my college instructors used tended to be full of formal-looking lists of reading references, content, deadlines, and grading criteria. I need some of that here, but I can't be too specific about dates and deadlines until I get into the course and see how things go. In college there were also a couple of paragraphs providing a rationale for the course. I should have something like that, but I've got to keep in mind that I'm dealing with ninth and tenth graders here—there's the matter of reading level and the danger of turning them off with a long narrative.

"I need to think more about the purposes. First, the syllabus should provide a guide for the course. Second, it needs to give them some idea about what to expect, which includes such things as classroom rules. I don't want to forget that. Then, there's the business of getting the class off to a good start—setting a businesslike tone and building some enthusiasm for algebra. And fourth, give them the impression I know what I'm doing. Seeing a well-organized syllabus will give them that idea a lot better than me preaching to them about how important and organized this course is!

"I'll start with an outline of what to include: name of course, basic information such as my name and the room number, a rationale, what the course is all about, a list of materials they need, classroom rules, an idea of what they'll be doing, goals of the course, the basis for their grades. Vanessa was right, writing this thing is going to force me to make some hard decisions that'll get me organizing the course!"

Further thought about how to format the syllabus leads Casey to an innovative idea. He decides to organize the syllabus around the questions that the document should answer for students—questions he would expect them to raise about the course. After another hour and a few false starts, he has the following list of questions, which will become the headings in the syllabus:

1. What is the course all about?
2. What is algebra?
3. Why should you learn algebra?
4. Are you ready to learn algebra?
5. With whom will you be working in this course?
6. Where will you be learning algebra?
7. How will you be expected to behave in this class?
8. What materials will you need for class?
9. What will you be doing for this class?
10. What will you learn from this class?
11. How will you know when you've learned algebra?
12. How will your grades for the course be determined?

Casey spends the next two days determining how to answer these 12 questions for this students and how to express the answers in the syllabus. The most taxing task is to answer the tenth question. Before he can do that he has to determine the sequence of teaching units for the course and formulate the learning goal for each. He finds the Teacher's Guide supplement to the textbook quite helpful in

determining the units and in estimating the number of days and lessons for each. The 17 units about which he ultimately organizes the course correspond to, but do not completely follow, 15 of the textbook's 16 chapters.

Once Casey completes the syllabus, much of his anxiety about teaching algebra I evaporates and his enthusiasm for the school year intensifies. He feels prepared to go to work. His algebra I syllabus with the 17 unit titles is displayed in Exhibit 11.3.

Third-Period Geometry. Pleased with the format of the algebra I syllabus, Casey writes the geometry syllabus for his third-period class in a similar manner. As with the algebra I syllabus, Casey cannot include some details until arrangements such as scheduling the computer lab an be worked out. For example:

- He plans to assign ongoing, unit-long assignments that utilize computers. But the plan depends on computers being available. He's considering designating one day a week on which the class will meet in the computer lab.
- After working out the sequence of teaching units, he notes a number of topics conducive to being taught in coordination with topics from other courses (e.g., a geometry unit on similarity with an art unit on perspective drawing). However, at this point the syllabus cannot reflect such an effort until he can make arrangements with other teachers who also teach a major share of his students.

Fourth-Period Geometry. Because Casey uses word processing, it's a trivial matter to modify the geometry syllabus he wrote for third period so that it is personalized for the fourth period.

Fifth-Period Consumer Mathematics. Unlike the textbook for his other three courses, the consumer mathematics text is not generally organized around mathematical topics, such as applications of addition on rational numbers and applications of solving open sentences, but rather around consumer and daily-living topics like Earning Money, Housing, and Taxes and Insurance. He considers this arrangement inconsistent with the NCTM *Standards* and the way he thinks the course should be organized. However, being less comfortable with the content of the consumer mathematics course than he is with the other three courses, he doesn't feel ready this first year to organize the course so that he cannot depend on the textbook for examples and exercises.

Taking Vanessa's advice, he patterns the teaching units so that the course will generally follow the book's sequence. However, he plans to build upon mathematical abilities, skills, and attitudes using the consumer and daily-living topic headings primarily as

Exhibit 11.3
Casey's syllabus for first-period algebra I.

**Course Syllabus
for
First-Period Algebra I**

WHAT IS THIS COURSE ALL ABOUT?

The course is all about *algebra* and

- Understanding how algebra is used to solve problems.
- Discovering and inventing ways to use algebra to solve your own problems.

What is Algebra?

When you learned arithmetic, you learned how to work with specific numbers. For example, you learned how to divide 3.45 by 0.82.

In algebra you learn to work with what are called *variables.* Being able to work with variables allows you to extend what you learn in one situation to countless other situations.

The question What is algebra? will be answered during the first few weeks of the course.

Why Should You Learn Algebra?

You should learn algebra because:

- Using algebra will help you solve many of the problems you face right now as well as later on in your life.
- Without algebra you cannot continue to advance in school for two reasons:

  Your success in other courses you take in high school, as well as in any vocational school, technical school, or college you might attend, depends on your understanding algebra.

  A full-year credit in algebra is required for a high school diploma in this state.

- An understanding of at least some algebra is expected of literate citizens in today's society and is needed in many occupations.

Are You Ready to Learn Algebra?

Absolutely yes, as long as

- You can do fundamental arithmetic.
- You want to solve problems that life tosses your way.

With Whom Will You Be Working in this Course?

You will be working with Casey Rudd, who is responsible for helping you and your classmates learn algebra. You will also be working with your classmates, each of whom will be making a unique contribution to what you get out of this course. In turn, you will contribute to what they learn by sharing your ideas, problems, discoveries, inventions and solutions.

Where Will You Be Learning Algebra?

You will draw your understanding of algebra from your entire environment, whether at home, school, or anywhere else. Your classroom, Room 213 at Malaker High, is the place where ideas about algebra are brought together and formalized. Room 213 is a place of business for learning algebra.

Exhibit 11.3
Continued

How Will You Be Expected to Behave in this Class?

You and your classmates have the right to go about the business of learning algebra free from fear of being harmed, intimidated, or embarrassed. Mr. Rudd has the right to go about the business of helping you and your classmates learn algebra without disruption or interference. Thus, you are expected to follow five rules of conduct:

1. Give yourself a complete opportunity to learn algebra.
2. Do not interfere with the opportunities of your classmates to learn algebra.
3. Respect the rights of all members of this class (they include you, your classmates, and Mr. Rudd).
4. Follow Mr. Rudd's directions for lessons and classroom procedures.
5. Adhere to the rules and policies of Malaker High as listed on pages 12–14 of the *Student Handbook.*

What Materials Will You Need for Class?

Bring the following with you to every class meeting:

- The course textbook
  Foster, A. G., Rath, J. N., and Winters, L. J., *Merrill Algebra One.* (Columbus, Ohio: Merrill, 1986).
- A four-part notebook
  1. Part 1 is for class notes.
  2. Part 2 is for homework and class assignments.
  3. Part 3 is for saving computer programs and flowcharts developed during the course.
  4. Part 4 is for definitions of vocabulary and symbols.
- A scratch pad
- Pencils, pens, and an eraser
- A hand-held, battery-operated calculator that includes the following features: (a) at least two memories; (b) x^n function key; (c) $\sqrt{}$ function key; (d) ( ) function key; (e) function key; and (f) π function key.
- A ruler (at least 12 inches but not more than 15 inches long)

You will also need five 5.25-inch computer diskettes in a storage case. You will not have to bring these to class every day, but have them available at school (in your locker).

A textbook has been checked out to you for the school year. You are responsible for maintaining it in good condition and returning it to Mr. Rudd on the last day of class. The other materials can be purchased at the Malaker High Bookstore or at other retail outlets.

What Will You Be Doing for this Class?

The course is organized into 17 units of about two weeks each. During each unit you will be:

- Participating in class meetings. Depending on the agenda you will be:
  Listening to Mr. Rudd speak and seeing his illustrations as you take notes on what is being explained.
  Listening to a classmate speak and seeing his or her illustrations as you take notes on what is being explained.
  Explaining things to the class as your classmates take notes on what you say and show them.
  Asking questions, answering questions, and discussing issues with members of the class during question/discussion sessions.
  Working closely with your classmates in small task groups.
  Working independently on assigned exercises.
  Taking brief tests.
- Completing homework assignments.
- Completing computer laboratory assignments.
- Taking a unit test.

Exhibit 11.3
Continued

What Will You Learn From This Class?

Each unit will either introduce you to a new algebraic topic or extend your understanding of a previous topic. During the unit you will:

- Discover an idea or relationship.
- Add to your ability to use the language of algebra.
- Acquire a new skill or polish previously acquired skills.
- Extend your ability to solve problems.

- Here are the titles of the 17 units:

1. Algebra and Its Language
2. Types of Numbers and Arithmetic Operations
3. Operations on Rational Numbers
4. Algebraic Inequalities
5. Powers
6. Polynomials
7. Factoring Polynomials
8. Quadratic Equations
9. Algebraic Functions
10. Extending Functions
11. Systems of Open Sentences
12. Extending Powers and Radicals
13. Extending Quadratic Functions
14. Operations with Rational Polynomials
15. Extending Work with Rational Polynomials
16. Special Functions with Natural Numbers
17. Extending What You've Learned

Units 1–8 are planned for the first semester; units 9–17 are planned for the second semester.

How Will You Know When You've Learned Algebra?

Everyone knows at least some algebra, but no one ever learns algebra completely. Algebra is being discovered and invented every day. You will use what you learn in this course to develop further your ability to use algebra to solve problems.

    The question is not whether or not you've learned algebra but how well you are learning it. During this course, you will be given feedback on your progress through comments Mr. Rudd makes about work you complete, scores you achieve on brief tests, and the grades you achieve based on unit, midsemester, and semester tests.

How Will Your Grades for the Course Be Determined?

Your grades for the first semester will be based on eight unit tests, a midsemester test scheduled between the fifth and sixth units, and a semester test. Your scores on these tests will influence your first-semester grade according to the following scale:

- The eight unit tests...60% (7.5% each)
- The midsemester test 15%
- The semester test..25%

Your grade for the second semester will be based on nine unit tests, a midsemester test scheduled between the twelfth and thirteenth units, and a semester test. Your scores on these tests will influence your second semester grade according to the following scale:

- The nine unit tests..60% (6.7% each)
- The midsemester test 15%
- The semester test..25%

motivation for learning mathematics rather than as an end in themselves. Casey plans for students to work with computers and calculators in every unit.

Sixth-Period Precalculus. Casey expects that all his students for the one-semester precalculus course are planning to attend college and will have already completed courses in algebra I, geometry, and algebra II with trigonometry. Thus, he is less concerned about using applications to real-life problems as a motivational strategy for engaging them in lessons. Compared with the other courses, he enjoys greater freedom in selecting content for units for the following reasons:

- Topics listed in the district's curriculum guide for precalculus (such as, exponential and logarithmic functions) are included in other Malaker High mathematics courses, primarily algebra II with trigonometry.
- From their experiences in previous courses, students should be familiar with the contents of the textbook's first three chapters. Those chapters are the only ones from the text upon which subsequent chapters depend. Thus, Casey does not feel bound to sequence units in the same order as the text chapters.
- The text is designed for a year-long course, allowing Casey to select topics from a textbook menu that is larger than he needs.

As with geometry and consumer mathematics, Casey follows the same 12-question outline to write the precalculus syllabus. Unencumbered by many restrictions, Casey plans the course so that students will not only discover and invent mathematics within well-defined content areas (as will also be the case in the other courses) but will also have ample opportunities to pursue unanticipated mathematical topics. Inserted throughout the textbook are exercises entitled Explore and Discover. Casey believes these and other activities (e.g., ones drawn from NCTM's *Addenda Series*) he plans will interest students and will lead them into areas of mathematics they can choose for themselves. Exhibit 11.4 is an example of one of the text's Explore and Discover exercises that might serve as a transition from a lesson on arithmetic and geometric series to one on fractal geometry.

Believing that the key to understanding calculus is the conceptualization and application of limit of a function, Casey feels that students in this course should engage in activities leading them to construct the concept of limits well before they are introduced to a formal definition of limit when they take calculus, either in high school or college. Casey is aware that although the calculus reform movement (Ferrini-Mundy & Graham, 1991; Rowley, 1995) is gradually impacting how calculus is taught, most calculus courses still have an algorithmic rather than a conceptual focus. Thus, he plans to include experiences that will lead students to begin to construct critical concepts such as continuity and limit for themselves. Noting that the textbook does not include a formal treatise on limits, Casey decides to select topics from units (e.g., partial sums of sequences) that will involve students in conceptualizing and applying limits, without needing to define formally the term "limit" in the conventional ϵ, δ sense.

Organizing the Classroom

With his course syllabi in hand, Casey is anticipating the opening day of school, still two weeks away. To begin organizing his classroom and working out a management plan for the year, he retrieves the textbook from the mathematics teaching methods course he took in college (the book you are now reading). Turning to Case 8.5, he carefully responds to each of the 15 questions under Classroom Organization and Ongoing Routines, to the 10 questions under One Time Only Tasks, and to the 3 questions under Reminders for the First Week's Learning Activities.

After a week of planning and organizing, he has those questions resolved and Room 213 now appears very similar to Mr. Haimowitz's room depicted in Exhibit 7.32. Unfortunately, he doesn't control Room 108 and it still appears as it looked originally.

Setting Up the Item Pool Files

Casey sets up his system for maintaining item pool files on his computer. He begins with one disk per course, with a directory for each unit and a file for each objective. He can begin writing items only for the first two units of each course because those are the only ones for which he has formulated objectives. However, he has the system ready to accept new objectives and new items for every unit as he develops them during the course of the school year. Casey is pleased to see that he will be able to draw many of the algorithmic-skill items and application-level items (with some minor modifications like adding extraneous data) from tests in the teacher's supplements accompanying his textbooks. However, he realizes he will have to originate the vast majority of items for the construct a concept and discover a relationship objectives.

Arrangements and Acquisitions

Although he spends much of the week before classes begin in meetings (e.g., a six-hour orientation meeting for all new teachers in the district and meetings of the school faculty and the Mathematics Department), Casey finds time to do the following:

Exhibit 11.4
An Explore and Discover exercise from Casey's precalculus textbook.

Explore and Discover

1. Square S_1 has vertex A_1 as shown in the diagram and each side of S_1 has length 1. Join the midpoints of the sides of S_1 to get another square S_2 with vertex A_2. Now join the midpoints of the sides of S_2 to get square S_3 with a vertex at A_3. Continue this process to obtain a sequence of squares $S_1, S_2, S_3, \ldots$.

   (a) Suppose $K_1, K_2, K_3, \ldots$ are the areas of the squares $S_1, S_2, S_3, \ldots$, respectively. Evaluate $K_1, K_2,$ and K_3. Make a guess about a formula for K_n, the area of the nth square. What type of sequence is $\{K_n\}$?

   (b) Let $a_1 = |\overline{A_1A_2}|$, $a_2 = |\overline{A_2A_3}|$, $a_3 = |\overline{A_3A_4}|$, $\ldots$. Evaluate $a_1, a_2,$ and a_3 and guess a formula for a_n. What type of sequence is $\{a_n\}$?

   (c) Does it make sense to talk about the total length of the path from A_1 to A_2 to A_3, and so on? That is, what is the sum of the infinite series $a_1 + a_2 + a_3 + \ldots$?

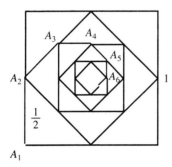

2. Follow a procedure similar to that in Exercise 1, taking points a third of the way along the side of the square rather than the midpoints, as suggested in the diagram. Answer questions **a**, **b**, and **c**.

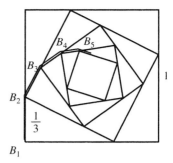

3. Consider a situation similar to that in Exercise 1, but using equilateral triangles instead of squares, as suggested in the diagram.

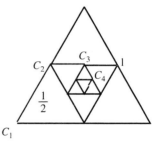

Source: From PRECALCULUS, 2nd Edition by Lawrence O. Cannon and Joseph Elich. Copyright © 1994 by HarperCollins College Publishers. Reprinted by permission.

- Visit with Mr. Tramonte to work out schedules and procedures for using the computer lab. Casey reserves the lab for his fourth-period geometry class every Wednesday during the year. Mr. Tramonte also gives him a schedule of the times each week during which Casey can send as many as six students into the lab to do independent work. As Armond had indicated, the lab is open to students and faculty for an hour before school and from 3:30 to 8 after school.

- Learn the ropes for obtaining supplies and equipment for his classroom at Malaker High. Surprising as it may seem, one of the more frustrating hindrances to classroom effectiveness faced by first-year teachers is the inability to obtain equipment and supplies for their classrooms (Duke, Cangelosi, & Knight, 1988). Each school seems to have a unique process to expedite such matters as obtaining colored board markers, replacing a burned-out lamp in an overhead projector, gaining access to a camcorder, and replacing lost books. Usually, it's a matter of identifying and befriending the right secretary or other staff member who knows how to get things done. Veteran teachers take such matters for granted and don't usually remember to inform beginning teachers of this informal network. Fortunately, Casey asked Vanessa about the process before wasting time going through formal channels.

- Obtain a set of 20 graphics calculators for use in the classroom, along with a display model for the overhead projector. Two years ago the Mathematics Department had applied for and received a grant for obtaining calculators. Don Delaney who hardly uses them for his own courses was happy to accommodate Casey's request to take them off his hands.
- Made arrangements with the bookstore to make graphics calculators available for student purchase at a discounted price.
- Coordinate plans for integrating curricula with other teachers, including the following:
  - Mr. Bosnick, an art teacher, agrees to have students apply geometric principles they learn from Casey to art projects.
  - Ms. Deere, an English teacher, and Casey plan a joint project in which students will use skills and principles developed in both consumer mathematics and communications classes to produce videotape programs.
- Show some of the other mathematics teachers how to set up a computerized item pool file and set up a computer network system for sharing measurement items with one another.

THE BEGINNING OF AN EVENTFUL SCHOOL YEAR

Opening Day

Casey bases plans for the first day's classes on the model exemplified by Mr. Krebs's in Case 8.4. However, unlike Mr. Krebs, Casey does not prepare videotape presentations. For each class he prepares name cards and a questionnaire/task sheet for students to work on as soon as they are seated in the classroom. The questionnaire/task sheets for the four courses are shown in Exhibits 11.5–11.8.

Casey designed the questionnaire/task sheets with the following purposes in mind:

- The students will immediately get busy doing mathematics while he takes care of some administrative chores like distributing textbooks. This, he feels, will help to establish the businesslike classroom learning environment that he read about in Chapter 8 of this book.
- The students will be both challenged by and successful with the tasks. The algebra students, for example, already know how to add simple fractions, but they've never before had to describe the process they use. Also, most of the items involve expressing opinions, describing observations, and reporting about themselves—things everyone can do, but which require thinking rather than only remembering.

- The students will begin to get the following impressions about the course they're starting under Mr. Rudd's direction:
  - The mathematics they will learn is related to their own individual interests.
  - They are expected to make judgments, and those judgments are valued.
  - They are expected to write about mathematics.
  - Their experiences in this course will be different from those they've had in previous courses.
- Students will pursue tasks they will later learn to accomplish more efficiently with mathematics planned for subsequent lessons in the course.
- Casey will be able to utilize students' responses to the questionnaires in a later session that helps students understand the nature of the course's mathematical content. This will be done in two ways:
  - As he discusses the course syllabus with the class, he will pick up on their responses to the question, What is algebra (geometry, consumer mathematics, precalculus)?
  - In subsequent lessons, he will occasionally make references to their responses to this questionnaire.
- Casey will make use of information gained from responses to the final question on the task sheet in planning lessons; he will be able to select topics for problems that will interest the students.

Just before each class, Casey places a name card and a questionnaire/task sheet on each student's desk. The 55-minute period is spent as follows:

1. He greets students at the door as they enter and directs each to locate the desk with her or his name card and to begin completing the questionnaire/task sheet.
2. As students answer the questions and work on the tasks, Casey distributes textbooks and course syllabi and takes the roll.
3. All students have an opportunity to work on the tasks, but no one completes them before Casey interrupts the work and goes through the course syllabus (see Exhibit 11.3). He uses the sections of the syllabus as an advance organizer for a presentation in which he communicates expectations, introduces some classroom procedures, and discusses the nature of mathematics. The students' work on the questionnaire/task sheet is utilized in discussions stimulated by the second section of the syllabus (What is algebra, geometry, consumer mathematics, or precalculus?). For example:

- In the algebra class he uses students' responses to set the stage for working with variables and generalizing rules of arithmetic.

Exhibit 11.5
Questionnaire/task sheet Casey uses with his algebra I class on the first day or school.

1. What is your name? _____

2. How many minutes does it take to listen to a rock Top-40 song six times from beginning to end?
_____

3. How many minutes does it take to listen to a rock Top-40 song six times from beginning to end?
_____

4. How many minutes does it take to listen to six different rock Top-40 songs from beginning to end?
_____

5. Simplify each of the following (showing two steps along the way):

   $\frac{3}{7} + \frac{2}{3}$ _____ _____ _____

   $\frac{2}{5} + \frac{1}{3}$ _____ _____ _____

   $\frac{1}{5} + \frac{3}{4}$ _____ _____ _____

Now, use the space just below to write a *description* of the process you used to find the three simplified sums of the fractions just given. Do *not* use the names of any specific numbers (such as 3/7, 3, or 7) in your description. Describe the *general* process you use for adding any two fractions like the ones above.

> Your description of the process:
>
>
>
>
>
>

6. Fill in the blank with one of the numbers that makes the following statement true:

$$7 - \rule{1cm}{0.4pt} > 3$$

The number you put in the blank is not the *only* one that will work. But not just any number will work. Make up a rule for choosing a number for the blank that makes the statement true. Write the rule in here:

> Your rule for picking a number that works:
>
>
>
>
>
>

7. Make a list of 10 important questions about which you're going to have to make a decision during the next 9 months:

   a. _____
   b. _____
   c. _____
   d. _____
   e. _____
   f. _____
   g. _____
   h. _____
   i. _____
   j. _____

Exhibit 11.6
Questionnaire/task sheet Casey uses with his geometry classes on the first day of school.

1. What is your name?_____

2. Carefully look at the photograph of the two trees. Write a *description* of how one tree looks different from the other.

_____
_____
_____
_____

Write a *description* of how the two trees look the same.

_____
_____
_____
_____

3. Carefully look at the photograph of the two people. Write a *description* of how one of the people looks different from the other.

_____
_____
_____
_____

Write a *description* of how the two people look the same.

_____
_____
_____
_____

- Modifying an idea he picked up from reading Case 8.4, Casey uses students' descriptions of figures in the photographs of Exhibit 11.6 to explain the focus of geometry.
- He raises the types of personalized problems the consumer mathematics students will be learning to solve throughout the course.
- With the precalculus class, he uses the peeking through a keyhole tasks to explain what he calls the "keyhole logic" of mathematics, in which we use our intellects to expand what we know beyond what we empirically observe.

4. Casey assigns homework that includes the completion of the questionnaire/task sheet.

Casey is generally pleased with how the first day goes. The students seem willing to cooperate, and most of them act friendly and try to follow his

Exhibit 11.6
Continued

4. Carefully look at the photograph of the two balls. Write a *description* of how one ball looks different from the other.

_____

_____

_____

_____

Write a *description* of how the two balls look the same.

_____

_____

_____

_____

5. Carefully look at the photograph of the two kites. Write a *description* of how one of the kites looks different from the other.

_____

_____

_____

_____

Write a *description* of how the two kites look the same.

_____

_____

_____

_____

6. Make a list of 10 important questions about which you're going to have to make a decision during the next 9 months.

a. _____

b. _____

c. _____

d. _____

e. _____

f. _____

g. _____

h. _____

i. _____

j. _____

Exhibit 11.7
Questionnaire/task sheet Casey uses with his consumer mathematics class on the first day of school.

1. What is your name? _____

2. What is something you bought during the month of August?
   _____
   Where did you buy it? _____
   About how much did it cost? _____
   Why did you make this purchase? _____
   _____

   When you decided to buy this thing, did you consider other options (like buying something else or buying another brand or not buying anything at all)? Describe the options.
   _____
   _____
   _____

   How do you know whether or not you selected the best option?
   _____
   _____
   _____

3. When people are deciding on objects to buy, what are some of the things they can do to figure out how to get the most for their money?
   _____
   _____
   _____
   _____

4. Suppose you're thinking about taking a job selling clothes in a store. Would you rather earn a salary that pays you by the number of hours you work or a salary based on the amount of sales you make?
   _____
   _____

   How would you go about finding out which way you would make more money?
   _____
   _____
   _____
   _____

5. In your opinion, who is currently the most successful singer in the world?
   _____
   Name another popular singer who, one of your friends might argue, should have been named in the above blank:
   _____
   Defend why you think the singer you chose is more successful than your friend's choice. Write out your argument in the blanks below:
   _____
   _____
   _____
   _____

6. Suppose you are going to be saving money over the next few years to buy something really expensive (like a CD player, motorcycle, or car). Where should you keep the money you save until you're ready to make the purchase—in a savings account, checking account, secure safe, in a bank at your home, in U.S. bonds, or where? Describe how you might go about making this decision for yourself.
   _____
   _____
   _____
   _____

7. Make a list of 10 important questions about which you're going to have to make a decision during the next 9 months.
   a. _____
   b. _____
   c. _____
   d. _____
   e. _____
   f. _____
   g. _____
   h. _____
   i. _____
   j. _____

Exhibit 11.8
Questionnaire/task sheet Casey uses with his precalculus class on the first day of school.

---

1. What is your name? _____

2. Suppose that you are by yourself in this unfamiliar building. You're in a hallway and come to a door. Before opening the door, you want to know what's on the other side. Fortunately, it's one of those old doors with the kind of keyholes you can look through. You peek through the keyhole and you see what appears in the picture below. *Describe* exactly what you *see* through the keyhole—and only what you can actually see.

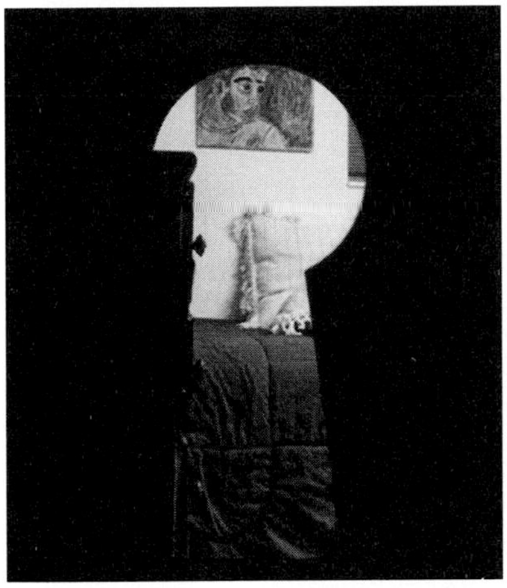

Your description: _____

_____

_____

_____

_____

_____

_____

_____

_____

_____

_____

_____

_____

_____

Now, *describe* what you would *infer* the room behind the door looks like, based on the limited view you had through the keyhole.

_____

_____

_____

3. Now you've arrived at the outside of another door. Again, you look through the keyhole. *Describe* exactly what you *see* through this keyhole as pictured below.

Your description: _____

_____

_____

_____

_____

_____

_____

_____

_____

_____

_____

_____

_____

Exhibit 11.8
Continued

Now, *describe* what you would *infer* the room behind the door looks like based on the limited view you had through the keyhole:

_____

_____

_____

_____

4. According to a particular hospital's records, the number of people treated in the emergency room for drug-induced traumas were as follows for the year 1991:

Jan: 31	Apr: 40	Jul: NA	Oct: 37
Feb: 33	May: 39	Aug: 48	Nov: 35
Mar: NA	Jun: 45	Sep: NA	Dec: 34

(NA indicates records not available for that month)

Does the given data suggest any possible pattern relative to the relation between frequency of drug-induced traumas and the time of the year? Explain your answer:

_____

_____

_____

_____

Based on the data, what would you guess March, July, and September would show if the records for those months were available? Explain the reasons for your answer.

_____

_____

_____

_____

Estimate the total number of drug-induced traumas treated at that hospital's emergency room during 1991. Explain how you arrived at your estimate.

_____

_____

_____

_____

5. Estimate the area of the rectangular region in terms of the number of ☐ units:

Your estimate: _____

Exhibit 11.8
Continued

6. Estimate the area of the rectangular region below in terms of the number of ☐ units:

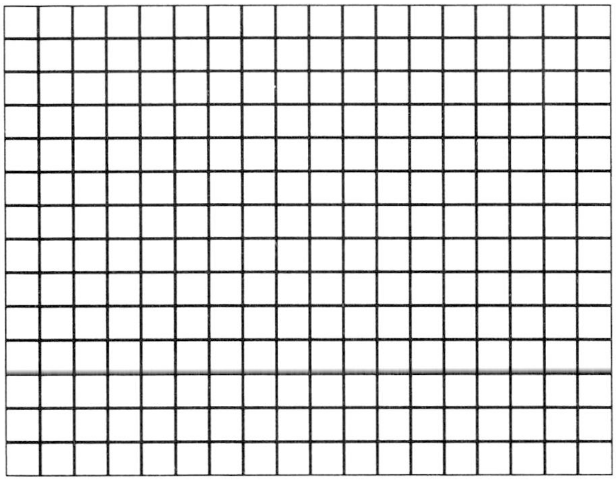

Your estimate: _____

7. Estimate the area of the region below in terms of the number of ☐ units:

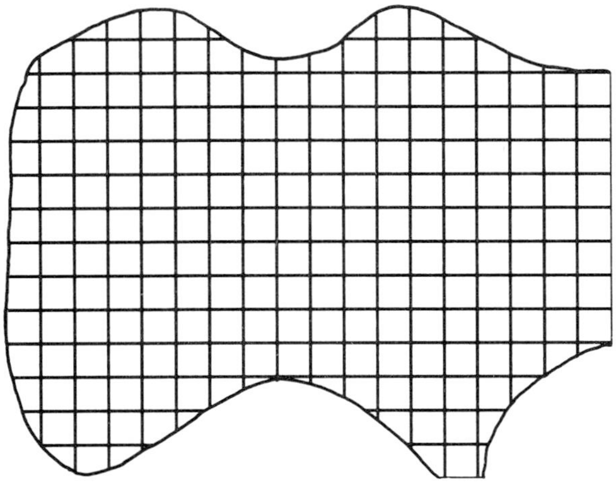

Your estimate: _____

8. Make a list of 10 important questions you're going to have to make a decision about which during the next 9 months.

   a. _____
   b. _____
   c. _____
   d. _____
   e. _____
   f. _____
   g. _____
   h. _____
   i. _____
   j. _____

directions. After the first few minutes of each period, his nervousness disappears and he surprises himself with his own glibness—speaking fluently and making the right responses to students' questions and behaviors. His energy level and enthusiasm peaks in the second half of each class.

Because many students are reluctant to fill out the questionnaire/task sheets without seemingly constant explanations and feedback from Casey, the administrative duties take longer in every class than he had planned. Thus, no class gets through its syllabus and Casey fears that the students are left hanging at the end of the period, without understanding course expectations and the meaning of algebra, geometry, consumer mathematics, or precalculus. He is especially anxious to meet with them on the second day to finish explaining the syllabi and get back on schedule.

After the fourth period went especially well, Casey concludes that dealing with the disadvantages of teaching in Room 108 may be easier than he had anticipated. However, after supervising lunch and arriving back in his own room just prior to fifth period, he discovers that the fourth-period health science class has left the room in disarray. The consumer mathematics class gets off to a rough start and he is flustered because he is unable to get the room back in order and the materials laid out by 1:30. The students don't appear surprised by the disorder nor do they seem to mind it. In fact, some of the students in his other classes are surprised by how well he has things organized.

Learning from Experiences

Becoming More Assertive. The ensuring weeks provide Casey with the richest learning experiences of his life. Possibly the most important lesson is that he must be *assertive* to be successful.

Early on, Casey discovers the need to be assertive with his colleagues. For example, just before the second day's homeroom period, Casey visits Ms. Bomgars, who teaches the fourth-period health science class in Room 213. Casey wants to discuss the problem her class created for him yesterday, but he would rather discuss it out of earshot of her homeroom students, some of whom are milling around the room. The conversation begins:

Casey: Hello, Ms. Bomgars, do you have a minute to talk?

Ms. Bomgars: Of course, Mr. Rudd—always glad to meet with a colleague! What can I do for you?

Casey: It's about your fourth-period class using Room 213. Could we step away from these students to discuss a problem I had yesterday with the room?

Ms. Bomgars: Oh, don't worry about these kids; they're not interested in what we're saying. What's your problem?

Casey: Well, it took me a long time to get the room ready yesterday for my fifth-period consumer mathematics class.

Ms. Bomgars: I thought all you math guys needed was a piece of chalk and you're ready!

Casey: (laughing with Ms. Bomgars) That's a common misconception, but really, I'd appreciate if you could—

A student comes up, interrupting Casey by asking Ms. Bomgars a question. She answers the student and they briefly converse as Casey waits.

Ms. Bomgars: Excuse me, Mr. Rudd—it's always something. You were saying?

Casey: I'd really appreciate it if you could have your students put things back as they were when they came into the room.

Ms. Bomgars: We took out all the extra chairs we brought in with us when we left. Were some left in?

Casey: No, that was great. It's just that—

Another student interrupts; because the bell is about to ring, Casey interrupts the student, to say, "Excuse me, Ms. Bomgars, I've got to get to my homeroom."

Ms. Bomgars: Thanks for coming by—I'm glad to help you out any way I can.

Casey: Thank you, I appreciate it.

The room is in no better shape when Casey arrives for fifth period than it was the first day; the problem persists for the remainder of the week. Realizing that he failed to tell Ms. Bomgars what he wanted out of fear of creating ill feeling, Casey is angry at himself for not communicating assertively.

Over the weekend he phones Ms. Bomgars:

Ms. Bomgars: Hello.

Casey: Hello, Marilyn, this is Casey Rudd. We spoke just before your homeroom Tuesday.

Ms. Bomgars: Oh, hi, Casey. How are things going?

Casey: Some things are going very well, others aren't. *We* still have a problem to solve regarding sharing *my* classroom. I'd really like to meet with you in my room so we can work out a solution.

Ms. Bomgars: You want to meet on Monday?

Casey: It has to be at a time when students won't be there to interrupt us. I can meet you any time today or tomorrow—or Monday at 7:15 in the morning would be okay too.

Ms. Bomgars: You seem pretty serious; I'd better meet you today. Would an hour from now be okay?

Casey: That would be great. See you in my room in an hour. Thank you very much.

Ms. Bomgars: Good-bye, Casey.

Casey: Good-bye, Marilyn.

Now that Ms. Bomgars understands that Casey is serious about the two of them solving what she now perceives as her problem as well as Casey's, she is very receptive to Casey's explanations of just how the room should be left after fourth period. In the classroom Casey readily points out exactly what he expects. Casey is pleased with the agreed upon arrangement and the way Ms. Bomgars leaves the room for the rest of the semester.

Casey also learns to communicate assertively with parents. After school one day, Casey passes one of his algebra students, Alphonse, walking with his father in the hallway:

Casey: Hello, Alphonse.

Alphonse: Hi, Mr. Rudd. Mr. Rudd, this is my dad.

Casey: Hello, Mr. Oldham, I'm Casey Rudd, very nice to meet you.

Mr. Oldham: So you're Alphonse's algebra teacher. You know, I tell my kids all the time, subjects like algebra and Latin—where you have to memorize—those are the subjects where you discipline the mind. Study algebra and you can make yourself do anything. Just because you don't use it much, today's kids don't want to learn it like the frilly subjects—but man needs to discipline his mind with stuff like algebra. It does for the mind what football does for the body! Isn't that right, Mr. Rudd; you tell him.

Smiling broadly at Mr. Oldham but quickly thinking to himself, "If only I had stayed in my room another 20 seconds, I would have avoided this dilemma. On the one hand Mr. Oldham has the best of intentions and I'm happy he's trying to encourage Alphonse to study algebra. He wants to support my efforts and I really appreciate that. But he's sending all the wrong messages about the value of algebra. I don't want Alphonse to believe what he's saying, but then I hate to contradict what a father says in front of his child!" Not wanting to appear insulting Casey only continues to smile and says, "I agree that algebra is surely important for everyone to learn. It's a pleasure meeting you, Mr. Oldham. Thank you for introducing me to your father, Alphonse."

The next day in algebra class, during a discussion about using open sentences to solve real-life problems, Alphonse says, "Yeah, but the real purpose of algebra is to train your memory. That's what my dad says, and Mr. Rudd agreed with him yesterday."

After diplomatically attempting to correct the record about his beliefs relative to the purpose of algebra, Casey resolves to be more assertive in communicating with parents and in responding to misconceived statements about mathematics.

Fortunately, Casey's resolve is still fresh in his mind as he meets with Ms. Minnefield about her daughter Melinda's work in geometry:

Ms. Minnefield: You know, Melinda really has a lot of respect for you; she raves about your class. That's why I thought you should be the one to help me with this problem.

Casey: What problem?

Ms. Minnefield: Well, Melinda has got herself involved with this boy who is much too old for her. She keeps seeing him even though she knows I don't like it.

Casey: I can see you're concerned.

Ms. Minnefield: I thought since she likes geometry so much, I could use that to get her to break it off.

Casey: I'm not following you.

Ms. Minnefield: Well, you know how math is harder for girls than boys. I told her if she keeps spending time with this boy, she was going to do bad in geometry. That's why girls don't do good in math because they get all goo-goo over boys. Do you see what I mean?

Casey: Not really, ma'am, but please go on.

Ms. Minnefield: Well, I thought you could back me on this—tell her she's going to flunk if she doesn't spend more time studying geometry and less time fooling around with that boy.

Casey: Ms. Minnefield, I really appreciate you sharing your ideas with me, and I appreciate your concern for Melinda's welfare. You, being Melinda's parent, know far more about this situation than I. I'll confine my remarks to what I do know about. First of all, research studies clearly point out that girls do *not* have any more trouble learning mathematics than boys. It's a common misconception that they do, but they absolutely don't.

Ms. Minnefield: But I had always heard that.

Casey: If you're interested, I can give you some journal articles that explain the facts about girls and women in mathematics.

Ms. Minnefield: Oh, that would be nice of you.

Casey: Second, and more to the point here, my job is to teach Melinda and the other students mathematics as professionally and responsibly as possible. I cannot in good conscience base Melinda's grade on anything other than how well she achieves the goals of the geometry course.

Ms. Minnefield: Well, I thought if you just told her, she'd listen.

Casey: I'm flattered that Melinda would have that much confidence in what I say. But if I start lying to her, I'll lose her confidence.

Ms. Minnefield: I don't mean for you to lie to her.

Casey: I know, Ms. Minnefield. You want what's best for your daughter.

In his classroom, Casey encourages more interaction among students than they had been used to in mathematics courses with previous teachers. Early in the year, some students tended to take advantage of their freedom of expression by drifting off the current topic. Casey, not wanting to alienate students or to discourage communications about mathematics, allowed some of the discussions to waste valuable class time. For instance, during a precalculus class, the difference between "negative x" and "x is negative" is being discussed:

Opal: If x is negative, then x has to be less than 0. But negative x could be a positive number.

Bernie: That's too picky. It's like in Spanish class, what's the difference between *temar* and *temer*? Mr. Waiters makes such a big deal over whether you say *ar* or *er!*" Who cares?

Rita: It gives him something to grade you on!

Bernie: He's not fair . . .

The discussion continues in this vein for several more minutes, with Casey worrying about the appropriateness of Mr. Waiters being the topic of conversation and about time being spent on the topic at hand.

After a few similar experiences, Casey resolves to be more assertive in such situations, and in subsequent weeks he is more likely to respond as he does in the following instance. During a geometry lesson about applying triangle congruence theorems to real-life situations, this conversation takes place:

Eric: In basketball there's a strategy you call the three-man game, in which you form a triangle. The triangle should be equilateral.

Casey: Yes, Damien.

Damien: Who cares about basketball? Eric's always got to talk about basketball. It's stupid!

Casey: Eric?

Eric: You've got to be better to play basketball than to—

Casey: Do not debate your opinions about basketball in here today. Even those that don't like basketball can learn something about equilateral triangles from Eric's example of the three-person strategy. Please repeat your example, Eric, without defending your opinion about basketball.

Addressing Behavior Management Problems. It is in meeting his most challenging responsibility of keeping students on-task and responding to off-task behaviors that Casey finds the greatest need to be assertive. At times, he resents having to work continually to maintain students' interest and to teach students who tend to get off-task to be on-task. He begins what turns out to be a productive conversation with Vanessa with an expression of frustration:

Casey: Some days I'd just love to walk into class and discuss mathematics without having to worry about Frankie over in the corner who is going to fall asleep unless I'm either right on top of her or we're discussing a problem that strikes within the limited range of what she fancies! Or just once, getting through a session without having to deal with Brad's showing off or Christi's yakking with anyone who'll listen to her—wouldn't that be nice? But that's too much to ask for!

Vanessa: Obviously, you're having one of those days!

Casey: It's just that we were getting into our first formal proof in third period today, and they seemed so enthusiastic. But then they started to get a little noisy—some off-task talking. I let it go at first because I didn't want to put a damper on their enthusiasm. But then it became obvious that Christi and Livonia's conversation had nothing to do with geometry—right in the middle of my explanation!

Vanessa: What did you do?

Casey: I kept on explaining the theorem, and just moved over to them and caught their eyes—that usually works for me.

Vanessa: But it didn't this time.

Casey: Oh, the two of them stopped as long as I stood there, but then other conversations broke out, and Christi and Livonia started up again as soon as I moved away. Five minutes later I'd had enough and made the mistake of threatening the class.

Vanessa: What did you say?

Casey: I told them if they didn't pipe down, they'd be sorry when the test came around. I knew that wasn't the right thing to say, but the noise just got to me and I reacted.

Vanessa: Did they quiet down?

Casey: Yes, but then Brad whispered something to Lin-Tau and she started giggling. That's when I jumped on them and called Brad a show-off. In other words, I handled it all wrong and made matters worse.

Vanessa: So you weren't Mr. Perfect. You let things go too far and reacted with hostility instead of assertiveness—the way most of us react when we feel we've lost control.

Casey: But I know better. I applied none of the stuff that's worked for me in the past—assertiveness, descriptive language, reinforcement principles—they all went out the window!

Vanessa: I don't think you threw your principles out of the window; I think you waited too long to respond decisively. Most teachers wait until they are too near their threshold for tolerating noise or other annoyances before dealing with students being off-task.

Casey: You're saying I should have stepped in and dealt with the early minor incidents before things escalated. I was passive in the beginning instead of being assertive. Then things got out of hand.

Vanessa: And when things get out of hand, it's natural to be hostile.

Casey: And that's why I'm really upset—at my own hostile behavior. I'm afraid I've lost some of the control and good will I've worked to build up to this point. I don't have much enthusiasm for tomorrow's class.

Vanessa: What do you have planned?

Casey: Before this, I was going to continue the session on proofs.

Vanessa: I think you have two choices. You either go on with your original plan and conduct the class as if none of this happened—but have an alternative plan ready to go to as soon as they become uncooperative—you know, one where they have to work on their own while you monitor their every move.

Casey: Yeah, I know what you mean. There was an example of that in my mathematics methods course from college. (See Case 8.30.)

Vanessa: The second choice is to start the period off by expressing your feelings about what happened, even indicating that you're disappointed in your own behavior for letting things go too far and then acting with hostility as a result. But if you use this tactic, make sure to assertively demand their cooperation. If it turns out you don't get it even after clearing the air, then go immediately to the alternative learning-activity plan.

Throughout the year, Vanessa and Casey regularly share ideas on handling discipline problems, as well as on other aspects of teaching. They even work out a plan by which Casey can send a student who behaves uncooperatively to Vanessa for custodial care until the end of the class period. Casey reciprocates by providing the same service for Vanessa.

Benefiting from Instructional Supervision. *Instructional supervision* is the art of helping teachers improve their teaching performances (Cangelosi, 1991, pp. 6–7). Vanessa serves as an instructional supervisor for Casey by sharing ideas on planning, managing student behavior, and other aspects of instruction. Working with Casey not only helps his classroom effectiveness, it also benefits Vanessa's teaching because conferring with Casey causes her to analyze problem situations and reflect on instructional activities more than she would otherwise. As the year progresses and Casey's confidence soars, Casey more and

more serves as an instructional supervisor for Vanessa as well. Consistent with research findings relative to instructional supervisory practices, Casey and Vanessa's cooperative partnership provides them with the most effective type of help with their teaching (Bang-Jensen, 1986; Brandt, 1989).

Accustomed to sharing ideas with Vanessa from his first day at Malaker, Casey seeks and listens comfortably to suggestions from other instructional supervisors as well (other teachers, his department head, principal, and the district mathematics teaching supervisor). Casey does not always agree with or take the suggestions he receives; however, everyone stimulates his ideas for everything from coping with individual differences among students to eliciting parents' cooperation.

Casey's most frustrating problem is finding enough time to do what he considers necessary for optimal classroom effectiveness. The following exchange with Armond Ziegler, Mathematics Department head, helps:

Casey: There are so many things I ought to be doing but never get to around to!

Armond: Like what?

Casey: I need to develop enrichment materials for some students who are ahead of the rest of the class. And there are parents I should be contacting. I haven't been entering items into my item pool file as regularly as I should.

Armond: Okay, slow down! I hear you. You have to realize that it's impossible to do everything you want to or should do. Make some difficult decisions and partition your time. Prioritize from what you must do—like sleep, eat, and show up for class—to what is critical, down to what you really want to do but could put off, and then finally to what isn't all that important. Put a high priority on things that will help you save time down the road—like keeping up with that item pool file. Neglect something else instead.

Casey: I try to keep to a schedule, but then students come in for tutoring, and then—wham!—time I schedule for formulating examples for class is used up!

Armond: Don't allow it to happen; take control. You wouldn't drop in on a lawyer or physician without an appointment. Don't let your clients do that to you.

Casey: What clients?

Armond: Your students are your clients. Also don't let parents, colleagues, or administrators abuse your schedule either.

Casey: What about you? Should I tell you to buzz off when you ask me to turn in my supply order while I'm in the midst of scoring tests? How about Harriet (the principal)? Can I put her off too?

Armond: You can tell me to buzz off anytime. And I know Harriet well enough to think she'll respect your businesslike approach, and understand that you've got your time scheduled.

Casey: But everything can't be scheduled. Unanticipated things have to be take care of.

Armond: Of course they do, but get a calendar anyway and use it as an organizational tool for your own convenience—not something you blindly follow.

Casey: Today is a case in point. I planned to phone a couple of parents during the B lunch period, but then we were short a supervisor, so I had to stay that period besides my usual A lunch period.

Armond: Those are the times when I take a triage approach. I decide where my time can be most efficiently spent. Some crises are beyond our reasonable control and others can wait.

Casey: So, now I have to find the time to schedule my time!

Preparing for Administrative Supervision. Instructional supervision is concerned solely with improving instructional practices. On the other hand, *administrative supervision* is concerned with quality control (Cangelosi, 1991, pp. 163–173). Malaker High and school district administrators are responsible for determining whether or not Casey teaches well enough to be retained as a teacher and given incentives to remain on Malaker High's faculty. The district has an administrative supervisory program in which the classroom instructional practices of each beginning teacher are evaluated three times a year. The outcomes of these evaluations hinge primarily on observational data gathered by a team composed of the school principal, the district subject supervisor, and a same-subject teacher from another school.

Vanessa helps Casey prepare for the scheduled visits from his observational team by doing the following:

- Advising him to use preobservational conferences to apprise team members of the instructional strategies they can anticipate seeing him employ.
- Suggesting that it is appropriate to utilize postobservational conferences not only for learning from the team's report but also to express his own needs regarding support services from the administration.
- Simulating a team visit, with Vanessa playing the role of the team in a preobservational conference, an in-class observation (during one of her nonteaching periods), and a postobservational conference.

In anticipation of the team visits, Casey is quite nervous. However, after the first few minutes of the first in-class observation, he relaxes and learns to enjoy the attention. It helps that he thinks of his visitors as colleagues whose goals of helping students learn mathematics are the same as his own. Although he feels the team never sees him at his best, his performances receive better than satisfactory ratings and his confidence continues to rise.

SAMPLE ALGEBRA I UNIT

Designing a Unit on Factoring Polynomials

Ten weeks have elapsed since the opening of school. Casey's algebra I class is in the early stages of Unit 6, Polynomials. Casey anticipates the class beginning Unit 7, Factoring Polynomials, in two weeks, and starts designing it.

It's nearly 10 p.m. as Casey sits in front of his computer. Strewn about are the algebra I course syllabus, algebra I textbook, reference books, a calculator, paper, pens, pencils, and his teaching notebook. Since August, as ideas occur to him that might be useful for future lessons, he has jotted them down in this teaching notebook. He reads the goal of Unit 7:

> Understands why certain factoring algorithms work and can use them in problem solving.

He thinks: "I need to define this goal with objectives. Let's see, why do I want to teach them about factoring polynomials in the first place? Primarily because they need to know how to factor and why factoring works in order to learn how to find roots of higher-degree equations, inequalities, and functions. So this unit should really emphasize discovery of relationships underlying certain factoring algorithms, as well as the development of their skills with those algorithms. The real application comes in Units 8, 9, and so forth. But I had better build at least one application objective in here, or I'll lose them before they even get to Unit 8.

"Okay, so I'll end with an application objective, but where do I start! Better first get them to conceptualize the role of factoring in problem solving—the value of undoing multiplication. This'll almost be like an affective objective—but, I'll stick with discover a relationship."

In a few minutes Casey formulates Objective A, as listed in Exhibit 11.9. He then reviews pages 210–243 of the textbook, which will be the primary reference for this unit. He plans to cover the four principal factoring algorithms included in those pages with two objectives each—one discover a relationship objective for the students to understand why the algorithm works and one algorithmic-skill objective for the students to execute it efficiently. After coming up with those eight objectives (listed as C, D, E, F, G, H, I, and J in Exhibit 11.9), he decides he should include an objective involving comprehension of the language related to factoring polynomials. He feels it is important to list it in order to guard against just assuming students follow and use communication conventions about the topic—a mistake he made with previous units. Consequently, he formulates Objective B, as listed in Exhibit 11.9. He notes that the terms specified as content for Objective B are all terms to which students were previously exposed—but only in the context of working with integer constants, not polynomials.

Like Objective B, Objective K is not a central objective of the unit, but computer programming is something he's trying to build into most units. Achievement of the application objective, L is to be the climax of the unit.

For purposes of the blueprint for the unit test, Casey weights the objectives. It is past midnight when Casey completes his plan for Unit 7 as it appears in Exhibit 11.9.

Day -1: Reviewing the Unit Test on Polynomials and Setting the Stage for the Unit on Factoring

It's Monday, the last day the algebra I class devotes to Unit 6. After reviewing the unit test, Casey calls attention to one of the items from the test—an item Casey had planted on the test just for this moment. The item as most students worked it out, appears in Exhibit 11.10.

Casey engages the students in a brief reasoning-level question/discussion session:

Casey: I'm just looking at the $-3ab$ and wondering what it means. What is it? Juaquin.
Juaquin: It's a number.
Casey: I agree. But what kind of number—large, small, what? Dustin.
Dustin: It's negative.
Casey: What do you want to say, Kevin?
Kevin: It wouldn't be negative if ab is negative or 0.
Casey: Raise your hand if you disagree with Kevin. So, everyone agrees that $-3ab$ could be negative, 0, or positive depending on a and b. Give us a number, Cassandra.
Cassandra: 24.
Casey: If $-3ab$ is 24, what would a and b be? Mary.
Mary: You still don't know, because the value of one would affect the other.
Casey: -3 times what equals 24? Dustin.
Dustin: 8—no! I mean -8.
Casey: So, what's ab if $-3ab$ is 24? Mary.
Mary: -8.
Casey: If ab is -8, what is a? Omar.
Omar: You don't know unless you know b. If b were 2 a would be -4.

Casey: Thank you. . . . I see quite a few of you still have something to contribute to this matter, but we're nearly out of time, so I'll explain the homework assignment and we'll start Unit 7 tomorrow.

Casey distributes the task sheet shown in Exhibit 11.11, without the numerals 24, 24, 10, and 0 written in the blanks. He gives them directions for completing the sheet for homework:

Casey: Look at item 1 of the tasksheet. Fill in the blank with the number Cassandra chose for us. What was it again, Russell?
Russell: 24.
Casey: Thank you. Now, plug the 24 into the two blanks of item 2. For the first item you need to find all possible integer *pairs* for a and b that make the statement true. That's really only one table; I split it up into two parts just to conserve space. For item 2, find three more pairs that work, but this time you aren't restricted to integers. Yes, Mary?
Mary: We have to use fractions?
Casey: Try fractions if you like—as long as they're real numbers. Now, since Cassandra got to choose the number for the blank in the first two items, I'm going to choose numbers for the third and fourth. Put 10 in the blank for item 3 and put 0 in for item 4. Yes, Blair?
Blair: That's not fair, we only got to pick one number—you get two!
Casey: (laughing with Blair and most of the other students) You're absolutely right, it isn't fair. That's one of the many great things about being a teacher—it's not always necessary to be fair!

Planning for Day 1

After school Casey works on lessons for Tuesday's five classes. He starts with plans for the first day of Unit 7 for algebra I. Casey thinks: "I hope that little homework assignment will turn their thoughts toward undoing multiplication. But for this first lesson on Objective A, I really need to grab their attention with a real-life problem that'll stimulate them thinking why we ever want to look at factors."

He checks his unit plan (Exhibit 11.9) and rereads the part pertaining to teaching for Objective A. Struggling to come up with the attention-grabbing problem to open the lesson, he considers using a bank interest problem in which the interest earned is a given and questions are raised about possibilities for the variables *principle* and *interest rate*. Trying to use that same idea, but shifting it to a more interesting topic, he thinks about a situation in which a politician brags that she has funneled so many thousands of dollars into a project that helps crime victims; he could then have the

Exhibit 11.9
Casey's plan for the algebra I unit on factoring polynomials.

Course: Algebra I

Unit No.: 7 (of 17)

Title: Factoring Polynomials

Goal: Understands why certain factoring algorithms work and can use them in problem solving.

Weighted Objectives:

(06%)   A. Explains how factoring polynomials can facilitate problem solving.   (*discover a relationship*)

(06%)   B. Translates the meaning of the following terms in the context of communications relative to algebraic polynomial expressions: "factor," "prime factorization," "greatest common factor," "difference of squares," "perfect square trinomial," and "prime polynomial."   (*comprehension*)

(09%)   C. Explains why the distributive property of multiplication over addition can be used to express a polynomial in factored form.   (*discover a relationship*)

(09%)   D. Factors polynomials expressible in the form $ax + ay$.   (*algorithmic skill*)

(09%)   E. Explains why polynomials expressible in the form $a^2 - b^2$ can be expressed in factored form as $(a + b)(a - b)$.   (*discover a relationship*)

(09%)   F. Factors polynomials expressible in the form $a^2 - b^2$.   (*algorithmic skill*)

(09%)   G. Explains why polynomials expressible in the form $a^2 + 2ab + b^2$ can be expressed in factored form as $(a + b)^2$.   (*discover a relationship*)

(09%)   H. Factors polynomials expressible in the form $a^2 + 2ab + b^2$.   (*algorithmic skill*)

(10%)   I. Explains why some polynomials expressible in the form $ax^2 + bx + c$, where x is a real variable and a, b, and c are rational constants, can be expressed in factored form as $(dx + e)(fx + g)$, where d, e, f, and g are rational constants, and others cannot.   (*discover a relationship*)

(10%)   J. Given a polynomial expressible in the form $ax^2 + bx + c$, where x is a real variable and a, b, and c are rational constants, determines if it can be expressed in factored form as $(dx + e)(fx + g)$, where d, e, f, and g are rational constants, and if so, does so.   (*algorithmic skill*)

(04%)   K. Writes and uses computer programs to execute the algorithms covered in the above listed objectives.   (*comprehension*)

(10%)   L. Given a real-life problem, explain how, if at all, factoring polynomials can be utilized in solving that problem.   (*application*)

Estimated Number of Class Periods: 12

Textbook Page References: 210–243. Unless otherwise indicated, page numbers referred to in the overall lesson plan are from the course textbook (Foster, Rath, & Winters, 1986).

Overall Plan for Lesson:

I will confront students with a problem either in class or as part of a homework assignment that will be designed to set the stage for an inductive lesson relative to **Objective A.** That inductive lesson should be designed to stimulate students to discover the need to "undo" multiplication and to generalize from constant expressions in factored form to variable expressions in factored form. I'll need to design examples and nonexample problems for the lesson, but some useful follow-up practice exercises, as well as needed definitions, are given in the text on pp. 211–213. (Estimated time needed: *1.5 class periods plus homework*)

For **Objective B,** direct-instructional and comprehension-level activities will be integrated within lessons for the other objectives to help students utilize the

Exhibit 11.9
Continued

vocabulary terms in communications. (Estimated time needed: *2–10 intermittent minutes each class period plus homework*)

For **Objective C,** I will conduct a relatively brief inductive lesson to help students discover the algorithm using their understanding of the distributive property. Examples on p. 214, the geometric paradigm on p. 216, and the Excursions in Algebra on p. 215 of the text should prove useful. (Estimated time needed: *0.5 of a class period plus homework*)

I will conduct a direct instructional lesson for **Objective D** as a natural extension to the previous lesson. Adequate practice exercises are on p. 215. (Estimated time needed: *0.4 of a class period plus homework*)

For **Objective K,** direct-instructional and comprehension-level activities will be integrated within lessons for Objectives D, F, H, and J to help students write programs and utilize computers in executing algorithms. (Estimated time needed: *Homework plus a total of 40 minutes intermittently distributed among different class periods*)

A brief test on objectives A and C and parts of objectives B and K will be given and reviewed with the class for purposes of formative feedback. Using the test review as a lead-in, lessons for **Objectives E and F** will be conducted following a design similar to that for Objectives C and D. The geometric model and the examples explained on pp. 217–218 will be utilized in the inductive activities, along with the Excursions in Algebra section on p. 220. The paper-folding and cutting up squares experiments from pp. 172–173 in Sobel & Maletsky (1988) may also be incorporated. For the direct instructional lesson, exercises on p. 219 as well as the Using Calculator section should prove useful. (Estimated time needed: *1.75 class periods plus homework*)

For **Objectives G and H** I will follow a similar inductive-direct instruction sequence as for prior conceptualization/algorithmic-skill pairs. Examples explained on pp. 224–226, as well as the paper-folding experiment on p. 171 from Sobel & Maletsky (1988) will be utilized in the inductive lesson, and exercises and examples from p. 223 for the direct lesson. (Estimated time needed: *1.75 class periods plus homework*)

A brief test on Objectives A, C, D, E, F, G, and H and parts of Objectives B and K will be given and reviewed with the class for purposes of formative feedback. (Estimated time needed: *0.5 of a class period*)

Again, the inductive-direct instruction sequence will be used, but this time for **Objectives I and J.** Cardboard models from Sobel & Maletsky (1988, pp. 174–175) for factoring trinomials will be utilized for the inductive lesson. Examples and exercises, including the Using Calculator sections from pp. 224–234, will be used in both lessons. (Estimated time needed: *2.5 class periods plus homework*)

I will conduct a deductive lesson for **Objective L,** drawing example and nonexample problems from a variety of sources, including prior units, references sources, and my head. (Estimated time needed: *0.75 of a class period plus homework*)

Using a practice test, I'll conduct a review session for the unit test for Objectives A–L. (Estimated time needed: *0.5 class period plus homework*)

A unit test for Objectives A–L will be administered and the results reviewed with the class. (Estimated time needed: *1.5 class periods*)

Extraordinary Learning Materials and Equipment Needed:

Cardboard for cardboard cutout models as explained in Sobel & Maletsky (1988, pp. 173–174).

Exhibit 11.10
One student's response to an item Casey planted on the Unit 6 test to set the stage for Unit 7.

Simplify the following polynomial:

$21a + 3a(b - 2b - 7)$

$21a + 3a(-b - 7)$

$21a - 3ab - 21a$

$-3ab$

students figure how that translates into help for individuals in terms of the number of crime victims needing the help. He likes that idea, but continues to think in hope of coming up with something easier to illustrate.

Problems involving finding possible dimensions of figures given the areas of their interiors are considered, as well as travel problems in which rate and time vary but distance is constant. Thinking about travel problems leads to the problem he finally decides to use for the opening lesson on Objective A. He selects it because it involves the mathematical content of Objective A and is also a topic in which many students have shown interest—namely, solving

Exhibit 11.11
Homework task sheet Casey assigned for the first day of Unit 7.

1. Use the given table to show all possible pairs of integers (a, b) that make the following statement true:

    $-3ab = \underline{\ 24\ }$

    Note: You may not need to use all the spaces in the table.

2. Find three more pairs for (a, b) that work for $-3ab = \underline{\ 24\ }$, but this time a and b don't have to be integers:

    $-3ab = \underline{\ 24\ }$

3. Use the given table to show all possible pairs of integers (a, b) that makes the following statement true:

    $-3ab = \underline{\ 10\ }$

    Note: You may not need to use all the spaces in the table.

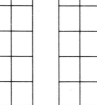

Exhibit 11.11
Continued

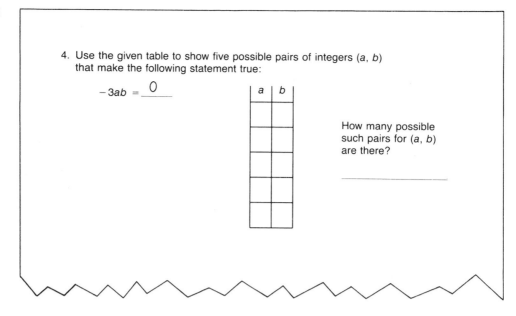

4. Use the given table to show five possible pairs of integers (*a*, *b*) that make the following statement true:

$$-3ab = \underline{0}$$

a	b

How many possible such pairs for (*a*, *b*) are there?

_____

crimes. The problem is explained in Exhibit 11.12

With the paramount problem for the day determined, Casey designs and schedules the activities. He thinks: "I want them working on the problem right away, but I also have to somehow respond to that homework assignment. It was really just to get them thinking about isolating and analyzing factors. I don't want to spend too much time discussing it, just enough to reinforce engaging in homework—and also to plant a few seeds that'll eventually help them discover some relationships down the road. 24, 10, and 0 are going to turn out to be great choices!

"We'll begin with an independent work session in which they deal with a problem I'll write out for them on a task sheet while I go around checking their homework. Then I can make comments about what I learned from reading the homework before we discuss the problem. But that won't work—some will finish the problem before I could possibly look through all their homework papers, and then they will be ready to discuss the problem and not be interested in the homework. I need another plan.

"I've got it! After quickly going over the homework, we'll deal with the problems in a large-group session. Oh, an even better idea! I'll introduce the problem by having them role-play the characters in the problem. It'll be easy for me to make out a script, pass that out, and assign the parts. As they go through the script, I'll put this diagram on the overhead (see Exhibit 11.12). After the problem is presented, should I have them discuss and solve it as a group or put them into the independent work session? Maybe I should have those who don't get to read parts make the judgment; I don't know. Okay, I'm going to go with the independent work session,

but I'll make it a writing exercise—they'll have to explain and argue for what they decide. That way, everybody will have a chance to at least put some thought into the problem before the fast ones with answers get restless. I should probably give them about a 12-minute writing assignment on the problem and then we'll discuss it.

For the in-class writing assignment, Casey develops the tasksheet shown in Exhibit 11.13.

He thinks: "There won't be much class time left after that—just time to do some summing up and vocabulary review—the ones in Objective B—and make an assignment. Better get the script written."

Within ten minutes, Casey has the script written. As it and the task sheet are being printed and then duplicated, he writes the agenda for Tuesday's class. Exhibit 11.14 contains the script; Exhibit 11.15 shows the agenda.

Day 1

On Tuesday, 24 of Casey's 26 algebra I students are in class. Four minutes into the class period, the students have their homework sheets (see Exhibit 11.11) in front of them as Casey conducts the planned reasoning-level question/discussion session.

Casey: How many pairs did you come up with for the first one, Alphonse?

Alphonse: 16.

Casey: Quickly, list them on the board for us—and while Alphonse is doing that, let's have Cassandra list hers for number 2, Kyle for number 3, and Abdul, 4. (Exhibit 11.16 displays what the students write.)

Exhibit 11.12
Problem Casey uses in the first lesson of Unit 7.

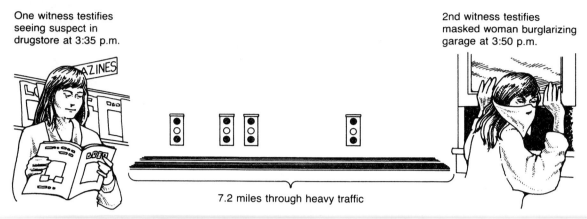

One witness testifies
seeing suspect in
drugstore at 3:35 p.m.

2nd witness testifies
masked woman burglarizing
garage at 3:50 p.m.

7.2 miles through heavy traffic

A woman is accused of burglarizing a garage at approximately
3:50 p.m. on a Tuesday. At 3:35 p.m. that day, she was seen
in a drugstore 7.2 miles west of the garage. The direct
route between the two locations is congested with traffic at
that time and has four traffic lights.

A traffic engineer testifies that:

Between 2 p.m. and 4 p.m. on the day of the crime, the
fastest average rate a vehicle could travel from a point
near the drugstore to the crime scene would be 30 mph.
The average rate at which traffic travels there at that
time is 20 mph. Unless there is an extraordinary event
(e.g., an accident) stopping traffic on that road,
traffic will move at 15 mph at the very least. On that
day, there was no such traffic stoppage.

The woman's defense attorney claims she could not possibly
have been at the crime scene at 3:50 since she was in the
drugstore at 3:35.

The question:

Is it possible for her to have been in the drugstore at
3:35 and be burglarizing the garage at 3:50? If so, is
it likely she was able to travel the 7.2 miles in the available
time?

Casey: Let's turn our attention to Alphonse's entries for the first one. Where are the rest of them, Alphonse?

Alphonse: What do you mean?

Casey: You said you had 16; I only see 8 pairs.

Alphonse: That's what I meant—I was counting numbers, not pairs.

Casey: Okay, any comments or questions for Alphonse? Do his entries match your own? Go ahead, Dick.

Dick: Did we have to repeat them like he did? 4 and -2 is the same as -2 and 4.

Casey: Direct your questions to Alphonse. He can either answer you himself or call on a volunteer.

Alphonse: I don't know. Okay, Dustin.

Dustin: You've got to do them both, because if like, ah, $a = 4$, then b has to be -2. But if a is -2, b has

to be 4. What I did was to solve for all the a's; then b had to be whatever it had to be.

Casey: Do you have a response to Dustin's explanation, Dick? No? Okay, anybody else? Put your hand up if you don't understand why Alphonse's 8 pairs are all possible ordered pairs of integers a, b in the case where $-3ab = 24$. Questions or comments for Cassandra? Ron.

Ron: You've only got two pairs up there, not three.

Cassandra: What do you mean—see, one, two, three?

Ron: The first and second are the same one; $^-\frac{1}{2}$ is -0.5!

Cassandra: Oh! Sorry, just switch the two—make the second row $(16, -0.5)$ instead. Edwin.

Edwin: I thought they all had to be fractions.

Cassandra: Here, does this make you happy?
(Cassandra modifies her entries so that they now appear as in Exhibit 11.17.)

Exhibit 11.13
Casey's task sheet for the independent work session to solve the problem given in Exhibit 11.12.

Your mission is to solve the problem by answering the following questions:

1. Based on the evidence, was it possible for the suspect to have been in the drug-store at 3:35 p.m. on the day in question and also to be burglarizing the garage at 3:50 p.m.?

   Yes ____ No ____. Explain exactly how the evidence supports your conclusion in the space provided.

2. If you answered Yes to the first question, was it likely or probable that she was able to travel the 7.2 miles in the available time?

   Yes ____ No ____. Explain exactly how the evidence supports your conclusion in the space provided.

3. If you answered No to the second question, how high would the fastest average rate given by the traffic engineer have to be before you would conclude that it is likely or probable to travel the 7.2 miles in the available time?

   ____ mi/h. Defend your answer with an explanation.

Casey: We'll allow any pair that works as long as they both aren't integers. All the numbers Cassandra has can be expressed as fractions, but she doesn't have to express them as fractions. Marlene.

Marlene: Are her answers right or not? None of mine agree with hers.

Casey: Raise your hand if you have exactly the same entries as Cassandra. . . . Nobody agrees with Cassandra! But her answers are exactly correct; so nobody else did this right. I'm shocked! Read yours, Sid.

Sid: (8/7, 7), and (8/9, 9), and (8/10, 10).

Casey: Well that would be right if Sid sticks in some negative signs here and there, but then it still wouldn't be the same as Cassandra's. Read yours, Omar.

Omar: (32, −¼), and (−¼, 32), and (16, −½).

Casey: Well that's surely right, but it's different from Cassandra's. Marlene.

Marlene: So, you're really saying that there's more than one correct answer to this one.

Casey: How many possible *a*, *b* pairs will work if we don't say *a* and *b* both have to be integers, Xavier?

Xavier: I don't know.

Casey: What three pairs did you put down for number 2, Xavier?

Xavier: I didn't do it.

As Casey redirects his initial question for Xavier to another student, he quickly writes on a slip of paper, "Xavier, please check with me later on in class

today right after I assign the homework for tomorrow. I want to speak with you briefly." He hands the note to Xavier as he continues.

Casey: How many possible *a*, *b* pairs will work if we don't say *a* and *b* both have to be integers, Juaquin?

Juaquin: There's no limit; you can keep going.

Casey: Let's go to item 3 and look at what Kyle put. . . . Blanks! All blanks! You were supposed to fill in the blanks, not leave them blank, Kyle! What do you have to say about this?

Kyle: There are no answers.

Casey: Do you think I'd give you an exercise with no answers?

Kyle: You do it to us all the time.

Casey: Explain to the class why this one has no answers.

Kyle: 3 doesn't go into 10, so there's no integer times 3 that'll give you 10. Mary?

Mary: But you could put in fractions, right?

Kyle: But we weren't supposed to for this one.

Casey: If nonintegers were allowed, how many answers would there be, Juaquin?

Juaquin: You could keep going and going.

Casey: Okay, that brings us to the last one. Do you agree with Abdul's entries? Alena.

Alena: I agree, but they're not the same as mine.

Casey: Super quick, write yours on the board, and while Alena is doing that, write yours also, Terri. Okay, does anybody want to quarrel with anything

Exhibit 11.14
Script for students to follow in role-playing the problem situation given in Exhibit 11.12.

Prosecutor Wilma Jones: (To witness Alvin Smith) Mr. Smith, at approximately 3:50 P.M. on Tuesday, January 26, tell us what you saw just outside the garage located at 821 North Street.

Alvin Smith: I saw a woman in a ski mask enter the garage. A couple of minutes later she came out of the garage carrying a television set and a small box. She put them into a car parked just outside the door. Then she made two more trips, taking what looked like auto equipment—speakers and tools and stuff.

Wilma Jones: And what kind of car was the suspect—ah, excuse me, I mean the person you observed—using?

Alvin Smith: A light green hatchback of some kind—maybe a Dodge or something.

Wilma Jones: (To suspect Alice Brown) Ms. Brown, what kind of car do you drive?

Alice Brown: A green 1987 Dodge hatchback, but I didn't—

Wilma Jones: That's all Ms. Brown; thank you.

Defense Attorney Willie Adams: (To witness Irene Johnson) Ms. Johnson, where do you work?

Irene Johnson: At Sitman's Drugstore on 5980 North Street.

Willie Adams: Ms. Brown, please stand up so this witness can take a good look at you. Thank you. Now Ms. Johnson, have you ever seen this person at any time before today?

Irene Johnson: Only once, and that was at Sitman's Drugstore where I work. She bought some gloves and I rang up the sale for her.

Willie Adams: And at what time and on what day did this occur?

Irene Johnson: At exactly 3:35 P.M. on January 26 of this year.

Willie Adams: You seem so sure of the date and time. How can you be so sure?

Irene Johnson: The date and time are right here on this cash register slip.

Willie Adams: (To traffic engineer Bob Moore) Mr. Moore, what position do you hold with our great city?

Bob Moore: I'm a traffic engineer. I study traffic patterns and basically work to keep traffic on our city streets flowing as smoothly as possible.

Willie Adams: Mr. Moore, how far is it between Sitman's Drugstore at 5980 North and the garage, allegedly burglarized at 821 North?

Bob Moore: 7.2 miles.

Willie Adams: Please tell us, based on your scientific studies, how long it would take someone to travel those 7.2 miles between 3:35 and 4 o'clock on Tuesday, January 26, a workday.

Bob Moore: The average rate at which traffic travels between those two points on a Tuesday at that time is 20 miles per hour. It's quite congested and there are four major traffic lights.

Willie Adams: That's the average. What's the fastest a car could average over that 7.2 miles?

Bob Moore: 30 miles per hour max.

Willie Adams: You say that's the most. Is it realistic to expect someone to average as high as 30 miles per hour over that 7.2 mile stretch at that time of day on a Tuesday?

Bob Moore: It would be a rare occurrence, to say the least.

---

that's on the board? How many possible correct pairs could we have? Salvador.

Salvador: Infinite.

Casey: Describe what must be true for a pair to work. You tell us, Salvador.

Salvador: You've got to have a 0.

Casey: We're going to be okay as long as a or b is 0. If a is 0, then b—what about b if a is 0, Mary?

Mary: It can be anything. And if b is 0, a can be anything.

Casey distributes copies of the crime-solver script and appoints individuals to play the roles. With the diagram from Exhibit 11.12 displayed on the overhead, the students read through the parts. As planned, they then complete the task sheet shown in Exhibit 11.13 as Casey circulates about the room selecting sample

Exhibit 11.15
Casey's agenda for the first day of the algebra I unit on factoring polynomials.

1. Transition period: start class and direct students to take out the worksheets they completed for homework (see Exhibit 11.11).
2. Intellectual-level question/discussion session in which students share homework responses leading to the idea of undoing multiplication.
3. Transition period: crime-solver problem scripts are distributed and roles are appointed.
4. Interactive lecture session: designated students play their characters from the crime-solver script and the problem is clarified.
5. Transition period: give directions and hand out worksheet for the independent work session.
6. Independent work session: students completing the worksheet (see Exhibit 8.13) and the teacher reads and selects sample responses to be read in the follow-up question/discussion session.
7. Transition period into question/discussion session.
8. Intellectual-level question/discussion session:
   - Selected contrasting responses are read aloud and analyzed.
   - Strategies for solving the problems are articulated.
   - Types of problems with solutions requiring the undoing of multiplication are characterized.
   - Additional example problems are compared to nonexample problems.
9. Transition period: students are directed to open the textbook to p. 210.
10. Interactive lecture session:
    - Review the textbook and notebook glossary definitions of factoring, prime number, composite number, and greatest common factor.
    - Explain the examples and directions for the textbook exercises on pp. 212–213.
11. Transition period: assign homework:
    - Think up and write out a real-life problem. Make it one that has a solution that requires the undoing of multiplication (such as the crime-solver problem we worked on in class today).
    - Work the following exercises from p. 213: 11, 15, 19, 20, 21, 25, 28, 33, 49,53, 54, 55
12. Independent work session: begin homework.
13. Transition period into the second period.

responses to use in the follow-up question/discussion session. Students enthusiastically engage in that session (listed as item 8 in Exhibit 11.15) until there are only seven minutes remaining in the period, at which time Casey terminates the discussion. Thinking quickly, he tries to summarize points made during the session, explaining that the type of problem on which they will be focusing in this unit involves situations in which they already have a product and want to look at different factor combinations that could have resulted in that product.

Lacking time to get to item 10 on the agenda, Casey shifts to item 11, explaining and assigning the part of the homework in which they think up and write out a sample real-life problem. He postpones the part of the assignment from the textbook.

Planning for Day 2

It's 4:30 when Casey gets around to reflecting on the day's classes. Regarding algebra I, he thinks: "I like the way they got into the two inductive activities to-

day. The trouble is, we didn't leave time to really get things summed up at the end and to go through the vocabulary. I'm sorry I didn't get to work in at least two more example-type problems and at least one nonexample problem. My attempt to tie things up at the end didn't work because we only had one problem to think about. They loved that crime-solver business—think I'll try that in the geometry classes. I'm glad I came up with that idea. . . . I wonder if it was a mistake to postpone the textbook assignment. Earlier in the year, I would've assigned it even though I hadn't gone through the vocabulary, but I've learned that usually doesn't work for most of this group—they see a word they don't know and just fold up the tent.

"Okay, so where do I go with this tomorrow? That'll be Wednesday, so three more days this week, and . . . Oh, we've got plenty of time; the extra time spent on the discover a relationship objective will make the rest of the unit go smoother. Okay, back to tomorrow. We need to get to the vocabulary. But first

Exhibit 11.16
Students' initial whiteboard entries for the activity reviewing the homework assignment with the task sheet of Exhibit 11.11.

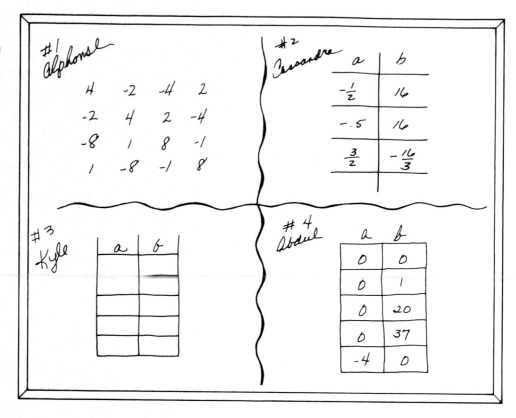

I need to hit them with example and nonexample problems and then try to do a better job of summing things up. Better jot down these problems I thought of at the end of class. . . . Let's see, one was on area, the other on money spent by the politician. Oh! It would be even better if I used the problems they bring to class from the homework assignment. I almost forgot about that. Some are bound to come up with super examples; others won't actually involve factoring—I can use some of those for nonexamples. I'm glad I made

Exhibit 11.17
Cassandra's modification to her entry shown in Exhibit 11.17.

#2 Cassandra

a	b
$-\frac{1}{2}$	$\frac{16}{1}$
$\frac{16}{1}$	$-\frac{.5}{1}$
$\frac{3}{2}$	$-\frac{16}{3}$

that assignment; it will work out well. Then, we tie up Objective A and go straight to the textbook and the vocabulary stuff planned for today." With the unit plan (Exhibit 11.9), Tuesday's agenda (Exhibit 11.15) and page 212 of the textbook in front of him, Casey calls up the computer file with Tuesday's agenda and begins modifying it into Wednesday's agenda, resulting in Exhibit 11.18. As Casey looks at it, he thinks, "We probably won't get through this one either, but I'd much rather have too much planned than not enough and be left with dead time."

When Casey first begins writing the agenda, he doesn't plan for the activities related to Objective A to be as elaborate as agenda items 1–4 suggest. Initially, he planned to quickly tie together the end of Tuesday's activities for that objective. However, as he thinks of how to make efficient use of the homework and the need to involve problems in addition to the crime-solver one, he ends up with a more elaborate plan. Although this should provide a stimulating start to the period, it will not leave him with enough time to do all the following:

1. Go through the vocabulary and set the stage for the textbook activities.
2. Provide students with needed exposure to and practice in factoring constant and variable expressions from page 213 (e.g., find the prime factorization of 112, and find the greatest common factor of $18a^2b^2$, $6b$, $42a^2b^3$).

Exhibit 11.18
Casey's agenda for the second day of the algebra I unit on factoring polynomials.

1. Transition period: I start class and distribute an overhead transparency and transparency (erasable) pen to each student and direct them to take out the problems they formulated for homework.
2. Independent work session: each student quickly copies her or his homework problem onto the transparency (make sure they display their names).
3. Transition period: I collect completed transparencies and the pens.
4. Interactive lecture session:
   - I quickly display each transparency on the overhead as the student who wrote it reads the problem aloud.
   - After each problem is shown, the students independently and quietly classify the problem on their worksheet as either an example or a nonexample.
   - After all the problems are shown, I select two example problems and two nonexample problems (assuming they exist in the sample—if not, use my own as a last resort) and use the contrast between the two types to sum up the need to undo multiplication to solve some types of problems.
5. Transition period: students are directed to open the textbook to p. 210.
6. Interactive lecture session:
   - Review the textbook and notebook glossary definitions of factoring, prime number, composite number, and greatest common factor.
   - Explain the examples and directions for the textbook exercises on pp. 212–213.
   - Call their attention to the purpose of the textbook section Factoring Using the Distributive Property on p. 214.
7. Transition period: assign the following homework:
   - Work the following exercises from p. 213: 11, 15, 19, 20, 21, 25, 28, 33, 49, 53, 54, and 55.
   - Study page 214, working through the four examples with the authors.
   - Work the following exploratory exercises from p. 215: 1, 2, 3, and 9.
   - Work the following written exercises from p. 215: 1, 2, 3, 5, 9, and 15.
8. Independent work session: begin homework.
9. Transition period into the second period.

3. Conduct the brief inductive lesson relative to Objective C as suggested in his unit plan (see Exhibit 11.9) and the follow-up lesson for Objective D.

He estimates that stopping with only the first two tasks completed will leave unused class time but not enough to complete the third task. The agenda of Exhibit 11.18 represents a compromise; he will plan to have the students get a jump on Objectives C and D by working ahead on textbook page 214, which is reproduced in Exhibit 11.19. He doesn't really like the idea of students being introduced to steps in an algorithm before experiencing a discover a relationship lesson on why it works, but he goes ahead with the agenda of Exhibit 11.18 because it seems to be the most efficient way to use the available time. Besides, he doesn't consider this particular algorithm, which is based on the familiar distributive property, to be conceptually complex for the students.

Day 2 and Planning for Day 3

Wednesday's algebra I class smoothly followed the agenda of Exhibit 11.18. Casey reflects on the day's events and makes plans for Thursday's classes. He thinks to himself: "That first part of algebra really went well. Flashing every one of their problems on the overhead screen reinforced their engagement in homework and exposed them to a variety of problems—examples and nonexamples—with them both seeing and hearing the problems. I'm going to use that tactic more often, but next time I need to think of it before I assign the homework. That way they can save class time by taking the transparencies home and have them prepared before coming into class.

"Even agenda item 6 went well—switching to direct instruction using the textbook was a nice change after all the lively inquiry activities. They can take only so much inquiry before needing some old-fashioned, straightforward here's something to memorize teaching. But I wonder just how much they got from studying page 214. I'd better start off tomorrow with a brief test to get some formative feedback on where they are and also to reinforce their work on the assignments. The test shouldn't take more than 20 minutes, but I ought to have one or two items on Objective A, items for the vocabulary we went over

Exhibit 11.19
Page 214 of Casey's algebra I
textbook.

Examples

1   **Use the distributive property to write $10y^2 + 15y$ in factored form.**

First, find the greatest common factor of $10y^2$ and $15y$.

$10y^2 = 2 \cdot \boxed{5} \cdot \boxed{y} \cdot y$
$15y = 3 \cdot \boxed{5} \cdot \boxed{y}$ *The GCF is 5y.*

Then, express each term as a product of the GCF and its remaining factors.

$10y^2 + 15y = 5y(2y) + 5y(3)$
$\qquad\qquad = 5y(2y + 3)$ *Use the distributive property.*

2   **Factor: $21ab^2 - 33a^2bc$**

$21ab^2 = \boxed{3} \cdot 7 \cdot \boxed{a} \cdot \boxed{b} \cdot b$
$33a^2bc = \boxed{3} \cdot 11 \cdot \boxed{a} \cdot a \cdot \boxed{b} \cdot c$ *The GCF is 3ab.*

Express the terms as products.

$21ab^2 - 33a^2bc = 3ab(7b) - 3ab(11ac)$
$\qquad\qquad\qquad = 3ab(7b - 11ac)$ *Use the distributive property.*

3   **Factor: $12a^5b + 8a^3 - 24a^3c$**

$12a^5b = 2 \cdot 2 \cdot 3 \cdot a \cdot a \cdot a \cdot a \cdot a \cdot b$
$8a^3 = 2 \cdot 2 \cdot 2 \cdot a \cdot a \cdot a$
$24a^3c = 2 \cdot 2 \cdot 2 \cdot 3 \cdot a \cdot a \cdot a \cdot c$ *The GCF is $4a^3$.*

$12a^5b + 8a^3 - 24a^3c = 4a^3(3a^2b) + 4a^3(2) - 4a^3(6c)$
$\qquad\qquad\qquad\qquad = 4a^3(3a^2b + 2 - 6c)$

4   **Factor: $6x^3y^2 + 14x^2y + 2x^2$**

$6x^3y^2 = 2 \cdot 3 \cdot x \cdot x \cdot x \cdot y \cdot y$
$14x^2y = 2 \cdot 7 \cdot x \cdot x \cdot y$
$2x^2 = 2 \cdot x \cdot x$ *The GCF is $2x^2$.*

$6x^3y^2 + 14x^2y + 2x^2 = 2x^2(3xy^2 + 7y + 1)$

Source: From *Merrill Algebra One* (p. 214) by A. G. Foster, J. N. Rath, and L. J. Winters, 1986, Columbus, OH: Merrill. Copyright 1986 by Merrill Publishing Company. Reprinted by permission of the publisher.

today, and some items similar to the textbook exercises relative to Objective D. A pretty easy item on Objective C should tell me if that little explanation at the top of page 214 helped them understand that the distributive property in reverse is the basis for the algorithm. . . . I'm afraid this brief test may not be as brief as I'd like!"

Casey spends nearly an hour entering items for Objectives A, B, C, and D into his item pool file. He longs for the day when he won't have to create new items every time he puts together a test—the second year of teaching should be easier than this one. After synthesizing the test, Casey works out the agenda given in Exhibit 11.20.

Day 3 and Planning for Day 4

Feedback from the brief test suggests to Casey that most students failed to achieve Objectives C and D well enough to be ready for Objectives E and F. Thus, he spends the majority of the class period on item 4 of the agenda (see Exhibit 11.20). Because he needs to have them complete the task sheet of Exhibit

11.21 before he spends class time on Objectives E and F, he postpones agenda items 5 and 6 and begins explaining and assigning the task sheet immediately after item 4. He does not give any other homework assignment, since there is no time at the end of the period for item 8.

For Friday, he plans quick coverage of items 5 and 6 from Thursday's agenda, and then will utilize the results of the homework (see Exhibit 11.21) to get them to discover that $a^2 - b^2 = (a + b)(a - b)$. He expects them to bring in a variety of square and rectangular regions, from which he'll use inductive questioning strategies to get them to generalize from their own examples to the general relationship for factoring difference of squares. He'll then assign written and calculator exercises from pages 215 and 218–219 in which they practice factoring algorithms from both Objectives D and F.

Day 4 and Planning for Day 5

On Friday Casey spends more time with the computer programming activities than he had planned.

Exhibit 11.20
Casey's agenda for the third day of the algebra I unit on factoring polynomials.

1. Transition period: start class and initiate a brief test.
2. Brief test relevant to Objectives A, B, C, and D.
3. Transition period from the test to the review of the results.
4. Interactive lecture and question/discussion session:
   - I call out the scoring key for each test item while students check and score their own responses.
   - Items about which students raise questions are discussed.
   - I explain any topics the test results suggest need to be explained.
5. Transition period: students are directed to take out their homework papers, open textbooks to p. 214, and open their notebooks to Part 3, where they keep computer programs and flowcharts developed during the course.
6. Interactive lecture session: walk the students through writing a basic program for factoring, using the distribute property.
7. Transition period: distributive homework worksheet (see Exhibit 11.21); explain worksheet; and assign homework to:
   - Complete the tasks for the worksheet
   - _____ (to be determined in class, depending on feedback from brief test).
8. Independent work session: begin homework.
9. Transition period into the second period.

The reasoning-level question/discussion session is quite lively, with students abstracting the general relationship for factoring the difference of two squares (see Exhibit 11.22) from the examples produced in the homework assignment (see Exhibit 11.21). However, Casey is able to get the students through only the first two and part of the third stage of the four-stage lesson: (1) experimenting, (2) reflecting and explaining, (3) hypothesizing and articulating, and (4) verifying and refining. He's unhappy that he has to stop the lesson with just enough time remaining to give the planned homework assignment. Most students appear disappointed that the class period is over.

The high point on which the first period ends leaves Casey so energized that he begins planning for Monday's algebra class during second period (see Exhibit 11.1 for his class schedule) instead of collecting his thoughts for periods 3 and 4, as he does on most days.

He locks his classroom door, gathers the unit plan and the day's agenda, sits at his computer, and thinks to himself: "I should've given them a computer assignment to follow up that programming session. They could've handled it with the weekend break. Wow! They really got into discovering why $a^2 - b^2 = (a + b)(a - b)$—I sure hate to wait until Monday to tie it all down. Let's see, page 217 gives them a pretty good explanation of a geometric model that's isomorphic to the one we discovered in class. Not many of them would understand it if I hadn't put them through the task sheet experience first (see Exhibit 11.21). Page 218 lays out the algorithm quite clearly with five examples and a variety of coefficients. Then the written and calculator exercises I assigned will give them skill work for this and the previous algorithm. I shouldn't feel badly about having had to cut the session short. It'll come together for those who put an effort into this homework assignment. That means I'd better start Monday's class off with a brief test to reinforce those who made the effort ."

Casey develops Monday's agenda, as shown in Exhibit 11.23, but he doesn't get the brief test completed until Friday evening.

Day 5

Monday's first period follows the schedule of Exhibit 11.23. Twelve minutes into the period, 6 of the 25 students present have completed the test shown in Exhibit 11.24 and are waiting at their places for the others to finish. Casey regrets not having made accommodations by having a stand-by assignment for students finishing at different times. Seven minutes later, most students are finished; Casey halts the test and begins calling out the key to the items:

Casey: Number 1, $6x(3x - 2)$—to prove that answer, let $a = 6x$, $b = 3x$, and $c = -2$. Number 2, the greatest common factor is $7a$. Number 3, $3xy(x^2y + 3y + 12)$. Number 4, $(5w + 9q^2)(5w - 9q^2)$. Number 5, $\frac{2}{3}(x + 2)(x - 2)$. And for number 6,

Exhibit 11.21
Task sheet assigned for homework as part of the lesson for Objective E (see Exhibit 11.9).

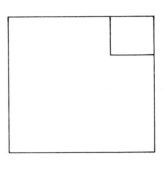

DIRECTIONS:

1. Take a sheet of cardboard (preferably) or a sheet of paper and cut it into a square region no smaller than 8″ by 8″.

2. Measure your square carefully and record the dimensions here:

   Length = _____   Width = _____   Area = _____

3. Now, measure a small *square* region out of the top right corner of your original square region as shown below:

---

your dimensions and rectangle might look something like this. He displays Exhibit 11.25 on the overhead.

Sid: I don't get number 5 on the test.

Casey: When you see "factor ⅔(x^2) ⁻⅞," what's the first think you think of doing, Sid?

Sid: Look for common terms, but first I got rid of the number at the bottom.

Casey: How?

Sid: By multiplying through by 3—that gives me $2x^2 - 8$ and now 2 is common.

Casey: Hold on, doesn't multiplying by 3 change the value of the expression?

Sid: It's okay to do it to both sides.

Casey: Both sides of what?

Sid: The equation.

Casey: I don't see an equation, just an expression standing for one number.

Sid: Oh, yeah.

Casey: What did Sid tell us he thinks about first when factoring an expression like this, Charlene?

Charlene: Look for a common term.

Casey: And is there a common term in this case, Sid?

Sid: They both have 3's on the bottom.

Casey: Divided by 3 is the same as multiplied by what, Sid?

Exhibit 11.21
Continued

4. Record the dimensions of the small square region here:

   Length = _____   Width = _____   Area = _____

5. Now, cut the small *square* region out and remove it from your original square region as shown below:

6. Now, divide the region pictured on the left below into two rectangular regions as shown:

Sid: 1/3.

Casey: So, what's common?

Sid: 1/3.

Casey: Using the distributive property, you take 1/3 out and you have 1/3 of what?

Sid: $2x^2 - 8$. . . . And now, 2 is common also, so you get $\frac{2}{3}(x^2 - 4)$. But that's not the answer you gave us.

Casey: Okay, Juaquin, you've been waiting to tell us something for a long time. You're up.

Juaquin: $(x^2 - 4)$ is the difference of two perfect squares, so you can factor that too, and you end up with your answer.

Sid: I see. Thank you.

Twelve minutes later, Casey has just talked the class through the paper-folding experiment shown in Exhibit 11.26 and completes agenda item 6 (see Exhibit 11.23) by listing the steps in the algorithm for factoring expressions of the form $a^2 + 2ab + b^2$. He talks the students through two examples and then assigns the homework. He leaves the algorithm's steps and illustrative examples displayed on the board as students begin their homework (agenda item 8). Although only seven minutes are left for the independent work session, Casey efficiently provides individual help to 12 students by applying techniques suggested in this book's section entitled "Ideas for

Exhibit 11.21
Continued

7. Carefully measure the two rectangular regions, both the top one and the bottom one. Record the dimensions here:

   Top rectangle:

   Length = _____   Width = _____   Area = _____

   Bottom rectangle:

   Length = _____   Width = _____   Area = _____

8. Carefully cut off the top rectangular region as shown below:

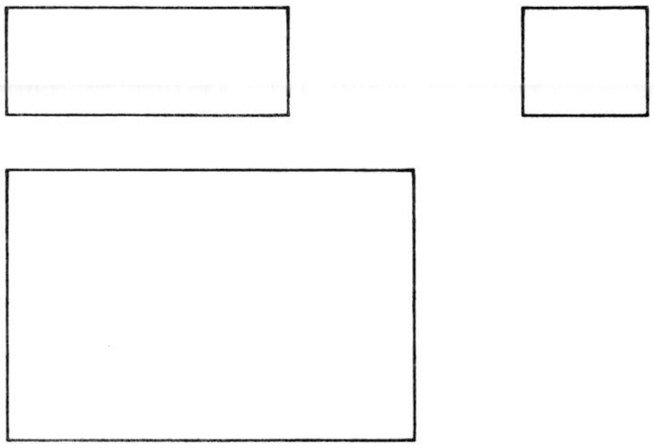

9. Now rotate the top rectangular region and attach it to the left side of the bottom rectangular region as shown below (it should fit exactly):

10. Carefully measure the rectangular region you just formed. Record the dimensions here:

   Length = _____   Width = _____   Area = _____

Exhibit 11.22
General model for $a^2 - b^2 = (a + b)(a - b)$ that Casey's algebra students abstracted from their examples based on the task sheet of Exhibit 11.21.

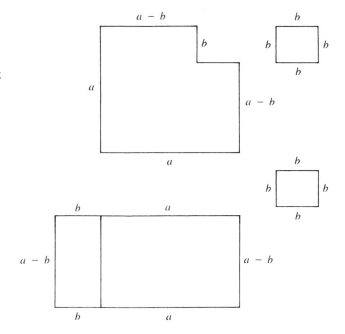

Exhibit 11.23
Casey's agenda for the fifth day of the algebra I unit on factoring polynomials.

1. Transition period: start class and initiate a brief test.
2. Brief test relevant to Objectives C, D, E, and F.
3. Transition period from the test to the review of the results.
4. Interactive lecture and question/discussion session:
   - I call out the scoring key for each test item while students check and score their own responses.
   - Items and homework exercises about which students raise questions are discussed.
   - I explain any topics the test results and questions suggest need to be explained (this may well require a direct-instructional learning activity on the algorithm for factoring the difference of perfect squares).
5. Transition period: a 10-in. by 10-in square-shaped sheet of colored paper is distributed to each student.
6. Interactive lecture session:
   - Demonstrate and work through the paper-folding experiment (see Exhibit 11.26) illustrating why $a^2 + 2ab + b^2$ can be expressed as $(a + b)^2$.
   - Use direct instruction to explain and provide practice with the algorithm for factoring $a^2 + 2ab + b^2$.
7. Transition period: assign the following homework:
   - Read the textbook section Perfect Squares and Factoring, pp. 221–222, and work through the accompanying examples.
   - Complete the following Exploratory Exercises from p. 222: 1–6 and 9–12.
   - Complete the following Written Exercises from p. 223: 5, 7, 9, 10, 12, 25, 34, 36, 39, 41, 42, 47, and 48.
8. Independent work session: begin homework.
9. Transition period into the second period.

Exhibit 11.24
Brief test for Objectives C, D, E, and F (see Exhibit 11.9) Casey uses on the fifth day of algebra I, Unit 7.

Algebra I — Brief Test 7–2

1. Write $18x^2 - 12x$ in factored form;

   $18x^2 - 12x = $ _____

   Prove your answer with the distributive property $ab + ac = a(b + c)$ by indicating what you let a, b, and c equal:

   $a = $ _____ , $b = $ _____ , $c = $ _____

2. What is the GCF of $14ac + 21a^3$?

   _____

3. Factor $3x^3y^2 + 9xy^2 + 36xy$

   _____

4. Factor $25w^2 - 81y^4$

   _____

5. Factor $\frac{2}{3}x^2 - \frac{8}{3}$

   _____

6. Illustrate why $100 - x^2 = (10 + x)(10 - x)$ for $x < 10$ by writing in dimensions for the region shown below and then by drawing a rectangle with the same area:

Exhibit 11.25
Casey's display in response to item 6 of the brief test of Exhibit 11.24.

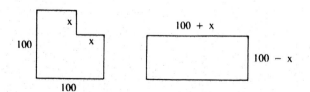

Independent Work Sessions", in Chapter 9. For example, he responds to Mary's request for help with Exploratory Exercise 5 from page 222 of the textbook:

> Determine if each trinomial is a perfect square trinomial. If it is, state its factors.
>
> 5. $n^2 - 13n + 36$

Mary: Mr. Rudd, I can't do this one.
Casey: Is the expression written in standard form?
Mary: Yes.
Casey: Are the first and third terms perfect squares?
Mary: Yes.
Casey: Then that means you are on which step on the board?

Mary: Ahh, 5.

Casey: Okay, go with step 5. I'll be back in 33 seconds. (Casey returns just in time.)

Mary: So, this middle term has to be $2ab$. But I still don't get it.

Casey: What's a in this case?

Mary: n.

Casey: n or $-n$, and what's b in this case?

Mary: 6 or -6.

Casey: Is there any way $-13n$ could be $2ab$ for any of those values of a and b?

Casey moves to another student as Mary completes the exercise and moves on to number 6.

Planning for Day 6

That evening, Casey plans for Tuesday's classes. He thinks about the algebra I class: "So up to this point, all of them—with the possible exception of Dick, Blair, and Delia—seem to be just fine as far as discovering the relationships underlying the three algorithms we've covered. Skillwise most of them are coming along. Let's see, next we go to the biggie—factoring $ax^2 + bx + c$—Objectives I and J. I'd better wait on those until they've had more practice with the distributive one, the difference of squares, and perfect square trinomials. Also, we haven't hit on any kind of real-life problem solving since the second day. I shouldn't go any longer without some application work, or else they'll lose that real-world connection we started with the crime-solver problem. Okay, better build some applications for tomorrow for the three algorithms, which means we'll begin working on parts of Objective L before getting to Objectives I and J. Also, I should work computer utilization into the practice and review lessons."

As Casey develops the detailed plan, he gets quite frustrated attempting to formulate or locate real-life problems in which the three factoring algorithms apply. Any problem he thinks will interest students and in which factoring is truly useful requires the upcoming algorithm for $ax^2 + bx + c$. He avoids problems solvable by finding roots to equations such as $x^2 - 25 = 0$, because he would rather have students use common sense to reason that x^2 is 25, so x can only be 5 or -5, than blindly adher to a factoring algorithm for solving such equations. Consequently, he reluctantly uses contrived rather than real-life problems for his lesson (for example, see the two word problems in the task sheet of Exhibit 11.27).

The agenda Casey develops is displayed as Exhibit 11.28.

Day 6

Twenty-five minutes into the class period, the class has completed the first five agenda items and Casey initiates the presentation session on item 6. Casey displays the transparency, shown in Exhibit 11.12, that he used one week ago when the class discussed the crime-solver problem.

Casey: I'd like for someone to come up here and quickly summarize the problem this reminds you of. Marlene.

Exhibit 11.26

Paper-folding experiment in which Casey engages students during the fifth class meeting of Unit 7. **Source:** Max A. Sobel/Evan M. Maletsky, TEACHING MATHEMATICS: A Sourcebook of Aids, Activities, and Strategies, 2e, © 1988, pp. 171-172. Reprinted by permission of Prentice Hall, Inc. Englewood Cliffs, New Jersey.

Paper Folding for $(a + b)^2 = a^2 + 2ab + b^2$

Material

One square piece of paper per student.

Directions

1. Fold one edge over at a point E to form a vertical crease parallel to the edge. Label the longer and shorter dimensions a and b.

2. Fold the upper right-hand corner over onto the crease to locate point F. Folding this way, point F will be the same distance from the corner as point E.

3. Now fold a horizontal crease through F and label all outside dimensions.

4. Find the areas of the two squares formed. Find the areas of the two rectangles formed. Show that these four areas together must equal $(a + b)^2$.

Exhibit 11.27
Homework task sheet Casey plans to assign on Day 6 of the algebra I unit on factoring polynomials.

1. Answer the following questions, assuming that a and b are two numbers such that $ab = 0$.
   If a is 19, what is b?_____
   If b is -3.74, what is a?_____
   If a is positive, what must be true about b?_____
   If b is negative, what must be true about a?_____
   If $a = 0$, what must be true about a?_____

2. Answer the following questions, assuming that c and d are two numbers such that $cd \neq 0$.
   What can you conclude about c?_____
   What can you conclude about d?_____

3. There are two numbers for which the following statement is true:
   Seven times the square of the number equals 14 times the number.
   For what two numbers is that statement true? Display your work and write the numbers in the blanks.
   _____ and _____

4. Sam's age times itself is the same as 30 times his age less 225. How old is Sam? Display your work and write Sam's age in the blank.
   _____

5. According to a principle of physics:
   If an object is launched from the ground into the air and allowed to fall back to the ground, its height above the ground during the trip is governed by the following formula:

$$h = vt - 16t^2$$

   where h is the number of feet above the ground the object is t seconds after launch and v is the velocity at which it left the ground in feet per second.
   Use this formula to assess how many seconds a golf ball will be in flight if it is hit so that it leaves the ground at a velocity of 64 feet per second.
   Hint: First solve for h by answering the following question: How high off the ground is the ball when it lands after being hit?
   Draw a picture illustrating the path of the ball, display your work and write your answer in the blank.
   _____

6. Enter, debug, and save on a disk the computer programs for factoring polynomials that we wrote in class.

7. For each of the following use the programs to determine if the polynomial can be expressed in factored form with integer coefficients; if so, factor it and print out the results.

$$3a + 54a^2 + 81a$$
$$70x^2 - 7x^2 - 2y(500y + 4y)$$
$$9b^2 + 16\,c^2 + 24bc$$
$$5x^2 - 24x + 10$$

Marlene: This woman was accused of stealing stuff from this garage here. But she was seen at the drugstore over here just before that. The problem was, did she have enough time to get from the drugstore to the garage to still commit the crime?

Casey: How far would she have had to travel?
Marlene: 7.2 miles.
Casey: Thank you. The day after we solved that problem we classified problems you people came up with for homework as either solvable by factoring or not. Here's a sample of those problems.

Exhibit 11.28
Casey's agenda for the sixth day of the algebra I unit on factoring polynomials.

1. Transition period: I start class and direct the students to do the following:
   - Take out their homework and display it on their desktops.
   - Begin working the mini-review exercise on p. 223 (a short exercise on topics from prior units).
2. Independent work session on the mini-review: I quickly check homework and direct some students to display selected homework exercises on the chalkboard.
3. Transition period: work on the mini-review is halted and attention is directed to the completed homework exercises now displayed on the board.
4. Interactive lecture and question/discussion session:
   - Students individually explain to the class how they completed the homework exercises displayed on the board.
   - Homework and mini-review exercises about which students raise questions are discussed.
5. Transition period: direct students to put away homework and to
   - Turn their notebooks to the pages relating to the first two days of the unit, during which we worked on the crime-solver problem and in which they developed problems and displayed them on transparencies.
   - Retrieve their completed homework worksheet for the first day (see Exhibit 11.11).
6. Interactive lecture session: I
   - Play upon their work during the first 2 days of the unit to get them to deduce how factoring can be used to solve open sentences.
   - Walk them through writing computer programs for factoring differences of perfect squares and perfect square trinomials.
7. Transition period: distribute and assign the homework worksheet (see Exhibit 11.27).
8. Independent work session: begin homework.
9. Transition period into the second period.

Casey begins showing a few problems from those transparencies, one at a time.

Casey: This one was a factoring problem. This one, was not. This one, yes, and this one, yes. . . . This one, no. This one, yes. Now, what is special about the problems where the solution required undoing multiplication, or factoring? Omar.

Omar: In all those we were given some product, like 7.2, and we had to find out different combinations that got you to it.

Casey: So, if you know the dimensions of a polygon and you wanted to find the area, would you have one of those factoring problems? Megan.

Megan: Yes, sir.

Casey: Why would it be?

Megan: I don't know.

Casey: What did Omar tell us we're given in one of those kinds of problems?

Megan: I don't remember.

Casey: Thanks for waiting; go ahead, Kyle.

Kyle: It wouldn't be a factoring problem, because you have to multiply—not undo multiplying.

Casey: Turn it around so it would be a factoring problem, Kyle.

Kyle: You would want to find the dimensions and you know the area.

Casey: How did I originally describe the type of problem, Megan?

Megan: Something about a polygon.

Casey: Cassandra?

Cassandra: You wanted the polygon's area and you knew its dimensions. Kyle reversed it, where you had the area but not the dimensions.

Casey: Write your statement on the upper right corner of the board, Omar—the one about describing the kinds of problem that are solvable using factoring. Thank you. We're now going to discuss using factoring to solve equations. We aren't switching topics; we're still going to be dealing with the kinds of problem Omar's statement describes. What we'll be doing is developing a more systematic approach to solving those kinds of problem. To get us started, turn your attention to the homework task sheet for the first day of this unit—it looks like this. You don't have yours, Xavier? . . . Magnolia, would you mind if Xavier looks on with you? Thank you. Everybody, look at what you have for item 4. Magnolia, read yours, giving us one a, b pair at a time.

Magnolia: $(0, 7)$, $(7, 0)$, $(0, 0)$, $(11, 0)$, $(1, 0)$.

Casey: How is yours different from Magnolia's, and how is it the same, Alena?

Alena: Well, I had $(1, 0)$ and then—

Casey: I didn't say what I meant. Don't give us your list. *Describe* how yours differs and how it's the same without actually listing your pairs.

Alena: Okay, . . . just a minute, let me think. This is hard. Okay! Mine's different because my numbers aren't all the same as hers. But mine's the same because, like Magnolia, every pair has at least one 0—it's got to!

Casey: Why does it have to, Megan?

Megan: You're picking on me today.

Casey: Possibly. Why does a or b have to be 0 if $-3ab = 0$?

Megan: Because the only thing you can multiply 3 by to get 0 is 0. So, ab is 0, and 0 times anything is 0.

Casey: Megan makes an important point for us. Zero times any number is 0, alright. For our purposes, let's turn that around. Okay, Salvador.

Salvador: The only way the product of two numbers can be 0 is if one of the numbers is 0.

Casey: Write that down for us under Omar's statement . . . Thank you. Consider how we might solve this equation:

Casey displays $3x(x - 8) = 0$ with the overhead

Casey: Jot down the solution. What did you put, Alphonse?

Alphonse: Zero.

Casey: If $x = 0$ as Alphonse indicates, what is $x - 8$? Delia.

Delia: I don't know.

Casey: Look at this equation. . .

Casey writes $ab = 0$ right under $3x(x - 8) = 0$

Casey: What is b if a is 0, Delia?

Delia: It can be any number.

Casey: So, let $b = x - 8$. Go back to the original equation, where $3x = 0$. So what about $x - 8$? Delia.

Delia: Any number.

Casey: But if $3x = 0$, then what's x? Megan.

Megan: Zero.

Casey: If $x = 0$ as Megan and Alphonse said, what is $x - 8$? Delia.

Delia: Anyth—Oh! Then $x - 8$ is $0 - 8$, which is just -8! I get it!

Casey: So for $3x(x - 8) = 0$, we have numbers multiplied together giving us a product of what? Xavier.

Xavier: Zero

Casey: So, for the equation to be true, . . . Juaquin?

Juaquin: One of the factors has to be 0. So either $3x = 0$, which means $x = 0$ or the other one can be 0.

Casey: Keep it going. What's true if the other one is 0—that is, if $x - 8 = 0$?

Juaquin: Then $x = 8$.

Casey: Dustin.

Dustin: I don't get it. How can $x = 0$ and $x = -8$?

Casey: Dustin, it can't. But x can equal 0, *or* x can equal -8. This equation happens to have two solutions. Kyle.

Kyle: I get it! It's like $ab = 0$. a is $3x$ and b is $x - 8$. Right?

Casey: You've got the idea, but technically what you said is not exactly right. And I'm not sure how to help you clear it up in the amount of time we have left. Let me try something. I don't know if it's going to help, but it's worth a try. We didn't run into this problem with $ab = 0$ because we were dealing with two different variables. So when we took the case that $a = 0$, b could be anything. Now, as Kyle pointed out to us $(3x)(x - 8) = 0$ works the same way with one difference; $3x$ and $x - 8$ are related, so the value of one affects the value of the other. So in the case of $3x = 0$, x must equal 0 and there's only one number x—it's the same x. . .

Looking at the sea of blank faces, Casey feels ambivalent. He feels that some of the students who tend to struggle in mathematics are on the threshold of conceptual-level understanding, but on the other hand, he realizes that the subtleties of what he is trying to explain are not coming across to them. Noticing that there are only 14 minutes remaining, he continues:

Casey: We have a point of confusion that we have yet to clear up. But instead of me rattling on about it, I think we should look at two more equations and then assign the homework. The experience should help the explanation make more sense tomorrow. Look at this equation:

Casey displays $x^2 - 7x = 0$

Casey: Let's find what, if any, values for x make this statement true. With the previous equation, $3x(x - 8) = 0$, we had a polynomial in factored from equal to 0. So, we knew that the equation held for an x value where one of the factors equals 0. But with this one, we have a binomial equal to 0. We're looking at the difference of two terms, not the product. Any suggestions? Does anyone see a way we could rewrite this binomial so that it's in factored form? Then we could find solutions by find-

ing values of x that make a factor equal 0. . . .
Okay, Mary.

Mary: Just factor the binomial.

Casey: Everybody, take Mary's suggestion—quietly, on the paper in front of you. Shhh, just do it please. Tell us what the equation looks like on your paper, Edwin.

Edwin: $x(x - 7) = 0$.

Casey: If one of two things is true, the statement is true. What are those two things, Magnolia?

Magnolia: If $x = 0$ or if $x - 7 = 0$.

Casey: And if $x - 7 = 0$, what's x in that case, Sid?

Sid: Seven.

Casey: We've got time for one or two more quick ones.

Casey writes and displays $12x^2 = 4x$

Casey: How about this one? Okay, Juaquin.

Juaquin: Just divide both sides by $4x$ and you get $3x = 0$. So x has to be 0.

Casey writes and displays the following:

$$12x^2 = 4x$$

$$\frac{12x^2}{4x} = \frac{4x}{4x}$$

$$3x = ?$$

Casey: What's $4x$ over $4x$?

Juaquin: Oh, yeah, it's 1 not 0. So then, $3x = 1$, and $x = \frac{1}{3}$.

Casey: Everybody, quickly try $\frac{1}{3}$ for x in the original equation and see if it works. Put your hand up if and when you find it does. Okay, so $x = \frac{1}{3}$ works. Does any other value for x work? . . . Sid.

Sid: $x = 0$.

Casey: Everybody, try it. Raise your hand if and when you find it works. Okay. So we've got two cases for x that work. Let me just raise a little caution flag about solving equations like this. Be careful when you divide through by the unknown variable for two reasons: One, you might lose a solution, and two, you need to watch that you don't try to divide by 0. By the way, we did nicely on that one, but I was surprised because I expected we'd do this:

Casey writes and displays:

$$12x^2 = 4x$$

$$12x^2 - 4x = 0$$

$$4x(3x - 1) = 0$$

Either $4x = 0$ or $3x - 1 = 0$

If $4x = 0$, then $x = 0$

If $3x - 1 = 0$, then $x = 1/3$

Casey: Let's squeeze in one more. I'm going to write it out quickly; you copy it and think about it as part of your homework.

Casey writes and displays:

$$x^2 + 25 = 10x$$

$$x^2 + 25 - 10x = 0$$

$$x^2 - 10x + 25 = 0$$

$$(x - 5)^2 = 0$$

$$x = 5$$

He then distributes the homework task sheet (see Exhibit 11.27) but assigns only items 1–5 because he did not get to the computer programming part of the day's agenda, which is the second part of item 6 in Exhibit 11.28. The bell sounds, and Casey is left pondering what happened in the class. However, he quickly turns his thoughts to the next business at hand—third period geometry.

Reflecting on Day 6 and Planning for Day 7

After school, Casey thinks about the day's algebra class and plans for Wednesday. He thinks: "That session was exciting, but it sure went a bit haywire when I tried to parallel $3x(x - 8) = 0$ with $ab = 0$. Next time, I'll anticipate some of them thinking that x in $3x$ is not equal to x in $x - 8$. I learn something every day! I don't think there's any way I can explain that nuance to them until they have more experience in factoring to solve real-life problems. Then they'll be able to make the connections. That's why I wanted to get into applications before we got to the really useful stuff—$ax^2 + bx + c = 0$. I hate waiting too long without touching real-life situations. As things went, my planned application lesson turned out to be more of a discover a relationship lesson!

"I hadn't realized that the little business we did with that homework task sheet (see item 4 of Exhibit 11.11) on the first day didn't do the discovery trick for them. It seems like such a straightforward idea—if $ab = 0$, then a or b must be 0! But I've got to remember these kids are just being introduced to this stuff; I've been using that relationship for years.

"The unit is going to work out fine. Even though I didn't spend enough time with discovery in the beginning, I'm making up for it now. There's still time to work on application—especially after we get through Objective J. Maybe today's activities, coupled with some review and practice tomorrow, will provide them with enough of a hint that factoring has real-world applicability. Of course, part of the difficulty is that the algorithms we've covered up to this point in the unit are included because they lead to something that's useful, not necessarily because they are all that useful in themselves. At least, the kids seems to be hanging in with me, and I've already given them more real-life applications of mathematics than I ever had in any six mathematics courses I took!

"I'd better stop trying to make myself feel better and start deciding where we go with the rest of this unit. First of all, I need to follow up with this homework assignment and use their work on it to further the discover stuff and give them more of an idea about applications of factoring. Most everybody will have done okay with items 1 and 2 (see Exhibit 11.27). Work with item 3 will help clear up that business about *x* being one number *and* another rather than one number *or* another. I doubt if too many of them will understand item 5, but it gets us into application. Actually, there's a nice progression in that task sheet from the discovery stuff of items 1 and 2 to the thought problems of 3 and 4 and then the heavy application word problem of 5. Not bad, Casey!

"After we get through the homework, I've simply got to walk them through writing the computer programs as planned for today. . . . Then I should give them practice with the algorithms to this point and wait until Friday or so to go on to the discovery lesson on factoring trinomials. If things go well tomorrow, we could get to that Thursday, but if I try to do that, we probably wouldn't start until the latter part of the period, and then could run out of class time and not reach closure. This unit may go a day or two longer than planned, but if I rush things, it'll just create difficulties in Unit 8 and on down the road."

Days 7 to 14

Day 7. On Wednesday Casey reviews the homework and then completes the computer program writing activity previously planned for Tuesday (i.e., the second part of agenda item 6 in Exhibit 11.28). For homework he assigns items 6 and 7 from Exhibit 11.27, as well as textbook exercises that will provide practice in factoring algorithms.

Day 8. After reviewing the homework on Thursday, Casey divides the class into three independent work groups. Some students go to the computer lab to complete the factoring exercises, using programs they had entered and debugged for homework. Another group utilizes the classroom computers to work on the same exercise. The remaining students engage in small-task-group sessions, working on word problems similar to item 5 of Exhibit 11.28.

Day 9. Casey finally gets to conduct the lesson on Objective I (see Exhibit 11.9) that he's been anticipating since the unit began. In a reasoning-level question/discussion session, he takes advantage of students' prior knowledge of the FOIL method for multiplying binomials (the **f**irst terms are multiplied, then the two **o**uter terms, followed by the two **i**nside terms, and then the two **l**ast terms) to lead them to formulate the algorithm for factoring trinomials.

A small-task-group session follows, with four subgroups of about six students each working with cardboard rectangular regions to develop geometric models for factoring different trinomials, for example, $2x^2 + 3x + 1 = (x + 1)(2x + 1)$. The activity, the idea for which Casey picked up from Sobel and Maletsky (1988, pp. 174–175), is illustrated in Exhibit 11.29.

The Weekend. Over the weekend Casey uses procedures explained in the section Designing Teacher-Produced Tests in Chapter 10 to develop a unit test for Objectives A–L in Exhibit 11.9. Exhibit 11.30 contains a copy of the test resulting from that effort. He also synthesizes a practice test to use in a review session he'll conduct the day before the unit test is scheduled.

Day 10. Monday's class is devoted to direct instructional activities on the algorithm for factoring trinomials (Objective J from Exhibit 11.9). Case 5.12 includes a list of the steps in the algorithm Casey explains during this session. An independent work session and a homework assignment provide students with skill-level practice with algorithms.

Day 11. On Tuesday Casey guides the students through the writing of a computer program for factoring trinomials, as he has done for previous algorithms. He then distributes a task sheet containing word problems to be solved. As suggested in the section Lessons for Application Objectives in Chapter 6, the task sheet contains example problems solvable by factoring, as well as nonexample problems solvable via methods from prior units. Assigning the task sheet is Casey's first step in conducting a deductive lesson for Objective L (see Exhibit 11.9).

Exhibit 11.29
An experiment Casey used.

Factoring a Trinomial

Material

A set of large squares measuring x by x, labeled by their areas as $x \times x$ or simply x^2.

A set of small squares measuring 1 by 1, labeled by their areas as 1×1 or simply 1.

A set of rectangles measuring x by 1, labeled by their areas as $x \times 1$ or simply x.

Directions

Monomials, binomials, and trinomials in x can now be represented by the appropriate geometric figures.

In factoring a trinomial, the various monomial parts are arranged in a rectangular shape. The dimensions of the rectangle give the factors.

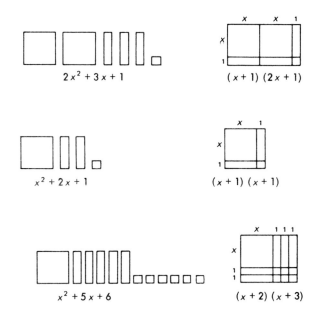

1. Show how to factor $3x^2 + 4x + 1$ using a model.
2. Show how to factor $4x^2 + 8x + 3$ using a model.
3. Show some other trinomials that can be factored using a model. Show some that cannot be factored.
4. Imagine a rectangular array of these pieces measuring $5x + 1$ by $2x + 3$. How many pieces are in it? How many of each size are there? What trinomial factorization does it represent?

Source: Max A. Sobel/Evan M. Maletsky, TEACHING MATHEMATICS: A Sourcebook of Aids, Activities, & Strategies, 2e, © 1988, pp. 174–175. Reprinted by permission of Prentice Hall, Inc., Englewood Cliffs, New Jersey.

During the remainder of the period, the class engages in an independent work session, with some students working at classroom computers to enter and debug their programs and others beginning work on the task sheet. All students are directed to complete both for homework.

Day 12. On Wednesday Casey conducts a reasoning-level question/discussion session relative to Objective L. His deductive questions focus on problems students addressed for homework and lead them through the first three of the four stages of an application lesson: (a) initial problem confrontation and

Exhibit 11.30
Casey's algebra I unit test for his first-period class.

Algebra I
1st Period
Unit 7 Test

1. What is your name?_____

2. Following is a list of questions. For each, determine whether or not analyzing the factors of a number would help to answer the question. If so, write Yes in the blank. If not, write No. Write one sentence explaining the reason for your answer.

   _____$5,378 was donated for a cause. How many people donated to the cause and what was the average donation?
   Reason:_____
   _____

   _____How large an area can I enclose with 60 meters of fencing?
   Reason:_____
   _____

   _____If I save $175 in a bank at an interest rate of 6%, compounded monthly for a year, how much interest will I have earned after 2 years?
   Reason:_____
   _____

   _____How long will it take me to travel 300 miles by car?
   Reason:_____
   _____

3. List all the factors of -18 that are integers.
   _____

4. Express 72 in a factored form using only prime numbers.
   _____

5. Which of the following two expressions represents a prime polynomial? Put an X in the blank in front of the prime polynomial and then use the space provided to explain why it is prime and the other one is not.
   _____ $80a^3b - 4ab^2$ _____ $80a + 17b$
   _____
   _____

6. Write $21x^3 + 6x$ in factored form._____
   Prove your answer with the distributive property $ab + ac = a(b + c)$ by indicating what you let a, b, and c equal:
   $a =$ _____, $b =$ _____, $c =$ _____

7. Illustrate that $x^2 + 4x + 3$ can be expressed in factored form as $(x + 3)(x + 1)$ by drawing a puzzle constructed from the following eight puzzle pieces:

   Label your finished puzzle to indicate the dimensions of the two-dimensional region it forms:

Exhibit 11.30
Continued

---

8. For each of the following that is factorable, factor completely; write not factorable under the others:

a.

$$11w^3 - 44w$$

b.

$$2x^2 + 11x - 30 + x^2 + 10$$

c.

$$t^2 + t + 2$$

d.

$$5x^2 - 80$$

9. A rectangle is 4 meters wide and 7 meters long. If the length and the width are increased by the same amount, the area is increased by 26 square meters. What are the dimensions of the new rectangle? Display your work and write your final answer in the blank.

_____

10. The difference between the square of a particular whole number and itself is 12. What is that whole number? Display your work and write your final answer in the blank.

_____

11. Smile.

analysis, (b) subsequent problem confrontation and analysis, (c) rule articulation, and (d) extension into subsequent lessons, as explained in Chapter 6.

For homework, Casey assigns the practice test he developed over the weekend.

Day 13. Thursday is review day. The practice test that students were directed to complete for homework is reviewed and questions relative to any of the unit topics raised by the review are addressed.

Day 14. Friday, the students take the unit test.

Scoring and Interpreting the Unit Test

Casey scores the test and, with the aid of his computer, generates the detailed results shown in Exhibit 11.31. Using the compromise method explained in Chapter 10, he converts the scores to grades for the unit, with scores greater than or equal to 74 assigned A's, scores between 65 and 70 assigned B's, scores between 40 and 60 assigned C's, the scores 22 and 24 assigned D's, and the score of 15 assigned an F.

The following are some of the conclusions he draws from his analysis of the item by item results:

- In general, students tended to have more trouble expressing themselves about mathematics than executing mathematics.
- Overall, students achieved at the application level—Objective L—better than expected.
- Students in general—but especially those who scored below 60—tended to have difficulty with item 2, which was designed to be relevant to Objective A.
- He should think about developing and using strategies to: (a) provide Magnolia and Juaquin with more advanced work; (b) keep Delia and Xavier engaged in learning activities—their lack of attention and effort seems to have led to their failure to achieve this unit's goal satisfactorily; and (c) remediate what appears to be significant learning gaps in Dick's understanding of mathematics.

Casey notes individual students' responses to certain items that he wants shared with the class on Monday when the test is reviewed. Since he plans to utilize small task groups as part of the review session, he organizes the subgroups so that each one has at least two students with high scores.

Day 15.

Casey reviews the test results with the class by following the four stages explained in the section Formative Feedback in Chapter 10. In the latter part of the class, Casey uses the discussion of items 9 and 10 to lead into Unit 8, Quadratic Equations.

SAMPLE GEOMETRY UNIT

Although preparing for, conducting, and evaluating outcomes for just the algebra I class could keep Casey busy every day, Casey must split his time among five classes. While preparing and orchestrating the algebra I unit on factoring polynomials, he is also busy with a third-period geometry unit on polygonal similarity. Exhibit 11.32 displays the overall plan Casey follows for that unit.

SAMPLE CONSUMER MATHEMATICS TEACHING UNIT

Reread the section Fifth-Period Consumer Mathematics in this chapter. Casey designed the consumer mathematics course with 16 units in mind:

1. Using Mathematics to Make Decisions
2. Measurements and Numbers
3. Calculating, Organizing Data, and Using Formulas
4. Using Statistics
5. Using Computers
6. Saving and Investing Money
7. Borrowing
8. Spending Wisely
9. Acquiring a Place to Live
10. Maintaining a Home
11. Construction and Trades
12. Taxes
13. Insurance
14. Transportation and Travel
15. Sports, Hobbies, and Recreation
16. Occupations and Employment

After completing the first 12 units, he is pleased with how the course has gone. However, he is concerned that virtually no new mathematics is introduced in Units 6–12, as those units focus on applying previously learned mathematics to new situations. He is now planning Unit 14, Transportation and Travel.

Chapter 8 of the course's textbook (Keedy, Smith, & Anderson, 1986, pp. 263–301) is the principal reference for the unit. Casey rereads the chapter section headings: Buying a Car, Buying a Motorcycle, Financing Your Purchases, Maintenance and Repair, Highway Safety, Planning a Trip, Renting a Car, Recreational Vehicles, and Air Travel.

He thinks: "If I follow the book, there are nine topics or situations that apply the same mathematics we've been applying for the last eight units. I'd like to break the monotony of the pattern I set for Units 6–13.

Exhibit 11.31
Detailed results from Casey's Unit 7 test shown in Exhibit 11.30.

Item (Max. Points)	2 (8)	3 (3)	4 (3)	5 (3)	6 (8)	7 (12)	8 (28)	9 (8)	10 (8)	Test Score (81)
Magnolia	8	3	3	3	8	12	28	8	8	81
Juaquin	8	2	3	3	8	12	27	8	8	80
Marlene	6	3	3	3	8	10	28	8	8	77
Alena	7	2	1	3	8	12	28	8	8	77
Cassandra	6	3	3	2	8	12	25	8	8	75
Kevin	5	3	2	3	7	10	28	8	8	74
Omar	3	3	3	3	3	10	28	8	8	69
Tawny	8	3	3	3	8	2	28	6	8	69
Edwin	7	1	3	3	8	12	20	6	8	68
Megan	4	3	3	3	8	12	28	3	4	68
Sid	5	3	2	3	4	9	26	8	8	68
Chevron	8	2	3	3	8	12	19	5	8	68
Salvador	8	3	3	3	4	10	24	6	6	67
Dustin	8	3	3	3	8	4	25	6	6	66
Mary	6	1	2	2	4	7	28	8	8	66
Kyle	4	3	3	1	6	10	22	4	6	59
Mylinn	1	1	1	0	8	10	22	8	8	59
Amad	2	2	2	2	7	10	19	6	6	56
Ron	3	3	3	3	8	10	15	4	6	55
Alphonse	2	3	3	3	4	6	26	4	4	55
Russell	6	3	3	3	8	2	12	4	5	46
Blair	5	3	3	3	4	4	13	4	5	44
Delia	2	2	3	0	1	6	5	2	3	24
Xavier	4	2	3	0	3	1	7	1	1	22
Dick	2	1	0	1	2	3	4	1	1	15
Ann	Has not taken test									

$n = 25$ $\mu = 60.32$ $\sigma = 17.51$ $r = 0.78$ SEM $= 8.21$

"Let's see, 28 students in the class—if I farm out these nine topics to cooperative small task groups, that'd give us eight groups of three and one group of four. Maybe if I make each group responsible for searching out information on how to apply the mathematics to the type of situation and teach the rest of the class. . . . It would really be nice to spice it up and somehow turn it into some sort of project. But what?

"I've got it! They love to perform in front of the video camera, and almost all of them are interested in television and videos. What if I assigned each group a topic for which they could develop a short, how-to-do videotape program—like plan a trip? I'd have to set some tight parameters to make sure they get to application of the relevant mathematics, limit the length of the programs, clearly define the audience—that stuff."

Deciding to try out the idea, Casey develops the overall unit plan shown in Exhibit 11.33.

At the conclusion of the unit, Casey judges that the cooperative group videotape program projects worked so well that he should use the approach more in the future and in other courses.

SAMPLE PRECALCULUS UNIT

Reread the section Sixth-Period Precalculus in this chapter. Exhibit 11.34 displays the overall plan for one of Casey's precalculus units. Note that the format Casey uses to capture his plan for achieving the objectives differs from those of Exhibits 11.9, 11.32, and 11.33. He modifies his planning methods as he learns what works best for him, according to his purposes at the time.

INSERVICE OPPORTUNITIES AND THE NCTM CONFERENCE

Throughout the school year Casey avails himself of opportunities to improve his teaching performances. Meetings of the local affiliate of NCTM

Exhibit 11.32
Casey's plan for the geometry unit on polygonal similarity.

Course: Geometry
Unit No: 10 out of 18
Title: Polygonal Similarity
Goal: Discovers and proves certain similarity relations and uses them in problem solving.
Weighted Objectives:

(15%)   A. Distinguishes between examples and nonexamples of similarity relations between two polygons.   (*construct a concept*)

(05%)   B. Defines the following terms: "similar polygons," "proportion," and "geometric mean."   (*simple knowledge*)

(05%)   C. Explains how the algebra of proportions relates to similarity between polygons.   (*comprehension*)

(33%)   D. Explains why each of the following relations holds:
   1. Side-splitting theorem
   2. Converse of the side-splitting theorem
   3. AAA similarity postulate
   4. AA similarity theorem
   5. Two right triangles are similar if an acute angle of one triangle is congruent to an acute angle of the other triangle.
   6. In a right triangle, the length of the altitude to the hypotenuse is the geometric mean between the lengths of the two segments of the hypotenuse.
   7. Given a right triangle and the altitude to the hypotenuse, each leg is the geometric mean between the length of the hypotenuse and the length of the segment of the hypotenuse adjacent to the leg.
   8. SSS similarity theorem
   9. SAS similarity theory
      (*discover a relationship*)

(20%)   E. Proves similarity theorems.   (*application*)

(02%)   F. Writes and uses computer programs to execute algorithms used in applying similarity relations to the solutions of problems. (*comprehension*)

(20%)   G. Given a real-life problem determines how, if at all, a solution to that problem is facilitated by using relations derived from the AAA similarity postulate or theorems listed for Objective E.   (*application*)

Estimated Number of Class Periods: 14
Textbook Page References: 308–357. Unless otherwise indicated, page numbers referred to in the overall lesson plan are from the course textbook (Burrill, Cummins, Kanold, & Yunker, 1993).
Overall Plan for Lessons:
   Throughout the unit, the students who are in both this class and Mr. Bosnick's art class (12 out of 23 students) will be applying what they learn about polygonal similarity to a perspective art project. Those students will be reporting on the progress of their project in class. (Estimated time needed: *A total of 1.5 class periods intermittently distributed over about 7 days*)
   For **Objective A,** I will conduct a four-stage inductive lesson using examples and nonexamples of similar pairs in the sorting and categorizing stage. (Estimated time needed: *1 class period plus homework*)
   For **Objective B,** direct instruction and exposure to word usage will be integrated within lessons for the other objectives to help students utilize the vocabulary terms in communications.   (Estimated time needed: *1–3 intermittent minutes each class period plus homework*)
   For **Objective C,** direct instruction will be used to help students comprehend the explanation and examples in the section Proportions on pp. 308–310. Exercises from pp. 307–307 will be assigned for an independent

Exhibit 11.32
Continued

work session and homework.   (Estimated time needed: *1 class period plus homework*)

Relative to the first two relations listed under Objective D (the side-splitting theorem and its converse), lessons for **Objectives D, E, and G** will be conducted according to the following pattern:

1. Inductive learning activities leading to the discovery of the relations.
2. Deductive learning activities leading to proofs of theorems deduced from the relations.
3. Deductive learning activities leading to application of the relations to problem solving.
4. Exercises assigned from pp. 316–320.
5. A brief test for formative feedback.

(Estimated time needed: *1.5 class periods plus homework)*

Relative to the third, fourth, and fifth relations listed under Objective D (AAA similarity postulate, AA similarity theorem, and the theorem on similarity of two right triangles), lessons for **Objectives D, E, and G** will follow the five-step pattern above, but with the exercises being assigned from pp. 328–335. (Estimated time needed: *2.25 class periods plus homework*)

Relative to the sixth and seventh relations listed under Objective D (the two that are relative to geometric means), lessons for **Objectives D, E, and G** will follow the five-step pattern above, but with the exercises being assigned from pp. 336–341. (Estimated time needed: *2 class periods plus homework*)

Relative to the eighth and ninth relations listed under Objective D (SSS and SAS similarity theorems), lessons for **Objectives D, E, and G** will follow the five-step pattern above, but with the exercises being assigned from pp. 346–348.   (Estimated time needed: *2.25 class periods plus homework*)

For **Objective F,** I'll conduct a direct-instructional lesson to walk students through writing a single program and have them enter, debug, and utilize it for homework. (Estimated time needed: *0.75 of a class period plus homework*)

Using a practice test, I'll conduct a review session for the unit test for Objectives A–G. (Estimated time needed: *0.75 of a class period plus homework*)

A unit test for Objectives A–G will be administered and the results reviewed with the class. (Estimated time needed: *1.75 class periods*)

Extraordinary Learning Materials and Equipment Needed:

No materials are needed that have not already been used in previous units.

provide opportunities to share ideas with colleagues and hear presentations on mathematics and on teaching mathematics. Although they rarely address his particular teaching situation, his creative thinking about teaching is stimulated by a graduate course he manages to attend one night a week and by several inservice workshops sponsored by the school district. Although he had enjoyed the journals *Mathematics Teacher* and *Mathematics Teaching in the Middle School* for several years, he finds the articles even more meaningful now that he has real students and actual courses to teach. His continuing struggles to come up with meaningful examples and real-world problems for his con-

struct a concept, discover a relationship, and application lessons motivates him to read about mathematics more than ever before. The seemingly endless need to respond to students' queries and thoughts helps him gain insights into mathematics and human behavior that he never before imagined.

He learns from interacting with colleagues and they learn from him. Vanessa Castillo's help is invaluable; even teachers with whom he disagrees on most pedagogical issues (e.g., Don Delaney) stimulate productive thought.

In April Casey takes three professional-leave days to attend the annual NCTM Conference. There, he interacts with colleagues from around the world,

Exhibit 11.33
Casey's plan for the consumer mathematics unit on transportation and travel.

Course: Consumer Mathematics
Unit No.: 14 out of 16
Title: Transportation and Travel
Goal: Applies fundamental relations from arithmetic, algebra, and statistics to solve problems related to transportation and travel.
Weighted Objectives:

    (10%) A. Translates the meaning of the following terms in the context of transportation/travel* related situations: "Cash price of a vehicle," "base price of a vehicle," "sticker price of a vehicle," "down payment," "amount financed," "finance charge," "deferred payment price," "parts and materials costs," "labor charges," "taxable items," "stopping distance," "drag factors," "nomogram," "base air fare," "discount air fare," "special rate air fare," and "excess baggage fare."   (*comprehension*)

    * For purposes of this unit, transportation/travel includes:
        1. Buying a car
        2. Buying a motorcycle
        3. Financing the purchase
        4. Maintenance and repair
        5. Highway safety
        6. Planning a trip
        7. Renting a car
        8. Recreational vehicles
        9. Air travel

    (25%) B. Explains the rationale underlying fundamental formulas used in solving transportation/travel related problems.   (*discover a relation*)

    (10%) C. Executes algorithms based on fundamental formulas used in solving transportation/travel related problems.   (*algorithmic skill*)

    (55%) D. Given a transportation/travel related problem, explains how, if at all, mathematical relations and algorithms learned in Units 1–5 can be used to solve the problem.   (*application*)

Estimated Number of Class Periods: 16
Textbook Page References: 263–301 and 336–39 (Keedy, Smith, & Anderson, 1986)
General Approach for Conducting the Unit:

The class will be subdivided into nine groups of three or four each, with each group being assigned one of the nine transportation/travel topics listed in the objectives. Each group is to undertake a project in which they produce a videotape program (approximately 25 minutes long) designed to help the rest of the class achieve the four objectives of the unit relative to the assigned topic. From design through production and presentation, I will supervise each group's project.

Overall Plan for Lessons:

In a large-group presentation, I'll (a) provide the class with an overview of the plans for the unit, (b) organize the nine subgroups (based on selections I make prior to class—ideally, each group will have a student who has had a relatively easy time with mathematics and one who does not but who is knowledgeable about the travel/transportation area), (c) distribute resources, and (d) explain and have them begin the initial assignment for each group (which will involve reading the relevant section of the textbook and gathering background information). (Estimated time needed: *1 class period plus homework*)

Each group will report results of the initial assignment to the class and then I will specify the parameters for the projects, explaining what is to be included and outlining each of the following phrases: information gathering,

Exhibit 11.33
Continued

analyzing, designing, script writing, evaluating/refining, and video program production. (Estimated time needed: *1.75 class periods plus homework*)

In small-task-group sessions, each group will develop, evaluate, and refine a data gathering, development, and production plan and have it critiqued and approved by me. (Estimated time needed: *1.5 class sessions plus homework*)

Students will engage in data-gathering activities, including visiting off-campus sites as necessary and practical. (Estimated time needed: *1 class period plus homework*)

In small-task-group sessions, each group will complete their production according to its approved plan. Productions are scheduled and presented to the class as a whole as soon as reasonably possible upon completion. Students observing a production are responsible for learning from the presentations in order to achieve the unit's objectives. I will conduct an question/discussion session on each of the nine topics after it is presented. Brief tests will be intermittently scheduled for formative feedback. (Estimated time needed: *10 class periods plus homework*)

A unit test will be administered and the results reviewed with the class. (Estimated time needed: *1.5 class periods*)

Extraordinary Learning Materials, Equipment, and Arrangement Needed:
(a) Informational resources (e.g., travel and buyers' guides), (b) arrangements for students to visit automobile dealers, motorcycle dealers, recreational vehicle dealers, travel bureaus, auto rental outlets, and motor vehicle safety office, and (c) equipment and supplies for videotaping in the classroom over a two-week period.

whose goals, problems, frustrations, and successes appear remarkably familiar after eight months in the profession. Although the school year is winding down, Casey is energized by the professional associations and the conference sessions. Some sessions include hands-on, take it with you activities; at others speakers present ideas or research findings. The quality of the sessions varies considerably from very boring to very exciting, but all leave Casey with thoughts that will improve his classroom effectiveness. At the conference Casey reviews exhibits of instructional resources, technology, and publications for mathematics teachers.

WINDING DOWN THE SCHOOL YEAR AND ANTICIPATING NEXT YEAR

The end of May is filled with clerical tasks like retrieving textbooks and completing scores of year-end forms and reports required by the school district office. Though feeling exhausted, Casey is already anticipating his second year. He thinks to himself: "If I had known in August what I know now, my students would have learned so much more! I'll be ready to do it right next year! Now, I know what to expect and what to prepare for. This year, I started from scratch. Now I have a wealth of resources—lesson plans, item pools, examples, nonexamples, real-world problems, contrived problems—all neatly stored on computer disks, quite a bit to build on. I know I can succeed in this profession. Even with all my mistakes, I managed to lead the vast majority of my students to do meaningful mathematics—to construct concepts, discover relationships, comprehend and communicate mathematically, develop algorithmic skills, acquire and retain information, solve real-world problems, create and invent mathematics, and develop healthy attitudes about mathematics!"

TRANSITIONAL ACTIVITIES FROM CHAPTER 11 TO CHAPTER 12 _____

1. With a group of your colleagues who have also read Chapters 1–11, engage in a discussion relative to the following questions or tasks:
   a. How important to his success was Casey's assertive behavior? What might have gone differently if he had not learned to be more assertive?
   b. Critique Casey's syllabus in Exhibit 11.3 with respect to readability for algebra I students, completeness, format, and inclusion of unnecessary material.

Exhibit 11.34
Casey's plan for the precalculus
unit on sequences.

Course: Precalculus
Unit No: 4 out of 8
Title: Sequences
Goal: Understands the language of discrete mathematics; discovers, proves, and
applies certain theorems about sequences; explores the idea of the limit of a
sequence; and associates discrete mathematics with some of its history.
Weighted Objectives:

(10%)   A. Interprets and uses the following terms, notations, and medi-
ums in communications about discrete mathematics: "Function
on the set of natural numbers," "sequence," "infinite sequence,"
"finite sequence," sequence notations (e.g., t_i), "recursive definition," "factorial notation," "partial sum, "summation notation,"
"sequence of partial sums," "arithmetic sequence," "geometric
sequence," "common difference of an arithmetic sequence,"
"common ration of a geometric sequence," "convergent
sequence," and "divergent sequence."   (*comprehension*)

(10%)   B. Distinguishes between examples and nonexamples of each of
the following concepts: (a) sequence, (b) finite sequence, (c)
infinite sequence, (d) convergent sequence, (e) divergent
sequence, (f) arithmetic sequence, (g) geometric sequence,
and (h) partial sum of a sequence.   (*construct a concept*)

(20%)   C. Explains why each of the following relations holds:

1. $a_n = a_1 + (n - 1)(a_2 - a_1)$ where a_n is the nth term of an
arithmetic sequence $(a_1, a_2, a_3, \ldots)$.

2. $\sum\limits_{i=1}^{n} (a_i) = (n/2)(a_1 + a_n)$ where $(a_1, a_2, a_3, \ldots)$ is an
arithmetic sequence.

3. $a_n = a_1(a_2/a_1)^{n-1}$ where a_n is the nth term of a geometric se-
quonoo $(a_1, a_2, a_3, \ldots)$.

4. $\sum\limits_{i=1}^{n} (a_i) = [a_1(1 - (a_2/a_1)^n]/[1 - (a_2/a_1)]$ where $(a_1, a_2,$
$a_3, \ldots)$ is a geometric sequence.

5. $\sum\limits_{i=1}^{\infty} (a_i) = a_1/[1 - (a_2/a_1]$ where $(a_1, a_2, a_3, \ldots)$ is an infinite geometric sequences such that $-1 < (a_2/a_1) < 1$.

(*discover a relationship*)

(10%)   D. Explains proofs for the five theorems listed in Objective C.
(*comprehension*)

(20%)   E. Formulates hypotheses based on the five theorems listed in
Objective C and explores relations relative to limits of sequences.
(*discover a relationship*)

(10%)   F. Proves corollaries to the five theorems listed in Objective C (e.g.,
0.999, . . . = 1).   (*application*)

(02%)   G. Writes and uses computer programs to execute algorithms used
in applying relations listed in Objective C.   (*comprehension*)

(05%)   H. Explains some episodes in the historical development of discrete
mathematics.   (*comprehension*)

Exhibit 11.34
Continued

(13%)　I.　Given a problem, determines how, if at all, a solution to that problem is facilitated by using relations derived from the theorems listed for Objective C.　(*application*)

Estimated Number of Class Periods: 15.5

Textbook Page References: 425–450. Unless otherwise indicated, page numbers referred to in the overall lesson plan are from the course textbook (Cannon & Elich, 1994).

General Day-by-Day Plans:

Day 1:　1.　Interactive lecture session to define discrete mathematics and set the stage for the unit.

2.　Independent work session to review needed definitions, notations, and special functions.

3.　Question/discussion session to review results of the independent work session.

4.　Homework assignment continuing the review (reference pp. 426–436).

Day 2:　1.　Brief test for formative feedback relative to parts of Objective A.

2.　Interactive lecture session to review the test results.

3.　Question/discussion session to discover the concepts of convergent and divergent sequences.

4.　Homework and computer laboratory assignment to examine properties of various sequences.

Day 3:　1.　Question/discussion session to review results of the homework and computer laboratory assignment.

2.　Question/discussion session to discover relations 1 and 3 listed in Objective C.

3.　Homework assignment from pp. 434–442.

4.　Independent work session to begin the homework.

Day 4:　1.　Small-task-group session to review the results of the homework.

2.　Question/discussion session to discover relation 2 listed in Objective C.

3.　Interactive lecture session to prove relation 2 listed in Objective C.

4.　Homework assignment to compute partial sums and make conjectures about partial sums of special sequences.

5.　Independent work session to begin the homework.

Exhibit 11.34
Continued

Day 5: 1. Brief test for formative feedback relative to parts of Objectives A, B, C, D, and E.

2. Interactive lecture session to review the test results.

3. Question/discussion session to discover relation 4 listed in Objective C.

4. Interactive lecture session to prove relation 4 listed in objective C.

5. Homework assignment to compute partial sums and make conjectures about partial sums of special sequences.

Day 6: 1. Small-task-group session to review the results of the homework.

2. Interactive lecture session to write computer programs for computing partial sums of arithmetic and geometric sequences.

3. Interactive lecture session to organize and schedule small task groups to study and report on the history of some special sequences.

4. Homework and computer laboratory assignment: (a) enter and debug programs for computing partial sums, and (b) read references relative to small-task-group reports on history of certain sequences.

5. Small-task-group and independent-work sessions to begin the homework.

Day 7: 1. Deductive-level question/discussion session relative to applications of the first four relations listed in Objective C to (a) proofs of theorems and (b) problem solving.

2. Application-level homework assignment.

3. Small-task-group and independent-work sessions to begin the homework.

Day 8: 1. Brief test for formative feedback relative to parts of Objectives A, B, C, D, E, F, and I

2. Interactive lecture session to review results of the test.

3. Homework assignment dependent on results of the test and also continue to work on historical reports according to the previously determined scheduled.

Day 9: 1. Question/discussion to review homework as necessary.

2. First group's historical report.

3. Question/discussion session to review the report.

4. Second group's historical report.

Exhibit 11.34
Continued

5. Question/discussion session to review the report.

Day 10: 1. Brief test for formative feedback relative to part of Objective H.

2. Interactive lecture session to review results of the test.

3. Question/discussion session to discover relation 5 listed in Objective C.

4. Interactive lecture session to prove relation 5 listed in Objective C.

5. Homework assignment selected from exercises on pp. 445–448.

Day 11: 1. Small-task-group session to review homework results.

2. Deductive-level question/discussion session relating application of the fifth relation listed in Objective C to (a) proofs of theorems and (b) problem solving.

3. Homework assignment relative to applications of the fifth relation listed in Objective C.

4. Independent works session to begin the homework.

Day 12: 1. Brief test for formative feedback relative to Objective I.

2. Interactive lecture session to review results of the test.

3. Third group's historical report.

4. Fourth group's historical report.

5. Homework assignment dependent on the results of the test.

Day 13: 1. Inductive/deductive question/session to explore the concept of limits of sequences.

2. Independent work session dependent on the outcome of the exploration activities.

3. Homework assignment to complete the practice test in preparation for the unit test.

Day 14: 1. Interactive lecture session to review the practice test results.

2. Fifth group's historical report.

3. Homework assignment to prepare for the unit test.

Day 15: Unit test

Day 16: 1. Review the results of the unit test.

2. Set the stage for Unit 5, beginning with binomial distributions.

c. The *Standards* (NCTM, 1989, p. 127) suggest that use of factoring to solve equations should receive less attention in algebra courses than it has in the past. In what ways does Casey's Unit 7, described in the section Sample Algebra I Teaching Unit, depart from this suggestion? In what ways is it consistent with this suggestion?

d. As indicated by Exhibits 11.9, 11.32, 11.33, and 11.34, each of Casey's four sample units included several brief tests prior to the unit test. In addition to providing him and the students with formative feedback, how do you suppose these brief tests enhanced the units?

e. What are the advantages and disadvantages of Casey's use of a practice test for purposes of review just before the unit test? Contrast this strategy to reviewing simply by fielding students' questions and summarizing salient points about each of the unit's topics.

f. During Day 5 of the sample algebra I unit, Casey is conducting an independent work session when he tells Mary, "Okay, go with step 5. I'll be back in 33 seconds." Why do you suppose Casey said "33 seconds" rather than "in a minute" or "right away" or even "half a minute"?

g. Rather than using a factoring algorithm, Casey prefers to have students solve equations such as $x^2 - 25 = 0$ by reasoning "25 from what number is 0? Obviously, 25. What number squared is 25? Either 5 or -5." Why do you suppose he feels this way?

h. On Day 6 of the sample algebra I unit, Casey directs Xavier, who doesn't have his own task sheet, to look at Magnolia's. What are some of the possible repercussions of that action by Casey?

i. Later in the same example noted in h above, Megan appears unprepared and unwilling to get involved in the question/discussion session. What are the advantages and disadvantages of the manner in which Casey attempted to help her be engaged?

j. Later in the same example alluded to in i above, Casey writes $ab = 0$ under $3x(x - 8) = 0$. How did this move backfire? How did it help? In the long run, do you think the strategy will turn out to be more helpful or more hurtful to the students' understanding of mathematics?

k. From the examples of question/discussion sessions described in the section Sample Algebra I Teaching Unit, does it appear that Casey managed to involve a satisfactory number of students in lessons? Compare his tactics with those of Mr. Citerelli, Mr. Grimes, Mr. Smart, and Ms. Cramer in Cases 4.8, 9.9, 9.10, and 9.11, respectively.

l. On Day 6 of the sample algebra I unit, Juaquin simplified the equation $12x^2 = 4x$ to be $3x = 0$. Critique the way Casey responded to the mistake.

m. Critique the homework task sheet of Exhibit 11.27 in light of Casey's purpose in assigning it.

n. No examples of Casey using games are included in this chapter. In light of the sample unit plan shown in Exhibits 11.9, 11.32, 11.33, and 11.34, where do you think Casey might have appropriately incorporated games in his lessons?

o. How consistently do Casey's four sample unit plans follow the suggestions in Chapters 4–6 for designing lessons?

p. What are the advantages and disadvantages of Casey guiding students through writing computer programs for executing the algorithms he taught in the four sample units?

q. What are the advantages and disadvantages of centering the transportation and travel unit on the videotaping projects (as indicated in the section Sample Consumer Mathematics Teaching Unit)?

r. In what ways did Casey depend on his personal computer to get things done? What things would he have not accomplished efficiently without ready access to a computer?

s. In light of the number of points per item indicated in Exhibit 11.31 and the weights assigned to his objectives in Exhibit 11.9, critique the unit test displayed in Exhibit 11.30.

t. Formulate two example problems Casey may have been able to use in a lesson for Objective G of Exhibit 11.32. Do the same for Objective D of Exhibit 11.33 and for Objective I of Exhibit 11.34.

2. Select a course typically included in secondary or middle school mathematics curricula. Acquire a textbook that might be adopted for that course. Now, develop a syllabus for that course. Compare your syllabus to that of a colleague who is also engaged in this activity.

3. Interview a first-year mathematics teacher. Include the following questions: (a) What are some of the more important things you've learned since you've started teaching? (b) At this point in your career, what has been the most satisfying surprise? (c) At this point, what has been the most frustrating surprise?

4. Prepare for your work with Chapter 12 by discussing the following questions with two or more colleagues:

a. What are some of the major issues presently confronting the mathematics teaching profession? How might those issues be addressed and possibly resolved over the next ten years?
b. What hope does the mathematics teaching profession have for markedly increasing the percentage of its practitioners who meet the re-quirements spelled out in *Professional Standards for Teaching Mathematics* (NCTM, 1991)?
c. What role should we as mathematics teachers play in the ongoing movement to reform mathematics curricula and the way mathematics is taught in school.

CHAPTER

12

A Profession in Transition

This chapter is intended to stimulate your thinking about the current movement to reform the way mathematics is typically taught in schools and to reflect on your professional role in that movement.

A MIXED HISTORY

Exemplary mathematics teaching consistent with research-based principles and the *Standards* (NCTM, 1989a, 1991) has been successfully practiced at least since the time of Socrates. The merits of teaching methods based on these principles were extolled in literary works as early as 1791, when Johann Pestalozzi wrote *Leonard and Gertrude* (Cubberley, 1962, pp. 394–397; Wilds & Lottich, 1961, pp. 292–293). In Skemp's (1973) classic *The Psychology of Learning Mathematics,* the fundamental principles by which students construct mathematical concepts and discover relationships are explicated. The efficacy of the model is supported by a myriad of research findings (see for example, Driscoll, 1982; Grouws, 1992; NCTM, 1988-1989; Suydam & Brosnan, 1993, 1994): Inductive lessons lead students to discover mathematics, direct instruction helps them remember information and improve their algorithm skills, comprehension lessons help them communicate about mathematics, and deductive lessons help them apply mathematics. Many mathematics teachers like Casey Rudd continue to practice these research-based methods successfully within the entire spectrum of middle, junior high, and senior high school mathematics classrooms.

However, such exemplary mathematics has never been typical (Jesunathadas, 1990; NCTM,

1991). With nearly 200,000 teachers estimated to be teaching mathematics courses in the middle and secondary schools of the United States, most students never have the opportunity to learn mathematics from a teacher like Casey Rudd. Consequently, the history of mathematics education is mixed, marked by the crowning achievements of a relatively few and missed opportunities for the masses.

THE NCTM-*STANDARDS* DRIVEN REFORMATION

In the minds of some teachers, a question still exists as to whether they should attempt to follow the research-based approaches recommended by the mathematics education literature (e.g., the NCTM *Standards* and this book). They argue that although inquiry instructions may work in theory, it is simply too difficult to implement in realistic classroom situations. Although agreeing that their own traditional approaches are unsuccessful with the majority of students, they contend that most people need only fundamental skills and that conceptual and application learning is possible only for the gifted. They point to the successful mathematicians, engineers, and scientists who profited from traditional instruction.

In the minds of both teachers who have successfully implemented research-based approaches and mathematics education specialists, the research-based approaches are clearly superior to the traditional approaches, not only in theory but also in practice with all students. At this point, the most critical issue facing mathematics education specialists is not how mathematics should be taught but rather how to increase the number of mathematics teachers who break from tradition and apply the research-based approaches. Because teaching is a complex of messy functions successfully executed only by professionals astute in pedagogy, cognitive science, mathematics, behavior management, and evaluation of student achievement, reformation of the practices of the majority of mathematics teachers is an ambitious goal to say the least.

A century of efforts to reform the teaching of mathematics has failed to impact the majority of practitioners. What, if anything, would lead anyone to believe that the current movement under the banner of the NCTM *Standards* would be any more successful than those in the past? First of all, on the heels of highly publicized reports of widespread mathematical illiteracy, the political climate seems ripe for reform (see e.g., Wallis, 1994). Furthermore, the movement is piggy-backing on at least three other curriculum-reform movements:

- One addresses the need to provide meaningful educational experiences to students from groups that historically have been discriminated against in traditional school programs. Disparities among various social classes relative to preparation for entry into mathematically oriented professions must be addressed (Secada, 1992). Success in beginning calculus courses often determine entry into these professions; concern for under-represented groups in such professions at least partially motivated the calculus-reform movement currently impacting the teaching of mathematics in colleges and universities (Rowley, 1995).
- Another involves developing a technologically literate citizenry. Advances in technology clearly impact upon how mathematics is done, not only by professional mathematicians, statisticians, scientists, and engineers, but also in everyone's everyday activities—in the way goods are purchased, money is managed, and data are reported to the public.
- Advances in cognitive science, especially those involving the constructivist perspective, are increasingly being filtered through inservice and preservice teacher preparation programs and to those who shape school curricula.

The greatest challenge for mathematics education professionals may not be to stimulate the reformation as much as to guide the direction of the movement.

There is cause for optimism. As indicated in Chapter 2, the *Standards* are being afforded a high profile supported by a solid coalition of learned and professional societies of educationists, mathematicians, scientists, engineers, school administrators, and instructional supervisors. Curriculum materials like NCTM's *Addenda Series* are now available to not only inform teachers of what should be done, but also to provide a myriad of examples of just how to implement the *Standards*. *Professional Standards for Teaching Mathematics* (NCTM, 1991), which describes the competencies mathematics teachers should demonstrate, has become the guide that agencies such as the National Council for Accreditation of Teacher Education (NCATE) use to assess how well colleges and universities prepare mathematics teachers.

By combining a strong preparation in mathematics and pedagogy with achievement of the objectives listed for Chapters 1–11, you meet these professional standards for teaching mathematics. It is assumed, of course, that through actual classroom experience you will develop your abilities to implement and improve upon what you now understand.

Recent widespread agreement on resolutions to some previously controversial issues should also hasten the reformation in a direction favorable to *Standards*-based curricula. Although resistance to the resolutions still exists in some influential circles, the following is generally accepted:

- *Virtually everyone needs to do meaningful mathematics to solve real-life problems and is quite capable of learning to do so.* Some people (for example, Don Delaney, to whom you were introduced in Chapter 11) continue to perceive mathematics as a mystical sequence of rules that most people can learn to follow but only the gifted can understand. Such an erroneous perception, coupled with prejudiced attitudes about the capabilities of various ethnic groups to learn mathematics, flies in the face of overwhelming evidence to the contrary (Leder, 1992). Fortunately, naiveté and prejudice can hardly stand up to the current movement favoring meaningful mathematics for all students.
- *A wealth of proven instructional strategies, techniques, resources, and technologies that heretofore were either unavailable or untested are now available to help teachers implement research-based approaches.* As illustrated throughout this book, there are now effective strategies for (a) integrating mathematics history to demystify topics, (b) utilizing reading, writing, and speaking activities to facilitate students doing meaningful mathematics, (c) integrating mathematical topics with each other and with other disciplines to facilitate application-level learning, (d) using cooperative learning activities to tap the vast wealth of experiences and teaching potential among students, (e) using computers, calculators, and other technologies to relieve much of the tedium of executing algorithms, generate examples, generate and ma-

nipulate models, make quality presentations, manage and maintain files, and facilitate experimentation, (f) managing student behavior, and (g) evaluating student achievement for both formative and summative purposes.

- *Teachers need in-depth preparation in both mathematics and teaching methods (which includes cognitive science, behavior management, pedagogical principles, and evaluation of student achievement).* In some naive circles, people contend that to teach mathematics one needs only to be very knowledgeable in mathematics and that there is no value in wasting time learning teaching methods. Others, in equally naive circles, argue that teachers can be effective without knowing mathematics beyond the levels they teach, as long as they practice sound teaching methods in other words, to teach algebra, you don't need to understand calculus. Such uninformed opinions have recently been countered by the joint forces of professional societies of both mathematicians and educators. For example, *Guidelines for the Continuing Mathematical Education of Teachers* (The Mathematical Association of America, 1988) and *Professional Standards for Teaching Mathematics* (NCTM, 1991) both emphasize the necessity of teachers having advanced work in mathematics, as well as in instructional methods. Mathematics and the teaching of mathematics are inextricably interrelated. In mathematics education the two are indistinguishable.

- *Teachers should no longer be expected to succeed without appropriate support services of administrators, without competent instructional supervision, and without continuing inservice education.* With nearly 200,000 teachers estimated to be conducting mathematics courses in the nation's middle and secondary schools, the reformation can hardly succeed unless inservice as well as preservice teachers are affected. The outmoded model by which teachers collected the tools of their profession—their understanding of mathematics and instructional methods—from their preservice preparation programs in colleges, and then were left unattended to learn how to use the tools during their first inservice years in the classroom, has proven ineffectual at worse and inefficient at best (Duke, Cangelosi, & Knight, 1988). In response to such findings, promising models for providing inservice teachers with necessary instructional supervisory support services have been developed and validated (Cangelosi, 1991, pp. 119–159). With the influence of the Association of Supervision and Curriculum Development, there is considerable hope that the inservice support and education so desperately needed by teachers will become widely available through implementation of these models. Wherever such services are available, they could become a vehicle for guiding mathematics teachers toward research-based practices.

YOUR ROLE

Clearly, the most important variable in determining the future of mathematics education is *you* and your colleagues who are also embarking on careers as mathematics teachers. How do you influence the success of the profession and the course of the reformation? You begin by teaching as well as you reasonably can. How you execute your messy teaching functions impacts the students fortunate enough to be under your tutelage. Sometimes teachers complain, "My students just aren't capable of learning mathematics at this level. With a more capable group, I could succeed, but not with this bunch!" But the capabilities of your students do not influence the success of your teaching performance. Your teaching success depends on how well you lead your students to extend their grasp of mathematics within their own capabilities. In other words, evaluate how far they reach not where they reach.

Avail yourself of inservice education opportunities. Mathematics and pedagogical discoveries and inventions occur every day. How well you execute your messy teaching functions depends on your continuing to learn from experiences, as well as staying abreast of current research findings. Your NCTM membership will serve you well in this area.

Our profession is represented by dedicated, highly competent teachers as well as by fools. As a member of the former category, be a protagonist in the reformation of the profession.

TRANSITIONAL ACTIVITIES FROM CHAPTER 12 TO INSERVICE TEACHER

1. Interview two currently active mathematics teachers. Include the following items:
   a. Have your read the NCTM *Standards?* If so, what is your opinion of the points it makes and how do you think it has and will impact upon what actually goes on in the classroom?
   b. I would like to compare the preservice college preparation program you had with my own. I'm interested in how they compare relative to mathematical content and teaching methods—especially mathematics teaching methods, field-based experiences, theory of educational psychology, classroom and behavior management, use

of technology, and evaluation of student achievement. Please describe your program and let's compare similarities and differences between yours and mine.

c. What did you learn in your preservice teacher preparation program that helped you succeed as a mathematics teacher?

d. What aspects of your preservice education program did not prove helpful to you as a teacher?

e. In what inservice education programs have you participated? In what ways have they been helpful to you?

f. What advice do you have for me as I start my own career as a mathematics teacher?

2. Have an enjoyable and productive teaching career.

Excerpt from *Mathematics Core Curriculum: Grades 7–12* Relative to Teaching Elementary Algebra

SIS Number: 5250
SIS Code: MO

Course Title: Elementary Algebra

Unit of Credit: 1.0

Prerequisite: Mastery of Prealgebra

COURSE DESCRIPTION

The Elementary Algebra course of study consists of three principal parts:

1. Review of previously learned mathematics concepts, including maintaining the previous mathematics core standards.
2. Mastery of core standards and objectives for Elementary Algebra.

Source: From *Mathematics Core Curriculum: Grades 7–12* by Utah State Office of Education, 1995, Relative to the Teaching of Elementary Algebra, pp 16–27. Reprinted by permission.

3. Introduction of new concepts and skills outlined in district curriculum guides and/or textbooks.

Students in Elementary Algebra explore a mathematical model for the real number system involving the study of straight lines and numerical relationships. The properties of the real number system are used to solve linear equations and inequalities. Simple operations with polynomials are introduced and the laws of exponents are studied.

CORE STANDARDS OF THE COURSE

Standard 5250-*01.* Mathematics as Problem Solving

Purpose: Mathematical problem solving is nearly synonymous with doing mathematics. The problem-solving strategies learned in the earlier grades should have become increasingly internalized to form a broad basis for doing mathematics, regardless of the topic. Problem solving is a process by which mathematics is both constructed and reinforced.

Objectives

5250-0101	Use, with increasing confidence, problem-solving approaches to investigate and understand mathematical content.
5250-0102	Apply integrated mathematical problem-solving strategies to solve problems from within and outside mathematics.
5250-0103	Recognize and formulate problems from situations within and outside mathematics.
5250-0104	Apply the process of mathematical modeling to real-world problem situations.

Skills and Strategies

1. Solve a variety of problems including open-ended, puzzles, application, patterning, and extended problem-solving projects.
2. Link problem solving to the short sequencing of steps in a proof and draw reasonable conclusions.
3. Represent problem situations with algebraic equalities, inequalities, or models.
4. Formulate a plan to solve a problem by using one or more strategies such as:

   - Drawing a picture or diagram.
   - Looking for a pattern.
   - Guessing and checking.
   - Using a list, table, graph, or equation.
   - Working backwards.
   - Examining possibilities.
   - Working a similar simple problem.
   - Making a model or simulation.

6. Estimate solutions to problems and determine the reasonableness of the answer by relating it to the estimate.
7. Solve multi-step, complex problems.
8. Choose an appropriate calculation method from: mental math, estimation, paper-and-pencil, calculator, and/or computer.
9. Solve non-routine problems.
10. Investigate and formulate questions from problem situations.
11. Represent problem situations verbally, numerically, graphically, geometrically, or algebraically.

Standard 5250-*02.* Mathematics as Communication

Purpose: At this level, methods of mathematical communication becomes more formal and symbolic.

Facility with the language of mathematics is an integral part of thinking mathematically, solving problems, and reflecting on one's own mathematical experiences. All students need extensive experience with listening, reading, writing, speaking, and demonstrating. Small group activities can enhance these experiences. These techniques can also focus students away from an emphasis on recall to deeper understanding. Continually encouraging students to clarify or elaborate will increase their facility with language.

Objectives

5250-0201	Reflect upon and clarify their thinking about mathematical ideas and relationships.
5250-0202	Formulate mathematical definitions and express generalizations discovered through investigations.
5250-0203	Express mathematical ideas orally and in writing.
5250-0204	Read written presentations of mathematics with understanding.
5250-0205	Ask clarifying and extending questions related to mathematics they have read or heard about.
5250-0206	Appreciate the economy, power, and elegance of mathematical notation and its role in the development of mathematical ideas.

Skills and Strategies

1. Visualize, formulate, and communicate problems involving appropriate algebraic situations.
2. Use technology to express algebraic ideas.
3. Discuss, read, and write about mathematical ideas and relationships including those found in books and media.
4. Clarify, paraphrase, and elaborate on the mathematical strategies used to solve problems.
5. Employ precise language in conjunction with algebraic notation.
6. Discuss and write about the economy, power, and elegance of mathematical notation and its connection to society.
7. Investigate and formulate questions from problem situations and discuss with a small group.

Standard 5250-*03.* Mathematics as Reasoning

Purpose: At this level, students should be encouraged to use deductive and inductive reasoning to validate a mathematical assertion. This more formal practice, traditionally addressed primarily in geometry, should be expanded to other mathematics topics. Generalizing from patterns of observations (inductive reasoning) can be tested using a logical verification (deductive reasoning).

Objectives

5250-0301	Make and test conjectures.
5250-0302	Formulate counter examples
5250-0303	Follow logical arguments.
5250-0304	Judge the validity of arguments.
5250-0305	Construct simple valid arguments.

Skills and Strategies

1. Formulate counter examples.
2. Construct simple, valid arguments.
3. Use the concepts of logic and deductive and inductive reasoning to draw conclusions.
4. Utilize relationships between problem structures based upon algebraic properties.
5. Explain logical relationships by writing accurate if/then statements.
6. Identify valid or invalid information and/or conclusions.
7. Solve multi-step problems based on disqualification of available options.
8. Use deductive or inductive reasoning to validate hypotheses.

Standard 5250-04. Mathematical Connections

Purpose: Connections should be made between mathematics topics and other disciplines or the real world. Also, it is important to make connections between two equivalent representations of mathematics ideas and between corresponding processes in each. Students who are able to translate among different representations of the same situation will have a powerful, flexible set of tools for problem solving.

Objectives

5250-0401	Recognize equivalent representations of the same concept.
5250-0402	Relate procedures in one representation to procedures in an equivalent representation.
5250-0403	Use and value the connections among mathematical topics.
5250-0404	Use and value the connections between mathematics and other disciplines.

Skills and Strategies

1. Use algebraic functions as a link to geometric transformations.
2. Use scaling and coordinate geometry to connect algebraic concepts to geometric concepts.

3. Connect abstract symbols, physical models, pictorial representations, and real-world applications.
4. Recognize and develop mathematical situations that arise in literature.
5. Recognize and develop the use of math skills and concepts in science.
6. Recognize and develop relationships between math and art such as shapes, proportion, scale drawings, tessellations, and mosaics.
7. Recognize and develop the use of mathematics in music.
8. Illustrate connections between verbal, analytical, algebraic, geometric, and graphic representations of mathematical problems.
9. Investigate historical and multicultural contributions to algebra via reports, research, projects, and presentations.
10. Find applications of algebraic concepts in newspapers, magazines, television, radio, or other sources to create picture books, collages, displays, etc.

Standard 5250-05. Algebra

Purpose: Algebra is a language through which most mathematics is communicated. The proposed algebra curriculum will move away from a tight focus on manipulative facility to include a greater emphasis on conceptual understanding, on algebra as a means of representation, and on algebraic methods as a problem-solving tool. Connections will be made to other representations such as numerical and graphing, and a graphing utility will be incorporated.

Objectives

5250-0501	Represent situations that involve variable quantities with expressions, equations, inequalities, and matrices.
5250-0502	Use tables and graphs as tools to interpret expressions, equations, and inequalities.
5250-0503	Simplify and operate on expressions and matrices, and solve equations and inequalities, using properties of equality and inequality.
5250-0504	Appreciate the power of mathematical abstraction and symbolism.
5250-0505	Use graphing technology to explore algebraic situations.

Skills and Strategies

1. Find the solutions set of an equation or a system of equations represented with a graph.

2. Represent and solve real-world situations with appropriate numerical and variable expressions, equations, inequalities, tables, or graphs.

3. Generate possible scenarios that would be represented by a given graph.

4. Generate equations and graphs from a table of values algebraically and graphically.

5. Solve linear equations and inequalities.

6. Explore solutions to quadratic equations graphically, numerically, and algebraically.

7. Identify properties used to validate each step in solving an equation or inequality.

8. Compare solutions of equations and inequalities, both algebraically and graphically including those with absolute value.

9. Evaluate formulas.

10. Multiply polynomials including special binomial products $(a+b)2$ and $(a-b)2$ interpreting with area models using manipulatives.

11. Create area models for factoring and demonstrate ability to solve factoring questions.

12. Using graphing technology, graph equations derived from real situations; identify the roots of the equation; and interpret the validity of these solution(s).

13. Compare area model factoring with identifying the roots of an equation on a graphing utility.

14. Simplify numerical expressions using the order of operations including those involving absolute value.

15. Evaluate algebraic expressions for a given value of each variable.

16. Simplify algebraic rational expressions and evaluate.

17. Form number patterns from models and real-life situations.

18. Generalize an equation from number or geometric patterns.

19. Use appropriate technology to investigate square roots and square root approximations.

20. Recognize when it is appropriate to use an approximation for a square root.

21. Use appropriate technology to graph and make predictions from functions that demonstrate variation.

22. Use the rules of exponents and roots to simplify radical and exponential expressions.

Standard 5250-*06.* Functions

Purpose: The concept of function is a unifying idea in mathematics as it ties together relationships between variables, sets, numbers, or geometric images. It also provides a way to describe many input-output situations in the real world. Students should have the opportunity to explore real-world relationships that can be depicted as functions numerically, algebraically, and graphically.

Objectives

5250-06*01*	Model real-world phenomena with a variety of functions.
5250-06*02*	Represent and analyze relationships using tables, verbal rules, equations, and graph.
5250-06*03*	Translate among tabular, algebraic, and graphical representations of functions.
5250-06*04*	Recognize that a variety of problem situations can be modeled by the same type of function.
5250-06*05*	Analyze the effects of parameter changes on the graphs of functions.

Skills and Strategies

1. Determine ordered pairs, domain, and range from a graph of a relation.

2. Identify when a relation is a function.

3. Determine the x- and y- intercepts from an equation of a line.

4. Using appropriate technology to graph families of lines and predict rules for slope and intercept.

5. Determine the slope of a line from a linear equation or its graph.

6. Determine the slope of a line given two ordered pairs or the slope and a point on the line.

7. Write an equation for a line given the graph.

8. Graph linear equations and inequalities using point plotting while also emphasizing other methods.

9. Identify perpendicular, horizontal, vertical, and parallel lines given the equations.

10. Given a scatter plot which approximates a linear graph, find a linear equation that best fits the graph.

11. Graph direct and inverse functions using appropriate technology and interpret the effect of parameter changes on the graph.

12. Given data in written or tabular form, create a graph and derive a formula that represents the relationship. (Examples: Fahrenheit to Celsius, ratio of circumference to diameter, volume and area relationships, etc.)

Standard 5250-*07.* Synthetic Geometry

Purpose: At this level, the geometry strand should provide experiences that deepen students' understanding of shapes and their properties with an emphasis on their applications in life. Physical models and examples in the real world should be used to provide a basis for development of intuitive and formal understanding.

Objectives

5250-0701   Represent problem situations with geometric models and apply properties of figures.

5250-0702   Classify figures in terms of congruence and similarity and apply these relationships.

5250-0703   Deduce properties of figures and relationships between them from given assumptions.

Skills and Strategies

1. Represent problem situations by constructing a geometric model and analyzing the properties of the figure.
2. Identify segment and angle congruence using physical models and drawings. (Example: paper folding, pattern blocks, compass/straightedge, etc.)
3. Identify polygons and understand properties of similarity in real-world situations.
4. Identify symmetry in real-world situations, plane geometric relationships, and coordinate geometry.
5. Explore measurement relationships among circles, and identify circles in the real world.
6. Use computers and calculators to illustrate triangle and quadrilateral properties.

Standard 5250-08. Geometry from an Algebraic Perspective

Purpose: The purpose of this level is to connect geometry with algebra. Relationships of geometry with algebraic expressions, equations, functions and coordinate geometry should all be emphasized at this level. The interplay between geometry and algebra helps students' ability to deal with problems both within and outside mathematics.

Objectives

5250-0801   Translate between synthetic and coordinate representations.

5250-0802   Deduce properties of figures.

Skills and Strategies

1. Calculate the perimeter of various polygons and circles.
2. Draw and illustrate perimeter of polygons in a coordinate geometry context (geoboard, calculator and computer utilities, etc.).
3. Illustrate polygons and circles in plane and coordinate geometry and determine the area (geoboard, calculator and computer utilities, etc.).

4. Explore and identify the properties of triangles and quadrilaterals in the real world and in coordinate geometry.

Standard 5250-09. Trigonometry.

Purpose: At this level, the study of triangle measurement is limited to understanding and applying the Pythagorean theorem and simple trigonometric ratios. Students should be given opportunities to explore applications in the real world for measuring right triangles to determine angles and sides. Graphing utilities should be used to enhance the understanding of triangle measurement and calculations.

Objectives

5250-0901   Apply trigonometry to problem situations involving triangles.

Skills and Strategies

1. Apply the Pythagorean Theorem to solve real-world problems involving right triangles using appropriate technology.
2. Calculate two unknown sides of special right triangles (30, 60, 90 and 45, 45, 90) given a known side, and relate these to real-world problems.
3. Solve real-world problems using isosceles right triangles.
4. Understand and use Pythagorean triples in real-world applications.

Standard 5250-10. Statistics

Purpose: Collecting, representing, and processing data are activities of major importance to contemporary society. At this level, students should be given opportunities at exploratory data analysis with real-world data. Students should gain appreciation for the value of statistical analysis and not reject the claim because it allows counter examples. Graphing utilities will enhance the analysis and presentation of the data and assist in making connections between numerical, algebraic, and graphical representations.

Objectives

5250-1001   Construct and draw inferences from charts, tables, and graphs that summarize data from real-world situations.

5250-1002   Use linear curve fitting to predict from data.

5250-1003   Understand and apply measures of central tendency.

Skills and Strategies

1. Organize a set of data by sorting and sequencing; and present it graphically, using a graphing calculator utility where applicable.

2. Determine the mean, median, mode, and range or a given set of data.
3. Present and analyze data graphically using tables, frequency distributions, stem-and-leaf plots, line graphs, circle graphs, box plots, and bar graphs using a graphing calculator utility where applicable.
4. Draw inferences and test validity of statistical data from the real world.

Standard 5250-*11*. Probability

Purpose: For beginning algebra, the focus of instruction should begin to shift from the selection of the correct counting technique to analysis of the problem and design of the procedure. Connections can be made to simple theoretical probability concepts and comparisons to experimental probability outcomes. Graphing utilities should be incorporated to enhance calculations and understanding.

Objectives

5250-11*01*	Use experimental or theoretical probability, as appropriate, to represent and solve problems involving uncertainty.
5250-11*02*	Use simulations to estimate probabilities.
5250-11*03*	Understand the concept of a random variable.

Skills and Strategies

1. Estimate the probability of an event using the results of experiments such as flipping a coin or rolling dice.
2. Predict the probability of an event based on given data using simple theoretical probability methods.

Standard 5250-*12*. Discrete Mathematics

Purpose: Modeling the non-material world of information processing such as computers should involve discrete or discontinuous mathematics. In beginning algebra, students will represent finite graphs or other sources of finite information in the form of a matrix and interpret simple operations on matrices.

Objectives

| 5250-12*01* | Represent problem situations using discrete structures such as finite graphs, matrices, sequences, and recurrence relations. |

Skills and Strategies

1. Write and interpret an information matrix from various sources such as directed graphs, weighted graphs, drawings, tables, and networks.
2. Interpret sums and products of matrices.

Standard 5250-*13*. Conceptual Underpinnings of Calculus

Purpose: This standard calls for opportunities for students to systematically, but informally, investigate the central ideas of calculus - limit (undefined), the rate of change, and slope.

Objectives

| 5250-13*01* | Investigate limiting processes by examining graphs and equations. |

Skills and Strategies

1. Identify slope as a rate of change.
2. Recognize when a rational expression is undefined.

Standard 5250-*14*. Mathematical Structure

Purpose: Students at this level should become aware of the overall structure of mathematics including the relationships of properties and the relationships of sets of numbers. It should be approached over time in context of various experiences instead of a list of properties. The degree of formalization should be consistent with the students' level of mathematical maturity.

Objectives

5250-14*01*	Compare and contrast the real number system and its various subsystems with regard to their structural characteristics.
5250-14*02*	Understand the logic of algebraic procedures.
5250-14*03*	Appreciate that seemingly different mathematical systems may be essentially the same.

Skills and Strategies

1. Identify sets as finite or infinite.
2. Describe natural numbers, whole numbers, integers, rational numbers, irrational numbers, and real numbers by using set notation.
3. Represent the relationship of real number subsets by using Venn Diagrams and other representations.
4. Associate rational numbers in a one-to-one correspondence with points on the number line.
5. Understand the basic properties of real numbers, demonstrate examples, and identify when these are used.

B

Example of an Article from *Mathematics Teacher:* "An Application of Quadratic Equations to Baseball"

In baseball, the primary objective of each team is to have the greatest winning percentage in its division at the end of the season. During the season, daily standings list the teams in order of decreasing winning percentages. Beside each team's percentage is the number of games it is behind, a measure of how many games that team trails the team with the greatest winning percentage. For example, consider the standings of National League teams on the morning of 8 August 1984, as shown in Table 1.

The number of games behind (GB) is calculated as follows: Suppose that the leading team has a won-lost record of (A, B) and the trailing team has a won-lost record of (a, b), where

$$\frac{A}{A + B} > \frac{a}{a + b}$$

Then the trailing team is $A - a$ wins behind (or "games behind in the win column") and $b - B$ losses behind (or "games behind in the loss column"). The number of games behind, *GB,* is calculated as the mean of these two quantities:

$$GB = \frac{(A - a) + (b - B)}{2}$$

Baseball fans and players know that "games behind" is not always a good measure of the deficit between the trailing team and the leading team. A New York Mets fan would look at the standings and think: *We're 3.5 games behind the Cubs but only 2 in the loss column.* That is, if the Cubs lose 2 games, the Mets can catch them by winning as many as the Cubs do over the rest of the season (to use a baseball cliche, the Mets would "control their own destiny"), so the Mets' deficit appears to be *less than* 3.5 games. In contrast, the Atlanta Braves trail the San Diego Padres by 10 in the loss column, although they are only 9.5 games behind. This means that San Diego must lose 10 more games than Atlanta over the rest of the season for the Braves to have a chance, so the Braves' deficit appears to be *greater than* 9.5 games.

Strangely, it is even possible for the leading team to be "behind" the trailing team in games. For example, consider the following standings:

Team	W	L	Pct.	GB
Leaders	18	13	.581	0.5
Trailers	22	16	.579	0.0

Because of the difference in the number of games played, the Leaders are 0.5 games behind the Trailers.

Let's define the deficit D of a trailing team as the number of times the trailing team would have to beat the leading team for them to be tied in the standings. If the two teams have played the same number of games (i.e., $A + B = a + b$), then GB is equal to D. However, if they haven't played the same number of games, GB and D are not equal. To illustrate, consider the standings of 8 August 1984 given in table 1.

Chicago and St. Louis have both played 112 games. St. Louis is 11 wins behind Chicago and 11 losses behind Chicago. If St. Louis beat Chicago 11 times, both teams would have records of 67–56 and they would be tied. Thus St. Louis has a deficit of 11 games, which is equal to the number of games behind listed in the standings.

In contrast, New York has played 109 games. New York is 5 wins behind Chicago and 2 losses behind Chicago. The mean of these, 3.5, is New York's games behind. But if New York beat Chicago 3.5 times (assuming that such a thing is possible), then New York would have a record of 65.5–47, whereas Chicago would have a record of 67–48.5. New York's winning percentage would be .582, whereas Chicago's would be .580, so New York would be ahead of Chicago rather than tied. Thus, the deficit between New York and Chicago is actually *less than* 3.5 games, confirming our intuitive judgment that was based on the loss column.

Now look at the situation in the Western Division between San Diego and Atlanta. Atlanta is 9 wins behind and 10 losses behind, which are averaged to give 9.5 games behind. But if Atlanta beat San Diego 9.5 times (again, assuming it's possible), then Atlanta would have a record of 67.5–54 and San Diego would have a record of 67–53.5. Atlanta's winning percentage would be .5556, but San Diego's percentage would be .5560, so Atlanta would still be behind. Thus, Atlanta's deficit is actually *greater than* 9.5 games, again confirming our intuition that was based on the loss column.

The examples of New York and Atlanta suggest that the relationship between a team's games behind and its deficit is this: *The direction of the inequality between the deficit and the games behind is the same as the direction of the inequality between losses behind and wins behind.* That is, if a team's losses behind are fewer than its wins behind, its deficit is less than its games behind, whereas if its losses behind are greater than its wins behind, its deficit is greater than its games behind.

Having established that games behind does not accurately describe the deficit between teams, we are faced with two mathematical questions: (1) How can we calculate the deficit between teams? (2) Can we use the answer to question (1) to *prove* the relationship between games behind and the deficit just described?

Earlier we said that a team's deficit is the number of times it would have to beat the leading team to become tied in the standings. (The two teams may not actually play that number of games in the remaining schedule.) Returning to the standings, suppose the New York Mets trail the Chicago Cubs by a deficit of D games. Then if the Mets had D more wins (and no more losses) and the Cubs D more losses (and no more wins), they would be tied, that is,

$$\frac{62 + D}{109 + D} = \frac{67}{112 + D}$$

Solving this proportion, we obtain the following:

$$(62 + D)(112 + D) = 67(109 + D)$$
$$6944 + 174D + D^2 = 7303 + 67D$$
$$D^2 + 107D - 359 = 0$$

Thus, the number of games by which the Mets really trail the Cubs is the solution of a quadratic equation. Solving by the quadratic formula, we have (ignore the negative root)

Table 1

	Eastern Division					Western Division			
Team	W	L	Pct.	GB	Team	W	L	Pct.	GB
Chicago	67	45	.598	—	San Diego	67	44	.604	—
New York	62	47	.569	3.5	Atlanta	58	54	.518	9.5
Philadelphia	60	51	.541	6.5	Los Angeles	55	58	.487	13
St. Louis	56	56	.500	11	Houston	52	61	.460	16
Montreal	53	58	.477	13.5	Cincinnati	47	65	.420	20.5
Pittsburgh	48	65	.425	19.5	San Francisco	44	65	.404	22

$$D \approx \frac{-107 + 113.512}{2} \approx 3.26.$$

Thus, the Mets trail the Cubs by 3.26 games. The result confirms that the Mets are actually closer to the Cubs than their 3.5 games behind would indicate.

Similarly, if the Atlanta Braves have a deficit of D games with respect to the San Diego Padres, then

$$\frac{58 + D}{112 + D} = \frac{67}{111 + D}$$

or

$$(58 + D)(111 + D) = 67(112 + D)$$
$$D^2 + 102D - 1066 = 0$$

and

$$D \approx \frac{-102 + 121.11}{2} \approx 9.56$$

So the Padres lead the Braves by 9.56 games. The result confirms that the Padres' lead is greater than the Braves' 9.5 games behind would indicate.

These two examples should whet any mathematician's appetite for a proof. Let us restate the relationship in the form of a proposition and try to prove it.

Proposition. *The direction of the inequality between a team's deficit and its games behind is the same as the direction of the inequality between its losses behind and its wins behind.*

Let's define some variables so we can express the proposition with algebraic inequalities. As before, let the leading team have A wins and B losses. Suppose the trailing team is x wins behind and y losses behind. Then its record is $a = A - x$ wins and $b = B + y$ losses. The proposition states that if $x > y$, then the team's deficit D is less than $(x + y)/2$, whereas if $x < y$, D is greater than $(x + y)/2$.

Now be definition, D is the solution to the equation

$$\frac{A - x + D}{A - x + B + y + D} = \frac{A}{A + B + D}$$

which simplifies to

$$D^2 + (A + B - x)D - (Ay + Bx) = 0$$

Using the quadratic formula and ignoring the negative root, we have

$$D = \frac{\sqrt{(A + B - x)^2 + 4(Ay + Bx)} - (A + B - x)}{2}$$

so

$$D < G = \frac{x + y}{2}$$

if and only if

$$\sqrt{(A + B - x)^2 + 4(Ay + Bx)} - (A + B - x) < x + y$$
$$\sqrt{(A + B - x)^2 + 4(Ay + Bx)} < A + B + y$$
$$(A + B - x)^2 + 4(Ay + Bx) < (A + B + y)^2$$

and

$$x^2 - 2(A - B)x < y^2 - 2(A - B)y$$

Now let $f(t) = t^2 - 2(A - B)t$. The proposition is equivalent to the following statement: If $x > y$, then $f(x) < f(y)$, and if $x < y$, then $f(x) > f(y)$. That is, the proposition is true if x and y belong to an interval on which $f(t)$ is a decreasing function. But $f(t)$ is a quadratic function; it is decreasing on the interval $t \le A - B$ and increasing everywhere else. Hence, the proposition is true if both x and y are less than or equal to $A - B$, the difference between the leading team's wins and losses. So we can restate the proposition as a theorem:

Theorem. *Suppose the numbers of games by which a team trails the leading team in the win and in the loss columns are both fewer than or equal to the difference between the leading team's wins and losses. Then the direction of the inequality between the team's deficit and its games behind is the same as the direction of the inequality between its losses behind and its wins behind.*

In most pennant races, this condition will hold. In major league baseball, the leading team usually has a percentage near .600, as both leading teams do in the example. That means that late in the season, the difference between the leading team's wins and losses will be greater than 20. So the relationship will hold for any team that is fewer than 20 games behind in both the win and loss columns. Looking back to the league standings, we see that Chicago's win difference is 22, so that for any team whose wins behind and losses behind are both fewer than or equal to 22, the conclusion of the theorem will apply. For San Diego, the corresponding number is 23.

A final note: If the deficit rather than the games behind is used as the measure of the distance between teams, the anomaly at the beginning of this article—a team trailing the leader by a negative number of games—cannot occur. The calculation of the deficit between the Trailers and the Leaders requires us to solve the equation

$$\frac{22 + D}{38 + D} = \frac{18}{31 + D}$$

or $D^2 + 35D - 2 = 0$, yielding $D \approx 0.06$, so the Trailers trail by 0.06 games.

In fact, it is easy to prove that D is always positive. Recall that D is the greater of the two solutions (the lesser solution is always negative) of the quadratic equation

$$D^2 + (A + B - x)D - (Ay + Bx) = 0$$

Replacing x by $A - a$ and y by $b - B$ yields the equivalent equation

$$D^2 + (B + a)D - (Ab - Ba) = 0$$

This equation has a positive solution if and only if

$$\sqrt{(B + a)^2 + 4(Ab - Ba)} > B + a$$

that is, $Ab > Ba$. But the relationship of the two teams' winning percentages is

$$\frac{A}{A + B} > \frac{a}{a + b}$$

which is equivalent to $Ab > Ba$. Thus, D is always positive for a team with a lower winning percentage than the leader. We can conclude that a team's deficit D is a better measure of its distance from the leader than its games behind.

List of Standards from NCTM's *Curriculum and Evaluation Standards for School Mathematics*

CURRICULUM STANDARDS FOR GRADES K–4

Standard 1: Mathematics as Problem Solving

In grades K–4, the study of mathematics should emphasize problem solving so that students can

- Use problem-solving approaches to investigate and understand mathematical content.
- Formulate problems from everyday and mathematical situations.
- Develop and apply strategies to solve a wide variety of problems.
- Verify and interpret results with respect to the original problem.
- Acquire confidence in using mathematics meaningfully.

Standard 2: Mathematics as Communications

In grades K–4, the study of mathematics should include numerous opportunities for communication so that students can

Source: Reprinted with permission from National Council of Teachers of Mathematics, "List of Standards," in *Curriculum and Evaluation Standards for School Mathematics.* Copyright 1989 NCTM.

- Relate physical materials, pictures, and diagrams to mathematical ideas.
- Reflect on and clarify their thinking about mathematical ideas and situations.
- Relate their everyday language to mathematical language and symbols.
- Realize that representing, discussing, reading, writing, and listening to mathematics are a vital part of learning and using mathematics.

Standard 3: Mathematics as Reasoning

In grades K–4, the study of mathematics should emphasize reasoning so that students can

- Draw logical conclusions about mathematics.
- Use models, known facts, properties, and relationships to explain their thinking.
- Justify their answers and solution processes.
- Use patterns and relationships to analyze mathematical situations.
- Believe that mathematics makes sense.

Standard 4: Mathematical Connections

In grades K–4, the study of mathematics should include opportunities to make connections so that students can

- Link conceptual and procedural knowledge.
- Relate various representations of concepts or procedures to one another.

- Recognize relationships among different topics in mathematics.
- Use mathematics in other curriculum areas.
- Use mathematics in their daily lives.

Standard 5: Estimation

In grades K–4, the curriculum should include estimation so students can

- Explore estimation strategies.
- Recognize when an estimate is appropriate.
- Determine the reasonableness of results.
- Apply estimation in working with quantities, measurement, computation, and problem solving.

Standard 6: Number Sense and Numeration

In grades K–4, the mathematics curriculum should include whole-number concepts and skills so that students can

- Construct number meanings through real-world experiences and the use of physical materials.
- Understand our numeration system by relating counting, grouping, and place-value concepts.
- Develop number sense.
- Interpret the multiple uses of numbers encountered in the real world.

Standard 7: Concepts of Whole-Number Operations

In grades K–4, the mathematics curriculum should include concepts of addition, subtraction, multiplication, and division of whole numbers so that students can

- Develop meaning for the operations by modeling and discussing a rich variety of problem situations.
- Relate any mathematical language and symbolism of operations to problem situations and informal language.
- Recognize that a wide variety of problem structures can be represented by a single operation.
- Develop operation sense.

Standard 8: Whole Number Computation

In grades K–4, the mathematics curriculum should develop whole-number computation so that students can

- Model, explain, and develop reasonable proficiency with basic facts and algorithms.
- Use a variety of mental computation and estimation techniques.
- Use calculators in appropriate computational situations.

- Select and use computation techniques appropriate to specific problems and determine whether the results are reasonable.

Standard 9: Geometry and Spatial Sense

In grades K–4, the mathematics curriculum should include two- and three-dimensional geometry so that students can

- Describe, model, draw, and classify shapes.
- Investigate and predict results of combining, subdividing, and changing shapes.
- Develop spatial sense.
- Relate geometric ideals to number and measurement ideas.
- Recognize and appreciate geometry in their world.

Standard 10: Measurement

In grades K–4, the mathematics curriculum should include measurement so that students can

- Understand the attributes of length, capacity, weight, area, volume, time, temperature, and angle.
- Develop the process of measuring and concepts related to units of measurement.
- Make and use estimates of measurement.
- Make and use measurements in problem and everyday situations.

Standard 11: Statistics and Probability

In grades K–4, the mathematics curriculum should include experiences with data analysis and probability so that students can

- Collect, organize, and describe data.
- Construct, read, and interpret displays of data.
- Formulate and solve problems that involve collecting and analyzing data.
- Explore concepts of chance.

Standard 12: Fractions and Decimals

In grades K–4, the mathematics curriculum should include fractions and decimals so that students can

- Develop concepts of fractions, mixed numbers, and decimals.
- Develop number sense for fractions and decimals.
- Use models to relate fractions to decimals to find equivalent fractions.
- Use models to explore operations on fractions and decimals.
- Apply fractions and decimals to problem situations.

Standard 13: Patterns and Relationships

In grades K–4, the mathematics curriculum should include the study of patterns and relationships so that students can

- Recognize, describe, extend, and create a wide variety of patterns.
- Represent and describe mathematical relationships.
- Explore the use of variables and open sentences to express relationships.

CURRICULUM STANDARDS FOR GRADES 5–8

Standard 1: Mathematics as Problem Solving

In grades 5–8, the mathematics curriculum should include numerous and varied experiences with problem-solving as a method of inquiry and application so that students can

- Use problem-solving approaches to investigate and understand mathematical content.
- Formulate problems from situations within and outside mathematics.
- Develop and apply a variety of strategies to solve problems, with emphasis on multistep and nonroutine problems.
- Verify and interpret results with respect to the original problem situation.
- Generalize solutions and strategies to new problem situations.
- Acquire confidence in using mathematics meaningfully.

Standard 2: Mathematics as Communications

In grades 5–8, the mathematics curriculum should include opportunities to communicate so that students can

- Model situations using oral, written, concrete, pictorial, graphical, and algebraic methods.
- Reflect on and clarify their own thinking about mathematical ideas and situations.
- Develop common understandings of mathematical ideas, including the role of definitions.
- Use the skills of reading, listening, and viewing to interpret and evaluate mathematical ideas.
- Discuss mathematical ideas and make conjectures and convincing arguments.
- Appreciate the value of mathematical notation and its role in the development of mathematical ideas.

Standard 3: Mathematics as Reasoning

In grades 5–8, reasoning shall permeate the mathematics curriculum so that students can

- Recognize and apply deductive and inductive reasoning.
- Understand and apply reasoning processes, with special attention to spatial reasoning and reasoning with proportions and graphs.
- Make and evaluate mathematical conjectures and arguments.
- Validate their own thinking.
- Appreciate the pervasive use and power of reasoning as part of mathematics.

Standard 4: Mathematical Connections

In grades 5–8, the mathematics curriculum should include the investigation of mathematical connections so that students can

- See mathematics as an integrated whole.
- Explore problems and describe results using graphical, numerical, physical, algebraic, and verbal mathematical models or representations.
- Use a mathematical idea to further their understanding of other mathematical ideas.
- Apply mathematical thinking and modeling to solve problems that arise in other disciplines, such as art, music, psychology, sciences, and business.
- Value the role of mathematics in our culture and society.

Standard 5: Number and Number Relationships

In grades 5–8, the mathematics curriculum should include the continued development of number and number relationships so that students can

- Understand, represent, and use numbers in a variety of equivalent forms (integer, fraction, decimal, percent, exponential, and scientific notation) in real-world and mathematical problem situations.
- Develop number sense for whole numbers, fractions, decimals, integers, and rational numbers.
- Understand and apply ratios, proportions, and percents in a wide variety of situations.
- Investigate relationships among fractions, decimals, and percents.
- Represent numerical relationships in one- and two-dimensional graphs.

Standard 6: Number Systems and Number Theory

In grades 5–8, the mathematics curriculum should include the study of number systems and number theory so that students can

- Understand and appreciate the need for numbers beyond the whole numbers.
- Develop and use order relations for whole numbers, fractions, decimals, integers, and rational numbers.
- Extend their understanding of whole-number operations to fractions, decimals, integers, and rational numbers.
- Understand how the basic arithmetic operations are related to one another.
- Develop and apply number theory concepts (e.g., primes, factors, and multiples) in real-world and mathematical problem situations.

Standard 7: Computation and Estimation

In grades 5–8, the mathematics curriculum should develop the concepts underlying computations and estimations in various contexts so that students can

- Compute with whole numbers, fractions, decimals, integers, and rational numbers.
- Develop, analyze, and explain procedures for computation and techniques for estimation.
- Develop, analyze, and explain methods for solving proportions.
- Select and use an appropriate method for computing from among mental arithmetic, paper and pencil, calculator, and computer methods.
- Use computation, estimation, and proportions to solve problems.
- Use estimation to check the reasonableness of results.

Standard 8: Patterns and Functions

In grades 5–8, the mathematics curriculum should include exploration of patterns and functions so that students can

- Describe, extend, analyze, and create a wide variety of patterns.
- Describe and represent relationships with tables, graphs, and rules.
- Analyze functional relationships to explain how a change in one quantity results in a change in another.
- Use patterns and functions to represent and solve problems.

Standard 9: Algebra

In grades 5–8, the mathematics curriculum should include explorations of algebraic concepts and processes so that students can

- Understand the concepts of variable, expression, and equation.
- Represent situations and number patterns with tables, graphs, verbal rules, and equations and explore the interrelationships of these representations.
- Analyze tables and graphs to identify properties and relationships.
- Develop confidence in solving linear equations using concrete, informal, and formal methods.
- Investigate inequalities and nonlinear equations informally.
- Apply algebraic methods to solve a variety of real-world and mathematical problems.

Standard 10: Statistics

In grades 5–8, the mathematics curriculum should include exploration of statistics in real-world situations so that students can

- Systematically collect, organize, and describe data.
- Construct, read, and interpret tables, charts, and graphs.
- Make inferences and convincing arguments that are based on data analysis.
- Evaluate arguments that are based on data analysis.
- Develop an appreciation for statistical methods as powerful means for decision making.

Standard 11: Probability

In grades 5–8, the mathematics curriculum should include explorations of probability in real-world situations so that students can

- Model situations by devising and carrying out experiments or simulations to determine probabilities.
- Model situations by constructing a sample space to determine probabilities.
- Appreciate the power of using a probability model by comparing experimental results with mathematical expectations.
- Make predictions that are based on experimental or theoretical probabilities.
- Develop an appreciation for the pervasive use of probability in the real world.

Standard 12: Geometry

In grades 5–8, the mathematics curriculum should include the study of geometry of one, two, and three dimensions in a variety of situations so that students can

- Identify, describe, compare, and classify geometric figures.
- Visualize and represent geometric figures with special attention to developing spatial sense.
- Explore transformations of geometric figures.
- Represent and solve problems using geometric models.

- Understand and apply geometric properties and relationships.
- Develop an appreciation of geometry as a means of describing the physical world.

Standard 13: Measurement

In grades 5–8, the mathematics curriculum should include extensive concrete experiences using measurement so that students can

- Extend their understanding of the process of measurement.
- Estimate, make, and use measurements to describe and compare phenomena.
- Select appropriate units and tools to measure to the degree of accuracy required in a particular situation.
- Understand the structure and use of systems of measurement.
- Extend their understanding of the concepts of perimeter, area, volume, angle measure, capacity, and weight and mass.
- Develop the concepts of rates and other derived and indirect measurements.
- Develop formulas and procedures for determining measures to solve problems.

CURRICULUM STANDARDS FOR GRADES 9–12

Standard 1: Mathematics as Problem Solving

In grades 9–12, the mathematics curriculum should include the refinement and extension of methods of mathematical problem-solving so that all students can

- Use, with increasing confidence, problem-solving approaches to investigate and understand mathematical content.
- Apply integrated mathematical problem-solving strategies to solve problems from within and outside of mathematics.
- Recognize and formulate problems from situations within and outside of mathematics.
- Apply the process of mathematical modeling to real-world problem situations.

Standard 2: Mathematics as Communication

In grades 9–12, the mathematics curriculum should include the continued development of language and symbolism to communicate mathematical ideas so that all students can

- Reflect upon and clarify their thinking about mathematical ideas and relationships.

- Formulate mathematical definitions and express generalizations discovered through investigations.
- Express mathematical ideas orally and in writing.
- Read written presentations of mathematics with understanding.
- Ask clarifying and extending questions related to mathematics they have read or heard about.
- Appreciate the economy, power, and elegance of mathematical notation and its role in the development of mathematical ideas.

Standard 3: Mathematics as Reasoning

In grades 9–12, the mathematics curriculum should include numerous and varied experiences that reinforce and extend logical reasoning skills so that all students can

- Make and test conjectures.
- Formulate counterexamples.
- Follow logical arguments.
- Judge the validity of arguments.
- Construct simple valid arguments.

In addition, college-intending students can

- Construct proofs by mathematical assertions, including indirect proofs and proofs by mathematical induction.

Standard 4: Mathematical Connections

In grades 9–12, the mathematics curriculum should include investigation of the connections and interplay among various mathematical topics and their applications so that all students can

- Recognize equivalent representations of the same concept.
- Relate procedures in one representation to procedures in an equivalent representation.
- Use and value the connections among mathematical topics.
- Use and value the connections between mathematics and other disciplines.

Standard 5: Algebra

In grades 9–12, the mathematics curriculum should include the continued study of algebraic concepts and methods so that all students can

- Represent situations that involve variable quantities with expressions, equations, inequalities, and matrices.
- Use tables and graphs as tools to interpret expressions, equations, and inequalities.
- Operate on expressions and matrices, and solve equations and inequalities.
- Appreciate the power of mathematical abstraction and symbolism.

In addition, college-intending students can

- Use matrices to solve linear systems.
- Demonstrate technical facility with algebraic transformations, including techniques based on the theory of equations.

Standard 6: Functions

In grades 9–12, the mathematics curriculum should include the continued study of functions so that all students can

- Model real-world phenomena with a variety of functions.
- Represent and analyze relationships using tables, verbal rules, equations, and graphs.
- Translate among tabular, symbolic, and graphical representations of functions.
- Recognize that a variety of problem situations can be modeled by the same type of function.
- Analyze the effects of parameter changes on the graphs of functions.

In addition, college-intending students can

- Understand operations on, and the general properties and behavior of, classes of functions.

Standard 7: Geometry from a Synthetic Perspective

In grades 9–12, the mathematics curriculum should include the continued study of geometry of two and three dimensions so that all students can

- Interpret and draw three-dimensional objects.
- Represent problem situations with geometric models and apply properties of figures.
- Classify figures in terms of congruence and similarity and apply these relationships.

In addition, college-intending students can

- Develop an understanding of an axiomatic system through investigating and comparing various geometries.

Standard 8: Geometry from an Algebraic Perspective

In grades 9–12, the mathematics curriculum should include the study of the geometry of two and three dimensions from an algebraic point of view so that all students can

- Translate between synthetic and coordinate representations.
- Deduce properties of figures using transformations and using coordinates.
- Identify congruent and similar figures using transformations.

- Analyze properties of Euclidean transformations and relate translations to vectors.

In addition, college-intending students can

- Apply transformations, coordinates, and vectors in problem-solving.

Standard 9: Trigonometry

In grades 9–12, the mathematics curriculum should include the study of trigonometry so that all students can

- Apply trigonometry to problem situations involving triangles.
- Explore periodic real-world phenomena using the sine and cosine functions.

In addition, college-intending students can

- Understand the connection between trigonometric and circular functions.
- Apply general graphing techniques to trigonometric functions.
- Solve trigonometric equations and verify trigonometric identities.
- Understand the connections between trigonometric functions and polar coordinates, complex numbers, and series.

Standard 10: Statistics

In grades 9–12, the mathematics curriculum should include the continued study of data analysis and statistics so that all students can

- Construct and draw inferences from charts, tables, and graphs that summarize data from real-world situations.
- Use curve-fitting to predict from data.
- Understand and apply measures of central tendency, variability, and correlation.
- Understand sampling and recognize its role in statistical claims.
- Design a statistical experiment to study a problem, conduct the experiment, and interpret and communicate the outcomes.
- Analyze the effects of data transformation on measures of central tendency and variability.

In addition, college-intending students can

- Transform data to aid in data interpretation and prediction.
- Test hypotheses using appropriate statistics.

Standard 11: Probability

In grades 9–12, the mathematics curriculum should include the continued study of probability so that all students can

- Use experimental or theoretical probability, as appropriate, to represent and solve problems involving uncertainty.
- Use simulations to estimate probabilities.
- Understand the concept of random variable.
- Create and interpret discrete probability distributions.
- Describe, in general terms, the normal curve and use its properties to answer questions about sets of data that are assumed to be normally distributed.

In addition, college-intending students can

- Apply the concept of random variable to generate and interpret probability distributions, including binomial, uniform, normal, and chi-square.

Standard 12: Discrete Mathematics

In grades 9–12, the mathematics curriculum should include topics from discrete mathematics so that all students can

- Represent problem situations using discrete structures such as finite graphs, matrices, sequences, and recurrence relations.
- Represent and analyze finite graphs using matrices.
- Develop and analyze algorithms.
- Solve enumeration and finite probability problems.

In addition, the college-intending students can

- Represent and solve problems using linear programming and difference equations.
- Investigate problem situations that arise in connection with computer validation and the application of algorithms.

Standard 13: Conceptual Underpinnings of Calculus

In grades 9–12, the mathematics curriculum should include the informal exploration of calculus concepts from both a graphical and a numerical perspective so that all students can

- Determine maximum and minimum points of a graph and interpret the results in problem situations.
- Investigate limiting processes by examining infinite sequences and series and areas under curves.

In addition, college-intending students can

- Understand the conceptual foundations of limit, the area under a curve, the rate of change, and the slope of a tangent line and their applications to other disciplines.
- Analyze the graphs of polynomials, rational, radical, and transcendental functions.

Standard 14: Mathematical Structure

In grades 9–12, the mathematics curriculum should include the study of mathematical structure so that all students can

- Compare and contrast the real number system and its various subsystems with regard to their structural characteristics.
- Understand the logic of algebraic procedures.
- Appreciate that seemingly different mathematical systems may be essentially the same.

In addition, college-intending students can

- Develop the complex-number system and demonstrate facility with its operations.
- Prove elementary theorems within various mathematical structures, such as groups and fields.
- Develop an understanding of the nature and purpose of axiomatic systems.

EVALUATION STANDARDS
Standard 1: Alignment

Methods and tasks for assessing students' learning should be aligned with the curriculum's

- Goals, objectives, and mathematical content.
- Relative emphases given to various topics and processes and their relationships.
- Instructional approaches and activities, including use of calculators, computers, and manipulatives.

Standard 2: Multiple Sources of Information

Decisions concerning students' learning should be made on the basis of a convergence of information obtained from a variety of sources. These sources should encompass tasks that

- Demand different kinds of mathematical thinking.
- Present the same mathematical concept or procedure in different contexts, formats, and problem situations.

Standard 3: Appropriate Assessment Methods and Uses

Assessment methods and instruments should be selected on the basis of

- The type of information sought.
- The use to which the information will be put.
- The development level and maturity of the student.

The use of assessment data for purposes other than those intended is inappropriate.

Standard 4: Mathematical Power

The assessment of students' mathematical knowledge should yield information about their

- Ability to apply their knowledge to solve problems within mathematics and other disciplines.
- Ability to use mathematical language to communicate ideas.
- Ability to reason and analyze.
- Knowledge and understanding of concepts and procedures.
- Disposition toward mathematics.
- Understanding of the nature of mathematics.
- Integration of these aspects of mathematical knowledge.

Standard 5: Problem Solving

The assessment of students' ability to use mathematics in solving problems should provide evidence that they can

- Formulate problems.
- Apply a variety of strategies to solve problems.
- Solve problems.
- Verify and interpret results.
- Generalize solutions.

Standard 6: Communication

The assessment of students' ability to communicate mathematics should provide evidence that they can

- Express mathematical ideas by speaking, writing, demonstrating, and depicting them visually.
- Understand, interpret, and evaluate mathematical ideas that are presented in written, oral, or visual form.
- Use mathematical vocabulary, notation, and structure to represent ideas, describe relationships, and model situations.

Standard 7: Reasoning

The assessment of students' ability to reason mathematically should provide evidence that they can

- Use inductive reasoning to recognize patterns and form conjectures.
- Use reasoning to develop plausible arguments for mathematical statements.
- Use proportional and spatial reasoning to solve problems.
- Use deductive reasoning to verify conclusions, judge the validity of arguments, and construct valid arguments.
- Analyze situations to determine common properties and structures.

- Appreciate the axiomatic nature of mathematics.

Standard 8: Mathematical Concepts

The assessment of students' knowledge and understanding of mathematical concepts should provide evidence that they can

- Label, verbalize, and define concepts.
- Identify and generate examples and nonexamples.
- Use models, diagrams, and symbols to represent concepts.
- Translate from one mode of representation to another.
- Recognize the various meanings and interpretation of concepts.
- Identify properties of a given concept and recognize conditions that determine a particular concept.
- Compare and contrast concepts.

In addition, assessment should provide evidence of the extent to which students have integrated their knowledge of various concepts.

Standard 9: Mathematical Procedures

The assessment of students' knowledge of procedures should provide evidence that they can

- Recognize when a procedure is appropriate.
- Give reasons for the steps in a procedure.
- Reliably and efficiently execute procedures.
- Verify the results of procedures empirically (e.g., using models) or analytically.
- Recognize correct and incorrect procedures.
- Generate new procedures and extend or modify familiar ones.
- Appreciate the nature and role of procedures in mathematics.

Standard 10: Mathematical Disposition

The assessment of students' mathematical disposition should seek information about their

- Confidence in using mathematics to solve problems, to communicate ideas, and to reason.
- Flexibility in exploring mathematical ideas and trying alternative methods in solving problems.
- Willingness to persevere in mathematical tasks.
- Interest, curiosity, and inventiveness in doing mathematics.
- Inclination to monitor and reflect on their own thinking and performance.
- Valuing of the application of mathematics to situations arising in other disciplines and everyday experiences.
- Appreciation of the role of mathematics in our culture and its value as a tool and as a language.

Standard 11: Indicators for Program Evaluation

Indicators of mathematics program's consistency with *Standards* should include

- Student outcomes.
- Program expectations and support.
- Equity for all students.
- Curriculum review and change.

In addition, indicators of the program's match to the *Standards* should be collected in the areas of curriculum, instructional resources, and forms of instruction.

Standard 12: Curriculum and Instructional Resources

In an evaluation of a mathematics program's consistency with the *Curriculum Standards,* the examination of curriculum and instructional resources should focus on

- Goals, objectives, and mathematical content.
- Relative emphases of various topics and processes and their relationships.
- Instructional approaches and activities.
- Articulation across grades.
- Assessment methods and instruments.
- Availability of technological tools and support materials.

Standard 13: Instruction

In an evaluation of a mathematics program's consistency with the *Curriculum Standards,* instruction and the environment in which it takes place should be examined, with special attention to

- Mathematical content and its treatment.
- Relative emphases assigned to various topics and processes and the relationships among them.
- Opportunities to learn.
- Instructional resources and classroom climate.
- Assessment methods and instruments.
- The articulation of instruction across grades.

Standard 14: Evaluation Team

Program evaluations should be planned and conducted by

- Individuals with expertise and training in mathematics education.
- Individuals with expertise and training in program evaluation.
- Individuals who make decisions about the mathematics program.
- Users of the information from the evaluation.

Example of an Article from *Mathematics Teaching in the Middle School*

Graphing Calculators Aren't Just for High School Students

GRAPHING CALCULATORS ARE REVOLUTIONIZing the learning and teaching of mathematics. Students can view and manipulate graphs of functions in a matter of seconds. Such features as "plot," "graph," "trace," and "zoom" offer opportunities for users to develop an understanding of the terms *variable* and *function*. According to the *Curriculum and Evaluation Standards for School Mathematics* (NCTM 1989), these concepts are vital aspects of the middle school curriculum. According to the standards document, "[A]n ideal 5–8 mathematics curriculum would expand students' knowledge of numbers, . . . patterns and functions, and the fundamental concepts of algebra" (pp. 65–66). In addition, "[T]echnology, including calculators, computers, and videos, should be used when appropriate" (p. 67). It stands to reason that tools to aid in understanding such concepts as variable and function, specifically graphing calculators, should not be reserved for high school juniors and seniors. This article discusses the use of graphing calculators by students of middle school age in an enrichment program for academically able, but economically disadvantaged, students. The exercises described helped students develop an understanding about variable and function. Students were actively engaged in problem solving that involved hands-on, real-life activities.

In this program, students worked with scientific calculators to aid in constructing tables representing relationships before they were introduced to the graphing calculator. Table-building activities were developed in a problem-solving situation in which the students investigated relationships that evolved from specific problems. After building tables, students approached the same or similar problems from a graphical point of view by hand plotting the pairs of numbers found in the table. According to Leitzel and Osborne (1985), this hand-plotting activity reinforces the concept of a graph's being a collection of points generated by the function. Table building naturally led to the concept of variable and was used as a device to create an algebraic expression that enabled the student to extend the table. Experiences using a computer spreadsheet in more extensive table building added to these students' concept and intuition of number sense. By the time the TI-81 graphing calculator was introduced, the students were proficient at building tables.

The *Curriculum and Evaluation Standards* (NCTM 1989) advocates "[b]ecoming confident in one's own ability" (p. 6). We observed this confidence in our students as they made some decisions about the mathematics they were doing. For example, students were given the task of setting the parameters of the graph. When asked, they gave reasonable suggestions for the scaling of the axes. At times it was necessary to extend the *x*-axis to view the function for larger values of *x*. With the graphing calculator, changes could be made without losing data or tediously redrawing the axes. The students seemed to become more assertive in their engagement with mathematics, and they eagerly offered suggestions and explanations for the changes.

> ## We observed confidence grow in our students

LINDA TAYLOR *teaches at the University of Cincinnati, Cincinnati, OH 45221-0002. She studies the uses of technology, especially the graphing calculator, to teach mathematics and is interested in equity issues.* JERI NICHOLS *teaches at Wright State University, Dayton, OH 45435. She is interested in teaching and learning mathematics with technology as well as the transfer of learning between mathematics and science.*

A Distance-Rate-Time Problem

A DISTANCE-RATE-TIME PROBLEM WAS CHOSEN FOR the initial exercise because it was easily understood, allowing students to focus on the keyboard and features of the TI-81. Students were asked, "How far can a person drive if she maintains a speed of 55 MPH for the designated number of hours listed in the table?" As a result of their past experiences, students easily constructed a table to match the problem (see **table 1**). The last line of the table contained a generalization of the distance traveled. Using the point-plotting feature of the calculator, the students entered into the calculator's statistical memory the points from the table of the form (hours driven, distance traveled). The students did not find labeling in this manner to be an obstacle.

A scatterplot of the points obtained from **table 1** was constructed using the statistical features of the graphing calculator. A discussion of the apparent shape of the graph ensued. The discussion was similar to the following sequence of questions and answers:

Q: Do you notice anything about these points?
A: They seem to be on a line.
Q: How can we find out if they are in a straight line?
A: Hold a ruler next to them.
Q: What do you find?
A: The points *are* on a line.
Q: What name do you think that we give to this kind of graph?
A: A line graph?
Q: That's close. We call it *linear.* Do you see where the word *line* is in the word *linear?* What if we choose more replacements for *x*?
A: The new points will be on the line with the rest of the points.

Additional points were found, including points between those in the table and points with hours greater than twenty. These data were entered into the calculator and plotted. The linear quality of the graph was very evident **(fig. 1).** Students overlaid the graph of the equation representing the generalized expression developed in the table. The visualization of the line going through the plotted points, similar to a Green Globs effect (Dugdale 1982), was dramatic **(fig. 2).** Once the line was graphed, the trace feature could be used to answer many questions, of which the following are examples:

> **They adjusted the parameters on the axes**

- How long will it take to drive 825 miles?
- After 8 hours, how far will she have traveled?
- If you drove at the same rate for 20 hours, how far would you go? (See **fig. 2.**)

TABLE 1

Table of Values of Hours Driven versus Distance Traveled

HOURS DRIVEN	CALCULATION	DISTANCE TRAVELED
$2 = X1$	2×55	$110 = Y1$
$4 = X2$	4×55	$220 = Y2$
$6 = X3$		
$8 = X4$		
$10 = X5$		
$20 = X6$		
$h = Xn$	$h \times 55$	$55h = Yn$

This activity built on students' earlier experiences with graphing and table building in which they knew that the *x*-component of the point represented the number of hours driven and the *y*-component represented the distance traveled.

To do this problem without the graphing calculator, continue the hand-plotting exercises. Using any calculator, determine the values for the distances driven. Plot the resulting points from the table, discuss the linear

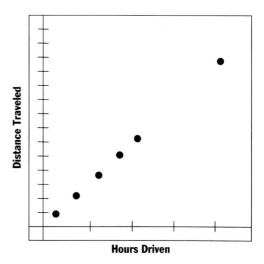

Fig. 1 Points graphed from the completed table with these range values:

$$Xmin = -1$$
$$Xmax = 25$$
$$Xscl = 5$$
$$Ymin = -100$$
$$Ymax = 1500$$
$$Yscl = 100$$

qualities, and graph the equation for the line. Have students find additional points for the table using *x*-values both between the given values and greater than 20. As these points are plotted, students will observe that they are on the graph of the line.

An extension of this problem is the comparison of graphs representing two different speeds on the same set of axes. Questions might include the following:

- How much farther would you have traveled if you had driven 65 MPH than if you had driven 55 MPH on your six-hour trip?

- How much quicker would you have gotten to the 250-mile destination if you had driven 65 MPH instead of 55 MPH?

Problems involving discount pricing constitute another linear example to build confidence in calculator skills. This type of problem requires students to make decisions about rounding to the nearest cent. The "trace" feature can be used to find the discount or wholesale price of a wide range of prices.

Population Problem

AN EXPONENTIAL RELATIONSHIP WAS EXAMINED IN THE context of a population problem. The population figures for the city in which the students live were researched in the *World Almanac* (1991), and a population decline of

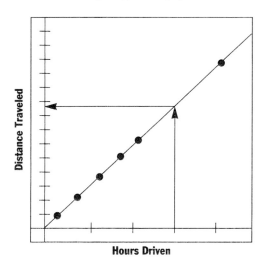

Fig. 2 Illustration of the line through the points with these range values:

$$Xmin = -1$$
$$Xmax = 25$$
$$Xscl = 5$$
$$Ymin = -100$$
$$Ymax = 1500$$
$$Yscl = 100$$

TABLE 2

Values of a 0.5 Percent Population Decrease per Year for the City of Cincinnati, Ohio

YEAR	POPULATION
1988	370 480
1989	370 480 (0.995) = 368 628
1990	(370 480 [0.995]) (0.995) = 370 480 (0.995)^2 = 366 785
1991	(370 480 [0.995]^2) (0.995) = 370 480 (0.995)^3 = 364 951
1992	(370 480 [0.995]^3) (0.995) = 370 480 (0.995)^4 = 363 126
1993	(370 480 [0.995]^4) (0.995) = 370 480 (0.995)^5 = 361 310
1994	(370 480 [0.995]^5) (0.995) = 370 480 (0.995)^6 = 359 504
YEAR *x*	370 480 (0.995)$^{(x-1988)}$

0.5 percent per year was determined. Students instantly became interested in this problem because it was about the population of *their* town. During the discussion of this problem, we found that the students' opinions about rounding differed from the traditional practices represented in their mathematics textbooks. For example, in the dialog about rounding, the students wanted to count any portion of a person as a whole person. That is, they rounded 335 140.090 7 to 335 141.

Similar to the activities described previously, a table of values was generated that included time in years and the corresponding population (see **table 2**). The data points were graphed and a pattern was observed. Time was allowed to investigate thoroughly the shape of the graph. The first few data points graphed caused the function to appear to be linear, since only a small portion of the graph was visible. Remember, the students were allowed to scale the axes. Students began asking questions that

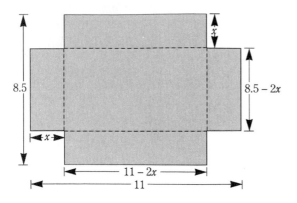

Fig. 3 Paper with corners removed

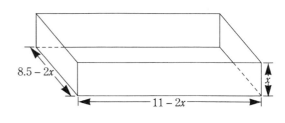

Fig. 4 Box formed by folding up the sides

could not be answered with the current view of the graph, which encouraged them to adjust the parameters of the axes. They asked questions such as these:

- What will be the population in the year 2000?
- What will be the population when I graduate from high school?
- What was the population the year I was born? The year my parents were born?
- Will the population ever be zero?

Setting more appropriate axes followed this query, and the students were amazed that the graph was not linear as compared with the graphs from the previous problems. Discovering the shape of the exponential curve took longer than exploring the linear graphs. The problem contained more intricacies, and students needed time to explore the possibilities. The exponential curve was an important concept for them to experience. They generated questions that could be answered

from the graphs, explored the graph for answers to those questions, and observed the shape of the curve. Let us not assume the concept of exponential relationships to be beyond the understanding of middle school students.

This activity could be approached without the graphing calculator by using hand plotting. Sheets of paper larger than eight-and-one-half-by-eleven inches would probably facilitate this process. Teachers can put students in groups with large sheets of graphing paper so the extension of the curve can be explored in all directions. It is possible to purchase graphing paper on rolls that are one meter wide.

The Box Problem

MAXIMIZING VOLUME WAS EXPLORED USING A PAPER-folding manipulative activity that led to developing an equation for volume, similar to that described in the NCTM's *Curriculum and Evaluation Standards* (1989,

TABLE 3

Values of Dimensions and Volume of Box

LENGTH OF ONE SIDE OF THE REMOVED SQUARE	LENGTH OF THE BOX	WIDTH OF THE BOX	HEIGHT OF THE BOX	VOLUME OF THE BOX
1 in.	$11 - 2(1) = 9$ in.	$8.5 - 2(1) = 6.5$ in.	1 in.	58.5 in.^{3}
1.5 in.	$11 - 2(1.5) = 8$ in.	$8.5 - 2(1.5) = 5.5$ in.	1.5 in.	66 in.^{3}
2 in.	$11 - 2(2) = 7$ in.	$8.5 - 2(2) = 4.5$ in.	2 in.	63 in.^{3}
x	$11 - 2x$	$8.5 - 2x$	x	$x(11 - 2x)(8.5 - 2x)$

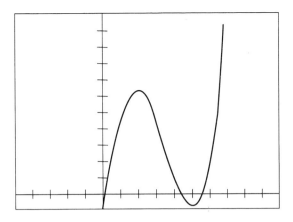

Fig. 5 Complete graph with these range values:

Xmin = –5
Xmax = 10
Xscl = 1
Ymin = –10
Ymax = 100
Yscl = 10

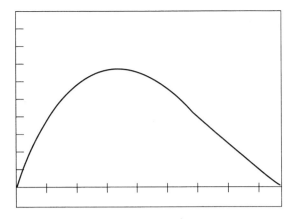

Fig. 6 Graph representing all possible volumes for the box problem with these range values:

Xmin = 0
Xmax = 4.25
Xscl = 0.5
Ymin = –10
Ymax = 100
Yscl = 10

80). A graph was generated and interpreted.

Students were asked to cut squares of equal size from the corners of an eight-and-one-half-by-eleven inch sheet of paper (see **fig. 3**). Students chose the size of the square, so many different cuts were represented. The sides of paper were then folded up and taped, creating a box with no top (see **fig. 4**). Students were asked to compare boxes to determine which cut would produce the box of greatest volume. Looking around, each student tried to decide whose box would likely hold the largest amount. After some discussion, the boxes were measured and a table of values (see **table 3**) was generated using the students' data. From the table, it was apparent whose box had the greatest volume. Students were asked to generalize the relationship between the size of the cut and the volume of the box in the last line of the table.

The graphing calculator was used to plot the points (size of cut, volume of box) as in the previous examples. Students quickly grasped the meaning of the x- and y-axes for this problem. In addition, they volunteered information regarding the restrictions for the value of x, for example, the size of the cut must be less than 4.25 inches. Their experiences with the concrete materials allowed them to have these insights into the situation. The equation for volume in terms of x was entered into the calculator, and the graph was superimposed over the previously plotted points. Students were asked whether a different box could be constructed to have the largest possible volume. Based on the graph, a discussion of the maximum volume followed.

The discussion was similar to the following sequence:

Q: If this graph represents all the volumes possible using the size of paper we started with, where do you think the greatest volume is represented on the graph?

A: At the hump.

Q: Why do you think it would be there?

A: Because it is the highest place on the graph.

Q: Why is the greatest volume at this highest place?

A: That is where the volume value will be the greatest.

Q: What variable are we using to represent volume?

A: The y-value.

Q: So please explain the "hump" in the graph.

A: (a spark of inspiration!) The y-values represent the volumes of the boxes formed from the different sizes of squares cut from the corners. So the place where the y-value is the greatest will correspond to the size of the square that was cut to form the box of the greatest volume.

Q: OK, we read the values to be x = 1.5 and y = 66. What does that mean?

A: That for a square whose side is 1.5 inches in length, the volume of the box is 66 cubic inches.

Q: Did anyone here make that box? Was anyone close to it? Let's see if it looks larger in volume than the rest of the boxes.

The students found creating the boxes, generating the table of values, and graphing the general equation to be an interesting activity. Students were heard to exclaim, "This was fun!" after the activity. They understood to a remarkable degree the relationship between the length of the side, x, of the cut-out square and the volume of the box, y. They also understood the difference between the complete graph of the equation **(fig. 5)** and the graph of the problem situation **(fig. 6)** and why the two were not the same. A *complete graph* is one in which all the important features, such as minimums, maximums, points of inflection, and end behavior, are visible; see Demana and Waits (1990). They verbalized the fact that the complete graph of the equation **(fig. 5)** included all values of x, including negative values, whereas they were merely interested in the portion of the graph including values of x between 0 and 4.25. When cutting the squares, they noticed that none could be larger than 4.25 inches on a side, and they knew they could not cut negative values. From this portion of the graph **(fig. 6)**, the students found a maximum volume of approximately 66 cubic inches when squares of side 1.5 inches are cut from the paper. Accuracy was not addressed with this group of students.

Many graphing-calculator activities are appropriate for middle school students, enriching their understanding of, and appreciation for, mathematics. Students' problem-solving abilities and their concepts of variable and function can be enhanced with this tool. Realistic problem situations and real data help students understand mathe-solving abilities while using numerical and graphical approaches to these problems. They build understanding about, and appreciation for, algebraic techniques, since they can investigate interesting problems while developing algebra skills.

Bibliography

Dance, Rosalie, Joanne Nelson, Zachary Jeffers, and Joan Reinthaler. "Using Graphing Calculators to Investigate a Population Growth Model." In *Calculators in Mathematics Education,* 1992 Yearbook of the National Council of Teachers of Mathematics, edited by James T. Fey, 120–30. Reston, Va.: The Council, 1992.

Demana, Franklin, and Bert K. Waits. *College Algebra and Trigonometry: A Graphing Approach*. Reading, Mass.: Addison-Wesley Publishing Co., 1990.

Dugdale, Sharon. "Green Globs: A Microcomputer Application for Graphing of Equations." *Mathematics Teacher* 75 (March 1982):208–14.

Hector, Judith H. "Graphical Insight into Elementary Functions." In *Calculators in Mathematics Education,* 1992 Yearbook of the National Council of Teachers of Mathematics, edited by James T. Fey, 131–37. Reston, Va.: The Council, 1992.

Kenelly, John W., and John G. Harvey. *Teaching Mathematics with Calculators: A National Workshop. The Graphing Calculator: Building New Models*. Washington, D.C.: Mathematical Association of America, 1992.

Leitzel, Joan, and Alan Osborne. "Mathematical Alternatives for College Preparatory Students." In *The Secondary School Mathematics Curriculum,* 1985 Yearbook of the National Council of Teachers of Mathematics, edited by Christian R. Hirsch, 150–65. Reston, Va.: The Council, 1985.

Mahoney, Carolyn, and Franklin Demana. "Filling the Math and Science Pipeline with Young Scholars." *Notices of the American Mathematical Society* 38 (February 1991):101–3.

National Council of Teachers of Mathematics. *Curriculum and Evaluation Standards for School Mathematics.* Reston, Va.: The Council, 1989.

Taylor, Linda J. C. "TI-81 Graphing Calculator Introductory Workshop." *Proceedings of the Fifth Annual International Conference on Technology in Collegiate Mathematics,* 136–39. Reading, Mass.: Addison-Wesley Publishing Co., 1994.

Vonder Embse, Charles. "Concept Development and Problem Solving Using Graphing Calculators in the Middle School." In *Calculators in Mathematics Education,* 1992 Yearbook of the National Council of Teachers of Mathematics, edited by James T. Fey, 65–78. Reston, Va.: The Council, 1992.

World Almanac and Book of Facts. New York: Pharos Books, 1991.

Example of an Article from *Teaching Children Mathematics*

Telling Tales: Creating Graphs Using Multicultural Literature

he focus in primary classrooms on children's literature through the whole-language approach to reading encourages the elimination of artificial divisions among subjects through such natural and desirable mixtures as mathematics and storybooks. Egan (1989) states that the use of stories is an excellent foundation for teaching all subjects. A setting or scenario in children's literature can be used as a direct lead-in to a mathematics exercise or can act as a catalyst to motivate students to pursue a related mathematical activity that includes the development of such mathematics process skills as problem solving and making inferences. When children are engaged in reading a book or story, they can become familiar with the characters and plot in sufficient depth that these literary elements can function as the nucleus for more authentic mathematics activities.

Mathematical problem solving based on familiar settings and contexts has been shown to increase the skills children need to make sense of their world. Research evidence consistently points out that students achieve higher levels of performance when

Tikki Tikki Tembo by Arlene Mosel, illustrations by Blair Lent Jr. Illustrations copyright © 1968 by Blair Lent Jr. Reprinted by permission of Henry Holt and Company, Inc.

confronted with problem-solving situations to which they can relate (Bradbard 1990; Davis-Dorsey 1991). Teachers must build bridges between settings with which their students are comfortable and the realm of mathematical ideas.

The Critical Link

In particular, mathematics skills involving examining problems, collecting and recording data, representing data, describing and interpreting data, and developing hypotheses and theories based on data are significant components of explorations in which elementary students will be engaged as envisioned in the National Council of Teachers of Mathematics's *Curriculum and Evaluation Standards for School Mathematics* (1989) and in the quantitative-literacy movement (TERC 1990). Linking these vital forms of representing mathematical concepts with literature gives students opportunities to communicate in mathematics on two levels. First, when students transform and analyze the information gleaned from the stories they are interpreting and enjoying in class, they develop skills in both critical thinking and mathematical reasoning. Second, such data collection based on stories enables students to increase their fluency in connecting written or oral language to mathematical language. Cultivating facility in communicating through multiple means equips students with the ability to "tell tales" through both traditional stories and graphic representations.

433

Stories can help students develop critical thinking

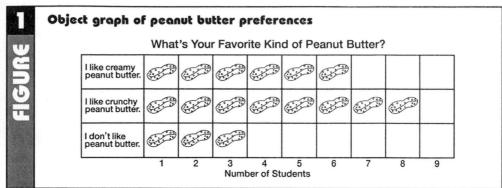

1 FIGURE

Object graph of peanut butter preferences

What's Your Favorite Kind of Peanut Butter?

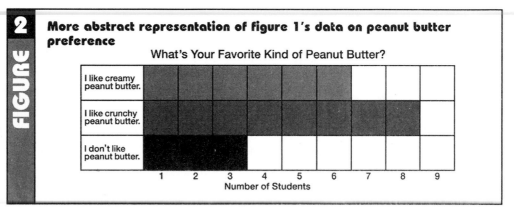

2 FIGURE

More abstract representation of figure 1's data on peanut butter preference

What's Your Favorite Kind of Peanut Butter?

The Need for Multicultural Literature

Although numerous books can be used for these purposes, multicultural literature is a rich source for encouraging students of all backgrounds to experience a variety of perspectives. Students need to have the "opportunity to benefit from the knowledge, perspectives, and frames of reference that can be gained from studying and experiencing other cultures and groups" (Banks 1989, 189). In light of the growing population of second-language learners, investigations of actual situations taken from their own real-world experience or an event described through the eyes of children from similar cultural backgrounds are critical for meaningful mathematics learning. In addition, a curriculum that neglects multicultural materials is moving away from achieving equity in learning mathematics, a goal that has been highly desirable yet equally evasive. Therefore, the following links between stories and data-collecting activities have the potential of meeting several points that represent the vision of the *Curriculum and Evaluation Standards for School Mathematics* (NCTM 1989).

Collecting peanut butter preferences

In a thematic, integrated unit on inventions, Eva Moore's book *The Story of George Washington Carver* (1990) generates fascinating information about Carver's discoveries involving peanut plants. In celebrating the accomplishments of this scientist, children recognize evidence of his original thinking that relates directly to their everyday eating experiences. This accounting of Carver's life was an ideal inspiration for a graph on peanut butter preferences. This activity included an actual taste test in which children decided whether they liked creamy peanut butter or crunchy peanut butter or that they didn't care for peanut butter at all. After the taste test, each student glued a peanut shell on a five-centimeter-square portion of an appropriate bar on poster paper to create a graph incorporating real materials. When all responses were recorded through this process, children totaled the frequency for each category by counting the peanuts (see **fig. 1**).

Next another poster-board graph organized in the same fashion as the first graph was incorporated to demonstrate how the data could be transformed into a more abstract representation. Instead of gluing peanuts on the graph, students colored in squares similar to those that held the peanuts to form single colored bars (see **fig. 2**). At this point, word problems based on the data were introduced. Then pairs of children were given an opportunity to create their own problems, which included such questions as "How many more children like peanut butter than those who do not?"

To extend the sample and create more possibilities for analysis, children in groups of three were assigned to poll other classrooms in the school to collect additional data on peanut butter preferences. The children passed out one peanut to each child in the classroom. Then the students were able to vote for their choice by placing their peanuts in an appropriately marked container (each group member was responsible for one of the labeled containers). When the data-collection team members returned to their own classroom, they continued to work in the small groups, tallying the peanuts by categories and illustrating the data on a graph. When all graphs were completed, they were posted in an area where they were interpreted by the class. A question such as "If a new child came into the school from a similar community, what would we expect that his or her choice would be?" was used to encourage predictions. Additional conclusions were drawn, and word problems comparing classes or grades were written by the students. Students were curious to examine the data for evidence that children's taste preferences change as they grow older. For example, are they more likely to have tried and enjoyed crunchy peanut butter by sixth grade as compared with the figure for kindergarten? The children were given a choice of writing a story about the project findings or creating a commercial appealing to their age group as suggested by the actual results.

Students can be further challenged by totaling the data from all the classroom graphs and compiling the information on another graph, using one-to-many correspondence through incorporating a one-to-five or one-to-ten icon. Taking advantage of the circumstance of dealing with such large numbers helps to demonstrate realistically the need for a representation other than one-to-one.

Reading knots

The intergenerational tale *Knots on a Counting Rope* by Bill Martin Jr. and John Archambault is a moving story of a Native American boy and his grandfather. The boy implores the old man to relate

the story of the boy's birth and early years, as is evident the grandfather has done many times before. The grandfather repeats these past events, including the challenges and trials the boy has already successfully faced in what appears to be an effort to nurture courage and confidence in the child. As this dramatic tale unfolds, the reader learns that the young boy is blind. Thus this tale is both a story of determination and a celebration of an individual's ability to overcome physical challenges. Consequently, the reader discovers that the title of the story represents the tactile way the boy is able to record the number of times his grandfather tells this story. Each knot made by the grandfather remains a permanent record of the storytelling experience.

A natural way that the author incorporated this concrete image into the classroom was to have children keep individual counting ropes to record the number of books that they had read. To represent the data accurately, the students' ropes were marked at ten-centimeter intervals so that the knots formed parallel number lines when they were hung vertically as a group graph from a bulletin-board strip (see **fig. 3**).

Cultivating cherries

The perfect opportunity to initiate both a science and mathematics activity through literature and multicultural characters is with the actual planting of cherry pits as suggested in the story *Cherries and Cherry Pits* by Vera B. Williams. Students measured the growth of their burgeoning seeds by using the edge of

Based on the graph, what if...?

Knots on a Counting Rope
By Bill Martin Jr. and John Archambault
Illustrated by Ted Rand

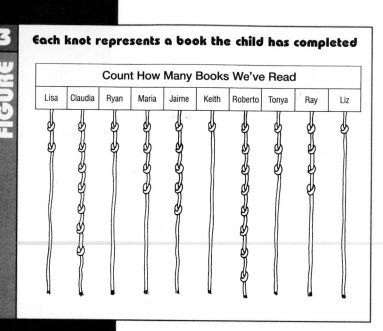

FIGURE 3

Each knot represents a book the child has completed

Count How Many Books We've Read									
Lisa	Claudia	Ryan	Maria	Jaime	Keith	Roberto	Tonya	Ray	Liz

Stories can lead to collecting data

computer paper that is interspersed with holes at equal intervals and matching it to the length of their plant's stem. At the point where they reached the top of the stem, they tore off the strip and used it as a record of the height of their plant. Recording measurements in three-day intervals, the resulting strips were placed on a continuum and thereby created a visual representation of the plant's growth. To connect to the theme of the story and make an appealing presentation, the strips were arranged on red paper so that the red color peeked through the holes and reminded the students of the small cherries in the story. The most critical component of this recording process was the analysis of the data. The students made comparisons of the graphs to generalize about successful plant care and environmental conditions best for growth.

Cherries and Cherry Pits copyright 1986 Greenwillow Books. Used with permission. All rights reserved.

Measuring baby

In another book, *She Come Bringing Me That Little Baby Girl,* Eloise Greenfield relates the gentle story of an African American boy's emotional dealings with the arrival of a new baby sister. Initially, the diminishing attention from all the adults turns the boy's world around for the worse. Eventually, his new role as big brother seems to garner appeal. With many students in the primary grades facing similar situations at home, this book is a welcome validation of their feelings as well as a foundation for a long-term graph.

To encourage positive feelings about a new sibling and to examine human growth over time, a graph of a new baby's length is an interesting class project. When a new baby was born to a family in the class, records of the baby's length were collected each month and recorded with a strip of paper cut to the same size as the baby's most recent measurement. As the newborn made monthly visits to the doctor, the sibling reported the actual growth to the class, and a corresponding strip of paper was added to the graph. The children enjoyed making regular predictions estimating the baby's length. Not surprisingly, this baby became a class favorite and received both invitations to visit—where comparisons to the graph were made—and an especially warm welcome.

Other books that invite follow-up experiences in the form of graphs are found in the **annotated bibliography** at the conclusion of this article. Surveys based on children's literature can also generate interesting graphing activities (see the **appendix**).

In the school day, fragmented with curricula ranging from the "three Rs" to moral development, the necessity for the intentional and rational integration of subjects is acute. The link between literature and mathematics can and should be encouraged and strengthened, capitalizing on the abilities, interests, and heritage of children who inspire connections between these subjects.

Appendix

Additional topics for graphing exercises might include literature-related surveys, such as the following:

- Which author do you like best—Donald Crews, Eloise Greenfield, or John Steptoe?

- Which Caldecott Medal winner did you enjoy most—*Arrow to the Sun: A Pueblo Indian Tale* by Gerald McDermott; *Why Mosquitoes Buzz in People's Ears: A West African Tale* by Verna Aardema; or *Lon Po Po: A Red Riding Hood Story from China* by Ed Young?

She Come Bringing Me That Little Baby Girl copyright 1974 by John Steptoe, selection reprinted by permission of HarperCollins Publishers, with the approval of the estate of John Steptoe. All rights reserved.

- Who is your favorite character in *"More, More, More," Said the Baby: Three Love Stories* by Vera B. Williams?

- Which version of the Cinderella story is your favorite? Select any three of the following: *Cinderella* (Italian) by David Delamare; *Yeh-Shen* (Chinese) by Ai-Ling Louie; *Rough Face Girl* (Native American) by Rafe Martin; *The Brocaded Slipper and Other Tales from Vietnam* by Lynette Vuong; *The Egyptian Cinderella* by Shirley Climo; or *Moss Gown* (Southern United States) by William H. Hooks?

Bibliography

Aardema, Verna. *Why Mosquitoes Buzz in People's Ears: A West African Tale.* New York: Dial Books, 1978.

Banks, James A. "Integrating the Curriculum with Ethnic Content: Approaches and Guidelines." In *Multicultural Education: Issues and Perspectives,* edited by J. Banks and C. M. Banks, 189–206. Boston: Allyn & Bacon, 1989.

Bradbard, Paula. "Improving Problem Solving through Writing Based on Children's Literature." Ph.D diss., University of Lowell (Mass.), 1990.

Climo, Shirley. *The Egyptian Cinderella.* New York: Harper Collins Publishers, 1989.

Crews, Donald. *Bigmama's.* New York: Greenwillow Books, 1991.

Davis-Dorsey, Judy. "The Role of Rewording and Content Personalization in the Solving of Mathematics Word Problems." *Journal of Educational Psychology* 83 (March 1991):61–68.

Delamare, David. *Cinderella.* New York: Simon & Schuster, 1993.

Egan, Kiernan. *Teaching as Story Telling.* Chicago: University of Chicago Press, 1989.

Greenfield, Eloise. *She Come Bringing Me That Little Baby Girl.* New York: HarperCollins Children's Books, 1990.

Hooks, William H. *Moss Gown.* New York: Clarion Books, 1987.

Louie, Ai-Ling. *Yeh-Shen.* New York: Philomel, 1982.

McDermott, Gerald. *Arrow to the Sun: A Pueblo Indian Tale.* New York: Puffin Books, 1977.

McKissack, Patricia, and Frederick McKissack. *George Washington Carver: The Peanut Scientist.* Hillside, N.J.: Enslow Publishers, 1991.

Martin, Bill, Jr., and John Archambault. *Knots on a Counting Rope.* New York: Henry Holt & Co., 1987.

Martin, Rafe. *Rough Face Girl.* New York: Putnam Publishing Group, 1992.

Moore, Eva. *The Story of George Washington Carver.* New York: Scholastic, 1990.

National Council of Teachers of Mathematics. *Curriculum and Evaluation Standards for School Mathematics.* Reston Va.: The Council, 1989.

Steptoe, John. *Mufaro's Beautiful Daughters: An African Tale.* New York: Lothrop, Lee & Shepard, 1987.

TERC (Technical Education Research Centers) and Lesley College. *Used Numbers.* Palo Alto, Calif.: Dale Seymour Publications, 1990.

Vuong, Lynette. *The Brocaded Slipper and Other Tales from Vietnam.* New York: HarperCollins Publishers, 1992.

Williams, Vera B. *Cherries and Cherry Pits.* New York: Greenwillow Books, 1986.

———. *"More, More, More," Said the Baby: Three Love Stories.* New York: Greenwillow Books, 1990.

Young, Ed. *Lon Po Po: A Red Riding Hood Story from China.* New York: Putnam Publishing Group, 1989.

Annotated Bibliography

Mosel, Arlene. *Tikki Tikki Tembo.* New York: Holt, Rinehart & Winston, 1989.

This Asian folktale about a boy with a dangerously long name lends itself to a graph of the lengths of children's names.

Yashima, Taro. *Crow Boy.* New York: Viking Books, 1976.

Children can use this story of a little Japanese child who has a significant distance to walk to school as a stimulus for a graph that communicates the length of their walk to school.

Baer, Edith. *This Is the Way We Go to School: A Book about Children around the World.* New York: Scholastic, 1990.

In a book that examines not only various regions of the United States but countries all over the world, we find descriptions of many different ways that children travel to school. A graph depicting students' mode of transportation to school would be a natural reply.

Cameron, Ann. *The Stories Julian Tells.* New York: Alfred A. Knopf, 1989.

This book contains a delightful chapter called "Because of Figs." On his fourth birthday the little African American boy in the story is given a fig tree that is to grow as fast as he grows. A graph representing children's heights might be a motivating response.

Brown, Marcia. *Stone Soup.* New York: Macmillan Child Group, 1986.

McGovern, Ann. *Stone Soup.* New York: Scholastic, 1986.

In a classic tale of trickery, soldiers turn a soup made from a stone into a vegetable soup fit for a feast. A graph representing students' favorite vegetables would be an appropriate link between this old French folktale and data collection and interpretation. 🌢

REFERENCES

Aaboe, A. (1964). *Episodes from the early history of mathematics*. Washington: The Mathematical Association of America.

Aleamoni, L. M. (1985). Review of *Stanford Achievement Test: Mathematics Tests*. In J. V. Mitchell (Ed.), *The ninth mental measurement yearbook* (pp. 1453–1455). Lincoln, NE: The Buros Institute of Mental Measurements and the University of Nebraska Press.

Allen, R. R., (1988, April). *Mathematics, reform, and excellence—Japan and the U.S.* A presentation at the annual meeting of the National Council of Teachers of Mathematics, Chicago.

Allen, R. R., Davidson, T., Hering, W., & Jesunathadas, J. (1984). *A study of the conditions of secondary school mathematics teacher education*. San Francisco: Far West Laboratory.

American Psychological Association, American Educational Research Association, & National Council on Measurement in Education. (1985). *Standards for educational and psychological testing* (5th ed.). Washington: Author.

Ames, C., & Ames, R. (Eds.). (1985). *Research on motivation in education: Vol. 1. Student motivation*. New York: Academic Press.

Amundson, H. E. (1989). Percent. In *Historical topics for the mathematics classroom* (pp. 146–147). Reston, VA: The National Council of Teachers of Mathematics.

Anderman, E. M., & Maehr, M. L. (1994). Motivation and schooling in the middle grades. *Review of Educational Research, 64,* 287–309.

Archibald, D. A., & Newman, F. M. (1989). *Beyond standardized testing: Assessing academic achievement in secondary school*. Reston, VA: Association of Secondary School Principals.

Arnold, D., Atwood, R., & Rogers, V. (1974). Questions and response levels and lapse time intervals. *Journal of Experimental Education, 43,* 11–15.

Ashlock, R. B. (1990). *Error patterns in computation: A semiprogrammed approach* (5th ed.). Columbus, OH: Merrill.

Augustine, D. K., Gruber, K. D., & Hanson, L. R. (1990). Cooperation works! *Educational Leadership, 47,* 4–7.

Azrin, N. H., Hake, D. G., & Hutchinson, R. R. (1965). Motivational aspects of escape from punishment. *Journal of Experimental Analysis of Behavior, 8,* 31–44.

Azrin, N. H., Hutchinson, R. R., & Sallery, R. D. (1964). Pain-aggression toward inanimate objects. *Journal of Experimental Analysis of Behavior, 7,* 223–228.

Ball, D. L. (1988a). *The subject matter preparation of prospective mathematics teachers: Challenging the myths*. (Research Report 88-3). East Lansing: Michigan State University National Center for Research on Teacher Education.

Ball, D. L. (1988b). *Unlearning to teach mathematics*. (Issue Paper 88-1). East Lansing: Michigan State University National Center for Research on Teacher Education.

Bandura, A. (1965). Behavior modification through modeling procedures. In L. Krasner & L. P. Ullman (Eds.), *Research in behavior modification* (pp. 310–340). New York: Holt, Rinehart, & Winston.

Bang-Jensen, V. (1986). The view from next door: A look at peer "supervision." In K. K. Zumwalt (Ed.), *Improving teaching* (pp. 51–62). Alexandria, VA: Association for Supervision and Curriculum Development.

Barnsley, M. (1988). *Fractals everywhere*. Boston: Academic Press.

Baroody, A. J. (1989). Kindergartners' mental addition with single-digit combinations. *Journal of Research in Mathematics Education, 20,* 159–172.

Barrow, J. D. (1992). *Pi in the sky: Counting thinking being*. Boston: Little, Brown.

Battista, M. T. (1994). On Greeno's environmental/model view of conceptual domains: A spatial/geometric perspective. *Journal of Research in Mathematics Education, 25,* 86–99.

Begle, E. G. (1958). The school Mathematics Study Group. *The Mathematics Teacher, 51,* 616–618.

Bell, E. T. (1965). *Men of mathematics*. New York: Simon & Schuster.

Beltrami, E. (1993). *Mathematical models in the social and biological sciences*. Boston: Jones and Bartlett.

Benjamin, A., & Shermer, M. B. (1993). *Mathemagics: How to look like a genius without really trying*. Los Angeles: Lowell House.

Bennett, D. (1993). *Exploring geometry with the Geometer's SketchPAD*. Berkeley, CA: Key Curriculum Press.

Berg, F. S. (1987). *Facilitating classroom listening*. Boston: College-Hill.

Berk, R. A. (1986). Performance standards on criterion referenced tests. *Review of Educational Research, 56,* 137–172.

Beyer, B. K. (1987). *Practical strategies for teaching of thinking*. Boston: Allyn and Bacon.

Beyer, W. H. (Ed.). (1987). *CRC standard mathematical tables* (28th ed.). Boca Raton, FL: CRC Press.

Bloom, B. S. (Ed.). (1984). *Taxonomy of educational objectives: The classification of educational goals. Book I: Cognitive domain.* New York: Longman.

Bloom, B. S., Madaus, G. F., & Hastings, J. T. (1981). *Evaluation to improve learning.* New York: McGraw-Hill.

Bolt, B. (1992). Mathematical cavalcade. Cambridge, England: Cambridge University Press.

Bongiovanni, A. F. (1979). An analysis of research on punishment and its relation to use of corporal punishment in schools. In I. A. Hyman & J. Wise (Eds.), *Corporal punishment in American education* (pp. 351–372). Philadelphia: Temple University Press.

Bourne, L. E., Dominowski, R. L., Loftus, E. F., & Healy, A. F. (1986). *Cognitive processes* (2nd ed.). Englewood Cliffs, NJ: Prentice Hall.

Boutte, G. S., & McCormick, C. B. (1992, Spring). Authentic multicultural activities. *Childhood Education,* pp. 140–144.

Bowden, R. (1993). Precision teaching in algebra. Dissertation, Utah State University, Logan.

Bowers, J. (1988). *Invitation to mathematics.* New York: Blackwell.

Boyer, C. G. (1991). *A history of mathematics* (2nd ed.). New York: Wiley.

Brandt, R. (1989). A changed professional culture. *Educational Leadership, 46,* 2.

Bridges, E. M. (1986). *The incompetent teacher.* Philadelphia: The Falmer Press.

Brophy, J. (1986). Teaching and learning in mathematics: Where research should be going. *Journal of Research in Mathematics Education, 17,* 323–346.

Brown, S. I., & Walter, M. I. (1990). *The art of problem posing* (2nd ed.). Hillsdale, NJ: Erlbaum.

Brown, S. T., Cooney, T. J., & Jones, D. (1990). Mathematics teacher education. In W. R. Houston (Ed.), *Handbook of research on teacher education* (pp. 639–656). New York: Macmillan.

Brubaker, D. L. (1982). *Curriculum planning: The dynamics of theory and practice,* Glenview, IL: Scott, Foresman.

Burrill, G. F., Cummins, J. J., Kanold, T. D., & Yunker, L. E. (1993). *Merrill geometry: Applications and connections.* Westerville, OH: Glencoe.

Business & Educational Technologies. (1994). *B. & E. Tech Technology Catalog for Mathematics.* Dubuque, IA: Author.

Cajori, F. (1985). *A history of mathematics* (4th ed.). New York: Chelsea.

Cangelosi, J. S. (1980). Four steps in teaching for mathematical application. *Mathematics and Computer Education, 14,* 54–59.

Cangelosi, J. S. (1982). *Measurement and evaluation: An inductive approach for teachers.* Dubuque, IA: Brown.

Cangelosi, J. S. (1984a). Another answer to the cut-off score question. *Educational Measurement Issues and Practice, 3,* 23–25.

Cangelosi, J. S. (1984b). *Teaching students to apply mathematics.* Paper presented at the meeting of the Research Council for Diagnostic and Prescriptive Mathematics. San Francisco, CA.

Cangelosi, J. S. (1989a). *Demystifying school mathematics.* Videotape program. Logan, UT: National Science Foundation and Utah State University Telecommunications Division.

Cangelosi, J. S. (1989b, April). *A video inservice program for underprepared mathematics teachers.* Presentation at the annual meeting of the National Council of Teachers of Mathematics, Orlando, FL.

Cangelosi, J. S. (1990a). *Cooperation in the classroom: Students and teachers together* (2nd ed.). Washington: National Education Association.

Cangelosi, J. S. (1990b). *Designing tests for evaluating student achievement.* New York: Longman.

Cangelosi, J. S. (1990c). *Using mathematics to solve real-life problems.* Videotape program. Logan, UT: National Science Foundation and Utah State University Telecommunications Division.

Cangelosi, J. S. (1991). *Evaluating classroom instruction.* New York: Longman.

Cangelosi, J. S. (1992). *Systematic teaching strategies.* New York: Longman.

Cangelosi, J. S. (1993a, April). *Cheating in elementary and secondary school classrooms.* Paper presented at the annual meeting of the American Educational Research Association and of the National Council on Measurement in Education, Atlanta, GA.

Cangelosi, J. S. (1993b). *Classroom management strategies: Gaining and maintaining students' cooperation* (2nd ed.). New York: Longman.

Cangelosi, J. S., Struyk, L. R., Grimes, M. L., & Duke, C. (1988, April). *Classroom management needs of beginning teachers.* Paper presented at the annual meeting of the American Educational Research Association, New Orleans, LA.

Cannon, L. O., & Elich, J. (1994). *Precalculus* (2nd ed.). New York: HarperCollins.

Canter, L., & Canter, M. (1976). *Assertive discipline: A take-charge approach for today's educator.* Seal Beach, CA: Canter and Canter.

Carpenter, T. P., Lindquist, M. M., Brown, C. A., Kouba, V. L., Silver, E. A., & Swafford, J. O. (1988). Results of the fourth NAEP assessment of mathematics: Trends and conclusions. *Arithmetic teacher, 36,* 38–43.

Chance, P. (1988). *Learning and behavior* (2nd ed.). Belmont, CA: Wadsworth.

Chase, A., & Wolfe, P. (1989). Off to a good start in peer coaching. *Educational Leadership, 46,* 37.

Chrisco, I. M. (1989). Peer assistance works. *Educational Leadership, 46,* 31–32.

Cieply, J. F. (1993). Parametric equations: Push 'em back, push 'em back, way back! *Mathematics Teacher, 86,* 470–474.

Cobb, P. (1988). The tension between theories of learning and instruction in mathematics education. *Educational Psychologists, 23,* 87–103.

Cobb, P. (Ed.). (1994). *Learning mathematics: Constructivist and interactionists theories of mathematical development.* Hingham, MA: Kluwer.

Cole, R. S. (1993). Why should we care about teaching calculus? *Washington Center News, 7,* 4–6.

College Board Publication. (1990). *Advanced placement course description in mathematics.* Princeton, NJ: Author.

Conference Board of the Mathematical Sciences. (1983a). *The mathematical sciences curriculum K–12: What is still fundamental and what is not.* Report to the National Science Board Commission on Precollege Education in Mathematics, Sciences, and Technology. Washington: Author.

Conference Board of the Mathematical Sciences. (1983b). *New goals for mathematical education.* Report. Washington: Author.

Connolly, P., & Vilardi, T. (Ed.). (1989). *Writing to learn mathematics and science.* New York: Teachers College Press.

Coolican, J. (1988). Individual differences. In R. McNergney (Ed.), *Guide to classroom teaching.* Boston: Allyn and Bacon.

Cooney, T. J., Davis, E. J., & Henderson, K. B. (1983). *Dynamics of teaching secondary school mathematics.* Prospect Heights, IL: Waveland Press.

Cooper, P. A. (1993). Paradigm shifts in designed instruction: From behaviorism to cognitivism to constructivism. *Educational Technology, 33,* 12–19.

Costa, A. L. (1989). Re-assessing assessment. *Educational Leadership, 46,* 2.

Coxford, A. F. (1991). *Geometry from multiple perspectives.* Reston, VA: National Council of Teachers of Mathematics.

Creative Publications. (1994). *Middle grades mathematics catalog.* Oak Lawn, IL: Author.

Cubberley, E. P. (1962). *Public education in the United States* (rev. ed.). Cambridge, MA: Riverside Press.

Cuisenaire Company. (1994). *Materials for learning mathematics and science.* White Plains, NY: Author.

Culotta, E. (1992). The calculus of education reform. *Science, 255,* 1060–1062.

Curcio, F. R., & Bezuk, N. (in press). *Understanding rational numbers and proportions: Addenda Series.* Reston, VA: NCTM.

Curwin, R. L., & Mendler, A. N. (1988). *Discipline with dignity.* Alexandria, VA: Association for Supervision and Curriculum Development.

Dale Seymour Publications. (1994). *Secondary mathematics.* Palo Alto, CA: Author.

Darling-Hammond, L., & Snyder, J. (1992). Curriculum studies and the traditions of inquiry: The scientific tradition. In P. W. Jackson (Ed.), *Handbook of research on curriculum* (pp. 41–78). New York: Macmillan.

Davis, R. B., Maher, C. A., & Noddings, N. (Ed.). (1990). *Constructivist views on the teaching and learning of mathematics.* Reston, VA: National Council of Teachers of Mathematics.

Delgado, J. M. R. (1963). Cerebral heterostimulation in a monkey colony. *Science, 141,* 161–163.

Delta Education. (1994). *Hands-on math.* Nashua, NH: Author.

Demana, F., Waits, B. K., & Clemens, S. R. (1992). *Precalculus mathematics: A graphing approach* (2nd ed.). Reading, MA: Addison-Wesley.

Devaney, R. L. (1990). *Chaos, fractals, and dynamics: Computer experiments in mathematics.* Menlo Park, CA: Addison-Wesley.

Devlin, K. (1993). Computers and mathematics. *Notices of the AMS, 40,* 1352–1353.

Devlin, K. (1994). A parade of errors. *Focus, 14,* 1–3.

Donley, H. E., & George, E. A. (1993). Hidden behaviors in graphs. *Mathematics Teacher, 86,* 466–468.

Dossey, J. A., Mullis, I. V. S., Lindquist, M. M., & Chambers, D. L. (1988). *The mathematics report card: Are we measuring up? Trends and achievement based on the 1986 National Assessment.* Princeton, NJ: Educational Testing Service.

Doyle, W. (1986). Classroom organization and management. In M. C. Wittrock (Ed.), *Handbook of research on teaching* (3rd ed.) (pp. 392–431). New York: Macmillan.

Drake, D. D. (1993). Student diversity: Implications for classroom teachers. *The Clearing House, 66,* 264–266.

Driscoll, M. (1982). *Research within reach: A research-guided response to the concerns of educators.* Reston, VA: National Council of Teachers of Mathematics.

Duke, C. R., Cangelosi, J. S., & Knight, R. S. (1988, February). *The Mellon project: A collaborative effort.* Colloquium presentation at the annual meeting of the American Association of Colleges for Teacher Education, New Orleans, LA.

Dunham, P. H., & Dick, T. P. (1994). Research on graphing calculators. *Mathematics Teacher, 87,* 440–445.

Dunham, W. (1994). *The mathematical universe: An alphabetical journey through the great proofs, problems, and personalities.* New York: Wiley.

Edwards, L. (1994). *Manipulating math for meaning via graphing calculators.* A workshop presentation sponsored by the Mathematics Teacher Network, Utah State University, Logan.

Eisner, M. P. (1986). An application of quadratic equations to baseball. *Mathematics Teacher, 79,* 327–330.

ETA. (1994). *A universe of math manipulatives.* Vernon Hills, IL: Author.

Evans, R. (1989). The faculty in midcareer: Implications for school improvement. *Educational Leadership, 46,* 10–15.

Evertson, C. M. (1989). Classroom organization and management. In M. C. Reynolds (Ed.), *Knowledge base for the beginning teacher* (pp. 59–70). Oxford, England: Pergamon.

Eves, H. (1983a). *Great moments in mathematics after 1650.* Washington: Mathematical Association of America.

Eves, H. (1983b). *Great moments in mathematics before 1650*. Washington: The Mathematical Association of America.

Ferrini-Mundy, J., & Graham, K. G. (1991). An overview of the calculus reform effort: Issues for learning, teaching, and curriculum development. *American Mathematical Monthly, 98*, 627–635.

Fey, J. G. (Ed.). (1992). *Calculators in mathematics education: 1992 yearbook*. Reston, VA: National Council of Teachers of Mathematics.

Fisher, C. W., Berliner, D. C., Filby, N. N., Marliave, R., Cahen, L. S., & Dishaw, M. M. (1980). Teaching behaviors, academic learning time, and student achievement: An overview. In C. Denham & A. Lieberman (Eds.), *Time to learn* (pp. 7–32). Washington: National Institute of Education.

Flato, M. (1990). *The power of mathematics*. New York: McGraw-Hill.

Floden, R. E. (1985). Review of Sequential Tests of Educational Progress, *Series III*. In J. V. Mitchell (Ed.), *The ninth mental measurement yearbook* (pp. 1363–1364). Lincoln, NE: The Buros Institute of Mental Measurements and the University of Nebraska Press.

Foster, A. G., Rath, J. N., & Winters, L. J. (1986). *Merrill algebra one*. Columbus, OH: Merrill.

Foster, A. G., Winters, L. J., Gordon, B. W., Rath, J. N., & Gell, J. M. (1992). *Merrill algebra 2 with trigonometry*. Westerville, OH: Glencoe.

Fowler, D. (1994). What society means by mathematics. *Focus, 14*, 12–13.

Froelich, G. W. (1991). *Connecting mathematics*. Reston, VA: National Council of Teachers of Mathematics.

Frye, S. M. (1989a). The NCTM Standards—Challenges for all classrooms. *Arithmetic Teacher, 36*, 4–7.

Frye, S. M. (1989b). The NCTM Standards—Challenges for all classrooms, *Mathematic Teacher, 82*, 312–317.

Fuson, K. C. (1992). Elementary mathematics education. In M. C. Alkin (Ed.), *Encyclopedia of educational research* (6th ed.) (pp. 776–785). New York: Macmillan.

Gagne, E. D., Yekovich, C. W., & Yekovich, F. R. (1993). *Cognitive psychology of school learning* (2nd ed.). New York: HarperCollins.

Gardner, M. (1969). *The unexpected hanging: And other mathematical diversions*. New York: Simon & Schuster.

Garner, R. (1990). When children and adults do not use learning strategies: Toward a theory of settings. *Review of Educational Research, 60*, 517–529.

Geddes, D. (1992). *Geometry in the middle grades*. Reston, VA: National Council of Teachers of Mathematics.

Geddes, D. (1994). *Measurement in the middle grades*. Reston, VA: National Council of Teachers of Mathematics.

Gibilisco, S. (1990). *Optical illusions: Puzzles, paradoxes and brain teasers, Number 4*. Blue Ridge Summit, PA: Tab.

Gilligan, L. G., & Marquardt, J. F. (1991). *Calculus and the DERIVE program: Experiments with the computer* (2nd ed.). Cincinnati: Gilmar.

Ginott, H. G. (1972). *Teacher and child*. New York: Avon.

Gipps, C. (1993, April). *Emerging models of teaching assessment in the classroom*. Paper presented at the national meeting of the American Educational Research Association, Atlanta, GA.

Goldberg, K. P. (1994). Using technology to understand the jury decision-making process. *Mathematics Teacher, 87*, 110–114.

Goldin, G. A. (1990). Epistemology, constructivism, and discovery learning mathematics. In R. B. Davis, C. A. Maher, & N. Noddings (Eds.), *Constructivist views on the teaching and learning of mathematics* (pp. 31–47). Reston, VA: National Council of Teachers of Mathematics.

Good, T. L., Grouws, D. A., & Ebmeier, H. (1983). *Active mathematics teaching*. New York: Longman.

Good, T. L., & McCaslin, M. M. (1992). Teaching effectiveness. In M. C. Alkin (Ed.), *Encyclopedia of educational research* (pp. 1373–1388). New York: Macmillan.

Good, T. L., Mulryan, C., McCaslin, M. (1992). Grouping for instruction in mathematics: A call for programmatic research on small-group processes. In D. A. Grouws (Ed.), *Handbook of research on mathematics teaching and learning* (pp. 165–196). New York: Macmillan.

Goodlad, J. I., & Su, Z. (1992). Organization of the curriculum. In P. W. Jackson (Ed.), *Handbook of research on curriculum* (pp. 327–344). New York: Macmillan.

Gordon, W. J. J. (1961). *Synectics*. New York: Harper & Row.

Gowan, J. C., Demos, G. D., & Torrance, E. P. (1967). *Creativity: Its educational implications*. New York: Wiley.

Gronlund, N. E., & Linn, R. L. (1990). *Measurement and evaluation in teaching* (6th ed.). New York: Macmillan.

Grouws, D. A. (Ed.). (1992). *Handbook of research on mathematics teaching and learning*. New York: Macmillan.

Guilford, J. P. (1959). *Personality*. New York: McGraw-Hill.

Guzzetti, B. J., Snyder, T. E., Glass, G. V., & Gamas, W. S. (1993). Promoting conceptual change in science: A comparative meta-analysis of instructional interventions from reading education and science education. *Reading Research Quarterly, 28*, 117–159.

Hall, N. (Ed.). (1991). *Exploring chaos: A guide to the new science of disorder*. New York: Norton.

Hall, R. S. (1973). *About mathematics*. Englewood Cliffs, NJ: Prentice-Hall.

Hambleton, R. K., & Swaminathan, H. (1985). *Item response theory: Principles and applications*. Boston: Kluwer Nijhoff.

Haney, W. (1985). Making testing more educational. *Educational Leadership, 43*, 4–13.

Hardy, G. H. (1992). *A mathematician's apology*. New York: Cambridge University Press.

Harvey, J. G. (1992). Mathematics testing with calculators: Ransoming the hostages. In T. A. Romberg (Ed.), *Mathematics assessment and evaluation: Imperatives for mathematics educators* (pp. 139–168). Albany, NY: State University of New York Press.

Hembree, R., & Dessart, D. J. (1986). Effects of hand-held calculators in pre-college mathematics education. *Journal for Research in Mathematics Education, 17,* 83–99.

Hiebert, J., & Carpenter, T. P. (1992). Learning and teaching with understanding. In D. A. Grouws (Ed.), *Handbook of research on mathematics teaching and learning* (pp. 65–97). New York: Macmillan.

Hirsch, C. R. (Ed.). (1986). *Activities for implementing curricular themes from the agenda in action: Selections from the Mathematics Teacher.* Reston, VA: National Council of Teachers of Mathematics.

Hoffman, P. (1988). *Archimedes' revenge: The joys and perils of mathematics.* New York: Fawcett Crest.

Hofmann, R. (1975). The concept of item efficiency in item analysis. *Educational and Psychological Measurement, 35,* 621–640.

Hogben, L. (1983). *Mathematics for the millions.* New York: Norton.

Hopley, R. B. (1994). Nested Platonic solids: A class project in solid geometry. *Mathematics Teacher, 87,* 312–318.

Hunter, M. (1982). *Mastery teaching.* El Segunda, CA: TIP Publications.

Hyman, I. A., & Wise, J. H. (Eds.). *Corporal punishment in American education.* Philadelphia: Temple Press.

James, W. (1890). *The principles of psychology,* Vols. I and II. New York: Holt, Rinehart, & Winston.

Jesunathadas, J. (1990). *Mathematics teachers' instructional activities as a function of academic preparation.* Dissertation, Utah State University, Logan.

Jones, F. H. (1979). *The gentle art of classroom discipline. Principal, 58,* 26–32.

Jones, P. S. (1989). The history of mathematics as a teaching tool. In *Historical topics for the mathematics classroom* (pp. 1–17). Reston, VA: The National Council of Teachers of Mathematics.

Joyce, B., Weil, M., & Showers, B. (1992). *Models of teaching* (4th ed.). Boston: Allyn and Bacon.

Kapaddia, R., & Borovcnik, M. (Eds.). (1991). *Chance encounters: Probability education.* Hingham, MA: Kluwer.

Kaput, J. J. (1992). Technology and mathematics education. In D. A. Grouws (Ed.), *Handbook of research on mathematics teaching and learning* (pp. 515–556). New York: Macmillan.

Karp, K. S. (1994). Telling tales: Creating graphs using multicultural literature. *Teaching Children Mathematics, 1,* 87–91.

Kasner, E., & Newman, J. R. (1989). *Mathematics and the imagination.* Redman, WA: Tempus Books.

Keedy, M. L., Smith, S. A., & Anderson, P. A. (1986). *Applying mathematics: A consumer/career approach.* Reading, MA: Addison-Wesley.

Keeves, J. P. (Ed.). (1988). *Educational research, methodology, and measurement: An international handbook.* Oxford, England: Pergamon Press.

Kellough, D. (Ed.). (in press) *Integrating mathematics and science for intermediate and middle school students.* Columbus, OH: Prentice Hall.

Kennedy, E. S. (1989). The history of trigonometry. In *Historical topics for the mathematics classroom* (pp. 333–364). Reston, VA: The National Council of Teachers of Mathematics.

Kidder, R. M. (1985). How a highschooler discovered a new math theorem. *The Christian Science Monitor, 75,* 19–20.

King, J. P. (1992). *The art of mathematics.* New York: Fawcett Columbine.

Kinney, L. B., & Purdy, C. R. (1952). *Teaching mathematics in the secondary schools.* New York: Holt, Rinehart, & Winston.

Koehler, M. S., & Grouws, D. A. (1992). Mathematics teaching practices and their effects. In D. A. Grouws (Ed.), *Handbook of research on mathematics teaching and learning* (pp. 115–126). New York: Macmillan.

Kohut, S., & Range, D. G. (1979). *Classroom discipline: Case studies and viewpoints.* Washington: National Education Association.

Kouba, V. L. (1989). Children's solution strategies for equivalent set multiplication. *Journal of Research in Mathematics Education, 20,* 147–158.

Kounin, J. (1977). *Discipline and group management in classrooms.* New York: Holt, Rinehart & Winston.

Krantz, S. G. (1993). *How to teach mathematics: A personal perspective.* Providence, RI: American Mathematical Society.

Krathwohl, D., Bloom, B. S., & Masia, B. (1964). *Taxonomy of educational objectives, the classification of educational goals, Handbook 2: Affective domain.* New York: Longman.

Lacampagne, C. B. (1993). *Transforming ideas for teaching and learning mathematics.* Washington: Office of Research, U.S. Department of Education.

Lamb, A. (1993). *IBM Linkway plus Linkway Live! Authoring tool.* Orange, CA: Career Publishing.

Lane, S. (1993, April). *Assessing performance assessments. Do they withstand empirical scrutiny?* A symposium presentation at the national meeting of the American Educational Research Association, Atlanta, GA.

Langer, J. A., & Allington, R. L. (1992). Curriculum research in writing and reading. In P. W. Jackson (Ed.), *Handbook of research on curriculum* (pp. 687–725). New York: Macmillan.

Leder, G. C. (1992). Mathematics and gender: Changing perspectives. In D. A. Grouws (Ed.), *Handbook of research on mathematics teaching and learning* (pp. 597–622). New York: Macmillan.

Leighton, M. S. (1994). Cooperative learning. In J.M. Cooper (Ed.), *Classroom teaching skills* (pp. 281–325). New York: Macmillan.

Lerman, S. (Ed.). (1994). *Cultural perspectives on the mathematics classroom*. Hingham, MA: Kluwer.

Lewis, R. B., & Doorlag, D. H. (1991). *Teaching special students in the mainstream* (3rd ed.). New York: Macmillan.

Linn, M. C. (1986). Science. In R. F. Dillon & R. J. Sternberg (Eds.). *Cognition and instruction* (pp. 155–204). San Diego, CA: Academic Press.

Livingston, S. A., & Zieky, M. J. (1982). *Passing scores: A manual for setting standards of performance on educational and occupational tests*. Princeton, NJ: Educational Testing Service.

Lowry, D. W., OcKenga, E. G., & Rucker, W. E. (1992). *Heath pre-algebra*. Lexington, MA: Heath.

Lucas, J. F., & Lucas, C. A. (1992). *A guided tour of the TI-85 graphics programmable calculator with emphasis on calculus*. New York: Ardsley House.

Lyman, L., & Foyle, H. C. (1990). *Cooperative grouping for interactive learning: Students, teachers, and administrators*. Washington: National Education Association.

Mathematical Association of America and the National Council of Teachers of Mathematics. (1980). *A sourcebook of applications of school mathematics*. Reston, VA and Washington: Authors.

Mathematical Association of America. (1988). *Guidelines for the continuing mathematical education of teachers*. Washington: Author.

Mathematical Sciences Education Board (1989). *Everybody counts: A report to the nation on the future of mathematics education*. Washington: National Academy Press.

McLeod, D. B. (1992). Research on affect in mathematics education: A reconceptualization. In D. A. Grouws (Ed.), *Handbook of research on mathematics teaching and learning* (pp. 575–596). New York: Macmillan.

McCleod, D. B. (1994). Research on affect and mathematical learning in the *JRME*: 1970 to present. *Journal of Research in Mathematics Education, 25,* 637–647.

McLeish, J. (1991). *Number: The history of numbers and how they shape our lives*. New York: Fawcett Columbine.

Merriam-Webster, Inc. (1986). *Webster's third new international dictionary*. Chicago: Author.

Miller, L. (1989). Radical symbol. In *Historical topics for the mathematics classroom* (pp. 147–148). Reston, VA: National Council of Teachers of Mathematics.

Miller, M. D., & Legg, S. M. (1993). Alternative assessment in a high stakes environment. *Educational Measurement: Issues and Practice, 12,* 9–15.

Millman, J., & Greene, J. (1989). The specification and development of tests of achievement and ability. In R. L. Linn (Ed.), *Educational measurement* (3rd ed.) (pp. 335–336). New York: American Council on Education and Macmillan.

Milosheff, E. M. O. (1992). *The influence of high school teachers' attitudes and behaviors on students' mathematics achievement*. Dissertation. Chicago: The University of Illinois at Chicago.

Müller, R. (1989). *The great book of math teasers*. New York: Sterling.

National Council of Teachers of Mathematics. (1940). *Fifteenth yearbook: The place of mathematics in general education*. New York: Teachers College Press, Columbia University.

National Council of Teachers of Mathematics. (1980). *An agenda for action: Recommendations for school mathematics of the 1980s*. Reston, VA: Author.

National Council of Teachers of Mathematics. (1988–1989). *Research agenda for mathematics education* (Volumes 1–5). Reston, VA: NCTM and Hillsdale, NJ: Laurence Erlbaum Associates.

National Council of Teachers of Mathematics. (1989a). *Curriculum and evaluation standards for school mathematics*. Reston, VA: Author.

National Council of Teachers of Mathematics. (1989b). *Historical topics for the mathematics classroom*. Reston, VA: Author.

National Council of Teachers of Mathematics. (1991). *Professional standards for teaching mathematics*. Reston, VA: Author.

National Council of Teachers of Mathematics. (1992a). *A core curriculum*. Reston, VA: Author.

National Council of Teachers of Mathematics. (1992b). *Data analysis and statistics*. Reston, VA: Author.

National Council of Teachers of Mathematics. (1993). *Assessment standards for school mathematics: Working draft*. Reston, VA: Author.

National Council of Teachers of Mathematics. (1994). *NCTM educational materials catalog*. Reston, VA: Author.

National Science Board Commission on Precollege Education in Mathematics, Science, and Technology. (1983). *Educating Americans for the twenty-first century: A plan for action for improving the mathematics, science, and technology education for all American elementary and secondary students so that their achievement is the best in the world by 1995*. Washington: National Science Foundation.

National Science Foundation. (1993). *Mathematics instructional materials: Preschool-high school*. Washington: Author.

Nunes, T. (1992). Ethnomathematics and everyday cognition. In D. A. Grouws (Ed.), *Handbook of research on mathematics teaching and learning* (pp. 557–574). New York: Macmillan.

Oosterhof, A. (1994). *Classroom applications of educational measurement* (2nd ed). New York: Macmillan.

Orlich, D. C., Harder, R. J., Callahan, R. C., Kauchak, D. P., & Gibson, H. W. (1994). *Teaching strategies: A guide to better instruction* (4th ed.). Lexington, MA: Heath.

Papert, S. (1972). Teaching children to be mathematicians versus teaching about mathematics. *International Journal of Mathematics Education, Science and Technology, 3,* 263–268.

Paulos, J. A. (1991). *Beyond numeracy: Ruminations of a numbers man*. New York: Knopf.

Peitgen, H., Jürgens, H., & Saupe, D. (1992). *Fractals for the classroom. Part One: introduction to fractals and chaos.* Reston, VA: National Council of Teachers of Mathematics.

Peterson, I. (1988). *The mathematical tourist: Snapshots of modern mathematics.* New York: Freeman.

Phillips, E. (1991). *Patterns and functions.* Reston, VA: National Council of Teachers of Mathematics.

Phye, G. D. (1986). Practice and skilled classroom performance. In G. D. Phye, & T. Adre (Eds.), *Cognitive classroom learning* (pp. 141–168). San Diego, CA: Academic Press.

Pintrich, P. R. (1990). Implications of psychological research on student learning and college teaching for teacher education. In W. R. Houston (Ed.), *Handbook of research on teacher education* (pp. 826–857). New York: Macmillan.

Pólya, G. (1977). *Mathematical methods in science.* Washington: Mathematical Association of America.

Pólya, G. (1985). *How to solve it: A new aspect of mathematical method* (2nd ed.). Princeton, NJ: Princeton University Press.

Posamentier, A. S., & Stepelman, J. (1990). *Teaching secondary school mathematics: Techniques and enrichment units* (3rd ed.). Columbus, OH: Merrill.

Post, T. R., & Cramer, K. A. (1989). Knowledge, representation, and quantitative thinking. In M. C. Reynolds (Ed.), *Knowledge base for the beginning teacher* (pp. 221–231). Oxford, England: Pergamon.

Poundstone, W. (1992). *Prisoner's dilemma.* New York: Doubleday.

Puhlmann, N. A., & Petersen, M. L. (1992, April). *The electronics teaching station of the future—today.* Presentation at the annual meeting of the National Council of Teachers of Mathematics, Nashville, TN.

Quina, J. (1989). *Effective secondary teaching: Going beyond the bell curve.* New York: Harper & Row.

Rahn, J. R., & Berndes, B. A. (1994). Using logarithms to explore power and exponential functions. *Mathematics Teacher, 87,* 161–170.

Raney, P., & Robbins, P. (1989). Professional growth and support through peer coaching. *Educational Leadership, 46,* 35–38.

Reys, B. J. (1991). *Developing number sense in the middle grades.* Reston, VA: National Council of Teachers of Mathematics.

Rogers, B. G. (1985). Review of *Stanford Diagnostic Mathematics Test.* In J. V. Mitchell, (Ed.), *The ninth mental measurement yearbook* (pp. 1457–1462). Lincoln, NE: The Buros Institute of Mental Measurements and the University of Nebraska Press.

Rogers, R. L., & McMillin, S. C. (1989). *Freeing someone you love from alcohol and other drugs: A step-by-step plan starting today!* Los Angeles: The Body Press.

Romberg, T. A. (1992a). (Ed.). *Mathematics assessment and evaluation: Imperatives for mathematics educators.* Albany, NY: State University of New York Press.

Romberg, T. A. (1992b). Problematic features of the school mathematics curriculum. In P. W. Jackson (Ed.), *Handbook of research on curriculum* (pp. 749–788). New York: Macmillan.

Romberg, T. A., & Carpenter, T. P. (1986). Research on teaching and learning mathematics: Two disciplines of scientific inquiry. In M. C. Wittrock (Ed.), *Handbook of research on teaching* (3rd ed.) (pp. 850–873). New York: Macmillan.

Romberg, T. A., Wilson, L., & Chavarria, S. (1990). *An examination of state and foreign tests.* Madison, WI: Wisconsin Center for Education and Research.

Romberg, T. A., Wilson, L., Khaketla, M., & Chavarria, S. (1992). Curriculum and test alignment. In T. A. Romberg (Ed.), *Mathematics assessment and evaluation: Imperatives for mathematics educators* (pp. 61–74). Albany, NY: State University of New York Press.

Rose, T. L. (1984). Current uses of corporal punishment in American public schools. *Journal of Educational Psychology, 76,* 427–441.

Rosenshine, B. (1987). Direct instruction. In M. J. Dunkin (Ed.), *The international encyclopedia of teaching and teacher education* (pp. 257–262). Oxford, England: Pergamon.

Rowley, E. R. (1995). Alternative assessments of meaningful learning of calculus content: A development and validation of item pools. Dissertation, Utah State University, Logan.

Russell, B. (1993). *Introduction to mathematical philosophy* (rev. ed.). London, England: Routledge.

Rust, J. O., & Kinnard, K. Q. (1983). Personality characteristics of the users of corporal punishment in the schools. *Journal of School Psychology, 21,* 91–105.

Ryan, K., & Cooper, J. M. (1992). *Those who can, teach* (6th ed.). Boston: Houghton-Mifflin.

Salem, L., Testard, F., & Salem, C. (1992). *The most beautiful mathematical formulas.* New York: Wiley.

Santa, C. M., & Alvermann, D. E. (Eds.). (1991). *Science learning: Processes and applications.* Newark, DE: International Reading Association.

Santa, C. M., & Havens, L. T. (1991). Learning through writing. In C. M. Santa & D. E. Alvermann (Eds.). *Science learning: Processes and applications* (pp. 122–133). Newark, DE: International Reading Association.

Santrock, J. W. (1984). *Adolescence* (2nd ed.). Dubuque, IA: Brown.

Schank, R. (1987). Let's eliminate math from schools. *Whole Earth Review, 55,* 58–62.

Schiffer, M. M., & Bowden, L. (1984). *The role of mathematics in science.* Washington: Mathematical Association of America.

Schoenfeld, A. H. (1985). *Mathematical problem solving.* San Diego, CA: Academic Press.

Schoenfeld, A. H. (1988). When good teaching leads to bad results: The disasters of "well-taught" mathematics courses. *Educational Psychologist, 23,* 145–166.

Schoenfeld, A. H. (1989). Teaching mathematical thinking and problem solving. In L. B. Resnick & L. E. Klopfer (Eds.), *Toward the thinking curriculum: Current cognitive research: 1989 Yearbook of the Association for Supervision and Curriculum Development* (pp. 83–103), Alexandria, VA: ASCD.

Schoenfeld, A. H. (1992). Learning to think mathematically: Problem solving, metacognition, and sense making in mathematics. In D. A. Grouws (Ed.), *Handbook of research on mathematics teaching and learning* (pp. 334–370). New York: Macmillan.

Secada, W. G. (1992). Race, ethnicity, social class, language, and achievement in mathematics. In D. A. Grouws (Ed.), *Handbook of research on mathematics teaching and learning* (pp. 623–660). New York: Macmillan.

Senk, S. L. (1992). Assessing students' learning in courses using graphics tools: A preliminary research agenda. In T. A. Romberg (Ed.), *Mathematics assessment and evaluation: Imperatives for mathematics educators* (pp. 128–138). Albany, NY: State University of New York Press.

Shuell, T. J. (1990). Phases of meaningful learning. *Review of Educational Research, 60,* 531–547.

Skemp, R. R. (1971). The psychology of learning mathematics. Middlesex, England: Penguin.

Skovsmose, O. (1994). *Philosophy of critical mathematics education.* Hingham, MA: Kluwer.

Slavin, R. E. (1991a). *Student team learning: A practical guide to cooperative learning* (3rd ed.). Washington: National Education Association.

Slavin, R. E. (1991b). Synthesis of research on cooperative learning. *Educational Leadership, 48,* 71–82.

Smith, F., & Adams, S. (1972). *Educational measurement for the classroom teacher* (2nd ed.). New York: Harper & Row.

Sobel, M. A., & Maletsky, E. M. (1988). *Teaching mathematics: A sourcebook of aids, activities, and strategies* (2nd ed.). Englewood Cliffs, NJ: Prentice Hall.

Stanley, S. J., & Popham, W. J. (Eds). (1988b). *Teacher evaluation: Six prescriptions for success* (pp. xi–xii). Alexandria, VA: Association for Curriculum and Supervision.

Steen, L. A. (1987). Mathematics education: A predictor of scientific competitiveness. *Science, 237,* 251+.

Steen, L. A. (1988). Out from underachievement. *Issues in Science and Technology, 10,* 88–93.

Steere, B. F. (1988). *Becoming an effective classroom manager: A resource for teachers.* Albany, NY: State University of New York Press.

Steffe, L. P., & Kieren, T. (1994). A radical constructivism and mathematics education. *Journal in Research in Mathematics Education, 25,* 711–733.

Stevenson, F. W. (1992). *Exploratory problems in mathematics.* Reston, VA: National Council of Teachers of Mathematics.

Stewart, I. (1992a). *Another fine math you've got me into . . . .* New York: Freeman.

Stewart, I. (1992b). *The problems of mathematics* (2nd ed.). Oxford, England: Oxford University Press.

Stewart, I., & Golubitsky, M. (1992). *Fearful symmetry: Is God a geometer?* Oxford, England: Blackwell.

Stewart, J., & Hafner, R. (1994). Research on problem-solving: Genetics. In D. L. Gabel (Ed.), *Handbook of research on science teaching and learning* (pp. 284–300), New York: Macmillan.

Stiggins, R. J. (1988). Revitalizing classroom assessment: The highest instructional priority. *Phi Delta Kappan, 69,* 363–368.

Stiggins, R. J., & Conklin, N. F., & Bridgeford, N. J. (1986). Classroom assessment: A key to effective education. *Educational Measurement: Issues and Practices, 5,* 5–17.

Stiggins, R. J., & Duke, D. (1988). *The case for commitment to teacher growth: Research on teacher evaluation.* Albany, NY: State University of New York Press.

Strike, K., & Soltis, J. (1986). Who broke the fish tank? And other critical dilemmas. *Instructor, 95,* 36–39.

Strom, R. D. (1969). *Psychology for the classroom.* Englewood Cliffs, NJ: Prentice Hall.

Struyk, L. R., Cangelosi, J. S., & Elhert, D. (1993, April). *The impact of a calculator-based mathematics teaching inservice program for elementary school teachers.* Paper presented at the annual meeting of the American Educational Research Association, Atlanta, GA.

Sulzer-Azaroof, B., & Mayer, G. R. (1977). *Applying behavior analysis procedures with children and youth.* New York: Holt, Rinehart, & Winston.

Suydam, M. N., & Brosnan, P. A. (1993). *Research on mathematical education reported in 1992.* Journal for Research in Mathematics Education, 24, 320 385.

Suydam, M. N., & Brosnan, P. A. (1994) Research on mathematical education reported in 1993. *Journal for Research in Mathematics Education, 25,* 375–434.

Swetz, F., & Hartzler, J. S. (Eds.). (1991). *Mathematical modeling in the secondary school curriculum.* Reston, VA: National Council of Teachers of Mathematics.

Taylor, L. J. C., & Nichols, J. A. (1994). Graphing calculators aren't just for high school students. *Mathematics Teaching in the Middle School, 1,* 190–196.

Texas Instruments. (1990). *TI-81 Graphics Calculator Guidebook.* Lubbock, TX: Author.

Thorndike, E. L. (1904). *An interpretation of the theory of mental and social measurements.* New York: Teachers College Press, Columbia University.

Thorndike, E. L., & Woodworth, R. S. (1901). The influence of improvements in one mental function upon the efficiency of other functions. *Psychology Review, 8,* 247–256.

Tobin, K., Tippins, D. J., & Gallard, A. J. (1994). Research on instructional strategies for teaching science. In D. L. Gabel (Ed.), *Handbook of research on science teaching and learning* (pp. 45–93), New York: Macmillan.

Torrance, E. P. (1962). *Guiding creative talent.* Englewood Cliffs, NJ: Prentice-Hall.

Torrance, E. P. (1966). Fostering creative behavior. In R. D. Strom (Ed.). *The inner city classroom: Teacher behavior* (pp. 57–74). Columbus, OH: Merrill.

Towers, R. L. (1987). *How schools can help combat student drug and alcohol abuse.* Washington, DC: National Education Association.

Tymoczko, T. (1986). *New directions in the philosophy of mathematics.* Boston: Birkhäuser.

Ulrich, R. E., & Azrin, N. H. (1962). Reflexive fighting in response to aversive stimulation. *Journal of Experimental Analysis of Behavior, 5,* 511–520.

United States Department of Education. (1994). *Eisenhower national clearinghouse for mathematics and science education: Guidebook to excellence. A directory of federal resources for mathematics and science education improvement for the Far West region.* Washington: Author.

U.S. students again rank near bottom in math and science. (1989). *Report on Educational Research, 23,* 1–4.

U.S. teens lag behind in math, science. (1989). *Education, USA, 31,* 161+

Utah State Board of Education. (1995). *Mathematics core curriculum: Grades 7–12.* Salt Lake City, UT: Author.

Van Horn, K. L. (1982, April). *The Utah pupil/teacher self-concept program: Teacher strategies that invite improvement of pupil and teacher self-concept.* Paper presented at the annual meeting of the American Educational Research Association, New York.

von Baravalle, H. (1989). The number π. In *Historical topics for the mathematics classroom* (pp. 148–155). Reston, VA: National Council of Teachers of Mathematics.

von Glasersfeld, E. (1990). An exposition of constructivism: Why some like it radical. In R. B. Davis, C. A. Maher, & N. Noddings (Eds.), *Constructivist views on the teaching and learning of mathematics* (pp. 19–29). Reston, VA: National Council of Teachers of Mathematics.

Voorhies, R. (1989). Cooperative learning: What is it? *Social Studies Review, 29,* 7–10.

vos Savant, M. (1993). *The world's most famous math problem.* New York: St. Martin's Press.

Wagon, S. (1991). *Mathematica in action.* New York: Freeman.

Wallis, C. (1994). A class of their own. *Time, 144*(18), 53–63.

Webb, N. L., & Coxford, A. F. (Eds.). *Assessment in the mathematics classroom: 1993 yearbook.* Reston, VA: National Council of Teachers of Mathematics.

Webb, N., & Romberg, T. (1992). Implications for the NCTM *Standards* for mathematical assessment. In T. A. Romberg (Ed.), *Mathematics assessment and evaluation: Imperatives for mathematics educators* (pp. 37–60). Albany, NY: State University of New York Press.

Weber, W. A. (1994). Classroom management. In J. M. Cooper (Ed.), *Classroom teaching skills* (5th ed.) (pp. 233–279). Lexington, MA: Heath.

Wickelgren, W. A. (1974). *How to solve problems: Elements of a theory of problems and problem solving.* New York: Freeman.

Weinstein, C. E., Goetz, E. T., & Alexander, P. A. (Eds.). (1988). *Learning and study strategies: Issues in assessment, instruction, and evaluation.* San Diego, CA: Academic Press.

Welsh, R. S. (1985). Spanking: A grand old American tradition? *Children Today, 14,* 25–29.

Whitney, H. (1987). Coming alive in school math and beyond. *Educational studies in mathematics, 18,* 229–242.

Wiggins, G. (1989). Teaching to the (authentic) test. *Educational Leadership, 46,* 41–47.

Wilds, E. H., & Lottich, K. V. (1961). *The foundations of modern education* (3rd ed.). New York: Holt, Rinehart, & Winston.

Wilford, P. (1993). *Peer collaboration in the Mathematics Teacher Network Project: A qualitative study.* Dissertation, Utah State University, Logan.

Wittrock, M. C. (1992). Knowledge acquisition and comprehension. In M. C. Alkin (Ed.), *Encyclopedia of educational research* (6th ed.) (pp. 699–705). New York: Macmillan.

Wolfe, D. P. (1989). Portfolio assessment: Sampling student work. *Educational Leadership, 46,* 35–39.

Wolpe, J., & Lazarus, A. A. (1966). *Behavior therapy techniques: A guide to the treatment of neuroses.* Oxford, England: Pergamon.

Wood, R. (1988). Item analysis. In J. P. Keeves (Ed.), *Educational research, methodology, and measurement: An international handbook* (pp. 376–384). Oxford, England: Pergamon.

Woolfolk, A. N. (1993). *Educational psychology* (5th ed.). Boston: Allyn and Bacon.

Yassin, S. A. J. (1992). *A study of achievement, retention, and transfer resulting from teaching absolute value by two definitional approaches,* Dissertation, Tallahassee, FL: Florida State University.

Zawojewski, J. S. (1991). *Dealing with data and chance.* Reston, VA: National Council of Teachers of Mathematics.

Zumwalt, K. (1989). Beginning professional teachers: The need for a curricular revision of teaching. In M. C. Reynolds (Ed.), *Knowledge base for the beginning teacher* (pp. 173–184). Oxford, England: Pergamon.

Index

ABOUT THE AUTHOR

James S. Cangelosi (Ph.D., Louisiana State University, 1972) has extensive experience teaching mathematics at the middle school, high school, and university levels. He specializes in mathematics education, data collection, assessment of student achievement, and behavior management at Utah State University, where he serves as a professor in the Department of Mathematics and Statistics as well as in the Department of Secondary Education. Among his publications are articles in journals such as *Journal for Research in Mathematics Education, Mathematics Teacher, Arithmetic Teacher, Phi Delta Kappan, Mathematics and Computer Education, Educational Measurement Issues and Practices, Contemporary Education, The Clearing House, NASSP Bulletin,* and *Delta Pi Epsilon,* and books including *Measurement and Evaluation: An Inductive Approach for Teachers* (1982), *Cooperation in the Classroom: Students and Teachers Together* (1984, 1986, 1990), *Classroom Management Strategies: Gaining and Maintaining Students' Cooperation* (1988, 1993), *Designing Tests for Evaluating Student Achievement* (1990), *Evaluating Classroom Instruction* (1991), and *Systematic Teaching Strategies* (1992), and videotape programs for mathematics teachers such as "Demystifying School Mathematics" and "Using Mathematics to Solve Real-Life Problems." Recent funded research and development efforts (e.g., the *Mathematics Teacher Inservice Project, Calculators in the Classroom Study, Mathematics Teacher Network, Calculator-Based Calculus Project, Mathematics Core Curriculum Project for Elementary and Middle School Teachers,* and *Regional Institute for Mathematical Sciences*) reflect Dr. Cangelosi's concern for narrowing the gap between typical teaching practices and research-based teaching practices.

457